From Your Gods to Our Gods

From Your Gods to Our Gods

A History of Religion in Indian,
South African, and British Courts

MARCO VENTURA

CASCADE *Books* • Eugene, Oregon

FROM YOUR GODS TO OUR GODS
A History of Religion in Indian, South African, and British Courts

Cascade Books
An Imprint of Wipf and Stock Publishers
199 W. 8th Ave., Suite 3
Eugene, OR 97401

www.wipfandstock.com

ISBN 13: 978-1-62032-778-4

Cataloguing-in-Publication data:
_____

Ventura, Marco.

    From your gods to our gods : a history of religion in Indian, South African, and British courts
/ Marco Ventura.

    xii + 384 pp. ; 23 cm. Includes bibliographical references and index.

    ISBN 13: 978-1-62032-778-4

    1. Church and State—India. 2. Church and State—Africa. 3. Church and State—England. I.
Title.

BR500 V200 2014
_____

Manufactured in the U.S.A.

Contents

Acknowledgments | vii

1   Explosive Gods (1979–1994) | 1
2   Imperial Gods (1857–1947) | 76
3   National Gods (1995–2000) | 132
4   Cold Gods (1948–1978) | 181
5   Global Gods (2001–2009) | 263

Bibliography | 349
Case Law | 359
Index | 363

Acknowledgments

Fɪʀsᴛ I ᴡɪsʜ ᴛᴏ honor the memory of Jean Schlick, who instilled in me the passion for the surprising trajectories of history. I am grateful to Marie Zimmerman, my supervisor at the time of explosive gods, for her tireless advocacy of critical thought, and methodological rigor. During the preparation of this book, my association with the research center on law, society and religion in Europe in Strasbourg, at the French National Research Council, has been a constant source of reflection. My visits, lectures, and teaching at the University of Strasbourg have allowed me to test and develop the methodological assumptions of this book. I wish to express my gratitude to Francis Messner, Anne-Laure Zwilling, Françoise Curtit, Anne Fornerod, Jean-Luc Hiebel, and Marc Aoun. Discussions with Laurent Kondratuk have nourished my curiosity about the intermingling of power and beliefs. Edoardo Dieni and Jean Werckmeister passed away too soon to see this fruit of their unique contribution to the study of religious laws in history and society.

Throughout the preparation of the book, colleagues, students, and the staff of the University of Siena have been indispensable companions. My Italian colleagues in law and religion have and always will be my family. Since 2004, I have greatly benefited from being a member of the European Consortium for Church and State Research: friends of the Consortium have decisively strengthened my knowledge of law and religion in Europe, while pushing me to explore colonial and postcolonial implications.

I started conceiving the project of this book during my visit to the Faculty of Laws at the University College of London in 2002. Conversations with Sir Basil Markesinis, David O'Keefe, Oliver Dawn, Andrew Lewis, Michael Freeman, Rodney Austin, Riz Mokal, and Colm O'Cinneide have been a crucial source of inspiration. Later encounters with Ronan McCrea, George Letzas, and Myriam Hunter-Henin have enhanced my admiration for the Faculty at Bentham House.

Since then, the Institute for Advanced Legal Studies Global Law Library has been an invaluable part of my project.

I am indebted to the Asia-Europe Foundation for the invitation to participate in the Talks on the Hill in February 2004 in Singapore: the workshop encouraged me to develop my research on interactions between Asia and Europe in law, politics, and religion.

Acknowledgments

My visit to the Centre for Socio-Legal Studies at the University of Oxford in 2004 has been seminal. I express my gratitude to Denis Galligan for his invitation to present my embryonic project in a talk on June 9, 2004, as well as for his ongoing encouragement. At the time, my encounter with Grace Davie was most inspiring.

The term I spent at the Université Libre de Bruxelles in 2007 enabled me to lecture extensively for the first time on the topics of this book, and to challenge my assumptions in the vibrant environment of the Centre interdisciplinaire d'étude des religions et de la laïcité. I offer my warmest gratitude to Jean-Philippe Schreiber, who has continued to be a close friend in my endeavor, and to the colleagues, staff, and students.

The School of Oriental and African Studies (SOAS) in London has been the main reference point during my research and writing. As is abundantly evident in this book, Werner Menski has profoundly influenced my work. I thank him for his passion, generosity, and humility in sharing his knowledge with me. Conversations with Andrew Huxley and Prakhash Shah have greatly contributed to shaping and testing my research. I am deeply grateful to Faris Nasrallah and Jeremy Brown, who have been my constant enthusiastic and caring friends. I am indebted to the staff of the SOAS Library, and to Chiara Lapi and Lorenzo Arditi for helping me with several sources.

Several British colleagues were significant in bringing this book to fruition. Mark Hill generously offered me insights, information, and clarifications, and he read early drafts of parts of the book. I also thank Mark and the Ecclesiastical Law Society for including me on the editorial board of the *Ecclesiastical Law Journal* at Cambridge University Press. Thanks to the *Ecclesiastical Law Journal* I had the privilege to meet Lord Rodger of Earlsferry, who sadly passed away before this book was completed. During this time Norman Doe was an energetic comrade and an indispensable source of knowledge on developments in the Anglican Communion. I also benefited from conversations and encounters with Bernard Jackson, Julian Rivers, Peter Cumper, Malcolm Evans, Linda Woodhead, Ian Leigh, Russell Sandberg, Javier Oliva, and Peter Petkoff. Peter's Oxford Law and Religion Society offered me many opportunities to refine my research, and in particular a groundbreaking lecture by David Robertson on case law and the global politics of religious freedom. Many thanks to Geri Della Rocca De Candal and to Lorenzo Braca for their support in Oxford. Conversations with John Madeley and Conor Gearty at the London School of Economics, and with Tariq Modood in Copenhagen were also very precious.

Andrew Ashworth helped me clarifying the common law offense of blasphemy.

I am indebted to the staff of the Asian & African Studies Reading Room at the British Library for their assistance during my hours of research there.

My thanks go to the British Board of Film Classification for allowing me access to the file on *International Guerillas*, and particularly to Fiona Liddell for her valuable assistance. The Tony Blair Faith Foundation helped me with Tony Blair speeches.

In many passionate conversations Elias Nasrallah was my mentor on global Islamic politics and on Britain's wrestling with Islam.

John Hooper helped me to gain a better view on contemporary British politics and religion.

Bruce Clark enhanced my awareness of the global implications of my topic, and on its potential beyond the legal dimension and the boundaries of academic research. David Pollock significantly contributed to my understanding of the position of the British Humanist Association.

I am grateful to the Supreme Court of India for granting me access to their resources, and for allowing me to attend hearings. My warmest thanks to the Office of the Attorney General, and in particular to Devadatt Kamat and Nitin Lonkar for facilitating my visit. Nitin has also been a constant support in my struggle with Indian case law. I have immensely benefited from my visit to the Indian Law Institute. I am particularly indebted to the students and colleagues who attended my lecture in February 2011, and to Lavanya and Alex Fischer for facilitating this opportunity. Many thanks to K. K. Venugopal and to Gopal Sankaranarayaran.

I hope this book does justice to the defining deconstruction of religion by Federico Squarcini. Federico earnestly warned me of the risk of oversimplifying Indian culture and beliefs. I am not sure he will endorse the outcome. However, our dialogue encouraged me to take the risk. Romila Thapar kindly accorded me the privilege of a personal conversation, which decisively drew my attention to the ties between Indian history and contemporary issues. With his impressive lucidity and depth, Siddharth Varadarajan enlightened me on contemporary developments in India and the challenge that lies ahead. I owe special thanks to Justice Kuldip Singh for meeting me in his home in Chandigarh, and for engaging in a fascinating and insightful conversation. Honest criticism of his opinion in the Sarla Mudgal is my best way to honor him.

Conversations with Henri Stern at the Nehru Library at Teen Murti House and with Arundhati Virmani at the Vielle Charité in Marseille greatly contributed to my awareness of the immense richness of Indian culture. Many thanks to Rina Verma Williams for her help.

Rajesh Kapoor and Vineeth Mathoor have been my esteemed mentors in Delhi as well an invaluable guides to me following my return to Europe.

Since our first meeting in Siena, my research on South Africa was deeply influenced by Alex Boraine's personality. My sincere thanks to Alex for inspiring my quest, and to Marcello Flores, who facilitated our meeting, and who was a constant supporter of my project.

This book would not have been possible without the assistance of the Faculty of Law at the University of Cape Town, and of the Brand van Zyl Law Library. I am particularly grateful to Tom Bennett for his warm assistance, advice, and useful insights. Special thanks to Gareth Prince for meeting me, and for trusting my genuine interest for his remarkable personal story. I would not have met Gareth without the kind assistance of Frans Viljoen and Trudy Fortuin. I am also most grateful to Albie Sachs for our short and yet very intense conversation.

Acknowledgments

Pieter Coertzen has been an indispensable source of documents and information. Patrick Lenta assisted me in many ways. His works played a considerable role in shaping my approach to South African law, religion, and literature. I am particularly indebted to Patrick for my reading of his publications, including "Executing the Death Sentence: Law and Justice in Alan Paton's *Cry, The Beloved Country* and Nadine Gordimer's *The House Gun*," *Current Writing: Text and Reception in Southern Africa* 13 (2001) 46–69, as well as to his "The *Tikoloshe* and the Reasonable Man: Transgressing South African Legal Fictions," *Law and Literature* 16 (2004) 353–79.

Although the encounter with John de Gruchy emphasized my limited knowledge of the religious struggle in South Africa, his intellectual energy, and the spiritual drive of the Volmoed community were pivotal to my investigation. Michael Donen and Werner Smit helped me situate the Ashley Forbes' trial.

Reverend Matthew Esau was extremely helpful in elaborating the role of churches and religions in current issues in South Africa.

Vivian Bickford Smith attracted my attention on the illuminating film *A Reasonable Man* and enhanced my awareness of the potential and implications of remaking history through films.

Many thanks to Marlyn Adriaanse for his recollection of memories of apartheid, and for his impressions on the present within the country. And thank you to Henry "Africa" for his tales and jokes.

This book is also the result of my encounters with American law, religion, and politics. I am indebted to Olivier Roy, Heddy Riss, and the Center on Institutions and Governance at the University of California at Berkeley for the opportunity to present a paper on Indian conversions in Berkeley on May 6, 2011, and to Pradeep Chhibber for his discussion of the paper. Our common research project on religious norms and the public sphere has been very enriching. It enabled me to meet Christopher Kutz, Peter Danchin, Yüksel Sezgin, and Ofrit Liviathan. I am most grateful to the staff at the Doe Library at Berkeley. Also at Berkeley, I gained richer insights into Islam and Islamic law, thanks to my conversation with Ebrahim Moosa.

I am most grateful to Noah Feldman, Mark Tushnet, and Sheila Jasanoff at the Harvard University for agreeing to meet with me and discuss their research. Although they work in different fields, their vision on Islamic law, critical jurisprudence, and science and law has influenced this book. Colleagues at Brigham Young University also accompanied me during these years. I am particularly indebted to Fred Gedicks and Cole Durham. During my visits to Provo I had the chance to meet Paul Diamond, in October 2004, and to discuss with Michael Perry, David Fontana, Andrew Koppelman, Pierre-Henri Prélot, Blandine Chelini-Pont, Winnifred Sullivan, Brett Scharffs and Francis Kirkham in March 2009.

My thanks to the Jimmy Carter Library & Museum for their assistance in my research on Carter's visit to India.

x

On many occasions Jeremy Gunn stimulated my work through his intellectual curiosity, friendly conversations, and challenging approach to law, religion, and society. His work on "spiritual weapons" has defined my approach to "cold gods." Calum Carmichael was decisive in his support of my project.

Resources from the International Consortium for Law and Religion Studies (ICLARS), and the research in law and religion by Silvio Ferrari have been very helpful. The ICLARS international meeting in Milan in January 2009 offered me invaluable insights from the lectures by Grace Davie and Tahir Mahmood.

I thank Olivier Roy, Pasquale Annicchino, and Nadia Marzouki for the many occasions when I could refer to parts of this book in the *Religio West* program at the European University Institute in Firenze. My conversations with Ran Hirshl, Ronan McCrea, Zachary Calo, Elizabeth Shakman Hurd, Jeroen Temperman, Kristina Stoeckl, and Tim Peace were particularly helpful.

I owe the Faculty of Canon Law at KU Leuven special gratitude for allowing me to test this book with an extremely challenging group of international students in a seminar, in November 2011. More generally I am deeply grateful for the warm support of Rik Torfs, Hildegard Warnink, Wim Decock, Eric De Wilde, Cécile Roelandts-Hermans, Ellen Vandenbroeck, and Gidey Seyoum Halibo. Many thanks also to James Mearns and Michele Hugonnet. In the final preparation of this book, my students at KU Leuven have been a challenging reminder that teaching is the best assessment of research.

Many people have supported my research, but only Jeff Shapiro has worked with me from the beginning on this text. He has always encouraged my project to complete a rigorous and yet readable book for the nonspecialist. Without his editing and comments, his sense of a novelist in the construction of the text, I could not have fulfilled my ambition.

I am also grateful to Anita Manderfield for her editing and to Ralph Grillo for his reading of the manuscript and for his remarks. My thanks also to Angela Jayne Bates for her reading of an early draft of this book concerning the case of Gareth Prince.

I wish to thank all those people at Wipf and Stock who made this book possible, and in particular K. C. Hanson, Jeremy Funk, and Ian Creeger.

Of course, none of the above-mentioned people is responsible for any of my deficiencies and misinterpretations.

Chapter 1

Explosive Gods (1979–1994)

God's Children

IN 2007 V. S. Naipaul wrote of the simultaneous presence of Aldous Huxley and Mahatma Gandhi on the rostrum of a 1925 Indian National Congress conference in Kanpur.

Huxley, the Englishman, saw Gandhi as the "complete" Indian saint and nationalist, the champion of Indian independence, the figure dressed in the dhoti and the shawl, who would conquer generations. Naipaul challenged the assertion by the English writer Huxley, then thirty-one, that Gandhi, then fifty-six, was a complete icon. "In fact," Naipaul observed, "there was no completeness" to Gandhi:[1]

> He was full of bits and pieces he had picked up here and there: his mother's love of fasting and austerities, the English common law, Ruskin's idea of labor, . . . the South African jail code, the Manchester No Breakfast Association. His strong political cause—in South Africa and India—gave an apparent unity to all these impulses, but there was no real unity; the pieces did not fit together; no piece was indispensable.[2]

At the end of the first decade of the new millennium, Naipaul's exposure of the lack of "real unity" and completeness of Gandhi was the metaphor of a much wider struggle with the "bits and pieces" of the postcolonial world. Underneath lay the need to re-articulate the memory of Indians, South Africans, and Britons.

However powerful it may have been, the role of Gandhi in the history of the three peoples was just the most visible of numerous connections and interactions. India and Britain were crucial templates respectively for the colonized and the colonizer, while South Africa stood as the unique overlap of both patterns. As a whole system of interrelated nations and histories, the three represented an extraordinary spectrum of achievements and failures in the transition from the colonial to the postcolonial age.

---

1. Naipaul, *A Writer's People*, 168.
2. Ibid., 168–69.

Yet Gandhi was a metaphor not only of the political and cultural venture of Indians, South Africans, and the British, but particularly of their peculiar experience with religion and the law. Naipaul's insistence on Gandhi the saint and Gandhi the lawyer was reminiscent of the civil struggle with faith occurring in India, Britain, and South Africa, as individual countries and as parts of a larger whole.

If India, Britain, and South Africa shared the sharpest divides (*your* gods versus *my* gods, West versus East, North versus South, White versus Black) and the most disturbing hybrids—like converts and Orientalists—, they also jointly experienced the extreme ambivalence of religion as the source for the best and the worst. One hundred fifty years before Naipaul's portrait of "incomplete" Gandhi, thousands of Indians and Britons slaughtered one another in what Savarkar defined the War of Independence, and the British called the Mutiny. Gods had been invoked on both sides to justify the massacre of the enemy. From 1857 to 2007 many found inspiration in the gods for the most courageous acts of reconciliation and redress, and many others continued murdering in the name of God.

Religious violence had a long history in the three countries, but it was specifically associated with the colonial encounter with the gods of the other, with *your* gods. The clash between the gods of the colonizer and the gods of the colonized reshaped identities on both fronts, while also strengthening religious exclusivism and antagonism. By contrast, postcolonial modernity in India, Britain, and South Africa coincided with the ideal of *our* gods, according to which all gods from any religion or ideology could belong to the same pluralist society and contribute to its advancement. This ideal nourished the vision of a secular and multireligious India; of the rainbow South African nation of God; and of liberal, multicultural Britain.

The passage from the colonial *your* gods to the postcolonial *our* gods responded to the harsh reality of religious conflicts through the ideal vision of a reconciliation of faiths and ideologies for the sake of freedom, justice, and equality. Gandhi embodied such a response. From the time of his early steps in India, England, and South Africa he encountered the reality of religious exclusivism and simultaneously the possibility of interreligious cross-fertilization. This contrast between *your* and *our* gods Gandhi learned from his traditional upbringing in Porbandar; his mother's Satpranami shrine, combining Hindu and Muslim elements; his education in London, with its introduction to the Bible; the reading from Edwin Arnold's translation of Bhagavad Gita; Mme. Blavatsky and the secular society; and his time in South Africa, with Muslim Gujarati merchants in Natal, Afrikaner Calvinism, Anglican missionaries, and "backward" black customs. These early expressions of the gods prompted Gandhi to learn how to digest the evolving variety of deities he met and to transform the multicolor lot into a source of inspiration for ideas and practices. Hence the powerful energy, but also the inherent ambiguities and contradictions of what Naipaul saw as the Mahatma's "bits and pieces."

Yet, if Gandhi embodied the ambition to pass from *your* gods to *our* gods, he also personified the formidable symbolic and practical role of the law in the process. Gandhi the saint was also Gandhi the lawyer. Both as barrister and as the accused, the Mahatma brought his contest to the colonial world of *your* gods in court; it was in court that he proclaimed his dream of *our* gods and fought for it.

Because Gandhi summoned the gods to the dock or advocated religion in his speeches in courtrooms, and because so many others did the same in the recent history of the three countries, Indian, South African, and British courts forged a common history of the attempted transition to *our* gods. Such a process was composed of a whole set of characters: judges witnessing their beliefs, and reshaping them in the process of giving judgments; counsels doing the same while advising and assisting their clients; applicants translating in their claims the language of the gods; and the public participating in the excitement of trials, putting pressure on the protagonists and supporting, or contesting, faith-based litigations.

If Naipaul's readers in 2007 wanted to go beyond the mere acknowledgment of a torn-apart postcolonial universe, if they wanted to make sense of *your* gods and of *our* gods, they had to retrace the different generations of gods and discern how they had been tried in Indian, South African, and the British courts.

Five subsequent generations of gods were out there, ready to disclose pieces of truth about the common struggle of the three peoples with *your* gods and *our* gods. Imperial gods in the colonial world, cold gods during the Cold War, explosive gods after the religious surge of 1979, national gods in the late 1990s, and, most recently, global gods who commanded a fresh look, across ages, borders, faiths, and laws, into the global making of law and religion.

In a 1998 novel about the South African Constitutional Court's ban of capital punishment, Nadine Gordimer, a Nobel laureate like V. S. Naipaul, saw law as "a paper-chase,"[3] with legal clauses having the potential to "lead through the forest."[4]

The interaction of law and religion in the shift from *your* gods to *our* gods was also a paper chase. Making sense of the gods on trial in the Indian, South African, and British macrocosm implied a measure of hazard and surprise. Nonlinear time traveling was necessary. Like gods, courts and claimants moved back and forth over time, bringing precedents back to life and injecting modern sensitivity into past judgments.

A new paper chase through the forest of law and religion in India, South Africa, and Britain began in the first decade of the 2000s, when Naipaul delivered his "incomplete" Gandhi. At that time, social scientists from the three countries contributed to a new knowledge of old and new gods, of *your* and *our* gods. "Bits and pieces" were dug out and placed in tentative orders.

This coincided with the three private litigations: Sushmita Ghosh in Delhi, Gareth Prince in Cape Town, and Shabina Begum in London.

3. Gordimer, *The House Gun*, 58.
4. Ibid.

Sushmita asked the Supreme Court of India to prevent her husband, who had married her as a Hindu, from taking another woman as a Muslim. Gareth, meanwhile, asked the Constitutional Court of South Africa to recognize that he was entitled to lawfully consume cannabis as part of his Rastafarian religion. Finally, Shabina asked the House of Lords to declare that she was entitled to wear a full jilbab to public school, in keeping with her Islamic worldview.

By trying the gods in the three cases, the judges of India, South Africa, and Britain opened the doors of their courtrooms to the paper chase, in which the five generations of gods, with their questions and answers, could be tracked down. Distinctive national features and cross-national influences emerged, along with the three countries' shared quest for *our* inspirational gods. Each single country and the three together as a whole were concerned. Indians, South Africans, and Britons had a lesson to learn about the ambivalent interaction of politics, society, and religion, and about the failures and achievements inherent in moving towards *our* gods. Indeed *our* gods were there not in their idealized purity, but in the everyday experience of mixed identities, hybrid deities, shared fears, and hopes. During a postmodern age in need of re-articulating the "bits and pieces" beyond the borders, this was an extraordinary contribution to global coexistence with the gods.

You Will Begin to Believe

The first step in the stories of Sushmita, Gareth, and Shabina came at the end of the 1970s, when a generation of explosive gods rose to challenge Indians, South Africans, and Britons and to supersede the cold gods of the Cold War age.

Both fronts of the bipolar Cold War era largely resorted to religion.

On the capitalist side, West-praised religious liberty was marketed as the reason why believers and churches should stand for the "free world." Economic freedom and religious freedom went together. As had occurred for centuries, Western traders and missionaries joined forces in order for the strongest player to export his economy and his God. In the thick of the Cold War, on June 14, 1954, President Eisenhower decreed the phrase "under God" would be included in the US pledge of allegiance: America needed all possible weapons in the struggle against Communism, including, as Eisenhower said, "spiritual weapons."[5]

Communists also used religion. Marxism-Leninism, Stalinism, and Maoism stood as faiths themselves. They worshiped an atheistic God whose mission in history was to emancipate the impoverished masses and lead oppressed nations to freedom. In 1931, shortly before the British hanged him for sedition, the twenty-four-year-old Punjabi Marxist Bhagat Singh wrote the pamphlet *Why I am an Atheist*. "Society has to fight out this belief [that God is helpful to man in distress] as well as the idol worship

---

5. Gunn, *Spiritual Weapons*, 2.

and the narrow conception of religion,"[6] he proclaimed. And closed by anticipating how he would relate to religion in his imminent last hours:

> One friend asked me to pray. When informed of my atheism, he said, "During your last days you will begin to believe." I said, No, dear Sir, it shall not be. I will think that to be an act of degradation and demoralization on my part. For selfish motives I am not going to pray. Readers and friends, "Is this vanity?" If it is, I stand for it.[7]

The Marxist faith underscored the deceptive nature of traditional gods, the instrument of landlords and colonialists, and endeavored to replace traditional creeds: religions were crushed whenever possible; alternatively, they were subjugated or infiltrated.

The Cold War era changed the colonial setting. Both sides used decolonization: support to national struggles was meant to push the new independent states into the Atlantic or the Soviet orbit. In the postcolonial countries, an inextricable mix of independent politics and renewed colonialism, of continuity and discontinuity, was spawned. Again, religion played a substantial part, through either a God-driven struggle for liberation or a perpetuation of the old pattern of alien domination, under the heel of the capitalist or of the Marxist gods.

A time of clear-cut divisions, the Cold War was also a time of apparently unnatural marriages. Throughout the seventies in South Africa, Marxists and Christians, Muslims and Jews joined in the anti-apartheid struggle under the umbrella of the African National Congress. At the same time, Indian Marxists, Muslims, and Hindu conservatives formed the Janata party to oppose the authoritarian leadership of Indira Gandhi. And in Britain, conservative Christians and atheist consumerists fed the rise of Margaret Thatcher for the sake of the capitalist free market. Cold gods, the gods of the Cold War, were at the same time extremely polarized and deeply intertwined.

After the end of the seventies, the picture underwent a substantial change. Major events made the role of religion in the bipolar world of the Cold War much more visible. While the alliance between Marxists and believers on a social justice agenda tightened in non-Communist countries like Britain, India, and South Africa, the Soviet empire found itself increasingly threatened by the cold gods. In Eastern Europe, following his election in 1978, a viscerally anti-Communist Polish pope was on the attack. Many other factors—the holy war against the Soviets in Afghanistan, the revolution in Iran, and the takeover of the ayatollahs, the Iran–Iraq war, General Zia ul-Haq's proclaimed intention to transform Pakistan into an Islamic state, the escalation of violence in Israel and Lebanon, the murder of Egyptian president Sadat by those Islamists whom he himself had backed—all contributed to a new international

6. Singh, *Select Speeches & Writings*, 66.

7. Ibid., 66.

scenario in which political Islam was increasingly influential, and religion in general seemed to explode.

In the Cold War era, Britain had developed a pragmatic partnership with radical Islam. From Saudi Arabia to Pakistan, from the Muslim Brotherhood in Egypt to Iranian mullahs, the British along with their American ally supported Islamists against international Communism and secular nationalism. These were clearly anti-capitalist and anti-British partners, but as journalist and author Mark Curtis noticed, there was a consolidated foreign policy in this sense, and Britain was "desperate" to "retain some influence in a post-war world where its power was on the wane."[8] After the Soviet invasion of Afghanistan, the pattern was reiterated and strengthened, with Anglo-Americans mobilizing their age-old ambiguous partnership with the Saudis and Pakistan, to feed the mujahideens' jihad against the Soviets in Kabul and beyond. According to Curtis, a defining moment came on December 18, 1979, in New York, when Margaret Thatcher downplayed the Islamic element in the crisis of US hostages in Iran and "robustly championed Islam as an alternative to Marxism."[9] She said:

> The Middle East is an area where we all have much at stake. It is in our own interests, as well as in the interests of the people of that region, that they build on their own deep religious traditions. We do not wish to see them succumb to the fraudulent appeal of imported Marxism.[10]

The following British involvement in covert military training and arms supplies, in Afghanistan, in Pakistan, and beyond, further shaped the collusion with radical Islam, which had characterized British foreign policy as a response to decolonization. Mark Curtis sums up that along with their American allies,

> British planners believed that their aims—to reshape the global economy in the interests of Western business and counter nationalist or Soviet-backed forces—could be achieved in alliance with the Islamist right, just as they had throughout the entire post-war period.[11]

Throughout the eighties, a new pattern emerged. This was no more the time of a substantial but discreet religious influence on politics, with the capitalist and the Marxist gods prevailing over any other deity. The gods at work in the world were no longer cold ones. Instead, it looked as though the winds of religion were blowing. The time of explosive gods was underway.

8. Curtis, *Secret Affairs*, 64.

9. Ibid., 136.

10. Ibid.

11. Ibid., 151.

Guardians of the Sacred

The end of the seventies coincided with a watershed in the political life of Britain, India, and South Africa. In 1978, after the 1977 United Nations' embargo on arms trade to Pretoria had been declared, apartheid hardliner Pieter Willem Botha was sworn in as prime minister in an increasingly divided South Africa. In 1979, Margaret Thatcher won the elections in Britain and started implementing her conservative, liberal agenda. At the same time in India, the Janata coalition failed, and Indira Gandhi returned to power after the elections of 1980.

The three countries were faced with deep change in the economy and society, in both the domestic and the international arenas.

South Africa was more and more isolated. Not only had Euro-Atlantic white solidarity dramatically declined since the Western public opinion had fallen in love with Gandhi and Martin Luther King Jr., but also, with the end of Portuguese rule in Angola and Mozambique and the close of white rule in Rhodesia, the apartheid regime was now a unique exception in a postcolonial Africa. Supporters of apartheid were also isolated within the country. With a weakened economy superseding the boom of the seventies, the Afrikaner community became less cohesive, while non-whites resorted to the fiercest resistance. Against this background, Botha's plan to make concessions on minor aspects while keeping the system intact opened a new phase of tensions and violence.

Nine thousand kilometers north, Thatcher's reforms prompted general unrest. The clash between the government and the trade unions went wild. The shock therapy applied to the economy in the name of monetarism and the dismantling of the welfare system heavily impacted on the more marginal sections of society. Explosive gods benefited from social and economic troubles. If in South Africa the theological justification of apartheid crumbled, with religion posing as a powerful motivation for opposing the tyrannous state, British churches dissociated themselves from conservative Christian liberalism. Sociologist Grace Davie observed that over the decade during which Margaret Thatcher was in power, the churches grew "more representative than any political party"[12] and "found themselves defending their ground against an increasingly separate or sectarian government."[13] The sociologist stressed the renewed social salience of religion:

> The guardians of the sacred became the defenders of the whole nation, paying particular attention to those least able to defend themselves; in many cases those, paradoxically, least likely to attend their churches.[14]

Particularly affected under the Thatcher's reformatting of British society were immigrant communities. If South Africa and India had been multicultural societies for

12. Davie, *Religion in Britain since 1945*, 39.
13. Ibid.
14. Ibid.

centuries—owing to their own multiplicity and also to colonial policies—the advent of multicultural Britain was the late fruit of the collapse of the British Empire. Only since the end of World War II had immigrants poured in, mainly from the former colonies. In the last decades, immigration had grown into a hot topic. As Thatcher's policies accentuated social inequalities, ethnic and cultural diversities combined with general grievances for social and economic injustice. In 1981, the death in Northern Ireland of IRA hunger striker and British MP Bobby Sands and the riots in Brixton and Toxteth brought into full light alienated communities within a divided country.

While triggering violence and blasting bombs among Roman Catholics and Protestants in Northern Ireland, explosive gods pushed British Christians to split. While Margaret Thatcher enrolled Christianity in her conservative agenda and championed for individuals and families, based on there being "no such thing as society,"[15] future prime ministers Gordon Brown and Tony Blair shaped their politics through the encounter with Christian socialism. More subtly, explosive gods also fueled the clash between liberals indulging in religious satire and defenders of sacred traditions. Over the 1970s Mary Whitehouse had struggled against offenders of faith, asking courts to try the blasphemous gods. In 1979 the House of Lords dismissed an appeal against the first conviction for blasphemy in fifty years, in the *Gay News* case. With *The Life of Brian*, the Monty Python cast stood as the boldest adversaries of religious conventions. In 1983, their last film *The Meaning of Life* exposed the crisis of traditional religiosity in the postmodern culture. The explosive gods were indeed a revised edition of what these actors ridiculed as an implausible faith:

> Chaplain: Let us praise God. O Lord . . .
> Congregation: O Lord . . .
> Chaplain: . . . Ooh, You are so big . . .
> Congregation: . . . Ooh, You are so big . . .
> Chaplain: . . . So absolutely huge.
> Congregation: . . . So absolutely huge.
> Chaplain: Gosh, we're all really impressed down here, I can tell You.
> Congregation: Gosh, we're all really impressed down here, I can tell You.
> Chaplain: Forgive us, O Lord, for this, our dreadful toadying, and . . .
> Congregation: And barefaced flattery.
> Chaplain: But You are so strong and, well, just so super.
> Congregation: Fantastic.[16]

---

15. McSmith, *No Such Thing as Society*, 4.

16 The Monty Python Partnership, *The Meaning of Life*.

Riding the Elephant

In India, the emergence of explosive gods was particularly perceptible. Like Roman Catholics in Northern Ireland, since the late seventies, Sikhs in Punjab heavily resorted to their religious identity in the struggle for better conditions and ultimately for the independence of Khalistan from the central government.

In other Indian states the social rise of the low castes, labeled OBC ("other backward classes") under the Constitution, and of the untouchables (labeled the "scheduled castes") prompted tensions. Both groups drew advantage from the system of reserved seats: they built up a strong collective self-awareness and turned increasingly active. Gandhi championed the emancipation of untouchables in a somehow paternalistic manner and termed them Harijans, "children of God." He wanted the Hindu community to undertake a spiritual conversion and make room for the Harijans in the name of the common brotherhood among the sons of God. But after independence, also thanks to the system of reservation, untouchables viewed their own struggle in more social and political terms and called themselves Dalits, from the Sanskrit "oppressed" or "crushed."

At the end of the 1970s, local governments in India started experiencing affirmative actions in governmental jobs. Southern states were used to it, but in states like Bihar and Uttar Pradesh this was very controversial. In Uttar Pradesh, where the rural policies of both Indira Gandhi and the Janata government had proved immaterial for the poorest, there was an open confrontation between the forward castes and Dalits. The Jatavs, a subcaste of Dalits, had grown overtly defiant towards the upper castes. Dalit processions had been a tool for mobilization and protest since well before independence. On April 14, 1978 in Agra, the Jatavs celebrated what they called the Ambedkar Jayanti, or the annual commemoration of the birthday of Bhimrao Ramji Ambedkar. Ambedkar, an untouchable political leader and prominent jurist who under Nehru had served as minister for justice and chairman of the drafting committee of the Constituent Assembly, had been the champion of a secular state promoting religious reform and enhancing Dalits' rights. Since his late conversion to Buddhism and his death in 1956, he had become the icon of Dalit consciousness and struggle for liberation. That day in Agra the "portrait of Ambedkar"[17] was carried on an elephant, a high symbol of Hinduism. When the procession passed through an upper-caste neighborhood, it was attacked. In the following riots, with the government and the police standing by, ten people were killed and many others were wounded.

In 1978 the Janata government decided to entrust a Commission with the task of preparing the extension of reserved seats to central-government jobs. Instituted on January 1, 1979, the Mandal Commission recommended in 1980 that exclusive access to a certain portion of government jobs and slots in public universities be given to the other backward classes as well as to the scheduled castes and tribes. The Commission recommended increasing quotas from 22.5 percent to 49.5 percent. Caste conflicts

17. Lynch, "Rioting as Rational Action," 1952.

were at the core of the report. The Tata Institute of Social Sciences in Bombay prepared a study for the Commission, which emphasized the British legacy and colonial continuity in caste issues:

> The British rulers produced many structural disturbances in the Hindu caste structure, and these were contradictory in nature and impact . . . Thus, the various impacts of the British rule on the Hindu caste system, viz., near monopolization of jobs, education, and professions by the literati castes, the Western concepts of equality and justice undermining the Hindu hierarchical dispensation, the phenomenon of Sanskritization, genteel reform movement from above and militant reform movements from below, emergence of the caste associations with a new role set the stage for the caste conflicts in modern India.[18]

The return of Indira to power froze the report for a decade, but policies to encourage the social promotion of the disadvantaged sectors of the population remained a hot topic in the political debate. No matter the inactivity of the government, the explosive gods of backward classes and Dalits raised their voice.

The struggle of backward castes coincided with another spectacular sign that Indian gods claimed a new place in politics: Hindu conservative mobilization. Hindu conservatism had a long history. In 1980, a new chapter was written when the Bharatiya Janata Party (BJP) was created from the ashes of the Janata Party. With the Hindutva ideology at its core, the BJP nurtured the ambition to federate the galaxy of Hindu nationalist movements and leaders. Hindu religious and political unity was advocated as a necessity in the present context, if the secular policies of Indira Gandhi, the activism of Indian Marxists, and the offensive of other religious communities like Christians and Ambedkarite Buddhists were not to disband the cherished traditions. Muslim politics were reshaped accordingly, with the emergence of a conservative agenda. The riots in Uttar Pradesh the same year announced a decade of increasing Hindu-Muslim polarization and violence.

An Ascetic Sudra

While exploding in politics, the gods also challenged the law. The new gods' ambition to rule and the resulting social tensions caused religion-related lawsuits to increase. Courts became the arena in which the forces clashed: old gods against the new; secular gods against religious gods. Judges found themselves confronted with the hard task of having to try the explosive gods.

In courts as in politics, religion was more openly an issue in India than in South Africa or in Britain. The social salience of Indian religion was unique. The status of religion in Indian law was also distinctive, because of the extraordinary variety of experiences and of the peculiar formation of the system in history.

18. Mandal Commission, *Report of the Backward Classes Commission*, 36–37.

When the East India Company took over, the British found themselves confronted by a huge variety of precepts and practices. If, under the Moghuls, the Qazis enforced Muslim law to Muslims and, quite erratically, Hindu law to Hindus, the reality varied a lot according to the different places, castes, customs, and religions. The British endeavored to impose some uniformity. The courts they set up in India and the Privy Council from London enforced common law, based mainly on general principles of equity and justice. New general acts were also passed, like the Code of Civil Procedure of 1859, the Indian Penal Code of 1860, and the Code of Criminal Procedure of 1861. The ambition to unify the Indian law in harmony with the British legal rationalism of the time and for the sake of efficient colonial rule spared family law and religious customs. Colonial rulers had different reasons to refrain from entering such territories. Not only did they deem it too perilous to interfere with the native populations' most sacred tenets, but also their own political and legal culture, and indeed the template of the established Church of England, made them believe that, though not entirely sheltered from state interference, religion deserved special protection. Hence in 1772, Warren Hastings's foundation of Anglo-Hindu law, based on a Judicial Plan, the heart of which was the famous principle providing for Indian religious communities to be ruled by their own laws in matters of "religious usages and institutions": "In all suits regarding marriage, inheritance and caste, and other religious usages and institutions, the laws of the Koran with respect to Mahomedans, and those of the Shaster with respect to the Gentus (Hindus) shall be invariably adhered to."[19]

Noninterference proved more of a slogan than a practice. On the one hand, Christian missionaries and conversions to Christianity became a substantial feature of the colonial setting; on the other, the British understanding of religious communities and laws failed to reflect the immense variety of local religions and customs. Colonizers simplified the preexisting multiplicity and reformatted Indian society through the creation of artificial religious personal laws. Britain created the parallel universe of legal India, irrespective of reality.

Historian Rina Williams explains the twofold British elaboration of religious communities and laws in India. First, "Warren Hastings' definition served to distill the incredible religious and regional diversity of India into two major 'communities', Hindu and Muslim."[20]

Second, the British "assumed neither any internal differences within these communities, nor any actual or practical overlap between them with regard to their social practices, customs or traditions."[21] Courts played a key role. In truth, informal and local justice remained the closest form of adjudication for most people, even under the British Raj. But as the British Indian administration endeavored to give shape to religious personal laws, it emerged that the civil courts, not independent religious bodies, were in

19. Rocher, "The Creation of Anglo-Hindu Law," 79.

20. Williams, *Postcolonial Politics and Personal Laws*, 14.

21. Ibid.

charge of their application. Civil judges, including the members of the Privy Council in London, determined Hindu, Muslim, Christian, and Parsi personal law.

Under British rule, Indian civil courts ended up applying different sets of norms, including the Indian statutes made by the British; the Indian religious personal laws, as codified or made up by the British; and common-law principles like equity and justice. In the princely states, formally independent states under the substantial control of Britain, different systems of justice applied.

After independence, legal uniformity under a secular state was the prevailing legal ideology: the princely states were swept away and the introduction of a uniform civil code was envisaged in the Constitution. In the fifties, under Nehru, the Indian Parliament kept religious personal laws alive but introduced a special form of marriage accessible to all, irrespective of religion, through the Special Marriage Act of 1954. In the same period the Parliament reformed Hindu law, with the resulting piecemeal Hindu Code Bill also applying to Sikhs, Jains, and Buddhists. While defeating Hindu nationalists, forcible modernization of Hindu law also defeated the preexisting informal, nuanced, and much richer customary law.

So-called religious personal laws were thus the result of the manipulation by both the British Raj and independent India of the preexisting variety of religions, castes, and customs. A huge gap existed between religious, caste, and customary precepts actually observed by people, and the religious personal laws laid out in the statutes and in courts.

The judiciary and the Supreme Court had posed since independence as the guardian of modern secular order and modernized religion, as opposed to backward chaos and fanaticism.

At the end of the seventies, the system was under pressure. In 1978, the Supreme Court ruled against the traditional understanding under Muslim law that divorced women were entitled to very limited maintenance rights.[22] In 1979, the same Court dismissed an appeal against Mathura Ahir. Himself a Sudra, the respondent claimed he was entitled, despite his low-caste status, to be ordained to an ascetic religious order and become a Sanyasi or Yati. The case scandalized traditionalists. In the decision, Justice Sen defended the autonomy of Hindu law and criticized that the first instance judge "could not introduce his own concepts of modern times, but should have enforced the law as derived from recognized and authoritative sources of Hindu law."[23] Clearly such sources did not "sanction or tolerate ascetic life of the Sudras."[24] But practice worked differently. And Justice Sen acknowledged that the existing practice all over India was "quite contrary to such orthodox views"[25] and concluded for

---

22. *Bai Tahira*.

23. *Krishna Singh*, 712 [17]. (In this work, a number in brackets—[ ]—is a paragraph number.)

24. Ibid., 717 [37].

25. Ibid.

the legitimate access of Mathura Ahir to the religious order, based on the following passage of Mukherjea's *Hindu Law of Religious and Charitable Trusts*:

> In cases . . . where the usage is established, according to which a Sudra can enter into a religious order in the same way as in the case of the twice born classes, such usage should be given effect to.[26]

If in the fifties Nehru had forced legislative reform onto the Hindus, in the seventies the Supreme Court allowed exceptions to the preservation of traditional Hindu customs for the sake of antidiscriminatory policies. While Nehru had not addressed Muslims, Indira Gandhi imposed upon the Muslim community more equal rights for women with the 1973 reform of the Criminal Procedure Code, paving the way for the Supreme Court to grant better maintenance rights to Muslim wives in the late 1970s.

In the 1950s, the debate on the Hindu Code Bill went together with the debate on the adoption of a uniform civil code. This happened again in the 1980s. In a case decided in 1982, Justice Venkataramiah for the Supreme Court opposed those who argued that the inaction of the Parliament obliged the Court to enforce a uniform civil code sweeping away religious personal laws. The judge's opinion read:

> Would this Court enforce a uniform civil code in respect of all citizens, without the aid of an appropriate legislation even though the concept of equality is enshrined in the Constitution and Article 44 specifically requires the State to endeavour to secure for all citizens a uniform civil code? It may not do so. The only solution for many of these social problems is to appeal to the appropriate organs of the State to do their assigned job in the best interests of the community. It is wrong to think that by some strained construction of law, the Court can find solution to all problems.[27]

Tension about what belonged to the different branches of the state reflected the broader crisis of India in the early 1980s. In his seminal 1982 book, law professor Upendra Baxi pointed toward the "crisis of the Indian legal system,"[28] with its increasing corruption, legal insecurity, and abuse of power. Baxi underlined the fundamental lack of a "moral or ethical attitude prescribing that the legal rules ought to be followed because they are rules of conduct."[29] The author linked the gap between people's real life and the legal system to the preservation of a "colonial mould and mode of law"[30] based on top-down lawmaking, and to the "limited access of Indians to legal information, legal services, and the courts."[31]

---

26. Ibid.
27. *National Textile Workers' Union*, 282 [53].
28. Baxi, *The Crisis of the Indian Legal System*.
29. Ibid., 5.
30. Ibid., 42.
31. Williams, *Postcolonial Politics and Personal Laws*, 16.

The crisis of the Indian legal system was particularly visible in the issue of religious personal laws. On April 23, 1985, the Supreme Court ruled in a case concerning maintenance rights under Muslim law. Contrary to the 1982 opinion by Justice Venkataramiah, the Court pleaded for the adoption of a uniform civil code. In addition, the all-Hindu bench interpreted Muslim law as allowing for maintenance rights in favor of a divorced woman beyond the traditional *iddat* period. Many Muslims, feeling that the noninterference doctrine was betrayed, mobilized to defend what they perceived as a community under siege. Though for a part of the Muslim community, the decision of the Court did not seem so unorthodox, and it even represented a step in the right direction of a more modern Indian Islamic law, the opponents of the ruling prevailed and asked the Parliament to pass a bill nullifying the decision and restoring the integrity of Islamic law. A difficult choice awaited Rajiv Gandhi, who had taken the office of prime minister after the assassination of his mother nearly four months earlier.

Bantu Courts

South Africa shared with India the same British colonial pattern. Rina Williams underlined that "India fell in a critical sense in the interstices of British colonialism, between the early colonies in North America and the later colonies in Africa."[32] This made India, according to Williams, "a template for colonial knowledge and practice."[33] In particular, the British carried from India to Africa "the social classification of the people—by religion and/or caste in India, or by tribe in Africa."[34] In this regard, Mahmood Mamdani wrote that "encased by custom, frozen into so many tribes . . . the subject population was, as it were, containerized. That imperative, the containerization of a subject people, was the core lesson that Britain learned from its Indian encounter."[35]

If South Africa experienced the same British colonial system as India, two factors made the South Africa context very different: first, the Dutch-Roman legal legacy; second, the peculiar set of creeds and beliefs presiding over the natives' customs. On the one hand, the forced cohabitation between the Dutch and the British gave birth to a legal system combining both Dutch-Roman law and British statutory and common law. On the other, colonial rulers, and later the apartheid regime, never bothered to acknowledge the laws of the Muslim, Hindu, or Jewish minorities; instead, they used customary law, the law of the Bantus, to pursue their goals. In appearance, Africans were allowed to follow their customs; in practice, the Dutch and the British neutralized or 'civilized' customary rules when they deemed it necessary in order to strengthen the subjection of the natives. Customary justice was also domesticated. Legal expert Thomas Bennett studied

32. Ibid., 4.
33. Ibid., 5.
34. Ibid.
35. Ibid.

the issue in the 1980s and explained in 1991 how "colonial courts in Africa were the beacons of imperial power."[36] Their task, he explained, was "not only to settle disputes but also to proclaim the reach of government and the values of western civilization."[37] Even when traditional chiefs and procedures were left in place, the Department of Native Affairs supervised the whole process.

Nelson Mandela's childhood was defined by his father's refusal to appear before the local white magistrate to respond of a complaint against him for a missing ox. Gadla Henry Mphakanyiswa was a Thembu chief by blood and custom. He refused to bow down. He stood against the colonial authority. Mandela described the episode in his autobiography:

> My father's response bespoke his belief that the magistrate had no legitimate power over him. When it came to tribal matters, he was guided not by the laws of the king of England, but by Thembu custom. This defiance was not a fit of pique, but a matter of principle. He was asserting his traditional prerogative as a chief and was challenging the authority of the magistrate.[38]

As a result, the magistrate deposed Mandela's father, "thus ending the Mandela family chieftainship."[39]

A threefold court system was framed in Southern Africa. Courts of chiefs and headmen represented the first instance. Subordinate and higher courts judged on appeals. Bodies with predominantly white personnel, in charge of the general administration of the Africans, oversaw the system.[40]

In 1927 the Bantu Administration Act formalized the colonial customary law—Bantu law as it was called at the time—as a separate jurisdiction. Thomas Bennett explained that rules and procedures were "manipulated to suit an offensive state policy,"[41] hence they were also "eradicated"[42] from the real life and culture of African peoples.

The British Raj and colonial South Africa adjudicated local religions and customs for the sake of divide-and-rule policies. Behind proclamations of promoting the natives' self-determination and of noninterference in their culture, colonial justice served the goal of dividing indigenous populations into secluded communities while securing the dominance of the separate white community.

After 1948, independent India dismantled the princely states and struggled in searching for a way to adjudicate religious personal laws in harmony with the new Constitution. South Africa created the homelands, formally independent states under

---

36. Bennett, *A Sourcebook of African Customary Law*, 55.
37. Ibid.
38. Mandela, *Long Walk to Freedom*, 7.
39. Ibid.
40. Bennett, *A Sourcebook of African Customary Law*, 55.
41. Bennett, "Re-introducing African Customary Law," 8.
42. Ibid.

the de facto control of the central government, and used customary law to demark separate communities while confirming the state's power to reshape traditions and impose them as invented customs. The alienation of customary law increased. So-called Bantu or Black courts adjudicated the customary law of the white oppressor. In the homelands it was possible in theory to legislate a form of customary justice in tune with the actual practice and the needs of the communities. But attempts made in 1978, when Transkei introduced a Marriage Act, and in 1982, when Bophuthatswana passed a Succession Act, proved that local chiefs were too conservative and too deferential towards policies of segregation to depart from colonial customary law.

By the early 1980s, both the democratic and postcolonial system of Indian personal laws and the customary law under apartheid South Africa were under pressure.

In the same period British courts also tried the early explosive gods. In 1978 the Court of Appeal dismissed the application of Iftikhar Ahmad, an Indian-born Muslim British teacher who claimed he should be entitled to pray on Friday afternoons in derogation of his contract of employment and with full pay. In 1984 Janis Khan, a twenty-three-year-old British citizen born and resident in Huddersfield, was sentenced to nine months imprisonment for abduction of and sexual intercourse with a girl under the age of sixteen, conduct that Janis claimed was legitimate under Islamic law.

Not only Muslim gods were in the dock. In 1982 the European Court of Human Rights condemned the UK for corporal punishment in Scottish schools, upholding the appeal by two mothers, Mrs. Campbell from Strathclyde and Mrs. Cosans from Fife, who opposed physical chastisement in the name of their nonviolent convictions. In 1983 for the first time a British court recognized Scientology as a religion for tax-exemption purposes.

The life stories and lawsuits of Sushmita Ghosh, Gareth Prince, and Shabina Begum encapsulated the hardship of trying the explosive gods in the three countries.

In India, Sushmita Ghosh married under Hindu law in 1984: eight years later her husband left her, converted to Islam, and took another wife under Islamic law. As Muslim-Hindu tensions increasingly polarized Indian society and politics, Sushmita resisted her husband's action and joined the struggle of Indian women for justice and rights. She claimed that her husband's was a sham conversion, and that he was not entitled to desert her and take a second wife. Eventually the Supreme Court of India decided her case in 1995 and again, on the appeal, in 2000.

In 1984, the same year that Sushmita wed, Gareth Prince was meanwhile a turbulent teenager in the area of Western Cape in South Africa. While at school, he embraced Rastafarianism and became an anti-apartheid activist. When he enrolled in law school, Gareth had the ambition to become a defiant nonwhite lawyer just like Gandhi and Mandela. Two convictions for possession and use of cannabis did not diminish Gareth's resolve. He completed his law degree and applied to the Cape bar to be enlisted as a barrister. In the application Gareth was not apologetic. He exposed the convictions and advocated the right to be exempted from the general prohibition of cannabis consumption on grounds of his religion. The Cape bar rejected the application, refusing to admit a lawyer who deliberately broke the law. Gareth started a momentous litigation. The Constitutional Court of South Africa decided the case in 2002. The African Commission of Human Rights in 2004 and the Human Rights Committee of the United Nations in 2007 decided on the appeal.

Shabina Begum was born on September 19, 1988, when the courtroom struggles of Sushmita and Gareth were about to start. During the eighties her family, of Bangladeshi origin, had settled in England. By the time of her birth, her future school, the Denbigh High School of Luton, had become a prime example of multicultural Britain, with its 90 percent Muslim student body in 1993. Yasmin Bevan was appointed head teacher in 1991. She was herself born into a Bengali Muslim family and had been raised in India, Pakistan, and Bangladesh. In 2002 Begun objected to the uniform policy of the school, which did not allow her to wear a full-length *jilbab* in compliance with what she understood as a Muslim obligation. In response, the school required her to accept the existing uniform code or to seek a place at another school. A highly publicized case ensued. In the end, the House of Lords decided in 2006.

The three cases of Sushmita, Gareth, and Shabina encapsulated the struggle of India, South Africa, and Britain with the explosive gods in courts, and more broadly in society. They also symbolized the troubled transition from the colonial *your* gods to the postcolonial *our* gods.

Inspirational Gandhi

As Naipaul stressed in 2007, nobody embodied the ties between India, South Africa, and Britain better than Karamchand Mohandas Gandhi. A Gujarati law student in London, a lawyer and a leader of the Indian community in Southern Africa, and finally the famous spiritual and political inspirer of Indian independence, the Mahatma had witnessed the colonial and imperial transformation of the Indian, Southern African, and British peoples into an interdependent universe of oppression and violence, of resistance and freedom.

An audacious interpreter of religion, politics, and the law, Gandhi was a precursor of God's children in court. In their original ways, Sushmita, Gareth, and Shabina followed his path. Sushmita resorted to legal tools against the use of religion to oppress women in Indian society, something Gandhi had also done in his time. Like Gandhi, Gareth fought for the right to be a lawyer of a different kind. Like Gandhi, Shabina tested the limits of British tolerance.

At the opening of the Festival of India, on March, 22, 1982, Margaret Thatcher welcomed her counterpart, Indira Gandhi. Liberal conservative Margaret Thatcher and socialist Indira Gandhi personified two alternative visions. In the age of rising explosive gods, Indira Gandhi opposed the use of faith in politics and championed secular India, while Margaret Thatcher advocated traditional Christianity as a basis for her ideology and policies. In the eyes of their respective opponents, however, the two prime ministers had many points in common. Catholics in Northern Ireland and Sikhs in Punjab fought the two leaders as the symbol of oppression and violence. Those who had opposed Indira Gandhi emergency rule in the seventies still regarded her as an autocrat. Critics of Thatcher's attack on the welfare state and of her military patriotism in the Falklands War also viewed the British prime minister as an anti-democratic leader.

As Indira Gandhi divided Indian Hindus, so Margaret Thatcher divided British Christians. The social and economic crisis was not the only reason for dissonance between the government and the churches. In 1982, at the end of the Falklands War, the Church of England and Downing Street wrestled over a service to be held in St Paul's Cathedral. The government wanted it to be a nationalistic victory celebration, but the Church authorities did not allow it, as sociologist Robert Bocock underlined, "because they thought that the loss of life on both sides was not something to give thanks for."[43]

The Festival of India in the UK was organized under the slogan "continuity and change." For eight months different expressions of Indian culture were performed and displayed in Britain. In her March 22, 1982, address at No. 10 Downing Street, Thatcher announced that "it was time the great achievements of India, both ancient and modern, were brought before as wide a section of the British public as possible."[44] India and Britain were global players, and their partnership was strategic. The common allegiance to parliamentary democracy and civil liberties should prevail over the conflicts of the past. It was time to get rid of *your* gods and to embrace *our* gods.

The film *Gandhi* was released in Britain on December 3, 1982, a few days after the closing of the Festival of India. If both the film and the festival celebrated the postcolonial harmony between the two countries, the message of the film was that the victory of Gandhi over the British testified to the morality of both the oppressed and the oppressor. In an article for *Time* sixteen years later, novelist Salman Rushdie underlined that the lesson of the film was that you could prevail through nonviolence "by being more moral than your oppressor, whose moral code could then oblige him to withdraw."[45] While the British public was reminded of colonial atrocities, it was also provided with a reassuring postcolonial narrative: Gandhi's morality could not have prevailed without the British moral code. The American screenwriter John Briley and the British director and producer Richard Attenborough created the illusion of a consensual narrative about a personality as controversial as Gandhi's had been. The much richer Indian discussion was not taken into account.

43. Bocock, "Religion in Modern Britain," 213.
44. Thatcher, "Speech at Lunch for Indian Prime Minister."
45. Rushdie, "Mohandas Gandhi," 71.

Rushdie labeled the film typical "unhistorical Western saintmaking,"[46] which produced "Gandhi-as-guru, purveying that fashionable product, the Wisdom of the East; and Gandhi-as-Christ, dying (and, before that, frequently going on hunger strike) so that others might live." Yet, the Anglo-Indian writer admitted, the Hollywood Gandhi and the inspirational Gandhi of the eighties stood together: "Such is the efficacy of this symbolic Gandhi that the film, for all its simplifications and Hollywoodizations, had a powerful and positive effect on many contemporary freedom struggles. South African antiapartheid campaigners and democratic voices all over South America have enthused to me about the film's galvanizing effects. This posthumous, exalted 'international Gandhi' has apparently become a totem of real inspirational force."[47]

The film's sequences on Gandhi as a young lawyer in South Africa made the general public aware that the father of the Indian nation and the fierce enemy of the British was also the pioneer of the struggle against white oppression in South Africa. Because Gandhi's experience was so entrenched in the history of the three countries, the Indian leader proved such an inspirational force for Indians, Britons, and South Africans throughout the 1980s.

The Oppressed and the Oppressor

The filmic sanctification of nonviolent Gandhi coincided with spreading political violence in India, South Africa, and Britain. Margaret Thatcher escaped an IRA bomb in Brighton on October 12, 1984. Three weeks later, on October 31, 1984, Indira Gandhi was murdered by two of her Sikh bodyguards in revenge for the bloody attack she had ordered on the Amritsar Temple, occupied by Jarnail Singh Bhindranwale and his Sikh nationalist followers. To those who had warned her about the danger of keeping Sikh bodyguards, Indira had objected: "Aren't we a secular country?"[48] In the ensuing anti-Sikh riots, 1,277 people were killed, with the army and the police accused of standing aside. Indira's son and successor Rajiv justified violence through his famous comment: "When a big tree falls, the earth shakes."[49]

With the conflict in South Africa turning increasingly violent in the 1980s, violence spilled over the borders. In March 1984 four South African arm traffickers were arrested in Coventry for breaching the UN ban on exports of military equipment to South Africa. When the Coventry four were allowed to leave Britain and obtain protection from the South African government so as to avoid trial, the attitude of Margaret Thatcher toward apartheid attracted strong criticism. The British prime minister maintained that a policy of dialogue was necessary to protect national commercial interests, as well as to enable the government to put pressure on Pretoria. She

46. Ibid.
47. Ibid.
48. Guha, *India after Gandhi*, 570.
49. Ibid., 571.

considered a step in the right direction the South African constitutional reform of 1983 providing for a tricameral Parliament with separate representation of Indians and "Coloreds." But, when in June 1984 she received the visit of P. W. Botha, her call for further change in South Africa proved unsuccessful.

The Anglican archbishop of Cape Town, Desmond Tutu, was featured among the critics of the canny attitude of the British government. In his Nobel lecture on December 11, 1984, Desmond Tutu blamed the "West" for being mild on the 1983 Constitution, which entrenched "racism and ethnicity": "The new constitution, making provision of three chambers, for whites, coloreds, and Indians, mentions blacks only once, and thereafter ignores them completely. Thus this new constitution, lauded in parts of the West as a step in the right direction, entrenches racism and ethnicity."[50]

If in India and Britain explosive gods attacked rival creeds, ideologies, and nations, Desmond Tutu's explosive God attacked the idea and practice of racial segregation. Drawing on the theology of apartheid as a heresy formulated in the 1970s, Tutu denounced in his Nobel lecture the apartheid system and its "ideological racist dream."[51] He deplored the violence of the state, the "dumping" of black people in the Bantustan homeland resettlement camps, the migratory labor policy that uprooted thousands from their homes, and the discriminatory Bantu education. Apartheid was built upon a "phalanx of iniquitous laws"[52]: the Population Registration Act divided people into race categories; the Prohibition of Mixed Marriages Act and the Immorality Act prohibited interracial sex. Tutu also attacked banning orders and security laws allowing for unlimited detention.

Gandhi's nonviolence was a source of inspiration, but not an absolute principle. After every peaceful attempt by the black population to respond to state violence—including passive resistance—proved unsuccessful, no moral equivalent to Gandhi's approach could be established. Tutu identified this difference on behalf of the South African Council of Churches:

> We in the South African Council of Churches have said we are opposed to all forms of violence—that of a repressive and unjust system, and that of those who seek to overthrow that system. However, we have added that we understand those who say they have had to adopt what is a last resort for them. Violence is not being introduced into the South African situation *de novo* from outside by those who are called terrorists or freedom fighters, depending on whether you are oppressed or an oppressor. The South African situation is violent already, and the primary violence is that of apartheid, the violence of forced population removals, of inferior education, of detention without trial, of the migratory labor system, etc.[53]

50. Tutu, *The Rainbow People of God*, 86.

51. Ibid.

52. Ibid., 87.

53. Ibid., 90.

Tutu closed his speech on a more spiritual tone, based on the fundamental equality of "God's children."[54] How could the blasphemy of apartheid be tolerated? he asked. How could it be theologically and politically justified? "When will we learn that human beings are of infinite value because they have been created in the image of God, and that it is a blasphemy to treat them as if they were less than this and to do so ultimately recoils on those who do this?"[55]

At the time of Tutu's Nobel Prize, Gareth Prince was a student at Knysna High School in Western Cape. Himself a descendant of the Khoikhoi, of the original population of the Cape area, the obtuse legal categorization based on skin color labeled him a colored man. From 1984 to 1987, while getting increasingly involved in his first demonstrations against apartheid, Prince became intrigued by Rastafarian imagery. Bob Marley had died only three years earlier. The powerful music, the rebellious energy, and the sense of black pride resonated deeply with Prince's anxiety. "Get Up, Stand Up," the legendary Marley's lyric from 1973, communicated that "Great God" will not "come from the skies" to "take away everything" and "make everybody feel high." Rather "almighty God" was a "living man" inviting you to "look for" your life on earth:

> And now you see the light,
> You stand up for your rights.[56]

If Tutu opposed apartheid in the name of the inherent equality of God's children, the correspondent universal brotherhood preached by Rastafarianism pushed teenager Gareth Prince to join in the struggle.

Doing Justice to the Quran

One week before Tutu's Nobel Prize acceptance speech on the "infinite value" of God's children, the world's largest industrial disaster occurred in India. On December 3, 1984, shortly after midnight, methyl isocyanate gas leaked from a tank at the Union Carbide India Limited Bhopal plant in the state of Madhya Pradesh. More than 10,000 people died and hundreds of thousand of others were condemned to permanent and partial disabilities.

In 1969, the construction of a plant for the production of pesticides in Bhopal had been saluted as yet another success of the green revolution, one of the best achievements of Indira Gandhi. The deadly effects of famine and drought had been seriously countered thanks to massive irrigation programmes and the use of fertilizers and pesticides. Fifteen years later, a few months after Indira's assassination, the Bhopal disaster pointed at failures and inefficiencies in the industrial modernization

---

54. Ibid., 92.
55. Ibid.
56. Marley and Tosh, "Get Up, Stand Up."

of India. The US-owned Union Carbide Corporation and the government of Madhya Pradesh bore the responsibility. If the design of the unit and the security system were inadequate, the poor management had made the situation progressively worse. Repeated and serious previous warnings had been ignored. Nobody was ready to react to a predictable accident.[57]

The Bhopal disaster had this in common with religious violence: not only were both the leak in Bhopal and the explosion of communal riots in many parts of India the fruits of heavy mismanagement and bad government, but they also called into question the secular and industrial modernization of India after the age of Indira Gandhi. In the following months, Indira's successor, her son Rajiv, endeavoured to lead the country beyond a socialist planned economy towards further industrial development in a free market system. And he also struggled to curb the explosive gods.

On April 23, 1985, the Supreme Court set a new balance between secular Indian law and Islamic personal law.[58] The legacy of Indira Gandhi's effort to strengthen secular India was essential to the case, as this was built on her 1973 reform of the Criminal Procedure Code providing wider maintenance protection to deserted wives. The respondent, Shah Bano Begum, had been married since the age of sixteen to her cousin Mohamed Ahmed Khan. The marriage was celebrated in 1932, two years after Gandhi's famous Salt March. Forty-three years later, in 1975, Mohamed left Shah Bano and married a second wife. At the time, Mohamed and Shah Bano had five children. In April 1978 Shah Bano resorted to Section 125 of the Criminal Procedure Code as amended in 1973, and claimed maintenance beyond the *iddat* period of three months. In November of the same year Mohamed Ahmed Khan, himself a lawyer, divorced Shah Bano by irrevocable *talaq*.

In 1980 the Madhya Pradesh High Court directed Mohamed Ahmed Khan to make maintenance payments of Rs. 179.20 per month. The husband appealed to the Supreme Court, submitting that he had fulfilled his obligations under Muslim law by paying for Shah Bano's maintenance during the three months of the *iddat* period and by giving her back her dowry, the Mahr.

As in the similar cases judged in 1978[59] and 1980,[60] the Supreme Court decided in favor of the wife. No matter the alleged prescriptions of his Muslim personal law, the husband was not allowed to avoid the payment of the maintenance beyond the *iddat* period. Justice Chandrachud stressed that the rationale of the 1973 reform was to extend to ex-wives the right to maintenance previously reserved to current wives on account of a policy supporting "suffering sections of the society."[61] The reform, as

57. Eckerman, *The Bhopal Saga*, 6.
58. *Mohd. Ahmed Khan.*
59. *Bai Tahira.*
60. *Fuzlunbi.*
61. *Mohd. Ahmed Khan*, 572 [29].

Justice Chandrachud wrote, "cut across the barriers of religion."[62] Section 125 was above personal religious laws. Equality of women from all sections of society mattered more than religious differences. In the words of Justice Chandrachud, "whether the spouses are Hindus or Muslims, Christians or Parsis, Pagans, or Heathens is wholly irrelevant in the application of these provisions."[63]

If the ruling followed the analogous decisions of 1978 and 1980, the argumentation differed significantly. On the previous occasions, the Court had been extremely cautious not to step into religious matters. The two decisions had been appealed against precisely on account of allegedly neglected Muslim law. But in both judgments, Justice Krishna Iyer had given strict application to the amended version of the Criminal Procedure Code, with no reference to Muslim law provisions.

Instead, in the Shah Bano judgment, the judges engaged heavily with religion. They stood to defend the threatened secular ethical agenda providing for women's rights and equality. The socialist gods nourished by the Nehruvian modernizing agenda clashed with the explosive gods. Justice Chandrachud reiterated the pattern of an Indian judiciary preventing religious backwardness from affecting the progress of the country: "the moral edict of the law and morality"[64] could not "be clubbed with religion."[65] Indeed, the judge asserted, there was a problem with religion:

> "Na stree swatantramarhati" said Manu, the Law giver: the woman does not deserve independence. And, it is alleged that the "fatal point in Islam is the degradation of woman" [*Selections from Kuran*, Edward William Lane 1843, Reprint 1982]. To the Prophet is ascribed the statement, hopefully wrongly, that "woman was made from a crooked rib, and if you try to bend it straight, it will break; therefore treat your wives kindly."[66]

Not only did the judgment establish the superiority of the Indian secular law, which could not be altered, not even for the sake of Muslim specificity, but it further bent Muslim law to the rationale of the Indian statutes. In the time of explosive gods, the Supreme Court rose as a God and gave a theological decision. The five judges, all of them Hindu, engaged in a detailed analysis of the divine sources of Islam. Hence Justice Chandrachud's conclusion in favor of the concordance between Indian statutes and the will of the Prophet as expressed in the Quran: several Aiyats, he wrote,

> leave no doubt that the Quran imposes an obligation on the Muslim husband to make provision for or to provide maintenance to the divorced wife. The contrary argument does less than justice to the teachings of Quran. As observed by

62. Ibid., 562 [7].
63. Ibid.
64. Ibid., 563 [7].
65. Ibid.
66. Ibid., 559 [1].

> M. Hidayatullah in his introduction to Mulla's Mahomedan Law, the Quran is
> Al-furqan, that is, one showing truth from falsehood and right from wrong.[67]

According to the Court, it was not Islamic law but rather inaccurate or interested interpreters standing on the side of unscrupulous men that prevented deprived ex-wives from receiving their necessary support.

By connecting the issue of women's rights to the question of national integration, though without articulating how the two aspects combined, the Court advocated the cause of the uniform civil code. Despite the "difficulties involved in bringing persons of different faith and persuasions on a common platform,"[68] Justice Chandrachud invoked the superiority of the state and the priority of the constitutional public policy: "a common Civil Code will help the cause of national integration by removing disparate loyalties to laws which have conflicting ideologies."[69] The judge criticized the view that it behoved the Muslim community "to take a lead in the matter of reforms of their personal law."[70] Instead he asserted the role of both the Court and the Parliament. Contrary to the attitude of restraint that Justice Venkataramiah had preached for in 1982, Justice Chandrachud argued that "inevitably, the role of the reformer has to be assumed by the courts, because it is beyond the endurance of sensitive minds to allow injustice to be suffered when it is so palpable."[71] But the judge agreed with Justice Venkataramiah that "piecemeal attempts of courts to bridge the gap between personal laws cannot take the place of a common Civil Code"[72] since "justice to all is a far more satisfactory way of dispensing justice than justice from case to case."[73]

A couple weeks later, on May 10, 1985, the Court ruled on the divorce between Jorden Diengdeh (from a "Khasi Tribe" of Maghalaya), who was born and brought up a Presbyterian, and her Sikh husband. Justice Chinnappa Reddy reiterated the Supreme Court's appeal to the Parliament in view of the framing of a uniform civil code: "Time has now come for the intervention of the Legislature in these matters to provide for a uniform code of marriage and divorce and to provide by law for a way out of the unhappy situations in which couples like the present have found themselves."[74]

By Thumbprint

As had happened twelve years earlier, when Indira Gandhi introduced the new maintenance provisions, some sections of the Muslim community mobilized and protested.

67. Ibid., 568 [22].
68. Ibid., 573 [32].
69. Ibid., 572 [32]
70. Ibid.
71. Ibid., 573 [32]
72. Ibid.
73. Ibid.
74. *Jorden Diengdeh*, 72 [7].

But this time the outrage was stronger. Many Muslims felt targeted. The integrity of their sacred law was threatened, their right to follow the divine precepts questioned. Strikes and demonstrations spread. Muslim MPs demanded that the Parliament intervene to render the Supreme Court's decision null and void. Syed Shahbuddin blamed the judges for having interpreted Islam's holy script "as if a new revelation had dawned"[75] upon them.

At first Prime Minister Rajiv Gandhi, together with his Muslim colleague in the cabinet Arif Muhammad Khan, defended the ruling. In his speech in Parliament of August 23, 1985, Khan conceded the Court had lacked "judicial discretion"[76] on the issue of the uniform civil code, but strongly defended the conformity to Islam orthodoxy of the Shah Bano judgment. Subsequently, a first version of a bill against the Shah Bano ruling was defeated.

In the following months, the political pressure increased, pushing Rajiv Gandhi and Shah Bano herself to change their minds. Conservative Muslims victimized Shah Bano, now a seventy-five-year-old, at her own home in Indore, Madhya Pradesh. The woman yielded to the pressure. On November 15, 1985, her thumbprint sealed a document in which "she disavowed the Supreme Court,"[77] donated maintenance rights to charity and opposed state interference in Muslim personal law. A few weeks later, the electoral defeats of the Congress Party in Bihar and Assam materialized the erosion of minority community support for the Congress. Fear that Muslims might desert the Congress because they felt alienated by its policy on personal laws pushed the prime minister to endorse the view of the conservative Muslim faction. Thus he delegated another Muslim minister, Zia-ur-Rahman Ansari, a fierce critic of the Supreme Court's decision on the case of Shah Bano, to take the initiative in issuing an act reassuring Muslims. The Muslim Women (Protection of Rights on Divorce) Bill was passed on February 25, 1986. Arif Muhammad Khan resigned the day after. It was doubtful whether the Act had the power to annul the effect of the Shah Bano decision. Certainly the bill had the clear political goal to reinstate a solid Muslim exception.

Both fronts were unhappy. Anti-Muslim Hindus felt confirmed in the prejudice that Muslims refused to integrate in the national community and to take part in the effort of social modernization. Muslims were not content either. Some of them were ready to accept a more modern personal law and felt the new legislation prevented the community from advancing. Justice Chandrachud stressed during the Shah Bano case that Islamic law expert Tahir Mahmood, in his 1977 book *Muslim Personal Law*, had gone as far as to ask his own Muslim community to fully endorse Indian secularism and "to begin exploring and demonstrating how the true Islamic laws, purged of their time-worn and anachronistic interpretations, can enrich the common civil code of India."[78]

75. Williams, *Postcolonial Politics and Personal Laws*, 141.

76. Ibid., 137.

77. Guha, *India after Gandhi*, 581.

78. *Mohd. Ahmed Khan*, 573 [33].

Among those Muslims who did not yield to the Muslim conservative position endorsed by the government, Danial Latifi, the prominent expert in Islamic law and the counsel of Shah Bano, challenged the Muslim Women Bill before the Supreme Court. If the Parliament had acted so as to neutralize the Supreme Court, Danial Latifi's petition offered the judiciary the opportunity to fight back.

At a time when Rajiv Gandhi's strategy of dialogue in Punjab seemed conducive to better relations between the Sikh minority and the central state, the prime minister's approach to Shah Bano made the issue of personal religious laws and the uniform civil code the catalyst of a deepening polarization between Hindus and Muslims. Rajiv Gandhi's strategy to defuse the explosive gods proved utterly unsatisfactory.

The effect of the Muslim Women Bill, Rina Williams wrote later, was "to marginalize the progressive Muslim viewpoint even further, and further entrench the construction of the Indian Muslim community as 'conservative' and 'resistant to reform or change.'"[79] Williams raised the difference between Nehru's strategy in the fifties and Rajiv Gandhi's in the eighties: "Where Nehru sided with progressive or pro-reform Hindu opinion, Rajiv sided with conservative or anti-reform Muslim opinion. Where Nehru held reform and codification were the right policies, even if only supported initially by a progressive minority, Rajiv marginalized the views of the progressive minority. Where the controversy of the 1950s, over the Hindu Code Bill did not lead to Hindu-Muslim tension, the controversy over Muslim personal law in the 1980s did."[80]

The rising Hindu nationalist movement strongly influenced Rajiv Gandhi's mismanagement of the Shah Bano case. In 1984, the year of Bhopal and of Indira Gandhi's murder, the Vishva Hindu Parishad, the champion of "Hindu pride and unity," launched a fatal campaign. Hindu nationalists urged the opening of the locks that sealed the Babri Mosque in Ayodhya, Uttar Pradesh, and prevented Hindus from celebrating religious functions there. While Muslims saw it as a holy place, Hindus considered the site the Ram Janmabhoomi, meaning the birthplace of Ram, an avatar of the God Vishnu, and the place of a *mandir*, a Hindu temple, which had been demolished in the sixteenth century to build the mosque. In the time of the British Raj, the matter was settled by allowing the Muslims to worship in the building and the Hindus to make offerings on a platform outside. In 1949, following independence, the situation worsened when a Hindu official surreptitiously put a statue of child Ram in the mosque. This was widely believed to be a sign that the God wanted Hindus to take over the disputed structure, demolish the mosque, and build a *mandir* in his honor.

For three decades the Indian government had not altered the British status quo: Hindus were only allowed in the mosque once a year, to worship the idol of Ram Lalla, child Ram. But under the pressure of Hindu conservatives, on February 1, 1986, the Faizabad district judge ordered the removal of the locks and allowed Hindus to freely worship in Ayodhya. Many reckoned that the decision, which coincided with

79. Williams, *Postcolonial Politics and Personal Laws*, 147.
80. Ibid.

the parliamentary debate over Shah Bano and the adoption of the Muslim Women Bill, had been orchestrated by the central government. The prime minister was seen as appeasing conservative Muslims in Parliament, by adopting the anti–Shah Bano Bill, while encouraging the project of traditionalist Hindus to put their hands on Ayodhya. Explosive gods imposed their agenda.

Hindu-Muslim enmity over the Shah Bano and Ayodhya cases escalated in communal violence in Maharashtra, Uttar Pradesh, and in Calcutta. In both the Muslim and the Hindu community, conservatives and extremists gained momentum. The secular emphasis of the Gandhis was less credible than ever. Rajiv preached secularism but legitimized Hindu and Muslim hardliners. Explosive gods led communities to a religion-driven identity. From January 1987 to July 1988, the spectacularly popular TV series *Ramayan* awakened India to the perspective of an alliance between the modern, developing country and the Hindu sources.

This was not confined within Indian borders. Also in 1987, Indian law professor at the School for Oriental and African Studies in London, Werner Menski, wrote about Hindus in Britain who adapted to the British compulsory registration of marriages while maintaining their "customary forms of marriage solemnization."[81] Allegiance to a dual set of norms was also a fruit of explosive gods. As Menski explained, "Whilst we cannot dispute that Hindus in Britain are subject to English law, there is evidence that the individuals concerned also continue to be guided by Hindu law and have been put under pressure to work out compromises between conflicting legal demands."[82]

In 1987, at the twilight of the Cold War, while Indians adorned TV sets like altars to celebrate the broadcasting of *Ramayan*, the modern avatar of their ancient epic, an English director caricaturized the divine foundation of the American crusade against communism. In his *Full Metal Jacket*, Stanley Kubrick made Gunnery Sergeant Hartman's speech to a group of marine recruits the illustration of the exploitation of God for the sake of Western global strategies:

> Hartman: Today . . . is Christmas! There will be a magic show at zero-nine-thirty! Chaplain Charlie will tell you about how the free world will conquer Communism with the aid of God and a few marines! God has a hard-on for marines because we kill everything we see! He plays His games, we play ours! To show our appreciation for so much power, we keep heaven packed with fresh souls! God was here before the Marine Corps! So you can give your heart to Jesus, but your ass belongs to the Corps! Do you ladies understand?
> Recruits: Sir, yes, sir![83]

In 1984, Desmond Tutu invoked the equality of God's children while denouncing the oppressor and standing with the oppressed. In his time Gandhi had called the

---

81. Menski, "Legal Pluralism in the Hindu Marriage," 189.

82. Ibid., 188.

83. Kubrick, dir., *Full Metal Jacket*, based on Hasford, *The Short-Timers*, 19.

untouchables "God's children." By doing so, both intended to stress that discrimination had no religious justification. Gandhi's children of God were the children of an even-handed God, commanding universal brotherhood and the equality of all human beings. After Independence, Indian politics, and religions repeatedly defeated Gandhi's vision. Untouchables learned to defend their rights through mobilization and politics of reserved seats and jobs rather than through Hindu gods. And indeed, over the 1980s, Indian explosive gods of almost any creed grew eager to ask their children to fight against the children of rival gods in the name of irreconcilable identities. This also applied to South Africa, in the deadly confrontation between white and black God's children.

The reference to "God's children" conveyed an ideal of equality and peace, but had been increasingly turned into a tool for division and enmity. Through Sergeant Hartman's Christmas speech, Stanley Kubrick emphasized how heavily this applied to Western God's children who felt legitimized to roam the world and kill in the name of Christian capitalist gods. No matter the cause, no matter the toll, explosive gods asked their Indian, South African, and British children to rise. And to fight.

Our Sin

Maputo, capital of Mozambique, April 7, 1988. Albie Sachs left his apartment dressed in a T-shirt and shorts and headed to the beach; it was a public holiday. On the way he stopped by the car and unlocked the door. "Oh shit. Everything has abruptly gone dark, I am feeling strange and cannot see anything. The beach, I am going to the beach, I packed a frosty beer for after my run, something is wrong. Oh shit, I must have banged my head."[84]

The car had blown up. The blast wave smashed all windows in the block and damaged the nearby Portuguese Embassy. A hole twelve inches deep and thirty-five inches wide was left in the tarmac. Still conscious, Albie Sachs was rushed to the hospital where his shattered right arm was amputated.

At the age of fifty-two, Sachs was a South African lawyer and a prominent member of the African National Congress. He had suffered imprisonment and torture in his country and left it in the early sixties. That morning in central Maputo he was the victim of a murder attempt. Agents of South Africa's security forces had rigged the car with an explosive device and detonator triggered by the opening of the door. In the explosion, Sachs lost not only his right arm but also his sight in one eye.

"The white foe of Pretoria," as the *New York Times* presented him the day after the blast,[85] Albie Sachs was a leading figure in the struggle to end apartheid. The son of "Solly" Sachs, a prominent communist trade-union leader, Albie Sachs was the perfect representative of a generation simultaneously divided by apartheid and the Cold War.

84. Sachs, *The Soft Vengeance of a Freedom Fighter*, 7.
85. Battersby, "White Foe of Pretoria Injured."

In his article for the *New York Times*, John D. Battersby underlined that Sachs moved to Mozambique in 1977 after the Marxist revolution, which overrode Portuguese colonial rule. At the time, he was still a member of the outlawed South African Communist Party. Since 1969, when whites were admitted for the first time, he had been a member of the African National Congress. An obvious connection pulled together his Marxist views and his opposition to racial segregation.

Since the birth of the Union of South Africa in 1910, colonialism, segregation, and capitalism formed a tight alliance. Historian Leonard Thompson underlines that in the first decades after the creation of the Union of South Africa, "whites . . . dominated every sector of the capitalist economy and did so with the use of cheap black labor."[86] According to Thompson, "the categories Race and Class coincided closely."[87] At the time of its founding in 1921, the South African Communist Party was the only organization in the country to recruit from all racial groups, and it even had a multiracial executive. The black struggle was an anticapitalist struggle. Many militants, like Albie Sachs himself, were members of both the Communist Party and the African National Congress.

Since the Marxist anticolonial revolution of 1976, Mozambique had been a communist country supported by the Soviet Union. Maputo and Pretoria, Mozambique and South Africa, represented the two hemispheres of the Cold War world. South African communists and militants of the African National Congress were welcome. For fifteen years after the takeover, civil war between the ruling Marxist party and the South-African-funded Renamo ravaged the country. Eventually, in the eighties, Mozambique started transforming into a multiparty free-market system and reached a compromise with Pretoria. When he was assaulted in April 1988, Albie Sachs was no longer a member of the South African Communist Party; he was taking an active part in the transition to a postrevolutionary socialist Mozambique while continuing to play a key role in South African affairs.

The anticapitalist struggle was deeply linked with the fight against colonialism. The house in which Thabo Mbeki, leader of the African National Congress and later president of South Africa, grew up (in the Republic of Transkei), contained "a bust of Marx on the mantelpiece and a portrait of Gandhi on the wall."[88]

The inextricable knot linking apartheid, colonialism, and the Cold War was behind the instability and violence in the area. All throughout the eighties, South African cities suffered sabotage from African National Congress guerrillas while South African forces invaded Angola and repeatedly made hit-and-run raids, not only into Mozambique, as in the case of the Albie Sachs car-bomb, but also in Lesotho, Zimbabwe, and Zambia.

---

86. Thompson, *A History of South Africa*, 155.
87. Ibid.
88. Gevisser, "ANC Was His Family."

The South African government stressed the Marxist connotation of the anti-apartheid movement, arguing that the preservation of apartheid and the fight against its opponents were justified by the capitalist free world's endeavor against international communism. Religion was mobilized to this effect. Christianity was used to legitimize both capitalism and apartheid as the two necessary sides of the same coin. The survival of civilized and wealthy South Africa was at stake. South African Christians could not compromise with black, colored, and Indian communists. White communists like Albie Sachs embodied the worst option: they were deserters, renegades.

The anti-apartheid activists were easily labeled communists, although they claimed that a fundamental line divided the African National Congress and the South African communists. Freedom fighters also rejected the accusation that the support they got from other African countries was subservient to Soviet interests in the area. In fact, many human rights militants did not feel as though their struggle against racism and segregation implied a definitive pro-Communist or procapitalist choice. Lots of them criticized capitalism without embracing either Marxism or the Soviet cause. Yet for the government, any opposition to apartheid was on the side of international communism: anti-apartheid militants were assumed to stand against national interest; and, of course, against the Christian legacy of South Africa.

The Absolute Authority of God

In the late seventies, Alex Boraine was a Methodist pastor and South African MP who opposed the regime. His brother-in-law used to rebuke him for his anti-apartheid stance, telling him, "You are a bloody communist."[89] From the time of his first election to the Parliament in 1977 for the Progressive Federal Party, Boraine challenged the government in the name of Christianity. Separation between theology and politics, he maintained, was the oxygen of apartheid. The privileged relationship of churches with the state, of Afrikaner churches in particular, also legitimized racial policies in the name of God.

In July 1987, Alex Boraine met Albie Sachs in Dakar, the capital of Senegal, when a group of mainly Afrikaans-speaking whites and blacks gathered with a delegation of the African National Congress in order to establish a common platform of action. By that time, Alex Boraine was no longer a pastor and Albie Sachs no longer a communist.

At the end of the eighties, the contribution of Marxism and religion to the fight against racial segregation in South Africa had changed. Marxism was losing momentum; those within the African National Congress who thought of the end of apartheid in terms of a Marxist revolution were decreasing in number and political influence. By contrast, religion was growing more influential. Alex Boraine anticipated in the seventies that theology had the potential to undermine the system. In South Africa

---

89. Boraine, *A Life in Transition*, 62.

at the time, Marxism seemed the most powerful source of sociopolitical inspiration, while religion appeared to be the passive accomplice of the racist state. Christianity was still a powerful legitimizing resource for racial discrimination in general, and for the system of apartheid in particular. But things changed. Over the seventies and the eighties, an increasing number of religious leaders rose against the government. The alliance between Christianity and capitalism against the common foe of communism was no longer a barrier against an anti-apartheid theology. Churches and faith communities promoted an alternative order. Social justice was central to Christianity. And on the whole, Christianity ceased backing an unequal society.

Desmond Tutu was just the tip of the iceberg. Christians and other religious communities followed Tutu's inspiration by and large. In 1986, the Nederduitse Gereformeerde Kerk, an offspring of the Dutch Reformed Church in the Netherlands that had stood as a stronghold of racial segregation, held a synod, a church council, in which it rejected the biblical foundation of racial policies. Two months after the blast in Maputo, in June 1988, twenty-four Christian leaders called for a general boycott of the upcoming racially segregated elections. Heavy intimidation ensued. On September 1, 1988, Khotso House, the headquarters of the South African Council of Churches, was destroyed by an explosion. A bomb was also set off in the headquarters of the Southern African Catholic Bishops' Conference and of the South African Council of Churches. In 1989, the Secretary General of the South African Council of Churches, the Reverend Frank Chicane, became seriously ill while on visit to the United States. He was brought to the hospital, where doctors discovered he had been poisoned by a chemical substance sprayed onto his underwear.

Since the late seventies, anti-apartheid Christian theologians and church leaders were witnessing the rise of a religious challenge to the regime. In 1979, at the dawn of explosive gods, John de Gruchy's *The Church Struggle in South Africa*[90] represented at the same time the first history of the church in South Africa, the formation of the church's alliance against the state, and the intellectual manifesto of the struggle ahead. In a powerful foreword, writer Alan Paton described the issue of Christian nationalism as "the fusion of love of nation with love of Christ,"[91] which the Afrikaner Nationalist identified with Christianity itself, and which provided for the theological justification of apartheid. In the preface de Gruchy declared he had written the book "out of the conviction that the Christian gospel contains the word of hope for present and future South Africans, irrespective of race or culture."[92] Twenty-five years later, in 2004, de Gruchy's son Steve, also a theologian, emphasized that the book "was written . . . not as an unconcerned analysis, but as a contribution to the struggle and an invitation to

---

90. De Gruchy, *The Church Struggle in South Africa*.

91. Paton, "Foreword," x.

92. De Gruchy, *The Church Struggle in South Africa*, xiv.

others to participate. In that sense John de Gruchy was not just being a historian, and not even just being a theologian—he was also being a preacher."[93]

In 1985, de Gruchy, together with Charles Villa-Vicencio, edited *Apartheid Is a Heresy*,[94] the ultimate theological challenge to the traditional understanding of church and state complicity in South Africa. The work further proved that Desmond Tutu, though unique in terms of personal charisma, was not alone in his theology.

Still, Christians were divided and the churches wary. Referring to the 1985 Kairos document, the momentous anti-apartheid statement by black theologians, Charles Villa-Vicencio would later recall that "the argument that came from black theology, the argument that came through contextual theology and those remarkable affirmations of the Kairos document, did not receive the extensive, explicit and whole-hearted support of the churches. Those were minority voices. They were a church within the church rather than the church itself."[95]

In November 1988, de Gruchy gave evidence in court in his capacity as professor of Christian studies at the University of Cape Town. Ashley Forbes and the "Cape Town Fourteen," who were on trial for terrorism, belonged to several different churches and religions. They were Muslims, Anglicans, and Lutherans; two were members of the NG Sending Kerk. Leon Scott belonged to the African Methodist Episcopal Church. Ashley Forbes was a former Anglican converted to Islam. De Gruchy was examined on the "attitude of the church to apartheid,"[96] and in particular, on the "attitude of the church to resistance to the apartheid state"[97] and on the "attitude of the church to the armed struggle."[98]

De Gruchy started by warning against the risk of generalization. He pointed out that the church was "a living organism,"[99] "a very diverse and complex institution, or set of institutions."[100] He declared that "It is not possible to generalize about the church, either to say the church is for something or the church is against something."[101]

Nevertheless, he believed, the churches' attitude toward apartheid was very clear: "I think all the churches—well, I know all the churches listed there have rejected apartheid as unjust and immoral."[102]

The expert referred to extensive documents attesting the opposition to apartheid: "[documents] have generally followed the same pattern in terms of theological

93. De Gruchy, "Postscript to the Third Edition," xxx.

94. De Gruchy and Villa-Vicencio, *Apartheid Is a Heresy*.

95. Villa-Vicencio, "God, the Devil, and Human Rights."

96. Quoted from the transcript of the evidence, courtesy of John de Gruchy, 1918.

97. Ibid.

98. Ibid.

99. Ibid., 1920.

100. Ibid., 1918.

101. Ibid.

102. Ibid., 1920.

basis, though there have been developments in that regard too, in the light of chang-es in legislation and in the history of the country. But there is extensive documenta-tion, not only of these churches, but one could here include other denominations such as the Baptist Union, and there are documents also emanating from the Dutch Reformed Church."[103]

De Gruchy underlined the difference to the eyes of Christians between the abso-lute authority of God and the relative authority of the state: "All the traditions make the point that the fact that humans are subject to authority does not give authority—does not give the state absolute authority over people. It is a relative authority, because absolute authority is God's only . . . the authorities are subject to God, and . . . there is always a higher law than the law of the state."[104]

When the witness commented on the opposition of Christians, especially the youth, to the apartheid state as a tyranny, the president of the court, Denys William-son, a Roman Catholic, objected. De Gruchy replied that he meant that the govern-ment did not provide basic necessities. The court insisted:

> Is it theologically regarded as the duty of the state to provide basic necessities?
>
> De Grouchy: What is theologically required, on the basis of moral theology, would be that the state should always act in the benefit of the people.
>
> Court: Yes, it is a pretty broad statement, obviously. Then it comes down to a value judgment.
>
> De Grouchy: Certainly. Yes.[105]

De Gruchy explained that resistance to injustice fully belonged to the mainstream Christian tradition, going back to the "just war" theory according, to which "Chris-tians may legitimately take up arms in the struggle against injustice or tyranny."[106] This even went to the extent of justifying the taking of another person's life; de Gruchy gave the English example of Cromwell and the Puritan divines arguing "on Christian grounds"[107] in favor of the death of the king. In the South African context, he further showed that the problem of armed resistance arose when the space for legal resistance was closed.

The situation was particularly resented by churches, because they had a majority of black members: "Therefore, you are not dealing with a matter that is outside of the church; you are actually dealing with a matter inside the church . . . now, the position of the church, through its official pronouncements, has been that we can understand why people are brought to that particular position, to use violence."[108]

103. Ibid., 1921.

104. Ibid., 1922.

105. Ibid., 1924–25.

106. Ibid., 1929.

107. Ibid., 1937.

108. Ibid., 1928.

The Court contested the reference to the churches' "understanding" of violence. De Gruchy explained: "Many of the people who are involved in the liberation movements and the armed struggle are members of churches . . . and therefore the churches have a pastoral responsibility towards such people."[109] De Gruchy made clear that if there was a nuance of approval or sympathy in the churches' attitude of understanding the armed struggle of their sons, this did not mean that "the churches are sympathetic to the use of violence. They are sympathetic to the—what the struggle is about—namely the ending of apartheid."[110]

In the final exchange with the judge on the issue of the proportionality of reaction against evil in Christian theology, de Gruchy stressed the importance of experience and emotions in the articulation of theological arguments. If "the use of violence against an overwhelming evil, which is experienced as violence, is morally justified,"[111] he said, this had to be placed in a specific context. Many theological documents were "written in the heat of the event"[112] and thus lacked more reflection. But, as de Gruchy stressed to the court, "in that situation, what needed to be said was what I said, and if I had qualified it, it would not have carried the moral conviction that was necessary."[113]

The explosive gods who challenged the racist state were not only Christian. The increasing consciousness that African native culture deserved praise and recognition also entailed an emphasis on the link between the anti-apartheid struggle and African religions. The Rastafari universe attracted Gareth Prince, then a student in his early twenties, because of its special connection with the original element of the land and with black consciousness as well. The Rastafari movement was deeply seated in the African culture. Its imagery, rites, and symbols belonged to Africa and opposed the colonial subjugation of Africans. Rastafarianism was a religion of the marginal, the oppressed, and the rebellious.

From his native Cape Town, the same city where Albie Sachs had been born thirty years before him, Gareth Prince started looking at the changing picture in South Africa through the mirror of Rastafarianism. He also realized that in order for a new country to rise from the ashes of racist South Africa, change in the law was necessary. To his eyes, during the early nineties, the transition to a new South Africa took the shape of a new religion and a new law. Prince experienced the first by becoming a practicing Rastafarian; the second, by entering the Law School at the University of the Western Cape.

109. Ibid., 1930.
110. Ibid., 1933.
111. Ibid., 1936–37.
112. Ibid., 1938.
113. Ibid.

Lawyers for Change

In his early twenties, Nelson Mandela experienced the combination of religion and law too. He enrolled at the South African Native College at Fort Hare. Methodist missionaries opened the college in 1916, four years after the founding of the African National Congress. It was the first college devoted to the higher education of blacks in the country. Mandela lived in John Wesley College, named after the founder of the Methodist Church. But in 1940, before the completion of studies, Mandela was expelled from Fort Hare for political activism. He was then employed as a clerk in a law firm and enrolled for a Bachelor of Laws at the Witwatersrand, which would have allowed him to become a barrister. Seven years later, he still had to pass the final year, which he had failed three times. In December 1949, he wrote to the dean of the Law Faculty, explaining his difficult living conditions and pleading to be admitted to a supplementary examination. The letter read:

> Even during the examinations I was compelled to work in order to maintain the only source of livelihood that I had. It is my candid opinion that if I had done my work under more suitable conditions I could have produced better results.[114]

The request was rejected. Mandela would never become a barrister. According to Mandela's biographer David James Smith, the dean, professor Hahle told Mandela that becoming a barrister was "beyond the ability of black people":[115] "To be a barrister, the dean had said to Mandela, you must be part and parcel of the mores and habits of the people—meaning white people—so in his opinion Mandela should really drop his personal ambitions and become a solicitor or an attorney, which did not require an LLB but a diploma in law."[116]

Indeed Nelson Mandela passed his law diploma and started practicing as an attorney in a Johannesburg white law firm in 1952. In 1953, the Mandela & Tambo law firm opened.

Albie Sachs was himself a lawyer. The Maputo car bomb in 1988 hit not only the energetic activist but also the clever legal strategist. Sachs's effectiveness in designing legal strategies scared the state. In the context of the Cold War, the confrontation between the pro- and antiapartheid militants was also made of legal technicalities, of trials and lawyers. Not dissimilarly, the struggle of the Indian minorities in Transvaal and Natal at the turn of the nineteenth century had involved Gandhi as both lawyer and political leader.

Albie Sachs was also known throughout the world as a legal scholar. Immediately after the attack in Maputo, the deans of Columbia and Harvard Law Schools issued a

---

114. Smith, *Young Mandela*, 69.

115. Ibid., 70.

116. Ibid.

statement praising Sachs's idealism, courage, and "unyielding struggle against apartheid," which "inspired thousands of American law students."[117]

With the bogus constitutional reform of 1983 proving incapable of answering the actual demand for a true constitutional change, Sachs welcomed the opportunity to combine constitutionalism and political action. While recovering from the blast, he focused on the opportunity ahead. "How many lawyers have the chance to participate both in the research leading up to the adoption of a new constitution and in the political struggles that will make its achievement possible?"[118] he wrote in his first book after the bomb of Maputo. The attack strengthened Albie Sachs's vision of the tie between the legal and the political, and it made him the living symbol of the South African transition towards the rule of law and fundamental rights. Some time after the explosion, he told a radio interviewer that if ever the person who had put the bomb in his car were to be caught, "my most fervent wish was that he or she be tried by due process of law in the ordinary civil courts, and if the evidence was not strong enough for a conviction, he be acquitted."[119]

Twenty years later, Sachs added a poignant account of the transformative value of the bomb blast.

> The bomb literally hurled me out of my legal routine, and freed me to recreate my life from the beginning. I learned to walk, to stand, to run . . . and to prepare for the writing of South Africa's new Constitution. Suddenly, joyously and voluptuously, the grand abstract phrases of the legal text books united with and embraced the palpable passion for justice of the disenfranchized. And far from the law constituting a barricade of injustice that had to be stormed and torn down for freedom to be achieved, it became a primary instrument for accomplishing peaceful revolution . . . If the process of making of a new basic law helped my country to heal itself, it also resolved my own deep internal contradiction.[120]

In the same months, another South African white lawyer stood as a protagonist in the legal struggle against apartheid. Since the early sixties, Arthur Chaskalson had been a prominent advocate in political trials. In a hostile legal environment, Chaskalson defended the rights of the accused by calling for the strict respect of procedures and the rigorous scrutiny of evidence. According to fellow human rights lawyer George Bizos, despite the dramatic conditions in which he operated, Chaskalson was

---

117. Battersby, "White Foe of Pretoria Injured."

118. Sachs, *The Soft Vengeance of a Freedom Fighter*, 147.

119. Ibid., 199.

120. Sachs, *The Strange Alchemy of Life and Law*, 3.

extremely clever in "putting pieces of evidence together,"[121] but due to his high legal ethics, he "would never make accusations when the evidence did not support them."[122]

In 1979, Chaskalson set up the Legal Resources Centre as a strategic place for enhancing the legal culture of human rights in the country. As in the case of Sachs, legal practice and scholarly work combined in the resistance against apartheid.

On April, 12, 1989, Arthur Chaskalson gave a speech at the Legal Resources Centre to celebrate its tenth anniversary. The end of apartheid still appeared distant. Chaskalson underlined the role law must have in the process. Legal roots of the apartheid regime were not only in the statutes but also in the judiciary's attitude of reverence for the legislature. Legal and political reasons converged in weakening the potential anti-apartheid role of South African judges. The Roman-Dutch tradition prevailed over the common-law heritage. The Parliament that issued the apartheid legislation was supreme. Charles Villa-Vicencio stressed the theological vision that made "the testing right of any laws of Parliament . . . a principle of the devil."[123] The South African theologian further explained that "Boer sovereignty, Afrikaner freedom was to be attributed to Divine Providence, and any talk of human rights or any talk of the Bill of Rights that violated that fundamental will of the people expressed through the vote was, indeed, a principle of the devil."[124]

South African judges were expected to obey the law and apply it in courts with no margin for discretion. Like Gandhi and Mandela before them, Sachs and Chaskalson experienced that most of the time the judiciary adhered with great zeal to the policy directives of the state. Kader Asmal, himself a barrister and later the minister of education in the 1999 Mbeki cabinet, portrayed the South African proapartheid judges as people "who craved elegance, refinement and erudition, yet who end up revealed as upholders of an appalling system, apartheid, that was a crime against humanity."[125]

Chaskalson experienced throughout his legal practice the complicity of the judiciary in the crimes of apartheid. Nevertheless, in his 1989 speech he affirmed that little could be gained "in lamenting the past,"[126] and paid tribute to the positive role played after all by South African judges in keeping alive the rule of the law:

> I believe that we will come to appreciate that we owe much to our judges, and a great deal to some of them. For despite all the paradoxes, they have somehow held to the infrastructure and have kept alive the principles of freedom and justice [that] permeate the common law. True, at times no more than lip service has been paid to these principles, and there have been landmark cases where opportunities to give substance to and uphold fundamental rights have

121. Bizos, *No One to Blame?*, 166.

122. Ibid.

123. Villa-Vicencio, "God, the Devil, and Human Rights."

124. Ibid.

125. Asmal, "Foreword," viii.

126. Chaskalson, "Law in a Changing Society," 295.

been allowed to pass without even an expression of discomfort, let alone a vindication of the right. Yet the notion that freedom and fairness are inherent qualities of law lives on, and if not reflected in all of the decisions, is nonetheless acknowledged and reinforced in numerous judgments of the courts.[127]

In his speech of 1989 at the Legal Resources Centre, Chaskalson defended the view that a neutral conception of the law was fundamental in order to achieve a successful transition to a democratic and pluralistic state. Legal philosopher David Dyzenhaus stressed how crucial the idea of "the rule of law as antipolitics"[128] was for Chaskalson: only by conceiving of the rule of law as neutrally as possible, Dyzenhaus noted, can judges "be seen to stand above the political fray of a transition, accountable only to the law."[129]

Referring to the outstanding record of Chaskalson in the sixties, Joel Joffe stressed that "he had done this as a lawyer, not as a politician, and as a personal duty, not as a protest against the state."[130] As Chaskalson, himself, recalled in 1989, the decision to launch the Legal Resources Centre ten years before had been driven by "belief in the value of law as an instrument of justice."[131]

In their quest for the best way to deal with the past, while heading towards the future, Chaskalson and Sachs faced the same conundrum churches were confronting. It was crucial for all to distinguish between the past complicity of the judiciary and the church with apartheid, on the one hand, and the present duties of judges and theologians in opening up a new phase, on the other hand. Like Sachs, Chaskalson envisaged the adoption of a new Constitution, which could bridge what was still alive in the South African rule of law to a new democratic, human-rights-based era.

Chaskalson's personal legal ethics and his vision of "law in a changing society" converged in the possibility to operate a radical change through the law. A new South Africa implied a new Constitution as well as a new judiciary. Chaskalson's speech in 1989 was all about the decisive role law could play in establishing a democratic new order in the country. In the aftermath of the assault in Maputo and notwithstanding it, Sachs was no less determined than Chaskalson to prevent the past from compromising the future. A year after the Maputo car bomb, in September 1989, a meeting was arranged in New York at Columbia University to discuss the constitution of post-apartheid South Africa. A few weeks before the fall of the Berlin Wall, the topic echoed a broader questioning of justice and law in the transition to democracy. The question arose of how to best approach those who had violated fundamental rights during the apartheid regime. A member of the African National Congress in exile suggested the violators would have to be treated like the Nazi criminals in Nuremberg.

127. Ibid.
128. Dyzenhaus, *Truth, Reconciliation and the Apartheid Legal Order*, 21.
129. Ibid., 22.
130. Joffe, *The State vs. Nelson Mandela*, 19.
131. Chaskalson, "Law in a Changing Society," 293.

The chairman, George Bizos, himself a South African lawyer and human rights activist, recognized in the audience Albie Sachs and gave him the floor. Sachs said that "calls for acts of revenge would delay the dawn of freedom."[132] Then, Bizos reported, Sachs instinctively raised his damaged arm across his chest to say, "Comrade, if I can forgive them I am sure many more will do so."[133]

On the Threshold of New Things

In April 1989, Arthur Chaskalson and his audience at the Legal Resources Centre were aware that a crucial phase had begun. Three months earlier, President Pieter Willem Botha had suffered a stroke. In June 1988, Ronald Reagan and Mikhail Gorbachev, then the presidents, respectively, of the United States and the Soviet Union, had agreed on ending the Cold War in Africa. Soviet military aid and Cuban soldiers were expected to withdraw from Angola. In exchange, South Africa was required to do the same in Namibia. In the twilight of the Cold War, the anticommunist fight no longer supported South African expansionism in Africa. Moreover, it no longer legitimated apartheid rule. Due to his poor health, President Botha could not supervise that momentous phase. In February, he resigned as the leader of the ruling National Party. In March 1989, the National Party elected de Klerk as state president.

On December, 6, 1989, Gareth Prince celebrated his twentieth birthday. In Berlin the *Mauerspechte*, the wall woodpeckers, had been carrying on with the demolition of the wall since November. Though the turning point may have ostensibly appeared to concern only those who, like East Berliners, were set free from communism, change actually reached far beyond. The entire spectrum of ideologies and strategies based on the capitalism-communism divide was undermined. The end of Nehruvian socialist India and of Thatcherite Britain coincided with the end of apartheid in South Africa. With the resignation of Margaret Thatcher, the apartheid government in Pretoria lost precious support. In turn, the struggle for freedom in South Africa inspired marginalized minorities and the underprivileged in both Britain and India.

Such a context was prepared on June 11, 1988, when the Free Mandela concert took place at Wembley, with a worldwide audience of six hundred million. Albie Sachs was also in London, recovering from the blast. He later recalled watching the concert on TV "for hours"[134] and rejoicing for the "70,000 young British people supporting our struggle and having fun at the same time."[135]

Frederick Willem de Klerk, Botha's successor as leader of the National Party, was sworn in as the new president on August 15, 1989. De Klerk led a dramatic change foreshadowed in his famous speech on February 2, 1990. The dismantling of apartheid

132. Bizos, *No One to Blame?*, 230.

133. Ibid.

134. Sachs, *The Soft Vengeance of a Freedom Fighter*, 158.

135. Ibid.

was to go well beyond the first steps taken in the eighties: the ban was lifted on the African National Congress and the South African Communist Party. The imminent release of Nelson Mandela was announced after twenty-seven years of imprisonment.

De Klerk's older brother, Willem, explained that the leader had "truly undergone a major political conversion."[136] Collapse of communism in Eastern Europe and Russia had pushed de Klerk to believe the African National Congress was no more the Trojan horse of Soviet expansionism. There was a religious side in de Klerk's realization. Willem described his brother as someone convinced that "God gives insight through human thought and emotions."[137] The crumbling of the Berlin Wall went beyond the human will. According to de Klerk, "it was as if God had taken a hand—a new turn in world history. We had to seize the opportunity."[138]

The role of the gods in the end of apartheid went well beyond the personal experience of the last white president.

From 1990, Beyers Naudé, the most prominent Afrikaner anti-apartheid churchman and theologian, started giving readings from the Bible at events of the National African Congress.

In November 1990, Christian leaders representing eighty-five different denominations met in Rustenburg, Transvaal, under the auspices of President de Klerk. The National Conference of Church Leaders in South Africa resulted in a historic moment. Theology professor Willie Jonker from the University of Stellenbosch publicly apologized on behalf of the Dutch Reformed Church for its complicity in apartheid:

> I confess before you and before the Lord, not only my own sin and guilt, and my personal responsibility for the political, social, economical, and structural wrongs that have been done to many of you, and the results [from] which you and our whole country are still suffering, but vicariously I dare also to do that in the name of the Dutch Reformed Church of which I am a member, and for the Afrikaans people as a whole. I have the liberty to do just that, because the DRC at its latest synod has declared apartheid a sin and confessed its own guilt of negligence in not warning against it and distancing itself from it long ago.[139]

Desmond Tutu, who was in the audience, took the floor to say he was touched and ready to reply "I forgive you." He then added, "That confession is not cheaply made and the response is not cheaply given."[140]

---

136. De Klerk, *F. W. de Klerk: The Man in His Time*, 55.

137. Ibid., 26.

138. Ibid., 27.

139. Jonker, "Understanding the Church Situation," 92.

140. Alberts and Chikane, *The Road to Rustenburg*, 99.

For many church members Jonker's confession sounded like betrayal. "You are the ones who taught us that apartheid was Biblical, moral, and Christian. How dare you suddenly change your minds, making sinners of us all?"[141]

The Conference issued a momentous Declaration. The transition of the country called for the responsibility of Christians: "we stand on the threshold of new things. There appears to be the possibility of a new dispensation and the promise of reconciliation between all South Africans as both black and white leaders begin to negotiate together for a new and liberated nation of equity and justice. In this context, Christians are called to be a sign of hope from God, and to share a vision of a new society, which we are prepared to strive for, and if needs be, suffer for."[142]

Church leaders gathering in Rustenburg needed a radical break with the past so that "new things" could come: "we acknowledge that this hope will elude us unless we can break completely with the past." Accordingly they issued a momentous "confession":

> As representatives of the Christian Church in South Africa, we confess our sin and acknowledge our part in the heretical policy of apartheid, which has led to such extreme suffering for so many in our land. We denounce apartheid, in its intention, its implementation, and its consequences, as an evil policy, an act of disobedience to God, a denial of the Gospel of Jesus Christ and a sin against our unity in the Holy Spirit.[143]

Confessing complicity in past injustice and atrocities opened the door to a shared, ecumenical anti-apartheid theology: "On this we are all agreed, namely the rejection of apartheid as a sin."[144]

The conference was a watershed in church-and-state relationships. Church leaders agreed upon the support of "separation of Church and State, with freedom of religion and association guaranteed equally to all."[145]

Apartheid had flourished thanks to a mixture of Afrikaner Christian legitimacy and British Christian blindness and cynicism. A Christian-based distinction between religion and politics prevented believers from attacking the system in the name of their ideals. On this specific point, the Rustenburg Declaration of 1990 included a profound apology:

> In the past we have often forfeited our right to address the State by our own complicity in racism, economic and other injustice, and the denial of human rights. We also recognize that in our country the State has often co-opted the Church. The Church has often attempted to seek protection for its own vested

141. Storey, "There Comes a Time."

142. National Conference of Churches in South Africa, *Rustenburg Declaration.*

143. Ibid.

144. Ibid.

145. Ibid.

interests from the State. Our history compromises our credibility in address-ing Church-State issues.[146]

Hanged and Burned

Church-and-state issues were not the main topic in Britain when the English pub-lisher Viking Penguin launched Salman Rushdie's *The Satanic Verses* on September 26, 1988. But massive protests among Muslims all over the world called into question in Britain how the very structure of its church-and-state relations allowed for blasphemy law to protect the established Church of England to the exclusion of any other faith, notably of Islam.

India was also involved in the mayhem around its son Salman Rushdie, the ac-claimed author of the novel on independence and partition, *Midnight's Children*. On October 5, 1988, the Indian Home Ministry banned *The Satanic Verses* on the grounds that the book was likely to offend the Indian community in its religious sentiment. The book was banned in South Africa as well. In February 1989, violent riots exploded in Pakistan. In demonstrations against the book, people died in Mumbai, Rushdie's birthplace; in Lahore; and in Kashmir. At this stage, Ayatollah Khomeini, the Supreme Leader of Iran since the revolution of 1979, stepped in. On February 14, 1989, Radio Tehran broadcast his *fatwa*:

> In the name of Him, the Highest. There is only one God, to whom we shall all return. I inform all zealous Muslims of the world that the author of the book en-titled "The Satanic Verses"—which has been compiled, printed, and published in opposition to Islam, the Prophet, and the Qur'an—and all those involved in its publication who were aware of its contents, are sentenced to death.
>
> I call on all zealous Muslims to execute them quickly, wherever they may be found, so that no one else will dare to insult the Muslim sanctities. God willing, whoever is killed on this path is a martyr.[147]

Because the book was published in London, and because Rushdie was a British resident, Britain was at the forefront of the crisis. As soon as Rushdie's volume was made available in British bookshops, news about a book offending the most cher-ished tenets of Islam spread rapidly all over the country. Muslims gathered at different places. The book was doused with paraffin and set on fire publicly for the first time on December 2, 1988, during a rally in Bolton attended by seven thousand protesters. In January 1989, the novel was "tied to a stake" in Bradford and "set alight in front of the police station."[148] Tensions in Bradford prompted high media coverage and intense de-bate. Abdul Quddas, joint secretary of the Council of Mosques in Bradford, declared

146. Ibid.
147. Malik, *From Fatwa to Jihad*, 8.
148. Ibid., ix.

to the press that "every good Muslim is after [Rushdie's] life. He has tortured Islam and has to pay the penalty. He deserves hanging."[149] W. H. Smith booksellers withdrew the book from public display in Bradford. On May 27, 1989, more than fifteen thousand protesters gathered in Parliament Square in London, calling for the book to be banned and the author and the publisher prosecuted. Rushdie's effigy was hanged and burned.

Ever since the publication in 1981 of *Midnight's Children*, Salman Rushdie had stirred deep controversies. The principal character of that book, Saleem Sinai, lived in India during the Emergency and was sterilized in a general vasectomy campaign, a reference to the involvement of Indira Gandhi's son Sanjay in a similarly disastrous program. Saleem Sinai's foe was named the Widow, a clear and unflattering reference to Indira Gandhi herself, who sued Rushdie for defamation in the British courts. The case was settled extrajudicially not long before Indira's murder, when Salman Rushdie agreed to amend the book. However, the Indian debate on censorship was renewed in 1983, when Rushdie's novel *Shame* was immediately banned in Pakistan for allegedly insulting Zulfikar Ali Bhutto and General Muhammad Zia-ul-Haq.

Britons were used to religious tensions in the former colonies, especially in the Indian subcontinent. They were familiar with the conflict setting Catholics and Protestants against one another in Ireland. Religious divides were very much part of British history.

Also, after ten years under the government of Margaret Thatcher, social conflicts were no surprise. Since the Brixton riots in 1981, the symbol of the breakdown in racial relations, it had become conventional wisdom that ethnic tensions were an inevitable issue of contemporary Britain.

But now, with *The Satanic Verses*, something new was happening. The UK Action Committee on Islamic Affairs was created immediately after the launch of the book in September 1988. Muslims were gathering and protesting in the streets. Those who expressed their genuine anger were neither Arabs nor Indians—nor were they Pakistanis or Egyptians or Iranians; they were Muslims: Muslims capable of unity, visibility, and common action. Immediately after the burning of the book in Bradford, Sher Azam, the chairman of the Bradford Council of Mosques, commented, "We used to have questions about who we are and where we were going. Now we know. We've found ourselves as Muslims. There are action committees in every city up and down the country. It's bringing us together. Muslims are becoming much more united."[150]

This was something new to the British public. This was new to the Muslims themselves. They discovered a different identity, and experienced the potential for a network they were hardly aware of. The use of terms like *fatwa* and *sharia* meant that an alternative normative order was available to express an alternative collective identity.

Confronted with the Rushdie crisis, British Muslims sought a political solution by turning to the Thatcher's administration. One month after the launch of the book,

149. Rule, "Khomeini Urges Muslims to Kill Author of Novel," A-10.

150. Malik, *From Fatwa to Jihad*, 29.

on October 20, 1988, the Union of Muslim Organisations of the UK urged the British government to ban *The Satanic Verses* on grounds of blasphemy.

Blasphemy was well known as a crime to Christians, and it was a punishable criminal offense to the British legal system. But were blasphemy laws applicable to Islam too? No precedents seemed to back the use of blasphemy laws to prevent *The Satanic Verses* from circulating. Blasphemy law had been shaped over the centuries in order to protect Christians, and especially the established Church of England; legal action, therefore, appeared likely to fail. Muslim leaders approached the government and the Parliament asking for the law to be amended.

The Best Armor

A few days after Khomeini's *fatwa*, on February 24, 1989, Home Secretary Douglas Hurd delivered a speech at the Central Mosque in Birmingham. He acknowledged British Muslims were "grieved and hurt"[151] by the book. But he drew the line between legitimate protest and unlawful violence or threat of violence: "the law gives you the freedom to express your protests, peacefully and with dignity . . . British Muslims are entitled to speak out in defence of their religious faith and to protest about a book which they believe denigrates and insults the Prophet of Islam. But to turn such protests towards violence or the threat of violence is wholly unacceptable."[152]

A Muslim British citizen resident in London, thirty-five-year-old Abdul Hussain Choudhury realized that complaining to the government was useless. Legal action seemed to him a better option. Explosive gods urged to be tried and heard.

The following month, on March 13, 1989, he applied to the Chief Metropolitan Magistrate of London at Bow Street Magistrates, asking for the author and the publisher of *The Satanic Verses* to be summoned and charged with blasphemy. Abdul Choudhury alleged that *The Satanic Verses* was "a blasphemous libel concerning Almighty God (Allah),"[153] which heavily offended Islam on no less than six counts. First, God was described as "The Destroyer of Man." Second, the prophet Abraham, Ibrahim, was vilified. Third, Muhammad was called by the name *Mahound*, a word suggesting a demonic influence. Fourth, some prostitutes were named as Muhammad's wives. Fifth, the companions of Muhammed were grossly insulted and called "some sort of bums from Persia" and "clowns." Sixth, Islam was ridiculed as an exaggeratedly normative religion.

Choudhury's arguments made sense in legal terms. But they concerned more the form than the substance. Instead *The Satanic Verses* attacked the very substance of Islam in particular and of religion in general.

---

151. Hazarika, "Twelve Die in Bombay," 3.

152. Ibid.

153. *R v Chief Metropolitan*, 429.

In his 1984 essay "Outside the Whale," Rushdie explained his belief that the interplay of literature with politics and history was unavoidable in a world lacking "not only hiding places, but certainties."[154] Now *The Satanic Verses* pointed at the clash between religion and modernity as it unfolded at the end of the eighties on the eve of the collapse of the Berlin Wall. The book exposed the explosive gods' defiance. Though deeply personal, religious sensitivities were increasingly collective. They shaped confronting identities. They fed conflicts. Rushdie exalted the new power of faith, denominations, and religions, but also underlined how threatening the immensely creative individual experience of faith might be for traditions and identities. This point of substance in the book—not the shocking but superficial reference to prostitutes and clowns—encapsulated Rushdie's provocation. In the context of the rising religious challenge to secular and multireligious Britain, he announced a new era. He exalted the fragility and the power of contemporary religion simultaneously. This was his true blasphemy.

Rushdie attacked Islam and religion. He attacked secular certainties too. By doing so, he shook society. Debate and unrest ensued. Alleged blasphemy could not be disjointed from alleged sedition. Consistently, Abdul Choudhury not only pointed to *The Satanic Verses* as a blasphemous book, but he also alleged it was a seditious libel, "in that it raised widespread discontent and disaffection among Her Majesty's subjects."[155]

Choudhury's counsel, Ali Mohammad Azhar, emphasized the point: the book "had created hostility between different classes or sections of Her Majesty's subjects, namely, between British Muslims who are against the publication of the book, on the one hand, and on the other, non-Muslim British citizens who are in favor of the publication of the book on the basis of freedom of opinion or expression."[156]

Diplomatic tensions between UK and Muslim countries, in particular the breakdown of diplomatic relations between the UK government and Iran, were also produced as evidence of the book's seditious character.

On March 13, 1989, the Chief Metropolitan Stipendiary Magistrate, Sir David Hopkin, refused to issue summonses on the grounds that the common-law offense of blasphemy protected Christians only, and that no convincing evidence had been given of the seditious character of the book.

Choudhury sought judicial review, and his application was admitted on June 19, 1989. Two weeks earlier, on June 3, after eleven days in a hospital, Ayatollah Khomeini had died of a heart attack.

Before the competent Queen's Bench Division could give its judgment on Choudhury's appeal, the UK government took a more articulated position on the British Muslims' request that *The Satanic Verses* be banned. On July 4, 1989, John Patten, minister of state at the Home Department, wrote to a group of influential British

---

154. Rushdie, "Outside the Whale," 137.

155. *R v Chief Metropolitan*, 429.

156. Ibid., 432.

Muslims. The amendment of the common law of blasphemy was deemed impossible. Agreement lacked "over whether the law should be reformed or repealed":[157] in such conditions, John Patten clarified that "an alteration in the law could lead to a rush of litigation which would damage relations between faiths."[158]

Explosive gods challenged the very structure of British common law. John Patten defended an ideal separation of faith from politics and the law. "I hope you can appreciate,"[159] he wrote to the Muslim leaders, "how divisive and how damaging such litigation might be, and how inappropriate our legal mechanisms are for dealing with matters of faith and individual belief."[160]

Faith and belief had no place in the law. "Legal mechanisms" were "inappropriate for dealing" with creeds. The Christian yielding to the logic of a secular society and free religious market was the best example. "Indeed," the minister explained, "the Christian faith no longer relies on"[161] the law of blasphemy, "preferring to recognize that the strength of their own belief is the best armor against mockers and blasphemers."[162]

British Christians felt less and less attached to denominations and faith-based claims. They felt comfortable in British secular society. But British Muslims were ready to fight in order for Islam not to melt and dissolve in post-Christian secular Britain. Political scientist Tariq Modood made this point in a comment published in April 1990:

> The Rushdie affair is not about the life of Salman Rushdie, nor freedom of expression—let alone Islamic fundamentalism, or book burning, or Iranian interference in British affairs. The issue is of the rights of non-European religious and cultural minorities in the context of a secular hegemony. Is the Enlightenment big enough to legitimize the existence of pre-Enlightenment religious enthusiasm, or can it only exist by suffocating all who fail to be overawed by its intellectual brilliance and vision of Man?[163]

Visions of Ecstasy

Tensions in Britain did not involve only Muslims and alien religions. The recasting of Christianity in a secularized, postmodern culture came constantly into play. On September 18, 1989, two months after minister of state John Patten's statement that "Christian faith no longer relies on" the law of blasphemy, the British Board of Film Classification refused a classification certificate for the video work *Visions of Ecstasy*,

157. *Wingrove* [29].
158. Ibid.
159. Ibid.
160. Ibid.
161. Ibid.
162. Ibid.
163. Modood, "British Asian Muslims and the Rushdie Affair," 160.

on the grounds that it depicted the figure of Jesus Christ in an outrageous manner and thus was likely to violate blasphemy law. The eighteen-minute video by director Nigel Wingrove focused on Saint Teresa of Avila, the sixteenth-century Carmelite well known for her ecstatic experiences. Centered on an ambiguous intermingling of eroticism and ecstasy in the relationship between Saint Teresa and Jesus Christ, the video was later described by the European Court of Human Rights as follows:

> one sees the body of Christ, fastened to the cross which is lying upon the ground. St. Teresa first kisses the stigmata of his feet before moving up his body and kissing or licking the gaping wound in his right side. Then she sits astride him, seemingly naked under her habit, all the while moving in a motion reflecting intense erotic arousal, and kisses his lips. For a few seconds, it appears that he responds to her kisses . . . Finally, St. Teresa runs her hand down to the fixed hand of Christ and entwines his fingers in hers. As she does so, the fingers of Christ seem to curl upwards to hold with hers, whereupon the video ends.[164]

The British Board of Film Classification conformed to a traditional understanding of blasphemy. The video offended the image of Jesus Christ and thus was blasphemous: "if the male figure were not Christ, the problem would not arise."[165] As the Board itself explained, the rejection was not based on the filmed action but on the characters involved:

> Because the wounded body of the crucified Christ is presented solely as the focus of, and at certain moments a participant in, the erotic desire of St. Teresa, with no attempt to explore the meaning of the imagery beyond engaging the viewer in an erotic experience, it is the Board's view, and that of its legal advisers, that a reasonable jury properly directed would find that the work infringes the criminal law of blasphemy.[166]

On December 23, 1989, by a majority of three to two, a panel of the Video Appeals Committee dismissed the appeal against the denial of the certificate on the grounds that the video was "contemptuous of the divinity of Christ."[167] The outcome was the same, but the Board made it explicit that although blasphemy was an offense relating only to Christianity, the Board was ready to apply it to any other religion. The Board's director commented that "although the Board's decision was based upon its view that the video is blasphemous (blasphemy being an offence which relates only to the Christian religion), it would take just the same stance if it were asked to grant a Certificate to a video which, for instance, was contemptuous of Mohammed or Buddha."[168]

164. *Wingrove* [9].
165. Ibid. [13].
166. Ibid.
167. Ibid. [19].
168. Ibid. [17].

In its decision, the British Board of Film Classification dismissed the views of the government. Blasphemy law was indeed applied as a means to protect Christianity, contrary to what minister of state John Patten had affirmed two months before. In the decision of the Video Appeals Committee, the government was disowned again in its view that blasphemy needed not be extended to Islam, for the Board declared its readiness to apply blasphemy law to any creed.

No judicial review in the UK was available to Nigel Wingrove after the second decision by the Video Appeals Committee. Thus he resorted to the European Court of Human Rights. On June 18, 1990, he addressed the Court, asking it to "produce a judgment which declares the British blasphemy laws as unnecessary in theory as they are in practice in any multi-cultural democracy."[169] The European Court of Strasbourg was asked to rule against Britain, but this in conformity with what the British government itself had stated a few months before, in the wake of the Rushdie affair.

The paradox reflected the inherent ambiguities of the shift from *your* gods to *our* gods. If equality among creeds was a growing issue, if antireligious criticism was increasingly baffling, the British witnessed the resistance of *your* gods and the crumbling of the ambition to make secular and multireligious Britain the successful champion of *our* gods.

Muslims of Good Character

The contention between Choudhury's and Rushdie's counsels, and the eventual dismissal of Choudhury's appeal a few months later on April 9, 1990, translated into legal arguments the clash between secular and religious Britain, between Christian and Muslim Britain.

Rushdie's lawyers emphasized the limited scope of blasphemy laws and recalled previous fruitless attempts to amend it. The July 1989 letter from the minister of state at the Home Department was produced as a milestone. Accusations depicting *The Satanic Verses* as a seditious libel were adamantly dismissed. "The crime of sedition is committed by the publication of words with a seditious intent,"[170] Rushdie's counsel pointed out. "The gist of this intention is the determination violently to disturb constituted authority."[171] Thus they concluded, "the raising of discontent among citizens and the promotion of class hatred are not in themselves unlawful, unless they are done with a seditious intent."[172] It was crucial for Rushdie's counsel to draw the line between the victim, Salman Rushdie himself, and the perpetrators, violent protesters:

169. Ibid. [34].
170. *R v Chief Metropolitan*, 433.
171. Ibid.
172. Ibid.

there have been violent demonstrations, and threats of murderous violence, against the author and publishers of *The Satanic Verses*. But it is a fundamental principle that persons who are acting lawfully cannot be held responsible for the unlawful and violent acts of others which are directed against them.[173]

Rushdie's counsel, Geoffrey Robertson, also adhered to the exclusivist protection of Christian feelings under blasphemy law. Ironically, Rushdie defended his right to expression by legitimizing unequal treatment of Muslims and Christians. As far as blasphemy law was limited to Christianity, Rushdie's counsel argued, it was under control. Its application was fair and precise. The extension to other religions would create a legal monster. Together with his colleagues, Geoffrey Robertson argued:

> Many religions or religious practices deserve criticism or ridicule in the sharpest terms, even though this may be insulting to their adherents. Some such practices have been prohibited by Parliament. The English courts would have no competence to decide what were the practices of religions other than Christianity and whether what has been written or said outraged that religion.[174]

Since we do not know of them, we cannot protect them. This was a sound argument in 1990. An argument Rushdie could subscribe to, while championing the cause of freedom of expression. As a matter of fact, equality and nondiscrimination were not absolute truths. The extension of blasphemy law to other religions, argued Robertson, would, in the end, "encourage intolerance, divisiveness and unreasonable interference with freedom of expression."[175]

Lord Justice Watkins gave the judgment for the Queen's Bench Division, together with Lord Justice Stuart Smith and Justice Roch on April 9, 1990. Watkins mentioned the book had been banned in several countries, including India and South Africa, and listed the alleged reasons why the book was deemed blasphemous, adding that according to the applicant, "insult was added to injury by the liberal use of an offensive four letter word."[176]

"There are two million of that faith here,"[177] Justice Watkins stated, and seemed almost surprised that problems could rise with that community "of good character"[178] in the United Kingdom: "Muslims, otherwise of good character, have been arrested and convicted of offences against public order arising out of those demonstrations, in particular where the demonstrations by Muslims against the book have encountered groups demonstrating in favor of the book."[179]

173. Ibid., 434.
174. Ibid., 434–35.
175. Ibid., 435.
176. Ibid., 437.
177. Ibid.
178. Ibid.
179. Ibid.

Justice Watkins acknowledged the transformation of Britain into a multireligious country, and the anger of British Muslims for what they perceived as an outrageous attack. Like many English judges before him—as well as parliamentary commissions and Law reports—the judge conceded that reform of blasphemy law was probably necessary. But in which direction? Was it better to abolish the offense or to extend it to all faiths? Following the opinion given in 1985 in the "Criminal Law Report on Offences against Religion and Public Worship," Justice Watkins agreed with the opinion of Anthony Lester, counsel for Viking Penguin, against the extension of the scope of the offense. The judge gave the following summary of his own position:

> If the offence is extended to cover attacks upon religious doctrines, tenets, commandments, or practices of religions other than Christianity, the existence of such an extended law of blasphemy would encourage intolerance, divisiveness, and unreasonable interference and interferences with freedom of expression. Fundamentalist Christians, Jews, or Muslims could then seek to invoke the offence of blasphemy against each others' religions, doctrines, tenets, commandments, or practices; for example, for denying the divinity of Jesus Christ; or for denying that the Messiah has yet to come; or for denying the divine inspiration of the Prophet Mohammed, and so on. An extended law of blasphemy, which applied to all religions, could be used as a weapon between Protestants and Roman Catholics in Northern Ireland, or by fringe religions, such as the Church of Scientology.[180]

Joining Viking Penguin's counsel, Justice Watkins expressed his opinion outright. Better to abolish the offense than to extend it and risk triggering more tensions and conflicts. "Extending the law of blasphemy would pose insuperable problems and would be likely to do more harm than good,"[181] he insisted. This was his position in the debate on how to change the law. But his duty was to apply the law as it was; as he made clear, "it is in that circumstance the function of Parliament alone to change the law."[182] Thus the strict application of the law led Justice Watkins to dismiss the application. The offense of blasphemy did not apply, since the book did not touch upon Christianity. And as the book was not meant to attack, obstruct, or undermine public authority, the offense of sedition did not apply either. Choudhury was wrong and Rushdie right. *The Satanic Verses* was free to carry on strengthening its best-selling sales figures.

She Will Listen

Three months after the decision on Choudhury, another case concerning Salman Rushdie exploded when, on July 17, 1990, the British Board of Film Classification

180. Ibid., 451.
181. Ibid., 452.
182. Ibid., 447.

rejected the application for a certificate allowing the Pakistani film *International Guerillas* to be projected in British theaters.

A typical product of Indo-Pak cinema, following the formula of revenge movies, the film portrayed a group of Muslim heroes after Salman Rushdie's life. Rushdie was depicted as the Punjabi villain, an international gangster who lived protected on an island among palm trees and swimming pools, and plotted for the destruction of as many Muslim lives as possible. At some point, Rushdie was seen killing Muslims with slashes from a curved sword and then wiping the blood on his handkerchief and sniffing it. When he managed to kidnap a Muslim woman, Rushdie conceived the worst possible torture and forced her to listen to an audio recording of his *Satanic Verses* time and again: "lay the tape of my book to her, those Satanic verses which Muslims consider a sin to repeat. She will listen to those verses, and listen to them all night."[183]

In the film the heroes were repeatedly defeated in their attempts to neutralize Rushdie. A devil, Rushdie could not be killed by humans. In the end, the Quran appeared from the heavens to strike Rushdie's hands, feet, and breast with lightning bolts until, finally, he was incinerated, for "God himself is the protector of the book which holds no room for doubt."[184]

Discussion among the examiners of the British Board of Film Classification was indicative of the anxieties and dilemmas of the time. The only Pakistani and practicing Muslim examiner expressed both his personal apprehension and the awareness the Board was facing a momentous decision, with the film being "perhaps as stern a test of the British Board of Film Classification examiner body's skill and integrity and ability to be objective as there ever will be."[185]

"In years to come," another examiner wrote in his report, "historians will (I hope) have access to examiners' reports on this video."[186]

Perception of the stakes, with the real Rushdie still badly threatened, led the majority of the examiners to stand for the rejection of the demand. One examiner made this particularly explicit: "This is the one time where our decision at the Board is going to concretely matter. We cannot pass this film, or we are in peril of not only being appallingly hypocritical, but cowardly as well. How would any of us feel if we were Salman Rushdie? Very, very fed up, I should think, and [he] could well do without feeling abandoned as well. Reject."[187]

Another examiner expressed the same paramount concern for Rushdie's position:

---

183. British Board of Film Classification. File *International Guerillas*. The file, including a transcript of the film and other documents, was reviewed by the author on August 16, 2011. The film is available on DVD. (See the bibliography.)

184. Ibid.

185. Ibid.

186. Ibid.

187. Ibid.

"A man lives in fear of his life because of this religious mania. Anything [that] so clearly incites violence against his person for what he has done perfectly legally and morally, and then invents generally-accepted-as-criminal acts, which he never committed, is especially reprehensible, illicit, and almost certainly illegal and actionable. This, in all conscience, must be a reject."[188]

Yet another examiner took the same pro-Rushdie stance from a peculiar, autobiographical British Indian perspective:

> I feel for Mr. Rushdie, as one who, for four years of my childhood, lived under the threat of death—my father was no. two on an assassination list drawn up by fighters for Indian independence, as also were his family. I also feel for those less famous Indians, Sikhs and Muslims who have already suffered and may in the future suffer abuse, injury or death for their political beliefs, or merely for being Indians, Sikhs, and Muslims.[189]

Other examiners shared the rejection, but expressed a more nuanced position. One underlined that British Muslims felt loyally "bound by British law." Three underlined that the failure of the guerrillas and the need for an ultimate intervention from God were the not-altogether-intolerant true message of the film. As one examiner wrote, "Good and true men may attempt to eliminate the blasphemer, Salman Rushdie, but in the end, God and only God will carry out the execution. The good people, therefore, must concentrate on prayer as demonstrated in the film, calling on the prophets to bring God to their rescue."[190]

Another examiner concurred: "The film's only saving grace is that the final message seems to be, 'leave it to Allah to kill Rushdie for you. Just pray.' Not much of a mitigation, but at least we don't see the guerrillas carrying out the fatwa."[191]

In this, the Muslim reading echoed medieval Christianity, as one examiner pointed out:

> Evil is ubiquitous. Man may attempt to destroy it but cannot. Only Allah can, aided and abetted by the honorifics. And this was also the message of the Medieval Mystery plays and moral interludes, at a time when the Bible informed the lives and politics of the English. In them, too, evil was comic, attractive even, but that as the hook to draw audiences into the entertainment, which would then propound the appropriate morality. God, the Virgin, and the saints were the conquerors of evil, mankind the interceders. So, too, in the present film. The prayers of the good are answered; evil is burnt out root and branch.[192]

188. Ibid.
189. Ibid.
190. Ibid.
191. Ibid.
192. Ibid.

Two more examiners stressed that this was all about the clash between Britain, "a secular democracy"[193] as one of the two wrote, and an intolerant and alien religious view. Prescient of the clash-of-civilizations rhetoric, one examiner simplified the two fronts and formulated the challenge of explosive gods in the following terms:

> Why should one set of cultures and values have to digest and readily accept the other? Regard for the Individual and his rights of free literary expression in one culture stands alongside a respect for the word of the Prophet, of religion, of God. Who is to judge the worthier or mightier tradition? Is it to be the Individual versus God? The Muslim population in Britain has to live with the uncomfortable fact that within a British framework, the Satanic book cannot be banned, as it does not violate any law. However unfortunate the anomaly over the blasphemy law continues to be. In a sense the book is for western consumption, just as this video is for consumption purely within the limits of an Urdu-speaking Muslim community.[194]

The decision to ban the film was not unanimous. Some examiners believed the prevailing argument had to be based on consistency in upholding freedom of expression. One examiner wanted the film to be allowed in order not "to exacerbate an alienation and hostility that already exists,"[195] while demonstrating that there was "a robustness within British society that will take criticism, however distorted, of its current icons."[196] Another member of the board put forward the need not to create "a sense of resentment that British society protects apostasy but disregards their sense of affront, while at the same time legally condemning blasphemy against Christianity."[197] Another examiner stated the rejection "would only confirm every suspicion that exists in the minds of a disaffected minority that the Crusades have been effectively revived with their HQ in 3 Soho Square."[198]

Extreme criticism came from a fourth examiner: "By banning this video we have acted as intolerantly as those who demanded Rushdie's death. *Satanic Verses* was deliberately satirical and offensive—and why not? This video responds in like manner—and the novelist would have been the first to defend its release."[199]

On July 25, 1990, the ban was appealed by the British distributor of the film before the Video Appeals Committee of the British Board. The appeal came on the grounds that "any reasonable viewer"[200] of *International Guerillas* "would not understand the video to be libellous of Salman Rushdie given the grossly exaggerated and

193. Ibid.
194. Ibid.
195. Ibid.
196. Ibid.
197. Ibid.
198. Ibid.
199. Ibid.
200. Ibid.

melodramatic nature of the work, which is unmistakably an entertainment, and which was intended to be so by its producer."[201]

On August 15, 1990, Rushdie's counsels sent a statement by the novelist to be placed before the Appeals Committee, asking for the ban to be lifted and the certificate delivered.

From the outset, Rushdie declared himself, "as a writer,"[202] opposed "in principle to the use of the archaic criminal laws of blasphemy, sedition, and criminal libel against creative works, whether by way of prosecution of their producers or distributors or as an excuse for imposing censorship by way of prior restraint."[203]

Rushdie had no doubts about the abusive content of a film that "quite plainly"[204] vilified him: "I have viewed the film *International Guerillas* (in Urdu, which I speak) which portrays me as a murderer and as a sadist. The producers of this film claim that my good name has already been so vilified as to make the issue of defamation irrelevant. This is manifestly untrue."[205]

However, the writer did not wish to seek "the dubious protection of censorship,"[206] which he considered to be "usually counter-productive"[207] and likely to "exacerbate the risks which it seeks to reduce":[208] "The truth is that I have more confidence than the BBFC (whose submissions I have read) in the ability of the film's audience, non-Muslims as well as Muslims, to recognize this film for the distorted, incompetent piece of trash that it is, and to understand that the 'Salman Rushdie' character is ludicrously unlike the real me."[209]

Hence Rushdie declared he did not wish "to take any legal action against the film's distributors"[210] and he was "in favor of this film being certified for open video sale,"[211] full disclosure of the film being, he wrote, "the surest way of revealing its shabbiness and of preventing it from becoming a "cause celebre."[212] He concluded that the banning of *International Guerillas*, "however well intended, can only damage the process of reconciliation, and I urge the Appeal Committee to reverse the existing ban."[213]

As a result, on August 29, 1990, the film was classified as suitable for viewing only by people at least eighteen years old.

201. Ibid.
202. Ibid.
203. Ibid.
204. Ibid.
205. Ibid.
206. Ibid.
207. Ibid.
208. Ibid.
209. Ibid.
210. Ibid.
211. Ibid.
212. Ibid.
213. Ibid.

Resourceful Mr. Azhar

The Rushdie affair awakened Britain to the explosive gods who attacked both the secular and the multireligious character of British society. At the end of Thatcher's decade in power, creeds were not just folklore reminiscent of a dead and buried past. The public dimension of faith could not be ignored. The disruptive potential of religious conflicts could not be disregarded. The task to replace *your* gods with *our* gods looked harder than ever.

In facing the explosive gods, Britain was not an island. Links established by the history of the British Empire had an impact on then-current relations between the British, Indians, and South Africans.

The Rushdie affair prompted a new look at the age of the British Empire and its legacy. Rushdie's "midnight's children" were the children of freedom and independence from domination and exploitation. But the legacy of the British Empire was also about continuity between imperial policies and postcolonial states. Long after independence, Indian midnight's children were still the children of religious divisiveness, of bloodbaths, and of the long-lasting effects of partition.

Decades after its dissolution, the British Empire still maintained transnational interactions. Strong ties continued to bind the three countries. On February 11, 1990, two weeks before the hearings of the case against Rushdie and Viking Penguin, Britons and Indians joined millions all over the world by tuning in to watch the live broadcast of Nelson Mandela's release from Victor Verster Prison in Paarl.

In order to attack Rushdie in court, Choudhury's counsel, a Mr. Azhar, emphasized the tie between contemporary Britain and the former British Empire. The making of a multireligious British Empire had turned Britain itself into a multireligious country. Mr. Azhar argued that English courts had to "adapt the common law of blasphemy to changing circumstances of society."[214] Contemporary, multireligious Britain, he underlined, was inevitably bound by the multireligious erstwhile British Empire, in particular by its legacy:

> The British empire included 200 million Muslims in India. It is inconceivable that, while a Christian had protection for his faith against insult, a Muslim had not. Blasphemy originated in the common law. The same law applied to all citizens and subjects of the British empire. In India and Pakistan the common law still obtains. It cannot be imagined that in those countries a Christian would be allowed to desecrate a mosque.[215]

The English judiciary did not buy into the argument. Choudhury's claim was dismissed. On July 11, 1990, Mr. Azhar was refused leave to appeal to the House of Lords. He then filed a suit to the European Court of Human Rights. British public opinion

214. *R v Chief Metropolitan*, 431.
215. Ibid.

and politics were discussing the place for the UK in a tighter European integration. The adhesion to the Treaty of Maastricht lay ahead. The decision on the case of *The Satanic Verses*—as well as on the case of *Visions of Ecstasy*—did not belong exclusively to the British judiciary any longer. Europe mattered. Europe had a say. Justice Watkins for the Queen's Bench Division was well aware of this and carefully justified his dismissal in light of the European Convention of Human Rights. In its decision on March 5, 1991, the European Commission of Strasbourg focused on religious freedom and declared the application inadmissible on the grounds that no evidence had been given of the direct interference "in the applicant's freedom to manifest his religion or belief."[216] Vilification of religion was deemed irrelevant as far as it did not impinge on the strict sphere of the freedom to manifest one's religion or belief.

The "resourceful"[217] Mr. Azhar, as Justice Watkins described him, was defeated. Freedom of expression prevailed. Blasphemy laws could not and should not be extended as to protect Islam.

The process would be completed twenty years later with the demise of blasphemy in the common law of England and Wales in 2008. In taking blasphemy law as a useful tool to arbitrate religious differences, Abdul Choudhury and his counsel Ali Mohammad Azhar were wrong. But in anticipating the twenty-year struggle to come with hatred speech and defamation of religion, especially of Islam, in secularized societies, and in awakening Britain to the post-1979 explosive gods, they were to be proven utterly right.

The traditional church-and-state fabric was challenged in both South Africa and Britain. It was easier in South Africa to discern the fruits of the explosive gods' transformational energy. This was about confessing "our sin" for the past and about preparing a future through national reconciliation and the transition to democracy. In Britain, explosive gods were blurred. They had no sin to confess, and no big ideals to stand for. They were reluctant to take responsibility for the past, and they were not ready to prepare the future. For both countries, India served as a template, with explosive gods showing the potential for either the best or the worse impact on social stability and advancement.

The Future of the Past

On September 3, 1992, a marriage was celebrated in Delhi before the Mufti Mohammed Tayyeb Qasmi. The groom was registered as Mohammed Carim Gazi, of 7 Bank Enclave, Delhi. The bride was described as Henna Begum, of D-152 Preet Vihar, Delhi. The witness, the bride's brother, Kapil, put his signature in English on the certificate.

That day changed the life of Sushmita Ghosh.

---

216. *Choudhury*, [2] the law.
217. *R v Chief Metropolitan*, 448.

Ostensibly the marriage did not concern the lady. She had married Shri G. C. Ghosh according to Hindu rites in 1984. No apparent connection existed between the two couples, other than Delhi itself, for indeed both the Muslim marriage between Mohammed Carim Gazi and Henna Begum in 1992 and the Hindu wedding between Sushmita and Shri Ghosh in 1984 had been celebrated in Delhi.

But a link between the two couples did exist, and it was substantial. Sushmita knew that only too well. Five months before, on April 1, 1992, her husband, Shri Ghosh, had announced he was going to leave. For him, their marriage was over. A divorce by mutual consent was the best solution for both, Shri argued. This was no April Fool's Day joke. He was going to marry another woman very soon.

Sushmita was not ready to give up. She knew that, legally, she could not be forced. Under Hindu law, her marriage was valid. Conditions were not fulfilled for a divorce to be imposed upon her. But she knew what her husband had in mind. He would convert to Islam and consider that his conversion automatically dissolved his Hindu marriage with Sushmita.

Both Sushmita's father and aunt tried to convince Shri to desist. They proved unsuccessful. He was adamant: he had already made plans to marry Vinita Gupta, a divorcee with two children. The wedding was scheduled for the upcoming summer.

In June 1992, Shri officially converted to Islam. The office of the Maulana Qari Mohammad Idris, called the *Shahi Qazi*, issued a certificate of the conversion on June 17, 1992. Sushmita immediately filed a petition to the Supreme Court asking the judges to stop her husband's second marriage, scheduled for July 10, 1992.

The day before the celebration, on July 9, 1992, Justice Venkatachaliah for the Supreme Court announced that if during the pendency of Sushmita's petition, Shri G. C. Ghosh proceeded to contract a second marriage while lacking the legal capacity to do so, such a marriage would be void. The wedding was rescheduled.

One week later, the Supreme Court took up the case. But before the judgement, the marriage was celebrated anyway on September 3, 1992, in Delhi, before the Mufti Mohammed Tayyeb Qasmi—on the same day, at the same place, and with the same Mufti as for the marriage between Mohammed Carim Gazi and Henna Begum. In fact it was the same marriage. Mohammed Carim Gazi was the new Muslim name of Shri G.C. Ghosh; Henna Begum was the new Muslim name of his lover, Vinita Gupta.

Heavy consequences awaited Sushmita. She lost her husband after having "happily lived"[218] with him for eight years, as she submitted in the application to the Court. She underwent "great mental trauma."[219] She lost financial support as well. She was thirty-four and unemployed.

218. *Lily Thomas*, 234 [2].
219. Ibid., 235 [2].

You Keep Your Religion

Mohandas Gandhi fought the theological justification for oppression of women while opposing Westernization. Indian nationalists saw abuse and discrimination of Indian women as a legacy of oppressive colonialism and backward traditions. The dilemma was still there at the time of explosive gods. If the past forged the chains that kept Indian women prisoners of a hostile society, it also conveyed the tools for liberation. How to give the past a future compatible with the dignity and rights of Indian women: this was the question now.

The *purdah*, the curtain isolating the women's quarters in the house, encapsulated the ambivalent past. If the purdah denoted seclusion and inferiority, it was also the symbol of women's protection and prerogatives. Colonialists simplified the picture in order to make sense of it. For the most refined among British observers, the oppression of Indian women went together with the oppression of Indians in general. In his *Passage to India* of 1924 E. M. Forster made the Muslim character of Dr. Aziz the example of the Indian fighter for both independence and the dignity of women. "The purdah must go . . . otherwise we shall never be free,"[220] said Dr. Aziz, who maintained "that India would not have been conquered if women, as well as men, had fought at Plassy"[221] when the British took control of India in 1757.

Accentuating customary gender inequalities, the strict colonial construction of religious laws made the conjugal status of women more rigid. Both repudiation under Islamic law and marriage dissolution under Hindu law often left women with no support or protection. On the other hand, time and again strict application of indissolubility locked women in situations of abuse and violence.

Different patterns collided. The Gandhian reconciliation between religious tradition and women's rights proved ineffective. The secular socialist vision of a new age of gender equality clashed with deep-seated cultural assumptions. After Indian independence, policies aimed at improving women's conditions crashed into the wall of tradition and poverty. Castes and classes proved terrible enemies of women's enfranchisement.

By the late 1970s, the project of gender equality through legal modernization along the Western—especially the British—model had failed. Duncan Derrett, Indian law professor at the School of Oriental and African Studies in London, urged India to follow the English path of family-law reforms. Then he realized the outcome was contradictory, with the same tools meant to empower women being turned against them by unscrupulous husbands. As his successor Werner Menski pointed out, "Applying the principle of gender equality in a patriarchally dominated legal system, where gender justice remains a dream for most women, was not a suitable progressive route."[222]

---

220. Forster, *A Passage to India*, 279.
221. Ibid.
222. Menski, "Asking for the Moon," 64.

In his 1978 book *The Death of a Marriage Law*, Derrett acknowledged that a different path should be taken. As Menski wrote, Derrett virtually admitted "defeat of his own modernizing prescriptions."[223]

In the early 1980s, India stopped following the English example of the 1970s, leading to the "quickie divorce" when the introduction of an act recognizing the conjugal breakdown as a legitimate ground for divorce was dropped.

Religious conversions interfered insidiously with women's matrimonial state and welfare.

By imposing the division of Indian society along religious lines well beyond traditions and customs, that is, by endorsing *your* gods, the colonial power dramatized conversions. Again, Forster's Dr. Aziz embodied the British construction of a presumed established wisdom that in India each believer had better stick to his or her community. "You keep your religion, I mine. That is the best,"[224] as Forster's Dr. Aziz sharply put it.

In the age of explosive gods, conversions became particularly sensitive and divisive. New Christian groups proselytized more aggressively. Dalits protested against Hindu caste exclusivism by converting to Buddhism or Islam. Muftis accepted Hindu husbands who converted to Islam for the sake of a new marriage. Hindu conservatives pushed for anticonversion legislation to prevent Christian missionaries from allegedly buying the conversion of impoverished tribals. Historian Romila Thapar denounced "syndicated Hinduism," pointing at the peculiar reshaping of Hinduism into a missionary religion. She regarded "Hindu missionary organizations,"[225] such as the Ramakrishna Mission, the Arya Samaj, the R.S.S., and the Vishva Hindu Parishad, as "taking their cue from Christian missionaries":[226]

> They are converting [the adivasis, mainly scheduled castes and tribes] . . . to a Hinduism as defined by the upper caste movements of the last two centuries . . . What is important for Hindu missionaries is that these communities declare their support for the dharma and be ready to be labelled as Hindus in any head count of either a census or a support to a political party. That this conversion does little or nothing to change their actual status and that they continue to be looked down upon by upper caste Hindus is of course of little consequence.[227]

Rising tensions on conversions in the 1990s pushed professor of comparative literature Gauri Viswanathan to write the capital essay *Outside the Fold*, published in 1998. In the preface, the author summarized the overarching nature of conversion:

223. Ibid.

224. Forster, *A Passage to India*, 135.

225. Thapar, *Cultural Pasts*, 1033.

226. Ibid.

227. Ibid.,1033–34.

Conversion is arguably one of the most unsettling political events in the life of a society. This is irrespective of whether conversion involves a single individual or an entire community, whether it is forced or voluntary, or whether it is the result of proselytization or inner spiritual illumination. Not only does conversion alter the demographic equation within a society and produce numerical imbalances, but it also challenges an established community's assent to religious doctrines and practices. With the departure of members from the fold, the cohesion of a community is under threat just as forcefully as if its beliefs had been turned into heresies.[228]

And conversions could have a double-edged impact on marriages and women. As changing religion could be used as a way to avoid obligations imposed via religious law, conversions could be exploited as a means to achieve a better conjugal status, depending on the interests of the parties. The husband might use it to secure what he saw as a better union or to avoid conjugal burdens. The wife could try conversion as an extreme remedy to escape abuse, but she might also use it to access a better marriage too.

Conversions could be the worst threat to women's welfare in terms of the stability of wedlock. But they might also turn out to be the only maneuvering space for women.

In practice, women were most often the losers in conversion cases, especially those involving Hindu husbands converting to Islam in order to marry a new partner without divorcing under the Hindu Marriage Act. The problem was an age-old one. In the time of explosive gods, it came again to the forefront in 1983, when the Delhi High Court decided the Vilayat Raj's case.[229] Justice Leela Seth ruled that the Hindu Marriage Act continued to apply to a man who was Hindu at the time of marriage despite his subsequent conversion to another religion. Of course the man was still free to seek divorce under the Hindu law, but not on the grounds of his own conversion.

The most prominent Islamic legal scholar, Tahir Mahmood, commented on the case in the *Hindustan Times* of October 27, 1983, condemning sham conversions to Islam as a "humbug":

> Well known is the fact that a Hindu husband who is fed up with his wife but is too impatient to wait till he has obtained a divorce under Hindu law, unscrupulously gets converted to Islam and contracts a second bigamous marriage believing (albeit wrongly) that Islamic law allows it unconditionally. The conversion in such cases is invariably a humbug and is generally followed by re-conversion of the newly-wed to Hinduism, at least in practice. This shuttlecock playing with various religions is not checked by our existing law, though it is neither allowed by the religion which is dishonestly adopted nor sanctioned by the one that is forsaken for selfish ends.[230]

---

228. Viswanathan, *Outside the Fold*, xxi.
229. *Vilayat Raj Alias Vilayat Khan*.
230. Mahmood, *Uniform civil code*, 63.

The Sarla Mudgal Case

The litigation in which Sushmita Ghosh engaged was originally of a private nature. She had no political purpose to accomplish. She was not a national star. But her struggle before the Supreme Court was not a solitary venture. The experiences of her friends and family, and stories reported by media already demonstrated that her case was far from unique. When she started her journey through the Indian judicial system, Sushmita realized she had traveling companions. Plenty of them.

Two such travel mates were Meena Mathur and Sunita Narula.

On February 2, 1978, Meena married Jitender Mathur. Three children were born from the union. At the beginning of 1988, Meena discovered that Jitender had converted to Islam and taken Sunita as his second wife.

Both women submitted a petition to the Supreme Court. In 1989 Meena Mathur filed a petition against her husband because of his second marriage. Sunita Narula, whose name was now Fathima since she had converted to Islam in order to marry Jitender, also filed a petition against the same Jitender in 1990. Of course, she had a different reason to sue him. Allegedly pressured to do so by his first wife, Meena, Jitender had reverted back to Hinduism on April 28, 1988, and had resumed living with his first wife and three children. Sunita, alias Fathima, remained a Muslim: in her petition she asked the court to recognize both her Muslim marriage and her right to be maintained by the legitimate husband.

Beyond their singularity, the cases of Sushmita, Meena, and Sunita (Fathima) had this in common: they were ordinary life stories expressing the general Indian struggle with religious diversity and equal protection of fundamental rights, especially in the spheres of family and marriage.

The cases eventually converged—along with others—upon a single judicial case. The case collected different petitions labeled after the first one filed in 1989 by another woman, Sarla Mudgal, the president of Kalyani, an Indian organization devoted to the welfare of needy families and women in distress. A bench of the Supreme Court formed by two judges, Justice Kuldip Singh and Justice Sahai, was called to decide on three related questions: "whether a Hindu husband, married under Hindu law, by embracing Islam, can solemnize second marriage? Whether such a marriage, without having the first marriage dissolved under law, would be a valid marriage qua the first wife who continues to be Hindu? Whether the apostate husband would be guilty of the offence under Section 494 of the Indian Penal Code [bigamy]?"[231]

Justice Sahai made explicit what the real issue was: "the problem with which these appeals are concerned is that many Hindus have changed their religion and have become convert [*sic*] to Islam only for purpose of escaping the consequences of bigamy."[232]

---

231. *Sarla Mudgal*, 639 [2].
232. Ibid, 652 [45].

The case arose from the petition of Sarla Mudgal in 1989. Sushmita climbed aboard in 1992. The Court decided in 1995. In those five years the judges of the Supreme Court studied and weighed the files, preparing a crucial decision. The same period witnessed the rise of Indian explosive gods, culminating in the 1992 demolition of the Babri Masjid mosque in Ayodhya and in the 1993 Bombay blasts, while proving a time of wide-ranging change for India in economy and politics.

Anarchy and Peyote

Demonstrating the worldwide reach of explosive gods, in the late eighties an American case anticipated, and later influenced, Rastafari Gareth Prince's trials in South Africa.

Alfred Smith and Galen Black, two members of the Native American Churches, were convicted for use of the hallucinogenic drug peyote, something they asserted was a part of their religion. Smith and Black were fired by their employer, a private drug-rehabilitation organization, and were excluded from unemployment compensation. They sued the Employment Agency of Oregon, claiming their religious freedom was violated if they were not free to use peyote for sacramental purposes. They maintained that the free exercise clause of the First Amendment to the US Constitution granted them an exemption from the application of the antidrug measures and, furthermore, should afford them access to the unemployment scheme. As in the case of Gareth Prince a few years later, religious freedom was understood in a new, much wider sense, encompassing the broadest range of performance of, or abstinence from, physical acts. American judges had to decide whether to uphold the enlarging scope of religious freedom or to put an end to its increasing expansion. The Oregon Supreme Court stood for the former and ruled that the denial of the unemployment treatment to Smith and Black violated the free-exercise clause.

For many years, the US Supreme Court had been sympathetic to exemption-seeking claims based on religion. But in 1990, the Court set a limit on the acceptability of religious difference and reversed the Oregon Supreme Court's decision. The Court judged lawful the denial of an exception to Smith and Black; religious freedom had not been violated in the case. In his opinion for the majority, Justice Antonin Scalia affirmed that, according to the First Amendment's protection of religious liberty, such an exception "would open the prospect of constitutionally required religious exemptions from civic obligations of almost every conceivable kind."[233]

According to Scalia, "we cannot afford the luxury of deeming *presumptively invalid*, as applied to the religious objector, every regulation of conduct that does not protect an interest of the highest order."[234]

Justice Scalia declared himself aware that his approach left no judicial remedies to groups suffering from discrimination through the political process, but he deemed

233. *Employment Division*, 888.
234. Ibid. (italics original).

this inevitable in a democratic, multireligious society: "it may fairly be said that leaving accommodation to the political process will place at a relative disadvantage those religious practices that are not widely engaged in; but that unavoidable consequence of democratic government must be preferred to a system in which conscience is a law unto itself."[235]

In his opinion Scalia refused to comply with the "strict scrutiny" doctrine elaborated by the US Supreme Court itself. According to this doctrine, the strict-scrutiny test was aimed at checking that no limitations to the free exercise of religion were admitted other than those required by a "compelling state interest."

The doctrine was refined in the Sherbert case of 1963. A member of the Seventh-Day Adventist Church and a textile-mill operator, Adell Sherbert lost her job because she refused to work on Saturday, the Sabbath Day to which she felt religiously bound. She then applied for unemployment compensation, but the Employment Security Commission denied her claim. A state trial court and the South Carolina Supreme Court upheld the denial.

In 1963, the US Supreme Court reversed the previous decisions because, in the words of Justice Brennan's opinion for the majority, no "compelling state interest" justified the restriction. In fact, the judge wrote: "it is basic that no showing merely of a rational relationship to some colorable state interest would suffice."[236]

The US Supreme Court upheld the doctrine of strict scrutiny in the sixties and the seventies. The compelling-interest, or Sherbert, test meant an extremely comprehensive recognition of religious motives. In their controversy with the Employment Agency of Oregon, respondents Smith and Black relied on it in order to secure the exception.

The minority of the Court also invoked the application of a less restrictive doctrine. In his opinion, Justice Harold Andrew Blackmun refused to accept "the repression of minority religions"[237] as, in Scalia's own words, an "unavoidable consequence of democratic government." "I do not believe," Blackmun added, "the Founders thought their dearly bought freedom from religious persecution a 'luxury,' but an essential element of liberty—and they could not have thought religious intolerance 'unavoidable,' for they drafted the Religion Clauses precisely in order to avoid that intolerance."[238]

In agreement with Justice Blackmun, Justice Sandra Day O'Connor also expressed bitter criticism against the Smith ruling. Although concurring in the order against Smith, she attacked the attempt to get rid of the compelling-interest test. Such a test, she stated, "reflects the First Amendment's mandate of preserving religious liberty to the fullest extent possible in a pluralistic society."[239]

235. Ibid., 890.
236. *Sherbert,* 406.
237. *Employment Division,* 909.
238. Ibid.
239. Ibid., 903.

In the decision delivered on April 17, 1990, however, the Court denied the applicability of the test in the case. Justice Scalia himself stated not only that "any society adopting such a system would be courting anarchy,"[240] but also that "danger increases in direct proportion to the society's diversity of religious beliefs, and its determination to coerce or suppress none of them."[241]

Thus Justice Scalia ordered the decision of the Oregon Supreme Court to be reversed: "Because respondents' ingestion of peyote was prohibited under Oregon law, and because that prohibition is constitutional, Oregon may, consistent with the Free Exercise Clause, deny respondents unemployment compensation when their dismissal results from use of the drug."[242]

Scalia's opinion in *Smith* marked the end of the liberal jurisprudence on religious minorities. The epoch of the Warren Court was over. Fear of religious diversity was more in tune with American politics in the era of President Reagan. This was no more the time for ruling in favor of the Amish refusal to comply with public-education regulations, as the Supreme Court did in 1972, arguing with Chief Justice Burger against "contemporary society exerting a hydraulic insistence on conformity to majoritarian standards."[243]

With alarm for anarchy replacing the favor for religious pluralism of the sixties and the seventies, a new American understanding of religious freedom was on the rise. Ten years later, in the decision on the case of Gareth Prince, South African constitutional judges would depart from Justice Scalia's jurisprudence.

The US Supreme Court decided the Smith case in the midst of the events leading up to the collapse of communism. Only one month before the Smith ruling, the Soviet Congress of People's Deputies, upon request by President Gorbachev, amended the USSR Constitution of 1977. The principle that the Communist Party of the Soviet Union, "armed with Marxism-Leninism," was the "leading and guiding force of the Soviet society and the nucleus of its political system, of all state organizations and public organizations" was repealed.

Shove Some More

When the Berlin Wall crumbled, Gandhi's dream of India as the country of a pre-industrial, village-based economy symbolized by the *charkha*, the spinning wheel, was long dead. The old-fashioned industrial India dreamed of by Soviet-friendly Congressmen like Nehru was also sinking in the abyss of free-market economics.

From his first budget in March 1985, Rajiv Gandhi endeavored to dismantle the system of a directed economy and open India to business. The example of economic

240. Ibid., 888.
241. Ibid.
242. Ibid., 890.
243. *Wisconsin*, 217.

reforms in China between 1978 and 1984 was powerful. Rajiiv brought deregulation in strategic industrial sectors and simplified the licensing policy. The success of Reliance Industries and similar achievements confirmed that Rajiv was on the right truck. Opponents, however, underlined that behind the increasing prosperity of the middle class, social conflicts persisted and poverty was far from defeated. Growing political corruption also coincided with the new age of business.

In the early 1990s, tensions over inequalities, the market economy, and communal conflicts dominated the debate. It was the time of the three *M*'s. The first *M* stood for the implementation of the Mandal Commission's recommendations of 1980, aimed at fostering the inclusion of the backward classes. The second *M* stood for the project of Hindu nationalists to build a temple, a *mandir*, in place of the Babri Mosque in Ayodhya. The third *M* stood for *market*.

After the 1989 general elections, a National Front government was formed. The government issued an order to implement the recommendations of the Mandal Commission and increase the quota of reserved jobs in the government for backward castes. This meant a reduction of the job opportunities for upper-caste Indians. Vibrant protests ensued, with hundreds of suicide attempts. At the same time, not all the underprivileged benefited from the Mandal formula, since the definition of backwardness ignored the heterogeneity of the category of the "other backward classes." Political scientist Bidyut Chakrabarty points out that the benefits deriving from the effort to redress the imbalance were "monopolized by the better-off and influential"[244] in the backward castes.

The debate proved excruciating for the rising Bharatiya Janata Party (BJP). For some, the implementation of the Mandal recommendations undermined the unity of Hindus; for others, on the contrary, it enlarged the constituency of the BJP. As historian Ramachandra Guha noticed, the discussion "threw the party into a tizzy."[245] The risk of infighting was such that the BJP leaders opted for dodging the issue. As Guha wrote, "the BJP chose to shift the terms of political debate, away from Mandal and caste and back towards religion and the mandir/mosque question."[246]

On September 25, 1990 the BJP launched the Ram Rath Yatra, a march from the temple of Somnath in Gujarat to Ayodhya, the place of the Babri Masjid. When the march reached the mosque one month later, the police prevented the most fanatic militants, the *kar sevaks*, literally the "volunteers," from destroying the mosque, during a three-day riot. About twenty kar sevaks died and were celebrated as martyrs by the Vishwa Hindu Parishad, the most active organization in the struggle for the construction of the Ram Mandir.

Against the background of the *mandir* mobilization, economic, social, and political issues intertwined in 1991. A Tamil suicide bomber killed Rajiv Gandhi on May

---

244. Chakrabarty, *Indian Politics and Society*. 66.

245. Guha, *India after Gandhi*, 635.

246. Ibid.

20, 1991, the day after the first round of polling for the general elections. Rajiv had started his electoral campaign in Ayodhya seven months earlier.

The BJP resorted to Hindutva rhetoric and actively campaigned for the construction of a temple in Ayodhya, commemorating the sacred place of Ram's birth. After the final vote of June, the BJP scored a record 20 percent, becoming the second national party after the Congress.

New Prime Minister Narasimha Rao was confronted with a massive balance-of-payment crisis. In the context of the collapse of the Soviet Union, acceleration of the transition to a market economy appeared inevitable. In July 1991, the Congress-led government issued the Industrial Policy Resolution. A new industrial licensing policy was envisaged, together with the endorsement of direct foreign investment and actions aimed at improving the performance of public-sector units.

The transition was full of obstacles. In April 1992, after a sustained bull run, the Indian stock market crashed. In the following two months, stock prices dropped by over 40 percent. Precisely at that time, Sushmita Ghosh's husband celebrated his Muslim marriage to Vinita Gupta, now known by her new Muslim name, Henna Begum.

The social instability prompted by reforms in the economy, and the increasing exposure of the country to global dynamics fueled the political exploitation of religious identities.

Starting in October 1991, Hindu nationalists under the umbrella of the Sangh Parivar (Family of Associations) carried on demolitions in Ayodhya, bought land around the mosque and built a concrete platform. The Vishva Hindu Parishad launched a campaign to start the building of the *mandir* in Ayodhya on the auspicious day of December 6. The creation of a BJP-led government in Uttar Pradesh after the 1991 elections encouraged the influx of activists from all over the country.

On December 6, 1992, some one hundred thousand kar sevaks, armed with tridents, bows, and arrows, endeavored to raze the mosque, with almost no opposition from the police. Ramachandra Guha gave this account of the demolition:

> By noon, volunteers were crawling all over the Masjid, holding saffron flags and shouting slogans of victory. Grappling hooks were anchored to the domes, while the base was battered with hammers and axes. At 2 p.m., one dome collapsed, bringing a dozen men down with it. "Ek dhakka aur do, Babri Masjid tor do!" screamed the radical preacher Sadhvi Ritambara ("Shove some more, and the whole thing will collapse!"). At 3:30, a second dome gave way. An hour later, the third and final one was demolished.[247]

Disputes about the real dynamic and the political responsibilities followed, together with serious riots. About two thousand people were killed in clashes in several Indian cities, including Mumbai and Delhi.

---

247. Guha, *India after Gandhi*, 639.

The either/or terms of the issue in Ayodhya—opposing the Babri Masjid (the mosque) to the Ram Mandir (the Hindu temple)—and the subsequent demolition of the Masjid, marked a turning point. The Masjid-Mandir divide became the symbol of communal violence and unrest that reached well beyond Hindus and Muslims. Explosive gods coincided with *your* gods. The ideal of *our* gods was becoming passé.

Bidyut Chakrabarty points out that the achievement of democracy in India, as opposed to Pakistan, was made possible by the fact that "religious divisions were cross-cut by numerous regional, language and caste cleavages."[248] The explosive gods of Hindu nationalists changed the picture and challenged as never before the ideal of a multireligious country under the principle of secularism.

The Supreme Court was at the center of tensions. On November 16, 1992, the Court upheld the government's order to implement the Mandal recommendations, though it ruled that reservations could not exceed 50 percent of the jobs. In the same weeks the chief minister of Uttar Pradesh, the BJP leader Kalyan Singh, managed to prevent the Supreme Court from intervening in the Masjid-Mandir conflict.

Sushmita's petition to the Court did not enjoy the publicity and coverage of the Mandal and the Ayodhya cases, but the stakes were very much the same. Was religion a vital force for the country? Or was it only a liability? Was the passage from *your* gods to *our* gods at all realistic? Would religions undermine secular India and prove the impossibility of a peaceful multireligious India? Or would they feed the old nationalist and modernist vision and renovate the country?

Similar questions were being asked in South Africa and Britain. The very same day as the demolition of the Babri Masjid in 1992, Gareth Prince celebrated his twenty-third birthday in Cape Town. When Sushmita Ghosh filed her suit, Prince was studying law at the University of Western Cape and taking an active part in the transition to democracy of his country. Shabina Begum had just been born in England, one week before the publication in Britain of *The Satanic Verses*. Her father, once a headmaster in Bangladesh, died shortly afterward. The elder brother took responsibility for her education. In 1993, the Denbigh High School of Luton, Shabina's future school, adjusted its uniform policy to the multicultural environment. In order to satisfy Islamic requirements of modest dress for girls, the governors consulted local imams and approved the wearing of the *shalwar kameeze* and of head scarves of a specified color and quality.

Thousands of miles separated Sushmita, Gareth, and Shabina. They belonged to different generations and shared no common cultural or religious background. Still they witnessed the same explosive gods and played substantial roles beyond their own intentions. As (respectively) a deserted woman, a marginal believer, and a woman representing a minority within the Muslim minority, Sushmita, Gareth, and Shabina fought for their rights, while taking a stand against what their gods regarded as unequal and unjust.

248. Chakrabarty, *Indian Politics and Society*, 34.

The Religious Experience of Democracy

With the dismantling of apartheid, explosive gods challenged South Africa. In the Rustenburg Declaration of 1990, church leaders committed themselves to the principle that "the State is always under God." But whose God, in such a multireligious context? And with what legitimacy in a heavily consumerist society?

The transformative energy of explosive gods intermingled with the violence of the transition to postapartheid South Africa. Alex Boraine, the former Methodist pastor and prominent MP, saw his office firebombed twice. He later recalled "wreaths were placed at our homes and threats were a daily occurrence, but somehow we managed to survive and continue the work that we had started, namely the encouragement and support of negotiations politics."[249]

From 1989 to 1994, the South African transition turned into a bloodbath. Political violence claimed 17,425 lives in that five-year period. As the declining gods of communism and the rising gods of Christianity played a substantial part in the foundation of the new country, many communists and Christians were also among the victims of the transition.

At fifty, the popular general secretary of the Communist Party, Chris Hani, exemplified the quest for a new Marxist inspiration in the post–Cold War age. His quest was the same as that of those many Indians who resorted to Marxism in order to oppose neoliberalism, particularly in West Bengal and Kerala. On April 10, 1993, a member of the Afrikaner Weerstand Beweging, the Afrikaner Resistance Movement, shot and killed Hani.

On July 25, 1993 four cadres of the Azanian People's Liberation Army attacked a congregation during a service at Saint James Church, Kenilworth, one of the most inclusive churches in Cape Town. Eleven members of the congregation were killed and fifty-eight wounded.

Violence also targeted sixty-six-year-old Johan Heyns, one of the most influential church leaders and anti-apartheid theologians. A prominent member of the Nederduitse Gereformeerde Kerk, he was at the forefront of the internal struggle to change the position of the church, which led to the creation of the Afrikaans Protestant Church. He played a key role in the 1986 Synod that rejected the biblical foundation of racial segregation, and in the Rustenburg Conference of 1990. The biography of Heyns also encapsulated the increasing tension between religion and secularization, as he firmly opposed liberal theological views on homosexuality. On November 5, 1994, a single rifle shot through an open window killed Heyns as he was playing cards with his wife and three grandchildren at his home in Pretoria.

In 1994, after the presentation of his book, *Dealing with the Past*,[250] Alex Boraine met Albie Sachs again. They had a conversation on how best to approach transition.

249. Boraine, *A Life in Transition*, 166.

250. Boraine et al., *Dealing with the Past*.

The subtitle of the book, *Truth and Reconciliation in South Africa*, sounded promising. Following the conversation, Boraine sent a paper to Nelson Mandela, proposing the constitution of a truth commission for South Africa. Boraine believed that "the legacy of apartheid still had to be dealt with. Nothing had been done to assuage the grief and anger of a pernicious racist system's hundreds and thousands of victims."[251]

Reconciliation was central to the construction of Mandela's leadership. The son of the Thembu chief emerged on the occasion of Chris Hani's murder as the true guide of the country. He succeeded in preventing further riots and protecting the negotiations thanks to a TV-broadcast appeal emphasizing the fact that Chris Hani's killer was a Polish immigrant, and that he had been arrested thanks to an Afrikaner eyewitness.

During this period, Mandela attended a service of the Nederduitse Gereformeerde Kerk in Pretoria, the very congregation of his fiercest enemies. Biographer Martin Meredith stressed the symbolic value of the episode: "[in] the church to which Verwoerd and Vorster, Strijdom and Malan had belonged, [Mandela was] surprised by the warmth of his reception from the congregation: 'If I had gone there four years ago, the security would have had to protect me against assault, against people who would want to kill me. This time they were there to protect me from being killed, out of love.'"[252]

On April 27, 1994, the first democratic, racially inclusive elections were held. "For former vote-less people, it was the experience of a lifetime,"[253] historian Leonard Thompson wrote; "for some it took on the aura of a religious experience."[254] In accordance with the interim Constitution voted in 1993, the Constitutional Court of South Africa was created in 1994. Religious change coincided with legal change. New courts were needed to try the new gods. In June 1994, President Mandela appointed Arthur Chaskalson, the celebrated human rights lawyer, as the first president of the Court. Following a selection supervised by the Judicial Service Commission, the man injured by the car bomb in Maputo, Albie Sachs, was also appointed a constitutional judge. Gareth Prince was about to cross paths with the two of them on his way to a new law and a new religion for South Africa.

Believing Without Belonging

By 1994, the three countries had undergone a fundamental change in economy and politics.

Thatcherism and Reaganomics, the fall of the Soviet Union and of its satellite regimes in Eastern Europe, and economic reforms in China had a strong impact on Indian economy and politics. While opening up to a market-oriented economy, India

---

251. Boraine, *A Life in Transition*, 167.
252. Meredith, *Nelson Mandela*, 527–28.
253. Thompson, *A History of South Africa*, 263.
254. Ibid.

moved to a regionalized, coalition-based system of government. The appointment of the Fifth Pay Commission in 1994 triggered a deep reform of public administration, according to the imperative of understanding customer needs. Global capitalism and neoliberalism affected not only the economy but also the whole governance of the country. Indian Marxists did not surrender: communist parties proved extremely resilient, especially in their strongholds of West Bengal and Kerala. In some regions, the underground activities and the military actions of Maoist Naxalites against land-lords and exploitation of natural resources kept attracting the sympathy of the poorest sectors.

From 1979 to 1994, South Africa also changed radically, by abandoning the still deeply seated apartheid system of the eighties. In March 1992, the last all-white ref-erendum in South Africa approved of de Klerk's process to end apartheid. The first racially inclusive elections of 1994 led to Mandela's presidency the following May.

In the same period, Britain too went through a phase of political transition, with Margaret Thatcher resigning from office in November 1990 and Tony Blair being elected Leader of the Labour Party in 1994. In 1991, Prime Minister John Major led the UK into the Gulf War after Saddam Hussein's invasion of Kuwait, a major chal-lenge to British geopolitics. In 1994, after twenty-five years of violence and the death of more than three thousand people, the IRA announced a cease-fire.

Explosive gods were a substantial part of the picture.

The demolition of the Babri Mosque showed that religious divisions were at the heart of Indian politics. The explosive gods of Hindu nationalists, conservative Mus-lims, jiadhists in Kashmir, turbulent Sikhs and Buddhists, and aggressive Christians challenged the Nehruvian fabric of secular, peacefully multireligious India.

In South Africa, explosive gods played a decisive role in the dismantling of apart-heid and in contributing to a new national cohesion. South Africa was undergoing rebirth as a secular state. Separation of church and state was meant to replace the civil religion of apartheid. The equality of all religions was meant to cement a multi-religious state: the only possible expression of a multireligious society. The age of Christian exclusivity, of a biblical foundation for racial exclusion, was over.

From 1979 to 1994, explosive gods also challenged the twofold secularized and multi-religious identity of Britain. In 1994, sociologist Grace Davie published a key essay on the altered British religious landscape. In the space of the last five decades, she argued, Britons had changed their approach to faith in response to modernity and postmodernity.

Contrary to numerous predictions that had followed Nietzsche's "God is dead" dictum, gods were alive and well, though they had undergone a fundamental muta-tion. Grace Davie gave the example of collective mourning rituals after the tragedy of Hillsborough: in April 1989, ninety-four Liverpool supporters lost their lives as they were crushed against the perimeter fence at the beginning of a Football Associa-tion Cup semifinal match in Sheffield. The subsequent pilgrimage of mourning to the

Liverpool stadium provided a crucial lesson for British sociologists about the persisting latent religiosity and the entanglement of religious, civic, and footballing rituals. The two Liverpool bishops, the Roman Catholic Derek Worlock and the Anglican David Sheppard, described the pilgrimage to Anfield Road Stadium in an article for the *Independent* on April 29, 1989:

> Over the goalpost and crush barriers hung red and blue scarves with flags and banners portraying the Liver Bird emblem and the inevitable assurance that "you'll never walk alone." On the turf below lay a field of flowers, more scarves and caps, mascots and souvenirs, and incredibly, kneeling amidst wreaths and rattles, a plaster Madonna straight from a Christmas crib. Blasphemy, unhealthy superstition, tawdry sentimentality. Or a rich blend of personal mourning, prayerful respect, and genuine faith?[255]

Grace Davie wrestled with the dilemma and formulated her theory that dissociation between belief, practice, and membership was the main feature of contemporary religion in the country. From 1990, the sociologist advanced the formula "believing without belonging"[256] as the most appropriate phrase to describe the persistent salience of religion in Britain, and the mismatch between "high levels of belief and low levels of practice."[257] An "active religious minority"[258] coexisted with a "less active believing majority."[259] Many people in Britain had come to experience faith without shared orthodoxy and obligations, religion without membership, God without churches. And yet, in Britain too, religion refused to be a merely private aspect of individual life. Faith-based public claims featured in politics, with an increasing need for morality, and in society at large.

In March 1993, in his foreword to a book on Christianity and socialism, Tony Blair delivered his vision of Christianity as a source of inspiration for a Labour Party in search of identity. The then Labour MP for Sedgefield, Blair underlined the close intertwinement between the values of Christianity and those "of democratic socialism, founded on a belief in the importance of society and solidarity."[260] The unity of the individual and the collective dimension of human beings was central to Blair's elaboration on political Christianity: "above all, [Christianity] is about the union between individual and community, the belief that we are not stranded in helpless isolation, but owe a duty both to others and to ourselves and are, in a profound sense, dependent

---

255. Davie, *Religion in Britain since 1945*, 90.
256. Davie, "Believing without Belonging."
257. Davie, *Religion in Britain since 1945*, 5.
258. Ibid., 75.
259. Ibid.
260. Blair, "Foreword," 11.

on each other to succeed . . . the Christian message is that self is best realized through communion with others."[261]

Hence, Blair's Christian socialism: the future prime minister concluded that Christianity was a "tough religion,"[262] placing "a duty, an imperative on us to reach our better self and to care about creating a better community to live in. It is not utilitarian . . . It is judgemental. There is right and wrong. There is good and bad. We all know this, of course, but it has become fashionable to be uncomfortable about such language. But when we look at our world today and how much needs to be done, we should not hesitate to make such judgements. And then follow them with determined action. That would be Christian socialism."[263]

Explosive gods took the shape also of new religious movements, of atheist militants and indeed of religions resulting from Britain's growing cultural diversity. Change in traditional churches was also a part of the picture. In 1992, ecclesiastical law of the established Church of England was reformed so as to allow for the access of women to the priesthood; on March 12, 1994, the first women ministers were ordained.

Definitely, Grace Davie was right in pointing at a new landscape combining secularization and faith.

If Christianity changed, and new religious movements blossomed, the Rushdie affair awakened the country to the complexity of British Islam and to the contradictions of governmental policies at home and abroad.

In the early 1990s, the retreat of the Soviets from Afghanistan and the victory of mujahideens were followed by three waves of Islamist mobilization. Through the first, the remaining Marxist forces in Afghanistan were crushed, this ultimately leading to the Taliban takeover in 1996. Through the second wave, Pakistan exploited the network and facilities set up during the Afghan jihad to expand influence in central Asia. While challenging Britain's partnership with Islamabad, this impacted India by means of a new Pakistani-backed offensive to "liberate" Kashmir. In 1992, the third wave of mobilization hit Bosnia. Though Britain played a very ambiguous role, it certainly did not oppose the jihadist indoctrination and military training of British nationals, mostly of Pakistani origin, who ended up fighting in the Balkans.

In 1993, the same year as the first attack on the World Trade Center in New York, British intelligence submitted a report on *Islamic Fundamentalism in the Middle East* to the Foreign Office. Though the report raised awareness of explosive Islamist gods to some degree, the old belief that radical Islam did not fundamentally threaten British strategic interests was reiterated: "Fundamentalism does not pose a coherent and monolithic threat to Western interests in the way that Communism once did. It is not supported by a superpower. Its appeal in Western countries is confined to Muslim minorities and the threat of subversion is, in the UK at least, minimal. Dealings with

261. Ibid., 10–11.
262. Ibid., 12.
263. Ibid.

extreme fundamentalist regimes would be highly unpredictable but not necessarily unmanageable."[264]

In 1994, two events announced the growth of Londonistan, which Mark Curtis defined "the principal administrative centre for the global jihad,"[265] with the connivance of the British government.

That July, Osama Bin Laden started his Advice and Reformation Committee in London, and during 1994, he personally stayed in town for some time. Aimed at spreading the anti-Saudi and anti-West word, the London base proved a crucial support to the construction of al-Qaeda, allowing bin Laden, according to Curtis, "to motivate his supporters around the world."[266] From Wembley, bin Laden publicized his statements, recruited future al-Qaeda militants, managed funds, and organized equipment and services. Curtis also reported that the Wembley headquarters "served as a communication centre for reports on military, security, and other matters from various al-Qaida cells to its leadership."[267]

Later in the year, Abu Hamza also set up the headquarters of his Supporters of Sharia in Britain. An Egyptian with British citizenship and a sympathizer of the Muslim Brotherhood, Abu Hamza provided assistance to wounded mujahideens in London during the war against the Soviets in Afghanistan. After the retreat of the Soviets, he settled in Afghanistan. In 1993 he lost both hands and one eye in a blast. After his experience in the Bosnian war, he became the symbol of Londonistan in the second half of the 1990s, the inflammatory sheikh radicalizing British Islam and recruiting jihadists in the Finsbury Park Mosque, but also the suspected agent of British services.

In an increasingly interrelated world, the impact of explosive gods was far from linear and unambiguous. While in India they seemed to prevent a plural society from growing peacefully, and while in South Africa they stood as one of the strongest assets for the renewal and the reconciliation of the country, Britain experienced both aspects at the same time.

Imperial Gods

In 1978, Trevor Ling, a comparative-religion scholar in Manchester, noticed that in the history of Britain and India, to varying degrees, "politicized religion"[268] had entailed "the suppression of spontaneous, charismatic, or prophetic groups."[269] Ling also underscored that, in contrast with the establishment of churches in England, Wales,

---

264. Curtis, *Secret Affairs*, 173.

265. Ibid., 223.

266. Ibid., 185.

267. Ibid., 181.

268. Ling, *Religious Change and the Secular State*, 97.

269. Ibid., 100.

and Scotland, India had "successfully withstood all attempts in modern times to conjoin state and religion."[270]

In the following fifteen years, from 1979 to 1994, "politicized religion" and the cross-national impact of explosive gods differentiated and united Britain, India, and South Africa. Because of their past ties within the British Empire and Commonwealth, and because of their ongoing relationships, India, Britain, and South Africa, which had rejoined the Commonwealth on June 1, 1994, after a thirty-four-year break, experienced renewed mutual influence.

Models and ideals, issues and solutions circulated from one country to the other. Desmond Tutu was an example for Christians in Britain and India. Salman Rushdie challenged Muslims in India, South Africa, and Britain alike: protests in Mumbai and Cape Town rebounded with protests in Bradford; the debate on censorship and blasphemy linked London, Delhi, and Pretoria. Well beyond Rushdie, the secular challenge to the gods was at stake, as was the gods' challenge to secular societies and free expression in a democratic setting. The demolition of Babri Mosque and the Masjid-Mandir controversy questioned not only the Indian multireligious and secular pattern, but also both secular and multireligious Britain and South Africa.

By 1994, Sushmita Ghosh was deep in her fight before the Supreme Court of India. Gareth Prince was being educated as a lawyer in Cape Town and grew into a convinced Rastafarian, for this encapsulated the ambition of new generations of South Africans to tighten the link with the land and with their black ancestors. Shabina Begum was a child in Britain, with a mother unable to speak English, experiencing the everyday struggle for identity and achievement in multicultural London. In their extremely diverse life stories, the three figures already were, or were about to become, religious fighters. Sushmita struggled to prevent Indian women's rights from being undermined by religious laws. She was a fighter for woman-friendly religion. Gareth was starting his fight for full rights as a Rastafarian in South Africa. He would be a fighter for marginal religion. Shabina would demand that her distinctive Muslim identity be integrally respected in Britain. She would be a fighter for different religion. In the context of the major religious conflicts experienced in their respective countries, the fights may have appeared minor or marginal. No political party or powerful religious community backed Sushmita, Gareth, or Shabina. They were no more than private individuals. But the three litigations would go on to become landmark cases before the respective highest jurisdictions of the three countries. Beyond their solutions, they would mark crucial steps in the changing interaction of law, politics, and the gods.

In the case against Rushdie and Viking Penguin, Choudhury's counsel, Mr. Azhar, argued that the legacy of the British Empire in India imposed full protection of all religions in Britain. India was put forward as an example of the standard to which the British judiciary should conform. Rushdie had to be condemned for blasphemy against Islam in London, because he would have been convicted on the same count

270. Ibid.

in Delhi. And Delhi was not just India. Delhi was the erstwhile Empire; Delhi was the living reminder of the imperial legacy.

The judges of the Supreme Court of India in charge of the case of Sushmita Ghosh were applying the same approach. They were studying precedents from the British Raj in order to determine their judgment on the case. An equivalent interdependency would feature in the South African case of Gareth a few years later and in the British case of Shabina ten years down the road.

British imperialism had shaped all three countries and had linked them together. Colonial ties still influenced their interaction in the early 1990s. Margaret Thatcher, Desmond Tutu, and Nelson Mandela could not be explained without Winston Churchill, Jan Smuts, and Mohandas Karamchand Gandhi. Judges in India, South Africa, and Britain still built upon the decisions taken by their predecessors in the nineteenth and early twentieth centuries. They might either reject or follow jurisprudence from the past, but never could they avoid making reference to it. The future was built out the past.

Indians, South Africans, and the British struggled with the gap between the re-emerging reality of *your* gods and the waning ideal of *our* gods. On December 24, 1995, in her address to the Jadavpur University, in Calcutta, historian Romila Thapar underlined "the most dramatic resurgence of ideologies and aspirations which have a distinctly nineteenth century feel to them."[271] The celebrated scholar and worldwide authority to warn: "these have brought back history—if ever it had indeed been ended—with a disquieting resonance."[272]

Four decades after the end of the British Empire, in a twisting world, the past resurfaced. In courts as well as in synagogues, churches, gurdwaras, temples, and mosques, memory of the colonial past was reshaped. Post-1979 explosive gods resuscitated the imperial gods who had dominated the three countries for ninety years, from 1857 to 1947. An age of interdependence had begun in 1857, when the Independence War, or the Mutiny as they preferred to call it, made the British aware of the fragility of their Indian conquest, and the Xhosa cattle killing showed the religious potential for the most dramatic events in Southern Africa. For ninety years—until Indian independence in 1947 and the electoral triumph of the National Party, leading to the establishment of apartheid in 1948—the story of India, South Africa, and Britain was based on the common experience of religion under the Empire. With their mixture of violence and heroism, faith and cynicism, gods under the empire, imperial gods, modeled the three countries and shaped the relationships among their peoples.

---

271. Thapar, *Cultural Pasts*, 1015.

272. Ibid.

Chapter 2

Imperial Gods (1857–1947)

A Picture of My Father

IN THE MID-1990S, JUDGES in Britain, India, and South Africa bore the burden of reconciling the harsh reality of *your* gods and the ideal of *our* gods.

As the Rushdie case dramatically signaled, wariness to react in Whitehall and Westminster meant that the onus of addressing tensions in multireligious Britain fell largely upon the judiciary. In this context, Shabina Begum grew up and her spectacular litigation on behalf of radical Islam was prepared.

Courts in South Africa and India were also solicited. South African judges had to rule on claims of religious diversity in the blossoming postapartheid society. Gareth Prince would soon challenge the whole fabric of South African law by his adherence to a rebellious legal and religious practice. In a rapidly changing India, through the judgment on Sushmita Ghosh's petition, the Supreme Court would be in charge of responding to the voices of women and of those in other discriminated social sectors.

Summoned to interpret the latest situation, British, Indian, and South African judges turned to the past in search of inspiration from both failures and achievements. Lord Justice Watkins, one of the judges in charge of the Rushdie case, acknowledged that the Rushdie issue reminded Britons of their past connections with Muslims in the context of the British Raj. The man injured by the car bomb in Maputo, Albie Sachs, now a judge of the newly appointed South African Constitutional Court, took a similar position in 1995, when he wrote in his first opinion for the Court that it was "instructive to look at the evolution of values in the colonial settlement as well as in African society."[1]

The bench of the Indian Supreme Court in charge of the Sarla Mudgal case, the case that had absorbed Sushmita's petition, also turned towards the imperial age. As

---

1. *S v Makwanyane* [384].

Justice Kuldip Singh stressed in his opinion for the Court, "it would be useful to have a look at some of the old cases on the subject."[2]

In the midst of deep transformations in their countries, Indian, British, and South African judges were in charge of drawing the line between what was to be retrieved from the past and what was to be changed. Deciding for present times implied assessing what their predecessors had done in the past. This went beyond the traditional importance of precedents in the common-law tradition. The utilitarian approach of Justice Singh in the case of Sushmita downplayed the importance of the past. "To have a look" at precedents served more than the goal of merely fishing for practical solutions.

Precedents told the common story of colonialism and racial segregation, of reinvented traditions, of east-west and north-south reciprocal influences. They encapsulated the evolution of each single country while inevitably connecting the three of them.

What first linked India, South Africa, and Britain was, of course, the British Empire. Religion strongly influenced the colonial and the imperial pattern. The British venture in the colonies also deeply affected religion both at home and abroad. Gods at the time of the Empire, imperial gods, accompanied the British takeover in India through the East India Company. They also accompanied the British expansion in Southern Africa against the indigenous populations and the Afrikaners alike. Imperial gods were central to a twofold transformation.

First of all, the global role of Britain prompted British Christianity to change at home. Evangelical Anglicans propelled a spiritual reform, which provided the British mission in the world with a moral foundation. British Protestants from other denominations also combined missionary impetus and social concern. Catholic Anglicans rather opposed what they saw as the secularization of the Church and the liberal turn in theology. They held fast to tradition, stressing the potential for unity with the Roman Catholic and Orthodox churches and promoting liturgical reform. Conversions from the Church of England to the Roman Catholic Church, as in the famous case of John Henry Newman in 1845, expressed the turbulent mutation of British Christianity. At the same time, Evangelicals endeavored to convert the native, and sought the conversion of the corrupt Anglican Englishman both at home and in the colonies. Conversions from one church to another, conversions within the "true church" and conversions from "paganism" to Christianity—all belonged to the same picture.

The second process of transformation concerned religion in the colonies. The Evangelical drive generated a massive effort for civilizing and converting. Age-old rivalries, along regional, religious and caste lines—including friction between the former ruling Muslims and the Hindus—were joined by new tensions between the religion of the colonizer and the religion of the colonized. The landscape could not but undergo deep transformation on all sides.

---

2. *Sarla Mudgal*, 641 [9].

Religion in Southern Africa also changed, as the result of the often lethal confrontation between the Dutch Reformed nationalist Christianity of the Afrikaners; the Anglican, Catholic, and Protestant gods of the British; and the indigenous gods.

"Ideas and conceptions," Rina Williams suggested, "moved back and forth between colony and metropole, each modifying the other in the process."[3] By clashing with each other, the conquerors' gods and the gods of the conquered participated in the same process of mutual change. The imperial age constituted ties and bonds between gods in India, South Africa, and Britain. In the process, the British Empire made *your* modern gods, but it also pulled the different gods together and ultimately triggered the ideal of *our* gods.

Killing the Cattle

At the end of the eighteenth century, evangelical Anglicanism developed as a powerful movement within the Church of England. Evangelicals emphasized the Anglican connection to Reformation and preached a spiritual and moral renewal. The religious revival they promoted had a fundamental impact on Britain and on the British colonial policy. The traditional principle of separation between the superior white race and the indigenous races clashed with the new missionary thrust. The "superior" British Christian race also had the mission to "civilize" the natives and possibly to convert them. But races had to stay separate. Conversions were not meant to invite anyone to cross the racial line.

South African history in the nineteenth century proved the ambivalence of British Christianity. Missionaries backed social and economic exploitation, but they also educated and, more or less voluntarily, empowered indigenous people.

After the occupation of the Cape and the creation of the British Cape Colony in the early nineteenth century, the London Missionary Society, an interdenominational Protestant organization, defended the Xhosa and the Khoikhoi, the so-called Hottentots. John Philip, a radical evangelical engaged with the London Missionary Society, struggled for the relief of the Hottentots. His effective lobbying in London led to a motion approved on July 15, 1828, by the House of Commons, according to which the colonial government was bound to "secure to all natives of South Africa the same freedom and protection as are enjoyed by other free people of that Colony, whether English or Dutch."[4]

Some twenty years earlier the British Parliament had already banned slave trade. They further passed measures against the degrading treatment of slaves, especially punishments. Historian Andrew Ross pointed to the special contribution of British nonestablishment Protestants, whose mission in South Africa and all the colonies was driven by "the belief that social and political issues were central to the concerns of a

3. Williams, *Postcolonial Politics and Personal Laws*, 37.

4. Thompson, *A History of South Africa*, 60.

Christian."[5] By educating and employing black people, missionary schools and organizations contributed to the creation of a black middle class.

In India, and especially in South Africa, the British did not only clash with the indigenous, for tensions also arose among whites. Missions divided Christians. British Protestant missionaries believed in the evangelization of the indigenous people and were against slavery and the degrading treatment of natives. Afrikaners instead viewed themselves as the pure Christians, whose mission was to avoid contamination and build a society respecting the will of God as to the natural hierarchy of races and creeds.

When, in 1837, Piet Retief launched the Great Trek and led the Afrikaners to the conquest of the land beyond the Vaal River, he denounced the hatred "cast upon us by interested and dishonest persons, under the cloak of religion, whose testimony is believed in England, to the exclusion of all evidence in our favor."[6] His niece, Anna Steenkamp, later claimed that the emancipation of slaves and the recognition of equal dignity for each man was so unbearable to Afrikaners as to push them to leave—"to trek" north, and settle in new lands in order "to preserve our doctrines in purity":[7]

> It is not so much [the Africans'] freedom that drove us to such lengths, as their being placed on an equal footing with Christians, contrary to the laws of God and the natural distinction of race and religion, so that it was intolerable for any decent Christian to bow down beneath such a yoke.[8]

Two years before the Great Trek, in 1835, Thomas Macaulay had summarized the different articulation of race and color in the British approach to India:

> We must at present do our best to form a class who may be interpreters between us and the millions whom we govern; a class of persons, Indian in blood and color, but English in taste, in opinions, in morals, and in intellect.[9]

Imperial gods caused the white and the black, the evangelizer and the evangelized, to intermingle and influence each other. Mission stations were set up to spread Christian civilization, to convert and educate, to transform the irrational, primitive blackness into "enlightened," rational whiteness. Missions were also meant to draw a clear line not only between good and evil, right and wrong, but also between races. Instead, they ended up facilitating intermixing well beyond the clear, abstract line drawn by Thomas Macaulay.

In 1850, Mlanjeni rose as a prophet and started the resistance of the Xhosa against the Cape Colony in the name of a God-given mandate, clearly influenced by Christian missionaries. Mlanjeni claimed God had told him that a stick from the

---

5. Ibid., 59.

6. Villa-Vicencio and Grassow, *Christianity and the Colonisation of South Africa*, 272.

7. Thompson, *A History of South Africa*, 88.

8. Ibid.

9. Macaulay, "Indian Education," 729.

plumbago plant would have rendered the Xhosa invulnerable. The sacred Christian history and the present war between whites and blacks had mingled in Mlanjeni's mind. He announced, as author and historian Johannes Meintjes wrote, that "he had been to heaven and had talked to God, who was displeased with the white man for having killed his Son . . . God would help the black man against the white."[10]

A few years later, in 1857, overlapping Christian and African imageries dramatically changed the course of the events for the Xhosa when lung sickness, a lethal cattle disease, arrived from Europe and spread rapidly. Already weakened by the wars with the whites, the Xhosa "sought answers,"[11] as Leonard Thompson wrote, "in their indigenous concepts of witchcraft, pollution, sacrifice, and the powers of the ancestors; but they also adapted concepts of sin and the resurrection from the teachings of the missionaries."[12]

Nongqawuse, a sixteen-year-old girl, announced she had received a message from two men who had died long before. According to the account left by William Gcoba, a Xhosa living at the time, this had been the message:

> tell that the whole community will rise again from the dead, and that all cattle now living must be slaughtered, for they have been reared by contaminated hands, because there are people about who deal in witchcraft. There should be no cultivation, but great new grain pits must be dug, new houses must be built, and great strong cattle enclosures must be erected. Cut out new milksacks and weave many doors from buta roots. So says the chief Napakade, the descendant of Sifuba-sibanzi. The people must leave their witchcraft, for soon they will be examined by diviners.[13]

The indigenous community split. Those who rejected the prophecy and preserved the cattle came to be known as the *amagogotya*, the "hard believers." Many others followed Nongqawuse's prophecy and pursued it to a dramatic extent. They were the *amathamba*, the "soft believers." About four hundred thousand head of cattle were slaughtered. Extensive destruction of grain also took place. The prophecy should have been fulfilled at the new moon on February 18, 1857, but the destruction continued throughout 1857. Eventually about forty thousand Xhosa starved to death. Resurrection and witchcraft, sacrifice and last judgment, Christianity and native cultures, merged. With the Archbishop of Cape Town of the time impressed about how much the prophecy "borrows from Christianity and the Bible,"[14] Jeff Peires concluded that "far from being a retreat into a pre-Christian shell, the Cattle-Killing owed its very existence to biblical doctrines."[15]

---

10. Thompson, *A History of South Africa*, 77.

11. Ibid., 78.

12. Ibid.

13. Peires, *The Dead Will Arise*, 99.

14. Ibid., 159.

15. Ibid.

Revolutionary Sepoys

Also in 1857, one century after Clive's victory at Plassey established the rule of the British East India Company, dramatic events took place in India, when native troops in the army of the Company killed British officers and started a large-scale rebellion. This army being made up of British officers and indigenous soldiers, called Sepoys, summarized the contradictions of the British venture in India. It was, as Mark Twain noted, "a club made by British hands to beat out British brains with."[16] The "Mutiny," or the "independence war" as the revolt was to be recorded in the Indian national struggle, challenged coexistence between the ruling British and the subject Indian.

A not-yet-famous correspondent from London for the *New York Daily Tribune* underlined the failure of the "divide and rule" pattern applied by the British Raj: "It is the first time," Karl Marx wrote on July 15, 1857, "that Sepoy regiments have murdered their European officers; that Mussulmans and Hindoos, renouncing their mutual antipathies, have combined against their common masters."[17]

Marx identified in the "antagonism of the various races, tribes, castes, creeds, and sovereignties"[18] what he called "the vital principle of British supremacy."[19] But something had changed. If Indian religious divisions in the past had favored the white conqueror, now Indians moved beyond the religious line that divided them. As Marx noticed, "Mussulmans and Hindoos . . . combined against their common masters.[20]

The Sepoy rebellion had profound social and political motivations, but Western imperialists were blind to the various highly dynamic and syncretistic Indian realities and preferred to credit the "Mutiny" to clear-cut religious identities. The British were struck by the fact that what ultimately triggered the Mutiny was the mandatory use of rifle cartridges greased with pig or cow tallow, which Hindu and Muslim Indian troops in the army were compelled to ready by mouth. Karl Marx himself underscored what he saw from London as the religious implications and motives of the "Sepoy Mutiny." He wrote for the *New York Daily Tribune* that

> the alleged cause of the dissatisfaction, which began to spread four months ago in the Bengal army, was the apprehension on the part of the natives lest the Government should interfere with their religion. The serving out of cartridges, the paper of which was said to have been greased with the fat of bullocks and pigs, and the compulsory biting of which was, therefore, considered by the natives as an infringement of their religious prescriptions, gave the signal for local disturbances.[21]

16. Nayar, *The Penguin 1857 Reader*, 246.
17. Husain, *Karl Marx on India*, 61.
18. Ibid.
19. Ibid.
20. Ibid.
21. Ibid.

In reality, the affair of the greased cartridges was just the tip of the iceberg. Grievances had been growing over the increasing activism of British missionaries and civil servants. The unity of Muslims and Hindus underlined by Marx was less a spontaneous reaction to an isolated religious affront than it was a long-brewing result of overall British policy during the first half of the nineteenth century.

Christian Government

Before that time, the religious attitude of the British in India had diverged from the attitude of the Afrikaners towards the African natives. In South Africa during the eighteenth century, the Dutch East India Company controlled the religious establishment. "The ministers were salaried officials," explained Leonard Thompson, "the Church Council was nominated by the governor and Council of Policy, and it, too, consisted largely of officials."[22] Christianity was central to the Company's settlements. A visitor observing the town growing at the Cape in Table Bay in 1702 would have noticed that "it now boasts of a Church, built in the Dutch fashion and adorned with a fair-sized tower, in which on Sundays the Word of Truth is preached."[23]

The Dutch farmers and burghers were called the Boers by the British, but they would rather have called themselves Europeans, Afrikaners, and even Christians. They held the teachings from the Bible as the basic structure for their lives in the new and threatening environment. God wanted them to conquer and civilize the new world. God wanted them to stay pure by avoiding "contamination" with idolatry and close relations with the "inferior" black race.

Instead, the British East India Company fought Christian missionaries and made its officers trustees of Hindu temples. In the first century of British rule through the East India Company, the main goal was to secure trade and to preserve public order. The status quo needed to be protected. There was room for chaplains in the army, as superbly witnessed by the adventures of Kipling's Kim. But there was no room for religious zeal. Indigenous religions and cultures were largely tolerated. Local authorities, especially in the princely states, were entrusted with the mission of controlling the masses.

The British evangelical revolution of the 1820s and 1830s changed everything. Imperial gods pushed the revivalists to reshape religion, both at home, with a more rigorous definition of the government's Christian allegiance, and overseas, with a missionary thrust aimed at redressing both the whites, who worshiped money, and the blacks, who worshiped idols. Indian religions were also construed as monolithic and homogenous identities irrespective of the extremely diverse Indian reality.

Reformers in the homeland were mostly concerned with the weakening of established Christianity, namely the Church of England. Increasing diversity and tolerance

22. Thompson, *A History of South Africa*, 41.
23. Ibid., 39.

were perceived as a dangerous treason against the nation. The expression "national apostasy" became a manifesto of the fear that England was losing its religious and civil identity. In a famous sermon preached at St. Mary's, Oxford, on July 14, 1833, John Keble pointed at national apostasy as the main danger for the country:

> One of the most alarming, as a symptom, is the growing indifference, in which men indulge themselves, to other men's religious sentiments. Under the guise of charity and toleration, we are come almost to this pass; that no difference, in matters of faith, is to disqualify for our approbation and confidence, whether in public or domestic life. Can we conceal it from ourselves, that every year the practice is becoming more common, of trusting men unreservedly in the most delicate and important matters, without one serious inquiry, whether they do not hold principles which make it impossible for them to be loyal to their Creator, Redeemer, and Sanctifier?[24]

The judge in charge of the Rushdie case in 1990 went back to this period, one hundred fifty years earlier, to retrace the modern grounding of blasphemy law as a principle meant to protect the established religion and the established religion only. In 1838, Justice Alderson B. addressed the jury in the Gathercole's case in the following terms:

> A person may, without being liable to prosecution for it, attack Judaism, or Mahomedanism, or even any sect of the Christian Religion (save the established religion of the country), and the only reason why the latter is in a different situation from the others is, because it is the form established by law, and is therefore a part of the constitution of the country. In like manner, and for the same reason, any general attack on Christianity is the subject of criminal prosecution, because Christianity is the established religion of the country.[25]

British Christianity needed to be protected and nourished in the homeland if it was to inspire the spreading of civilization across the Empire.

In South Africa, a clash with the Afrikaners was inevitable inasmuch as the evangelical revolution had brought about the abolition of the slave trade, the reform of the penal code and the Poor Laws. In the name of the same God, British Christians freed the slaves and rejected degrading punishments while the Afrikaner Christians affirmed a God-given right over their slaves and held cruelty as an indispensable means of government.

In 1995, in its first decision ever, the South African Constitutional Court faced the issue of the death penalty. Justice Albie Sachs explained for the Court how the Dutch and the British had progressively diverged in the way they approached torture and punishment. Under Dutch rule, not only were executions practiced, but, as Justice Sachs pointed out, "the judges specified in detail gruesome modes of execution designed to produce maximum pain and greatest indignity over the longest period of

24. Keble, *National Apostasy*, 12–13.
25. *R v Chief Metropolitan*, 441.

time. The concept of a dignified execution was seen as a contradiction in terms. The public was invited to witness the lingering death, the mutilation and the turning of human beings into carrion for the birds."[26]

For the British, Albie Sachs observed, capital punishment served to civilize the indigenous culture: the local system based on cattle fines for murders was replaced by executions, the pedagogy of which was that a man's life is priceless. For the indigenous culture a cattle fine was a fair response to a murder. For the British, it was not enough: paradoxically, life was so precious that a murderer deserved to be killed.

Yet the British who took over in Southern Africa in the nineteenth century were against torture and cruel modes of execution. A divide arose not only between the British and the Afrikaner, but also between the British coming from the homeland and the British already settled in the Cape Colony or in Natal. British settlers found, Sachs recalled, "that whatever might have been appropriate in Britain, in the conditions of the Cape, to rely merely on hangings, corporal punishment, and prison was to invite slave uprisings and mayhem."[27] Albie Sachs summed up the confusion of those times in a powerful image: "the public executioner was so distressed that he hanged himself."[28]

In India, reformers aimed at evangelizing their own government. In Edwardes's words, "the Evangelicals thought the government of India was a Christian government that had discarded Christian morals."[29] A new rule, even more imperial and even more Christian, was needed. Consequently, a true evangelical revolution was experienced through the reforms of Lord William Bentinck in the 1830s and Lord Dalhousie in the 1840s, with the prohibition of self-torture of the Hindus, of infanticides, of the Sati, of the burning of widows, and of self-immolation under the wheels of Jagannath during the Rath Yatra festival at Puri. This widened the gap between the rulers and the ruled. The propagation of Christianity further exacerbated spirits. Since the Charter Act of 1813 first opened the doors of India to private individuals, both missionaries and teachers had flooded in, and from America as well. British schools and churches spurred conversions to Christianity.

The law was involved, too. The son of a fervent evangelical and abolitionist, Thomas Macaulay included legislative reform in his colonial vision of British India. If English was to be the new language of the Indian elite, English legal rationality had to replace what the colonizer saw as the confused and arbitrary multiplicity of customary and religious precepts. In his speech to the House of Commons of July 10, 1833, four days before John Keble's sermon on national apostasy, Macaulay drew a dramatic picture of the Indian legal landscape.

26. *S v Makwanyane* [384].

27. Ibid. [385].

28. Ibid.

29. Edwardes, "The Mutiny and Its Consequences," xix.

> We have now in our Eastern empire Hindoo law, Mahometan law, Parsee law, English law, perpetually mingling with each other and disturbing each other, varying with the person, varying with the place . . . The consequence is that in practice the decisions of the tribunals are altogether arbitrary. What is administered is not law, but a kind of rude and capricious equity.[30]

Consequently, a uniform legal code imposing superior British rationality was needed. It was necessary, in Macaulay's own words, "to digesting and reforming the laws of India."[31] Colonial laws, Rina Williams wrote, "simultaneously served to justify European colonial rule and also to assure its implementation and success."[32] The Evangelical drive pushed not only to reinvent Indian religions and customs, but also to establish a uniform colonial law encompassing customs, castes, and religions. Both the plural faiths and cultures and the plural legal universe of Indians were threatened. The same Christian, imperial gods that struggled with humanizing and converting the Western colonialists also sought to redraw the religious and legal map of India.

Landlords and the Faithful

In a three-hour speech delivered in London on July 27, 1857—in the midst of the Mutiny—future Prime Minister Benjamin Disraeli blamed the recent change of policy in India as the ultimate cause of the uprising. He carefully avoided any overt mention of the Evangelical thrust, which he believed had led to the revolt. He emphasized that for almost one century the British had applied the Roman principle of "*divide et impera*," divide and rule, in a manner that was respectful of property rights, of "the different nationalities of which India consisted,"[33] as well as of the different creeds. Then the principle of "destroying nationalities"[34] was adopted and realized, Disraeli maintained, "by the forcible destruction of native princes, the disturbance of the settlement of property, and the tampering with the religion of people."[35]

The link between land revenue policies, property rights, and religion was not easy for the British to grasp. Disraeli did not address the question openly. But he emphasized that the British had deeply affected property rights by denying the application of the Hindu law of adoption on which every Hindu landowner in the country relied. In the following years, Indian Muslims would also come to complain about the negative impact on the old Mughal ruling elites of revenue policies and, in particular, of the abolition of the taluqdari rights, the privileges of the landlords.

---

30. Macaulay, "Government of India," 713–14.

31. Ibid., 713.

32. Williams, *Postcolonial Politics and Personal Laws*, 36.

33. Husain, *Karl Marx on India*, 67.

34. Ibid., 68.

35. Ibid.

Karl Marx reported Disraeli's analysis in his correspondence for the *New York Daily Tribune* of August 14, 1857. Marx embraced Disreali's idea that this was not a military mutiny, but a "national revolt."[36] If Indians went beyond divisions in caste, status, and creed, he believed, if they became a nation, then British rule was in serious jeopardy.

Marx did not sympathize with the East India Company. Protectionist readers in New York appreciated his critique of the British free traders. But he also despised Indian religion based on the Hegelian assumption that India was a passive civilization. He considered India a "strange combination of Italy and Ireland, of a world of voluptuousness and of a world of woes,"[37] as he wrote in the *New York Daily Tribune* of June 25, 1853. In the same article, he depicted traditional Indian society as negatively affected by distinctions of caste and by slavery. To him, religion was a substantial part of that picture. In the religion of India, he wrote, "never changing natural destiny,"[38] combined with "a brutalizing worship of nature, exhibiting its degradation in the fact that man, the sovereign of nature, fell down on his knees in adoration of Hanuman, the monkey, and Sabbala, the cow."[39]

Therefore, in the name of emancipation from superstition and bigotry, Marx could endorse the revolution in the Indian economy imposed and fueled by the Company. He stressed not only the role of the British tax-gatherer and the British soldier, but in particular the effect of English steam-powered industry and English free trade. The British distanced the spinner from the weaver, underlined Marx, putting "the spinner in Lancashire and the weaver in Bengal,"[40] or swept away both spinner and weaver from India, thus sapping the traditional village-based Indian economy. This Marx supported. "We must not forget," he wrote "that these idyllic village-communities, inoffensive though they may appear, had always been the solid foundation of Oriental despotism, that they restrained the human mind within the smallest possible compass, making it the unresisting tool of superstition, enslaving it beneath traditional rules, depriving it of all grandeur and historical energies."[41]

The Reformers emphasized the British mission of evangelizing and civilizing. Marx conceptualized an Indian national unity prompted by the British dismantling and rebuilding of the whole structure of Indian economy and society. He and the Reformers shared the common foe of what they saw as the backward and superstitious Indian system of beliefs. Marx was aware of the hostility between Hindus and Muslims, but he thought the crucial divide was rather between Indians and Christians. In his view, the distinction between premodern indigenous creeds and modern secularized Christianity was at the foundation of the uprising, the very explosion of which

36. Ibid., 70.
37. Ibid., 11.
38. Ibid., 16.
39. Ibid.
40. Ibid.
41. Ibid.

depended on those "wild, aimless, unbounded forces of destruction," wrote Marx, that "rendered murder itself a religious rite in Hindostan."[42]

The Finger of God

The confrontation between Indian religions and British evangelical zeal grew silently until it exploded in Meerut in 1857, when Indian troops shot their British officers. Michael Edwardes emphasized the religious implications of the British fury, after British women and children held prisoners at Cawnpore in the residence of Nana Sahib were murdered and their bodies thrown into the well of the house:

> The reaction of the British to the Mutiny was one of Evangelical fury. They insinuated God into every one of their actions, smugly quoting Holy Writ as a justification for the most abominable tortures. John Nicholson, the "Hero" of Delhi . . . wrote: "We are told in the Bible that stripes should be meted out according to faults" and suggested that hanging was too good for the mutineers, and proposed "a Bill for the flaying alive, impalement, or burning of the murderers of women and children."[43]

General Neill, responsible for the subsequent indiscriminate killing of Indians—the "second massacre" of Cawnpore—ordered that "each miscreant . . . will be taken down to the house in question . . . and will be forced into cleaning up a small portion of the blood stains; the task will be made as revolting to his feelings as possible . . . After properly cleaning up his portion, the culprit is to be immediately hanged."[44]

Neill himself later recalled that "Mahomedan officer of our civil court, a great rascal . . . he rather objected, was flogged, made to lick part of the blood with his tongue."[45]

The British saw God in the "Mutiny." In the trial against the former king of Delhi, Muhammad Bahadur Shah, they accused the leader of the insurgence of having urged the chief police officer to proclaim "throughout the city, by beat of drum that this is a religious war, and is being prosecuted on account of the faith, and that it behoves all Hindu and Mussalman residents of the imperial city."[46]

In Kipling's novel *Kim*, first published forty-four years after the "Mutiny," the Lama asked about the "black year" of 1857: "What madness was that, then?"[47] Proud of his loyalty to the British, the old Indian soldier replied, "The gods, who sent it for a plague, alone know."[48]

---

42. Ibid.

43. Edwardes, "The Mutiny and Its Consequences," xvi–xvii.

44. Ibid., xv.

45. Ibid.

46. Garrett, *The Trial of Muhammad Bahadur Shah,* 248.

47. Kipling, *Kim,* 73.

48. Ibid.

In 1857, imperial gods served as justification for the massacres following the "Mutiny"; also, on the other side of the Indian Ocean, gods warranted the Xhosa cattle killing.

But religion did not drive "superstitious" Xhosa in South Africa and "miscreant" Indian natives only. General Neill himself gave a God-based explanation for his cruel Christian punishments: "No doubt this is strange law, but it suits the occasion well, and I hope I shall not be interfered with until the room is thoroughly cleansed in this way . . . I will hold my own, with the blessing and help of God. I cannot help seeing that His finger is in all this."[49]

For other British soldiers, who also were taking part in the ruthless vengeance, Christian gods indeed played a role, but a different one. As William Howard Russell, a war correspondent for the *Times* mentioned in his diary of the Mutiny, the right to inflict the worst punishment might spring from a different theological articulation: "We are not Christians now, because we are dealing with those who are not of our faith."[50]

In fact, what Russell saw was the ambivalence not only of the Indian but also of the British. To whites, the Indian was both "monkey and tiger,"[51] peaceful and lethal. But the trees festooned with Indians hanged on the side of the roads proved that the Briton was no less "monkey and tiger" than the Indian. Russell wrote:

> They are the true composite of monkey and tiger, those Orientals. Any one of those amicable kite-flyers would probably disembowel you—cut off your head if you fell into his hands and could not defend yourself. We tortured our Jews once on a time as the Hindus and Mohammedans mutilate their Christians now, and I presume our Crusaders—if not the knights, at least their barbarous followers—gave scant grace to the Moslem.[52]

Carried on in the name of a typically Victorian self-righteousness, the "Christian" revenge undertaken by the British after the Mutiny announced the failure of the evangelical revolution, which had started some thirty years before. The changes in the law, blamed by Disraeli and suffered by the Indians, had failed to serve the religious goal: "The excrescences of Hinduism had been legislated away, but the great conversion had not taken place,"[53] Edwardes wrote. And he added: "In the Mutiny, Satan had rebelled."[54]

In the meantime, in South Africa, the black nations also resisted the conversion, civilization, and domination of the whites. If in the British Empire "a black skin was

49. Edwardes, "The Mutiny and Its Consequences," xv–xvi.

50. Russell, *My Indian Mutiny Diary*, 198.

51. Ibid., 80.

52. Ibid.

53. Edwardes, "The Mutiny and Its Consequences," xvii.

54. Ibid.

the mark of a murderer,"[55] as Michael Edwardes claimed in regard to British brutality in the wake of the Mutiny, this was because the superior Christianity of the colonizer had not delivered that "great conversion" of both whites and blacks that the Bibles of the Afrikaners and of the British Reformers alike, though in different terms, had promised.

The Solace of Religion

The cattle killing had proved decisive in weakening indigenous resistance against both Afrikaner and British whites, ultimately leading to the military defeat of the indigenous nations and to the Anglo-Boer war. Similarly, the War of Independence of 1957 changed the Indian landscape forever.

The British reestablished their order in India through bloodshed. But their military superiority and the divisions among Indians were not enough. A different policy was necessary. After one hundred years, the rule of the East India Company was over. The English crown took direct control of India. A viceroy of India would replace the governor-general and act in the name of the Queen. The British Raj was born.

Gods could not be bypassed. Not only had the Mutiny demonstrated the tremendous potential for a war of religion between Indians and the British, but it had also shown that tensions were still high among religious communities in India.

In fact, at the time, Muslims and Hindus were already at odds in Ayodhya around the Masjid, the mosque that Hindu nationalist kar sevaks would demolish 135 years later, in 1992. Intercommunal unity prompted by the insurgence slowed down tensions, but the issue remained as hot then as at the time of Sushmita. Immediately after the war, the British built an enclosure in front of the Masjid. The Hindus were prevented from entering the inner yard and instead raised a platform outside on which to perform their rites. In 1858, some Hindu monks occupied the Masjid, and local Muslims complained to the British government. While arbitrating the conflict between Hindus and Muslims, the British kept exploiting its extraordinary potential for a divide-and-rule policy.

Queen Victoria took upon herself the task of setting the new framework for India. In the proclamation of November 1, 1858, she announced the birth of the British Raj and further declared the principle of religious policy on which rested the Queen's rule in India and beyond:

> Firmly relying Ourselves on the truth of Christianity, and acknowledging with gratitude the solace of Religion, We disclaim alike the Right and the Desire to impose our Convictions on any of Our Subjects. We declare it to be Our Royal Will and Pleasure that none be in any wise favoured, none molested or disquieted, by reason of their Religious Faith or Observances; but that all shall alike enjoy the equal and impartial protection of the Law: and We do strictly charge and enjoin all those who may be in authority under Us, that they abstain from

---

55. Ibid., xviii.

all interference with the Religious Belief or Worship of any of Our Subjects, on pain of Our highest Displeasure.[56]

For the time, the assertion of "the equal and impartial protection of the law" was quite a political and legal achievement. Restraint from "interference," renewing Warren Hastings's promise, was noticeable. The combination of state religion and tolerance of other creeds was also remarkable. Yet in practice Indians remained skeptical about the doctrine and untouched by it. War correspondent William Howard Russell noticed that although the East India Company was replaced by the Queen's rule, Indians "will lie under the same machinery of finance, of justice, and they will be subjected to the same grievances in the courts of law, and to the same oppressive system of police."[57]

The governor general read the proclamation on November 1, 1858, in Allahabad. Fireworks were set off in celebration. William Howard Russell was present and reported an anecdote that encapsulated how difficult the new system of government looked in the light of the deep-seated habits of Victorian arrogance: "I was greatly amused . . . to hear a sergeant who was on duty at the foot of the staircase, call to one of the men and say to him, 'I'm going away for a moment: do you stay here and take care that no nigger goes up.'"[58]

The gods were not appeased. In his *History of the Indian Mutiny* of 1859, Charles Ball published a translation of the counterproclamation issued immediately after the release of Queen Victoria's by the Begum of Oude, the native state annexed by the East India Company before the Mutiny and a hot spot of the ensuing war:

In the [Queen Victoria's] proclamation it is written, that the Christian religion is true, but that no other creed will suffer oppression, and that the laws will be observed towards all. What has the administration of justice to do with the truth or falsehood of religion? That religion is true which acknowledges one God, and knows no other. Where there are three Gods in a religion, neither Mussulmen nor Hindoos—nay, not even Jews, Sun-worshippers, or Fire-worshippers can believe it true. To eat pigs and drink wine—to bite greased cartridges, and to mix pig's fat with flour and sweetmeats—to destroy Hindoo and Mussulman temples on pretence of making roads—to build churches—to send clergymen into the streets and alleys to preach the Christian religion—to institute English schools, and to pay a monthly stipend for learning the English sciences, while the places of worship of Hindoos and Mussulmans are to this day entirely neglected; with all this, how can the people believe that religion will not be interfered with? The rebellion began with religion, and, for it, millions of men have been killed. Let not our subjects be deceived; thousands

56. Victoria, "Proclamation."

57. Russell, *My Indian Mutiny Diary*, 207.

58. Ibid., 209.

were deprived of their religion in the North-West, and thousands were hanged rather than abandon their religion.[59]

In 1858, the first analysis of the Mutiny by a native Indian was published by Benares Medical Hall Press. The book circulated among the elite, in India and in London. The author was Syed Ahmed Khan, the father of Indian Islamic modernism. Unlike the Begum of Oude, Syed Ahmed Khan praised the Queen's proclamation. Faced with "such ample redress or every grievance which led up to that revolt,"[60] he "felt his pen fall from his hands."[61] Yet Syed Ahmed Khan took upon himself the task of representing the viewpoint of the "native of the country."[62] To him this meant representing the Muslims, notably the old ruling class, asserting their loyalty to the crown and defending them from the accusation of having been the true conspirators behind the Mutiny. He also spoke out of his own experience: relatives killed in the British revenge, his mother dead because of the privations after the recapture of Delhi, the targeting of Muslims, his personal effort to save British lives in the Bijnor district, his own life at risk. The whole experience, he wrote, "made an old man of me. My hair turned white."[63]

Throughout his pamphlet, Syed Ahmed Khan endeavoured to make the point that the catastrophe had resulted from the British failure to hear the voice of the people. No Indian representative had been appointed to the Legislative Council. No Indian claim had been taken seriously. This had caused the disaster, since, Syed Ahmed Khan pleaded, "a needle may dam the gushing rivulet. An elephant must turn aside from the swollen torrent."[64]

When Syed Ahmed Khan's book circulated in London, Charles Darwin's theories were being widely discussed as well. *On the Origin of Species*, the foundation of evolutionary biology, was published on November 24, 1859. British society was changing. Its gods were transforming. The debate on national apostasy and blasphemy was also affected. The English judges in charge of the Rushdie affair in 1990 noticed that by the time of the Mutiny, "as a result of the revolution in thought brought about by Darwin and others . . . it was no longer blasphemous to make a sober reasoned attack on the Christian religion."[65] No reasonable critique, but only a scurrilous vilification of religion was recognized and punished as blasphemy.

In his early thirties, Thomas Macaulay was very active in the debate on religious equality. In his maiden speech, April 17, 1833, on Jewish disabilities, he approached blasphemy in terms of equal dignity and treatment of all creeds. "If I were a judge in

59. Ball, *History of the Indian Mutiny*, 543.

60. Ahmed Khan, *The Causes of the Indian Revolt*, 1.

61. Ibid.

62. Ibid.

63. Ibid., ix.

64. Ibid., 12.

65. *R v Chief Metropolitan*, 442.

India,"[66] he said to the House of Lords, "I should have no scruple about punishing a Christian who should pollute a mosque."[67]

In the wake of the birth of the British Raj, Macaulay, now in his late fifties, applied the principle of tolerance of Queen Victoria's proclamation when he drafted his Indian Penal Code, later enforced in 1860, immediately after his death. As Lord Justice Watkins emphasized in 1990 when delivering judgment on the case of *The Satanic verses*, "when Macaulay became a legislator in India, he saw to it that the law protected the religious feelings of all."[68]

The Indian code of 1860 provided for the punishment of intentional insults to religious feelings, whatever the faith involved. Section 296 punished disturbances to a religious assembly. Section 298 punished utterances and words "with deliberate intent to wound the religious feelings of any person." A reminder of the tensions in Ayodhya, Section 295 punished the act of injuring or defiling a place of worship.

The new system was taking shape. Contrary to Macaulay's wishes in 1833, and despite his Penal Code, the Code of Civil Procedure of 1859, and the Code of Criminal Procedure of 1861, legal uniformity had not been achieved. Religions, castes, and customs kept ruling society of their own right, parallel to the largely immaterial codified law. Macaulay's ambition of ordering the messy Indian legal landscape collided with Indian resilience as well as with the new British vision of tolerance and restraint.

The new system was soon tested in courts. Another Victoria, this time an ordinary young English lady whose father had been killed during the Mutiny, offered the British judiciary the occasion to assess the real meaning of Queen Victoria's proclamation.

Separate Communities

Victoria Skinner's father, a British Christian, died during the Mutiny. After his death, Victoria lived with her mother, who in the meantime had started cohabiting with a married Christian, John Thomas John. The man and Victoria's mother converted to Islam and married under Islamic law. The conversion and the subsequent Muslim marriage represented their extreme attempt to transform an illicit concubinal liaison into a licit conjugal relationship.

At the age of fourteen, Victoria also decided to convert to Islam. This prompted the relatives of Victoria's father to rise against what they saw as an irregular and dangerous situation for Victoria and to ask the judge of Meerut to remove the child from the custody of the mother. Meerut was the same town where the first British officers had been shot fourteen years earlier, at the beginning of the Mutiny. The judge and the High Court of Judicature for the North-Western Provinces at Allahabad accepted the petition and ordered the removal of the girl. In his decision of December 1871, for

66. Ibid., 445.

67. Ibid.

68. Ibid.

Her Majesty's Privy Council in London, Lord Justice James confirmed the judgments as given by the lower courts.

Lord Justice James displayed his faith in the pattern of the British Raj, as laid down in Queen Victoria's proclamation. Equality and impartiality were emphasized on one hand as the modern principles globally spread by the British Empire; on the other hand the rights of local cultures and habits were also recognized.

This was the British Raj. Natives were now to be handled more nicely. In 1862, Ahmed Khan's complaint was finally heard, and the first Indian was appointed to the Legislative Council, thus opening the era of elective Indian representatives on local boards. Indian religions were to be respected as well. Justice James brought the Indian diversity of cultures, customs, and traditions into British modernity, using the language of the "nation" and of "political rights":

> In India . . . all or almost all the great religious communities of the world exist side by side under the impartial rule of the British Government. While Brahmin, Buddhist, Christian, Mahomedan, Parsee, and Sikh are one nation enjoying equal political rights and having perfect equality before the tribunals, they co-exist as separate and very distinct communities having distinct laws affecting every relation of life.[69]

One same nation, separate and distinct religious communities. One encompassing British common law for all, one specific religious law for each community. Lord James's statement summarized the conundrum of British India after the Crown's takeover. The language of political modernity—rights, impartiality, equality—struggled with the otherness of Indian cultures and religions. The principle deduced by Lord James from the 1858 proclamation was particularly true in family matters where the private and the public converged. According to the judge, "the law of husband and wife, parent and child, the descent, devolution, and disposition of property are all different, depending, in each case, on the body to which the individual is deemed to belong; and the difference of religion pervades and governs all domestic usages and social relations."[70]

The lesson of the Mutiny was tangible. The judge appeared eager to use the law to neatly demarcate the different communities while emphatically purporting not to interfere with religious traditions. The pre-Reformers' pragmatic pattern of tolerance and public order resurfaced. But the case of Victoria was more challenging. Conversion was at stake. And converts were challenging inasmuch as they trespassed the line dividing the whites from the "coolies." Whatever the reason—to escape bigamy, to achieve a more convenient social status, to sincerely embrace a more convincing faith or to please one's family, husband, or wife—conversions blurred the borders between the communities and the relevant laws. When the boundaries were broken, religious communities and laws could not "coexist side by side" anymore. They overlapped

69. *Skinner*, 323.

70. Ibid.

and conflicted. British common law and traditional religious laws could no longer be peacefully articulated.

The conversion of Victoria's mother and of Victoria herself made this blatant.

The common-law principle to be applied in the controversy was that the only ground legitimizing a change in the custody of children was the manifest immorality of the parent. This was not easy to establish under the circumstances. Victoria's mother claimed she was simply a widow who legitimately married a second time. The problem was that the second husband was already married. Was she morally living with a man in a legitimate marriage, or was she immorally the concubine of a man married to another woman? Did the conversion of both to Islam and the celebration of a Muslim marriage make the union legitimate? Was that Muslim marriage valid despite the previous wedlock of John Thomas John? The immorality of Victoria's mother and the change of custody depended on the validity of the Muslim marriage between her and John.

This was a very difficult judgment to give in 1871, as it would be more than one century later for the Supreme Court of India to rule in the case of Sushmita Ghosh.

Faced with the disturbing reality of a Mutiny victim's widow who converted to Islam in order to save an adulterous relationship, Victorian morality prevailed.

However, the judge did not pay any attention to the difference between an adulterous union and a valid Muslim marriage, which would have constituted a regular relationship between Victoria's mother and her partner: "their Lordships can entertain no doubt, that when the connection between John Thomas John and the Widow was formed, whether it was merely adulterous or under the cover of a Mahomedan marriage, the home was no longer a fit home for a Christian young girl."[71]

Arguments were not needed. The interpretation of Muslim law did not matter. Muslim law itself was not worth taking into account. The only relevant point was the superior interest of a Christian girl not to be diverted from her natural education. That made perfect sense to the judge, to "their Lordships" and to white society as a whole.

I Am Studying the Koran

The crux of the decision—the heart of the principle proclaimed by Lord Justice James—was that morality meant allegiance to one's own community. And that conversion from one community to another was synonymous with immorality when a person converted from the superior Christian faith to a barbarous native religion.

By converting to Islam, Victoria's mother overstepped the bounds. She betrayed her community; she betrayed the patriarchal pattern. She was twice to blame. First, she had moved from the superior community of the rulers to the inferior community of the ruled over. She had broken the natural order determining the way different

71. Ibid., 325.

communities coexisted in the colonial environment. Second, she had done so in order to start a substantially adulterous relationship with a partner who was still (morally if not legally) bound by his previous marriage, indissolubility being, at the time, the distinctive feature of Christian civilization.

This was the real meaning of the principle according to which all creeds could coexist "under the impartial British rule:" such coexistence was possible only insofar as the colonial pattern was preserved. The autonomy of the different groups was acknowledged in order to fuel division among them and to erect a wall between the ruled communities and the rulers. The preservation of the natural order was the fundamental guarantee that white Christian colonizers would not lose their superiority: that their principles—such as the patriarchal reverence owed to fathers and the indissolubility of marriage—would not fade away in the hostile environment.

The proclaimed "equality" and "impartiality" counted insofar as the rulers and the native indigenous people were kept separate by the law. Recognizing the different religious communities was not about bringing non-Christians in, but about keeping them out. Belonging to the same British Raj was not about integration and inclusion, but rather about exclusion and separation in secluded communities. The distinctive civil and social status of the white Christian colonizer had to be preserved. The "Mutiny" had demonstrated—and not only to Karl Marx and his readers in New York— how dangerous the national unity of the Indian communities could be for Britain. The safeguard of both indigenous divisions and Christian British rule stood behind the apparently anodyne statement of Lord Justice James, according to which "a child in India, under ordinary circumstances, must be presumed to have his father's religion, and his corresponding civil and social status."[72]

The outcome in court was coherent with these social and political priorities. The Muslim marriage of Victoria's mother was not recognized. She was deemed adulterous and socially expelled from the white Christian community. She lost custody of her daughter. Victoria was forced to abandon her family and home environment. She was not allowed to become a "Mahommedan"; she could not shift from her dead father's Christian faith to her living mother's new one.

The evidence given by Victoria herself in the trial was the best example of how harmful the entangling of conversions, families, and identities could be for the ruling British Christians:

> I am studying the Koran with a teacher. There was a picture of my father, and there were several other pictures; but as I had heard that it was strictly forbidden to keep pictures by our religion, I, therefore, destroyed them with my own hands. The picture was on paper in a frame with glass.[73]

---

72. Ibid., 323.

73. Ibid., 326.

Nothing could be more telling than Victoria destroying her father's image. The betrayal of the paternal faith was the betrayal of the community: the patriarchal and the colonial patterns were at stake. Conversions and immorality intertwined. The dark had to be separated from the light, the black from the white. Lord Justice James could conclude "the case of the appellant, in fact, rested on this deposition."[74]

The principle of separateness and unevenness applied by Lord Justice James, also presided over the census operations started in 1872, one year after the decision on Victoria's custody. As sociologist Van der Veer noticed, "the collection of data on caste and the division of the population into religious communities"[75] mirrored "indigenous and pre-colonial divisions."[76] However, it now served the divide and rule strategies of the British Raj. Also in 1872, gold was discovered in the Lydenburg district of the Zuid-Afrikaanse Republiek. This, of course, attracted more and more workers from Britain and ultimately the British army for the campaign of occupation, which led to the Boer War. Meanwhile, the mining industry in southern Africa also brought ethnic and racial exploitation and discrimination.

The picture of Victoria's father was the symbol of imperial gods. Afrikaners, South African British settlers, African native nations like the Xhosa and the Zulu, British colonialists, Indian Muslims, Hindus, and Parsis, all were haunted by the traumatic end of the world of the fathers. They all were overwhelmed by the new coming age, no matter how powerful their weapons or how numerous their possessions. The more the fathers were venerated, the more their image was blurred and even destroyed, as in the case of Victoria. The more the Empire erected walls between creeds, the more religions intermingled. The more *your* gods were worshiped, the more *our* gods marched in.

In the mid-1990s, Edward Said emphasized Kipling's idea of the complex functioning of the Indian society under the Empire. Said made Kim himself the symbol of Kipling's colonial society, which could be "neither rigidly run by "structures" nor completely overrun by marginal, prophetic, and alienated figures":[77] "That Kim himself is both an Irish outcast boy and later an essential player in the British Secret Service Great Game suggests Kipling's uncanny understanding of the workings and managing control of societies."[78]

Indeed Kipling placed gods—intermingling, syncretic gods, *your* and *our* gods— at the center of Kim's universe. What the Roman Catholic chaplain of the Mavericks Father Victor taught Kipling's young hero sounded to Kim like "an entirely new set of Gods and Godlings—notably of a Goddess called Mary, who, [Kim] gathered, was one

74. Ibid., 327.

75. Van der Veer, *Religious Nationalism*, 21.

76. Ibid.

77. Said, *Culture and Imperialism*, 170.

78. Ibid.

with Bibi Miriam of [Kim's Muslim mentor] Mahbub Ali's theology."[79] Imperial gods announced preservation and purity; they brought fusion and change.

Terrible Judgment

Tensions both with imperial gods at the end of the nineteenth century and with explosive gods one century later concerned the Christian struggle with both alien creeds in the colonies and an increasingly secular society in the homeland.

When Lord Justice Watkins wrote the opinion for the Queen's Bench Division on the Rushdie case in 1990, he faced two contradictory claims, both challenging the sense of blasphemy law in contemporary Britain. Rushdie's defense argued that blasphemy law was meant to protect Christians only, and that freedom of expression deserved absolute protection anyway. Anti-Rushdie activists rather claimed that the law should extend to nonconformists and ultimately protect British Muslims as well.

In search of inspiration, Justice Watkins went back to the debate on atheism that had taken place in Parliament a century earlier, in the late 1880s. In the time of imperial gods, the opposition between those who upheld the Christian vocation of Britain and those who promoted militant atheism went beyond Britain and influenced the whole Empire, including India and South Africa. Mohandas Karamchand Gandhi, who spent three crucial years in London around this time, and then brought his experience to South Africa and India, became a special witness of the conjunction between religious tensions and Imperial politics.

The Empty Oath

In the second half on the nineteenth century, after the "Mutiny," a new religious challenge arose in England.

So far, the opposition between evangelicals and Anglo-Catholics had occupied the stage. Meanwhile, the problem of non-Anglican Christians, or nonconformists, as they were called at the time, had stirred divisions. Civil disabilities of the Jewish and the Roman Catholics prompted a tense political and parliamentary debate; Macaulay himself had touched upon the issue of blasphemy in India during his maiden speech at the House of Commons in 1833 while advocating the necessity to abandon the system of Jewish disabilities. Religion was also inextricably linked to the Irish problem, with Charles Stewart Parnell, the Protestant Irish nationalist leader, being elected to Parliament for the first time in 1875.

After the proclamation of Queen Victoria in 1858, a new problem with religion emerged: traditional Christianity was made the object of fundamental criticism. Some, like the theosophists, criticized institutional religion and preached a universal

---

79. Kipling, *Kim*, 158.

syncretistic faith bridging Western and Eastern creeds. Others engaged in a more radical confutation of theism and campaigned for the legitimacy and virtue of atheism. The old and the new religious tensions influenced British politics both in the homeland and overseas. Evangelical Anglicanism was responsible for more active policies in India, which had exacerbated problems with the natives and ultimately resulted in one of the causes of the war of 1857. It had also widened the gap with racist Calvinist Afrikaners in southern Africa. Theosophists and atheists, though from two opposite perspectives, both undermined the Christian foundation of British imperialism and provided native Indians and Africans with the vision of independence and the tools to pursue it.

Elected to the Parliament in 1880, Charles Bradlaugh made a decisive case for the right to be a public atheist in England. The president of the London Secular Society at the time of the "Mutiny" and the founder in 1866 of the National Secular Society, together with Annie Besant Bradlaugh, personified the secular turn of Britain and the breakthrough of freethinkers and atheists. While entering Parliament, Bradlaugh refused to take the traditional oath of allegiance, which included the words "so help me, God." He asked to "affirm" his allegiance instead. In fact "affirmation" was the alternative for those who objected in conscience to taking an oath. The Parliament refused. Then Bradlaugh offered to take the oath "as a matter of form," making clear that such an act was devoid of any substantial meaning to him. On May 24, 1880, as Bradlaugh was about to be sworn in, some English MPs objected. Winston Churchill's father, Randolph, emerged as the fiercest contender. The same day he gave a sulphurous speech and urged the Parliament not to allow Bradlaugh's mocking oath. If the House of Commons, said Randolph Churchill, accepted that the words "so help me, God" were transformed in "a ridiculous and superstitious invocation, utterly devoid of any moral force, then the whole connection between the proceedings of Parliament and a Divine sanction was in danger; and the idea, [I] might almost say the faith, which had for centuries animated the House of Commons that its proceedings were under the supervision and would be guided by the wisdom of a beneficent Providence, lost all its force."[80]

At the end of the speech, Randolph Churchill hurled a pamphlet by Bradlaugh on the floor and crushed it under his feet. In the end, Bradlaugh was not allowed to take the oath and could not take his seat at the House as the honorable member for Northampton.

Bradlaugh's struggle continued through a cycle of electoral victories, four in a row, and parliamentary rejections. His case was not limited to English religious and political quarrels. His fight for nonconformists and nonbelievers was also a fight for the unpaired and the exploited. To him, British home politics and imperial strategies were the two sides of the same coin. In fact, his atheism was strictly linked to a radical criticism of British imperial gods. Charles Bradlaugh was stigmatized in Parliament as the "member for India," as he actively stood for Indian self-rule. Randolph Churchill became himself increasingly interested in colonial affairs and visited India in early

80. Churchill, "Speech in Parliament."

1885. On February 22, in Benares on a boat on the Ganges, he encountered Indian religiosity: "The water is very dirty," he wrote, "but they lap it up in quantities as it is very 'holy.'"[81] Once back in England, in June, he was made Secretary of State for India; immediately after, he declared: "without India, England would cease to be a nation."[82] The same conviction would steer his son Winston throughout the whole of his political career.

Precisely at the same time, in 1885, Courtney Stanhope Kenny, later a law professor at Cambridge, entered Parliament and proposed to abolish the common-law offense of blasphemy. One century later in the Rushdie affair, Justice Watkins underlined this momentous step.

Darwin had died in 1882, three years before Kenny's proposal. In the wake of the scientific and social success of evolutionism, Professor Kenny represented the increasing portion of English society that assumed free discussion on issues of religion should prevail over the conformist supremacy of the Church of England. Evolutionism challenged religion. The status quo was under threat. Professor Kenny believed that the introduction of a statutory offense concerning intentional insults to any sort of religious feeling was more appropriate for the new British society than the old-fashioned, Church of England–centered, blasphemy law. The equalitarian protection of all beliefs was preferable to the sole protection of Christians. His model was the Indian Penal Code drafted by Macaulay nearly thirty years earlier.

In 1889, during Gandhi's first year as a law student in London, Kenny's project failed. In the Choudhury-Rushdie case of 1990, Justice Watkins explained that Kenny's project "was dropped in favor of Bradlaugh's Bill . . . abolishing all laws relating to blasphemy and not replacing them."[83] In 1886, Bradlaugh had been allowed to take his pro forma oath; in 1888, he definitively won his case when a new Oaths Act recognized the right of members of both Houses "to affirm" in place of taking the oath. Bradlaugh's Bill against blasphemy law was meant to go beyond the victory on the oath, but, as Justice Watkins pointed out, the Bill was, in effect "not carried."[84]

A Severe Punishment

When the judges of the Indian Supreme Court in charge of the case of Sushmita studied the case between 1989 and 1994, they time-traveled back to the early British Raj. The oldest case they took into account, going back one century earlier, concerned Ram Kumari, a girl sentenced to prison for bigamy on December 2, 1890, by the judge of Alipore, a town in the outskirts of Calcutta. Ram Kumari was sixteen years old—the same age as Shabina Begum was when she objected to the uniform policy of the

---

81. Herman, *Gandhi & Churchill*, 39–40.

82. Ibid., 50.

83. *R v Chief Metropolitan*, 447.

84. Ibid.

Denbigh High School, starting the case that would end up before the House of Lords in 2005.

Though already married to Dukhi Singh under Hindu law, Ram Kumari converted to Islam and, at the age of twelve, got married—or rather her mother gave her in marriage, to a Muslim man, Guzaffer Ali. The judge in charge, Justice Beveridge, accused her of taking a second husband while she was still bound to the first. The defense of Ram Kumari objected that the Hindu marriage was invalid for caste reasons. Her Hindu husband was a genuine Chattri, while she was an illegitimate child: her mother had been turned out of the house when pregnant with Ram Kumari because the husband suspected her of infidelity. The argument of caste difference as a ground for the nullity of the marriage under traditional Hindu law did not persuade the British judge, who stressed that Ram Kumari was socially accepted as a Chattri anyway.

The defense of Ram Kumari advanced a second reason why the first marriage should be considered invalid: since she converted to Islam and her first husband did not, Ram Kumari was not bound by the first Hindu marriage any more.

This meant, as the judge put it, that it had to be decided "whether Ram Kumari's Hindu marriage did not become dissolved by her conversion to Mahomedanism."[85] Justice Beveridge had no doubt about the answer: under the specific circumstances of the case, neither Hindu law nor Muslim law provided for conversion to imply the invalidity of the previous marriage. Both marriages celebrated by Ram Kumari were valid. Neither caste reasons nor Muslim marriage law could help the girl. She was guilty of bigamy.

The judge took the sincerity of the girl in her conversion to Islam as a reason not to apply a "severe punishment:"

> I do not think that she deserves a severe punishment. There is nothing to show that the conversion to Mahomedanism was not conscientious, or that she became a Mahomedan merely in order to be free, as she supposed, from her marriage with Dukhi. The whole family turned Mahomedan, and I daresay that Ram Kumari's account of the motive is the correct one. I sentence her to be rigorously imprisoned for one month.[86]

Ram Kumari appealed to the High Court at Calcutta. Two judges were appointed: Justice Macpherson and the native Indian Justice Banerjee. In the 1890s, it was normal for an Indian to sit as a judge, but the status of indigenous Indian judges was controversial. Eight years before, in 1883, under the supervision of Viceroy Lord Ripon, the Ilbert Bill was passed. Named after Courtenay Ilbert, the legal adviser to the Council of India, the bill provided for the power of native Indian judges to try British offenders in criminal cases. The step caused bitter protest among the British in India and at home, resulting in what came to be known as the White Mutiny.

---

85. *Ram Kumari*, 266.
86. Ibid., 266–67.

Such reaction made evident that racial stereotypes and uncontrolled emotions had grown since 1857. The British were still divided between those who, like Macaulay, and now Lord Ripon and Ilbert, believed Indians could achieve a certain degree of self-administration, and those who thought that self rule would lead India back to the chaos from which Britain had rescued the subcontinent. Seditious "pencil-pushing baboons" became the symbol of Indians progressively taking control and threatening the English domination. For example, the idea of English women appearing before an Indian judge in a trial for rape was unbearable to British sensibilities. Forster's *A Passage to India* revived that image forty years later, with the trial of suspected rapist Dr. Aziz, in which the Indian judge, Das, examines the English alleged victim, Miss Quested. In the novel, the British officials and friends of Miss Quested followed her onto the platform of the court hall. When Dr. Aziz's counsel from Calcutta objects to that illegitimate and intimidating action, the Indian judge, Mr. Das, "hiding his face desperately in some papers,"[87] decided that the British "should be so excessively kind as to climb down."[88] Through the iconic up and down of the British group in the court hall, Forster represented for generations of Britons the tragic rise and fall of British supremacy in India.

In an 1883 pamphlet in favor of the Ilbert Bill, Arthur Hobhouse stigmatized the "panic, terror and rage"[89] that had "displaced common sense."[90] He recalled a public meeting in 1836 at the time of a previous reform of the Indian judiciary, when a speaker drew the following grim, extravagant picture:

> I have seen at a Hindoo festival a naked, dishevelled figure, his face painted with grotesque colours, and his long hair besmeared with dirt and ash. His tongue was pierced with an iron bar, and his breast was scorched by the fire from the burning altar which rested on his stomach. This revolting figure, covered with ashes, dirt and bleeding voluntary wounds, may the next moment ascend the Sudder Bench, and in a suit between a Hindoo and an Englishman think it an act of sanctity to decide against law in favor of a professor of the true faith.[91]

A rigid racial separation presided over the welfare of the British Raj. Any proposed bridge between the white and the black posed a threat. In the end, a light version of the bill was passed. The whites were unhappy anyway. The effigy of Ilbert was publicly burnt. The native elites were no less bitterly disappointed. They realized no real autonomy was in sight. The following year, 1885, the Indian National Congress was founded.

---

87. Forster, *A Passage to India*, 208.
88. Ibid.
89. Hobhouse, *Native Indian Judges*, 11.
90. Ibid.
91. Ibid.

In this atmosphere, Justice Banerjee and Justice Macpherson took the case of Ram Kumari for the High Court of Calcutta. With Ram Kumari's being an Indian, no particular problem existed with a mixed Indo-British bench. But Ram's conversion was itself highly problematic.

The young age of the girl at the time of the marriage—she had yet to reach twelve—was not taken into account. The caste issue was also left aside. The two judges focused only on what respectively Hindu law and Islamic law provided for in the relevant matter. The Court concluded that no argument whatsoever could be found in either law to support the claim of Ram Kumari. It was true that according to the "Mahomedan Law," when the wife becomes a convert to Islam and the husband is an unbeliever, the former marriage can be dissolved. But that could not take place automatically. The Islamic authority should call upon the non-Muslim husband to embrace Islam, and only after his refusal to do so could the authority declare the end of the marriage. This was not the case of Ram Kumari and her husband. No Islamic authority had been involved at any stage except for the celebration of the marriage, nor had Ram Kumari given any notice to the first husband regarding her conversion and subsequent Islamic marriage. Therefore, declared Justice Macpherson and Justice Banerjee, Ram Kumari's first marriage "was not dissolved by reason of her change of faith according to the Hindu law or the Mahomedan law."[92] Ram's second, Islamic marriage, with Guzaffer Ali, had taken place during the life of the former husband and thus was void and bigamous. Ram Kumari was guilty of bigamy for the High Court of Calcutta as well. The first precedent considered by the Supreme Court of India in the case of Sushmita, one century later, was against a woman, but in favor of Sushmita's claim that conversion could not be used to nullify a marriage.

A Spectacular Funeral at Brookwood

When the conviction of Ram Kumari was confirmed in Calcutta on February 18, 1891, Mohandas Karamchand Gandhi was completing his law degree at University College London and qualifying as a barrister at Inner Temple. Not even one month earlier, on January 30, 1891, Charles Bradlaugh, the freethinker who tried in vain to sweep blasphemy law away from common law, had died. Bradlaugh's funeral in London, on February 3, was attended by a crowd of three thousand people. In his autobiography, Mohandas Gandhi remembered he stood among them, "as I believe every Indian in London did,"[93] to celebrate the courageous advocate of atheism and the rights of Indians.

Charles Bradlaugh was a reference point for the community of counterculture intellectuals who forged Gandhi's personality in the three years he spent in London. Helena Blavatsky and the Theosophists taught Gandhi the essential unity of all

92. *Ram Kumari*, 271.
93. Gandhi, *An Autobiography*, 78.

religions and set him free from what Gandhi himself called "the notion fostered by the missionaries that Hinduism was rife with superstition."[94] The same environment led Gandhi to encounter the Bhagavad Gita in Edwin Arnold's translation. Political experiments with civil disobedience were also linked to Gandhi's discovery of Henry David Thoreau's writings and his personal contact with Annie Besant, who had already organized in 1887 a mass demonstration of civil disobedience in Trafalgar Square against British rule in Ireland, which resulted in the famous "Bloody Sunday," with three people killed and hundreds arrested.

In London, Gandhi realized that an alternative to Western industrial and colonial modernity was possible. Westerners themselves could dream of a better age to come after awful modernity. His friends expressed their vision in the title of their magazine, the *New Age*.

Militant atheist Bradlaugh and panreligious Blavatsky converged in the anticipation of a New Age of spiritual awakening. Sixty years after Keble's alarm on national apostasy, the secular and liberal foundation of English counterculture combined with a syncretistic religious inspiration. Contradictions were unavoidable. The day of Bradlaugh's funeral, Gandhi witnessed an atheist attacking a clergyman on the platform at North Station while waiting for his return train from the cemetery of Brookwood. The episode, Gandhi wrote more than thirty years later, "further increased my prejudice against atheism."[95] If religion separated the whites from the blacks, it also divided the whites themselves. London counterculture made Gandhi aware of the opposition between secular and religious claims, between *your* secular and religious gods. Both, he realized, could help the Indian cause.

Four months after Bradlaugh's funeral and Ram Kumari's sentence, on June 10, 1891, Gandhi passed the bar exam. The day after, his New Age friends gave him their farewell. On the 12th, he sailed back to India.

Gandhi had knowledge of English common law, but "had not the slightest idea of Hindu and Mahomedan law."[96] The legal landscape he found back in India was perfectly illustrated by the approach of the High Court of Calcutta to the Ram Kumari case. The methodology of the two judges, based on the application of Islamic and Hindu laws as the personal laws of the party, adhered to the new pattern of the British Raj based on a uniform civilizing law and community boundaries reinvented through rigid and monolithic religious laws.

During the rule of the East India Company, religious laws applied because the British did not think of imposing a different legal standard on the peoples of India. At the time of the Lord Hastings's principle, the Regulations of 1772 and 1781 on the administration of civil justice for the native population delegated rule over the various Indian communities to what the British construed as the traditional religious

94. Ibid., 77.
95. Ibid., 78.
96. Ibid., 88.

laws. From the 1830s and 1840s, British common law began to rather erode religions and customs, thus deepening the Indian rejection of British rule. In the decades after the "Mutiny," the evangelical reforming impetus, which had led to Bentinck and Dalhousie's reforming activism, was replaced by a pragmatic combination of tolerance towards cultural and religious Indian "traditions" and programs aiming at industrializing the country while improving material conditions. British technological superiority had a tremendous impact on communications, thanks to bridges, railways, and roads. Sanitation and antifamine programs were also widely implemented. Factories and mines modelled a new productive and social landscape.

This was Kipling's India: the place and time where, in Edward Said's words, British imperialism "had almost lost sight of the unfolding dynamics of a human and secular truth: the truth that India had existed before the Europeans arrived, that control was seized by a European power, and that Indian resistance to that power would inevitably struggle out from under British subjugation."[97]

The British Raj imposed artificial boundaries on Indian religion and society, while proclaiming that the colonial power was ready to settle and indulge. The religious laws applied by the High Court of Calcutta in the Ram Kumari case expressed this approach. Separation of native religious communities was necessary to prevent them from allying against the British, as happened at the time of the "Mutiny." Separation was also needed in order to separate the black community from the white.

In 1871, Victoria Skinner changed custody because Lord James refused to apply Islamic law to one born Christian. Twenty years later, the application of Hindu law and "Mahomedan Law" led the High Court of Calcutta to convict Ram Kumari for bigamy. Both judgments were grounded on the principle set by Lord James in 1871, based on the 1858 Proclamation, according to which religions coexisted in the British Raj "as separate and very distinct communities having distinct laws affecting every relation of life."[98]

The recognition and application of religious laws endorsed a vision of racial and religious separation. The British contentedly adhered to what they saw as the traditional Indian pattern of Hindu caste seclusion and Muslim exclusivism as far as it perpetuated the divide-and-rule system and erected a wall that protected the white island from the surrounding "black" Indian ocean. But political interests and fear were not the only reasons why Britain embraced racial separation. Ideology also mattered, since social Darwinism provided a narrative that justified Christian and British white rule as the domination by the socially and racially superior.

---

97. Said, *Culture and Imperialism*, 195–96.

98. *Skinner*, 323.

Face to-Face with Militant Mohammedanism

Social Darwinism had a great impact on Winston Churchill's mind. In his early twenties, during his service in India as a subaltern, the future prime minister absorbed social Darwinism especially through the reading of Winwood Reade's *The Martyrdom of Man*. The British Empire ruled over India not because of its force and technology, but because of its superior vision and mission. "The evolutionist," young Churchill wrote, "will not hesitate to affirm that the nation with the highest ideals would succeed."[99]

The deep influence of Edward Gibbon's *Decline and Fall of the Roman Empire*, which Churchill read in the pink-and-white stucco bungalow he shared with two comrades in Bangalore, made him feel that, in India, he was face-to-face with the supreme threat to the British Empire. Barbarism and fanaticism, the same kind of enemy that led Rome to collapse, was now jeopardizing the British Empire. Indian religions, Indian superstition and backwardness, were the enemy. Karl Marx would have fully agreed, though from an anti-British and anticapitalistic perspective. In 1897, Churchill served in military action for the first time during the Malakand campaign against the Pathan rebels in the Northwest Frontier province. As a correspondent for the *Daily Telegraph* embedded in the British army, he experienced the fire of the Muslim tribesmen and shot at them himself. He wrote he had understood, in a nutshell, that "civilization was face to face with militant Mohammedanism."[100]

For his father, Randolph, the fight against atheist Bradlaugh in Britain and the fight against uncivilized religions in India were both needed to preserve Britannia. To Winston Churchill, the enemy was Indian magic and fanaticism. This led him to secularize Christianity and transform it into a superior moral standard fitting into the narrative of social Darwinism and conferring upon Britain the destiny of the dominator.

Historian Arthur Herman observed that "his years [in India] were an intellectual, even spiritual, awakening for Churchill, as much as Gandhi's years in New Age London had been."[101] But India taught Churchill that the British Empire was the only religion that mattered; for him, it encapsulated the superior moral standard of which Christianity consisted. Conversely, London taught Gandhi that true faith, whether the atheists' faith in one's own conscience, the theosophist's and Tolstoy's nonconformist faith, or his own renewed and blossoming Hindu faith, mattered more than any empire.

At the turn of the century, both Gandhi and Churchill consolidated their vision. Churchill definitively identified with the British mission in the world. Gandhi came to reject the British Empire and to shape his ideal of universal peace and of Indian self-rule. To this effect, the experience of southern Africa, of the Boer War and the Zulu Wars, played a crucial part.

99. Herman, *Gandhi & Churchill*, 97.

100. Ibid., 106.

101. Ibid., 92.

A British Subject in Natal

Mohandas Karamchand Gandhi spent twenty-one years in South Africa. When he arrived, in 1893, the country was still divided into British colonies and Afrikaner republics. A London-educated lawyer, proud to be a subject of the Empire, Gandhi had been hired to protect the interests of rich Indians, especially Gujarati merchants in Natal. Indian trade and free Indian immigration threatened the tiny minority of European settlers, whose number equaled one-tenth of the Africans and half the population of Indians in Natal.

When he arrived in Natal, twenty-four-year-old Gandhi immediately realized that racial differences were dealt with differently in southern Africa than they were in England. On his first day in court in Durban, he was shocked when the judge summoned him to take off his turban, a respectable and harmless mark of identity. Shortly thereafter, on May 31, 1893, Gandhi was thrown off a train at the station of Pietermaritzburg in Transvaal after claiming he had the right to travel first class. During the famous cold night in the waiting room of the station, his awareness of the discrimination of Indians in the British Empire began to take shape.

In his South African years, Gandhi experienced violence and witnessed death while transporting wounded and killed soldiers from the battlefields of South Africa. During the Boer War and the repression of Zulu insurgence, he organized an ambulance corps for the British army and commanded a Red Cross unit. This was part of his vision and strategy. Between March and December 1900, some seven thousand Indian soldiers and officers fought in the Boer War. Indians, Gandhi believed, were now more then ever entitled to assert their rights as subjects of the British Empire. Queen Victoria's benevolent proclamation of 1858 should have been applied not only in British India but also in the British territories of Natal and Cape Colony. At the same time, the British should push the Afrikaners, by force if necessary, to recognize the respectable status of Indians.

Over the twenty-one years he spent in South Africa, Gandhi was to change his vision and to reverse his loyalty to the cause of the British Empire. South Africa also led Gandhi to civil disobedience, nonviolence, and a different way of life as an individual, as well as the leader of a community. The influence of the New Age circle he had met in London had been strengthened by his acquaintances in Johannesburg. Many elements forged his personal and public persona, including theosophy, nonviolence, the rejection by the English counterculture of both industrial modernity and institutional Christianity, and Tolstoy's *The Kingdom of God is Within You*, a work that inspired the "Tolstoy farm," Gandhi's first experiment of modern ashram. After his years in England, South Africa built the adult Gandhi.

From 1908 on, Gandhi resorted to the theory and practice of *Satyagraha* as the best way to advance claims on behalf of South African Indians. Satyagraha was a Sanskrit expression made of two parts, which suggested the ideas of truth and enduring soul force. Gandhi's experience with the Natal Indian Congress and successive organizations led him towards new means of challenging the government. As a barrister, he knew that law alone was insufficient to promote real change in society; effective social mutations depended rather on deep shifts in attitudes and practices. But this did not make him skeptical about the law. Rather it pushed him to innovate: he facilitated arbitration instead of litigation whenever possible. As the acclaimed leader of the Indian community, he proved highly creative in handling legal tools. Civil disobedience was the best example: by turning a prison conviction into an opportunity to oppose the system from inside, Gandhi showed that maneuvering space within legal structures—British legal structures at least—was always great.

Expectations nourished by the Anglo-Boer war dissolved, since discriminatory acts and measures were adopted afterwards. White domination was embodied in the 1909 Constitution, with membership in Parliament being limited to white men. Specific threats to nonwhite populations rose in the first years after the birth in 1910 of the Union of South Africa. In 1964, Nelson Mandela explained to the Supreme Court of South Africa, which was trying him for sedition and sabotage, that the very creation of the African National Congress responded to that climate: "The African National Congress was formed in 1912 to defend the rights of the African people, which had been seriously curtailed by the South Africa Act, and which were then being threatened by the Native Land Act."[102]

The Steamer Is Leaving

One year before Gandhi's definitive departure from South Africa, on March 14, 1913, Justice Searle, for the Cape Supreme Court, ruled that marriages not celebrated according to Christian rites and/or not registered by the Registrar of Marriages were invalid.

The Indian community was shocked: the decision was taken to mean that all Muslim and Hindu marriages were to be deemed invalid. That "terrible judgment,"[103] Gandhi wrote later, had set aside the practice of forty years and "nullified in South Africa, at a stroke of the pen, all marriages celebrated according to the Hindu, Musalman and Zoroastrian rites. The many married Indian women in South Africa in terms of this judgement ceased to rank as the wives of their husbands and were degraded to the rank of concubines, while their progeny were deprived of their right to inherit the parents' property."[104]

The decision originated from the case of an Indian resident in South Africa, who married under Muslim law during a visit to India and, once back, applied to the authorities in order for his wife to be recognized and authorized to land. Justice Searle acknowledged he would have liked to go more in depth in the case. "I should have

---

102. Mandela, *The Struggle Is My Life*, 157.

103. Gandhi, *Satyagraha in South Africa*, 276.

104. Ibid.

been glad,"[105] he wrote in his opinion, "to have had a little more time in regard to giving judgment in this matter so as to have been able to go into it somewhat more fully, but on account of the departure of a steamer it is of urgency and thus requires to be disposed at once."[106]

Bal Mariam, the Muslim wife of the applicant, was on the steamer, waiting for Justice Searle to judge on her status. The decision had to be given quickly as the steamer was about to leave and sail back to India. Justice Searle did not dispute that a marriage had actually taken place in India. Rather, this was a Muslim marriage, and thus potentially polygamous: "this so-called marriage was what is commonly known as a polygamous one; in other words . . . the applicant was free to enter into other unions of similar nature during the subsistence of the marriage with Bal Mariam."[107]

As a consequence, it would not have been possible to recognize the status of proper "wife" to someone like Bal Mariam, "who might legally be repudiated the next day after the arrival by the husband entering into a lawful union in this country with someone else, or even without his doing so."[108]

This was why, Justice Searle stated, "courts of this country have always set their faces against recognition of these so-called Mahommedan marriages as legal unions."[109]

Given the impossibility of applying the status of wife generally recognized in South Africa to Bal Mariam because she was wed under Muslim law, the judge ruled that she was not allowed to land unless she accepted to legalize her marriage according to the law of South Africa. The Muslim marriage she had celebrated in India was not valid. She could not land unless she was ready to celebrate a new Christian or civil marriage.

Justice Searle's was a terrible decision because it touched upon an extremely difficult and tense situation. It was also terrible in the sense that it was exceptionally painful and frightening for those who were involved.

"When Marriage is Not a Marriage"[110] was the title Gandhi chose in 1928 for the chapter he consecrated to Justice Searle's decision in his book *Satyagraha in South Africa*. Gandhi recalled how the judgment prompted him to launch a Satyagraha, to which women were for the first time associated:

> We decided to offer stubborn Satyagraha irrespective of the number of fighters. Not only could the women now be not prevented from joining the struggle, but we decided even to invite them to come into line along with the men. We first invited the sisters who had lived on Tolstoy Farm. I found that they were only too glad to enter the struggle.[111]

105. *Esop*, 134.
106. Ibid.
107. Ibid., 135.
108. Ibid.
109. Ibid.
110. Gandhi, *Satyagraha in South Africa*, 276.
111. Ibid., 277.

Gandhi saw women's sacrifice as the accomplishment of Satyagraha. As he wrote, those illiterate women, and later his wife Kasturba herself, "knew that a mortal blow was being aimed at the Indians' honour, and their going to jail was a cry of agony and prayer offered from the bottom of their heart, was in fact the purest of all sacrifices. Such heart prayer is always acceptable to God. Sacrifice is fruitful only to the extent that it is pure."[112]

Gandhi believed that his fight was successful in any case. Whatever the political or legal reaction of South African authorities, truth triumphed: "Satyagrahis may rest assured that even if there is only one among them who is pure as crystal, his sacrifice suffices to achieve the end in view. The world rests upon the bedrock of *satya* or truth."[113]

The Satyagraha started in the name of Indians' honor, and continued as a struggle to support workers in coalmines and sugar plantations. The combined issues of marriage and labor mobilized thousands. Restrictions on immigration, pass laws, and unfair administration also heated the community. Gandhi's grievances before General Smuts, the then colonial secretary of Transvaal and later Prime Minister of South Africa, included the repeal of the three-pound tax on indentured laborers and the "legalization of the marriages celebrated according to the rite of Hinduism, Islam, etc."[114] Ultimately the Indians' Relief Bill was passed. The tax was repealed. Marriages held to be legal in India were validated in South Africa. In exchange, Indians accepted that, as Gandhi wrote, "if a man had more wives than one, only one of them would at any time be recognized as his legal wife in South Africa."[115]

General Smuts and the government did not consider the Indians' Relief Bill as a defeat. Indians remained in a subordinate position. The Bill was one more step towards the apartheid regime and the consolidation of a policy based on separate communities and subsequent discrimination of Coloreds, Indians, and Africans. South African historian Leonard Thompson underlined that Gandhi's fight produced little results and always remained racial in character. According to the historian, "Gandhi's movement won minor concessions for the Indian population but fought no battles on behalf of the Africans."[116] In her reconstruction of Gandhi's years in South Africa, Maureen Swan saw Gandhi as "a racial purist, and proud of it."[117] Arthur Herman gave a severe report of Gandhi's thought at the time:

> "We believe in the purity of race as much as we think" whites do, Gandhi wrote. "If there is one thing which the Indian cherishes more than any other, it is the purity of the [racial] type." Gandhi felt "strongly" that blacks and Indians should not be forced to live in the same Johannesburg suburbs. "I think it is

112. Ibid., 284.
113. Ibid., 285.
114. Ibid., 331.
115. Ibid., 335.
116. Thompson, *A History of South Africa*, 171.
117. Swan, *Gandhi: The South African Experience*, 112.

very unfair to the Indian population," he said. In fact, many of Gandhi's proposals in Indian Opinion pushing separate facilities for separate races would make him an early architect of apartheid.[118]

Gandhi wrote to General Smuts that the Relief Bill would be regarded as a step in the right direction, not as the final settlement: "complete satisfaction cannot be expected until full civic rights have been conceded to the resident Indian population."[119] In his *Satyagraha in South Africa*, Gandhi interpreted the Bill as a momentous achievement. From his viewpoint, Satyagraha had proved successful; he had accomplished his task in South Africa. Yet, as Robert Huttenback wrote, if "Gandhi had left South Africa optimistic about the future of his countrymen there . . . his optimism was ill-founded."[120]

Gandhi was to leave the country with a clear awareness of the importance those twenty-one years had had for him: "it was a great wrench for me to leave South Africa, where I had passed twenty-one years of my life sharing to the full in the sweets and bitters of human experience, and where I had realized my vocation in life."[121]

On July 18, 1914, Gandhi himself took a fateful steamer. He first sailed for England and, after a short visit, went back to India. His struggle for Swaraj, Indian Home Rule, was to begin. The struggle of Indians, Coloreds, and Africans in South Africa continued.

The twenty-one years spent by Gandhi in South Africa created a fundamental bond between the three countries. That bond was revitalized in the 1990s when British, South African, and Indian judges found themselves confronted by explosive gods and looked at the past in search of inspiration. British judges in charge of Rushdie's case became aware that since the nineteenth century their predecessors had struggled with the issues of blasphemy and equality of beliefs, while the legislature had proved unable to reform the system along the multireligious, equalitarian line experienced with the Indian Penal Code. In their first cases, prior to the decision on Gareth Prince's application, the South African constitutional judges went back to the foundation of the monolithic legal system that marginalized Indians, Coloreds, and blacks. In the meantime, the Indian Supreme Court found precedents in favor of Sushmita's claim and traced back to the British Raj and *your* imperial gods the foundation of the social and legal structure, which made common law and religious laws compete in the adjudication of family rights. It was now up to them—to the Indian, South African, and British judges of the 1990s—to give judgments on terribly complicated cases. Would they prove clever enough not to give terrible judgments?

118. Herman, *Gandhi & Churchill*, 131.
119. Gandhi, *Satyagraha in South Africa*, 336.
120. Huttenback, *Gandhi in South Africa*, 331.
121. Gandhi, *Satyagraha in South Africa*, 338.

Knights Errant

Until 1857, the year of the war in India and of the cattle killing in southern Africa, imperial gods—gods at the time of the British Empire—featured heavily in both Christian colonial expansion and the resistance of indigenous creeds. From the proclamation of Queen Victoria in 1858 to the onset of World War I, imperial gods shaped the separation of communities in response to growing interchange, and conversions. Faced with a colonial setting based on brutal segregation and violence, in the first half of the twentieth century natives engaged in the process leading to independence in India and embarked on the struggle for equality and freedom in South Africa.

After 1979, and especially during the 1990s, British and South African judges were confronted by the ultimate outcome of the processes triggered at the end of World War II, when the British Empire collapsed, Indian partition resulted in a bloodbath and the South Africa of apartheid took on its distinctive configuration, thanks to the electoral victory of the National Party in 1948.

During the last years of the British Empire, a handful of Indian cases once more brought conversions and conjugal conflicts to the fore. In the final arm wrestling between the colonial British power and Hindu and Muslim Indian leaders, judges in India struggled yet again with the application of personal religious laws. Their decisions were apparently outstripped by the historical turning point as the end of the war came closer and independence and partition approached. But when Indian judges in the 1990s time-traveled back to the midforties, they discovered how seminal those decisions were. In fact, those decisions provided the basic arguments for the judgment on Sushmita's case fifty years later. They also anticipated the themes and the solutions that would occupy British and South African judges half a century later.

The Survival of Christian Civilization

Between the return of Gandhi to India in 1914 and World War II, the British Empire dramatically changed. Those thirty years coincided with the prominent development of the Indian struggle led by the National Congress and Gandhi himself, as well as with the increasing activism of the Muslim League. The massacre of Amritsar in 1919, the formulation of Purana Swaraj, complete independence in 1929, the Salt March of 1930, and the Poona Pact between Gandhi and Ambedkar on the status of untouchables in 1932 all led to the opening of the final stage. In the Government of India Act of 1935, the gradual emergence of India as a self-governing entity was envisioned for the first time, if only partially. With the outbreak of World War II, in 1939, the Congress endorsed Nehru's manifesto offering Indian cooperation to the British war effort in exchange for independence; in 1940 in Lahore, the Muslim League called for an independent Pakistan.

At that occasion Muhammad Ali Jinnah, the British-educated leader of the Muslim League, proclaimed his final vision of the "real nature of Islam and Hinduism"[122] as two distinctive civilizations that could not constitute one same nation under one state since they "are not religions in the strict sense of the word, but are, in fact, different and distinct social orders."[123] In his speech at Lahore, on March 22, 1940, he definitively declared that

> it is a dream that the Hindus and Muslims can ever evolve a common nationality, and this misconception of one Indian nation has gone far beyond the limits and is the cause of more of our troubles and will lead India to destruction if we fail to revise our notions in time. The Hindus and Muslims belong to two different religious philosophies, social customs, and literature[s]. They neither intermarry nor interdine together, and indeed they belong to two different civilizations, which are based mainly on conflicting ideas and conceptions . . . To yoke together two such nations under a single state, one as a numerical minority and the other as a majority, must lead to growing discontent, and final destruction of any fabric that may be so built up for the government of such a state.[124]

The Lahore Resolution was aimed at protecting the independence and unity of Muslims: since the 1923 Treaty of Lausanne, the Ottoman Empire had ceased to exist, and concern was great for the future of the "Muslim nation." Indian Muslims knew perfectly well that the British Empire had a paramount role in the end of the Caliphate. Pakistan was, first of all, meant to settle Muslim grievances with Britain in India. At the same time, the Lahore Resolution represented the political defeat of the Congress as a multireligious actor, as well as the personal defeat of Gandhi, whose political action, since his first experiments in Natal, had been driven by the idea of a common Indian struggle beyond lines of caste and religion. Despite his inclusiveness and his opposition to the anti-Ottoman British geopolitics, Muslims increasingly viewed Gandhi as a threat. His biographer Arthur Herman underlined that the more Gandhi enjoyed his status of holy man among Hindu masses, the more the Muslims lost trust in him. In fact, Herman wrote, Gandhi's "emergence as the Mahatma had solidified his support among Hindus and, step by step, made him the spiritual authority of an entire nation. But, step by step, it had also alienated Muslims."[125]

At the same time, in South Africa, white power consolidated while segregation and discrimination spread pervasively throughout the economy and society. As Christian domination shrank in India, due to the struggle for independence, Christian predominance strengthened in South Africa through an increasingly purist regime, in terms of race and faith. The rising National Party relied heavily on the Christian

122. Jinnah, "Presidential Address at the All-India Muslim League," 177.

123. Ibid., 177–78.

124. Ibid., 178.

125. Herman, *Gandhi & Churchill*, 453.

legitimacy provided by the biblical rhetoric of the Afrikaners. White superiority encapsulated the superiority of Christian civilization. Black culture and religions were anathematized. Thirty years after Gandhi's departure, the Indian community and Indian creeds still faced discrimination.

In Europe, World War II also challenged Christianity. The pope signed concordats with Mussolini in 1929 and Hitler in 1933, opting for a defensive deal between Catholicism, Fascism, and Nazism. In his famous "This was their finest hour" speech on June 18 in the House of Commons, two months after Jinnah's speech on Muslim and Hindu civilizations, Winston Churchill proclaimed that the defense of the British Empire against Nazi-Fascism went together with the preservation of "Christian civilization": "I expect that the Battle of Britain is about to begin. Upon this battle depends the survival of Christian civilization. Upon it depends our own British life, and the long continuity of our institutions and our Empire."[126]

In Churchill's mind, the "survival of Christian civilization" depended on the defeat of the Nazis, but also on the preservation of the Empire, first of all in India. Churchill's "Christian civilization" corresponded to Jinnah's vision of the two Hindu and Muslim "civilizations." More than four decades before Samuel Huntington's "clash of civilizations," this was yet another example of the continuity between the imperial and the explosive gods.

In 1947, independence and partition followed, while the United States and the Soviet Union emerged as the new superpowers. The Great Game, the epic rivalry between the British Empire and the Russian Empire for supremacy in central Asia, was replaced by a new conflict, with rising international socialism and communism transforming Karl Marx's Indian chronicles and analysis into plans for a secular, socialist India.

The Ornaments of Ayesha Bibi

The participation of Indians in the British effort in World War II and the prospect of independence influenced the general attitude of judges in India and, in particular, their approach to cases of conversion and divorce. With the independence of India appearing inevitable, judges were increasingly concerned with the unity of Indian law and with the adjudication of religious laws.

Judges also appeared more sensitive to the social reality with which they interacted. In family controversies where injustice and unbalance were at stake, some judges seemed driven less by the legal arguments than by the distress of the party, usually a woman, seeking relief from abuse at the hands of her husband. Such was the case of Justice Ormond, who, on March 2, 1945, declared the dissolution of a Hindu marriage based on the plaintiff's conversion to Islam. The judgment of Justice Ormond in the case of Ayesha Bibi was strongly influenced by the abuse and cruelty suffered by the

126. Churchill, "Alone: 'Their Finest Hour,'" 177.

applicant, a young girl whose awful and violent husband had been selected by her distinguished Brahmin family.

Justice Ormond delivered a detailed report about the distress of the girl: "from immediately after the marriage [the husband] used continuously to be demanding money from his wife, the plaintiff . . . When the defendant found that he could not obtain more money from his wife, he at once began to treat her badly. He used to abuse her and frequently strike her and kick her."[127]

When the husband brought the young woman, fifteen years old at the time of the marriage, to stay with his family for one week, she realized that the family expected her to bring in heavy money: "when she could not procure any money for them they treated her very badly and with cruelty, confining her in her room, and curtailing her food."[128]

At home, the abuse continued. One day the husband "struck her so violently that she fell down senseless."[129] Ayesha was later to go to visit her husband's family for a second time. Again, when she proved unable to supply as much money as expected, "they beat her, and took her ornaments away from her; and turned her out of the house."[130]

Eventually the father took her back home. At the end of June 1943, two years after the wedding, conjugal cohabitation was definitively interrupted. A couple months later, on September 12, 1943, the seventeen-year-old girl converted to Islam.

Justice Ormond decided the case on March 2, 1945, during the battle of Mandalay and the clearing of the road to Rangoon, which resulted in a decisive step towards the defeat of the Japanese in Burma and changed the destiny of Britain and India. The defeat was in sight of those Indian nationalists who dreamed of using the Japanese invasion to get rid of the British.

Justice Ormond made plain from the beginning that the judiciary had limited competence in assessing whether a conversion was genuine or not. Since "no Court can test or gauge the sincerity of religious belief,"[131] the judge stuck to the objective evidence that the plaintiff actually changed her religion and performed the rite of conversion; he was not at all ready to go "into the question of motives for the conversion or their relative religious or ethical values."[132]

Circumstances of the conversion proved nevertheless crucial and Justice Ormond quite contradicted himself when he stressed more then once that Ayesha's conversion was bona fide. Indeed, he underlined the link between her conversion and the woman's quest for a better condition:

> when she was so badly treated by her husband, and did not get any sympathy
> from the Hindu society to which she belonged, some of her Muslim friends

127. *Musstt. Ayesha Bibi*, 441.
128. Ibid.
129. Ibid.
130. Ibid.
131. Ibid., 442.
132. Ibid.

began to talk to her about their religion, and also gave her books on their religion to read . . . Then, as she puts it, she "came to the conclusion that in the Muslim faith and society, the position of unfortunate girls like herself was not so low as that." She says, in effect, she found that in Muslim society, there existed a sufficient degree of freedom and independence of thought and action for women.[133]

Justice Ormond knew that the social reasons the girl gave for her conversion could be a counterproductive argument. She stepped into the Muslim faith not for merely spiritual reasons, but in order to avoid her personal and social obligations. This risked making her case worse. But the judge explained why the social motives of the girl did not undermine the sincerity, solidity, and effectiveness of her conversion:

> if she chooses to consider that the principles of conduct governing the relation in human society of a woman with her fellow men and women are superior in merit as ordained under Islam to those ordained under Hinduism and chooses to be converted to Islam, principally for that reason, then since those social principles are themselves part of the very fabric of the Islamic religion, she is to my mind making an effective change of religion; and for entirely bona fide reasons: and moreover reasons which it is impossible not to subscribe as bona fide religious reasons. To my mind she is just as entitled to come to a bona fide decision to be converted for these reasons as for any other reasons of mystical faith or belief, or any other reasonings of theoretical theology or intellectual processes, or disputations of higher criticism.[134]

At a time when Hindus and Muslims were increasingly at odds which each other, with partition on the horizon, the judge stood for the individual. Adjudicating rights was not about preserving and separating distinctive communities, but about personal rights and case-specific situations. The right of the woman to improve her poor condition, as well as her freedom of religion, combined in shaping Justice Ormond's mind. Of course, technicalities and legal arguments abounded in the judge's opinion. He said he gave judgment according to "justice and right."[135] But his sympathetic understanding of the claim was decisive in order to shape the judgment. In the end, the case was decided on the basis of the principle that if a Hindu wife, upon conversion to Islam, presented her new faith to her husband, and if the husband failed to convert as well, then the marriage was to be considered dissolved. Conversion proved an effective tool in liberating an abused woman from hideous marriage. Ayesha was free.

Justice Ormond was a different kind of British judge in India. Ayesha was a different kind of Indian wife. In his evidence, her father told how vigorously she had countered his opposition to conversion. She said to him, "you have spoilt my life once,

133. Ibid.
134. Ibid., 444.
135. Ibid., 460.

you have no right to spoil my life any longer, you should allow me in all fairness to act according to my determination."[136]

In the context of British victory in the Second World War and of British failure in India, Justice Ormond's decision favored conversions on the one hand and Islam on the other, as it conferred upon Muslim converts the power to avoid the obligations they had contracted under Hindu law.

However, considerations of legal rationality and colonial policy mattered less to the British judge than did Ayesha Bibi herself. Faced with the Hindu-Muslim storm, and with the relevant British ambiguities and collusions, Justice Ormond handled religious laws for the sake of the deprived, for the sake of Ayesha. He simply stood for the relief of the individual who had turned to him in search of a better life.

Unhappy Marriages

Justice Ormond's decision was attacked and his approach reversed a few months later in the two cases of Sayeda Khatoon and Robasa Khanum.

The case of Sayeda Khatoon was decided on August 10, 1945, by Justice Lodge. The case concerned a Jewish couple, the Obadiahs, who married in November 1943 at the Bethel Synagogue in Calcutta. A few weeks later, the husband deserted the wife, leaving her with no remedies under Jewish law, since requirements for a Jewish divorce were not met, and thus imprisoned in the marriage. In May 1945, the wife, Annie Moses, converted to Islam in the presence of the imam of the Nakhoda Mosque in Calcutta. This was the same mosque where Ayesha Bibi had converted from Hinduism two years earlier. Annie took the name of Sayeda Khatoon. She then wrote three times to the husband calling him up to convert to Islam. The husband did not reply, and after the third letter the woman asked the civil court in Calcutta to apply the provisions of Islamic law on the dissolution of a marriage after conversion. This was the issue Justice Lodge had to decide upon: was the Jewish marriage dissolved because of the conversion to Islam of Sayeda? Was she "entitled to a declaration that she is no longer the lawful wife of the defendant and that her status and legal character is that of a single woman"?[137]

Justice Lodge refused to declare the Jewish marriage dissolved. He gave two reasons for that. First, Sayeda's husband had refused to convert, and thus he was not a Muslim to whom Muslim law might apply. The system of personal religious laws implied the religious homogeneity of a couple. The common religious membership of the spouses was the condition for the application of religious laws in India. As soon as the religious homogeneity of a couple was broken by conversion, a matrimonial law of general application was needed. But, Justice Lodge explained,

136. Ibid., 442.
137. *Sayeda Khatoon*, 747.

there is no matrimonial law of general application in India. There is a Hindu law for Hindus, a Mahomedan law for Mahomedans, a Christian law for Christians, and a Jewish law for Jews. There is no general matrimonial law regarding mixed marriages other than the statute law, and there is no suggestion that the statute law is applicable in the present case.[138]

As a result, Muslim law could not be taken as the new religious law of the former Jewish couple. Why, Justice Lodge wrote, should "the Mahommedan law . . . be preferred to the Jewish law in a matrimonial dispute between a Mahommedan and a Jew, particularly when the . . . marriage was created under the Jewish law?"[139]

Second, India was not a Muslim country and Muslim law was not the law of the land. Had India been a Muslim country, of course Muslim law could rule a mixed couple, and the plaintiff would be entitled to her desired declaration, "but this is not a Mahommedan country,"[140] Justice Lodge said, "and the Mahommedan law is not the law of the land."[141]

Justice Lodge affirmed that the effect of conversion should not be exaggerated: "If the two are happy in their marriage, would the Courts consider it just and right to declare the marriage dissolved by the mere fact of conversion?"[142] he asked. "I think not,"[143] was his reply. What counted in the step taken by Annie Moses, alias Sayeda Khatoon, was not her conversion but her will not to be bound by her Jewish marriage any longer: "the dissolution of the marriage would seem to depend not on the fact of conversion but on the voluntary act of the wife seeking to dissolve the marriage."[144]

The decision to convert and the decision to dissolve a marriage were not inevitably linked. Justice Lodge concluded:

> It seems to me that except in the case of unhappy marriages, it would be neither just nor right to hold that a marriage was automatically dissolved by the conversion of one of the parties to another religion; and in the case of unhappy marriages, the "justice and right" depends on the discontent of the parties and not on the conversion.[145]

In a similar case one year later, in August 1946, Justice Chagla for the High Court of Bombay further elaborated on the distinction introduced by Justice Lodge between the decision to convert and the decision to end an unhappy marriage. He upheld the fundamental difference between the religious and the existential dimensions of a marriage:

138. Ibid., 748.
139. Ibid.
140. Ibid.
141. Ibid.
142. Ibid., 749.
143. Ibid.
144. Ibid.
145. Ibid.

The bond that keeps a man and woman happy in marriage is not exclusively the bond of religion. There are many other ties which make it possible for a husband and wife to live happily and contentedly together. It would indeed be a startling proposition to lay down that although two persons may want to continue to live in a married state and disagree as to the religion they should profess, their marriage must be automatically dissolved.[146]

An increasing awareness was emerging that conversions were used as the only means to give voice to the discontent of the parties and their desire to quit current unions and enter new relationships. Conversion was not the reason why a marriage could not stand, but the tool through which people in good or bad faith sought relief from an undesired matrimonial bond. Such an awareness was new, compared to the time of Victoria Skinner and Ram Kumari: the will of the parties now mattered. Choices mattered. The matrimonial bond was no longer absolutely beyond the freedom of the spouses, women in particular. This did not automatically open the way for conversions to nullify marriages. According to Justice Lodge's approach, conversion should not replace the "discontent" of the spouses. For these reasons, contrary to the decision given by Justice Ormond, Justice Lodge decided in August 1945 that Sayeda Khatoon was not entitled to the dissolution of her Jewish marriage simply because of her conversion to Islam.

Dreaming of Muhammad

A few months later, on December 14, 1945, in the Robasa Khanum case, another British judge in India, Justice Blagden, took the same position as Justice Lodge. He refused to accept that by means of a change in religion a spouse could force the newly acquired personal law "on a party to whom it is entirely alien and who does not want it."[147] In his emphatic style, Justice Blagden declared himself not ready to endorse "so monstrous an absurdity."[148]

The Robasa Khanum case was occasioned by a Zoroastrian marriage celebrated in Iran, the failure of which led the wife to look for an opportunity to escape from wedlock. She converted to Islam and called upon the husband to convert as well. The man did not reply, and Robasa assumed she was entitled to the dissolution of her Zoroastrian marriage under the Muslim law; this she asked in her petition to Justice Blagden.

The mingling of the British Indian law and the different religious laws was inevitable. Some new pieces of legislation were playing considerable roles in making the judiciary more exigent and precise. The Government of India Acts of 1915 and 1935 had come to regulate when and to what extent personal religious laws were to

---

146. *Robasa Khanum*, 879.

147. Ibid., 869.

148. Ibid.

be enforced. The Shariat Act of 1937 and the Muslim Marriages Act of 1939 also had clarified and restricted the enforcement of Muslim law in the British Raj. Paradoxically, through these acts the British rulers and the Muslim nationalist elite shared the same goal of building, noted Rina Williams, a "traditionalist and uniform"[149] Muslim law as opposed to "syncretic, local or ambiguous identities."[150] As Scott Kugle points out, "British jurisprudence had defined Islam as a rarefied and monolithic identity, and now Muslims accepted this definition as a vehicle to agitate for political rights and nationalist agendas."[151]

Still British lawyers felt that the problematic cohabitation of religious laws undermined the certainty of the law as it had at the time of Thomas Macaulay one century earlier. In the Robasa Khanum case, bewildered Justice Blagden asked himself, "Under what law am I to try it?"[152]

Justice Blagden's approach strongly differed from the sympathetic stance taken by Justice Ormond in the Ayesha Bibi case. When Robasa Khanum advanced her life story and reported on her own conversion, Justice Blagden patronized her. He found that the report on the adulterous relationship of the woman with her new partner Abdul Taqui after the alleged desertion of the husband was "lacking in candor."[153] Furthermore, the judge gave a sarcastic interpretation of the circumstances of the conversion:

> The plaintiff says she had, in or about April 1944, a dream. Therein, Mahomed appeared to her in the guise of a very tall handsome man with a beard and a face as bright as the sun—I strongly suspect, though she says he had nothing to do with it, that this is an idealized form of Abdul Taqui—and invited her to become a Muslim.[154]

Following the analysis of Justice Lodge in the Sayeda Khatoon case, Justice Blagden eventually denied Robasa Khanum the dissolution of her Zoroastrian marriage because of the conversion. His methodology was based on a strict legal scrutiny excluding any concern for the sake of the parties. He referred to Justice Ormond's decision in the case of Ayesha Bibi and distanced himself from it:

> A damsel in distress has always been considered a proper object for the attention and the activities of a Knight errant, but hardly, I should have thought, for those of a Judge as such. If the latter attempts to go out of his way to her rescue, "errant" is apt to be the operative used. A Judge as such is ill-qualified for an itinerant career rescuing distressed damsels.[155]

149. Williams, *Postcolonial Politics and Personal Laws*, 88.
150. Ibid.
151. Kugle, "Framed, Blamed, and Renamed," 303.
152. *Robasa Khanum*, 867.
153. Ibid.
154. Ibid.
155. Ibid., 875–76.

The dichotomy was set between Justice Ormond, the "knight errant" in Blagden's words, and Blagden himself, the true judge who stuck to the law instead of riding, again in his words, the "unruly horse"[156] of public policy. Of course, Justice Blagden, too, cared about the actual outcome of his decision for Robasa Khanum. But he claimed he also cared about the outcome for any other woman in India:

> to refuse the plaintiff relief serves, in my opinion, no useful purpose. But to grant it means . . . to give the approval of this Court to a doctrine under which the matrimonial right of Christians and Parsis are largely abrogated by a change of faith on the part of their spouses, and innocent Hindu wives could be consigned to a limbo (quite unknown to the ideas of their community) in which, to use a popular expression, they would be "neither fish, nor fowl, nor good red herring."[157]

The judge eventually denied the dissolution of Robasa's marriage on the grounds of her conversion. Essentially, Justice Blagden was no less concerned than Justice Ormond with the actual outcome of the decision. But he did not focus on Robasa Khanum only. He contemplated that the use of conversion, which would help a woman today, might be turned against her tomorrow. Half a century later, Sushmita Ghosh would benefit from Justice Blagden's foresight.

An Intelligent Visitor from Another Planet

For a long time, British judges in India stuck stubbornly to their job, despite their mental and cultural distance from the host environment. In *A Passage to India*, first published in 1924, E. M. Forster famously described in these terms the typically colonial solitude and superiority of the Chandrapore City Magistrate Ronny Heaslop:

> Every day he worked hard in the court, trying to decide which of two untrue accounts was the less untrue, trying to dispense justice fearlessly, to protect the weak against the less weak, the incoherent against the plausible, surrounded by lies and flattery. That morning he had convicted a railway clerk of overcharging pilgrims for their tickets, and a Pathan of attempted rape. He expected no gratitude, no recognition for this, and both clerk and Pathan might appeal, bribe their witnesses more effectually in the interval, and get their sentences reversed. It was his duty.[158]

At the end of World War II, not only were judges in India more sensitive to the social outcome of their decisions, but they also had achieved a better perception of the complexity of their context. Also, their experience of different ways of interaction

---

156. Ibid., 876.

157. Ibid., 876–77.

158. Forster, *A Passage to India*, 45–46.

between law and religion made them aware of the relativity of legal systems. Justice Blagden openly acknowledged the diversity of religious approaches to marriage and marriage failure. He underlined the difference between English law, still influenced by the Christian doctrine of indissolubility, and Indian religious laws, which, in many communities, recognized as a marriage "a union of opposite sexes, which is dissoluble at the will of the male person concerned and admits of polygamy."[159] In a context where such diversity was contemplated and legalized, the general application of the "justice, equity, and good conscience" clause was clearly problematic. In fact Justice Ormond believed that it was "just and right" to free Ayesha from her wedlock, while Justices Lodge and Blagden thought it "just and right" not to dissolve Sayeda's and Robasa's Hindu marriages because of their conversions to Islam.

After the certainties of the Victorian age, in the twilight of the British Empire, judges discovered that it was impossible to assert any universal principle beyond the relative historical and cultural context. The impregnable superiority of Christian values, or of any other religion or culture, succumbed to the rise of a diverse, interconnected world.

On this point, Justice Ormond and Justice Blagden stopped representing two opposite approaches and instead expressed the same conscience of the cultural and legal relativity accompanying the fall of imperial gods in the colonies and in the homeland alike.

While judging the case of Ayesha, Justice Ormond acknowledged that, compared to England, the intermingling of religion and law made India a completely different legal landscape

> in India the legal principles . . . both in regard to Hinduism and Mohamedanism are interwoven with, and wrapped up in, the religious side of these systems . . . In England . . . where the legal system is separate from the religious system, the position is very different. In England it is possible for the view of the law Courts to differ in particular respects from the view of the Church on matters of marriage. In India, the legal system and the religious system of Hinduism are largely the same thing.[160]

In turn, Justice Blagden admitted that the Christian and Hindu construction of marriage as "something more than a mere civil contract rescindable at the will of the parties"[161] was far from absolute: "If I had sitting by me an intelligent visitor from another planet I might find it difficult to justify, on the grounds of public morality, the enforced countenance of a marriage which has ceased to be one in all but the name."[162]

---

159. *Robasa Khanum*, 872.

160. *Musstt. Ayesha Bibi*, 443.

161. *Robasa Khanum*, 870.

162. Ibid.

Changes in matrimonial law in England also played a part, with women being allowed to use the same grounds as men for divorce since 1923. Whether in India or in the homeland, the indissolubility of marriage was nothing more than one possible cultural understanding of wedlock. "Justice and equity" did not require indissolubility more than any other solution, including repudiation or divorce. Justice Blagden concluded that "justice and equity" did not automatically imply "that a marriage, once validly celebrated, should be judicially dissoluble or otherwise capable of being terminated, except by death."[163] Indissolubility was not absolutely and universally "just and right" any longer.

Judges in India tried to swim in the turbulent sea of preindependence. For those like Justice Ormond, substantial justice prevailed over legal technicalities. Those like Justice Blagden and Justice Lodge believed that public policy concerns must be kept rigorously out of the judiciary. Justice Ormond concentrated on the social justice aspects of the specific case and recognized in conversion the power to change a person's status. Justices Lodge and Blagden denied conversions the power to influence rights already acquired by the parties.

When, between 1989 and 1995, the Supreme Court of India looked back at the case law of the forties, the judges found themselves confronted with two alternative solutions.

In March 1945, Justice Ormond set Ayesha Bibi free from her Hindu wedlock, recognizing her conversion to Islam as the ground for the dissolution of the previous Hindu marriage. Contrary to this "knight errant" approach, the opposite decision was made, both in August 1945 by Justice Lodge and in December 1945 by Justice Blagden, who decided, respectively, that Sayeda Khatoon and Robasa Khanum were still bound by their previous marriages irrespective of their conversion to Islam.

In 1995, in their decision on Sushmita's case, the judges of the Supreme Court did not even mention Justice Ormond and the Ayesha Bibi case. Instead they largely referred to Justice Lodge and Justice Blagden.

In 1945, strategies and interests were leading the British colonial power to what historian Stanley Wolpert, recalling a famous expression of Winston Churchill's, called "Great Britain's hasty, shameful flight"[164] away from India. Justice Ormond, the "knight errant," opposed the tyranny of personal religious laws by giving conversion legal effect for the sake of the "damsel in distress." Justice Blagden and Justice Lodge opposed the same tyranny of personal religious laws by denying conversion any legal effect. Judges did not share the same legal doctrine, but they did share the responsibility of standing at the junction between the path of normal people and the destiny of nations.

163. Ibid., 869.
164. Wolpert, *Shameful Flight*, 193.

Fifteen Thousand Protesters in Durban

American journalist and Gandhi-biographer Louis Fischer visited the Mahatma in July 1946. Gandhi, Fischer reported, was concerned about the increasing violence: "'First,' he said, 'there is South Africa. A man has been killed there in connection with the recent disturbances. He was innocent. Also, they have tied Indians to trees and whipped them. This is lynch law. And now these riots in Ahmedabad between Hindus and Moslems.'"[165]

Thirty years after his departure from South Africa at the time of Justice Searle's "terrible judgment," Gandhi was still connecting in his mind, as well as in his action, the two sides of the Indian Ocean. Violence in South Africa and in India had the same imperial history.

During World War II, racial policies in South Africa pushed the Native Representative Council, the African National Congress, the Natal Indian Congress, the Transvaal Indian Congress, and other organizations united to campaign against white supremacy.

The Asiatic Land Tenure and Indian Representation Bill was passed on June 2, 1946. The bill offered some political representation to Indians, but, in essence, it restricted Indian land ownership and residence to limited areas. Gagathura "Monty" Naicker, the president of the Natal Indian Congress, condemned it as the Ghetto Bill.

Indians all over the country mobilized in a passive resistance campaign. Over fifteen thousand protesters gathered in Durban and marched on a parcel of municipal land at the intersection of Umbilo Road and Gale Street. Once there, several passive militants pitched tents in defiance of the Ghetto Bill and prepared to resist.

On June 16, white assailants armed with knuckle-dusters, bicycle chains and belts tore down the tents and attacked the protesters while the police stood by. Several acts of intimidation and violence against the resisters ensued in the following days. On June 30, an Indian policeman, Krishensamy Pillay, died as the result of an assault on the night of June 21, when he was beaten unconscious and left in the gutter with lacerations on the head. Krishensamy Pillay was the "innocent man" mourned by Gandhi in the conversation with Louis Fischer.

The cycle of protest and repression went on for months, with more episodes of violence and many people arrested. Protesters appealed to the British Indian government and to the newly instituted United Nations, a decisive founder of which had been Jan Smuts himself, former counterpart to Gandhi, now prime minister of South Africa. Some whites joined as well. Reverend Michael Scott, a Scottish Anglican anti-apartheid activist from Johannesburg, joined the passive resisters and was himself involved in assaults, arrested, tried, and convicted. Together with the other arrested campaigners, he marched to the police station, waving to the crowd, his prayerbooks carried with him in full view. In a public meeting the day before, the court sentenced him to three months in jail. Scott responded by challenging the Christianity of the

---

165. Fischer, *The Life of Mahatma Gandhi*, 526.

apartheid supporters and called true Christians to action: "South Africa must wake up before immense harm is done by such false religious doctrines and such evilly inspired legislation against a whole race without constitutional means of redress . . . True statesmanship can and must find other way, for there will be many like myself, who hold the faith for which Christ paid the penalty, who will never be reconciled to kind of legislation."[166]

Protests were so strong and pervasive that in August 1946 the government, led by Jan Smuts, established the Fagan Commission to recommend that socioeconomic inequalities be redressed and that rigid segregation of Indians, blacks, and Coloreds be replaced by a more flexible system of cohabitation side by side. "The idea that the Natives must all be removed and confined in their own kraals," Jan Smuts declared, "is in my opinion the greatest nonsense I have ever heard."[167]

Complete Religious Neutrality

Also in August 1946, in the appeal to the Robasa Khanum case, Justice Chagla and Justice Stone for the High Court of Bombay upheld Justice Blagden's approach and affirmed that it was "not in accordance with justice and right that on the conversion of one of the parties to the marriage to Islam it should be held that the marriage stands dissolved."[168] Robasa's strategy to invoke conversion in order to deem the first marriage invalid and thus avoid her conjugal obligations was rejected by the High Court of Bombay as well.

One week before the decision, on August 16, Jinnah had proclaimed a Day of "direct action" to achieve Pakistan and to mobilize the Muslims for the coming struggle. Ensuing fights between Muslims and Hindus in Calcutta resulted in a blood bath, with five thousand murdered and fifteen thousand injured.

In this climate, Justice Chagla, in his opinion for the High Court, established a clear framework for coexistence between general Indian law, statute law, and religious personal laws: "Complete religious neutrality obtains in our country and Courts administer laws irrespective of the creed of the parties who appear before them. The Courts do not administer the laws of any particular community, but they administer such laws as are valid in British India."[169]

In 1946, on the eve of the end of the British Raj, the "complete" religious neutrality preached by Justice Chagla played the twofold role of emphasizing national identity irrespective of religion while pushing the different communities to adjust to a common Indian standard. This approach was to become the model for independent India. But it further scared Muslims who felt exposed to the arbitrary will of the Hindu majority.

166. Scott, "Statement in Court."
167. Barber, *South Africa in the Twentieth Century*, 134.
168. *Robasa Khanum*, 882.
169. Ibid., 877.

According to Justice Chagla, religious laws could not afford to stand as islands on their own. They were filtered by general Indian law; they were codified by statute law. They applied where and how Indian law provided for their application. If needed, they were submitted to reform by Indian law. In Justice Chagla's words, "Courts in British India administer(ed) Muslim law as altered and amended by statute law."[170]

Rather than an almost untouchable Muslim law in India under British rule, an Indian Muslim law was forged. Civil powers in British India had the ambition to force ancient Muslim law to modernize. Justice Chagla explained this process in 1946 in his opinion in the Robasa Khanum case:

> Under Muslim law, apostasy from Islam of either party of the marriage operates as a complete and immediate dissolution of the marriage. But s. 4 of the Dissolution of Muslim Marriages Act (VIII of 1939) provides that the renunciation of Islam by a married Muslim woman or her conversion to a faith other than Islam shall not by itself operate to dissolve her marriage. This is a very clear and emphatic indication that the Indian legislature has departed from the rigour of the ancient Muslim law and has taken the more modern view that there is nothing to prevent a happy marriage notwithstanding the fact that the two parties to it professed different religions.[171]

Chagla announced that independent India would not get rid of Muslim law, but that Muslim law would be molded according to Indian specificity and needs. Acts and court decisions forced religious laws, and in particular Muslim law, to modernize. Nothing could have been more threatening for Indian Muslims, with the Hindu majority menacing the integrity and tradition of Muslims. The departure of the British could only make things worse. The "complete religious neutrality" advocated by Justice Chagla looked like an artificial establishment of a Hindu despotism. Modern socialist, secular India appeared as the deceptive carapace of an absolutist Hindu Raj.

While interreligious violence was spreading all over the country, dying British India was the laboratory for both the British postcolonial and the Indian national future. So far the recognition of religious communities had basically been about preserving the boundaries separating them, especially those between the Christian rulers and the indigenous religions. The "equal and impartial protection of the Law" promised by Queen Victoria in 1858 proved more a matter of political correctness and paternalistic imposition of the British supremacy than an effective guideline.

The different visions of independent India in the mid-1940s depended on the role assigned to religious communities in the national struggle. The project of the Indian National Congress implied that the various religious communities had to be equally involved in the identity building process. Swaraj, the self-rule of Indians, meant the full involvement of Hindus and Muslims in the struggle for independence.

170. Ibid.
171. Ibid., 879.

For Gandhi, this entailed the subordination of religions to the common effort so that Hindus, Muslims, and all other communities could merge in a united Indian nation. But of course, the generosity of Hindu leaders, including Gandhi, was not enough to encourage Muslims. After all, Hindus represented the majority, and all they could offer to the minorities was their own volatile benevolence. In a democratic state, numbers prevailed. And numbers favored the Hindus.

For the Muslim League of Jinnah, and for many purist Hindus too, true independence could only be achieved through the separation of Muslim India from Hindu India. In their "shameful flight," the British hesitated, but came to believe that separation between the two communities was the only viable option, and the one that was most likely to best guarantee British interests in the area. Divide and rule had been the principle of the British Raj. It was now the principle that guided the British in handing the power over.

Fast unto Death

On December 11, 1946, the Constituent Assembly met for the first time in order to draft a Constitution for India. On June 15, 1947, through the Indian Independence Act, the British Parliament enforced partition and the independence of the two dominions of Pakistan and the Union of India, due to remain formally under the crown until the adoption of the respective constitutions.

On August 15, 1947, the saffron, white, and orange Indian flag was hoisted at the Red Fort. British rule was over.

In the same period, South Africa also underwent a fundamental transformation. The rising Herenigde National party reacted to Smuts's moderate politics, attacked his connection to Britain, and appointed the Sauer Commission to design a straightforward policy of apartheid. The Sauer Report described Indians as a foreign community the integration of which was simply impossible. Rigorous segregation of blacks and Coloreds as well as the consolidation of African reserves were recommended. No representation of natives in councils had to be granted. The missionary influence on natives, especially in the field of education, had to be curtailed.

In this climate, antigovernment militants strengthened the cooperation already experienced during the protests against the Ghetto Bill. On March 9, 1947, Transvaal and Natal Indian Congress groups signed a pact of cooperation with the African National Congress. The increasing polarization would dominate the general elections of May 1948. Ultimately, the National Party would prevail, thanks to the proactive Afrikaner churches, which posed as the key agencies for the inoculation of a culture based on white supremacy and racial purity, and to the alliance among Afrikaner workers worried about competition with African laborers, farmers, and businessmen for whom the exploitation of black labor was essential. Between 1947 and 1948, with the passage from the British-friendly Smuts government to the Afrikaner nationalist government led by Daniel François Malan, the political conditions for the most radical enforcement of apartheid came to be fulfilled.

Meanwhile, since the electoral win of the Labor Party in 1945, Clement Attlee's government was reforming Britain, with the view that British socialism could be built upon the solid democratic and liberal foundation of the country. The creation of the national health system and the development of a national economy exalted the abnegation of Attlee's team, but also ended up draining its momentum by 1947.

Through the Constituent Assembly, independent India was also shaping its future. The constitutional process started in December 1946 would only be completed a few years later with the adoption of the Constitution in 1949 and the birth of the Republic of India in 1950. India's first independent minister of justice and the chairman of the Constitution draft committee, Bhimrao Ramji Ambedkar, became crucial, especially in stirring the constitutional approach to the issue of personal religious laws, of conversions and marriages.

Since the early twenties Ambedkar had played a key role in the struggle for independence. His program included emancipation and equality for the deprived Indian masses—women and untouchables in particular—in a modern, Westernized, secular India. While pointing at the failure of British rule, Ambedkar was also very critical of Hindu leaders and the Indian National Congress. In particular, Ambedkar resisted Gandhi's methodology and principles. He stood against the rural, traditional, religious India that Gandhi championed. If Gandhi felt for the syncretistic new age of Tolstoy and Blavatsky, nurtured by the English and South African acquaintances of the Mahatma, Ambedkar was driven by his own pragmatic, secular education in economics at Columbia University in New York and at the London School of Economics. To Gandhi's benevolent and sentimental Hinduism, Ambedkar responded by opposing the claim that religion had to withdraw for the sake of a modern, civil Indian society.

The issue of caste privileges and discrimination divided the two men. Since deciding at eighteen years of age to sail to London, despite his caste elders' disagreement, Gandhi had engaged in an energetic fight against caste-based discrimination. Gandhi called the untouchables *Harijan*, children of God and said he was one of them. He preached a substantial conversion of the heart, leading to respect and inclusion. But he considered untouchability an issue the solution to which belonged to the Hindus as a whole and to Hindus only. The fight for the relief of the untouchables did not belong to the British or to Muslim or Sikh or Christian Indians. Neither did it belong to the state.

Himself of untouchable descent, Ambedkar was more radical: as only an outcast exposed to the Western and especially American culture could be, he wanted the caste system to be completely swept away—by any means, including civil legislation. Ambedkar rejected the term *Harijan* as patronizing; he preferred the term *Dalit*, which encapsulated the sense of oppression. Instead of relying on the goodwill of people from the upper caste, he believed the caste system had to be challenged by raising a Dalit leadership. Reservation of electoral seats for the untouchables and a separate electorate were the indispensable tools. Dalits had to be treated differently in order to be promoted in society. They had to be sure they could vote in Councils. They had to be sure they could elect their own representatives.

After World War I, the British government proved more open to the rights of Indian minorities. In August 1932, the MacDonald cabinet presented the Communal Award, a charter project on the status of minorities in view of the future Constitution of India. Drafted with the support of many Indian liberals, the project gave the untouchables a separate status and electorate. Gandhi rose against the plan in the name of Hindu unity and started a "fast unto death" while still in detention at Yerawda Jail in Poona. The move was meant to be the continuation of the creative and heroic South African Satyagraha, but to Ambedkar, the fast was nothing more than blackmail.

After a few days Ambedkar realized he had no alternative than to visit the Mahatma and settle. The Poona pact was sealed on September 24, 1932. Gandhi accepted the principle of reserved seats for the untouchables, but achieved his main goal of striking out the principle of separate electorates. Untouchables should be elected. But untouchables could not elect their own separate representatives.

Religious Reform

The defeat in 1932 further convinced Ambedkar that the independence and unity of India depended on a deep social and religious reform. He believed socialism could be beneficial if adapted to the Indian peculiarity. But he openly opposed the Marxist view subordinating the social and the religious spheres to the economic. He argued that social reforms in general were quintessential and that reforms in religion were particularly indispensable. In his book *Annihilation of Caste*, prepared in 1936 for the meeting of a group of liberal Hindu caste-reformers in Lahore, he wrote:

> Religion, social status, and property are all sources of power and authority, which one man has to control the liberty of another. One is predominant at one stage, the other is predominant at another stage. That is the only difference. If liberty is the ideal, and if liberty means the destruction of the dominion which one man holds over another, then obviously it cannot be insisted upon that economic reform must be the one kind of reform worthy of pursuit. If the source of power and dominion is, at any given time or in any given society, social and religious, then social reform and religious reform must be accepted as the necessary sort of reform.[172]

When charged to preside over the drafting of the Constitution in 1947, Ambedkar brought to the task his reformist vision. He wanted India to be a modern socialist state with the mission to reform religion so as to eradicate backwardness and oppression. This implied first the construction of India as a neutral, secular, nonconfessional

---

172. Ambedkar, *Annihilation of Caste*, 11.

state protecting religious freedom; secondly, the abolition of caste privileges, namely of untouchability; thirdly, the passage from personal religious laws to a uniform civil code for all citizens in family matters.

Both as a London-trained barrister familiar with legal mechanisms and as an experienced politician aware of the symbolic power of a foundational charter, Ambedkar knew a compromise was necessary. He bore in mind that the support of the leaders of the Congress, including Gandhi, was determinant.

Eventually, Ambedkar would succeed in framing a Charter, which proclaimed religious freedom as the basic principle of India. He would also succeed in somehow infusing in the Constitution his struggle against untouchability. But he could not achieve his third goal, the replacement of the personal laws system by a uniform civil code applicable to all, regardless of their religious affiliation. Article 44 of the Constitution would only provide for a directive principle of public policy, according to which "the State shall endeavour to secure for the citizens a uniform civil code throughout the territory of India."

Ambiguities and conflicts on caste separation, women's rights, and the status of religious communities in India were at the core of partition and independence. Ambedkar's constitutional struggle from 1947 onwards would result in a fundamental reference for the Supreme Court of India in the case of Sushmita fifty years later. It summarized the vital energy of a country entering in a new age, as well as the heavy colonial legacy of imperial gods. The same melange challenged India after 1989, when the country gave up its socialist, planned economy and found itself, once again, face to face with communal, religion-based hatred and violence. Precedents from the late forties and the constitutional debate itself proved seminal for the Indian judiciary in the early nineties. They were a source of arguments and solutions; also they were a reminder of historical turns and contradictions.

Towards Cold Gods

In 1947, the page was turned. Ninety years after the "Mutiny" in India and the cattle killing in South Africa, imperial gods were over and a new phase had begun.

In India, the Constituent Assembly started preparing the Charter of a socialist, secular, one-nation country.

In Britain, while the socialist drive produced its formidable reforms, but also the backlash, which would ultimately bring Churchill back to power, the British realized they had won the war but lost the Empire. It was time for the British Commonwealth and decolonization to step in, with the British Nationality Act of 1948 recognizing the subjects of the colonies as equal citizens of the United Kingdom and Colonies. The doors were open for the massive immigration, which would result in the later multicultural and multireligious Britain.

In South Africa, the social tensions following World War II weakened the position of pro-British Commonwealth Jan Smuts and blew in the sails of Afrikaner nationalists; the elections of 1948 would see the National party gain the majority on which the definitive apartheid regime would be built in the fifties.

The Cold War was about to shape religion differently. Cold gods were being born from the ashes of imperial gods. Not only had the imperial age featured the clash between the gods of the colonizer and gods of the colonized, but imperial gods had also introduced a fundamental division between believers and non-believers, which would prove quintessential in the age of cold gods, when capitalist religious freedom would confront communist atheism.

After the Poona Pact had denied the untouchables the right to a separate electorate, not only did Ambedkar further hated Gandhi's reference to religion, but Jawaharlal Nehru, the first prime minister of independent India, confessed that Gandhi's "continual references to God irritate me exceedingly."[173] For historian Arthur Herman, the clash between Gandhi and Churchill had been prominently about the place of God in politics:

> For Gandhi, God is everywhere and the starting point of everything. For Churchill, He is nowhere. In a universe without God, or at least without the immanent presence of divinity, Churchill found redemption in the unfolding of history itself, as the story of man's biological and cultural ascent.[174]

The triangular relationship between India, Britain, and South Africa was reactivated when South African Prime Minister Jan Smuts himself wrote to Churchill and underlined the difference between the two of them and Gandhi: "He is a man of God . . . You and I are mundane people. Gandhi has appealed to religious motives. You never have. That is where you have failed."[175]

Imperial gods coincided with an age of Christian supremacy challenged by the emergence of atheistic claims on the one hand and by inter-Christian, religious, and nationalist conflicts on the other. After imperial gods, the gods of the Cold War would split the world into pro- and anti-God factions. Socialism and nationalism did not make religion disappear in Britain, India, and South Africa, but faith was apparently confined to the edge of politics. Then religion gradually climbed again to center stage. The undercurrent of cold gods mutated into the visible power of post-1979 explosive gods.

For the judges of India, South Africa, and Britain who found themselves confronted with the post-1979 religious challenge, the imperial age between 1857 and 1947 resulted in a powerful heritage of unsolved puzzles and hidden resources. Were they also going to be judged "knights errant" in their quest throughout history for a sound response to the gods of their time?

173. Herman, *Gandhi & Churchill*, 389 and 450.
174. Ibid., 98.
175. Ibid., 506.

The judgment on the case of Sushmita given by the Supreme Court of India in 1995 attempted to sensibly bridge imperial gods and the post-1979 explosive gods. The first decisions given by the newly established Constitutional Court of South Africa, including the one on Gareth Prince's claim, also went in the same direction. From the midnineties on, British judges also handled imperial gods as they dealt with cases of blasphemy and multireligious conflicts. Though in very different contexts, Indian, British, and South African judges shared the need to find an appropriate response to the same post-1979 explosive gods, and, from 1995 to 2000, to national gods. In doing so, they partook in the task of reinventing the common legacy of imperial gods.

Chapter 3

National Gods (1995–2000)

The Victory of Sushmita Ghosh

The case of Sushmita Ghosh was finally decided on May 10, 1995. The Supreme Court of India allowed the petition and recognized Sushmita's right not to be deserted by her husband following his conversion to Islam. Sushmita, the "unfortunate lady"[1] as the Court presented her, was still the legitimate wife of Shri Ghosh. Conversion to Islam did not imply the dissolution of a previous Hindu marriage. At thirty-seven years of age, Sushmita won the battle she had started three years before, when Shri urged her to consent to divorce and she refused, only to see her husband convert and take a new wife under Muslim law.

Of course Shri Ghosh was free to convert to Islam, free to become Mohammed Carim Gazi. But conversion did not entitle him to marry another woman without first obtaining a proper divorce. Based on the Hindu Marriage Act of 1955, the statute law for Hindu marriages, Justice Kuldip Singh stated for the Court that "assuming that a Hindu husband has a right to embrace Islam as his religion, he has no right under the [Hindu Marriage] Act to marry again without getting his earlier marriage under the Act dissolved. The second marriage after conversion to Islam would, thus, be in violation of the rules of natural justice and, as such, would be void."[2]

The two judges composing the bench of the Supreme Court, Justice Kuldip Singh and Justice Sahai, converged on the principle that a religious marriage cannot be dissolved "by the application of another personal law to which one of the spouses converts and the other refuses to do so."[3]

---

1. *Sarla Mudgal,* 640 [6].
2. Ibid., 647 [24].
3. Ibid., 645 [14].

Consequently, not only was the second marriage of Shri Gosh with Henna Begum null and void, but also Shri, the "apostate husband,"[4] as Justice Kuldip Singh qualified him, was guilty of the criminal offense of bigamy since he had married while still bound by a previous monogamous marriage.

Sushmita had thus achieved a twofold victory. Justice Kuldip Singh for the Court summarized both the civil and the criminal sides of the judgment on Sarla Mudgal, as the case of Sushmita was called after the name of the first applicant: "we hold that the second marriage of a Hindu-husband after conversion to Islam, without having his first marriage dissolved under law, would be invalid. The second marriage would be void in terms of the provisions of Section 494, Indian Penal Code and the apostate-husband would be guilty of the offence under Section 494, I.P.C."[5]

Through the victory of Sushmita, the Court reasserted its doctrine on the Indian nation. Since the struggle for independence, three different ways of understanding the nation had featured in Indian politics. The Congress stood for a multireligious single Indian nation, to be guided by a secular state. The one-nation theory was meant to encompass all differences and to give every Indian citizen or community the same status. Hindu nationalists shared the one-nation vision but claimed the one nation had to be Hindu. India was Hindu, Indian Muslims were Hindu, and the Indian nation could not be other than a Hindu nation. A third way of understanding the nation came from those sectors within the minorities who felt that the unity of the nation threatened their specificity. Many Muslims in particular felt alienated because of their double allegiance to both the Indian and the Muslim nation. The two-nation or three-nation vision expressed the frustration of those communities, for they held that neither version of the one-nation theory—neither the multireligious nor the Hindu—would allow room for them.

In the context of the 1990s, the traditional, multireligious, and secular one-nation vision promoted by the Court was highly problematic. Gandhi's multireligiosity and Nehru's secularism sounded to many like an old formula belonging to the past. Religious nationalism was the present state of the country, with the rhetoric of Hindu nationalism and the Muslim nation having been invigorated by post-1979 explosive gods. Yet, as the Supreme Court looked at the case of Sushmita through the lens of the secular state of India serving the multireligious Indian nation, many Indians believed, along with the judges, that this was the only option available in the march towards the future.

As post-1979 explosive gods generated a renewed debate on Hindu India, Muslim India, and secular or multireligious India, the conflict over how to combine religion and the nation monopolized Indian public life in the midnineties. National gods were rising.

4. Ibid., 639 [2].
5. Ibid., 651 [39].

Similarly, in Britain and South Africa, a debate started over how religion and the nation should combine in the new era. In the final years of John Major's government, the place of religion in British public life was under scrutiny. As British multireligious society proved increasingly turbulent, the traditional establishment of the Church of England came to be challenged. In January 1995, legal action began in Warwickshire, which would result in the milestone Aston Cantlow case and the redefinition of the status of the Church of England. In the second half of the nineties, the local breakthrough of the British National Party, with Nick Griffin joining in 1995 and being prosecuted for anti-Semitism, also witnessed a new mode of articulating religion and the nation.

National gods played a major part in South Africa too. With the institution of the Truth and Reconciliation Commission, also in 1995, the postapartheid nation-building process came to involve religion on many levels. By marking the end of a Christian preference and pulling all faiths together for the sake of the rising nation, the leadership of Desmond Tutu offered South Africa the vision of the "rainbow nation of God," a multireligious society to be realized through a religiously neutral state.

In India, Britain, and South Africa, various expressions of national gods represented the response to the explosive gods. Most Indians, Britons, and South Africans saw themselves as part of multireligious nations, but not all of them felt happy with that. Millions took the multireligious character of their societies as the reason why those same societies did not work. Minorities aimed to conquer more and more reserved spaces—majorities to push the outsiders out while reestablishing identities and traditions within.

From 1995 to 2000, new nations and new religions took shape in the global world. The intermingling of national and religious elements gave rise in the three countries to different variations of national gods. It also represented the ultimate effect of both imperial and cold gods.

The new context influenced the biography not only of Sushmita Ghosh but also of Gareth Prince and Shabina Begum. In 1995, when Sushmita won her case, Gareth had just completed his legal education and applied to the bar of The Cape, the application resulting in the controversy that would plunge him in a lengthy legal procedure. Also in 1995, when Shabina Begum was only six years old, her future school, the Denbigh High School of Luton, planned a decisive effort for coping with increasingly multi-religious classes. Tensions lay ahead, the tensions that would bring Shabina before the House of Lords ten years later.

How Many Nations?

While preparing their 1995 decision on Sushmita Ghosh, Justice Kuldip Singh and Justice R. M. Sahai time-traveled throughout precedents in the case law of the British Raj, back to Victoria Skinner in 1871, Ram Kumari in 1891, and other converted petitioners in the 1940s. They utterly ignored the solution provided by Justice Ormond, the "knight errant." Instead they extensively quoted Justice Lodge, Justice Blagden, and Justices Stone and Chagla, whose approach, though fifty years older, perfectly suited the Supreme Court of India. Continuity between the colonial and the post-colonial framework was blatant. In 1995, grounding their reasoning on the authority of the predominant view of 1945 and 1946, Justices Kuldip Singh and R. M. Sahai concluded that conversion was not a legitimate ground for dissolving a marriage.

In his opinion for the Supreme Court, Justice Kuldip Singh sympathized with Justice Blagden and quoted his very words from 1945 as the quintessence of both the problem and its solution. "Do then the authorities compel me,"[6] Justice Blagden asked himself, "to hold that one spouse can, by changing his or her religious opinions (or purporting to do so), force his or her newly acquired personal law on a party to whom it is entirely alien and who does not want it?"[7] The British judge gave the following answer:

> In the name of justice, equity, and good conscience or, in more simple language, of common sense, why should this be possible? If there were no authority on the point I (personally) should have thought that so monstrous an absurdity carried its own refutation with it, so extravagant are the results that follow from it. For it is not only the question of divorce that the plaintiff's contention affects. If it is correct, it follows that a Christian husband can embrace Islam and, the next moment, three additional wives, without even the consent of the original wife.[8]

Like Justice Blagden fifty years earlier, Justice Kuldip Singh in 1995 refused to apply Muslim law to a Hindu marriage and considered "the second marriage of a Hindu husband after embracing Islam"[9] void because it was "violative of justice, equity, and good conscience."[10] The silence of the law of the land on the issue could not be taken as allowing for the automatic application of Muslim Personal Law. Rather, as Justice Chagla clarified in 1946, the case had to be judged on the basis of "justice, right, and equity." Likewise, in 1995, Justice Kuldip Singh claimed, "the conduct of a spouse who converts to Islam has to be judged on the basis of the rule of justice and right or equity and good conscience."[11] And added:

> A matrimonial dispute between a convert to Islam and his or her non-Muslim spouse is obviously not a dispute "where the parties are Muslims" and, therefore, the rule of decision in such a case was or is not required to be the

---

6. *Robasa Khanum*, 869.

7. Ibid.

8. Ibid.

9. *Sarla Mudgal*, 647 [23].

10. Ibid.

11. Ibid.

"Muslim Personal Law." In such cases the Court shall act and the Judge shall decide according to justice, equity, and good conscience.[12]

Apparently there was no difference between cases of conversion and remarriage in 1945–46, on the eve of Independence, and in 1995, after almost fifty years of independent India. Arguments were reiterated. The legal jargon was pretty much the same. Sushmita could have been any deserted Indian wife of the 1940s. However, in reality, the parallel between the cases was only apparent. The two seemingly identical decisions responded to two distinct contexts and hid two different visions.

Judges like Justice Blagden served the administration of the British Raj. But in 1945 and 1946 British rule in India was politically moribund. As Independence neared, with Hindu-Muslim violence spreading and British and Indian leaders arranging partition, judges had no clear political vision to uphold. They simply stood for the coherence of the law with the colonial pattern and, sometimes, for the rights of the deprived sectors of society. Justice Blagden and his colleagues saw in conversions and remarriage the savage, undisciplined, and chaotic face of India. They observed unruly India triumphing through the prevailing rule of religious communities. All the judiciary of the British Raj could do was to bridle religious laws, Muslim law in particular. By denying conversion and remarriage the power to alter conjugal status, they did their best to protect colonial legal rationality.

In 1995, the Supreme Court of India responded with the same means to a different context. Widespread protests against the entry of "junk food chains" in India, with a Bangalore court closing a Kentucky Fried Chicken outlet as it breached regulations on additives, witnessed the difficult marriage between Indian sensibilities and global trade. The country was opening to market economy and exploring the possibilities of the postbipolar world. Indian Muslims were more and more concerned with the growth of Hindu nationalism: the Bharatiya Janata Party was becoming so popular as to challenge the Congress party. Intercommunal violence and global terrorism spread. In the eyes of the Supreme Court, conversions to Islam with the aim of avoiding conjugal obligations hindered the supremacy of the state and the unity of the Indian nation. Unlike Anglo-Indian judges in 1945–46, the judges of the Supreme Court put forward a clear and strong political vision. They applied the law so as to substantiate the principles the judiciary stood for. In 1945–46, subordination of Muslim law to the law of the land was meant preserving the abstract coherence of the law and what remained of the colonial pattern. In 1995, the same subordination was meant to enhance the multireligious Indian nation, the secular state, and the constitutional vision of the judges.

In the Sarla Mudgal decision, the Supreme Court took its legal arguments from the case law of 1945–46 and its political vision from the almost five decades of independent India. Beyond the private biography of Sushmita Ghosh, the legal and the

12. Ibid.

political were inextricably knotted in the decision of the Court. If denying conversion the power to prejudice the conjugal status was the legal side of the judgment, the subjugation of all religious communities to the same national legal standard was the political one.

The case of Sushmita Ghosh encapsulated the conflict between the two faces of independent India. On the one hand, India was modeled after the Western central-ized nation-state, the legendary unity and solidity of which was supposed to depend on the unification of the legal system: following the pattern of English law, a unified common law of the land should dominate and impose uniformity. This vision urged for religious laws to be reformed and limited by the state for the sake of the nation. Nationalization of religious laws was inevitable, as social engineering and social wel-fare combined.

On the other hand, India was an inherently pluralistic society, hence the inevi-table legal pluralism and the persistent salience of religious personal laws, no matter what this meant for the rights of the individuals and for general legal uniformity.

In the Sarla Mudgal decision, Justice Kuldip Singh overtly addressed the tension between the unity and plurality of India and dictated the "one-nation" vision of the Court: "[The] territory of India was partitioned by the British Rulers into two States on the basis of religion. Those who preferred to remain in India after the partition fully knew that the Indian leaders did not believe in two-nation or three-nation theory and that in the Indian Republic there was to be one Nation—Indian nation—and no com-munity could claim to remain a separate entity on the basis of religion."[13]

Cold Storage

The intrinsic tension between one-nation India and multi-nation India was expressed in the long-lasting debate on the application of Article 44 of the Constitution on the uniform civil code.

Ambedkar had injected into the article his dream of religious reform—that a uniform civil code would impose equality and unity upon unjust and unruly religious laws—but he had been forced to accept a compromise, the provision being not im-mediately applicable. In essence, legal uniformity would be enforced only if and when Indian minorities came to feel comfortable with the Hindu majority.

Through the adjudication of Sushmita Ghosh's case, the Supreme Court vigor-ously stepped into the debate on the uniform civil code. Justice Kuldip Singh affirmed that "there is no necessary connection between religion and personal law in a civilized society."[14] Article 44, the judge summed up, sought "to divest religion from social relations and personal law."[15]

13. Ibid., 650 [35].
14. Ibid., 649 [33].
15. Ibid.

The Court stood for the absolute need to give Article 44 full application, as the judges held a unified personal law for all Indians, regardless of their religious affiliation, to be an unalterable necessity. Justice Singh considered the "unequivocal mandate"[16] of Article 44 "a decisive step towards national consolidation"[17] and affirmed that "there is no justification whatsoever in delaying indefinitely the introduction of a uniform personal law in the country."[18] Justice Sahai joined in, underlining that a unified code was "imperative both for protection of the oppressed and promotion of national unity and solidarity."[19] National unity prevailed over religious identities. Sushmita's victory was the victory of a secular and multi-religious one-nation India.

The judgment of the Supreme Court on the case of Sushmita and the other women was thus vicarious in character, as it took the action the government was reluctant to take. The Court had to act because the Parliament and the Government proved unable to act: "governments," wrote Justice Singh, "till date have been wholly remiss in their duty of implementing the constitutional mandate."[20] Therefore the Court asked the Government "to have a fresh look."[21] Not the Courts, case by case, but the law, once and for all, should protect the rights of Sushmita and of the thousands of Indian women like her. For Kuldip Singh it was time to retrieve the uniform civil code "from the cold storage where it is lying since 1949."[22]

The Court's pro-unified-code position and the decision to allow Sushmita Ghosh's petition followed the same rationale. By deciding the case according to the principle that religious personal laws could not impinge on basic rights, the judges intended to limit how far each community could go within the national framework. Granting rights regardless of the religious membership of citizens and fighting for a civil status of general application regardless of personal laws were two sides of the same coin.

While pleading for the application of Article 44, the Court stepped into the issue of Hindu-Muslim tensions. Justice Kuldip Singh interpreted Sushmita's hardship as proof that Muslims were unfairly using polygamy in order to push Hindus to convert. In the lack of a unified code, the judge wrote, "there is an open inducement to a Hindu husband, who wants to enter into second marriage while the first marriage is subsisting, to become a Muslim. Since monogamy is the law for Hindus and the Muslim law permits as many as four wives in India, errant Hindu husband embraces Islam to circumvent the provisions of the Hindu law and to escape from penal consequences."[23]

16. Ibid., 639 [1].
17. Ibid.
18. Ibid., 649 [32].
19. Ibid. 652 [45].
20. Ibid. 650 [36].
21. Ibid., 651 [37]
22. Ibid., 639 [1].
23. Ibid., 640 [8].

Again, a link existed between the case law of the forties and that of the nineties. In 1946, Justice Chagla for the High Court of Bombay affirmed the supremacy of Indian law over Muslim law, and wished for a modernized Indian Muslim law. In 1995, the Court blamed Muslims for their surreptitious inducement to conversions, but more generally for their reluctance to take part in the national endeavor.

If the mandate of Article 44 had remained unfulfilled since 1950—while Nehru himself limited his reformist action to Hindu law—the Court suggested that this was because Muslims always defended in the firmest way their prerogatives and isolation under the umbrella of untouchable Islamic law. Justice Kuldip Singh underlined that by progressively agreeing to reform their own religious laws, "the Hindus, along with Sikhs, Buddhists, and Jains"[24] had "forsaken their sentiments in the cause of national unity and integration."[25] Other communities, like Muslims themselves, but also Christians, had not. Now, if a common standard of rights protection in modern India was a common interest and goal for all, Muslims themselves, Justice Singh affirmed, should be willing to adjust. The judge appealed to the sense of morality of the Muslims and urged them to counter the use of conversion in order to gain practical advantages:

> It is not the object of Islam, nor is the intention of the enlightened Muslim community that Hindu husbands should be encouraged to become Muslims merely for the purpose of evading their own personal laws by marrying again.[26]

The judge wanted Muslims to consent to some form of adjustment to the common standard. If not the uniform civil code itself, a legislative step of another kind was needed in order to foster the harmonization of rights irrespective of religious laws. Justice Sahai agreed that "the first step should be to rationalize the personal law of the minorities to develop religious and cultural amity."[27]

Bathing the Idol

The Sarla Mudgal decision appeared strongly pro-Hindu and anti-Muslim. To minimize that problem, Justice Sahai emphasized secularism and linked the cause of the uniform civil code to the idea of secular India embodied in the Constitution. "The Constitution," he wrote in his opinion, "was framed with secularism as its ideal and goal."[28] The construction of the secular state of India was the condition for the Indian nation to be multireligious and for religious freedom to be recognized and fostered.

24. Ibid., 650 [33].
25. Ibid.
26. Ibid., 647–48 [25].
27. Ibid. 652 [45].
28. Ibid., 651 [43].

After independence, the Supreme Court took on itself the mandate of enforcing secular India while expanding religious liberty. This, Justice Sahai stressed, allowed India to give the most comprehensive answer to the crucial question, "What is religion?"[29]

> Religion is more than mere matter of faith. The Constitution, by guaranteeing freedom of conscience, ensured inner aspects of religious belief. And external expression of it were [sic] protected by guaranteeing right to freely practice and propagate religion. Reading and reciting holy scriptures, for instance, Ramayana or Quran or Bible or Guru Granth Sahib, is as much a part of religion as offering food to deity by a Hindu or bathing the idol or dressing him and going to a temple, mosque, church, or gurudwara.[30]

Religion was not limited to rites and liturgies though. And religious freedom could not be limited to those dimensions either. On this point concerning the nature of religion, Justice Sahi departed from his colleague, Kuldip Singh, who in the same Sarla Mudgal decision dissociated religion from family and marriage. According to Indian constitutional jurisprudence, Justice Sahai responded, family life was also a matter of religion: "Marriage, inheritance, divorce, conversion are as much religious in nature and content as any other belief or faith. Going round the fire seven rounds or giving consent before Qazi are as much matter of faith and conscience as the worship itself."[31]

In Justice Sahai's approach, the assumption that religion was inherently present in all aspects of life came with the sister assumption that religion was inevitably about passions and emotions, divisions and conflicts. As the judge wrote, religious freedom was about setting foot on a land where "reason and logic have little role to play:"[32]

> When a Hindu becomes a convert by reciting Kalma or a Muslim becomes Hindu by reciting certain Mantras, it is a matter of belief and conscience. Some of these practices observed by members of one religion may appear to be excessive and even violative of human rights to members of another. But these are matters of faith. Reason and logic have little role to play.[33]

Throughout history, the judge also stated, India struggled with the need to both recognize and limit the power of faith: "The sentiments and emotions have to be cooled and tempered by sincere effort. But today there is no Raja Ram Mohun Roy, who single-handedly brought about that atmosphere which paved the way for Sati abolition. Nor is a statesman of the stature of Pt. Nehru, who could pilot through, successfully, the Hindu Succession Act and Hindu Marriage Act, revolutionising the customary Hindu Law."[34]

29. Ibid., 651 [43].
30. Ibid., 651–52 [43].
31. Ibid., 652 [44].
32. Ibid.
33. Ibid.
34. Ibid.

This lesson was drawn from history: in colonial India, as in Independent India, religions and the state could not avoid a painful quest for a viable compromise. For the two judges who granted Sushmita Ghosh her victory, the uniform code was a necessity, but it could become a reality, Justice Sahai made clear, only when the "social climate" was "properly built up by elite of the society, statesmen among leaders who, instead of gaining personal mileage, rise above and awaken the masses to accept the change."[35] Contrary to Kuldip Singh's activism, a cautious approach to the uniform code, Justice Sahai believed, was necessary to protect religion. "Freedom of religion is the core of our culture,"[36] the judge wrote, "even the slightest deviation shakes the social fibre."[37]

Swallowing the Camel

On May 28, 1995, two weeks after the decision, Tahir Mahmood commented on it for the *Hindu*. The famous Islamic law scholar applauded the decision on the "concrete issue":[38] "Derecognising bigamous marriages of non-Muslim husbands contracted in such a fraudulent manner indeed enforces Qur'anic justice. On this point the Supreme Court ruling is unassailable."[39]

But Tahir Mahmood strongly criticized the position taken by Justice Kuldip Singh on the uniform code. The Court, Mahmood argued, had shared "with the masses the myth regarding the non-enactment of a uniform civil code by way of 'appeasement' of the minorities, despite the majority community's clear option and commitment in its favor."[40]

This "myth," Mahmood maintained in *The Hindu*, was simply false. Codification of Hindu law under Nehru in the 1950s had far from satisfied "the Constitutional ideals of secularism, gender justice, and legal equality and uniformity."[41] In the eyes of the prominent Muslim law professor, Kuldip Singh's activism ignored "the ground realities."[42] Conditions were not fulfilled for a uniform code to be meaningfully created. In fact, such a code, "may only emerge, through an evolutionary process, out of the extremely rich composite legal heritage of the Nation, of which all the personal laws are equal constituents."[43]

35. Ibid.
36. Ibid., 652 [45].
37. Ibid.
38. Mahmood, *Uniform civil code*, 17.
39. Ibid., 18.
40. Ibid., 14.
41. Ibid., 16.
42. Ibid., 17.
43. Ibid.

The final judgment by Mahmood on Sushmita Ghosh's victory was thus that Sarla Mudgal amounted to a "judicious ruling" with an "invidious obiter."[44] The verdict against Sushmita's husband was correct; the plea for the uniform code was not.

In the following weeks, Mahmood reworked his article in the *Hindu* and made a pamphlet out of it: *Uniform civil code: Fictions and Facts*. From the outset, the author pointed out the anti-Muslim attitude of the Supreme Court and of Kuldip Singh in particular. Mahmood informed the reader that the Sarla Mudgal case was decided "on the eve of the Muslim festival of Id-ul-Azha—on which day, incidentally, was also burned down in Kashmir the shrine of Charar-e-Sharif."[45]

Mahmood reiterated his tribute to the ruling. He exposed the strategy of sham conversions to Islam by bigamist Hindus and expressed the strongest condemnation: "I strongly oppose this dirty game. I hold the imams doing the 'job' as much guilty as the dishonest Hindu husbands. What married Hindu men do and are helped with is a fraud on Hinduism, a disgrace to Islam, a cruel joke on the freedom-of-conscience clause in the Constitution of the country, and a criminal scheming against the law of the land."[46]

Coherently, he credited Kuldip Singh's understanding of the negative Muslim judgment on sham conversions as "the most sensible, the most gratifying and the most appreciable sentence in the whole judgment."[47]

At the same time, the author attacked the "myth" of the uniform code. Article 44 of the Constitution should not be taken as "the Alladin's lamp hoping for a *genei* called 'uniform civil code' to come out of it and do the magic trick."[48] Politicized religious identities had transformed the project of secular uniformity into a "stick" with which "to beat chosen sections of Indians."[49] Exploitation of the uniform code hindered, not encouraged, Muslim reform. According to Mahmood,

> The biggest hold-back factor in the context of necessary reform of the practice of Muslim law in India is the ongoing highly irresponsible talk about a uniform civil code by motivated communalists, self-serving politicians, fun-seeking media-men and—not too infrequently—ignorant or careless law-men, most of whom protect the code only as a death-knell of Islamic religio-legal traditions in India.[50]

In his article for the *Hindu*, Mahmood proposed a threefold approach to the calamity of conversions and unlawful bigamy. The solution would lie "in suitably amending

44. Ibid., 11.
45. Ibid., 11.
46. Ibid. 60.
47. Ibid., 66.
48. Ibid., 181.
49. Ibid., 41.
50. Ibid., 179.

the Hindu Marriage Act, improving the now cumbersome and vexatious judicial process for divorce, and properly codifying true principles of the Muslim personal law."[51]

Mahmood's pamphlet exposed the political exploitation of religion to the detriment of "the hapless Indian woman."[52] Sushmita Ghosh's victory was deserved, but very limited. Much more remained to be done to prevent women from being the true victims of the "tug-of-war . . . between the so-called 'pro-reform' and 'anti-reform' groups: between 'communalists' and 'secularists,' between 'pseudo-secularists' and 'religious secularists,' between the majority and the minorities, between Hindutva and Shari'a."[53]

Hence the Muslim author's vision of a healthy and progressive interpretation of Indian secularism: "What the Constitution insists on is not eradication of religion itself from the society, but eradication of abuse and exploitation of religion by anybody—by men against women, by politicians against masses, by bigots against the enlightened, by one community against another, by the majority against the minorities."[54]

Tahir Mahmood's analysis would influence interpreters in the following years. Commenting on Sarla Mudgal in 2003, U.S. law professor Gary Jeffrey Jacobsohn took inspiration from Mahmood for his critique of Kuldip Singh. Jacobsohn blamed Singh for the Supreme Court's "grossly misplaced conceptualization of the secular ideal of India"[55] and regarded Singh's approach to the uniform code as a "broader failure of imagination" on what "one might conceptualize [as] legal uniformity in the Indian context."[56]

Healing the Nation

In the beginning of 1995, on the eve of the decision of the Supreme Court of India on the case of Sushmita Ghosh, South Africa welcomed its first Constitutional Court. Immediately after its inauguration by President Nelson Mandela on the morning of February 14, 1995, the Court started examining the case of Themba Makwanyane and Mvuso Mchunu, two convicted prisoners previously sentenced to death on four counts of murder. The Court was asked whether the death penalty, still in the Statute Book despite the moratorium of 1990, was in contravention of the 1993 interim Constitution. A tougher kickoff was impossible. The Court had to decide whether the state in turn had the right to murder a murderer or not.

Religion had always nourished legal and illegal violence in South Africa. The relationship between creeds, faiths, morality, and violence was particularly at stake

51. Ibid., 18.
52. Ibid., 164.
53. Ibid., 163–64.
54. Ibid., 169.
55. Jacobsohn, *The Wheel of Law*, 117.
56. Ibid., 116.

now, as new South Africa endeavored to pass from the brutal society of the past to the harmonious society of the future, from *your* gods to *our* gods. Apparently religion did not play any part in the issue, but the decision on the death penalty was also a decision on how to articulate faith and killing.

In his 1991 book, *Shots in the Streets: Violence and Religion in South Africa*, religious studies scholar David Chidester retraced in South African history the roots of a tight relationship between violence and religion. What for centuries had been ritual killing ended up persisting in modern South African society in three ways: "it was an offering to a violent God; it was a ritual of elimination to restore purity; it was a ritual of incorporation to gain power."[57] Religion fueled individual and collective violence; it also played a remarkable role in state-administered violence, with Afrikaner Christian nationalism representing a fundamental factor for legitimizing the violence of apartheid and the death penalty itself.

After 1979, explosive gods challenged the place of faith and transcendent values in postapartheid South Africa. Deciding on the retention of the death penalty automatically implied deciding on the new place for religion and ethics in the country. Was the Afrikaner biblical foundation of capital punishment still acceptable? Was the death penalty to be retained on a secular rather than religious basis? Or did religion itself require the new South Africa to abolish the death penalty?

With the decision on the case of Sushmita Ghosh, the Supreme Court of India replied to explosive gods by rearticulating the relationship between the nation and religion. The nation came first; "national unity" was the supreme goal. In their Indian incarnation, national gods translated into the subordination of any single religion to a multireligious nation by way of a secular state. One month after the Indian judgment, South African judges themselves had to decide on the relationship between religion and the nation in postapartheid South Africa. The problem for Indian judges had centered the questions of what protection women deserved, regardless of religious specificities; and what measure of religious diversity was acceptable within one single nation. The problem for South African judges was how to redefine national morality itself after the transition from apartheid to democracy, human rights, and the rule of law.

Within the South African Constitutional Court, Justice Mahomed represented the Indian community for which Gandhi had fought in the age of imperial gods. Ismail Mahomed, the son of Indian shopkeepers, was a living reminder of the Indian struggle in the country. His turbulent legal practice had emblematically expressed the discrimination to which Indians were subject. Because of his Indian ancestry, he was denied admission to the bar in Pretoria, and only in the late 1950s was he admitted to the bar of Johannesburg, but with no right to rent an office of his own. Using his colleagues' offices, Ismail Mahomed became one of the most prominent lawyers and scholars in the country. In 1974, he was the first nonwhite to "take silk" and become a senior counsel.

---

57. Chidester, *Shots in the Streets,* 164.

In 1991, he was appointed the first nonwhite permanent judge of the Supreme Court of South Africa. In 1995, he was appointed to the Constitutional Court.

A member of the bench in charge of the death penalty case, Justice Mahomed clarified in his opinion that the challenge ahead was about the "aspirations"[58] of the nation as well as about "the moral and ethical direction which [the] nation has identified for its future":[59]

> All Constitutions seek to articulate, with differing degrees of intensity and detail, the shared aspirations of a nation; the values which bind its people, and which discipline its government and its national institutions; the basic premises upon which judicial, legislative and executive power is to be wielded; the constitutional limits and the conditions upon which that power is to be exercised; the national ethos which defines and regulates that exercise; and the moral and ethical direction which that nation has identified for its future.[60]

Indian judges openly addressed religion and religions; South African judges rather dealt with "the moral and ethical direction" of the nation. From 1995 onwards, national gods emerged in both India and South Africa, as the two countries redefined the place of religion in the national endeavor.

The Collective Morality of a Nation

In the struggle against apartheid, lawyers like Albie Sachs and Arthur Chaskalson believed that constitutionalism was the key. The new South Africa required a new fundamental Charter. The new country would produce a Constitution. The Constitution would produce the new country.

With its foundation in February 1995, the Constitutional Court came to embody such a dramatic change. In June 1994, Nelson Mandela appointed Arthur Chaskalson president of the Court, the first to serve in that newly established office. Albie Sachs, the man injured by the car bomb in Maputo seven years earlier, was also appointed to the Court following a selection supervised by the Judicial Service Commission.

New rules created a new game. The interim Constitution of 1993 already encapsulated the principles of substantial and procedural democracy that the final Constitution would consecrate in 1996. Parliament would no longer enjoy unlimited power as it had in the years of segregation and apartheid. The Constitution prevailed over the Parliament, over politics, over voters themselves. If the activism of the Supreme Court of India was meant to revitalize the Constitution of 1950, the South African constitutional judges endeavored to prevent emotional popular feelings from threatening the will of the nation, as expressed in their new charter. In his first opinion for the Court,

58. *S v Makwanyane* [262].

59. Ibid.

60. Ibid.

in the death-penalty case, Albie Sachs pointed out that "the function given to this court by the Constitution is to articulate the fundamental sense of justice and right shared by the whole nation, as expressed in the text of the Constitution."[61]

South African novelist Nadine Gordimer had received the Nobel Prize four years earlier. The discussion of the death-penalty case prompted her to write a novel on the subject. In *The House Gun*, a character underlined the novelty of a Constitutional Court prevailing over the contingent will of the people: "The question faced by the Court is whether the Death Penalty is constitutional, not whether it is justified by popular demand."[62] The president of the Court, Arthur Chaskalson expressed himself in the same terms in the opinion he wrote for the unanimous Court: "the question before us,"[63] he explained, "is not what the majority of South Africans believe a proper sentence for murder should be. It is whether the Constitution allows the sentence."[64] Chaskalson put "constitutional adjudication"[65] above the mere recognition of what would "find favour with the public:"[66]

> Public opinion may have some relevance to the enquiry, but in itself, it is no substitute for the duty vested in the Courts to interpret the Constitution and to uphold its provisions without fear or favour. If public opinion were to be decisive there would be no need for constitutional adjudication . . . This Court cannot allow itself to be diverted from its duty to act as an independent arbiter of the Constitution by making choices on the basis that they will find favour with the public.[67]

The Constitutional Court, a body of judges representing the highest instance of the national judiciary, was necessary to apply the supreme principles in the specific political and social circumstances.

In a country where "the contrast between the past which it [the Constitution] repudiates and the future to which it seeks to commit the nation is stark and dramatic,"[68] as Justice Mahomed stated, the Constitutional Court was in charge of articulating the repudiation of the past and the construction of the future. The task was macroscopically difficult in the judgment on the case of Makwanyane and Mchunu, where South Africa's harsh history was under judgment together with the spreading of violence in the South Africa of the present.

---

61. Ibid. [362].
62. Gordimer, *The House Gun*, 137.
63. *S v Makwanyane* [87].
64. Ibid.
65. Ibid. [88].
66. Ibid. [89].
67. Ibid. [88–89].
68. Ibid. [262].

Past violence, especially state-orchestrated violence, was a huge obstacle in the search of national unity. Nadine Gordimer set the everyday "cruelty enacted in the name of the State"[69] as the antecedent of her crime fiction on the death-penalty debate: "so many fatal beatings, mortal interrogations, a dying man driven across a thousand kilometres naked in a police van; common law criminals singing through the night before the morning of the execution, hangings taking place in Pretoria while a second slice of bread pops up from the toaster."[70]

The violence of the present was also terrible. The country was awash with murder, as it was with rapes, robberies, and hijackings. Communal violence was also spreading. In his opinion for the Constitutional Court in the death-penalty case, Justice Didcott recalled the national aspiration to get rid of both past and present violence: "South Africa has experienced too much savagery. The wanton killing must stop before it makes a mockery of the civilized, humane, and compassionate society to which the nation aspires and has constitutionally pledged itself."[71]

Abolitionists and retentionists challenged the Court, not only regarding the power of the death penalty to deter criminals, but all the more so concerning the consistency of such punishment with the right to life and the supreme values of the nation.

President Chaskalson left religion out of his discourse, but religious implications were obvious and ubiquitous. Death-penalty supporters and detractors had copiously speculated on theological arguments. Church leaders had taken positions. The decision had to be made, in Gordimer's words, "on the collective morality of a nation, which is the substance of a constitution."[72] The supreme value of life crossed the border between the religious and the secular. Nadine Gordimer summarized the two key principles at stake: "One, the sacred injunction, Thou Shalt Not Kill, two, the secular code, human life is the highest value to be respected."[73]

Both the secular and the sacred demanded to be included in the new South Africa. The "sacred injunction" and the "secular code" could be taken as the reason to lift the penalty or, at the opposite, as the reason to retain it. Nadine Gordimer captured the entanglement of God's will and man's will. She stressed the opposition between the strong divine commandment and the fragile human decision: "The Death Penalty . . . will be decided in this Court, reversed under another constitution in some future time, under some other government. God knows. God only knows how man has twisted and interpreted, reinterpreted, his Word, thou shalt not kill."[74]

---

69. Gordimer, *The House Gun*, 126.
70. Ibid.
71. *S v Makwanyane* [190].
72. Gordimer, *The House Gun*, 128.
73. Ibid., 98–99.
74. Ibid., 138.

Chaskalson's overview of death-penalty provisions around the globe illustrated how men "twisted and interpreted" God's word. The issue transcended borders and nations. The American case was, of course, an embarrassing reference, with the death penalty so often opposed or endorsed in biblical terms. Chaskalson also studied the provision of Macaulay's Indian Penal Code, which provided for the death sentence in cases of murder. In its amicus brief, the South African Police relied on the Indian case to support its retentionist view. In fact, a landmark decision of 1980 by the Indian Supreme Court had confirmed the constitutionality of the penalty. Commenting on the relevant case of *Bachan Singh v. State of Punjab*, Chaskalson emphasized the constitutional difference between South Africa and India. The "unqualified right to life vested in every person by section 9 of our Constitution,"[75] Chaskalson wrote, was decisive in assessing that "the death sentence is cruel, inhuman or degrading punishment within the meaning of section 11 (2) of our Constitution."[76] "In this respect,"[77] he concluded, "our Constitution differs materially from the Constitutions of the United States and India."[78]

The difference between India and South Africa was an example that the one absolute word of God gave different outcomes when filtered through the relative appreciation of men. The one word of God corresponded to the many different judgments of men. The oneness of God did not guarantee human unanimity.

Religion could be at the same time the cause of violence or its antidote. In Gordimer's crime fiction on capital punishment, the protagonist Duncan, a young man detained for murder waiting to be sentenced, wanders through the library of the prison, checking what was deemed suitable for criminals to read. The selection of books fitting into the correctional scheme amazes him. Duncan is confronted with "plenty of religious stuff; as if religion has never roused murderous passion, and is not doing so again, outside the walls."[79]

What the Nation Should Strive For

Chaskalson kept silent on the religious implications of the decision, but Albie Sachs openly addressed the connection between beliefs and executions. In his opinion for the Court, he answered the question of where to find "the source of values"[80] in order for the jurisprudence of the Court "to take account of the traditions, beliefs, and values of all sectors of South African society,"[81] including "unpopular minorities."[82]

75. *S v Makwanyane* [80].
76. Ibid.
77. Ibid.
78. Ibid.
79. Gordimer, *The House Gun*, 292–93.
80. *S v Makwanyane* [358].
81. Ibid. [361].
82. Ibid. [369].

In turn, Justice Mokgoro referred to the notion of *ubuntu* enshrined in the Constitution:

> Generally, *ubuntu* translates as *humaneness*. In its most fundamental sense, it translates as *personhood* and *morality*. Metaphorically, it expresses itself in *umuntu ngumuntu ngabantu*, describing the significance of group solidarity on survival issues so central to the survival of communities. While it envelops the key values of group solidarity, compassion, respect, human dignity, conformity to basic norms, and collective unity, in its fundamental sense, it denotes humanity and morality. Its spirit emphasises respect for human dignity, marking a shift from confrontation to conciliation.[83]

Justice Pius Langa, a township resident in his early life, recalled the historical antagonism between violence and *ubuntu*: "during violent conflicts and times when violent crime is rife, distraught members of society decry the loss of *ubuntu*. Thus heinous crimes are the antithesis of *ubuntu*. Treatment that is cruel, inhuman or degrading is bereft of *ubuntu*."[84]

For Pius Langa, *ubuntu* was not just a code cherished by a sector of the population. As a principle proclaimed in the preamble of the Constitution, *ubuntu* belonged to the whole nation and needed to be recognized by all as "a commendable attribute which the nation should strive for."[85]

The religious challenge to South Africa was not limited to the past and future place of Christianity. Recognition of indigenous beliefs was also crucial. In southern African indigenous cultures, Justice Sachs observed, capital punishment was understood in a peculiar way. It mainly applied to cases of suspected witchcraft, and "was normally spontaneously carried out after accusation by the diviners."[86] The death penalty was not applied as the punishment for murder; it was rather performed with "frenzied, extra-judicial killings of supposed witches, a spontaneous and irrational form of crowd behaviour that has unfortunately continued to this day in the form of necklacing and witch-burning."[87] Exceptions were documented. The Sotho king Moshoeshoe seemed to have opposed executions even in case of witchcraft.

Justice Sachs excluded that every aspect of indigenous traditions was to be automatically taken up as a source of values. A wary assessment was also required based on what part of the common-law heritage could be regarded as a source of values for contemporary South Africa. In the time of imperial gods, the Dutch and the British themselves had changed in the way they approached torture and punishment,

83. Ibid. [308].
84. Ibid. [225].
85. Ibid. [227].
86. Ibid. [377].
87. Ibid. [381].

including capital punishment. As in the case of the Supreme Court of India, imperial gods were an inevitable reference for those judges who struggled with new national gods.

On June 6, 1995, one month after the decision on the case of Sushmita in India, the Constitutional Court of South Africa unanimously declared the death sentence unconstitutional.

According to President Chaskalson, by providing that "every person shall have the right to life," section 9 of the Constitution recognized an "unqualified right to life."[88] Thirty years before, in the Rivonia trial of 1964, the clever human-rights lawyer Chaskalson saved Nelson Mandela from being sentenced to death. Now, the same man erased the death sentence itself from the statutes, in his capacity as the president of the Constitutional Court.

An adamant Albie Sachs concurred with Chaskalson's opinion: "Everyone, including the most abominable of human beings, has the right to life, and capital punishment is therefore unconstitutional."[89] Section 9, "every person shall have the right to life," had to be interpreted "to mean exactly what it says":[90] prohibition of the death penalty was inherent in it. If not, Sachs specified, "the killer unwittingly achieves a final and perverse moral victory by making the state a killer too, thus reducing social abhorrence at the conscious extinction of human beings."[91]

In the final pages of Gordimer's novel, *The House Gun*, Duncan, the convicted murderer, escapes execution thanks to the ruling of the Constitutional Court. So the fictional character Duncan also concurs with Chaskalson and Sachs: "Violence is a repetition we don't seem able to break . . . Can you break the repetition just by not perpetrating violence on yourself. I have this life, in here. I didn't give it for his. I'll even get out of here with it, some year or other. The murderer has not been murdered. My luck, this was abolished in my time."[92]

The "collective morality of the nation" consisted of the constitutional right to life, the protection of which demanded the abolition of death sentence. Both the "sacred injunction" and the "secular code" proclaimed by Nadine Gordimer were included in the judgment. The secular approach of Arthur Chaskalson and the multireligious approach of Albie Sachs responded for the South African nation to the need for new gods, for *our* gods.

88. Ibid. [27].
89. Ibid. [392].
90. Ibid. [357].
91. Ibid. [357].
92. Gordimer, *The House Gun*, 294.

Balm on the Wounds

On July 26, 1995, nearly two months after the decision on the death penalty, the Truth and Reconciliation Commission was created by the Promotion of National Unity and Reconciliation Act.

The first black archbishop of South Africa, Nobel Prize–winner Desmond Tutu, was appointed to chair the Commission. Former Methodist pastor and anti-apartheid activist Alex Boraine was appointed vice chairperson. Among the seventeen members, two others were priests and two belonged to the Indian minority.

The Commission was appointed with the mission of building the new South African nation upon the acknowledgment of past conflicts. The temptation of amnesia was rejected. Dealing with the past and coming to terms with history was the first, fundamental step in the path towards a new nation. President Mandela warned against the risk of "festering wounds," infecting the future of the country. Desmond Tutu used the same expression when he stated that reconciliation could only be the result of memory and truth:

> However painful the experience, the wounds of the past must not be allowed to fester. They must be opened. They must be cleansed. And balm must be poured on them so they can heal. This is not to be obsessed with the past. It is to take care that the past is properly dealt with for the sake of the future.[93]

If national amnesia was fought, judicialization was also rejected. The Commission was not a court of justice. South Africa did not want to repeat the Nuremberg Trials against Nazi criminals. Victor's justice would prove inexpedient.

The route of trials, Desmond Tutu stressed, would be an inappropriate solution: it "would have stretched an already hard-pressed judicial system beyond reasonable limits . . . It would have rocked the boat massively and for too long."[94] Instead, a completely different kind of justice was envisaged in tune with what the preamble of the founding act of the Commission defined as the constitutional acknowledgment of "a need for understanding but not for vengeance, a need for reparation but not for retaliation, a need for ubuntu but not for victimization."[95] A shared memory had to be established not through the opposition between the state, the victims and the perpetrators, but through a common effort to tell the truth. As a result, the proposal of blanket amnesty was jettisoned. Rather, a special committee would grant individual amnesty to those who fully disclosed their crimes.

The clash between traditional court-based justice and the consensual truth-telling procedure of the Commission was momentous. Many denounced the "amnesty for truth" scheme as a betrayal of justice. But for most South Africans, the two-year-long

---

93. Tutu, "Foreword by Chairperson," 7 [27].
94. Ibid., 5 [23].
95. Ibid., 8 [32].

work of the Commission proved fruitful. And the legal framework Alex Boraine accurately shaped was acclaimed worldwide as the cornerstone of transitional justice, the promising asset for the global advancement of democracy.

Pervasive religious implications accompanied the effort of the commissioners. The spiritual emphasis on truth and reconciliation and the activism of religious people and organizations made the Commission the most powerful witness of national gods in South Africa.

When, on April 16, 1996, the first public hearing took place, vice chair Alex Boraine witnessed the performance of "a ritual, deeply needed in the healing of a nation"[96]:

> As I walked into the East London City Hall with Tutu on that first morning, the curtain was raised on a drama that would unfold over the next two and a half years. I think what helped enormously, from the very beginning, was that the commission didn't consist of stern-faced officials cloistered in a private chamber, but rather a stage with a handful of black and white men and women who listened intently to stories of horror, sorrow, amazing fortitude, supreme heroism, and anger, . . . It was theatre, perhaps; it was certainly a ritual, deeply needed in the healing of a nation.[97]

Many wounds were open and cleansed. Despite the rigorous, rational organization supervised by Alex Boraine, emotions exploded. The hearing of Nomonde Calata, the widow of Fort Calata, one of the Cradock Four murdered in 1984, proved an extreme example. As Boraine recalled, in the middle of her testimony the woman "broke down, threw her head and entire upper body back and let out a cry that seemed to come from her very soul. It was like a howl in the darkness, an expression of all the horror of the apartheid years, that transformed the hearings from a litany of suffering and pain to an even deeper level."[98]

Through individual and collective emotions, religion often achieved a substantial part in the hearings. In the hearing on the 1992 Boipatong massacre, in which forty-eight people had been murdered—mainly women and children—the commissioners experienced the intertwining of sorrow and spirituality. Alex Boraine remembered he felt intimidated by the emotional pressure in the hall:

> I stood outside for a long while, trying to summon the courage to enter the hall, but, as we entered the bleak room, we heard the sound of singing. Quite spontaneously and in no way thanks to us, these poor people who had experienced so much sorrow and loss had started singing a well-known hymn. It filled the hall, bringing with it at least some measure of light and hope,

96. Boraine, *A Life in Transition*, 186.

97. Ibid.

98. Ibid., 187.

reminding me, not for the first time, how often religion . . . had given succour and comfort to so many black people.[99]

I Forgive You Unconditionally

Desmond Tutu encouraged the intermingling of spirituality and pain, truth and prayer. "The emotional reaction was so much part of Tutu,"[100] Boraine observed. Human-rights lawyer George Bizos underlined the mix of spiritual and civil leadership that characterized Archbishop Tutu's management of the Truth and Reconciliation Commission: "Archbishop Desmond Tutu, the chairperson of the Commission, occupied center stage, consoling the witnesses, offering them some comfort as they relived their tales of horror. Diminutive, robed in purple, the Archbishop invested the hearings with a mystical element, repeatedly invoking the grace of God, a solvent to wash away the pain of the past."[101]

According to historian and biographer Martin Meredith, Tutu sought "to imbue the search for truth and reconciliation with a Christian sense of mission."[102] The archbishop, Meredith stressed, "opened the proceedings with prayers, a hymn, and the lighting of a tall white candle in remembrance of those who had died and disappeared during the struggle against apartheid."[103]

Criticism was expressed on the excessive religious tone of the Commission. Historian Leonard Thompson blamed the Commission for having an "overridingly emotional and religious tone, rather than a legal one."[104] Anti-apartheid militant Marius Schoon wrote to a Sunday newspaper to complain: "As a religious leader, the Archbishop is completely entitled to make this type of appeal to his faithful. However, as chairperson of an important government commission, it is important that the Christian ethics is not viewed as the law of the land. Not all of us are Christians."[105]

Despite doubts over his purple cassock and insisted prayers, the archbishop confirmed he was a true leader. He might hide his face in his hands and weep as occurred on the second day of hearings, but he carried on. Boraine acknowledged Tutu's leadership within the group as he "was undoubtedly the cement that held the commission together."[106] But first of all, the chairperson of the Commission distinguished himself as the brave and effective defender of the Commissioners from the attacks they suffered from all sides. He fought relentlessly for the independence and fairness of the

99. Ibid., 193.
100. Ibid., 188.
101. Bizos, *No One to Blame?*, 2.
102. Meredith, *Coming to Terms*, 3.
103. Ibid.
104. Thompson, *A History of South Africa*, 275.
105. Meredith, *Coming to Terms*, 25.
106. Boraine, *A Life in Transition*, 188.

Commission. He held fast to his vision that violations counted no matter the political color or aim of the perpetrator: "a gross violation,"[107] he wrote in the Final Report, "is a gross violation, whoever commits it and for whatever reason."[108]

Tutu led the Commission to face the tragic truth that the anti-apartheid camp had been contaminated with the most toxic poison: apartheid itself. The testimony of Peter Storey provided the best and most grievous evidence. A former Methodist bishop, Storey was heard on the crimes Winnie Madikizela-Mandela ordered while under the protection of the Methodist Church, and concluded: "The primary cancer may be and was and always will be the apartheid oppression, but the secondary infection has touched many of apartheid's opponents and eroded their knowledge of good and evil. One of the tragedies of life is that it is possible to become like that which we hate most, and I have a feeling that this drama is an example of that."[109]

The Commissioners stood firm in the face of the pressure of the African National Congress and the Inkatha Freedom Party, both of which assumed their militants' violence was justified by the anti-apartheid struggle. Commissioners also resisted the pressure of former white officers. After decades of deceptive trials before powerless or biased judges, the Commission tried to set the opposite example. As Alex Boraine put it, "we were greatly encouraged that we had incurred the wrath of De Klerk and Mbeki, because it underscored the impartiality of the Commission."[110]

Invincible limits were experienced, but significant bits of reality were told and heard. One such case was the findings of the Commission on the attack on the congregation of St James Church in Kenilworth, Cape Town, on July 25, 1993. One thousand people of mixed origins and races were attending the evening service when two men entered, threw hand grenades, and, for about thirty seconds, opened fire with automatic rifles. They left eleven people dead and fifty-eight injured.

The Azanian People's Liberation Army, the armed wing of the anti-apartheid Pan-Africanist Congress, had orchestrated the operation. Gcinikhaya Christopher Makoma, one of the killers, seventeen years old at the time of the assault, applied for amnesty. When heard by the Commission, Makoma and his two accomplices justified the attack on the grounds that whites "took our country using churches and Bibles."[111]

Dawie Ackermann, a church official who lost his wife in the attack, offered his personal forgiveness but opposed amnesty. During the hearing, he asked the applicants to publicly apologize:

> Ackermann: I would like to hear from each of you, as you look me in the face, that you are sorry for what you have done, that you regret it and that you want to be personally reconciled . . .

107. Tutu, "Foreword by Chairperson," 12 [52].

108. Ibid.

109. Boraine, *A Life in Transition*, 197.

110. Ibid.

111. South Africa Truth and Reconciliation Commission, "Political Violence," 688 [475].

Makoma: We are sorry for what we have done. It was the situation in South Africa. Although people died during that struggle, we didn't do that out of our own will. It is the situation that we were living under. We are asking from you, please do forgive us . . .

Ackermann: I want you to know that I forgive you unconditionally. I do that because I am a Christian, and I can forgive you for the hurt that you have caused me, but I cannot forgive you the sin that you have done. Only God can forgive you for that.[112]

The religious legitimacy of the apartheid state as a necessary barrier against aggressive international communism could not survive the end of the Cold War. A different religious legitimacy was sought during the transition to democracy. In 1995, with the Constitutional Court ruling out the death penalty, and in 1996, with the Truth and Reconciliation Commission, South African national gods were summoned to heal the nation while contributing to a peaceful multireligious future. Your *gods* were discarded, *our* gods endorsed.

A United Bharat

In May 1995, with the decision on Sushmita Ghosh's case, the Supreme Court of India affirmed that in the field of family and marriage national legal uniformity had to be imposed upon religious communities, especially Muslims.

Eight months later, in January 1996, the Court took a milder position in its decision on the case of Pannalal Bansilal Pitti. Faced with state measures aiming at rationalizing the administration of Hindu religious and charitable institutions and endowments, some Hindu hereditary trustees asked the Supreme Court to declare that those secular restrictions were against the religious freedom of the Hindu majority. "It is impermissible,"[113] they argued, for

> an outside agency or the party like the State to determine as to which activity is essential part of religion and which part is not. It would not, therefore, be open to the State to restrict or prohibit, under the guise of its secular power, the administration of the religious or charitable institutions or endowments, contrary to what the followers of the religion believe to be the religious duty. The administration of religious or charitable institution and endowments as part of the religious practice, perceived and rigorously followed by Hindus cannot, therefore, be divested by legislation.[114]

---

112. South Africa Truth and Reconciliation Commission, "The Pan Africanist Congress," 400 [127].

113. *Pannalal*, 503 [4].

114. Ibid., 503–4 [4].

The Supreme Court replied that it was correct that the state should not intrude in the religious sphere of the population. But no intrusion subsisted if the state regulated the administration of Hindu trusts since the administrative sphere did not belong to "religious belief or faith."[115] Accordingly, the Court asserted that

> the right to establish a religious institution or endowment is a part of religious belief or faith, but its administration is a secular part, which would be regulated by law deemed appropriate by the legislature. The regulation is only in respect of the administration of the secular part of the religious institution or endowment, and not of beliefs, tenets, usages, and practices, which are an integral part of that religious belief or faith.[116]

In the case of Sushmita Ghosh, Justice Sahai was very cautious on the distinction between what belonged to religion and what did not: divorce or inheritance, bathing the idol or going around the fire seven times, he said in his opinion, were "as much matter of faith and conscience as the worship itself."[117] This awareness did not prevent the Court from imposing a minimum civil standard. Similarly, in the Pannalal case, the Court argued that religious freedom was not violated if the state imposed its standard on the administration of Hindu trusts, precisely because administration was secular and not religious.

As in the case of Sushmita, the cause of national unity was praised again in 1996. But in the Pannalal case, Justice Ramaswamy was more explicit in his acknowledgment of the peculiar Indian way to national harmony between diverse cultures and religions:

> The founding fathers, while making the Constitution, were confronted with problems to unify and integrate people of India professing different religious faiths, born in different casts, sex or sub-sections in the society speaking different languages and dialects in different regions and provided a secular Constitution to integrate all sections of the society as a united Bharat. The directive principles of the Constitution themselves visualize diversity and attempted to foster uniformity among people of different faiths.[118]

The difficult balance between national unity and diversity, so Justice Ramaswamy believed, demanded a prudent approach to legal uniformity. In the case of Sushmita Ghosh, Justice Singh's absolute call for the uniform code was mitigated by Justice Sahai's warning that the code could only be enacted when "social climate is properly built." Justice Ramaswamy further stated that a uniform law could be "counter-productive to unity and integrity of the nation:"[119]

---

115. Ibid. 513 [20].
116. Ibid.
117. *Sarla Mudgal,* 652 [44].
118. *Pannalal,* 510 [12].
119. Ibid.

A uniform law, though is highly desirable, enactment thereof in one go perhaps may be counter-productive to unity and integrity of the nation. In a democracy governed by rule of law, gradual progressive change and order should be brought about. Making law or amendment to a law is a slow process and the legislature attempts to remedy where the need is felt most acute. It would, therefore, be inexpedient and incorrect to think that all laws have to be made uniformly applicable to all people in one go. The mischief or defect which is most acute can be remedied by process of law at stages.[120]

Five months after, in May 1996, the Bharatiya Janata Party (BJP), the Hindu nationalist party, did remarkably well in the elections for the eleventh Lok Sabha. The BJP finished second behind a Congress Party that lost ninety-two seats, and had now a strong voice in a hung Parliament. While the judiciary defended secular India, many voters wanted the Parliament to reflect instead a Hindu nation. Whit both secular and Hindu nationalists invoking *Bharat*, the Sanskrit name for the Republic of India, the contrast between multiform, informal, bottom-up India and legally uniformed, top-down India emerged as the major challenge. Was a "united Bharat" to be pursued by leaving space for everyday, chaotic India, in which pervasive religion played such a decisive part, or through the legal top-down imposition of social progress? Did national gods push towards a compromise in society between abstract rights and real conditions and beliefs? Or rather, were they asking the state to enforce ideal standards, against religions if needed?

The Blasphemy of Europe

In the same period, greater European integration came to represent the highest challenge to British national identity, with the creation of the European Union through the Maastricht Treaty in 1992. Prime Minister John Major claimed he succeeded in negotiating favorable conditions for the place of Britain in the European Union, in particular by excluding the Social Chapter. He had won, a member of staff arrogantly said, "game, set, and match."[121] Despite this, if not because of this, Euroskepticism played again a substantial part in British politics when the negotiations started for greater European unity through the Amsterdam Treaty.

The defense of British national identity and interests was an issue in politics, in society, and in the economy. Seemingly, religion did not feature as a significant part of the picture. But in November 1996, the impact of European integration on British national religion was certified by two European courts' decisions in Luxembourg and in Strasbourg.

120. Ibid.
121. Major, *The Autobiography*, 288.

On November 12, the European Court of Justice partially upheld the action of the British government against the directive of the European Community, which imposed common standards upon the member states in the organization of working time. John Major's government opposed the very legal basis of such interference. As a consequence, Britain also stood against the identification of Sunday as the conventional resting day to be respected in all countries for the welfare of the workers. The Court of Luxembourg upheld the British position. The identification of Sunday as the resting day did not belong to the European competence, and had to be left to the appreciation of the states: "the question whether to include Sunday in the weekly rest period is ultimately left to the assessment of Member States, having regard, in particular, to the diversity of cultural, ethnic, and religious factors in those States."[122]

The relevant provision of the directive had to be annulled also in the merits. In effect, the European authorities had "failed to explain why Sunday, as a weekly rest day, is more closely connected with the health and safety of workers than any other day of the week."[123]

National gods prevailed and Britain successfully resisted the pressure of Europe. But Europe was there. And Britain needed to equip for the struggle between its national approach to religion and the increasingly intrusive European law.

As a confirmation, on November 25, 1996, the European Court of Human Rights decided the case of Nigel Wingrove and the ban on his film *Visions of Ecstasy,* deemed blasphemous. In 1990, Wingrove had asked the Court to condemn "the British blasphemy laws as unnecessary in theory as they are in practice in any multi-cultural democracy."[124] In particular the film director summoned the Court to declare the nonexistence of the "hypothetical right held by some Christians to avoid disturbance at the prospect of other people's viewing the video work without being shocked."[125]

In its judgment of 1996, the Court dismissed the application and endorsed the position of the British authorities.

Indeed the Court noticed that the application of blasphemy law only to the Christian religion was an "anomaly . . . in a multidenominational society"[126] like England; but the European judges dismissed the argument since "the extent to which English law protects other beliefs is not in issue before the Court which must confine its attention to the case before it."[127]

Justice De Meyer displayed his preference for the objection posed to anti-Rushdie Muslims by Minister John Patten: that for believers "the strength of their own

122. *UK v Council* [37].
123. Ibid.
124. *Wingrove* [34].
125. Ibid. [45].
126. Ibid. [50].
127. Ibid.

belief is the best armor against mockers and blasphemers."[128] The other judges did not follow. In the end, the Court of Strasbourg could not find any reason to reverse the decision of the national authorities. The Court opted for the same approach taken by the Court of Luxembourg in the case of Sunday as the resting day. No European consensus existed in the field of blasphemy. The increasingly rich religious landscape made it more and more difficult to assess in theory, from above, what precisely offended believers. According to the Court, "what is likely to cause substantial offense to persons of a particular religious persuasion will vary significantly from time to time and from place to place, especially in an era characterized by an ever growing array of faiths and denominations."[129]

No European standard could be imposed upon Britain. No general concept of religious freedom or freedom of expression could prevail on the British assessment of what in practice was gratuitously offensive, insulting, and blasphemous. National authorities were better placed to give a sound judgment, because "a wider margin of appreciation is generally available to the Contracting States when regulating freedom of expression in relation to matters liable to offend intimate personal convictions within the sphere of morals or, especially, religion."[130]

The Court held by seven votes to two that British blasphemy law was legitimate and that its application in the relevant case did not violate Nigel Wingrove's rights.

The year 1996 was not a happy one in the relationship between Britain and Europe, with the European ban on British beef because of "mad cow disease" causing deep concern among Her Majesty's subjects. But in November 1996, the British national approach to religion succeeded in the clash between Britain and Europe. In both the Wingrove and the Sunday-closing cases, Britain prevailed over Europe in the defense of its national interests and prerogatives. In Luxembourg, Britain won against Christianity and the imposition of Sunday as the conventional resting day; in Strasbourg, Britain won against blasphemers and the vilification of Jesus Christ. As in India and in South Africa, national gods responded to explosive gods in a deeply ambivalent manner.

Gareth Prince's Fight

In 1997, twenty-eight-year-old Gareth Prince completed his legal education and applied to the Bar. There was just one more condition for him to fulfill to become an attorney: he had to perform a period of community service with the Law Society of the Cape of Good Hope. The procedure was usually linear, but Gareth Prince was not a usual candidate. He was a Rastafari who scrupulously practiced his creed. He respected all commands, including those that resulted in practices breaching the law.

128. Ibid. [3].
129. Ibid. [58].
130. Ibid.

At the moment of applying to the Law Society of the Cape of Good Hope, he already had two previous convictions for possession of cannabis. In his application, Gareth Prince not only disclosed his previous convictions, but he also stated clearly that he had no intention of changing his lifestyle. He said he felt compelled to fully endorse and practice his faith to the extent of regularly using cannabis at ceremonies or privately by either burning it as an incense or smoking, drinking, or eating it at home. He mentioned he used about five grams of cannabis daily for purposes of meditation; and that he preferred "not to puff the holy herb before work and use it maximum twice per day after work."[131] Using cannabis was a fundamental part of his faith, and he was not ready to give it up.

The Law Society declined to register Prince's contract of community service on the grounds that a person declaring his intention to continue breaking the law was not "a fit and proper person to be admitted as an attorney."[132]

Prince could not accept a decision hindering at the same time his religious and his legal practice. He resorted to filing an application to the Cape High Court for review of the Law Society's decision.

Gareth Prince's fight expressed the struggle for diversity in postapartheid South Africa. The Constitutional Court and the Truth and Reconciliation Commission were trying to articulate the unity of the nation and the multiplicity of South African society. This was not enough for Prince. For him, the healing of the nation was not just about past violations; it had to be first of all about a tolerant society and an inclusive administration of justice now.

In Britain meanwhile, as the era of Tories came to an end, many Britons believed an updated articulation of the British nation was indispensable. Opposing Europe was not enough. A different understanding of culture and religion was needed. On April 7, 1996, in the *Sunday Telegraph*, Tony Blair attacked politicians "who wear God on their sleeves."[133] The New Labour advanced the promises that enabled Blair to triumph on May 1, 1997 with the largest Labour majority ever and the largest swing since 1945, when Churchill had been defeated. Religion was prominent in the biographies and political vision of both the Anglican Tony Blair and the Presbyterian Gordon Brown. The renewed emphasis on education characterized the schooling of young Shabina Begum and the progress of the Denbigh High School as an increasingly successful multicultural state school.

In the meantime, Sushmita Ghosh experienced the volatility of Indian national gods. Her application had been allowed, but the merits of the Sarla Mudgal decision and the activism of the Supreme Court in calling for a uniform code had stirred widespread discontent. Muslims felt outraged across the country. Two Indian Muslim associations, the Jamiat-Ulema Hind and the Muslim Personal Law Board, sought

131. *Prince*, 2002 [100].

132. Ibid. [2].

133. Chapman, *Doing God*, 12.

judicial review of the decision. The Supreme Court of India was going to take the case one more time. Sushmita's struggle wasn't finished yet.

Religion Is Not a Commodity

From 1995 to 2000, the African National Congress, the New Labour, and the Indian judiciary sponsored a renewed pact between the gods and the nation.

Two different ways of nationalizing gods coexisted in India. The first took inspiration from the secularist leaders of the past, like Nehru and Ambedkar, along with the classical Indian nationalism of Congress. In the 1995 Sarla Mudgal decision, and again in the 2000 judgment on the appeal, the Supreme Court of India endorsed this version: while valuing religion, the Court stood for the ultimate superiority of the secular state over faith communities. The second version of Indian national gods was politically impersonated by the rising Bharatiya Janata Party (BJP) and coincided with the call for Hindutva. Hindu nationalism stigmatized the decline of Hindu identity under the alleged arrogance of Indian Muslims and other minorities, and meanwhile exploited the secular state in the interest of its cause. As witnessed by the polls in 1996, and especially with the victory of the BJP in 1998, when the Congress was defeated for the first time, Hindu nationalism was now a true rival for old-fashioned Indian nationalists in the competition to shape Indian secularism and the new Indian gods.

In Britain, also, different forms of national religion were experienced from 1995 to 2000. In 1995 and 1996, John Major's "back to basics" civic and moral platform failed as a wave of scandals ravaged the government. The New Labour took over in the name of a new vision of the nation and a different route to national prosperity. In a time of increased competition and shared acceptance of market economy, ideology was useless. Ideas and ideals, not ideology, would unite and propel the British nation. A pragmatic search for "what works" would make Britain a postmodern, diverse, and cohesive nation. In such a comprehensive and inclusive program, the place for religion was implicit: new British national gods would be assessed on their capacity to provide common ideas and ideals and, most of all, on their social effectiveness. It was time to move from *your* gods to *our* gods. Tony Blair perfectly embodied such a secularized and yet religion-friendly approach. But the picture was more nuanced. During the same period, gods also fueled the British National Party in its campaign against the multicultural and communal corrosion of British identity.

Apparently, in South Africa, *our* national gods took on a more univocal meaning. In principle, all religions—the formerly persecuted and privileged alike—came together in the national effort. Desmond Tutu, the struggler and the healer, the spiritual and the civil leader, incarnated the new promise. But even in South Africa, national religion was far from unproblematic. Antagonistic minorities like Gareth Prince's Rastafarians felt discriminated against. Through their active propaganda and their strong institutions, Christians and Muslims tended to overwhelm informal and deinstitutionalized African religion. However "rainbow" it might appear, the "nation of God" was far from having solved the tension within the general cross-border African nation and the specific South African nation.

Beyond differences, beyond articulations, many political and religious forces in the three countries shared a similar vision about the possible, and possibly fruitful, partnership between religion and the renewed national effort. The hope was that tolerance and pluralism, recognition, and inclusion might foster the common good. The acknowledgment of religious diversity and a free religious competition might neutralize the creeds' potential for division and conflict. The state might safeguard all opinions and beliefs, while standing for even-handedness and integration. The outcome might be a wealthier nation, able to cope with the global market without jettisoning its identity and tradition. Contrary to the divisive nationalist gods of the Afrikaner, the BJP, or the British National Party, propitious national gods might reconcile religious freedom, secular societies, and the new economy. By contrast with *your* gods, *our* national gods might bring stability, cohesion, and growth.

In reality, the gods proved extremely knotty. After a while, not only Indians but also Britons and South Africans realized that explosive gods could not be disarmed. Religion could not be easily mastered and exploited. While challenging the dream of pacified multireligious nations, gods opposed secular postmodernity and defied global capitalism, which, ten years after the collapse of international communism, dictated development and growth.

Religion-based sectors of society could not be brought under the same roof. Minorities were reluctant to obey the interest of the nation. Majorities resisted claims that the Indian, British, and South African nations should be plural and equal. Nonbelievers felt increasingly uncomfortable with the gods' pressure on society.

Our national gods of tolerance, peaceful coexistence, and inclusiveness failed to replace *your* explosive gods of *The Satanic Verses* and of the Ayodhya Mosque. The strongest confirmation came in August 1996, when Osama Bin Laden's fatwa declaring war against the "Americans Occupying the Land of the Two Holy Places" was published in *Al Quds Al Arabi*, a London-based newspaper.

As the end of the millennium approached, the struggles of Sushmita Ghosh, Gareth Prince, and Shabina Begum coincided with the concoction of explosive and national gods. Sushmita discovered that Indian Muslims actively campaigned against her victory: Islamic associations appealed against the Sarla Mudgal decision and brought her case once more before the Supreme Court. Meanwhile, Gareth took part in the effort of marginal Rastafarians to push South Africa to be an open society reconciled with the African tradition, and started fighting in courts for his right to be different, as both a barrister and a believer. In turn, Shabina experienced the schizophrenic upbringing of a little girl from a Muslim Indian family in the context of Blairite England, with a non-English-speaking mother, which would prepare her to struggle for the full recognition of her right to strictly obey Sharia.

A Sectarian Christian Conception?

In the death-sentence case of 1995, the South African Constitutional Court focused on Gordimer's "collective morality of the nation" and on Sachs's "sources of values." Religion was not overtly handled. A couple years later, Gareth Prince explicitly claimed the right of a marginal believer to act in accordance with his creed. He injected a high dose of religion into the judicial agenda of postapartheid South Africa.

The Rastafari was not the first to test religion in court after the new Constitution. A few months prior to the Cape High Court's verdict on Gareth's petition, the case of one Magdalena Solberg urged the constitutional judges to establish whether Christianity still enjoyed a privileged position in South Africa, or whether the new state had to instead observe strict neutrality. Again, both Arthur Chaskalson and Albie Sachs were on the bench.

Magdalena Solberg's case arose from her conviction for selling wine at a Seven Eleven store on a Sunday, a closed day for sales of wine by holders of grocers' wine licences, according to Section 90 of the Liquor Act of 1989. The woman objected that the prohibition infringed upon her religious freedom. She contended that the purpose of prohibiting wine selling by grocers on "closed day[s]" was "to induce submission to a sectarian Christian conception of the proper observance of the Christian Sabbath and Christian holidays or, perhaps, to compel the observance of the Christian Sabbath and Christian holidays."[134]

Therefore, Magdalena Solberg maintained, individuals were forced "to affirm or acquiesce in a specific practice solely for a sectarian Christian purpose."[135] This, she argued, infringed upon the freedom of religion of those not holding such beliefs and not wishing to embrace them.

As the case of Prince did, so the case of Solberg could seem a marginal case, a bizarre claim. An anarchic Rastafari featured there, a dishonest seller here. Justice Sachs underlined that the law should not concern itself with trifles "in the area of belief and conscience."[136] Nevertheless, no matter how serious the claim, for the first time, a bench of the Constitutional Court needed to lay down the constitutional doctrine on religious equality, religious liberty, and the neutrality of the state. Explosive gods took the shape of faith-based personal claims. The new national gods enshrined in the Charter were tested.

Instead of engaging in his own definition of religious freedom, President Chaskalson referred back to Canadian Chief Justice Brian Dickson. In his opinion for the Supreme Court of Canada in the 1985 Big M Drug Mart case, Chief Justice Dickson had captured "the essence"[137] of religious freedom in "the right to entertain such re-

---

134. *S v Lawrence* [85].
135. Ibid.
136. Ibid. [139].
137. Ibid. [92].

ligious beliefs as a person chooses, the right to declare religious beliefs openly and without fear of hindrance or reprisal, and the right to manifest religious belief by worship and practice or by teaching and dissemination."[138]

President Chaskalson acknowledged he couldn't offer "a better definition than this,"[139] but he believed that religious freedom additionally implied "an absence of coercion or constraint and that freedom of religion may be impaired by measures that force people to act or refrain from acting in a manner contrary to their religious beliefs."[140] He declared himself "not unmindful"[141] that constraints on the exercise of freedom of religion "can be imposed in subtle ways."[142] He recognized that "the choice of Christian holy days for particular legislative purposes may be perceived to elevate Christian beliefs above others; and that, as a result, adherents of other religions may be made to feel that the state accords less value to their beliefs than it does to Christianity."[143]

But was this the case? Should the restriction imposed upon Magdalene Solberg not to sell alcohol on Sundays be considered as this sort of constraint?

In his opinion for the Court, President Chaskalson pointed out that Sundays had come to have a purely "secular nature."[144] Many people respected the weekly pause "because it has become the most convenient day for such purpose, and not because of any wish to observe the Christian Sabbath."[145] Therefore, he believed that the regulation in question did not violate Magdalena Solberg's freedom. In fact, he wrote in his opinion, section 90 of the Liquor Act did not

> interfere with the appellant's freedom of religion or the freedom of religion of any other person, or serve any other religious purpose. It is difficult to discern any coercion or constraint imposed by section 90 of the Liquor Act on the religious beliefs of holders of grocers' wine licences or any other person, or any religious purpose served by such prohibition. The section does not compel licencees or any other persons, directly or indirectly, to observe the Christian sabbath. It does not in any way constrain their right to entertain such religious beliefs as they might choose, or to declare their religious beliefs openly, or to manifest their religious beliefs. It does not compel them to open or close their businesses on a Sunday.[146]

138. Ibid.
139. Ibid.
140. Ibid.
141. Ibid. [93].
142. Ibid.
143. Ibid.
144. Ibid. [96].
145. Ibid.
146. Ibid. [97].

He then concluded that "whatever connection there may be between the Christian religion and the restriction against grocers selling wine on Sundays at a time when their shops are open for other business, it is . . . too tenuous for the restriction to be characterized as an infringement of religious freedom."[147] Indeed the contested restriction was legitimate.

Chaskalson outlined his theory but opted for a concrete analysis of the case coherent with the South African specificity. As in the death-penalty case, he discarded the American model, in this case separation of church and state: "our Constitution," he wrote, "deals with issues of religion differently to the US Constitution."[148]

Justice Kate O'Regan wrote a dissenting opinion to which Justices Goldstone and Madala also concurred. The main point of dissension between Justice O'Regan and President Chaskalson concerned the relation between religious freedom and the religious neutrality of the state. For Arthur Chaskalson, only the restriction of rights and freedoms mattered. He believed that, as long as rights and freedoms were not substantially infringed, the religious neutrality of the state was not an issue. For Justice O'Regan, however, religious neutrality was a problem indeed:

> In my view, the requirements of the Constitution require more of the legislature than that it refrain from coercion. It requires, in addition, that the legislature refrain from favouring one religion over others. Fairness and even-handedness in relation to diverse religions is a necessary component of freedom of religion.[149]

Albie Sachs proved sympathetic with Kate O'Regan. Though endorsing the difference made by Chaskalson between the US and the South African constitutions, he took inspiration from the US Supreme Court. In particular, he recalled the 1984 case of *Lynch v. Donnelly*, when Justice Sandra Day O'Connor focused on the constitutional prohibition against the government's identification with any particular religion. "Government can run afoul of that prohibition in two principal ways,"[150] Justice O'Connor explained in 1984:

> One is excessive entanglement with religious institutions, which may interfere with the independence of the institutions, give the institutions access to government or governmental powers not fully shared by nonadherents of the religion, and foster the creation of political constituencies defined along religious lines . . . The second and more direct infringement is government endorsement or disapproval of religion. Endorsement sends a message to nonadherents that they are outsiders, not full members of the political community, and an accompanying

147. Ibid. [105].
148. Ibid. [100].
149. Ibid. [128].
150. Ibid. [138].

message to adherents that they are insiders, favored members of the political community. Disapproval sends the opposite message.[151]

Albie Sachs embraced the basic distinction drawn by Sandra Day O'Connor between religious "insiders" and "outsiders." In his opinion in the Solberg case, he expressed the wish that the nation not be divided "into insiders, who belong, and outsiders who are tolerated:"[152]

> By endorsing a particular faith as a direct and sectarian source of values for legislation binding on the whole nation, [the state] exceeds the competence granted to it by the Constitution. Even if there is no compulsory requirement to observe or not to observe a particular religious practice, the effect is to divide the nation into insiders who belong, and outsiders who are tolerated.[153]

The antidiscrimination struggler Albie Sachs stood for the outsiders. Gareth Prince also claimed he was discriminated as an outsider. Was Sachs's approach heading toward the allowance of Magdalena Solberg's claim, thus paving the way for Gareth's appeal to be allowed as well?

Marginalized Hindus and Muslims

The divergence between Arthur Chaskalson on the one hand, and Kate O'Regan and Albie Sachs on the other was not just a matter of principles and theories. The place of history in the discussion of the case was also at stake. Arthur Chaskalson restrained himself to strict legal analysis and did not take history into account. By contrast, Albie Sachs took the case, first of all, as a matter of history; Kate O'Regan shared this view when she underlined that religious equality was proclaimed in the Constitution as a "rejection of our history, in which Christianity was given favoured status by government in many areas of life regardless of the wide range of religions observed in our society."[154]

The history of the country was at stake, as were the preconstitutional pro-Christian bias and, consequentially, Christian Afrikaner nationalism. Imperial and cold gods were still impacting the present. At the time of the Empire, Christianity legitimated colonial supremacists in the name of a civilizing mission amongst savage tribes. During the Cold War, Christianity legitimated the apartheid state in the name of the fight against communism. As in the public sessions before the Truth and Reconciliation Commission, the private struggles of Gareth Prince and Magdalena Solberg opened the wounds of the past and revealed the many ways and times in which Christianity inflicted such wounds.

---

151. Ibid.
152. Ibid. [179].
153. Ibid.
154. Ibid. [123].

"Religious marginalization"[155] was a substantial part of the history of the country, Justice Sachs wrote in his opinion for the Solberg case, and "coincided strongly with racial discrimination, social exclusion, and political disempowerment."[156] The judge recalled the Christian national education, the Sunday ban on horseracing in Natal and the prohibition of dancing "with a partner to the accompaniment of music"[157] in the Orange Free State according to the Control of Dancing Ordinance of 1957. He also recalled blasphemy laws protecting only Christians, this sounding as an impressive reminder of the Rushdie affair and the latest struggle of British judges with blasphemy.

In the Fraser case, judged by the Constitutional Court in February 1997, a few months before the Solberg decision, Justice Mahomed underlined the anti-Muslim bias implicit in the denial of recognition of Muslim law in family matters. Albie Sachs took Justice Mahomed's reference to Muslim marriages as a reminder of the marginalization of religious minorities throughout the history of South Africa, from Gandhi's time to the more recent developments. Justice Sachs stated:

> The marginalization of communities of Hindu and Muslim persuasion flowed from and reinforced a tendency for the norms of "Christian civilization" to be regarded as points of departure, and for Hindu and Muslim norms to be relegated to the space of the deviant "Other." Any echo today of the superior status in public law once enjoyed by Christianity must therefore be understood as a reminder of the subordinate position to which followers of other faiths were formerly subjected.[158]

Albie Sachs recalled Gandhi's fight against Justice Searle's "terrible judgment" of 1913. He also mentioned the decision of 1917, when Chief Justice Innes identified Christianity with what he called "civilized peoples,"[159] thus emphasizing, Sachs noticed, "the role of the Christian religion as a specific source of values for the interpretation and development of the law."[160] This was a completely different South Africa. Contemporary to the Fraser case, in the *Ryland v. Edros* case of 1997, the Cape Town High Court enforced a solely Muslim marriage. For the first time, legal scholar Ebrahim Moosa commented, a court in South Africa acknowledged that "the marriage contract in Muslim law was functionally similar to a contract in Roman-Dutch and common law."[161] Judge Ian Farlam for the Court awarded the repudiated woman, Mrs. Edros, an amount of arrears maintenance and a consolatory gift since the husband had unjustifiably terminated the marriage. Himself a South African Muslim of Indian

---

155. Ibid. [152].
156. Ibid.
157. Ibid. [149] at footnote 29.
158. Ibid. [152].
159. Ibid. [151].
160. Ibid.
161. Moosa, "Muslim Family Law in South Africa," 346.

descent, Moosa credited the momentous step to "imaginative lawyering and the ethos of the new constitution."[162]

In the Solberg case, President Chaskalson formulated his principles on church and state relationships in a discreet way. But for Sachs, the issue at stake inevitably asserted the need for the eradication of the preconstitutional bias. No Christian supremacy could be tolerated any longer. No association between the country and a specific belief or religion could be allowed under the Constitution. According to Sachs, the new South Africa had to be built as "an open and democratic society with a non-sectarian state that guarantees freedom of worship."[163] Sachs envisioned a country which "is respectful of and accommodatory towards, rather than hostile to or walled-off from, religion; acknowledges the multi-faith and multi-belief nature of the country; does not favour one religious creed or doctrinal truth above another; accepts the intensely personal nature of individual conscience and affirms the intrinsically voluntary and non-coerced character of belief; respects the rights of non-believers; and does not impose orthodoxies of thought or require conformity of conduct in terms of any particular world-view."[164]

For Justice Sachs, the lesson to learn was that in the new constitutional environment, "no official orthodoxy or faith"[165] could be endorsed by the state anymore. Well beyond President Chaskalson's reserve, Albie Sachs set the tune for an extensive change in the attitude of South Africa towards religion:

> The Constitution, then, is very much about the acknowledgement by the state of different belief systems and their accommodation within a non-hierarchical framework of equality and non-discrimination. It follows that the state does not take sides on questions of religion. It does not impose belief, grant privileges to, or impose disadvantages on adherents of any particular belief, require conformity in matters simply of belief, involve itself in purely religious controversies, or marginalize people who have different beliefs.[166]

Sachs's rich elaboration on even-handedness and equality, impartiality and fairness—the best example of *our* pluralistic national gods—turned out to be deeply disappointing for Magdalena Solberg, as well as for Gareth Prince himself, if only indirectly. When the case was decided on October 6, 1997, Magdalena Solberg's application was rejected. In the end, for all his different approach, Sachs was nonetheless brought to concur with Chaskalson in the order, claiming he shared the "spirit of realism and common sense"[167] of President Chaskalson.

162. Ibid.
163. *S v Lawrence* [148].
164. Ibid.
165. Ibid. [146].
166. Ibid. [148].
167. Ibid. [179].

Gandhi Modeling for Apple

On March 23, 1998, Gareth Prince's application to the Cape High Court was dismissed. Gareth decided not to yield. He pursued his struggle by filing an appeal to the Supreme Court of Appeal. His personal, solitary fight looked as untimely and quixotic as many of Gandhi's campaigns.

Three weeks later, on April 13, 1998, Gandhi became the object of an article by Salman Rushdie in the magazine *Time*. Ten years after the publication of *The Satanic Verses*, the acclaimed novelist commented on a photo of Gandhi used for the latest "Think Different" campaign of Apple Inc. "Once, a half-century ago, this bony man shaped a nation's struggle for freedom. But that, as they say, is history. Now Gandhi is modelling for Apple. His thoughts don't really count in this new incarnation. What counts is that he is considered to be 'on message,' in line with the corporate philosophy of Apple."[168]

Rushdie denounced the manipulation of Gandhi and the disrespect for historical truth and complexity: "Gandhi today is up for grabs. He has become abstract, ahistorical, postmodern, no longer a man in and of his time but a freeloading concept, a part of the available stock of cultural symbols, an image that can be borrowed, used, distorted, reinvented to fit many different purposes, and to the devil with historicity or truth."[169]

Instead, Rushdie praised "the real man"[170] Gandhi, with his contradictions and weaknesses. He underlined that Gandhi began by believing that civil disobedience would have worked in any case, even against Hitler, but at last he was brought to admit, in Rushdie's words, that "while the British had responded to such techniques because of their own nature, other oppressors might not."[171]

The real Gandhi did not interest Apple, just as he did not interest India, Rushdie argued. Both new global consumerism and new India, he believed, used Gandhi with no accurate consideration for his personality, his life, or his politics. The same spirit rendered advertising agencies for global companies and contemporary Indians incapable of grasping Gandhi's real ambiguity and complexity: "these are hurried, sloganizing times,"[172] Rushdie wrote for *Time*, "and we don't have the time or, worse, the inclination to assimilate many-sided truths."[173]

India, the writer believed, was particularly reluctant to acknowledge "the ambiguous nature of [Gandhi's] achievement and legacy, or even the real causes of Indian

168. Rushdie, "Mohandas Gandhi," 71.
169. Ibid.
170. Ibid.
171. Ibid., 72.
172. Ibid.
173. Ibid.

independence:"[174] "The harshest truth of all is that Gandhi is increasingly irrelevant in the country whose 'little father'—Bapu—he was."[175]

Such irrelevance of Gandhi was linked to his otherness with regard to both secularism and Hindu nationalism. "India came into being as a secularized state,"[176] Rushdie pointed out, "but Gandhi's vision was essentially religious. However, he "recoiled" from Hindu nationalism. His solution was to forge an Indian identity out of the shared body of ancient narratives."[177] Gandhi's ideas had "scarcely been mentioned"[178] in the recent elections, with the rising star of Hindu nationalism in the form of the BJP bearing witness to how far India was from Gandhi's path to inclusive and tolerant national gods.

Global capitalism and emerging India neglected the true Gandhi or used a "sloganized"[179] version of him. But even in this new version, Rushdie suggested, Gandhi had the potential for changing India and for changing the world: "Gandhi, who gave up cosmopolitanism to gain a country, has become, in his strange afterlife, a citizen of the world: his spirit may yet prove resilient, smart, tough, sneaky and, yes, ethical enough to avoid assimilation by global McCulture (and Mac culture too). Against this new empire, Gandhian intelligence is a better weapon than Gandhian piety."[180]

State Theology

In the summer of 1998, the thirteenth Lambeth Conference of the Anglican Communion, gathering all Anglican churches, took place. For the first time in the history of Anglicanism, eleven women were amid the 749 bishops who gathered in London from all over the world.

Explosive gods challenged the capacity of British Christians to stay in tune with postmodern British society while keeping a leading role in a world increasingly at odds with the secular West. Within the Church, explosive gods divided those who defended traditions from those who pushed for a compromise with modernity. In the context of the worldwide Anglican Communion, national episcopates dramatically split and Anglican unity was threatened.

The famous Resolution 1.10 was passed, declaring that "homosexual practice" was "incompatible with Scripture." But reaching a substantial consensus on such a controversial issue was impossible. In the aftermath of the Conference, 182 bishops from all countries issued an apology to homosexual Anglicans. The primate of South Africa figured among the eight primates who signed the document.

174. Ibid.
175. Ibid., 72, 74.
176. Ibid., 74.
177. Ibid.
178. Ibid.
179. See ibid. The term "sloganized" is adapted from Rushdie's reference to "sloganizing times."
180. Ibid., 74.

By the end of the Conference on August 9, 1998, a momentous declaration on apartheid was also issued. Anglican bishops welcomed the first democratically elected government led by Nelson Mandela and gave "thanks to God for the end of apartheid rule and of centuries of colonial oppression in South Africa."

Shortly after, on October 28, 1998, the Truth and Reconciliation Commission presented its final Report, which condemned both the state and the liberation movements for the atrocities of the past and called upon true national reconciliation.

Based on the hearings, the Commission devoted a separate chapter of the Report to drawing an ambivalent portrait of faith communities, all of which "contained victims, beneficiaries and perpetrators of apartheid."[181] The proceedings registered that "all the religious groups who appeared before the Commission acknowledged their complicity with apartheid."[182]

Faith communities were thus condemned as "agents of oppression,"[183] in particular for propagating "state theology,"[184] defined as the theology that gave legitimacy to the apartheid state. "The world Christian community,"[185] Archbishop Tutu wrote in his foreword, "has declared that the theological justification of apartheid is a heresy."[186]

Churches, the report read, built and perpetuated apartheid as both "a moral and Christian initiative in a hostile and ungodly world."[187] Faith communities were also blamed for failing to support "dissident ministers, priests, imams, rabbis, and lay persons who found themselves in confrontation with the state."[188]

The Report did not fail to celebrate faith communities as "victims of oppression"[189] and to praise them as "opponents of oppression."[190] The Commission was able to shed light on the 1988 bombing of Khotso House, the headquarters of the South African Council of Churches. General van der Merwe admitted that he received orders directly from Adriaan Vlok, the Minister of Law and Order, to render Khotso House inoperative. In his own application for amnesty, Vlok stated that President Botha personally ordered him to destroy the "house of evil."[191] The president, according to Vlok, told him in July 1988: "I have tried everything to get them [the South African Council

---

181. South Africa Truth and Reconcilation Commission, "Institutional Hearing: The Faith Community," 59 [3].

182. Ibid. 91 [119].

183. Ibid., 65 [28].

184. Ibid., 69 [45].

185. Tutu, "Foreword by Chairperson," 15 [62].

186. Ibid.

187. South Africa Truth and Reconcilation Commission, "Institutional Hearing: The Faith Community," 91 [121].

188. Ibid., 91 [119].

189. Ibid., 65 [28].

190. Ibid.

191. Pauw, *Into the Heart of Darkness*, 76.

of Churches] to other insights; nothing helped. We cannot act against the people, you must make that building unusable."[192]

Colonel Eugene de Kock told the Commission he executed the orders by "placing the rucksacks of explosives in front of the two lifts"[193] in the basement; "the operational teams withdrew in the direction of Hillbrow,"[194] he added, "and waited for the devices, activated by electronic time devices, to detonate."[195] The Commission also found that President Botha congratulated Vlok "on work well done."[196] Both Vlok and Vand der Merwe testified that President de Klerk was aware of their role in the sabotage.

Based on the investigations and on the amnesty application of Henri van der Westhuizen, the Commission also threw light on the car bombing in Maputo against Albie Sachs. The involvement of South African Special Forces was confirmed, as the Commission believed "the attack on Mr. Sachs to have been the work of a covert unit under the control of a senior Special Forces operative."[197] Yet it was discovered that Albie Sachs was not the target of the attack. According to the Truth and Reconciliation Commission's Report, "van der Westhuizen suggests that the target of the operation was not Sachs but Mr. Indres Naidoo, ANC diplomat in Maputo. The bomb was placed in Naidoo's car which, unbeknownst to the operatives, Sachs had borrowed on this particular day . . . The operative who placed the bomb was paid R 4000 for his work."[198]

The Report encapsulated the multiple implications of national gods between 1995 and 2000. Religion-based nationalism was denounced as the cause of "inter-religious suspicion, distrust and strife,"[199] ultimately leading to "religiously inspired conflict."[200] In response, devotion of faith communities to the cause of the nation was vigorously required:

> The nation has a right to expect of [faith communities] a commitment to mutual respect between religious groups; the building of communities that include people of different religious, racial, and ideological persuasions; and the promotion of peace and justice.[201]

The national process of reconciliation demanded much from religions. They were required to limit their competitive instinct and strategies. They were also asked

192. South Africa Truth and Reconciliation Commission, "The State inside South Africa," 291 [522].

193. Ibid., 292 [525].

194. Ibid.

195. Ibid.

196. Ibid., 292 [528].

197. Ibid., 121 [317].

198. Ibid.

199. South Africa Truth and Reconciliation Commission, 'Institutional Hearing: The Faith Community', 92 [122].

200. Ibid.

201. Ibid.

to reject any colonial assumption and to acknowledge the African element they had so often despised and persecuted: "The reaffirmation of *ubuntu* . . . requires other established religions to gain a new understanding of traditional African religious symbols and beliefs."[202]

By the end of 1998, through the Truth and Reconciliation Commission and the Constitutional Court, South Africa was actively engaged in getting rid of its former nationalist gods and becoming home to the pluralistic and multifaith, and thus confident and optimistic, national gods.

The Second Victory of Sushmita Ghosh

In 2000, while India celebrated the birth of its billionth citizen, Salman Rushdie visited the country. It was the first time since the publication and the ban of *The Satanic Verses* twelve years earlier. Only two years earlier the Iranian government had declared that it would "neither support nor hinder assassination operations on Rushdie,"[203] this being, as Kenan Malik commented in 2009, the closest the government "ever get to disowning the fatwa, which still stands."[204]

A few days after Rushdie's visit, on May 5, 2000, the Supreme Court of India decided on the appeal of the Sarla Mudgal decision. Again Sushmita was victorious. The new bench, composed of Justice Saghir Ahmad and Justice Sethi, judged that the 1995 decision was in accordance with the Constitution and thus stood. Justice Saghir Ahmad reiterated the refusal to grant the dissolution of a marriage and the right to remarry simply on the grounds of conversion from Hinduism to Islam:

> Mere conversion does not bring to an end the marital ties unless a decree for divorce on that ground is obtained from the court. Till a decree is passed, the marriage subsists. Any other marriage, during the subsistence of first marriage would constitute an offence . . . and the person, in spite of his conversion to some other religion, would be liable to be prosecuted for the offence of bigamy.[205]

The specificity and scope of Muslim personal law was not denied. Rather, as Justice Saghir Ahmad underlined, "prosecution [for bigamy] in respect of a second marriage under Mahommedan Law can be avoided only if the first marriage was also under Mohammedan law and not if the first marriage was under any other personal law where there was a prohibition on contracting a second marriage in the life-time of the spouse."[206]

---

202. Ibid., 92 [123].
203. Malik, *From Fatwa to Jihad*, 10.
204. Ibid.
205. *Lily Thomas*, 244 [35].
206. Ibid., 244–45 [36].

The Court energetically rejected the objection of the Muslim petitioners that "making a convert Hindu liable for prosecution under the Penal code would be against Islam, the religion adopted by such person upon conversion."[207] Justice Sethi responded that such claim demonstrated "the ignorance of the petitioners about the tenets of Islam and its teachings."[208] The judge pointed out the true principles of Sharia and lectured the Muslim petitioners that "it would . . . be doing injustice to Islamic Law to urge that the convert is entitled to practice bigamy notwithstanding the continuance of his marriage under the law to which he belonged before conversion."[209] Severely, Justice Sethi defended the true Indian Muslim law from the misleading interpretation of the applicants, the Jamat-e-Ulema Hind and the Muslim Personal Law Board:

> The progressive outlook and wider approach of Islamic law cannot be permitted to be squeezed and narrowed by unscrupulous litigants, apparently indulging in sensual lust sought to be quenched by illegal means.[210]

The verdict was the same as in 1995, but the approach significantly differed. In the 1995 decision, the formal validity of the first wedlock was central; in the 2000 appeal, the focus was rather on the lack of a genuine conversion.

Allegations that the conversion of Sushmita's husband was not genuine were quintessential in the strategy of the counsel appearing for Sushmita Ghosh. After the conversion Shri Ghosh had kept his Hindu name in the electoral roll. In 1995, he even applied for a Bangladeshi visa describing himself as Gyan Chand Ghosh and declaring that his religion was Hindu. Also, Sushmita's counsel had obtained the birth certificate of a son born to Shri G. C. Ghosh from the second wife in 1993. In the birth certificate, the name of the child's father was given as G. C. Ghosh and his religion was again indicated as Hindu; the mother's name was listed as Vanita Ghosh and her religion was also described as Hindu.

Evidence that Shri Ghosh's conversion was a fake did not play a major role in the 1995 decision. Now it proved crucial, as Justice Ahmad announced that it was in such evidence that the Court sought "the answer to the real question involved in the case."[211]

The exploitation of conversion by Shri Ghosh prompted the Supreme Court to praise the high value of religion and to describe, with Saghir Ahmad, its significance:

> Religion is a matter of faith stemming from the depth of the heart and mind. Religion is a belief, which binds the spiritual nature of man to a super-natural being; it is an object of conscientious devotion, faith, and pietism. Devotion, in its fullest sense, is a consecration and denotes an act of worship. Faith, in

---

207. Ibid., 254 [62].
208. Ibid.
209. Ibid., 255 [62].
210. Ibid.
211. Ibid., 239 [16].

the strict sense, constitutes firm reliance on the truth of religious doctrines in every system of religion.[212]

The brilliance of religion threw unambiguous light on the immorality of Shri's conduct. Again Justice Saghir Ahmad to stress the point:

> Religion, faith, or devotion are not easily interchangeable. If the person feigns to have adopted another religion just for some worldly gain or benefit, it would be religious bigotry. Looked at from this angle, a person who mockingly adopts another religion where plurality of marriage is permitted so as to renounce the previous marriage and desert the wife, he cannot be permitted to take advantage of his exploitation, as religion is not a commodity to be exploited.[213]

In 2000, the Supreme Court asserted Sushmita Ghosh's rights on the grounds of public morality and respect for religion. Sushmita was entitled to her full status as a legitimate wife, because, as Justice Saghir Ahmad proclaimed, "the institution of marriage under every personal law is a sacred institution."[214] The Indian nation, as the Court understood it, wanted religion to be respected. By warning that religion was not "a commodity to be exploited,"[215] the Court stepped in as the guardian of religion. Religion could contribute to the unity and welfare of the nation, the Court put forward, because the nation, by means of the state, acknowledged and preserved the sacredness of faith. With mounting Hindu nationalism and the increasing victimization of Muslims, this was hardly disinterested celebration of true religiosity in all its possible forms.

In 1995, the Court called upon the ideal of secularism; in 2000, not only was secularism absent in the decision, but the Supreme Court stepped back on the issue of the uniform civil code. In fact, though underlining the continuity between this decision and the earlier ruling, Justice Sethi actually reversed the position taken by his colleagues in the 1995 Sarla Mudgal case. He declared that "this Court has not issued any directions for the codification of a common civil code, and the Judges constituting the different Benches had only expressed their views in the facts and circumstances of those cases."[216]

The Court parted ways with the judicial activism of 1995. By 2000, a deeper awareness had emerged that law could be more usefully operated step by step, instead of by imposing top-down, traumatic revolutions. The opinion of Justice Ramaswamy in the 1996 decision of the Supreme Court on the Pannalal Bansilal Pitti was taken as the reference. A uniform law could be "counter-productive to unity and integrity of the nation";[217] it would be wrong to make the law "uniformly applicable to all people in

---

212. Ibid., 245 [38].
213. Ibid.
214. Ibid.
215. Ibid.
216. Ibid., 258–59 [68].
217. Ibid., 258 [68].

one go."[218] Bottom-up, gradual change was more appropriate for India. Again in 2000, the Court's statement in the Pannalal Bansilal Pitti resonated, "the mischief or defect which is most acute can be remedied by process of law at stages."[219]

The change that occurred in the period from 1995 to 2000 was double-sided. If the Supreme Court bowed to religion and brought to a halt the call for a uniform civil code, it also asserted the state's jurisdiction over what could be deemed true or false religiosity. Religion was praised as the essence of India, but the autonomy of religious laws and bodies, and the state's impartiality vis-à-vis minorities were seriously threatened. The victory of Sushmita coincided with the Supreme Court's advancing both less secularism and more religious power of the Indian state.

Five Strokes With a Cane

On May 25, 2000, three weeks after the second victory for Sushmita Ghosh, the South African Supreme Court dismissed Gareth Prince's appeal. The final available option was now an appeal to the Constitutional Court.

On August 18, 2000, a unanimous Court, which also included Arthur Chaskalson, held, through the opinion of Justice Sachs, that the 1996 South African Schools Act, prohibiting corporal punishment in schools, did not violate the rights of parents who, in line with their religious convictions, consented to it. The case originated from a network of 196 independent schools that claimed corporal "correction" to be an integral part of their evangelical Christian ethos, further insisting that its blanket prohibition through the 1996 Schools Act impinged on their individual, parental, and community rights to practice their religion freely. Biblical verses, they argued, imposed a divine duty to correction, which might lead to "five strokes"[220] given by the principal with a "cane, ruler, strap, or paddle."[221]

Justice Sachs stressed the constitutional "right of people to be who they are without being forced to subordinate themselves to the cultural and religious norms of others."[222] He also provided a passionate hymn to the salience and to the constructive potential of religion:

> The right to believe or not to believe, and to act or not to act according to his or her beliefs or non-beliefs, is one of the key ingredients of any person's dignity. Yet freedom of religion goes beyond protecting the inviolability of the individual conscience. For many believers, their relationship with God or creation is central to all their activities. It concerns their capacity to relate in an intensely meaningful fashion to their sense of themselves, their community

218. Ibid.
219. Ibid.
220. *Christian Education,* 5 [5].
221. Ibid.
222. Ibid., 25 [24].

and their universe. For millions in all walks of life, religion provides support and nurture and a framework for individual and social stability and growth. Religious belief has the capacity to awake concepts of self-worth and human dignity, which form the cornerstone of human rights. It affects the believer's view of society and founds the distinction between right and wrong. It expresses itself in the affirmation and continuity of powerful traditions that frequently have an ancient character transcending historical epochs and national boundaries.[223]

Such was the range of religion that it was impossible to separate it from the secular. The religious and the secular constantly overlapped and interpenetrated one another. Sachs wrote, "religious and secular activities are, for purposes of balancing, frequently as difficult to disentangle from a conceptual point of view as they are to separate in day-to-day practice. While certain aspects may clearly be said to belong to the citizen's Caesar and others to the believer's God, there is a vast area of overlap and interpenetration between the two."[224]

Genuine complexity of religion led Justice Sachs to emphasize the need for special protection of those beliefs that "the majority regard as unusual, bizarre, or even threatening."[225] Indeed, section 31 of the Constitution not only granted everybody the right "to enjoy their culture, practise their religion and use their language," but also it protected an interest, which in Sachs's words was "not a statistical one dependent on a counter-balancing of numbers, but a qualitative one based on respect for diversity."[226]

Still Sachs was not ready to accept the applicants' argument that corporal punishment had to be allowed in the name of religion. He reached such conclusion by applying a proportionality test and by weighing the impact of the contested legislation on the beliefs of the applicants. The test demonstrated that not only did the ban serve fundamental purposes, but also that, as Sachs pointed out, it did not force the parents "to make an absolute and strenuous choice between obeying a law of the land or following their conscience."[227] Chaskalson adhered to Sachs's view that the 1996 Constitution prescribed "the use of a nuanced and context-sensitive form of balancing."[228] As in the case of Magdalena Solberg, national legislation and values prevailed over the exception sought in the name of a specific understanding of faith. The Court dismissed the Christian schools' appeal.

In November 2000, Gareth Prince filed his appeal to the Constitutional Court of South Africa. As the country celebrated the adoption of the Promotion of Equality and Prevention of Unfair Discrimination Act, more commonly known as the

223. Ibid., 40 [36].
224. Ibid., 38 [34].
225. Ibid., 28 [25].
226. Ibid.
227. Ibid., 56 [51].
228. Ibid., 34 [30].

Equality Act, Prince's application challenged the constitutionality of the decision of the Law Society, which prevented him from becoming a lawyer because of his ritual, unlawful use of cannabis. He invoked, in particular, "his rights to freedom of religion, to dignity, to pursue the profession of his choice, and not to be subjected to unfair discrimination."[229]

According to the statute of the Constitutional Court, nine judges were appointed to hear the appeal. Both Arthur Chaskalson and Albie Sachs were sitting on the same bench with Justice Mokgoro, the judge who defined *ubuntu* for the Court in 1995. On December 12, 2000 the Court granted leave to Gareth Prince to provide further information on the creed and practices of the Rastafari community.

The Taj Mahal Like the Berlin Wall

Ten years after the collapse of international communism, nations struggled with their new place in the global world. Capitalism, the uncontested winner of the post-1989 age, imposed a kind of uniformity, which neither nations nor national gods could put up with. Though gods could not be easily handled, religion constantly risked being "a commodity" to be exploited. The national interest easily hid the expediency of divisive and shortsighted politics. However, like global capitalism, faiths were also increasingly global. They crossed boundaries and rendered national religious policies more and more ineffective.

In India, the call for national unity beyond religious lines was failing mainly because of that Hindu nationalism that monopolized the national discourse, hence the fear of many Muslims and Christians of being dissolved into the Bharat. On January 22, 1999, the murder of the Australian Christian missionary Graham Staines, burnt with his two children while they were sleeping in a station wagon in Keonjhar district in Orissa, epitomized the heavy atmosphere. Gandhi's vision of a united Indian nation beyond religious divisions was dead and buried. Nehru's ambition to absorb religious communities into a secular, socialist India was also more and more obsolete. From 1995 to 2000, the Supreme Court of India held firm on the national effort and on the state's power to regulate social implications of faith, but slowed down its secular agenda.

To those who recalled the fall of the Berlin Wall and urged them to give in, Indian Marxists countered with the example of the Taj Mahal, the famous temple erected to celebrate love. The Taj Mahal could crumble, their slogan was, but love never will. They meant that even though the Berlin Wall had crumbled, the sentiments of Indian Marxists for social justice and equality could not be demolished.

In Britain, the construction of a multicultural and multireligious nation under the New Labour looked increasingly problematic. Churches were under pressure from within, because of internal dissent and reforms, and from without, because

229. *Prince*, 2002 [6].

of an increasing competitive religious and social market. From the recognition of women priests in 1995 to the tensions of 1998–2000 on homosexuality, the Church of England exemplified the hardship of British Christianity in keeping in tune with postmodernity. At the same time, through the Anglican Communion, the Church of England preserved its global leadership. The incorporation of the European Convention of Human Rights through the Human Rights Act of 1998 injected new principles and tools into the British adjudication of religious claims. British gods in courts were about to become more European.

In the "millennium issue" of December 23, 1999, the *Economist* offered a provocative obituary of God. Trying the gods was ultimately about the encounter between the creator and the creature: "The test will come on Judgment Day," the *Economist* read, "when man, we are told, will meet his maker. Or will it be God meeting his?"[230] In a dramatic reply, one year later, December 2000, Mohammad Bilal became the first British Muslim suicide bomber to die in a blast in Srinagar, Kashmir.

In South Africa, the nationalist gods of apartheid were defeated, but the time did not yet appear ripe for *our* gods to contribute to the nation-building process invoked by Desmond Tutu. The status of Christianity was uncertain while minorities sought more revenge than responsibility. From the death penalty decision of 1995 to the decision on the Christian education case of 2000, the Constitutional Court elaborated a doctrine on sources of values and religious freedom, which pointed to a visionary future but fell short of addressing the problem-ridden present of the nation. When Thabo Mbeki succeeded Mandela as the new president in June 1999, a new phase for the place for religion in the country was also about to begin.

The personal trajectories of Sushmita Ghosh, Gareth Prince, and Shabina Begum epitomized the change the three countries underwent over the five years.

From 1995 to 2000, the legal action of Sushmita enjoyed success. With a husband still bound to another woman and to another child, though not lawfully, the achievement in court did not dramatically change her life, but at least she was proved right. The Indian struggle with religious personal laws, discrimination, abuse, and violence continued, with Indian women now in charge of taking advantage of Sushmita's endeavour.

During the same period, Prince started his fight in court, lost the first leg, and ultimately resorted to the Constitutional Court, his last hope to become a barrister, thus perpetuating the spirit of Gandhi's legal practice in South Africa and avenging the exclusion of Mandela from the Law School in 1949.

In 2000, Shabina Begum registered at Denbigh High School, though her family lived outside the school district. Her father had died in the meantime, and Shabina lived with her mother, a sister two years older, and her brother Rahman. For the first year the girl seemed happy with the new environment. Outwardly she may have appeared comfortable with her Islamic obligations, as she wore the *shalwar kameeze*

---

230. "God." *The Economist*, Millennium Special Edition, December 31, 1999, 135.

according to the school's uniform policy set under the Indo-British guidance of Mrs. Bevan. In fact, troubles were still ahead.

Ten years had passed since the crumbling of the Berlin Wall, the collapse of the Soviet Union and the defeat of communism. The Cold War seemed to have vanished in a quickly forgotten past. While recalling the tight connection between the apartheid state and the Cold War, Archbishop Tutu resisted the generalized temptation to get rid of the past too hastily. In his 1998 foreword to the Report of the Truth and Reconciliation Commission, he emphasized the importance of understanding "the nature of the Cold War period,"[231] when "the attitude towards Communism defined who one's allies and enemies were."[232] Supporters of apartheid, Tutu recalled, believed they "were defending their country and what they understood to be its Western Christian values against the atheistic Communist onslaught."[233]

Without acknowledging the past, the country could not step into the future. This concerned the colonial age too, as Tutu himself suggested when he underlined the link between the colonial and the Cold War roots of violence and discrimination. Imperial and cold gods had to be summoned from the past, and acknowledged, in order to build the "rainbow nation of God."

By the end of the millennium, it was clear in the three countries that inclusive and tolerant national gods lacked the power to extinguish the fire of explosive gods. Nations shrank because of globalization. Faiths struggled with galloping secularization. Rather than fuelling the all-encompassing and civilized alliance between the nation and the faiths, which Gandhi dreamed of, national gods often turned into nationalist gods.

The end of the Cold War and the "end of history" theory pushed religious and political actors hastily to forget about the past roots of their present. In fact, the Cold War had been removed too quickly. The New Labour in Britain, socialists and communists in India, Soviet-trained leaders in South Africa—they all had the problem of reconciling their past with the present world of global business and the free market. Colonialism and communism were apparently dead, but they still deeply influenced India, South Africa, and Britain. Although gods were now more visible than before, they had already been there during the Cold War. The wrestling of explosive and national gods in 2000 resurrected the cold gods, the gods who had inhabited the Cold War from 1948 to 1978.

231. Tutu, 'Foreword by Chairperson', 15 [63].
232. Ibid.
233. Ibid., 14 [56].

Chapter 4

Cold Gods (1948–1978)

An English Band

AT THE END OF the 1990s, the Cold War seemed as though it had belonged to a different geological age. The ten years that had passed since the fall of the Berlin Wall appeared transformational enough to have swept the previous world away. Under New Labour, Britain had virtually forgotten both the trade-unionist Labour of the seventies and the Thatcherism of the eighties. New India was uncertain about how to combine the free market, the gigantic central state and the multitude of regional and communal actors, but she did feel certain she had left Gandhi's village-based anti-industrialism, as well as Nehru's planned economy far behind. Former communists of the African National Congress, now in power in Cape Town and Pretoria, eagerly played the game of global capitalism.

The seeming worldwide acceptance of the free market pushed Francis Fukuyama to shape his "end of history" theory, according to which the end of the Cold War marked "the end point of mankind's ideological evolution and the universalization of Western liberal democracy as the final form of human government."[1]

Over the nineties, Fukuyama's optimism over Western liberal democracy wobbled, as the victory of the free market manifestly did not coincide with the "'universalization of Western liberal democracy.'" While neoliberalists and free-marketers stayed on the high, liberal democracies seemed to perform poorly and were certainly not spreading. The classical model associating free enterprise and free speech was challenged, not only from outside the West, but also from within.

The stories of Sushmita Ghosh, Gareth Prince, and Shabina Begum proved the ambivalence of liberal democracies and human rights. Even after her victory in court, Sushmita witnessed the continuing struggle for women rights and social justice in India. The Indian state's adoption of the European vision of a state law enforcing values

---

1. Fukuyama, "The End of History," 3.

upon society had proved symbolically powerful but practically immaterial. In South Africa, Gareth's championing marginalized minorities pointed at the fragility of both the Western individualism at odds with increasing social diversity, and the non-Western leaning toward social conformity. In the first decade of the 2000s, Shabina's claim not to abide by school regulations in the name of her Muslim radicalism would soon encapsulate the struggle of Western liberal democracy not only with the universalization of Western values but also with the crisis of Western principles in the homeland.

Another theory, also formulated in the aftermath of the fall of the Berlin Wall, proved more resilient than Fukuyama's. According to Samuel Huntington, after the Cold War pattern, dominated by economy and ideology, the "next pattern of conflict" would be along religion-fed cultural "fault lines." A war between civilizations would replace the Cold War, with religion playing a crucial role as a fundamental ingredient of one people's culture.

In one of his most cited passages, Huntington's outlook on culturally and religiously based conflicts was formulated in the following terms: "It is my hypothesis that the fundamental source of conflict in this new world will not be primarily ideological or primarily economic. The great divisions among humankind and the dominating source of conflict will be cultural."[2]

Huntington's theory seemed consistent with the evidence of the explosive and national gods that came after 1989. As religion exploded and challenged the old fabric of capitalist secularization and socialist egalitarianism, it also featured as a vital component in the identity of nations swallowed up by the global world. The association of religion and culture was as crucial after 1989 as economy and ideology had been before.

As the struggle pitting capitalist freedom of religion against communist atheism progressively faded away, the replacement of a God-free Cold War with a God-driven war between civilizations became received wisdom. Apparently, the Cold War had stepped out while religion was stepping in. Of course, this was an oversimplification; the Cold War had not been God free. But, after 1989, it was easy to think that it had been. If the economy and politics of the Cold War had been wiped out, so too had been the cold gods, the gods of the Cold War.

Indeed, as Fukuyama and Huntington perfectly knew, present conflicts were profoundly rooted in the post–World War II age. The Cold War had generated those religious developments that challenged New Labour–led Britain; the fast-growing, contradictory India of the nineties; and postapartheid South Africa. Salman Rushdie and Bin Laden would not have become who they were without the capitalist/communist divide, the Soviet invasion of Afghanistan, and the Anglo-American partnership with Saudi Arabia and Pakistan. Desmond Tutu himself warned that no rainbow nation of God could be born if people forgot that the Cold War, like Imperialism before it, had been the habitat for the religious justification of apartheid.

2. Huntington, "The Clash of Civilizations?" 22.

The response to the post-1979 explosive gods was based on the legacy of the thirty years from 1948 to 1978. Following the era of imperial gods, the cold gods had generated a mixture of explosive and national religion, which dominated the scene at the dawn of the new millennium. The Cold War had shaped the minds and the instincts of those who faced the task of responding to explosive gods and national gods. During the litigations of Sushmita Ghosh, Gareth Prince, and Shabina Begum, the counsels, judges, journalists, and scholars all used arguments and strategies established during the Cold War. From 2001 onwards, cold gods would substantially influence the Indian aftermath of the two judgments of 1995 and 2000 on the case of Sushmita Ghosh, the South African constitutional ruling on the case of Gareth Prince, and the discussion of Shabina Begum's case in Britain.

Soil Erosion, Soul Erosion

In the last week of November 1947, as bloodshed fueled by Partition worsened, Gandhi and Sheikh Muhammad Abdullah met in Delhi and together took part in the celebration of the anniversary of the birth of Guru Nanak, the founder of Sikhism. Abdullah was the Muslim leader of Kashmir, then an independent kingdom squeezed between the Pakistani-backed "tribal invasion" and the Indian military aid, the eventual price of which was the accession of Jammur and Kashmir to the Union of India. Gandhi saw Abdullah as a champion of interfaith peace and a witness that India could overcome communal strife and inter-religious violence. The Mahatma acknowledged the "great gulf between the Hindus and the Sikhs on one side, and the Muslims on the other"[3] but played to Indian nationalism and stressed that Sheikh Abdullah "has won the hearts of both, by making them forget that there is any difference between the three . . . Now the Muslims and the Hindus and the Sikhs . . . are fighting together to defend the beautiful valley of Kashmir."[4]

Contrary to the expectations of Gandhi and Sheikh Abdullah, fights would last for at least one more year, when a cease-fire was finally enforced and Kashmir became the unending witness to the tragedy of Partition and the Indo-Pakistani conflict.

But by the time of the cease-fire, Gandhi was no longer there. Two months after the meeting with Sheikh Abdullah, on January 30, 1948, the Hindu Mahasabha activist Nathuram Godse fired three shots at point-blank range on the grounds of Birla House in Delhi and killed Gandhi.

A new age began for Indians, British, and South Africans. Gandhi was no longer present to interact with the politics of the three countries. But his legacy would prove as vital and challenging for them as his life had.

A few months after Gandhi's death and the worldwide mourning surrounding the funeral, as the Constituent Assembly of India prepared the Constitution, and as

3. Guha, *India after Gandhi*, 71.
4. Ibid.

Attlee's Labour government started reforming Great Britain, crucial elections took place in South Africa, resulting in the victory of the proapartheid National Party.

On June 1, 1948, party leader Daniel François Malan was in Pretoria to celebrate the electoral win in May: this was the beginning of the transition from the segregation of the thirties and the forties to the apartheid of the fifties. When he proclaimed that "today, South Africa belongs to us once more,"[5] he referred first of all to the struggle for Afrikaner independence against British imperialists. This, for Malan, was the main implication of the defeat of the rival United Party, led by Jan Smuts. The inflexible rival of the early Gandhi, Jan Smuts was an Afrikaner who supported racial segregation and led commandos against the British in the Anglo-Boer War. But he also worked for a strategic alliance between South Africa and Britain in the new world; thus he played a crucial part in the creation of the League of the Nations. He wrote the preamble to the United Nations Charter, and in a speech given during the war in the Royal Gallery of the House of Lords, he used, for the first time, the term "British Commonwealth of Nations," referring to the "future constitutional relations and readjustments in the British Empire."[6] In February 1948, the Fagan Report issued by Smuts's government stated that strict segregation was counterproductive. The ensuing Afrikaner nationalist backlash condemned Smuts's party to the dramatic defeat in May, which Malan saw as the defeat of British intrusion, of any intrusion in Afrikaner interests.

The superiority of the Afrikaner over the African element was also at stake, and Malan's slogan on the occasion would haunt apartheid South Africa for the decades to come: "South Africa is our own for the first time since Union, and may God grant that it will always remain our own."[7]

The new government of the Union of South Africa intended to cut its ties with Britain. Britain itself was ready to reshape its relationships with the colonies, and with the ex-colonies such as South Africa as well, though the Empire remained very much part of the British self-perception and outlook. According to Jan Smuts's vision, the British Commonwealth was the instrument for a new British global sovereignty, and since South Africa was still a member, South Africans remained British subjects. In 1948, the Parliament of Westminster approved the British Nationality Act. The status of citizen of the United Kingdom and colonies was introduced, embracing all nationals from the United Kingdom and from the British colonies. This opened the door to immigrants, but no alarm was generated at the time, as Britons saw free access to Britain from the colonies as a rather obvious consequence of the new world order. They hardly predicted the massive influx of immigrants, which would dramatically change the country.

The first signals came very quickly. On June 21, 1948, a few weeks after Malan took office as prime minister, the ship *Empire Windrush* landed at the London

---

5. Giliomee, *The Afrikaners*, 487.

6. Hancock and van Der Poel, *Selections from the Smuts Papers*, 750.

7. Giliomee, *The Afrikaners*, 487.

Terminal of Tilbury Docks, resulting in the first big wave of immigrants from the British colonies in the West Indies to the English homeland.[8]

Only three days later, the Cold War erupted with the actualization of the Berlin Blockade. Starting on June 24, 1948, the Soviet Union blocked all railway and road access to the sectors of Berlin controlled by the Western Allies. Soviets aimed at gaining control over the whole of Berlin. The Blockade was eventually overcome thanks to an Airlift made possible through cooperation between the Royal Air Force and other air forces of the Commonwealth, including the South African Air Force.

During the Berlin crisis, in July 1948, an energetic Anglican priest gave a speech in his capacity as the president of the Cape branch of the African National Congress. James Calata was used to mixing his faith and his political activism. In the speech he addressed the religious immorality of apartheid as it was envisaged in the political program of the successful National Party. Racial segregation, Calata believed, was detrimental first of all for the economy and the welfare of the community, as, he said, "the state of the farm usually reflects the life of the labourers."[9] Calata pointed at the lack of concern for both the material and the spiritual needs of laborers and their families and predicted the "erosion" of soil and soul alike:

> Good farmers who provide their labourers with facilities, health, education, and religion usually get better fruits of labour. I have come to the conclusion that factors which contribute to the breakdown of health and moral and religious lives of communities are detrimental to pastoral and agricultural people. Soil erosion is very often the result of soul erosion.[10]

Calata also criticized the Afrikaner use of the Bible to legitimize racial policies and more specifically Malan's rhetorical reference to God and the church. During his first speech as prime minister, Malan mentioned that in South Africa's Constitution, God's sovereignty over the destiny of the country was specially acknowledged; he then declared that "in exercising our Governmental functions we wish to act in conformity with that confession"[11] and called upon the support of the church. To this, Calata responded by anticipating the rising involvement of anti-apartheid Christians in the struggle of the African National Congress:

> We have to accept the Government that is in power and find a way to cooperate with it in promoting our welfare. If Dr. Malan expects the Church to support him, he must abandon his apartheid policy, for the Church of God should not be a party to a policy of Colour Bar . . . I am one of those who have been preaching that Christianity is a world brotherhood, and that a European Christian is a nearer person to me than an African Mohammedan, but I am

8. Brooke, *Reform and Reconstruction,* 125–26.
9. Calata, "Presidential Address."
10. Ibid.
11. Ibid.

185

beginning to wonder if my European brethren preach a similar doctrine to their people. Well, there is your chance, Reverend Dr. Malan. Prove to the world that you stand by the principles of Christianity which involve the Fatherhood of God and brotherhood of man. God bless Africa.[12]

Christians within the Nederduitse Gereformeerde Kerk, the Afrikaner Dutch Reformed Church, held the opposite view. In their journal, *Die Kerkbode*, of February 23, 1949, one could read:

> The day is coming when the non-white races and powers will stand mobilized against the white for their supposed rights. So also will the time come that the mobilized powers of unbelief under the leadership of the Prince of Darkness will rise up in bloody strife against the real Christendom. These events summon us as Church today. Mobilize. Mobilize to the utmost![13]

Malan's government was elected precisely to protect the Afrikaner from the threat of both British neoimperialism and African claims, and further from the communist threat of "unbelief" and the black proletarian revolution. The government immediately endeavoured to enforce apartheid measures, starting from the Prohibition of Mixed Marriages Act of 1949. Also in 1949, South African citizenship was introduced, absorbing the preexisting category of the Union nationals. As a result, most of those who belonged to the Union of South Africa as British subjects were prompted to shift to South African citizenship.

The Tyrannous Code

In 1948 the Constituent Assembly of India examined two proposals related to religious diversity in the country. Both embodied the reformist and modernist vision of the Congress's elite, led by Prime Minister Nehru.

The first proposal aimed at committing the state to a uniform civil code bringing under the same personal law all Indian citizens, regardless of their religion, caste, or gender. In case the uniform civil code failed, the second proposal offered a plan B: the reform of Hindu law in personal matters as a step towards general legal uniformity. Both proposals were based on the conviction that legal reform would build the Indian nation, modernize the country, and advance socioeconomic justice and equality. The underlying belief was that, as Rina Williams put it, "uniform laws could build unified communities, and eventually a unified nation."[14]

Legal uniformity and reform of religious laws were the two sides of the same coin. The legislative activism of the Congress's socialist elite used legal unification to protect the nation from religious divide, and legal reform to change society for

12. Ibid.

13. Paton, *Apartheid and the Archbishop*, 189–90.

14. Williams, *Postcolonial Politics and Personal Laws*, 107.

the sake of discriminated social sectors, especially women and low-caste or outcaste people. Religion would be forced to move on in order for a more equal and modern Indian society to be shaped.

In April 1948, the reform of Hindu law was introduced, when the 1941 project of the Rau Commission was resumed and submitted to an ad hoc Select Committee of the Constituent Assembly. The Dalit leader and minister of Justice Bhimrao Ramji Ambedkar presented the Hindu Code Bill as a highly needed step towards a clearer and fairer personal law for the majority of Indians. Speaking a Western legal language, which could have belonged to Macaulay one century earlier, Ambedkar first recalled that his aim was "to codify the rules of Hindu law, which are scattered in innumerable decisions of the High Courts and of the Privy Council, which form a bewildering motley to the common man and give rise to constant litigation."[15]

He then illustrated the many provisions of the Bill, which innovated against the previous Hindu law in the direction of a more equal status for women and untouchables. Six points, Ambedkar summarized, encapsulated the reform:

> First, the abolition of birth-right and to take property by survivorship. The second point . . . is the giving of half-share to the daughter. Thirdly, the conversion of the women's limited estate into an absolute estate. Fourthly, the abolition of caste in the matter of marriage and adoption. Fifthly, the principle of monogamy, and sixthly the principle of divorce.[16]

The Code also recognized two distinct forms of marriage; one was called sacramental marriage and the other civil marriage.

A dramatic change of traditional Hindu law was thus envisioned. Members of the Committee sympathetic with the Bill stressed that reform was so badly needed because the British had crystallized Hindu law for the past 150 years. Supporting this view, Pattabhi Sitaramayya underlined the conservative role of Christian missionaries and clergymen in freezing customs, and explained, the British

> were afraid of any interference with the socio-religious structure, which was a delicate structure almost like a chemical balance and bore the repercussions of the smallest change coming from abroad and from adventitious sources. They were afraid that such repercussions would be ruinous to the stability of their empire in this country, and therefore they adopted the plausible and seemingly reasonable attitude of not interfering with the religion or the custom of the land. In this manner, the Judges of the High Courts always helped to register the custom as it had existed for long centuries behind, and never registered a change in the custom as marking a progress in society. Thus custom became petrified, and when custom became petrified, progress became

15. Ambedkar, "Speech on the Hindu Code Bill."
16. Ibid.

impeded altogether, and for a hundred and fifty years our society has not been able to make any progress.[17]

Indeed, neither the reformist thrust nor the allegation that Hindu backward orthodoxy was the result of British rule could appease those members of the Assembly who saw in the Bill an attack on the most cherished Hindu traditions.

The perspective of either a uniform civil code wiping out the system of personal laws or the Hindu Code Bill codifying and modernizing Hindu law triggered a negative reaction within the Assembly and in society.

On November 23, 1948, in a speech to the Constituent Assembly, B. Pocker Sahib Bahadur transformed the British noninterference and enforcement of personal laws into an argument in support of the preservation of the system:

> one of the reasons why the Britisher, having conquered this country, has been able to carry on the administration of this country for the last 150 years and over was that he gave a guarantee of following their own personal laws to each of the various communities in the country. That is one of the secrets of success and the basis of the administration of justice on which even the foreign rule was based.[18]

Personal laws were defended as a pillar of peaceful cohabitation. Mohammad Ismail Sahib, a Muslim from Madras, told the Assembly: "if people are allowed to follow their own personal law, there will be no discontent or dissatisfaction. Every section of the people, being free to follow its own personal law will not really come in conflict with others."[19]

A crucial point was the tight relationship between personal laws and religion. A uniform code or a reform of Hindu personal law would touch upon matters—such as marriage, the family, and inheritance—which were deemed to belong to the religious sphere. Enforcing monogamy or divorce or equal shares of inheritance for women was like changing a rite or a religious truth. Reforming the system of personal laws or a single personal law entailed reforming religion itself. Mohammad Ismail Sahib pleaded in front of the Assembly that "the right to follow personal law is part of the way of life of those people who are following such laws; it is part of their religion and part of their culture."[20] If the uniform code impinged on personal laws, B. Pocker Sahib Bahadur declared, it would interfere "with the religious rights and practices," and thus, "it will be tyrannous."[21]

The consequence of such tyranny, opponents of reform maintained, would be increased tension among communities, in the case of a uniform code obliterating

---

17. Pattabhi Sitaramayya, "Speech on the Hindu Code Bill."
18. B. Pocker Sahib Bahadur, "Speech at the Constituent Assembly," 544.
19. Mohammad Ismail Sahib, "Speech at the Constituent Assembly," 541.
20. Ibid., 540.
21. B. Pocker Sahib Bahadur, "Speech at the Constituent Assembly," 545.

personal laws, or, in the case of a new revolutionary Hindu law, the breakdown of the family, the economy and Hindu society.

Opponents not only played to Hindu traditions and beliefs; they also spoke the language of modern, democratic politics. The reform was criticized as an elitist attack on the people. No effective demand for change emerging from the Hindu community justified the intervention of the state against the noninterference principle. B. Pocker Sahib Bahadur rebuked Ambedkar for lying when he argued that his constitutional article on the uniform code enjoyed the support of the majority: "if the framers of this article say that even the majority community is uniform in support of this, I would challenge them to say so. It is not so."[22]

Also contested was whether the initiative was consistent with the secular character of the state. Mahboob Ali Baig Sahib Bahadur asked the Constituent Assembly to reject the reform precisely because it entailed a pervasive, all-encompassing mission of the state, which betrayed the true meaning of a secular state:

> People seem to have very strange ideas about secular State. People seem to think that under a secular State, there must be a common law observed by its citizens in all matters, including matters of their daily life, their language, their culture, their personal laws. That is not the correct way to look at this secular State. In a secular State, citizens belonging to different communities must have the freedom to practice their own religion, observe their own life, and their personal laws should be applied to them.[23]

Uniform India

At the end of 1948, it became clear to Ambedkar that his dream of replacing the personal laws system by a uniform civil code for all could not be realized. In the context of postpartition, he observed that the imposition of a uniform civil code would upset religious communities, especially the Muslims—not to mention the hostile conservative Hindus who did not want the legislature to intrude on Hindu law. Ambedkar could not afford to push his reformist action that far. But he could force a milder solution on his opponents: the Constitution would not immediately enact such an inflammatory change, but would include the future adoption of a uniform civil code among the directive principles of state policy at Article 44: "The State shall endeavour to secure for the citizens a uniform civil code throughout the territory of India."

Such was the compromise: the adoption of the uniform code was somehow envisaged, but directive principles were guidelines not enforceable in a court of law. Article 44 had very limited efficacy. This was the political message Ambedkar wished to transmit in the speech he gave at the Constituent Assembly on December 2, 1948.

22. Ibid.
23. Mahboob Ali Baig Sahib Bahadur, "Speech at the Constituent Assembly," 544.

The minister of justice and president of the Draft Committee reassured the opponents without giving up his own secular vision. Article 44 was not about prejudicing the state; it was about Parliament's freedom to legislate, about the possibility to change for the better in keeping with the people's wishes. "I should like," Ambedkar said, "to point out that all that the State is claiming in this matter is a power to legislate. There is no obligation upon the State to do away with personal laws. It is only giving a power. Therefore, no one need be apprehensive of the fact that if the State has the power, the State will immediately proceed to execute or enforce that power in manner that may be found to be objectionable by the Muslims or by the Christians or by any other community in India."[24]

Conditions were not fulfilled in the present context for giving up on personal laws and for embracing a new codified system of legal uniformity. Still, the general constitutional aim was to overcome communitarian differences and to foster national identity and unity. In this respect, the adoption of a common unified civil code to replace the different religious laws was prospected.

The article discontented everybody. Minorities, many Muslims in particular, felt targeted. Traditionalist Hindus also feared that Hindu law could be asked to set an example on the way towards uniformity. Socialists who viewed personal laws as the legacy of the British Raj were not happy either. They had believed that the independence of modern, secular, and equalitarian India would imply the end of personal laws and the triumph of a uniform law for a united nation. Now they discovered that the colonial construction of separate religious communities through personal laws was not likely to be swept away with colonialism.

The question of the uniform code was somehow fixed for the time being, with Article 44 included in the final draft of the Constitution. But the question was to haunt the future life of India. In 1995 and 2000, the Supreme Court in the case of Sushmita would still be struggling with the constitutional mandate. Ambedkar's speech of December 1948 would be quoted by the judges in the second decision of 2000 on Sushmita Ghosh's case, as a reference for their key argument that the Jamat-e-Ulema Hind and the Muslim Personal Law Board had no reason to worry, and that "this Court in Sarla Mudgal's case had not issued any direction for the enactment of a civil code."[25]

Although Article 44 on the uniform code was the best possible achievement under the circumstances, Ambedkar was perfectly aware that nothing had changed in the legislation yet. He thus returned vigorously to the Hindu Code Bill. If a change for everybody was still impossible, the Congress should promote reform for the largest part of the population. The Bill was framed accordingly as an Act addressed not only to the strictly Hindu but generally to all those who were not Muslims, Parsis, or Christians. As a result, not only was Hindu law sought to be radically reformed, but also Hinduism was very broadly defined as to include, in particular, the Sikh,

24. *Lily Thomas*, 246 [42].
25. Ibid,

the Jain, and the Buddhist. Hindu law was used as the quasi-synonym of Indian law. Beyond appearances, continuity was tightening between the imperial and the cold gods. Following the British pattern, "the postcolonial Indian government's definition" of religion "suppressed difference within," Rina Williams noticed, "and sharpened difference between religious communities so defined."[26]

In March 1949 the All India Anti–Hindu Code Bill Committee was created. Protests spread. Members of the Delhi Bar declared that "the mass of the Hindus believe in the Divine origin of their personal laws."[27] The Hindu Mahasabha featured among the fiercest foes of the Bill, with "black flag" demonstrations staged outside the Parliament and clashes with the police. Resolutions were passed, protesting that "the present Hindu Code Bill is against the basic principles of the Hindu Dharam Shastras . . . the revolutionary changes proposed in marriage, joint family system, inheritance . . . are opposed to the Hindu outlook, Hindu culture and are based on such conceptions, which . . . would lead the Hindus to destruction."[28]

Opposition to the Hindu Code Bill was so acute and widespread as to paralyze the Constituent Assembly. In 1949, as the Constitution took its final shape, it became clear that Article 44 was all that Ambedkar and the government could achieve in the struggle against personal laws. On the other hand, Ambedkar's fight against untouchability was going to have a happier outcome, with Article 14 of the Constitution proclaiming in plain terms the abolition of the system of the untouchables: "'Untouchability' is abolished and its practice in any form is forbidden. The enforcement of any disability arising out of 'Untouchability' shall be an offence punishable in accordance with law."

By abolishing untouchability and by envisaging the adoption of a uniform code sweeping away religious personal laws, Indian reformists intended to fight against deep-seated, detrimental cultural and social customs. The degrading conditions of millions of women and deprived people in the country should be given the priority, not religious sensitivities. But the ambition to promote change through the law would prove symbolically too heavy and practically too light. The secular, reformist and modernist vision of Ambedkar and Nehru would stir too much opposition and would fall too short of affecting real India.

A Great and Powerful Nation

In that same year, 1949, on his journey to the US, Nehru was conferred the degree of Doctor of Laws at Columbia University, New York. General Eisenhower greeted him personally, in his capacity of president of Columbia University. Some decades before, influenced by his reading of political and legal literature at the Low Library of Columbia, Ambedkar had developed his conviction that he was entitled to stand as a free

26. Williams, *Postcolonial Politics and Personal Laws*, 104.

27. Guha, *India after Gandhi*, 231.

28. Williams, *Postcolonial Politics and Personal Laws*, 111.

man, equal to any other, regardless of his untouchable descent. Also at Columbia, in September 1989, Albie Sachs showed up with the fresh signs of the attack he had just suffered in Maputo, and suggested that the transition to postapartheid South Africa could not be achieved without a pact with the enemy.

In his address of October 17, 1949, Nehru warned never to subordinate means to ends. "If the end is right but the means are wrong," he observed, this "will vitiate the end."[29] This was, he suggested, the lesson to draw from the Indo-British struggle:

> After a generation of intense struggle with a great and powerful nation, we achieved success and, perhaps, the most significant part of it, for which credit is due to both parties, was the manner of its achievement. History hardly affords a parallel to the solution of such a conflict in a peaceful way, followed by friendly and cooperative relations. It is astonishing how rapidly bitterness and ill will between the two nations have faded away, giving place to cooperation. And we in India have decided, of our own free will, to continue this cooperation as an independent nation.[30]

The "great and powerful nation" was, of course, Britain. The lesson Nehru drew from the conflict and the partnership between the Indians and the British was applied to the Cold-War divide between the States and the Soviet Union. In this regard, Nehru emphasized, India struggled "to combine idealism with national interest."[31] India pursued peace and justice "not through alignment with any major power or group of powers but through an independent approach to each controversial or disputed issue."[32]

The doctrine of nonalignment was thus announced to America in the very same speech in which Nehru paid his tribute to his own double British and Indian identity and to the Indo-British partnership. In the speech at Columbia, Nehru also raised the problem of "racial relations," with a view that again linked imperial and cold gods in Britain, India, and South Africa:

> In Asia and Africa, racial superiority has been most widely and most insolently exhibited. It is forgotten that nearly all the great religions of mankind arose in the East and that wonderful civilizations grew up there, when Europe and America were still unknown to history. The West has too often despised the Asian and the African and still, in many places, denies them not only equality of rights but even common humanity and kindliness.[33]

The example of Abraham Lincoln was clear to Nehru; he reminded his audience at Columbia that "one of your greatest men said that this country cannot exist

29. Nehru, "Ends and Means," 396.

30. Ibid., 396–97.

31. Ibid., 398.

32. Ibid.

33. Ibid., 400.

half-slave and half-free."[34] The Indian leader pleaded for coherence as he asked for the application of that lesson to the world divided by the Cold War.

The Music of Veena and Sitar

As Nehru tried to avoid India's being squeezed between the two superpowers, and as the final vote on the Constitution got closer, the gap widened between the political project and the dramatic present reality. Some members of the Assembly thought that the British tone of the Constitution betrayed the ideal India of the anticolonial struggle and framed a legal structure inappropriate to cope with the real India of traditional inequalities and postpartition instability. On November 17, 1949, Shri K. Hanumanthaiya gave a speech before the Constituent assembly, blaming the members of the draft committee for being "very well versed in case law and code law,"[35] but unmindful of the struggle for independence and of the Indian particularity. After a three-year debate, he observed, the final draft of the Charter framed a strongly centralized state. Gandhi had advised a broad-based, pyramid-like structure, Shri K. Hanumanthaiya recalled, but the Constitution was a reverse pyramid:

> The initiative from the Provinces and States and from the people has been taken away and all power has been concentrated in the Centre. That is exactly the kind of Constitution Mahatma Gandhi did not want and did not envisage.[36]

Shri K. Hanumanthaiya believed this was the effect of a prevailing British political and legal culture: "we wanted the music of *Veena* or *Sitar*, but here we have the music of an English band."[37]

The memory of Indians dressed and trained to look and perform like a band in Hyde Park was still strong. Three years of debates had not been enough for the Constituent Assembly to wash that sound and memory out of the text of the future Constitution. But the same three years had proved enough for Indian courts to try and convict Nathuram Godse, the murderer of Gandhi. On that very same November 17 on which Hanumanthaiya complained about a Constitution that was not Gandhian enough, Godse was executed.

Eight days later, on November 25, 1949, as the final draft of the Constitution was about to be voted on, Ambedkar made a "moving speech"[38] stating his vision on how India could flourish as a modern, developed nation. The old rivalry with Gandhi, whose fast in 1932 had forced Ambedkar to renounce his pro-Dalit claims and concede the Poona Pact, resurfaced as he declared that India should first of all get rid of

---

34. Ibid.

35. Shri K. Hanumanthaiya, "Speech to the Constituent Assembly," 616.

36. Ibid, 617.

37. Ibid, 616.

38. See Guha, *India after Gandhi*, 121.

Gandhi's Satyagraha. Ambedkar bore in mind anti–Hindu Code Bill protesters from the Rashtriya Swayamsevak Sangh or the Hindu Mahasabha blocking the streets. If applied against the legitimate government of independent India, Satyagraha would, in Ambedkar's view, represent an anarchic threat to democracy. In independent and democratic India, he believed, civil disobedience and noncooperation were "nothing but the grammar of anarchy."[39] He accepted faiths but feared that the tradition of Bhakti, the path of devotion or hero-worship, would pollute the young Indian democracy: "Bhakti in religion may be the road to the salvation of a soul. But in politics, Bhakti or hero-worship is a sure road to degradation and to eventual dictatorship."[40]

For Ambedkar, politics and religion had to stay separate. The United States were, at the time, the strongest advocate of separation. In the latest, seminal decision in the case Everson v. Board of Education of 1947, the US Supreme Court had famously proclaimed: "The First Amendment has erected a wall between church and state. That wall must be kept high and impregnable. We could not approve the slightest breach."[41]

In 1946, Justice Chalga for the High Court of Bombay had decided the case of Robasa Khanum, on conversion and remarriage, in the name of "complete religious neutrality." Ambedkar agreed. He wanted the Charter to oppose the most tenacious resistance to religious fanaticism.

When the Indian Constitution was passed on, November 26, 1949, its preamble proclaimed religious freedom in the following terms: "We, the people of India, having solemnly resolved to constitute India into a sovereign democratic Republic and to secure to all its citizens . . . liberty of thought, expression, belief, faith, and worship."

Article 25 further articulated a threefold right to freedom of conscience and religion as to include profession, practice, and propaganda: "Subject to public order, morality, and health, and to the other provisions of this Part, all persons are equally entitled to freedom of conscience and the right freely to profess, practise and propagate religion."

This was not the music of Veena and Sitar, with so much British and American sound in the text, nor was it the music of an English band, with a combination of worship, different religions, and republicanism unknown to the British constitution. Because it interwove so many rich and intricate voices, this was indeed a unique piece of polyphonic counterpoint.

No Irish, No Blacks, No Dogs

The Indian Constitution came into effect on January 26, 1950, exactly twenty years after Purna Swaraj, the declaration of independence proclaimed by the Congress.

---

39. Ibid.
40. Ibid.
41. *Everson,* 18.

India was now a republic, but, according to the London Declaration of April 28, 1949, it still accepted the British Sovereign as a "symbol of the free association of its independent member nations and, as such, the Head of the Commonwealth."[42]

At the time, the British postwar socialist experiment with Labour was at an end. Britons were glad for the achievements in the building of a welfare system, but they also wanted their country to depart from the austerity of the gloomy postwar years. British society was reacting to immigration as well. Outside shops, signs warning "No Irish, No Blacks, No Dogs" were common, encapsulating the growing social tension.

Britain was becoming a postimperial power, reconverting its economy, and sealing pacts with a new range of allies. The Commonwealth and the United Nations, along with its Universal Declaration of Human Rights of 1948, framed new geopolitics. Europe was crucial. In a broadcast to the nation during the war, Winston Churchill, who would be back as prime minister in 1951, anticipated that a Council of Europe would be needed. The Council was actually created on May 5, 1949, with the Treaty of London. On November 4, 1950 Britain figured among the first subscribers to the European Convention on Human Rights. Like the Indian Constitution, Article 9 of the European Convention recognized religious freedom, including freedom to change religion:

> Everyone has the right to freedom of thought, conscience, and religion; this right includes freedom to change his religion or belief, and freedom, either alone or in community with others and in public or private, to manifest his religion or belief, in worship, teaching, practice, and observance.

Fifty years later, Shabina would rely on this article, in her claim against Denbigh High School.

During the fifties, the South African government pushed apartheid to the extreme through hammering legal reforms and through pervasive social control. As Leonard Thompson notes,

> From 1948 on, "Whites Only" notices appeared in every conceivable place. Laws and regulations confirmed or imposed segregation for taxis, ambulances, hearses, buses, trains, elevators, benches, lavatories, parks, church halls, town halls, cinemas, theatres, cafes, restaurants, and hotels, as well as schools and universities. It was also official policy to prevent interracial contacts in sport.[43]

The Immorality Act of 1950 made sexual relations between whites and nonwhites unlawful. The same year, the Population Registration Act categorized the population according to a racial principle.

The creation of the homeland system, with enclaves formally controlled by indigenous "nations," further enhanced apartheid. The independence of the homelands was

---

42. De Smith, "The London Declaration," 353.
43. Thompson, *A History of South Africa*, 197.

fictitious, and the rhetoric of their development into true nation-states deceptive. Their construction on an ethnic basis destroyed families and communities. The National Party made the recognition of ethnic groups in South Africa the tool for the exploitation of black labor and for the pervasive control of the nonwhites, with forced removals and hundreds of thousands of Africans arrested each year "under the pass laws."[44]

The governments of London, Delhi, and Pretoria established heavily bureaucratic, all-encompassing administrations in the respective states. Indian and British rulers, confident as they were in their freedom-based socialism, attempted to force society towards uniformity, this resulting in a backlash of particularistic pride. South African nationalists developed a policy of racial fragmentation aimed at building a society of separated communities under the supremacy of whites.

In 1948 and 1949, as Mao took power in China, Nehru crashed a communist insurrection in Hyderabad. In the meantime, the communist party, led by Ranadive, succeeded in the Telengana region: this success was considered the first step toward a Red India.[45] One century earlier, working as a correspondent in London, Karl Marx had analyzed tensions in colonial India and pointed at the failures of imperial gods. White Christianity legitimized the British oppressor while Indian religions delayed the oppressed on their way towards freedom. Moving from this critique, Marxism had become the alternative to the imperial gods of both the colonialist and the colonized. At the end of the forties, Marxism was prominent in the construction of cold gods. It inspired British socialists and South African anti-Nationalists. In India, it stirred both the clashing projects of Nehru's benevolent socialism and Ranadive's subversive communism.

Hindu nationalism responded. In a theatrical tour of anti-communist propaganda, J. N. Chaudhuri, the military governor of Telengana, was portrayed as a Hindu God, while communists were portrayed as demons.[46] Himself a former admirer of postrevolutionary Russia, Nehru traveled to Moscow in 1955 to defend nonalignment from the pressure applied by Bulganin and Khrushchev. In 1950, while British soldiers were fighting communism in Korea, China invaded and annexed Tibet. In 1954, India recognized the annexation, and in that same year, Nehru visited China for the first time, meeting Zhou Enlai and Mao himself. Two years later, Zhou Enlai returned the visit and went to India. The Dalai Lama was with him and spoke to Nehru about seeking asylum in India if troubles were not settled in Tibet.

Also in 1950, the Suppression of Communism Act banned the Communist Party of South Africa and made the fight against communism an official aim of the state. The Act of 1950 gave such an extensive definition of communism that it stretched to cover any anti-apartheid fighter and opponent of the regime.

---

44. Ibid., 193.

45. Guha, *India after Gandhi*, 96.

46. Ibid., 97–98.

Until the Last Breath of My Life

By 1951, it became clear to Ambedkar that neither the uniform code nor his Hindu Code Bill could be realized. In September, Nehru announced that he was ready to compromise on a certain number of aspects of the Hindu Code Bill and to break it into separate bills. Ambedkar, who had already made some concessions, refused to follow and resigned from the cabinet in October 1951.

Nehru was aware that even a compromise on the content of the Bill would be of no use without a stronger popular mandate. With the first general elections ahead and Hindu nationalists overtly contending his leadership, he campaigned for a secular, progressive India while endorsing the struggle to improve the conditions of the deprived sectors of society. In a speech in Parliament on May 5, 1955, he criticized the way traditions and customs imposed different standards of morality on men and women. "It is only the women who have to behave like Sita and Savitri," he said, "the men may behave as they like."[47]

Nehru made the point that reform of Hindu law on personal matters was quintessential to his design of a modern India. He declared: "I have owned this Code, and I will continue to support it until the last breath of my life. If anybody says he will not vote for the Congress because of the Code, then I say he is free to cast his vote as he pleases. We won't bother about his vote."[48]

Opposition to the Hindu Code Bill coincided with opposition in the elections, with Hindu nationalists featuring on one side and anti-Congress socialists and communists on the other.

In his constituency of Allahabad, Nehru was elected only after a bitter contest with a sadhu, a Hindu holy man named Prabhu Dutt Brahmachari. Hindu Mahasabha lawyer Nirmal Chandra Chatterjee complained that the Bill would be enforced on the Hindus only and not on every community. Socialist Jivatram Bhagwandas Kripalani used the same argument. In general, communists and socialists joined Ambedkar in blaming Nehru's wariness and criticizing the Bill for being "not radical enough."[49]

Electoral victory in 1952 made Nehru stronger, but not strong enough to apply Article 44 and give shape to the uniform civil code. In 1954, he declared, "I do not think that at the present moment, the time is ripe in India for me to try to push it through."[50] Justice Kuldip Singh would recall this passage in 1995, in the first decision of the Supreme Court on the case of Sushmita Ghosh, as the expression of the ruler's reluctance to move on in the application of the Constitution.

---

47. Nehru, "Changing Hindu Society," 451.

48. Williams, *Postcolonial Politics and Personal Laws*, 105.

49. Guha, *India after Gandhi*, 238.

50. Ibid., 241.

Instead, the prime minister accelerated the passage of the Hindu Code Bills, the adoption of which he took as "the first step towards bringing some uniformity."[51] In his speech to the Lokh Sabha of September 14, 1954, he further explained:

> If you do not break down the barriers, first of all in the Hindu Community it-self—these caste barriers and the rest that keep each group apart, and secondly as between the Hindus and the Muslims, and the Christians, and the Parsis, and the Buddhists, and the Jains, and all others who live in this great country, you will never build up that . . . national concept.[52]

Despite the electoral defeat of Hindu conservatives, the opposition to the Bills did not slow down. In a speech to the Rajya Sabha on December 9, 1954, Radha Ku-mud Mookerji condemned the Bills' attempt "to change popular psychology as to the sanctity of marriage and family," and the risk that new legislation might compromise "the future of the race."[53]

But Nehru's leadership was now much stronger and the majority in Parliament much more committed, including dedicated women MPs, such as Subhadra Joshi and Sucheta Kripalani. Finally, four major pieces of legislation were passed in 1955–56: the Hindu Marriage Act of 1955, the Hindu Succession Act of 1956, the Hindu Minor-ity and Guardianship Act of 1956, and the Hindu Adoptions and Maintenance Act of 1956. Concessions were made, in particular on the retention of the Mitakshara, the joint family system, the reduction of the share of inheritance to daughters, the exclusion of agricultural land from the scope of the Bills, the drop of provisions on adoption and maintenance. Also, customary law was reestablished.

The background was set for Sushmita Ghosh's personal and legal trial thirty years later, the main features of which would be the system of personal laws still in place; the difference of marital status and provisions between Hindu and Muslim wives; cus-tomary, informal regulation outplaying modern, Western-fashioned bills; the political stakes; and the communal discourse prevailing over the real needs of people.

A new generation of Indian, British, and sometimes American scholars would be brought by the 1955–1956 Bills to study Hindu law. At the time in his thirties, future leading scholar in Hindu law, Englishman Duncan Derrett was preparing a book on the Hoysalas, a dynasty of medieval southern Indian kings.[54] The Bills, which he saw as an "experiment in social legislation,"[55] captured his attention. He was later to write that "for width of scope and boldness of innovation, [the Bills] can be compared only with the Code Napoleon."[56]

51. Williams, *Postcolonial Politics and Personal Laws*, 107.
52. Ibid.
53. Guha, *India after Gandhi*, 237.
54. Derrett, *The Hoysalas*.
55. Derrett, "The Hindu Succession Act," 485.
56. Derrett, *Religion, Law and the State in India*, 326.

Post-1979 explosive gods and post-1995 national gods prompted a new reflection on the Hindu Code Bills. In 1989, American Marc Galanter reiterated his 1968 depiction of the Bills as a "wholesale and drastic reform" entirely supplanting "the *sastra* as the source of Hindu law."[57] On the other hand, historical and anthropological research provided interpreters with evidence that the impact of reform on the life of women had been very limited. In 1994, Indian historian and classical singer Reba Som suggested this was the "victory of symbol over substance"[58] and the ratification of a deeply polarized Hindu community: "all those ranged on the side of the Bill were branded as ultra modern, westernized and not good Hindus, whereas those against the Bill were branded as being orthodox and reactionary."[59]

The price for modernization of Hindu law was a widened gap between the myth of a rational, uniform law and messy reality. In 2000, Nivedita Menon, a political scientist in Delhi, observed that the Bills had codified, not reformed Hindu law, and argued that an end had been put "to diversity of Hindu law as it was practised in different regions, in the process destroying existing, more liberal customary provisions in many cases."[60]

In 2006 Rina Williams underlined continuity between the colonial and the post-colonial state, but also the different aims and means:

> The British colonial government sought to reform and codify Hindu personal law for reasons of administrative and judicial clarity and convenience: the approach of piecemeal legislation had reached its logical limit and ended in a judicial-legal mess. For Nehru, however, the reform and codification of Hindu personal law was imperative to beginning the process of modernization, setting India on the path to national unification and social progress. Nor were the means the same . . . the British colonial government did not rest on any pretensions to representing the will of the Indian people. Nehru's Hindu Code Bill, on the other hand, for all the controversy surrounding it, was passed by the duly elected representatives of those people.[61]

"By privileging progressive Hindu opinion on the Hindu Code Bills," Williams added,

> the myth was perpetuated that significant reform of Hindu personal laws had been accomplished, when in fact by many standards (and certainly by standards of women's rights and gender equality), the Hindu Code Bills fell far short of achieving real, meaningful change. This myth, in turn, has added weight to the Hindu nationalist argument that the Hindu community has

---

57. Galanter, *Law and Society in Modern India*, 29.
58. Som, "Jawaharlal Nehru and the Hindu Code," 165.
59. Ibid., 178.
60. Menon, "State, Community, and the Debate on the Uniform civil code in India," 80.
61. Williams, *Postcolonial Politics and Personal Laws*, 115.

moved forward with their personal law, and the Muslim community is "lagging behind" and needs to catch up.[62]

The fifties handed over to future Indian politics two stereotypes of conflicting ideologies: progressive versus conservative Hindus on the one hand, advanced Hindus versus backward Muslims on the other. The cold gods' split between progressive and traditional religious inspiration replaced the traditional divide of imperial gods between the faith of the colonizer and the faith of the colonized.

Tensions over conversions and women's rights, epitomized by the story of Sushmita Ghosh, would be deeply affected by such a scheme.

Ambedkar's Conversion

On October 14, 1956 Ambedkar officially converted to Buddhism and led a mass conversion of Dalits from Hinduism to Buddhism at Deekshabhoomi, Nagpur. For many years Babasaheb (as he was called after converting) Ambedkar had been digging into his origins as a Mahar, eventually coming to believe that Mahars, once a Buddhist community, were condemned to be outcaste because of their refusal to give up their identity. By reverting back to the tradition and dignity of the fathers, by embracing an "egalitarian creed,"[63] Ambedkar bore witness once more to his struggle for the dismantling of the caste system.

That same month, October 1956, Britain, together with France and Israel, attacked Egypt in reaction to the nationalization of the Suez Canal. At the beginning of November, the British were forced to accept a cease-fire and to withdraw, defeated by the alliance between the rampant Arab nationalism of Nasser and the hegemonic America of Dulles. The British Empire was definitely over. Anthony Eden was replaced by Harold Macmillan, who accelerated decolonization, and antiwar demonstrations in London anticipated the marches against the Vietnam War in the sixties, and against Tony Blair's Iraq War in 2003. The American and Western oil alliance with the Saudis started drawing a map on which Saddam Hussein and Osama Bin Laden would later find their places.

In the same weeks, the Soviet repression of the Hungarian revolution also contributed to testing Nehru's nonalignment. The Indian prime minister attacked the British for the colonial raid on Port Said, but when a United Nations resolution condemning the Soviet Union's occupation of Budapest was put to the vote, his representative, V. K. Krishna Menon, abstained. As the polarization of the Cold War turned more savage, the credibility of Nehru's nonalignment suffered a serious blow.

---

62. Ibid., 119–20.

63. Jaffrelot, *Dr. Ambedkar and Untouchability,* 131.

On the eve of 1957, with the second general election ahead, and the celebration of the centenary of the 1857 War of Independence, and the bicentenary of the Battle of Plassey, Ambedkar died in his house in Delhi. It was December 6, 1956.

Death of an Archbishop

The anniversary of the War of Independence of 1857 coincided with the anniversary of the 1857 cattle killing in South Africa, and also with the decision of the Synod of the Dutch Reformed Church in South Africa to "authorise the separation of Coloured from white congregations."[64]

That step resonated one hundred years later in the context of the tightening of apartheid, when the government, now led by Hendrik Verwoerd, introduced a Native Laws Amendment Bill, the "church clause," of which gave the minister of native affairs the discretionary power to forbid natives to attend worship at a white church in a white residential area if whites in the area objected. Nonwhites were compelled to worship in their own churches. Mixed congregations were regarded with hostility by the government, and now, with the passage of the Bill, they would be made unlawful.

Faced with policies of apartheid shaping the whole of South African society and affecting their own life, churches reacted timidly. The state was still regarded as a protector of Christianity in society, as Albie Sachs would later recall in his opinion in the Solberg case of 1997, when he wrote about the prohibition of dancing "with a partner to the accompaniment of music"[65] according to the Control of Dancing Ordinance of 1957.

At the time, Alex Boraine, later a key actor of the Truth and Reconciliation Commission, was preparing to become a Methodist minister while growing increasingly aware of the situation: "When I tried, rather tentatively, to raise these issues with members of my congregation, they told me to steer clear of politics and stick to my job as a preacher and pastor."[66] Once ordained and sent to Pietermaritzburg, Boraine discovered more about apartheid and real South Africa. An Indian friend in the church told him about the difficult history and conditions of Indians. When Boraine raised the question with the other white ministers, "they played it down, one saying, 'Well, of course he is exaggerating. They do very well, actually, and sometimes the Indian people, you know, can be quite difficult.' I was quite staggered at that, stored it away and continued to think about it."[67]

All denominations opposed the Bill with the exception of Afrikaner Churches. But their silence was not monolithic. A letter from A. S. Geyser, Professor of Christian Ethics at Pretoria University, was published in *Die Vaderland* on July 24, 1957,

64. Thompson, *A History of South Africa*, 66.
65. *S v Lawrence* [149] at footnote 29.
66. Boraine, *A Life in Transition*, 30.
67. Ibid., 36.

underlining that "the silence of the Afrikaans Churches on this clause," did not mean that they could give "defensible support of the legislation on Biblical grounds."[68] "The Bible," Professor Geyser cautiously explained, "says nothing in favor of or against *apartheid* as a social matter and therefore as an arrangement which falls within the competence of the State."[69]

At the same time, he continued, "the Bible permits no separation on the grounds of race and descent in the community of the believers—i.e., in the Church."[70]

Roman Catholic archbishops of Durban, Pretoria, and Cape Town declared their churches would remain open to all members, "regardless of their race."[71] The Anglican Church strongly objected to the 1957 "church clause." A major player since the forties was the Anglican bishop Geoffrey Clayton. Born in Leicester, England, he was appointed bishop of the diocese of Johannesburg in 1933. Still, at that time, all but one Anglican bishop of what was known as the Church of the Province of South Africa were imported from Britain. They went "to the colonies" and then returned "home" to serve in the Church of England or to retire. The worldwide Anglican Communion had developed as the religious equivalent to the British Empire. In South Africa, *die Engelse Kerk*, the English Church, despised by the Afrikaners, was inevitably a part of the Anglo-Afrikaner struggle.

Bishop Clayton was voted to become the new Archbishop of Cape Town on November 17, 1948, only a few months after the electoral win of the National Party. For the following years, Clayton was at the forefront of Christian opposition to the tightening of apartheid legislation. When the church clause was envisaged, South African writer Alan Paton, a close friend of the archbishop, wrote that "for the first time in his life," the seventy-three-year-old Clayton "contemplated, not only defiance of the law, but the urging of others to defy the law, the penalties for which were extremely heavy."[72]

Clayton summoned the bishops of Grahamstown, Johannesburg, Pretoria, and Natal to meet with him at his residence. On March 6, 1957, the four bishops agreed on the letter to the prime minister, drafted by Clayton, making plain that the law containing clause 29 (c), the "church clause," could not be obeyed. The letter regarded the issue as pertinent to questions of religious freedom and freedom of worship. Solemnly, the letter said that "the Church cannot recognise the right of an official of a secular government to determine whether or where a member of the Church of any race (who is not serving a sentence which restricts his freedom of movement) shall discharge his religious duty of participation in public worship or

---

68. Bernstein, "Union of South Africa," 367.

69. Ibid.

70. Ibid.

71. Paton, *Apartheid and the Archbishop*, 276.

72. Ibid., 277.

to give instructions to the minister of any congregation as to whom he shall admit to membership of that congregation."[73]

In such circumstances, disobedience to the law had a theological justification. Clayton's letter to the Prime Minister addressed the point straightforwardly:

> We recognize the great gravity of disobedience to the law of the land. We believe that obedience to secular authority, even in matters about which we differ in opinion, is a command laid upon us by God. But we are commanded to render unto Caesar the things which be Caesar's, and to God the things that are God's. There are therefore some matters which are God's and not Caesar's, and we believe that the matters dealt with in Clause 29 (c) are among them.[74]

The letter to Prime Minister Verwoerd concluded on a dramatic note:

> It is because we believe this that we feel bound to state that if the Bill were to become law in its present form we should ourselves be unable to obey it or to counsel our clergy and people to do so.
>
> We therefore appeal to you, Sir, not to put us in a position in which we have to choose between obeying our conscience and obeying the law of the land.[75]

Before the bishops left, Clayton took the bishop of Johannesburg aside, holding him by the arm—"which was unusual for him," Paton commented[76]—and told him, "I don't want to go to prison. I'm an old man. I don't want to end my days in prison. But I'll go if I have to."[77]

According to Paton's account, the day after, on the afternoon of March 7, 1957, the head gardener and assistant Mr. Ackermann

"saw the Archbishop leave the window and, soon after, heard the sound of a chair moving, and what seemed to be books falling, followed by a cry."[78]

Ackermann was accustomed to Clayton's exuberance and did not pay attention. Only later in the evening, Clayton's curate Roy Cowdry went to the study and found him: "The Archbishop was lying on the floor between his desk and the bookcase. Cowdry thought that he was playing a game, and said, "Get up, your Grace." Then with great shock he realized that the Archbishop was dead."

On March 8, 1957, the letter was sent to the prime minister. No notice was given. The Bill was redrafted, in order to keep the substance, while avoiding an open confrontation with the churches. A Machiavellian solution was found: the African worshiper, not the church would be guilty of the offense.

---

73. Ibid., 279.
74. Ibid., 280.
75. Ibid.
76. Ibid.
77. Ibid.
78. Ibid., 280–81.

The House of Assembly passed the Native Laws Amendment Bill by a vote of 79 to 48 on May 1, 1957. The Senate approved the Bill on 15 May. The "church clause" forbidding interracial intermingling in churches was finally enacted.

Ten years after Independence, one hundred years after the "Mutiny," general elections consolidated India as a democracy. Ten years after the victory of the National Party in the 1948 elections, apartheid featured as the distinctive character of South African law and society. In the same ten years, immigration from the colonies to Britain grew at a steady pace; the Notting Hill racial riots in 1958 would expose an alarming tension. The background for the struggle of Sushmita Ghosh, Gareth Prince, and Shabina Begum was set through the passage from imperial gods (when the religion of the colonizer prevailed over the religion of the colonized) to cold gods (when religion was the hostage of the divide between the capitalist West and the communist East).

In his 1949 speech before the Indian Constituent Assembly, Shri K. Hanumanthaiya complained that the Indian Constitution sounded like an English band. On July 6, 1957, a Saturday evening, Paul McCartney met John Lennon for the first time in St. Peter's Church, Woolton, in Liverpool, "where the sixteen-year-old Lennon's skiffle group, the Quarry Men, was performing."[79] In 1949, the Indian constituents had only recently lost their father Gandhi. In 1957, both Lennon and McCartney had already lost their mothers. A new kind of English band was about to emerge. In the sixties not only the sound of Britain but the sound of India and South Africa as well was destined to change.

Man's Law above God's

From 1948 to 1957, the background was set for the struggle of Sushmita, Gareth and Shabina fifty years later. Apartheid was heavily legislated in South Africa; independent India started floating between the secular, reformist, modernist dream and a contradictory, diverse, complex reality; from the ashes of the Empire, socialists and Tories redesigned the institutions for a wealthier and increasingly consumeristic British society.

In the sixties, the background was further defined.

As the dignity of nonwhite people and nonwhite cultures became central in the anti-apartheid struggle, the conditions for Gareth Prince's fight started to take shape. At the beginning of the nineties, Gareth would identify with the cause of the free, pluralistic society that new generations of South Africans in the sixties had dreamt of. Over the same period, the judges who would decide Prince's case in 2002 lived through crucial years: future constitutional judge Albie Sachs experienced detention, torture, and exile; future president Arthur Chaskalson stood in courts to defend Mandela and other freedom fighters against prosecution by the racist state.

---

79. MacDonald, *Revolution in the Head*, 45.

The case of Sushmita Ghosh was also prepared as no consensus emerged in India for the enactment of the uniform civil code, and as the dramatic problems of Indian women were unaffected by legal reforms.

Shabina Begum's Britain was still impossible to imagine. But the multiethnic country of the future was already emerging, together with tensions and violence, and the debate began over how to deal with immigration, cultural diversity, and a social landscape reshaped by successful libertarian claims.

Crucial legal developments took place over this period. The clash between the racist South African state and the anti-apartheid activists was not confined to the streets, the townships, or prisons. The struggle in the courts was also central. The Rivonia trial of 1964 against Nelson Mandela and other members of the African National Congress showed the huge potential of the law in general, and of trials and courts in particular, not only as the means through which apartheid was secured, but also as a place where opposition to the state could be organized and publicized.

On the other side of the Indian Ocean, the states of Orissa and Madhya Pradesh enacted anticonversion regulations. The controversial spread of Christianity in the poorest states and the tribal areas was the alleged reason for the Acts, but growing Hindu fundamentalism played a crucial role. The adoption of the uniform civil code was frozen, other religious laws were left untouched, and the application of the new Hindu law had almost no impact on gender and caste inequalities.

In Britain, free immigration from the former colonies was halted. Limits to immigration were sweetened by measures to counter racism and protect new cultures and faiths. With the Commonwealth Immigrants Act of 1962 the age of free entry into Britain from the colonies came to an end: the number of admitted immigrants per year was limited, and the admission requisites were tightened. By way of compensation, the British Race Relations Act of 1965 made racial discrimination unlawful in public places, this including, for the first time, hate speech. As the law reacted to an increasingly multicultural Britain, legislation also adjusted to a more permissive and secularized country, with new regulations sweeping away traditional restrictions in morally sensitive areas like divorce, abortion, censorship, and homosexuality.

With the Cold War escalating, and the construction of the Berlin Wall starting in 1961, the three countries faced deadly conflicts. The general framework was set by the ideological and strategic confrontation between the US and the USSR, and between their respective allies. Religion interplayed in various ways.

The Indo-Pakistani wars contributed to defining multireligious, secular India in contrast with the all-Muslim enemy, but also nourished Hindu fanaticism and fed Sikh anxieties, both of which would explode in the eighties. Hindu-Muslim violence resurfaced again at the beginning of the sixties and continued throughout the decade.

At the end of the sixties, the intensification of the conflict in Northern Ireland provided tangible proof that Christians could transform their identity into a lethal weapon just as effectively as Hindus and Muslims.

South Africa fought wars in the name of the God of the Afrikaners, against the expansion of anti-God communism; in return many anti-apartheid fighters defied the state in the name of the God of Christian social justice. Capitalist and communist atheism both justified violence. But torture and killings also appeared to be religiously legitimized, alternatively by the God of the oppressor or by the God of the oppressed.

God sent many different avatars to inhabit the Cold War era. Five featured prominently, namely, the God of science, the God of liberation, the God of Marxist atheism, the God of religious conservatism, and the God of capitalism. These cold gods proved a powerful force, which interacted with the changing world of the sixties and turned out as hot and influential in their time as the explosive and national gods would be from 1979 to 2000. Cold gods also arose out of an increasing intermingling of faiths and cultures, with the renewed spread of Christianity in India and South Africa, and the dissemination of Asian and African religions in Britain.

Religion as such did not feature as a prominent subject in the global debate on the future of the world. Economy and ideology, real politics of war and oppression, and ideals of peace, equality, and freedom all starred in the time of the Cold War. Religion was often an undercurrent force, the positive or negative impact of which was not clearly recognized or articulated. Frequently, religion was taken as a secondary factor compared to major developments in the economy, ideology, national interests, or the commitment to peace, freedom, and justice. Advocacy of religion in politics would only grow in the seventies.

This was a time when man's law prevailed over God's law. Though secularization affected Britain, India, and South Africa at different paces and to different extents, materialism and consumerism were underway in all three countries. Society mattered more than spirituality. Communities grew less concerned with the mere worship of God and more keen on buying into politics and ideology. Believers were not satisfied with God's eternally immutable law; they aimed at controlling man's law. A less secular man's law, a civil law robustly shaped by Hindu or Muslim or Christian elements, would be the best achievement of God's law itself.

These developments would characterize cold gods and would bridge the imperial gods inherited from Victoria, Smuts, Gandhi, and Churchill with the post-1979 explosive and national gods of Sushmita Ghosh, Gareth Prince, and Shabina Begum.

The Wind of Change

Between the end of the fifties and the beginning of the sixties, communities violently clashed in Britain, South Africa, and India.

Since the War ended and the first immigrants arrived in Britain from the colonies, minor tensions had occasionally pitted newcomers against the local working-class youth. But in September 1958, when, in Notting Hill, "large crowds"[80] assaulted black immigrants of Caribbean origin, it became clear that Britain could not afford its post-war policy of no restrictions. No one was killed during the attacks, but the display of hundreds of Teddy boys "nigger-hunting" or "black-burying," and the streets littered with "Keep Britain White" signs, marked a turning point. Two opposite consequences emerged: as the open-door policy was publicly opposed, and eventually ended in 1962, immigrant communities engaged more actively in self-defense and self-promotion, with the Notting Hill Carnival starting a few months after the riots. From the Southern states of the United States, black consciousness and black power were exported not only to Cape Town, but also to London.

Over the same period, India faced renewed communal tension, with religion again featuring as the source or the pretext for unrest and violence. A decade of escalating religious violence in the country was inaugurated in early 1961, when some fifty people, mainly Muslims, were killed in riots in Jabalpur.

Meanwhile, South African tensions on apartheid had been growing since 1948 and exploded on March 21, 1960, when police opened fire on a crowd protesting the pass laws at the police station of Sharpeville. Sixty-seven were killed and 186 wounded. The Sharpeville Massacre resulted in an international blow for the reputation of South Africa and in a turning point for the anti-apartheid opposition. The camp of the anti-apartheid campaigners enlarged both within and without the country. With the ban of the African National Congress being issued by the government in the aftermath of the massacre, the idea that Gandhian nonviolent methods could pay off in South Africa as they had done in India lost momentum; violent resistance was resorted to as the only available option.

A few weeks before the Sharpeville Massacre, on February 3, 1960, British Prime Minister Harold Macmillan had visited South Africa, where he gave the famous "Wind of Change" speech to the Parliament in Cape Town. He did not mention race issues, but focused on the Cold War and on the nationalist movement in Africa. Macmillan argued that, as a loyal member of the "Free World," South Africa should not oppose African nationalism. In order to attract the nonaligned countries, he affirmed the "Free World" had to make room for self-government and set the example for new nations to join in the global struggle against communism. History, Macmillan said, was asking a crucial question in Asia and Africa: "will the great experiments in self-government that are now being made in Asia and Africa, especially within the Commonwealth, prove so successful and, by their example, so compelling that the balance will come down in favour of freedom and order and justice?"[81]

---

80. Karapin, "Major Anti-Minority Riots," 327.
81. Macmillan, "Speech to the South African Parliament."

For the British prime minister, this was "a struggle for the minds of men,"[82] which went beyond the "military strength or . . . diplomatic and administrative skill."[83] India had responded through the formidable democratic effort of the fifties. South Africa was cheating on the issue of self-government in the homeland. Macmillan did not say this, but when he talked of a "wind of change," everybody understood he meant that South Africa should revise the traditional position of the National Party in both its foreign and its home policy in order for nonaligned countries like India to put aside neutrality and join the right camp.

Nobody listened to the not-disinterested call of Downing Street. The government of South Africa was not willing to set any example of multiracial inclusivity. India was not prepared to take a lesson either from the British neoimperialists, whose axis with the US benefited Pakistan, or from the South African racialists.

Giving the Devil Benefit of Law

On July 1, 1960, five months after Macmillan's speech in Cape Town, Robert Bolt's play *A Man for All Seasons* premiered at the Globe Theatre in London. The play staged the clash between Henry VIII and Sir Thomas More, leading to the beheading of the former chancellor and future Roman Catholic saint. The West End audience was transported back to the birth of the Church of England, independent from Rome and under the absolute power of the sovereign, and to the dispute over Henry's divorce. More emerged in his full capacity as the martyr of the ultimate allegiance to conscience, guilty of defending the principle that divorce should be in the hands of the pope, with the Church standing independent from the state.

The dialogue between Chancellor Cardinal Wolsey, seeking to secure the divorce by any means, and Thomas More, adamant about the pope's indisputable right to decide the matter, epitomized the clash between politics and morals, between state reasons and the reasons of conscience. Such a clash proved as essential in the 1530s as in 1960. Cardinal Wolsey rebukes More for his lack of common sense and his "horrible moral squint."[84] The king needs the male heir the queen is unable to bear him. There are no grounds for objection. Reality is simple. But More refuses to see the facts as Wolsey would want him to. The cardinal reproaches him, "If you could just see facts flat on, without that horrible moral squint; with just a little common sense."[85]

Thomas More is concerned with the law. Chancellor Wolsey is concerned with securing the King's descent. Catherine is the legitimate wife, More insists. But she is

---

82. Ibid.

83. Ibid.

84. Bolt, *A Man for All Seasons*. 10.

85. Ibid.

"barren as a brick,"[86] Wolsey replies. "Are you going to pray for a miracle?"[87] he erupts. With irony Thomas More observes, "There are precedents."[88]

Two different worlds are face-to-face:

> Wolsey: Yes. All right. Good. Pray. Pray by all means. But in addition to Prayer there is Effort. My effort's to secure a divorce. Have I your support or have I not?
>
> More: A dispensation was granted so that the King might marry Queen Catherine, for State reasons. Now we are to ask the Pope to—dispense with his dispensation, also for State reasons?
>
> Wolsey: I don't *like* plodding, Thomas—don't make me plod longer than I have to. Well?
>
> More: Then clearly all we have to do is approach His Holiness and ask him.[89]

Bolt's was not a play on church-and-state relationships; the author was not interested in defending Roman Catholicism or the sovereignty of the pope. Agnostic, socialist Robert Bolt gave voice to the increasing portion of British society that was abashed at the deterioration of public morality and felt that social conservatism and the authority of the state in private matters like abortion and homosexuality should be challenged in the name of individual conscience. When Bolt wrote of King Henry VIII that "only the levity with which he handles his absolute power foreshadows his future corruption,"[90] the hint to the ruling Tories of the Macmillan years was obvious; when he said of Thomas More that "the life of the mind in him is so abundant and debonair that it illuminates the body,"[91] the playwright yearned for a generation of liberators in the name of conscience, the task of whom would be to institute private moral freedom and public social justice.

In the play, Thomas More is made as righteous and principled as the rest of the surrounding world is conventional and cynical. Cardinal Wolsey, the prelate turned chancellor, is thus described by Bolt as follows: "An almost megalomaniac ambition unhappily matched by an excelling intellect, he now inhabits a lonely den of self-indulgence and contempt."[92] The duke of Norfolk was characterized by "rigid adherence to the minimal code of conventional duty."[93] Thomas Cromwell's face did not express "inner tension, but the tremendous outgoing will of the renaissance;"[94] his

86. Ibid., 11.
87. Ibid.
88. Ibid.
89. Ibid., 11–12.
90. Ibid., 26.
91. Ibid., 2.
92. Ibid., 10.
93. Ibid., 4.
94. Ibid., 13.

"self-conceit"[95] could "cradle gross crimes in the name of effective action."[96] The honest individual morals of More and the absolutist politics of his rivals could not be more vividly juxtaposed.

During the Cold War, religion was used by capitalists to affirm that God has blessed the free market and its social inequalities, and by communists to put their faith higher than any other. But in Bolt's play, a different kind of religion is followed. This was the religion of the individual, in which conscience opposes conformity and customs; this was the postmodern, liberated religion of the future, as opposed to the Machiavellian religion of the past.

History consecrated Thomas More as the saint, the pious Catholic and the truly faithful. Robert Bolt and the audience of the West End rather valued More's devotion to conscience and to the distinction between man's law and God's law. Throughout the theatrical action, More's attitude toward conscience is the mirror of British society in the early sixties and the anticipation of postmodern Britain. When More refuses to take the oath supporting the supremacy of the king over the Church of England, as well as the divorce from Queen Catherine, alleging respect to his own soul, Chancellor Thomas Cromwell blames him for confusing the soul and the self. "Yes,"[97] More then proclaims, "a man's soul is his self!"[98] And when Cromwell accuses More of being "a shrill incessant pedagogue about its own salvation,"[99] but with "nothing to say of your place in the State,"[100] More's protest announces the revolution of the sixties:

> Is it my place to say good to the State's sickness? Can I help my King by giving him lies when he asks for truth? Will you help England by populating her with liars?[101]

Bolt's More was not an anarchist. He claimed himself the staunchest, most faithful servant of the Church and the most loyal subject of the Crown. But he also was perfectly in tune with a time when the *I* was to be exalted. As he says to his friend the Duke of Norfolk,

> what matters to me is not whether [the Apostolic Succession of the Pope] is true or not, but that I believe it to be true, or rather, not that I *believe* it, but that *I* believe it.[102]

And to his beloved daughter:

95. Ibid.
96. Ibid.
97. Ibid., 83.
98. Ibid.
99. Ibid.
100. Ibid.
101. Ibid.
102. Ibid., 49.

When a man takes an oath, Meg, he's holding his own self in his own hands. (*He shows her, cupping his hands*) Like water. And if he opens his fingers then—he needn't hope to find himself again. Some men aren't capable of this, but I'd be loath to think your father one of them.[103]

Such exaltation of the individual conscience was not meant to make an ascetic purist of Bolt's More. More was a lawyer, and a refined one at that. Bolt's Britain badly needed a reflection on the role of law in a changing society.

In the play, two answers were provided: the first stressed the fundamental distinction between man's law and God's law; the second regarded the law as the "causeway" that keeps a man free from the abuse of the state.

More discusses the link between man's law and God's law with his son-in-law, William Roper, an admirer of Luther and a harsh critic of the corruption of both the church and the monarchy. When William urges him to arrest Richard Rich (the traitor and perjurer who will ultimately condemn More to the scaffold) on the grounds that Rich is a "bad" man, More replies:

> More: There is no law against that.
>
> Roper: There is! God's law!
>
> More: Then God can arrest him.
>
> Roper: Sophistication upon sophistication!
>
> More: No, sheer simplicity. The law, Roper, the law. I know what's legal not what's right. And I'll stick to what's legal.
>
> Roper: Then you set Man's law above God's!
>
> More: No, far below; but let me draw your attention to a fact—I'm *not* God. The currents and eddies of right and wrong, which you find such plain-sailing, I can't navigate. I'm no voyager. But in the thickets of the law, oh, there I'm a forester. I doubt if there's a man alive who could follow me there, thank God.[104]

Quite a strange Catholic saint, this Thomas More of 1960, who knew not "what's right"—certainly not the same More canonized by the pope in 1935, only two years after the Catholic Church's Concordat with Hitler. In the play, Roper seems as peeved at his father-in-law's exaltation of man's law as the pope who canonized the true Thomas More would have been:

> Roper: So now you'd give the Devil benefit of law!
>
> More: Yes. What would you do? Cut a great road through the law to get after the Devil?
>
> Roper: I'd cut down every law in England to do that.

103. Ibid., 76.

104. Ibid., 36.

> More: Oh? And when the last law was down—and the Devil turned round on you—where would you hide, Roper, the laws all being flat? This country's planted thick with laws from coast to coast—Man's laws, not God's—and if you cut them down—and you're just the man to do it—d'you really think you could stand upright in the winds that would blow then? Yes, I'd give the Devil benefit of law, for my own safety's sake.[105]

This Thomas More, famously brought to the stage by Paul Scofield in the Summer of 1960, represented a specimen of believer who would flourish in British society and beyond in the following years. The many who would share More's struggle as interpreted by Robert Bolt would not react to secularization by getting rid of religion. Indeed, they would badly want religion, a deep, uncompromising religion, rooted in the individual conscience and commanding private and public liberation. These believers of the sixties would praise the conscience above all, and use the law not to reflect the image of God, but to resist the authority of the state and bring about further social justice. These believers would prepare the ground for the social and conscientious struggle of Sushmita Ghosh, Gareth Prince, and Shabina Begum a few decades later.

Far from the perfect architecture of God's law, man's law would be the imperfect realm of human autonomy and heroism. Until the end, Thomas More hides behind his legal skills, "in the thickets of the law,"[106] making his silence the famous symbol of extreme resistance to the absolute will of the tyrant. Only a rigged trial would outdo him. And then, with the capital sentence proclaimed, Robert Bolt put in More's mouth the words of human dignity and freedom, of respect towards God and reverence towards the conscience:

> Cromwell: I put it to the court that the prisoner is perverting the law—making smoky what should be a clear light to discover to the court his own wrongdoing!
>
> More: The law is not a "light," for you or any man to see by; the law is not an instrument of any kind. The law is a causeway upon which so long as he keeps to it a citizen may walk safely. In matters of conscience . . .
>
> Cromwell: The conscience, the conscience . . .
>
> More: The word is not familiar to you?
>
> Cromwell: By God, too familiar! I am very used to hear it in the mouths of criminals!
>
> More: I am used to hear bad men misuse the name of God, yet God exists. In matters of conscience, the loyal subject is more bounden to be loyal *to* his conscience than any other thing.[107]

105. Ibid., 37.
106. Ibid., 36.
107. Ibid., 83.

After More's execution, the "common man," the character in charge of the last words of the play, delivers the ultimate message of the time. "It isn't difficult to keep alive, friends,"[108] he says, "just don't *make* trouble—or if you must make trouble, make the sort of trouble that's expected."[109] With growing numbers of admirers of Thomas More around, this would indeed be a time of unexpected troubles.

Britons on Holiday

In 1960, while West End audiences received Bolt's Thomas More with passion, Alex Boraine was a freshly appointed twenty-nine-year-old Methodist minister who planned to leave South Africa and go to Oxford with the aim of refining his theology. Then the Sharpeville Massacre and the ensuing turmoil made him consider canceling the trip. With the African National Congress banned and Prime Minister Hendrik Verwoerd suffering an assassination attempt, the country was boiling. The sight of thousands of protesting blacks parading down West Street in Durban shocked Boraine.

In the end, the future protagonist of the anti-apartheid struggle and vice chair of the Truth and Reconciliation Commission resolved to go. The decision changed Boraine's life. At Oxford he matured his conversion into advocacy of the anti-apartheid struggle. "Gazing at my country from a distance," he later wrote, "was a transforming experience":[110]

> I realised as never before that our racist policies were totally wrong and evil. The feelings I had about loving God and loving one's neighbour had crystallised. Seth Mokotimi's words became my reality: how could you possibly say you loved God, when you were treating the vast majority of people like third-class citizens?[111]

Challenging academic discussions in Oxford and the ebullient early sixties in England served to open Boraine's eyes. The blindness of Britons for apartheid in South Africa also contributed to his awareness:

> I tried to warn people in England that they should be far tougher on South Africa and its policies rather than simply going along with them. Trade between the two countries was highly developed and many people from Britain went to South Africa on holiday. They didn't see the townships; they didn't see what apartheid was doing to so many people. They simply enjoyed the climate and the people they came in contact with, the fine hotels, good roads and infrastructure.[112]

108. Ibid., 89.
109. Ibid.
110. Boraine, *A Life in Transition*, 43.
111. Ibid.
112. Ibid.

While Britons enjoyed the fine hotels and nice weather of South Africa, the South African coast featured as one of the ideal locations for the quickly developing Indian cinema. But contrary to Downing Street, New Delhi was growing increasingly critical of apartheid and started pushing the Commonwealth to take a stance against the policy of Pretoria.

The early sixties marked a turning point in the relationships between Britain, India, and South Africa.

In October 1960, an all-white referendum determined that South Africa would be a Republic, ousting the Queen as the head of state, and thus threatening the ties with Britain and the Commonwealth. In March 1961, the prime ministers of the Commonwealth countries met at Lancaster House in London. The impression left by the Sharpeville killings was still strong and some kind of action against the prosegregation and murderous government of South Africa seemed inevitable. Nobody wanted to undermine the unity of the Commonwealth. Especially not Macmillan, for whom the organization represented Britain's last chance to remain a global player; nor Nehru, who saw in the Commonwealth an opportunity for his policies of nonalignment. Nehru joined in the Canadian proposal to issue a simple communiqué urging South Africa to relinquish race segregation. South African Prime Minister Verwoerd staunchly opposed the initiative and proved uncompromising over the full right of South Africa to pursue its policy of apartheid. After a final private conversation with Macmillan on Wednesday night, March 15, 1961, Verwoerd came back to the green baize table with a statement in his hand, reading that the Union of South Africa would withdraw from the British Commonwealth to become the independent Republic of South Africa.

Two days later, before flying back to South Africa, Verwoerd unfolded his decision in an address to the South African Club in London. He reported that the Afro-Asian countries had threatened to adopt a joint resolution condemning South Africa for its policy of "separate development." For those countries the multiracial character of the Commonwealth, "should not only be respected in the relationships between nations, as is done by all of us, South Africa included, but . . . must apply to the internal policies of constituent members as well."[113] This, Verwoerd explained to his audience, "would have to apply in such a way that full integration could be the only form which would do justice to such a principle."[114] Under such conditions, he claimed, "the disappearance of the rights of the white man and of the minority coloured groups in South Africa"[115] would be inevitable; hence the dramatic conclusion: he "could not accept this for South Africa."[116]

Verwoerd's speech confirmed what Alex Boraine had realized at Oxford. White South Africans and the British had a problem with the reality of apartheid. Involuntarily

113. Verwoerd, "Address to the South African Club in London."
114. Ibid.
115. Ibid.
116. Ibid.

echoing Boraine's comment about Britons on holiday in exotic and orderly South Africa, Verwoerd opened his address in London by calling forth the "beauty of the South African scenery,"[117] the white beaches, the vineyards and orchards, "the giraffe and the elephant."[118] Moreover, not only did the prime minister deny the actual social failure of South Africa, but he also reversed it into the myth of the land of opportunities and achievements. Verwoerd went as far as to blame envious nations, like India, for falling behind "the achievements of South Africa . . . with regard to her Bantu."[119]

Finally, Verwoerd warned Britain of the dangers ahead. One global "multi-racial state"[120] would undermine the position of the whites, and the strength of the United Kingdom itself. Rather, India would rule through its multitudes of non-Europeans:

> Would anybody in the United Kingdom accept as his ideal for the Commonwealth that it should became one state with one central government, controlled solely by numbers and not by the merit of your country as leader state, smaller in numbers but great in experience and knowledge?
>
> That one multi-racial state, including the province which Great Britain would then be, would of necessity be governed from India under the majority control of those hundreds and hundreds of millions of non-Europeans concentrated there, bolstered by others scattered over the earth.[121]

"Of course you thrust this aside as nonsense,"[122] Verwoerd concluded, seeking the complicity of the white audience. He further pleaded for his government's policies:

> Why must South Africa accept just that for herself in a smaller way? We prefer each of our population groups to be controlled and governed by themselves, as nations are. Then they can co-operate as in a Commonwealth or in an economic association of nations where necessary.
>
> Where is the evil in this?[123]

The right of South Africa to "separate development," and the right of Pretoria to impose apartheid, Verwoerd hinted, were the same right of Great Britain not to be ruled one day by the multitudes of African blacks and Indians. Feelings in Britain were mixed. The link with South Africa was too strong to let the crisis be pushed too far. But apartheid was impossible to swallow, and will of the multiracialist majority of the Commonwealth, including India, could not be ignored.

Two months later, on May 31, 1961, the Republic of South Africa was declared and Queen Elizabeth ceased to be the head of state of South Africa. Unlike in India,

117. Ibid.
118. Ibid.
119. Ibid.
120. Ibid.
121. Ibid.
122. Ibid.
123. Ibid.

the transformation of South Africa into a Republic coincided with the end of its Commonwealth membership.

Not only Nehru himself, but also the British press and intellectuals welcomed the isolation and "expulsion" of South Africa from the Commonwealth as the natural consequence of apartheid and the government's refusal to accept a multiracial society. Britons were now facing the challenges of multiracialism at home, with immigration resented as a mounting problem. In 2000, political scientist and historian Randall Hansen published a thorough analysis of immigration to Britain. He threw particular light on the end, in the early sixties, of the policy of "exceptional liberality and expansiveness"[124] practiced since 1948, thanks to which, according to Hansen's calculation, eight hundred million individuals had "enjoyed the right to enter the UK."[125] This was reversed on April 18, 1962, when the Tory government enacted the Commonwealth Immigrants Act, imposing, for the first time, severe restrictions on the admittance of immigrants to Britain. Labour leader Hugh Gaitskell stigmatized the act as a piece of "cruel and brutal anti-colour legislation."[126] Tories and Labour alike offered antiracial politics, but social anxiety over immigrants escalated, ultimately provoking, in 1968, Enoch Powell's "Rivers of Blood" speech, in which the end of Britain was prophesied as the result of barbarous immigration. When they took over in 1964, the Labour Party could tender anti-racism measures, but could not enforce a U-turn on restrictions to immigration. In 1962 the age of the free entry policy was closed forever.

It's a Miracle

During the sixties the popular perception of the colonial past was reshaped in Britain. In 1963, two British films encapsulated the mixed feelings for a colonialism characterized by glory and oppression, heroism and violence.

The first, *Nine Hours to Rama*, depicted the murder of Gandhi; the second, *Zulu*, restaged the famous resistance of a British company against a Zulu army at Rorke's Drift in 1879 during the Anglo-Zulu wars.

Nine Hours to Rama was a fictionalized account of the last nine hours of Nathuram Godse before his lethal assault on Gandhi at Birla House. Stanley Wolpert, the American author of the novel of the same name on which the film is based, was a marine engineer who, on his first visit to India, immediately after Gandhi's funeral, saw the immersion of Gandhi's ashes in Bombay's Back Bay. He was so shaken by the "multitude of grieving mourners"[127] of the Mahatma that he devoted himself to the study of Indian history, subsequently becoming a prominent scholar and one of the foremost experts on Anglo-Indian relationships. Forty years later, when Randall

124. Hansen, *Citizenship and Immigration in Post-war Britain*, v.
125. Ibid.
126. Pearce and Stewart, *British Political History*, 483.
127. Srinivasan, "Interview to Stanley Wolpert."

Hansen's history of immigration to Britain was printed, Wolpert published a seminal biography of Gandhi and then in 2006, *Shameful Flight*, a book stressing the heavy responsibility of the British government in the tragic events of partition.

When he published *Nine Hours to Rama* in 1962, the thirty-five-year-old Wolpert reopened the wound of Gandhi's murder at the very moment of India's defeat in the war against China. The Indian government banned first the book, then the film, presented in 1963.

Mark Robson, the Canadian-born director of the film adaptation, was known for his 1949 *Home of the Brave*, one of the first American films to deal with racism. But with *Nine Hours to Rama*, he failed to go beyond conventions. Gandhi's holiness, the popular reverence of the great man, the Hindu sect plotting to murder the Mahatma, the madness of Partition's bloodshed, the helpless effort of the secular police officer who despised the astrologists and yet used them in his manhunt, all such ingredients adhered closely to the Anglo-Saxon stereotype. The character of Nathuram Godse was himself a concession to Hollywood; the murderer was presented as a lunatic conservative, shocked by the rape and assassination suffered by his child wife. The fictional love story between Godse and a sophisticated, modern, and already engaged Indian lady gratified the Western convention of contradictory Indians. Clearly, no attention had been paid to the rich Indian cinema, with masterpieces like *Mother India* of 1957 and *Jis Desh Men Ganga Behti Hai* of 1960.

With white actors in brownface playing the roles of all the main Indian characters except Gandhi himself, the film fell well within the established tradition of de-contextualized, colonial movies. For decades, American movies had done the same with American Indians. Berliner Horst Buchholz played an improbable Nathuram Godse, while Californian Diane Baker was an imperceptibly Indian Sheila. This was all very colonial. And yet, the colonialist viewpoint coexisted at times with a new kind of illustration of the Indian context. Like the sixties themselves, the film was solidly rooted in the imperial age but also announced a post-colonial era.

Though *Nine Hours to Rama* was deeply Anglo-Saxon in the making, it nevertheless focused on the history of India as an independent nation. But in *Zulu*, the other British film shot in 1963, the focus was Britain itself, its imperial myth and the colonial relationship with South Africa. Filmed partly in Natal, nearly two years after the departure of the Republic of South Africa from the Commonwealth, *Zulu* represented the clash between the three actors of the South African wars: the British, the Zulu, and the Boers, though the Boers were somehow on the margin. The very fact that the film had been made possible—and its historically untrue final tribute of the defeated Zulus to the victorious Britons assisted by the hero Boer—expressed the rhetoric of a war finished long ago and replaced in present times by collaboration in filmmaking and beyond. The production credited the South African army. Credit was also given to Mangosuthu Buthelezi who was the actual leader of the Zulus. Buthelezi played the role of his own maternal great-grandfather, the Zulu king Cetshwayo. Of course, the

British shooting of native troops who left the station before the clash did not figure in the film. Neither did the killing by the British of hundreds of wounded Africans after the battle.

Indeed, film historian Sheldon Hall underlines that the conjunction of three factors made box-office success of the film possible: an American company eager to follow the pattern of investment on British-based productions of international scope, the South African government's favor, and "the British public's appetite for imperial nostalgia, coupled with its acceptance of a more sceptical, a more questioning attitude to the colonial past than had hitherto prevailed in popular cinema."[128]

In tune with an age of heavy Americanization of both Britain and South Africa, the model for the film was the American western. The American director Cy Endfield, had moved to Britain in 1951, escaping the censorship he had incurred in the US after being blacklisted as a communist. To the seven hundred Zulu extras who had never seen a film before, Endfield showed a western, from which they were expected to learn how to perform. As Michael Caine, then in his first major role, would recall later, the director

> set up a screen and a sixteen-millimetre projector and they [the Zulu extras] all gathered to watch and see what they were supposed to be doing. The film was an old Roy Roger's [sic] western, and when it first came on there was a gasp from everybody at the wonder of it. As the film progressed they quickly settled down and almost immediately started jeering at anything that looked ridiculous and shouting lines in Zulu that I am sure were "Look out! He's behind you!" when the villain crept up on Roy . . . The biggest laugh came when Roy sang as he rode along. They obviously could not understand why a man would want to sing riding a horse alone on a prairie and were puzzled about where the music was coming from. But after ten minutes they figured it out and their reaction was the same as anyone else's would have been.[129]

If the "communist" director Cy Endfield, who exported westerns to Britain and South Africa, was a living witness of the Cold War mindset, the derogatory representation of the missionary Reverend Witt, the stubborn pacifist compromising with the enemy, and the strenuous military resistance and heroism of the British regiment were metaphors of the anticommunist hardliners' vision at the time of Cold War.

When it was transformed into a supply depot and a hospital, Rorke's Drift was a mission station run by Reverend Witt, a Swedish missionary. In the film, Witt is depicted as a drunk and a cowardly pacifist who attempts to undermine the morale of the defendants in the moments preceding the assault by the overwhelming Zulu forces. The missionary succeeds in making the native troops escape and tries hard to push the regular soldiers to leave as well. Over and over he repeats that killing is against the will of

128. Hall, *Zulu*, 377–78.
129. Caine, *What's It All About?*, 148.

God and that they will all die. "You have made a covenant with death, and with hell you are in agreement,"[130] his anathema resounds. Joining forces with her father, the daughter of the missionary challenges the intrepid commander, who is ready to fight in the extreme. "Are you a Christian?"[131] she asks him. In fact, the true Reverend Witt had not opposed the transformation of the mission into a military base and actively supported the British expansion into the territory of the Zulu. In addition, he collaborated with the chaplain of the Regiment, a character omitted in the film. In a time when religion was meant to support the free man's struggle against the communists, the alliance of religion and pacifism was stigmatized. This was not the conscientious and nonviolent religion of Bolt's Thomas More or of Alex Boraine's theology at Oxford. This was the imperial religion of the erstwhile colonial power, now reviving and transforming into the cold religion of the anticommunist defender of the Western free world. In order for the concept to emerge in *Zulu*, the negative religion of the missionary was pitted against the positive religion of the British army, made of courage and abnegation, of strength and cleverness, of patriotism and scientific modernity. In the confrontation between the commander of the post, Lieutenant Chard, played by the star, Stanley Baker, and the missionary, Mr. Witt, two worldviews clashed. On one side, Lieutenant Chard represented the clear-minded distinction between the temporal and the spiritual, on which the wealth of Britain was built; on the other side, Mr. Witt embodied the arrogance of the religious pacifist standing on the wrong side of the river. In *Zulu*, the dialogue between the two characters stages this opposition:

> Mr. Witt: Cetewayo is coming with two impies [regiments] to destroy you . . .
>   I am ready to take away your sick and wounded. Please supply the wagons.
>   Daughter, tell the men to get ready.
>
> Lieutenant Chard: One moment . . . Mr. Witt? I don't suppose you hold the
>   Queen's commission.
>
> Mr. Witt: I'm a man of peace, sir.
>
> Lieutenant Chard: Allow a Queen's officer to give orders to her soldiers. Now,
>   how do you know what Cetewayo is doing?
>
> Mr. Witt: We have just come from his kraal. He's a member of my parish.
>
> Lieutenant Chard: Your parish? Are you sure you're on the right side of the
>   river?
>
> Mr. Witt: I am here to do my duty. I expect your cooperation.[132]

At the Lieutenant's resolve to stay and fight, a clash becomes inevitable:

> Mr. Witt: Sir, the book says, "There is no king that can be saved by the multi-
>   tude of a host . . ."

130. Transcript by the author of audio from Endfield, *Zulu*.
131. Ibid.
132. Ibid.

> Lieutenant Chard: Mr. Witt? When I have the impertinence to climb into your
> pulpit and deliver a sermon, then you may tell me my duty.[133]

After the battle, the famous exchange between Color-Sergeant Bourne and Lieutenant Chard celebrates Western, secularized, religion, and the marriage between this religion and the Victorian imperial gods:

> CS Bourne: Mr. Chard, Sir! Patrol has come back, Zulus have gone, all of 'em.
> It's a miracle!
>
> Lieutenant Chard: If it's a miracle Colour Sergeant, it's a short chamber Boxer
> Henry, point 4–5 calibre miracle.
>
> CS Bourne: And a bayonet, Sir! With some guts behind it![134]

Such a miracle of technology and resolve also encapsulated one more kind of cold god. This was the god of the socialist scientific revolution, as championed by Labour in Britain and, to some extent, by Nehruvian India. A perfect illustration was given on October 1, 1963, the eve of the release of *Zulu*, when Harold Wilson gave a famous speech presenting British socialism as a "scientific revolution" meant to permeate the "whole system of society:"

> In all our plans for the future, we are re-defining and we are re-stating our Socialism in terms of the scientific revolution. But that revolution cannot become a reality unless we are prepared to make far-reaching changes in economic and social attitudes, which permeate our whole system of society. The Britain that is going to be forged in the white heat of this revolution will be no place for restrictive practices or for outdated methods on either side of industry.[135]

However glorious the imperial past, and however promising the socialist future, the British still struggled with their new place in the world. Like those Britons on holidays in South Africa to whom Alex Boraine wished to explain the harsh reality of the country, Michael Caine and the others "had no preconceived notions about . . . politics of racial policy."[136] The brutality of the Afrikaner foremen taught the cast and crew of *Zulu* what apartheid was about: when a black worker made a mistake, an astonished Caine witnessed, "the foreman didn't reprimand him; he smashed a fist into his face instead."[137] Further evidence came with the troubles met by a white workman. An ordinary Cockney from London, the man "went native" and fraternized with the black extras. He was eventually accused of interracial sex, a crime punishable with seven years hard labor. In his memoir, *What's It All About?*, published in 1992 during the transition to postapartheid South Africa, Caine recalled the disturbing experience of 1963:

133. Ibid.
134. Ibid.
135. Wilson, "Speech at Labour Party Conference," 139–40.
136. Caine, *What's It All About?*, 153.
137. Ibid.

The helicopters landed and several policemen got out. The leader demanded to know who was in charge. Stanley [Stanley Baker, the star of the film] stepped forward. Apparently, our Cockney had gone a little more native than we all thought. He had moved out of the hotel into a mud hut, and had taken with him three Zulu wives. The policeman told Stanley that the man was under arrest. Later on we realized that one of our white Afrikaans foremen was in fact a police spy, placed with us for exactly this purpose. Worst of all, the policeman told Stanley that the production was closed down and we would have to leave the country. Stanley went to work on him immediately, and after much argument they made a deal: the unit could stay, provided that Stanley guaranteed to get the criminal out of the country by midnight.[138]

Here was a lesson for Caine and the others to learn: "Now I realized that apartheid was not a personal prejudice but a government-sponsored form of civil terrorism. I vowed there and then never to return to that country until they changed the system, and to this day, I haven't."[139]

Contrary to what the film seemingly entailed, the conflict between the Afrikaner, the British, and the blacks in South Africa was not solved. Reality was different, not only for the cast and crew of *Zulu*. Opposition to apartheid was growing; in response, repression was increasingly wild. During the making of the film, Nelson Mandela was serving his second year in prison, following his arrest in 1962. On October 15, 1963, Albie Sachs was arrested. When *Zulu* was released in 1964, the future constitutional judge was still in solitary confinement. At the premiere in South Africa, the Zulu extras who had taken part in the film were not allowed in the white-only theater where the projection took place. The South African minister of the interior explained that such a film could not be made accessible "to a race that has not yet reached the level of civilization that we have reached."[140] Certain films, the minister further maintained, "can be exhibited more safely to a white child of fourteen years than to an adult Bantu."[141]

By that time, Alex Boraine was in the US to pursue his studies. In England he had realized that a new theology and a new Christianity were on the move. In the United States, he experienced how such a liberating version of religion could transform society: Jesus Christ, he felt, "was no longer a prisoner of the written word, no longer confined to Nazareth, I encountered him in my neighbour."[142]

On August 28, 1963, Boraine found himself among the over two hundred thousand people in Washington DC who witnessed Martin Luther King's "I Have a Dream" speech: "It affected me deeply," he later recalled, "and I began to see what was happening

---

138. Ibid., 154.

139. Ibid.

140. Hall, *Zulu*, 267.

141. Ibid.

142. Boraine, *A Life in Transition*, 48.

in America, through a South African lens."[143] The American public somehow did the same thing, when the film *Zulu* was released in the States in the crucial summer of 1964, just before the adoption of the US Civil Rights Act. On July 8, 1964, Bosley Crowther attacked in the *New York Times* this "strangely archaic and indiscreet"[144] movie. Not that the formula of the memorable frontier film was not well interpreted. The point was rather the context, the spirit of the time. "The question," Crowther wrote,

> is whether such a picture, coming at this time, with tensions and discords so prevalent, is discreet or desirable. Is it a contribution to the cause of harmony to show so much vicious acrimony between black men and white, to wallow in blood-spurting slaughter, to make an exciting thing of firing rifles into the faces of charging warriors and sticking bayonets into them? And is the ideal of the white man's burden, which this picture tacitly presents (for all its terminal disgust with the slaughter), in the contemporary spirit?[145]

Rivonia Trial

On July 20, 1963, the South African police raided a farm at Rivonia, near Johannesburg. The people arrested were put on trial together with the already-detained Nelson Mandela; the group was accused of being the high command of the armed wing of the African National Congress. The state accused Mandela and the others of fighting apartheid under the influence of international communism.

According to *New York Times* critic Bosley Crowther, the film *Zulu* presented the African warriors as "wild, audacious, and remarkably easy to kill."[146] Mandela and his partners were certainly as audacious as the African warriors in the film, but the Rivonia trial would prove they were not so "easy to kill."

On April 20, 1964, at the opening of the trial in Pretoria before the Supreme Court of South Africa, Mandela took his own defense and gave a memorable speech from the dock. Against the Cold-War pattern and the Christians-vs.-Communists schemata, he stressed the authenticity of his African background and motivation. No external inspiration moved him. The antiracist fight was not commanded by any external force—namely, not by international communism—conspiring against the country. This was a genuine African struggle:

> I have done whatever I did, both as an individual and as a leader of my people, because of my experience in South Africa and my own proudly felt African background, and not because of what any outsider might have said. In my youth in the Transkei, I listened to the elders of my tribe telling stories of the

143. Ibid., 49.
144. Crowther, "It's British vs. Natives in Action-Filled 'Zulu,'" 38.
145. Ibid.
146 Ibid.

old days. Amongst the tales they related to me were those of wars fought by our ancestors in defence of the fatherland. The names of Dingane and Bambata, Hintsa and Makana, Squngthi and Dalasile, Moshoeshoe and Sekhukhuni, were praised as the glory of the entire African nation. I hoped then that life might offer me the opportunity to serve my people and make my own humble contribution to their freedom struggle. This is what has motivated me in all that I have done in relation to the charges made against me in this case.[147]

In the context of decolonization, opposition to apartheid was driven by the momentous international rise of racial justice, which Alex Boraine was witnessing in the United States. Mandela was aware that he risked being seen as a mere local executor of strategies devised by others. In response, he claimed from the dock that he was not the puppet of international communism: he was a true African leader. His resistance to the court equaled his ancestors' resistance to white colonists and imperialists.

By the midsixties, as the local and the international blended, identities were mobilized. The pure and distinctive Afrikaner identity was advocated to support the cause of apartheid, white supremacy, and racial segregation, against international communism. In turn, pure and distinctive African descent was mobilized against neocolonialism and imperialism. Appropriating the "fatherland" was crucial to success. Yet the "fatherland" had lost its purity long before. Purity was advocated from all sides, but no side was pure. The Afrikaners and the "Hottentots," the British and the Zulu, the "Bantu" and the "Kafir," the Colored, the Indians, and the Chinese, all possible original characters and identities had been, at the same time, mixed up and sealed. Wars had divided, but also united. Communities had more or less effectively resisted contamination, assimilation, and annihilation. As historian Leonard Thompson noticed, novelists like Es'kia Mphahlele and Mongane Serote pointed out that the resistance of Africans to the horror of apartheid policies depended on their ability to mingle across ethnic lines, regardless of governmental measures aiming at fostering ethnic divisions. New generations, Thompson wrote, started identifying themselves "as Africans (or even, comprehensively, as Blacks, thus including Coloreds and Indians) rather than as Xhosa, Zulu, Sotho, Pedi, or Tswana."[148]

The writer Alan Paton, a prominent Christian, accepted the invitation to give evidence at the trial in favor of Mandela and the other accused members of the African National Congress. A close friend of Archbishop Clayton, and the future author of the archbishop's biography, Paton was chosen by Mandela's defense team, as lawyer Joel Joffe later wrote, because of "his reputation as a reformer and liberal thinker . . . both inside and outside the country,"[149] and also because "he could not be accused of being a communist, concealed or otherwise."[150] Paton pleaded for clemency in the name of

---

147. Mandela, *The Struggle Is My Life*, 155.

148. Thompson, *A History of South Africa*, 201.

149. Joffe, *The State vs. Nelson Mandela*, 228.

150. Ibid.

the genuine desire of the accused "to see that South Africa became a country in which all people participate."[151] Christian racists accused Mandela of being a communist; a liberal Christian was called upon to neutralize the attack. The two cold gods—on the one hand the anticommunist, Western-centered, and on the other the progressive, liberationist, and anticolonialist—clashed many times during the Rivonia trial. When prosecutor Percy Yutar urged the accused Ahmed Kathrada to stay true to the oath and give evidence, and Kathrada replied that he was "honour-bond not to,"[152] Yutar tried bringing God into the argument:

> Yutar: Honour-bound to whom?
>
> Kathrada: To my conscience, my political colleagues, to my political organization, to all of whom I owe loyalty.
>
> Yutar: What about being honour bound to the Almighty?
>
> Kathrada: I am not telling any lies.
>
> Yutar: You are not honour-bound to that, are you?
>
> Kathrada: Well I don't know if the police are doing the Almighty's work![153]

Charged with conspiracy to overthrow the government by violent revolution, the accused of 1964 faced the grim prospect of being sentenced to death. Nelson Mandela was qualified to defend himself as a practicing attorney in Johannesburg, and he started the trial with his speech on his African ancestors.

He was not alone. A team of lawyers assisted him, the pillar being Arthur Chaskalson, the future president of the Constitutional Court. Joel Joffe, another lawyer of the defense team, recalled Chaskalson's standing up for the closing speech in June 1964: "Suddenly the court was no longer a forum for third-rate amateur theatrics, but became a court of law."[154]

In any event, mainly thanks to Chaskalson, Nelson Mandela and the other accused, managed to escape the death penalty. Thirty years later, in 1997, the same Chaskalson, in his capacity as the first president of the Constitutional Court of South Africa, would lead the Court to declare capital punishment unconstitutional.

A page was turned: Mandela still had to serve a life sentence, but anti-apartheid lawyers and the judiciary itself, despite its connivance with the system, had scored an important point.

151. Ibid., 249.
152. Ibid., 184.
153. Ibid.
154. Ibid., 237.

Five Cold Gods

By the end of the sixties, five different cold gods had taken a clear shape. Five different, but often overlapping, gods were worshiped.

One was shared by all, beyond the lines of the Cold War. This was the cold God of innovation and modernization, of technology and progress. Everybody venerated this god: old guard Labour Harold Wilson; young Tory MP Margaret Thatcher; Indira Gandhi, succeeding both Nehru, who had died during the Rivonia trial, and her fierce opponent J. P. Narajan; the South African government; as well as the many anti-apartheid strugglers who were trained in the USSR and who dreamt of a Sputnik-like industrial, communist liftoff. The antimodern, village-based, imperial gods of Gandhi were dead. The cold god of modernization was thriving ubiquitously and with unanimous support.

The second cold god was the alliance between faith and liberation, justice and equality. Such a cold god of liberation pushed to fight against oppression, to stand for the poor and the deprived. Believers in this kind of cold god wanted their religious traditions to be challenged. Some, like Indira Gandhi, embraced socialism without jettisoning religion. Many in South Africa or in some parts of India turned towards Christianity for the potential of Jesus as a liberator. Many in Britain looked at a radically new spirituality, coming from the East. For the first time Britons traveled to India, not for trade, exploration, or acquisition, but for a spiritual quest. For the first time, Indians traveled to Britain not as students or laborers but as gurus.

The cold god of liberation was deeply individualistic but also had a popular dimension and a social-reformist agenda. It had much in common with the Marxist struggle for a postcolonial age and with the socialist worldwide effort.

In this sense, the cold god of liberation often overlapped with the third cold god: the god of atheist secularism. The antireligious doctrine of Marxism was widely preached and practiced. In India, hard-liner atheists already featured in the struggle for independence, the brightest example being Bhagat Singh, who, in 1931, before being hanged for sedition, ostentatiously read Lenin instead of mumbling ancient prayers. The Nehrus had deeply imbibed the secularism of the French *philosophes* and of the Spanish republican cause, not to mention the impact on Jawaharlal and Indira of the followers of those British atheists, who had influenced young Gandhi thirty years earlier. But never had the Nehrus and the Congress dismissed religion. Never did they fight creeds or faith. Their secularism consisted rather of the idea that religion should not be exempt from the general push toward modernization, and that faiths ought not to determine politics.

From the sixties onward, the communists of Kerala and West Bengal followed the pattern: their Marxism was about the cause of the deprived and the opposition to the state, but they did not take any specific interest in fighting religion. Even Naxalites did not attack the religious side in the life of people.

In South Africa, many anti-apartheid strugglers embraced atheism, but this remained largely a private fact, also because of their attachment to the traditional religious element in the African culture and the increasing anti-apartheid activism of the churches.

In British society, the atheist God proved stronger, but affected churches more than it did individuals, many of whom remained somehow attached to personal forms of belief. In India, South Africa, and Britain, the cold God of atheism expanded with the spread of socialism and communism, but it did not always coincide with a deliberate antireligious struggle. In fact, the cold God of liberation and the cold God of atheism often overlapped and mutually interacted.

The fourth and the fifth cold gods, the God of religious conservatism and the God of capitalism developed as counterbalances to both the God of liberation and the God of Marxist atheism.

Religious conservatism and fundamentalism grew during the sixties. In Britain, the state-centered vision of socialists was increasingly opposed, as was the liberal action of the left in the private sphere. After the death of Churchill in 1965, a young Margaret Thatcher advanced a vision of Christian conservatism, advocating the liberation of the individual from the state and less indulgent policies affecting private behaviors. In South Africa, the Dutch Reformed Church increasingly applied a fundamentalist reading of the Bible to defend the apartheid system against the threat of unappeased black multitudes. In India, after Nehru's death, the Indo-Pakistani War of 1965 strengthened the pattern of Hindu-Muslim enmity and the opposition between the Muslim state of Pakistan and the secular state of India. After the war, Indian prime minister Lal Bahadur Shastri defined the difference between Pakistan and India in the following terms: "Whereas Pakistan proclaims herself to be an Islamic State and uses religion as a political factor, we Indians have the freedom to follow whatever religion we may choose [and] worship in any way we please."[155] When Indira Gandhi became prime minister, religious groups featured among those who opposed her authoritarian socialism. Sikhs developed a program of regionalism and separatism. Muslims and other minorities feared the secular state would attack their specificities. Hindu politics gained visibility and popular support. On November 6, 1966, one hundred thousand Hindu marchers surrounded Parliament House in New Delhi, calling for a ban on the killing of the sacred cow all over India. Mounted police faced the crowd of *sadhus*—Hindu holy men holding their traditional emblems, "tridents and spears"[156]—and heavy riots ensued. Increasing tensions between conflicting faiths were experienced in the poorest states, where Christian missionaries proved particularly active in their endeavor to convert tribal members. With the Orissa Freedom of Religion Act of 1967, a prohibition was issued preventing anybody from converting or attempting to convert "either directly or otherwise, any person from one religious faith to another

155. Guha, *India after Gandhi*, 401.
156. Ibid., 413.

by the use of force or by inducement or by any fraudulent means." Another Act, the Madhya Pradesh Dharma Swatantrya Adhiniyam of 1968, followed the same lines.[157]

In Britain and South Africa, the fourth cold god, religious conservatism, coincided with the strongest advocacy of capitalism, the free market, and consumerism. Indeed, this was a distinctive fifth God, which could also be embraced and supported by non-Christians and more generally by nonreligious people. The worship of capitalism was indeed widespread on the Western side of the bipolar world, together with the correspondent worship of anticommunism. In fact, capitalists who wanted a morally conservative society, and leftists who advocated moral liberation but opposed capitalism, both contributed to building the success of unrestrained consumerism and free morals. Britain distinguished itself as the example of an increasingly free society, resorting to massive shopping with the blessing, deliberate or involuntary, of free marketers and statists alike.

Five gods featured in the polytheist era of Cold War: the God of science, the God of liberation, the God of Marxist atheism, the God of religious conservatism, and the God of capitalism. They personified five distinct deities, but they also intermingled and overlapped.

No One Was Saved

The sixties in Britain proved an extraordinary laboratory for the growth of the five cold gods and for their interaction.

The passage from the postwar time to the new Britain of swinging London was encapsulated in the famous Beatles' song "Eleanor Rigby," released in 1966. The loneliness of Eleanor Rigby and Father McKenzie evoked dull, poor postwar England and the old religion of depressive parishes and solitary priests: a world that the youth revolution was wiping away. This Father McKenzie "writing the words of a sermon that no one will hear" was invented to exalt a generation, the words of which had to be heard by everybody. The cold God of social activists and pop consumerists was about a vital and optimistic self, constantly shopping for new rights, new goods, and new experiences. In this sense, Ian Macdonald saw the Beatles' lives and works as "prototype models of post-Christian 'nowness.'"[158] "What mass society unconsciously began in the Sixties,"[159] Macdonald argued, Thatcher and Reagan would have risen to the level of ideology in the eighties: "the complete materialistic individualization—and total fragmentation—of Western society."[160] Hence a "restless sense of urgency headily combined with unprecedented opportunities for individual freedom."[161] Somehow,

---

157. Heredia, *Changing Gods*, 81.

158. Macdonald, *Revolution in the Head*, 21.

159. Ibid., 32.

160. Ibid.

161. Ibid., 30.

the Beatles announced that "once the obsolete Christian compact of the Fifties had broken down, there was nothing—apart from, in the last resort, money—holding Western civilization together."[162] Macdonald concluded:

> Abandoning a Christian world of postponed pleasure for a hungry secularism fed by technological conveniences, [ordinary people] effectively traded a hierarchical social unity in which each "knew his place" for the personal rewards of a modern meritocracy.[163]

The "British invasion," as the worldwide success of British bands during the 1960s came to be known, expressed the potential of this Britain for the construction of a new, completely different, empire. The law was modified accordingly, with Labour chancellor Roy Jenkins playing a key role: abortion was legalized and homosexuality was decriminalized in 1967, theater censorship was abolished in 1968, and a more permissive regulation of divorce was introduced in 1969.

If Eleanor Rigby kept her face "in a jar by the door," thus masking according to Ian MacDonald "the despair inadmissible by English middle-class etiquette,"[164] Roy Jenkins the Welshman believed the average Englishman was too poor an example for new Britain. In a famous speech at the London meeting of the National Committee for Commonwealth Immigrants, on May 23, 1966, Jenkins delivered his vision of a culturally diverse country:

> I do not think that we need in this country a "melting pot," which will turn everybody out in a common mould, as one of a series of carbon copies of someone's misplaced vision of the stereotyped Englishman . . . I define integration, therefore, not as a flattening process of assimilation but as equal opportunity, accompanied by cultural diversity, in an atmosphere of mutual tolerance.[165]

Roy Jenkins explicitly referred to recent arrivals from India and Pakistan and pointed at the opposition between a conservative and a progressive view on immigration: "There are some people, many of them by no means illiberal, who believe that if everybody would only stay at home in their own countries, the world would be a much easier and better place. From this view I firmly dissent. Easier it might conceivably be, but certainly not better or more civilized or innovating."[166]

The loneliness of Eleanor Rigby was not only about the past of austere postwar Britain. There was also something terribly incumbent in it: yes, this new generation was electrified by the social experience of individual liberation and choice, but, the Beatles sensed, that same generation was also somewhat scared that the new super

---

162. Ibid., 32.

163. Ibid., 30.

164. Ibid., 204.

165. Jenkins, "Racial Equality in Britain," 267.

166. Ibid., 268.

individual, saturated with rights and goods, could end up desperately alone. Through the lonely death of Eleanor Rigby in the church, and the terrible closing verdict of the lyric, "no one was saved," the end of old Britain was announced. A hint to the deep uncertainty of new Britain was also present: the country was abandoning the pillars of the past—the local community, the church, parents, traditional morals, and faiths—and was still far from finding a new identity. "McKenzie's sermon won't be heard," Ian Macdonald suggested "because religious faith has perished along with communal spirit."[167]

In 1966, the same year as the release of "Eleanor Rigby" and of Jenkins's endorsement of immigration, Bolt's play about Thomas More was made into a film with Orson Wells superbly playing Cardinal Wolsey and the same Paul Scofield transferring his More from the stage to the screen. The potential of the theatrical text to exalt the liberating religion of the individual was fully developed in the film. The idea that the church must be independent from the state was also stressed. One of Scofield's most impressive moments comes when More "discharges" his mind after the verdict condemning him to death, and proclaims the Christian truth about the independence of the church from the state:

> The indictment is grounded in an Act of Parliament, which is directly repugnant to the Law of God and his Holy Church the supreme government of which no temporal person may, by any law, presume to take upon him. This was granted by the mouth of our Saviour Christ himself to St Peter and the Bishops of Rome whilst he lived and was personally present here on earth. It is therefore insufficient in law to charge any Christian to obey it. And more than this the immunity of the Church is promised both in *Magna Carta* and in the King's own coronation oath.[168]

Interestingly, Bolt's original text of 1960 was shorter than the film script: "The indictment is grounded in an Act of Parliament which is directly repugnant to the Law of God. The King in Parliament cannot bestow the Supremacy of the Church because it is a Spiritual Supremacy! And more to this the immunity of the Church is promised both in Magna Carta and the King's own Coronation Oath."[169]

The Second Vatican Council had just stated, in 1965, that the Catholic Church opted for relationships with the states based on the independence of both subjects and the cooperation between the spiritual and the temporal powers. An increasing number of Roman Catholics believed that secular states were more fit for modernity than Catholic states. In Britain, an independent, self-governed Church was advocated as the best response to a democratic and reformist society. This was no longer a time for clerics to mingle with mundane powers, like Orson Wells's Cardinal Wolsey. The

---

167. Macdonald, *Revolution in the Head*, 204.

168. Transcript by the author from the audio of Zinneman, *A Man for All Seasons*.

169. Bolt, *A Man for All Seasons*, 87.

time called for reformists and dissidents to step in and challenge the old institutions of both the church and the state. The response of English Anglicans was contradictory. They did not relinquish establishment, but they accepted a higher degree of internal democracy. Through the Synodical Government Measure of 1969, the Parliament provided for a more independent and collegial government of the Church of England. By investing priests and the laity with a portion of power, the newly created tricameral Synod limited the House of Bishops and democratized the leadership of the Church. The slogan "episcopally led but synodically governed" was coined to attenuate a momentous reform. In fact, the governance of the Church had been completely changed.

In 1966, finally released after three years in prison, Albie Sachs flew to England and started studying law at the University of Southampton. The icon of imprisonment and liberation met the generation of "Eleanor Rigby" and *A Man for All Seasons*. The same year, Desmond Tutu received his master's degree in theology from King's College London, and the future President Thabo Mbeki—the black gentleman who wore tweed suits, fancied "a pint of bitter,"[170] smoked pipes, and recited English poetry— was granted a master's degree in economics from Sussex University.

That same year, Alex Boraine came back to Durban from the United States. Confronted as he was with the opposition between Christians involved in the civil rights movement and "right-wing Christians, who believed that they were the chosen race and that Negroes, as they were called in the 1960s, were subhuman,"[171] Boraine made his choice. He acknowledged that Martin Luther King Jr.'s was "the authentic voice."[172] He became "a Christian humanist, with far greater emphasis on the need to serve humankind."[173]

In 1968, the Beatles went to India to follow the path of the Maharishi Mahesh Yogi, the most famous sample of those Indians who had successfully sold their spirituality in Britain during the sixties. Did they experience a genuine spiritual quest? Or was their time in Rishikesh just a fraud? And as they undoubtedly came back making different music, was the Indian influence merely superficial, was George Harrison using the sitar without understanding what traditional Indian music was really about, or had something deeper happened? Certainly, a band freshly mixing the Indian and the British sounds had replaced the British band evocated by deputy Hanumanthaiya at the Constituent Assembly in 1949.

All five of the cold gods promoted a clear vision, supplied a cause to stand for— or an enemy to fight against—and promised a better world. They offered individuals and communities a path that might save them. The seventies and the eighties would frustrate the expectations of all sides. International communism and Marxism would suffer a terrible blow, and faith-based social justice would be seriously damaged by

---

170. Gevisser, *Thabo Mbeki*, 183.

171. Boraine, *A Life in Transition*, 47.

172. Ibid.

173. Ibid.

religious fundamentalism and the capitalist breakthrough. Capitalism would apparently prevail, with neoliberalism spreading, but the financial crisis of the nineties would disillusion optimists and speculators. The religious support to free-marketism would also be weakened by increasing globalization, and by a religious Right obsessed with identities and protectionism. The most universally worshiped cold God itself, the God of industrial progress and modernization, would also step aside. "No one was saved," sang the Beatles in "Eleanor Rigby." Nothing was saved of old postwar Britain after the sixties. By the time of Sushmita Ghosh, Gareth Prince, and Shabina Begum, none of the five cold gods that thrived in the sixties had been spared. And yet their echo would resonate in courts when the three cases were heard.

God's Violence

At the end of the sixties, a wave of violence challenged the five cold gods.

In his defense from the dock at the Rivonia trial in 1964, Mandela explained that Gandhi's methods had been the first choice and constant model of the African leaders. Nevertheless, faced with the brutal response of the state, Mandela had been constrained to accept that "fifty years of non-violence had brought the African people nothing but more and more repressive legislation, and fewer and fewer rights."[174] Therefore, Mandela stated, "I, and some colleagues, came to the conclusion that as violence in this country was inevitable, it would be unrealistic and wrong for African leaders to continue preaching peace and non-violence at a time when the Government met our peaceful demands with force."[175]

This, the leader underlined, did not mean that the African National Congress departed from the traditional policy of nonviolence, but simply that it would tolerate specific actions of sabotage under the control of its armed wing, the Umkhonto we Sizwe. As a result, a moral radical and violent opposition to apartheid developed during the sixties.

In 1969, the social conflict in Northern Ireland deteriorated and transformed into a violent clash in which religion and politics blurred. Britain was awakened from the optimistic growth in the economy and the social reforms of the sixties and was reminded of its responsibility in an underdeveloped area with heavy anti-Catholic discrimination in housing, jobs, schooling, and local elections. Inspired by the anti-apartheid struggle in South Africa, Irish civil-rights protesters grew more and more defiant in 1967 and 1968. In August, the Battle of the Bogside in Derry and the riots in Belfast, with seven casualties and hundreds of wounded, started a violent conflict. Only at the end of the nineties would a solution be found. Confronted with the violence of the Protestant loyalists and the Ulster constabulary, British public opinion was deeply impressed. The troops sent by Prime Minister Wilson were meant to protect

174. Mandela, *The Struggle Is My Life*, 159.
175. Ibid., 160.

the Catholic community, but soon they would come to be identified with Protestant oppression. Founded in December that year, the Provisional Army Council of the IRA—the "Provos"—started their war to separate Northern Ireland from Britain, which would deeply affect the life of Britons in the twenty years to come. At the same time, the socialist policies of Indira Gandhi succeeded in the economy, with the green revolution and the nationalization of banks in July 1969, but failed in removing social unrest: the rhetoric of secular India proved powerless when faced with communal hatred. Hindu-Muslim violence raged again all over India and, in particular, in the states of Bihar and Uttar Pradesh. In September 1969, Hindu-Muslim riots exploded in Ahmedabad. During one week of fights, according to the Jaganmohan Reddy Commission of Inquiry, 660 were killed, of which four hundred thirty were Muslims.

Did such widespread troubles derive from the choice to put man's law above God's? After all, secular India, apartheid South Africa, and socialist, permissive Britain had all departed from traditional religion and from the supreme law of God. Hindu, Sikh, and Muslim good social morals were marginalized in India as the result of a pervasive state devoted to the socialist top-down reshaping of society. In South Africa, Christian social justice and African traditions had been sacrificed on the altar of white supremacy, and the Dutch Reformed Church was subservient to the almighty state. British atheists, liberals, and secularized Christians had built an omnivorous and intrusive state while undermining the authority of the family, the church, and the community.

So, was the prevailing law of man during the sixties the origin of unrest? Or was it the other way round? Might the troubles be evidence that religious fanaticism and the manipulation of God's law prevented secular modernity from delivering its goods? God-backed castes and customs were still the main social factor all over India, with the inevitable consequence of oppression and inequalities. South African white supremacists exploited God's law to justify, impose, and tighten the policy of apartheid. Immigrants to Britain could not integrate because their God's law was stronger than the British man's law; the mild but steady belief that their Christian God was with them prevented the Britons from giving up the habits of the colonialist at home and abroad.

For all their oversimplification, both visions were partly right. There were many failures on either side. And there was inspiration too. In many different ways and with different outcomes, man's law and God's law were wrestling in the age of the Cold War. Seemingly with the five cold gods—the God of science, the God of liberation, the God of Marxist atheism, the God of religious conservatism, and the God of capitalism—the law of man had prevailed. Some of these gods even alleged there was no longer room for God in society or religion in the public square. Never before had the death of God seemed so plausible. And yet God had not died. During the seventies, the boundary between right and wrong was redefined. This brought on the stage new believers, new beliefs, and new gods.

Right and Wrong

The cold gods grew increasingly contradictory over the seventies. Indian secular politics mounted spectacularly: limitations on personal Muslim law were first enacted in 1973 and then enforced by the Supreme Court in 1978. In 1976, India was proclaimed a socialist, secular state; in 1977, a substantially Marxist government was formed. Well beyond religion, the big question was how to make a state-controlled economy deliver, while addressing social inequalities. In a country where state policies fell short of impacting real social dynamics, this was a very serious problem. In Britain, too, the main focus was on the economy, with religion looking quite marginal. The same could be said for South Africa, where Marxism inspired the socioeconomic views of freedom fighters, and apartheid was defended in the name of Capitalism.

As politics seemed to veer toward the secular, religion systematically fought back. Indian society remained deeply religious, and religious politics challenged the Congress Party from all sides. In South Africa, the confrontation between proapartheid and anti-apartheid Christians became tenser. Finally, though apparently absent from the political arena, religion kept solid roots in British society.

Indeed, it was increasingly difficult to draw the line between the religious and the secular. The cold gods were blurring that boundary, as they were blurring the traditional boundary between right and wrong.

Demands of Pluralism

Over the seventies, British public life grew increasingly contradictory in matters of religion. Faith seemed to have lost its salience in a profoundly secularized society, and the debate focused predominantly on issues in the economy, with the trade unions and an expanding public sector challenging the Labour and the Tory governments alike. But there was another side of the picture: troubles in Northern Ireland stood as a reminder that appalling conflicts along religious lines were still possible in a secular age; and the rise of Margaret Thatcher showed that the advocacy of convictions deeply rooted in a traditional Christian upbringing made sense in modern times. On top of that, social issues went beyond the economy: frightening tensions with immigrants posed a basic question about what Britain wanted to be. In 1968, Enoch Powell had warned against the "canker" of communalism under the form of Sikhs' claims "to maintain customs inappropriate in Britain."[176] Over the course of the seventies, anxieties extended to the many others who were exposing the country to new habits and demands: to Indians and Pakistanis who asked to integrate without renouncing their origins, and also to Caribbean youth who fought for better conditions in the suburbs of London and Liverpool, not unmindful of the parallel fight of their brothers in South African hometowns.

176. Manzo, *Creating Boundaries*, 130.

As it struggled with going multicultural at home, Britain was also at odds with its former empire abroad. Postcolonial countries like India raised their voice in the Commonwealth. The oil crisis of 1973 stressed a daunting British dependency on the Arab world. In the end, their splendid erstwhile isolation was replaced by the inevitable accession of Britain to the European Community. Europe would now affect Britain in a direct way, through ties in the economy and in the law.

The British religious landscape underwent a threefold change. First, traditional Christianity featured a widening gap between the defenders of threatened traditions and morals, and the secularized and liberal Christians flourishing especially among the Anglicans, who advocated reform and modernization. Conservatives and liberals also clashed within the Jewish community, in a conflict that turned highly political after the Arab-Israeli war of 1973. Second, non-Christian believers, in particular Hindus, Sikhs, and Muslims, became a permanent and visible part of the landscape. Third, new religious movements imported from Asia and from the United States turned into an important aspect of British religiosity; Britons grew acquainted with Hare Krishna and Mormons, Jehovah's Witnesses and Scientologists.

The new socioreligious context prompted belief-based claims of a new kind, fought for in a new legal environment shaped by the competition between the British and the European courts. The struggle of five people, in particular, reshaped religion and law in the seventies. These were three women: Yvonne Van Duyn, Pat Arrowsmith, and Mary Whitehouse, and two men: Richard Handyside and Denis Lemon. Their fight in courts paved the way for the litigation of the nineties, with the Rushdie and the Wingrove cases, and ultimately provided the background for the case of Shabina Begum in the 2000s.

Richard Handyside was a publisher in London, where, in 1968, he started Stage 1, a house publishing books on counterculture movements and international Marxism. He planned to translate and disseminate a Danish book, the *Little Red Schoolbook*, which promoted freer morals among children and adolescents. Before the release of the book, during March 1971, alarmed reports were published in the *Daily Mirror*, the *Sunday Times*, the *Sunday Telegraph*, and the *Daily Telegraph*. As a result of preventive protests against the book, with vibrant campaigner Mary Whitehouse urging for action, the Director of Public Prosecutions instructed the Metropolitan Police to intervene. Richard Handyside's premises were searched, and about one thousand copies of the book were provisionally seized. On the basis of the Obscene Publications Act of 1959, amended in 1964, Handyside was summoned for possession of some 1,200 "obscene books entitled 'The Little Red Schoolbook' for publication for gain."[177]

On July 1, 1971, the Lambeth Magistrates' Court found Handyside guilty. He was fined £50 and ordered to pay £110 costs. The court also made a forfeiture order for the destruction of the books. On October 29 of that same year, the Inner London Quarter Sessions confirmed the judgment. With the Tories back in power after the elections

177. *Handyside* [16].

point:19,88

of 1970, the trade unions on the attack, and the conflict in Northern Ireland more and more worrying, the case ignited a clash between social liberals and the defenders of traditional British morals. The battle of experts in court, over whether or not masturbation was harmful, and the rest, staged the conflict between the two Englands that the sixties had set apart. In vain, John Mortimer, the famous barrister and writer, advocate of civil rights, pleaded in favor of Richard Handyside before the Sessions. Handyside's conviction was saluted as the victory of dignified and ordered England. Backward hypocrisy had won, complained those who stood for the brave publisher.

Conviction was based on the conclusion that the publication undermined the relationship between youngsters and educators. The boundary between right and wrong was at stake, together with the prerogatives of parents and churches in setting crucial boundaries for their children. A much-criticized passage of the book read as follows: "Don't feel ashamed or guilty about doing things you really want to do and think are right just because your parents or teachers might disapprove. A lot of these things will be more important to you later in life than the things that are 'approved of.'"[178]

Should "things you really want to do and think are right" be upheld no matter what the grown-ups think? For the Inner London Quarter Sessions, the answer was no. Judges deemed the *Little Red Schoolbook* inimical to good teacher/student relationships and "subversive, not only to the authority but to the influence of the trust between children and teachers."[179] Thus, the judges found, the book "would tend to undermine, for a very considerable proportion of children, many of the influences, such as those of parents, the Churches and youth organizations, which might otherwise provide the restraint and sense of responsibility for oneself which found inadequate expression in the book."[180]

Yet, this was not enough for Handyside to be convicted under the terms of the Obscene Publications Act of 1964. In fact, in order for a book to be deemed obscene, the Act required that it have the tendency "to deprave and corrupt." Indeed London judges could not deny the book contained "dispassionately and sensibly, and on the whole completely accurately, a great deal of advice which ought not to be denied to young children;"[181] nonetheless they concluded that "looked at as a whole," the book tended "to deprave and corrupt a significant number, significant proportion, of the children likely to read it."[182]

On April 13, 1972, Richard Handyside appealed to the European Commission of Human Rights, in one of the first British cases brought before the judges of Strasbourg. Handyside submitted that the United Kingdom had breached his right to freedom of thought, conscience and belief, protected under Article 9 of the European

178. Ibid. [32].
179. Ibid. [31].
180. Ibid. [52].
181. Ibid. [34].
182. Ibid. [33].

Convention, as well as his right to freedom of expression, protected under Article 10. According to the procedure, the Commission had to judge first on the admissibility of the application and then on the merits. The case could be then passed on to the main tribunal of Strasbourg, the European Court of Human Rights.

Two years later, on April 4, 1974, the Commission accepted to examine Handyside's application as far as freedom of expression was concerned, but dismissed the claim that freedom of conscience and belief had been violated. On September 30, 1975, the Commission decided that there had been no violation of Handyside's freedom of expression. On January 12, 1976, the case was referred to the European Court of Human Rights.

In the meantime, British accession to the European Economic Community had been confirmed by 70 percent of British voters in the referendum of 1975, with Margaret Thatcher actively campaigning in favor of joining. Britain was now twice legally tied to Europe: first, through the European Convention of Human Rights and the Strasbourg tribunals, where the case of Handyside and the *Little Red Schoolbook* was under scrutiny; second, through the law of the European Community and its judicial system, with the European Court of Justice in Luxembourg competing with domestic courts. Conflicts over British morals were a matter for Europe, and the European understanding of freedoms was a matter for Britain.

Before the Court of Strasbourg could decide on the case of Handyside, the case of a Dutch national, Yvonne Van Duyn, also challenged British authorities.

A member of the Church of Scientology in the Netherlands, Yvonne Van Duyn had been denied access to Britain as a pastoral worker by the Home Office on the grounds that her Church pursued "socially harmful" activities. Van Duyn's case was referred by the Chancery Division of the High Court of Justice in London to the European Court of Justice in Luxembourg. Judges in London were taking the new European obligations seriously. They had two fundamental issues to check with Luxembourg. First, there was a problem with the extent to which the law of the European Community applied in Britain. In response, the European Court of Justice asserted the direct applicability of the EEC (European Economic Community) Treaty, which conferred on individuals "rights enforceable to them in the courts of a member state."[183] The second question referred to the specific case of Yvonne Van Duyn. Under the European principle of free circulation of workers, could the British authorities restrict the freedom of Van Duyn based on her affiliation with an organization that the Home Office considered contrary to the public good but did not make unlawful in Britain? And could Britain deny Yvonne Van Duyn employment in the Church of Scientology, while the same employment was not denied to British nationals?

The European Court of Justice proved friendly toward the British. On December 4, 1974, the European judges upheld the position of the Home Office and condemned

---

183. *Yvonne van Duyn* [4].

Van Duyn's appeal to failure. The Court of Luxembourg decided that the norms of the European Community were to be interpreted

> as meaning that a member state, in imposing restrictions justified on grounds of public policy, is entitled to take into account, as a matter of personal conduct of the individual concerned, the fact that the individual is associated with some body or organization the activities of which the member state considers socially harmful but which are not unlawful in that state, despite the fact that no restriction is placed upon nationals of the said member state who wish to take similar employment with these same bodies or organizations.[184]

In the Van Duyn case, Britain clashed with both the new religion and the new law of the seventies—the new religion being exemplified by Scientology, and the new law by British obligations within the European Community. This time, British prerogatives were successfully defended in court. But a religious and legal challenge of a new kind was on the attack.

The Pacifist Belief

The new nature and structure of belief-based conflicts in the seventies was also witnessed by the case of Pat Arrowsmith. In the aftermath of the Bloody Sunday of January 30, 1972, when the British army killed twenty-six people during a protest in Derry, Pat Arrowsmith joined in the pacifist campaign against the deployment of British troops in Ulster. In May 1974 she was convicted at the Central Criminal Court, London, to eighteen months of prison for distribution of leaflets to soldiers stationed at an army camp. Leaflets urged soldiers to desert or to refuse to obey orders if they were posted to Northern Ireland: "soldiers who believe, as we do, that it is wrong for British troops to be in N. Ireland are asked to consider whether it is better to be killed for a cause you do not believe in or to be imprisoned for refusing to take part in the conflict."[185]

When the Court of Appeal confirmed the conviction on December 4, 1974, the very same day as the judgment in Luxembourg on Van Duyn's case, Pat Arrowsmith appealed to the European Commission of Human Rights in Strasbourg.

While the *Little Red Schoolbook* advocated new morals, and Yvonne Van Duyn belonged to a new church, Pat Arrowsmith adhered to a new belief. In fact, she claimed that her freedom of thought, conscience, and religion had been violated, the conviction crushing the mere expression of her belief in pacifism. "The dissemination of the leaflet," she submitted to the Commission of Strasbourg, "was a moral imperative flowing from her life-long commitment to the pacifist cause."[186]

---

184. Ibid. [24].

185. *Arrowsmith* (1977) 124.

186. Ibid., 124.

Pat Arrowsmith was a fiercer rival than the drunken pacifist missionary of the film *Zulu* ten years earlier. The British government did not deny that pacifism could be regarded as a "belief," but argued that Pat Arrowsmith concerned herself with the defeat of the British in Northern Ireland more than she cared for peacemaking. The British government further submitted that Article 9 of the European Convention on Human Rights did not protect all manifestations related to a belief, but only those who had "some real connection with the belief."[187] According to the government, "the question whether or not a particular manifestation falls within the protection afforded by Art. 9 (1) has to be determined by an objective, not subjective, test. In the present case, it has to be determined on the face of the leaflet itself: whether or not the contents of that leaflet and the act of its distribution were in fact a manifestation of the belief of pacifism. In fact, the contents of the leaflet and its distribution did not amount to the manifestation of a belief and so did not enjoy the protection of Art. 9 (1)."[188]

Objectivity was invoked at a time when believing was increasingly a matter of subjectivity. Pat Arrowsmith insisted on the moral imperative springing from her belief, which had pushed her to act. She provided the following "correct definition"[189] of pacifism as: "the commitment, in both theory and practice, to the philosophy of securing one's political or other objectives without resort to the threat or use of force against another human being under any circumstances, even in response to the threat of use of force."[190]

Moral philosophy and practical action, she maintained, "form an integrated conception."[191] Under such inspiration, political action should be considered a "moral imperative flowing from the pacifist cause."[192] Pat Arrowsmith declared her source was "the work of pacifists of the stature of the late Mahatma Gandhi and of the late Reverend Martin Luther King."[193] The cold God of liberation was worshiped here. The Indian experiment with nonviolence and the anti-apartheid struggle in South Africa were imported to Britain and fed the pacifist fight against the British "occupation" of Ulster.

The case of Pat Arrowsmith was discussed in Strasbourg at the same time as the case of Handyside. The Court of Strasbourg decided on Handyside on December 7, 1976, concluding that no violation of fundamental rights could be found in Handyside's criminal conviction, or in the seizure and subsequent forfeiture and destruction of the matrix and of hundreds of copies of *The Little Red Schoolbook*.

187. Ibid., 127 [3].
188. Ibid.
189. Ibid., 129 [I, 1].
190. Ibid.
191. Ibid.
192. Ibid.
193. Ibid.

The European judges proved sensitive to the argument of the British government that the debate on the case of Handyside was the result not of an antimodern "dark plot,"[194] but rather of the "genuine emotion felt by citizens faithful to traditional moral values."[195] The European Court acknowledged the lack of a "uniform European conception of morals"[196] in an era "characterized by a rapid and far-reaching evolution of opinions on the subject."[197] Europe should therefore refrain from imposing a view.

Still, the European judges had in mind a clear definition of freedom of expression, a definition applicable to all of Europe. "Freedom of expression," the judges wrote, "constitutes one of the essential foundations of [a democratic] society, one of the basic conditions for its progress and for the development of every man. [Freedom of expression] is applicable not only to 'information' or 'ideas' that are favourably received or regarded as inoffensive or as a matter of indifference, but also to those that offend, shock, or disturb the State or any sector of the population. Such are the demands of that pluralism, tolerance, and broadmindedness without which there is no "democratic society."[198]

Indeed, Europe sounded very British. Nothing better then this definition could have summed up sociopolitical developments in Britain from the sixties onwards. In 1976, both the Race Relations Act, which introduced measures to fight racial discrimination, and the Act recognizing the wearing of the turban as an unavoidable article of the Sikh faith and exempting Sikhs from the obligation of wearing crash helmets when riding motorcycles fitted perfectly into the "pluralism, tolerance, and broad-mindedness" preached by the Court. So did the removal from the statutes of the prohibition of acts of worship behind locked doors a few months later.

What then about Richard Handyside? Did the European judges use British demands of pluralism to condemn Britain? Did they uphold Handyside's demand of freedom? No, they did not. English judges would not be subjected to any lectures from Strasbourg. "In these circumstances," the Court of Strasbourg concluded, "despite the variety and the constant evolution in the United Kingdom of views on ethics and education, the competent English judges were entitled, in the exercise of their discretion, to think at the relevant time that the Schoolbook would have pernicious effects on the morals of many of the children and adolescents who would read it."[199]

A few months later, on May 16, 1977, the Commission of Human Rights declared the application of Pat Arrowsmith admissible. Only on October 12, 1978, a decision on the merits was given, when the same Commission issued a report dismissing the appeal on the ground that "the term 'practice,' as employed in Article 9.1, does not cover

194. *Handyside* [52].
195. Ibid.
196. Ibid. [48].
197. Ibid.
198. Ibid. [49].
199. Ibid. [52].

each act which is motivated or influenced by a religion or belief."[200] The Commission accepted the British argument that there was no necessary connection between the pacifist belief and the allegedly illegal leaflets: "when the actions of individuals do not actually express the belief concerned," the Commission concluded, "they cannot be considered as such protected by Article 9, even when they are motivated by it." In consequence, the Commission did not refer the case for a further judgment to the Court of Strasbourg, as it had done in the case of Handyside, but to the Committee of Ministers of the Council of Europe, which endorsed the position of the Commission. Pat Arrowsmith had lost her legal contest.

Again, as in the precedent cases of Yvonne Van Duyn and Richard Handyside, the European judges did not cross the British judiciary. Both British and European courts were now challenged with a new kind of human-rights claim, in which traditional religion barely appeared, and beliefs and ethics in the public sphere were reshaped. Though defeated in courts, the Church of Scientology, the belief of pacifism, and the ethics of free love and sexual awareness encapsulated the new Britain, in which traditions and authority were defied. Resistance in the name of traditional morals, the sort of resistance that would spur Margaret Thatcher's fight for good against evil, developed as the response to new times.

Sleeping on the Side of the Road

The boundary between right and wrong had been clearly drawn in South Africa along racial lines. White supremacy was yet another cold God, worshiped by the racist state via the theology of apartheid. In the context of the Cold War, this all-white God was championed as the best ally to the God of capitalism.

It was no surprise then that, in the seventies, the clash exploded between the all-white God and the God of liberation, with the breakthrough of the latter increasingly tangible abroad and at home.

Alex Boraine strived to import the lesson learned in the United States, when he had helped "desegregate a barbershop and a small soda fountain,"[201] and had ketchup and chairs thrown at him. He was now general secretary of the Youth Department of the Methodist Church, which he renamed the Christian Education Department. Methodists were changing in India as well, with a Methodist Church increasingly sensitive to Indian cultures, and in England, where the Methodist upbringing of Harold Wilson and Margaret Thatcher was bearing significantly different fruits.

The more Boraine transfused in his mission what he had learned from Oxford's new theologians and from black American preachers, the more he clashed with the state. The security police frequently raided his training courses, though agents

---

200. *Arrowsmith* (1978) 71 [33].
201. Boraine, *A Life in Transition*, 49.

"seemed to be more concerned about whether or not black and white students were sleeping with each other than with the political content of the course."[202]

Through his endeavor in education, Boraine came to meet Steve Biko, a student leader who had founded in 1968 the all-black South African Students' Organization and who was also involved in the Youth Christian Movement. "I remember," Boraine later wrote, "the two of us travelling to various youth rallies, sleeping at the side of the road, because he was black and I was white, and we could not stay in hotels together."[203]

In October 1970, to his "utter astonishment,"[204] Boraine was elected the youngest ever president of the Methodist Church in South Africa, and he pushed his community towards a greater engagement in the anti-apartheid struggle. The God of liberation was acting through him as he challenged "both religious and secular authorities."[205]

Troubles were ahead, but he found it natural for Christians to be in trouble because of their revolutionary stance. Like so many times in the past, uncompromising followers of Jesus "were called disturbers of the peace, meddlers in business and politics, irreligious disturbers of worship, law breakers."[206]

Far from stopping Boraine from being a "meddler" in politics, his new office pushed him to develop a radical opposition to the separation of religion and politics. "If you want to separate religion and politics," he wrote, "you have to reach for your scissors and start excising major sections of the Bible."[207]

Conflict with the state worsened when international Christians mobilized. In 1971, Boraine went to see Prime Minister John Vorster and tried to persuade him to permit a meeting of the anti-apartheid World Council of Churches to take place in Johannesburg. Vorster said he would let the delegates come, but they could not leave the airport. "The World Council of Churches refused to accept these restrictions," Boraine later recalled, "and opposition against apartheid escalated from Christian churches throughout the world."[208]

A meeting of church leaders with John Vorster revealed the very tense nature of church and state relationships at the time. "We sat in front of him," Boraine described, "almost like a bunch of schoolboys facing the headmaster."[209] Vorster blamed the leaders for hiding behind church vestments while doing politics. Boraine witnessed the imbalance between the almighty state and the powerless clerics: "I saw an archbishop reduced to silence when questioned by Vorster about statements that he had allegedly made. Vorster gave the other side and demanded to know why the archbishop had

---

202. Ibid., 56.
203. Ibid., 57.
204. Ibid., 60.
205. Ibid., 65.
206. Ibid.
207. Ibid.
208. Ibid., 59.
209. Ibid., 66.

made his statements without having all the facts. I was staggered that tough, good church leaders would succumb so easily to the overt power of the prime minister and his cabinet members."[210]

If the voice of church ministers was coy or deterred, the God of liberation found other ways to make itself heard. In Steve Biko's 1971 manifesto of black consciousness, God appeared as the creator of black people and the inspirer of a new awareness that racialism really had no religious legitimacy:

> Black Consciousness . . . takes cognizance of the deliberateness of God's plan in creating black people black. It seeks to infuse the black community with a new found pride in themselves, their efforts, their value systems, their culture, their religion, and their outlook to life. The interrelationship between the consciousness of the self and the emancipatory programme is of a paramount importance. Blacks no longer seek to reform the system, because so doing implies acceptance of the major points around which the system revolves. Blacks are out to completely transform the system and to make of it what they wish.[211]

Black consciousness conveyed a new political theology of "God's plan." God had planned to create the blacks. He had wanted them to be and, according to Biko's famous slogan, to be "beautiful." More than Marxist atheism, the religion of the black community was becoming a powerful inspiration for strugglers. Also in 1971, historian Johannes Meintjes published the story of Mlanjeni, the prophet who mixed the teaching of Christian missionaries and traditional native religion, and rose in 1850 as the leader of the Xhosa against the Cape Colony.[212]

Though generally in heavy collusion with the racist state, South African courts were not entirely immune to the new winds of black self-awareness. The African native culture could not be ignored any longer. On March 17, 1972, the Transvaal Provincial Division of the High Court of South Africa, later the North Gauteng High Court, ruled on whether and under which circumstances a conviction for dealing, use, or consumption of drugs could be suspended. In their analysis of the circumstances in which drugs were marketed or used, the three judges admitted that it was "relevant to consider the traditions and attitude of different groups of the population towards the use of a drug such as dagga."[213] The white perception of drugs was not the whole picture. The court recognized that "it is general knowledge that some sections of the Bantu population have been accustomed for hundreds of years to the use of cannabis, both as an intoxicant and in the belief that it has medicinal properties, and do not regard it with the same moral repugnance as do other sections of the population."[214]

210. Ibid.
211. Biko, *I Write What I Like*, 49.
212. Meintjes, *Sandile*.
213. *S v. Nkosi*, 763.
214. Ibid.

Albeit with much wariness, the court introduced a groundbreaking new principle: legal measures had to be graduated according to fundamental cultural assumptions. As the judges wrote, "In making these observations, we do not, of course, intend to minimize the fact that the use of dagga is a great social evil in South Africa. Nevertheless, the long-standing indulgence in the use of this substance by a group to which an accused person belongs may well constitute a circumstance to be taken into account in mitigation at any rate where he has been convicted of the use or possession of a small quantity."[215]

A light turned on for those who nourished the dream of a law mindful of indigenous culture. This decision would be recalled thirty years later, both by Gareth Prince's counsels and by Justice Albie Sachs himself in his opinion for the Constitutional Court.

Farewell to Innocence

In the early seventies, a sense grew among those who opposed apartheid that years of struggle were now met with a stronger anti-apartheid culture, and with inspiring examples from within and without the country. It was time for tougher action. The 1973 strike in Durban demonstrated that the black labor force was not passive any longer. The Christian community and the World Council of Churches turned bolder. Other religious communities mobilized as well. It was not a coincidence that writer Alan Paton, the Christian patron for the accused at the Rivonia trial, and the fervent disciple of the archbishop, who died of a heart attack while opposing the "church clause" in 1957, now published *Apartheid and the Archbishop*, his 1973 biography of Geoffrey Clayton.

In 1974, Alex Boraine vacated his position in the church and ran successfully in the electoral campaign for the Progressive Party. From his seat, he did not refrain from bringing the theological discourse into the political arena. As he later wrote, he adopted "a strong moral and religious line"[216] in his arguments "against the government's racist policies."[217] And more than that: "At every opportunity, I tried to show the contradictions of the National Party's claim—supported by the policies and practices of the Dutch Reformed Church, which was really the party at prayer—to be a godly people. A strong moral line, backed up with religious arguments, must inevitably focus on concern for people rather than on policies, so, wherever possible, I tried to highlight the impact of apartheid on individuals or families as well as on institutions."[218]

Boraine held that "religious conviction was the National Party's Achilles' heel":[219] "a large number of cabinet members and ordinary MP's firmly believed that God

215. Ibid.

216. Boraine, *A Life in Transition*, 95.

217. Ibid.

218. Ibid., 95–96.

219. Ibid., 95.

was on their side, and frequently invoked his blessing on the iniquitous laws they constantly imposed."[220]

That church leaders with strong personalities such as Desmond Tutu, Alan Boesak, and Beyers Naudé now "dared to take a stand against the immorality of apartheid, some openly denouncing the policy as a sin against God and his Creation,"[221] was in Boraine's view "the most bitter pill for the National Party to swallow."[222]

When the government attacked the eminent minister of the Dutch Reformed Church, Beyers Naudé, who had refused to give testimony to the Schlebusch/Le Grange Commission, Boraine spoke in Parliament in his defense and paid tribute to the ultimate allegiance to God, as opposed to the allegiance to the state. Bolt's Thomas More could not have done it better:

> Beyers Naudé has dared to test the apartheid ideology by his Christian faith. As a consequence, he has opposed discrimination on the grounds of race and colour with every fibre of his being. Beyers Naudé's real sin in the eyes of the Schlebusch/Le Grange Commission was that his ultimate allegiance was not to a political party, to a language, to skin colour, or even to the state, but to God. History will judge Dr Naudé not as a danger to the state, but as an urgent warning to South Africa.[223]

Boraine's mix of theology and politics elevated him to the prime minister's Enemy No. 1. "Who will deliver me from this turbulent priest?"[224] John Vorster once muttered at him. But friends were also scared. In the Party many feared the boomerang effect of his "preaching." In the church, his double role of ordained minister and Member of Parliament was met with increasing criticism. After some time Boraine received a letter indicating to him that he was no longer a "minister in good standing."[225]

He was less and less interested in the life of the church anyway. The more his Christian inspiration pushed him to fight for justice and freedom, the more he felt uninterested in the disincarnate spirituality of the congregations he was expected to join on Sundays.

In 1976, the decision to impose upon black schools the requirement to provide education in Afrikaans prompted the protests, which led to the riots in Soweto. In fact, demonstrators had much broader grievances. The awful conditions of education for blacks went well beyond the imposition of the Afrikaans language. And yet the Soweto killings of June 16, 1976, reached farther. They were about students and

220. Ibid.
221. Ibid., 96.
222. Ibid.
223. Ibid.
224. Ibid., 95.
225. Ibid., 97.

workers, blacks and whites opposing the state more openly and courageously than ever before.

June 16, 1976, marked a turn point. According to Alex Boraine, "after Soweto, it became clear that nothing less than equal rights and an end to racial discrimination at every level would suffice."[226] As Alan Boesak captured in a 1976 book on black theology and black power, this was the time of "farewell to innocence."[227] The evolution of black consciousness into black power was the signal for the Nationalists that the global war on freedom strugglers was legitimate. The violence of the state escalated. The security police arrested Steve Biko. He was tortured and murdered on September 12, 1977.

The government accused the opposition of being in collusion with the black-power movement, and thus with revolutionary communists and terrorists. The Christian capitalist God was mobilized against Godless revolutionaries. One month after Biko's death, theologian Charles Villa-Vicencio published a momentous accusation against the "theologized Nationalism" of the state.[228]

This was a crucial moment in the history of the three countries. In India, where Indira Gandhi had instituted Emergency rule, the supremacy of a centralized, militarized, authoritarian state clashed with the self-government of the innumerable Indian communities and with mass revolutionary movements. In Britain, where almighty trade unions and heavy public spending, together with leftist permissive morals, were triggering an age of privatization and patriotism, faith in the welfare state conflicted with faith in entrepreneurial values. In South Africa, patterns of economy and society were hidden behind the main contentions over white and black power. Again, the cold gods were central. Indira's secularism clashed with both Marxist revolutionaries and Hindu nationalists, not to mention adversarial Muslims and Christians. The socialist and the capitalist gods clashed in Britain. The God of liberation and the God of white supremacy collided in South Africa.

Accused of complicity with black power and the enemies of the state, Alex Boraine stood in Parliament during the third reading of the Appropriation Bill in 1977 and pleaded for a historical interpretation of the roots of the South African tragedy: "The seeds of black consciousness and black power are to be found in the history of South Africa and were planted at a prodigious rate by the wielders of white power. The thesis is white power, the antithesis is black power, and what we need to struggle for is a synthesis which will resolve the basic conflict between white and black power."[229]

Twenty years later, this vision of history and memory would nourish the Truth and Reconciliation Commission and the struggle for a unifying alliance between religion and the nation. The cold gods prepared the national gods. At the same time,

226. Ibid.

227. Boesak, *Farewell to Innocence.*

228. Villa-Vicencio, "South Africa's Theologized Nationalism," 373.

229. Boraine, *A Life in Transition*, 110.

Boraine's religion was also a reminder of imperial gods, since, as he stated in his speech, the South African conflict

> did not start in 1948, the 1960s, or the early seventies. This is the conflict which is inherent in the South African situation and with which we have to come to terms if we are going to have any kind of development in the future at all. White power results in black power . . . It is a long, long story.[230]

An individual but extremely relevant chapter of this "long, long story," was played at the Warehouse Theatre, London, on June 15, 1978, when the Royal Shakespeare Company brought onto the stage Albie Sachs's *Jail Diary*. If British politicians and businessmen might still be reluctant to break with the South African partner, British intellectuals had taken their stand on the side of anti-apartheid strugglers.

Mother and Witch

With her proclamation of 1858, Empress Victoria aimed to shape imperial religion as the peaceful coexistence among the different creeds under the domination of the colonizer. During the Cold War, two outstanding women, Margaret Thatcher and Indira Gandhi, emerged with two characteristic religious visions. Over the sixties and the seventies, Margaret Thatcher rose as the Christian advocate of traditional morals, capitalistic free enterprise, individual responsibility, the struggle against the communist evil, and the need for a less intrusive state. At the same time, after Nehru's death and the first war against Pakistan in 1965, Indira Gandhi featured for almost two decades as the secular leader who carried India from the fervor of the postindependence years to the divisions of the eighties.

Emergency rule characterized her experience in power. On June 24, 1975, Justice Krishna Iyer for the Supreme Court judged Indira's appeal against the decision of Allahabad High Court to render her election to the Lok Sabha void on two minor counts of electoral malpractice. Justice Krishna Iyer gave a conditional stay allowing her to remain a member of Parliament but ruled she could not take part in the parliamentary proceedings or vote until the final judgment on the appeal. In 2000, after he had retired, the judge recalled the very nature of his decision: "I referred to the dharma of politics and insisted that equal protection of the law could not make a difference in favour of the Prime Minister, the great proposition being: 'Be you ever so high, the law is above you.'"[231]

The day after Krishna Iyer's decision, the state of emergency was proclaimed. Democracy in India was halted, with political opponents arrested, fundamental rights suspended, the judiciary obstructed, and free press intimidated. Only in 1977 would full democracy and rule of law return.

230. Ibid.
231. Krishna Iyer, "Emergency."

Over her two terms in power as prime minister, from 1966 to 1977 and from 1980 to her murder in 1984, Nehru's daughter stirred opposite emotions. She was the Mother of the nation for the masses who loved her and cast their vote in her favor. But for many, Indira Gandhi was the enemy of democracy, civil rights, and Indian multiplicity. This was the case for the Hindu nationalists and for the Marxists. Both of them opposed the prime minister so effectively as to persuade her that Emergency was the only way out, and they eventually joined to defeat Indira in the 1977 elections. She was also the "old witch" for Richard Nixon, who could not stand her anticapitalist bearing; and later, in the early eighties, the "widow" for early Salman Rushdie, and the "wicked witch of the East," for revengeful Sikhs after the massacre of Amritsar.

Contrasting feelings about Indira Gandhi also spread in Britain. The day after the proclamation of the state of emergency, a number of prominent British personalities published a page of protest in the *Times*; at the top of the list was Ernest Huddleston, a bishop of the Church of England actively involved in the South African fight against apartheid.[232] Others had more moderate feelings.[233] Labour's Michael Foot sympathized with Indira's socialism. Margaret Thatcher admired the strong woman who somehow anticipated her own resolve.

For all her complexity, Indira Gandhi represented a unique version of religion in the Cold War, with her genuine interest for all faiths coinciding with her determination to advance a secular vision.

The secular agenda of Indira Gandhi was twofold. In the name of equality, justice, and social welfare, her program included on the one hand, continuity with the fathers of the nation; and on the other, a reformist impetus vis-à-vis a country that she believed was still badly in need of modernization.

Thus it came as no surprise that the issues of women's rights and religious personal laws came prominently into account. Indira Gandhi inherited the discussions of the fifties on the Hindu Bill and the uniform civil code and pushed them forward. By doing so, she prepared Sushmita's Ghosh's struggle against the sham conversion of her husband in the early nineties.

The time for legislative action came after the war with Pakistan, the consequent birth of the state of Bangladesh, and the 1971 electoral triumph of Indira, the victorious commander.

If the antipoverty effort, encapsulated by the slogan *garibi hatao*, "remove poverty," lay at the heart of Indira's campaign, the Congress Party government also grew increasingly concerned about the systemic infringement of the obligation to maintain destitute and deserted wives under Section 125 of the 1898 Criminal Procedure Code. Within the Muslim community, men resorted to divorcing their wives, thus escaping Section 125, which protected current "wives" only. Divorce allowed Muslim men to avoid applying the Code and to obey the more expedient Muslim law, according

232. Guha, *India after Gandhi*, 496.

233. Ibid., 508.

to which the ex-wife should be supported for the three months of the *iddat* period only. For a secular government that brandished the flag of social equality and women's rights, this was unacceptable. In 1973 Parliament reformed Section 125 so as to include any woman who had divorced but not remarried within the definition of destitute "wife." The question was now on the table: would Muslim personal law be preserved, or would it be interfered with? Were Muslim women expected to receive maintenance beyond the traditional *iddat* period, thanks to the statutes, or should their religion prevail and exempt them from the law of the land? The tensions of the fifties over the reform of the Hindu personal law and the uniform civil code resurfaced.

Tenants of the Muslim exception claimed that other forms of protection were available for ex-wives, and complained that Muslims were targeted. Faced with protests from the Islamic community, the government watered down the reform and amended Section 127 of the Criminal Procedure Code, allowing that the judge could cancel an order for maintenance if the divorcee had been granted "the whole of the sum which, under any customary or personal law applicable to the parties, was payable on such divorce." By granting the judiciary the power to graduate the application of the Code, the Parliament attempted to strike a balance between noninterference in Muslim affairs and the need for the Congress to secure a symbolic achievement in the direction of uniformity and women's rights.

As a result, pressure on the Indian judiciary to adjudicate religion-based claims augmented. Family law and women's rights were not the only reason for such pressure. Tensions over conversions were also increasingly at stake, with the 1967 Orissa Anti-conversion Act struck down by the Orissa High Court in 1972[234] and the equivalent legislation of 1968 for Madhya Pradesh upheld by the Madhya Pradesh High Court in 1974.[235] Changing one's religion and changing one's wife was increasingly contentious in India; such a knotty mix would explode in the case of Sushmita Ghosh fifteen years later.

You Shall Go to Hell

Since Independence, conversions had turned increasingly controversial. In 1957, immediately after Ambedkar's spectacular conversion to Buddhism, a fact-finding commission had been appointed to inquire into the activities of Christian missionaries in the state of Madhya Pradesh. Hindu nationalists opposed not only Nehruvian secularism and Muslims suspected of disloyalty, but also allegedly fraudulent or forced conversions to Christianity.

As Christian proselytizing came under attack, the constitutional definition of religious freedom was automatically challenged. In 1954, while Nehru fought his crucial battle on the Hindu Code Bill, the Supreme Court ruled in the Ratilal Panachand

234. *Mrs. Yulitha Hyde.*
235. *Rev. Stainislaus* (1974).

Gandhi case that freedom of propaganda was inherent in "the right freely to profess, practise, and propagate religion" proclaimed by Article 25 of the Indian Constitution. Justice Mukherjea wrote in his opinion: "every person has a fundamental right under our Constitution not merely to entertain such religious belief as may be approved of by his judgment or conscience but to exhibit his belief and ideas in such overt acts as are enjoined or sanctioned by his religion, and further to propagate his religious views for the edification of others. It is immaterial also whether the propagation is made by a person in his individual capacity or on behalf of any church or institution."[236]

This came together with a clear caveat regarding the state's interference in religion. According to Article 25 (2 a) of the Constitution, the state was fully entitled to regulate or restrict "any economic, financial, political, or other secular activity which may be associated with religious practice." Justice Mukherjea emphasized the point for the court: the Constitution did not commit the state to regulate religion as such, but only those activities "which are really of an economic, commercial, or political character, though they are associated with religious practices."[237]

The 1954 ruling of Justice Mukherjea, as later confirmed by the Supreme Court,[238] represented the background against which in 1972 the Orissa High Court overturned the Anti-conversion Act of 1967.

The case was brought by one Protestant theologian and seven Roman Catholics, three of them priests, who accused the 1968 Orissa anticonversion act of infringing upon religious freedom, as enshrined in the Constitution. Petitioners contended that the Anti-conversion Act created a grey area in which the inoffensive spreading of the Christian faith could be easily assimilated to forceful and treacherous conversion and thus prosecuted. The widespread concern for Christians taking advantage of extreme poverty and marginality to enlarge their flock was behind the Act, together with disapproval for the Christian depiction of other religions as untrue and idolatrous.

Christian exclusivism was indeed a problem. The Court underlined that Christians included "mild threats"[239] in their preaching: "The preacher says: 'You (non-Christians) shall go to hell' or 'You shall not obtain salvation.' The preacher also often says: 'Wrath of God shall come down upon you' or 'God will be displeased with you.'"[240]

The intermingling of poverty, marginalization, and conversions was also an issue. Truly it was impossible to separate the spiritual from the sociopolitical reasons why people in Orissa converted to Christianity. Evidence provided by the applicants led the High Court to establish a connection between social disadvantage and conversions: "People of the depressed classes in Society feel that they are hated and despised

---

236. *Ratilal*, 391 [10].

237. Ibid.

238. *Durgah Committee*.

239. *Mrs. Yulitha Hyde*, 118 [4].

240. Ibid.

by the well-placed section of people. People of the depressed classes embrace Christianity voluntarily as an escape."[241]

Petitioners cited the documents of the Second Vatican Council. Eight years earlier, in 1965, the momentous gathering in Rome of Catholic bishops from all over the world had directed Christians to work "especially in the developing nations, . . . toward the uplifting of human dignity, and toward better living conditions."[242] The passage belonged to the Decree on the Mission Activity of the Church, *Apostolicam Actuositatem*, n. 12, but Indian judges quoted it as generally derived "from the sixteen documents of Vatican II." Judges pointed out that according to the Catholic documents submitted to the High Court, Christians in places like Orissa should "take part in the strivings of those peoples who, waging war on famine, ignorance, and disease, are struggling to better their way of life and to secure peace in the world. In this activity, the faithful should be eager to offer prudent aid to projects sponsored by public and private organizations, by governments, by various Christian communities, and even by non–Christian religions."[243]

As in Britain and in South Africa, in India, too, the Roman Catholics' awakening to the social justice of the sixties was having an impact. The God of liberation was on the attack, though many Indians rather called him the God of bought conversions.

As laid out in the Orissa Act, the prohibition regarded "forcible" conversion, namely, conversion "by the use of force or by inducement or by any fraudulent means." Further definition provided in the Act made boundless the area of potentially illegal behavior: conversion by "force" included "threat of divine displeasure or social excommunication," while conversion by "fraud" included "misrepresentation or any other fraudulent contrivance." "Inducement" to conversion covered "the offer of any gift or gratification either in cash or in kind" or "the grant of any benefit, either pecuniary or otherwise." Against such definitions, the Christian applicants argued that words like *force* and *fraud* were already defined in criminal law and that "by giving extended meaning to the words, interference with the Christian religion has been caused."[244]

Finally the court shared the applicants' view that general criminal law was sufficient against the risk of abusive conversions, and that the special definitions of *force* and *fraud* provided in the Anti-conversion Act were likely to impinge on constitutional freedoms. Having ascertained, after a lengthy analysis of Christian tenets, that "it is the religious duty of every Christian to propagate his religion,"[245] the Orissa High Court concluded that conversion was part of the constitutional right to religious freedom: "The true scope of the guarantee under Art. 25 (1) of the Constitution . . . must be taken to extend to propagate religion and as a necessary corollary of this proposi-

241. Ibid.
242. Ibid.
243. Ibid.
244. Ibid., 120 [7].
245. Ibid., 119 [4].

tion, conversion into one's own religion has to be included in the right so far as a Christian citizen is concerned."[246]

On October 24, 1972, the Orissa High Court accepted that religious freedom guaranteed that "propagation of religion and conversion is a part of the Christian religion."[247] The applications succeeded; the Anti-conversion Act was quashed.

Two years later, in 1974, the Madhya Pradesh High Court gave the opposite judgment. The Madhya Pradesh Act of 1968 was upheld on the grounds that it was fully compatible with the constitutional understanding of religious freedom. The Constitution, wrote the judges, "establishes the equality of religious freedom for all citizens by prohibiting conversion by objectionable activities such as conversion by force, fraud, and by allurement."[248]

Socialist Secular

On the eve of Emergency rule, the two opposite interpretations—in Orissa and Madhya Pradesh—of the right to propagate religion and the "right to conversion" encapsulated two different visions of religious liberty and secularism in India.

Secularism had always remained a loose concept, not proclaimed in the Constitution and not defined in any legal text. Yet politicians and judges resorted to it profusely. Most remarkably, Justice Krishna Iyer advocated secularism in 1973, in his opinion for the Supreme Court on the case of Paras Ram. The applicant had been convicted of the murder of the four-year-old son whom he had ceremonially beheaded in a sacrifice to Devi, the Hindu Goddess. Justice Krishna Iyer refused to grant special leave on grounds of mental insanity. The judge displayed the staunchest resolve in arguing that primitive "superstitions" needed to be crushed beneath the scientific ethos of modern India:

> The poignantly pathological grip of macabre superstitions on some crude Indian minds in the shape of desire to do human and animal sacrifice, in defiance of the scientific ethos of our cultural heritage and the scientific impact of our technological century, shows up in crimes of primitive horror such as the one we are dealing with now, where a bloodcurdling butchery of one's own beloved son was perpetrated, aided by other "pious" criminals, to propitiate some blood-thirsty deity.[249]

By showing no mercy towards Paras Ram and his "blood-thirsty deity," the court gave voice to "secular India" for the sake of social justice and reform. In doing so, Justice Krishna Iyer magnified the "secular and civilizing role" of the judiciary:

246. Ibid., 120 [6].
247. Ibid., 123 [12].
248. *Rev. Stainislaus* (1974) 173 [27].
249. *Paras Ram*, 509 [2].

Secular India, speaking through the Court, must administer shock therapy to such anti-social "piety", when the manifestation is in terms of inhuman and criminal violence. When the disease is social, deterrence through court sentence must, perforce, operate through the individual culprit coming up before court. Social justice has many facets and Judges have a sensitive, secular, and civilizing role in suppressing grievous injustice to humanist values by inflicting condign punishment on dangerous deviants.[250]

Three years later, in the thick of the Emergency, on August 28, 1976, the Forty-second Amendment changed the preamble to the Constitution of 1950. Thus far a "sovereign democratic republic," India was proclaimed a "sovereign socialist secular democratic republic." The addition of "socialist" and "secular" encapsulated the program of Indira Gandhi and her ambition to bridge the secular socialism of her father with the current struggle against those who, in her view, were pulling the country apart: in particular the Hindu nationalists and the leftist revolutionaries. Indeed, the amendment also provided for the expression "unity of the Nation" to be replaced by "unity and integrity of the Nation." In the Statement of Objects and Reasons for the amendment, reference was made to the danger that was threatening India. Democratic institutions, the amendment read, "have been subjected to considerable stresses and strains," as "vested interests have been trying to promote their selfish ends to the great detriment of public good." Indira Gandhi imposed a clear pattern: as Emergency rule was necessary to defend democracy from its enemies, socialism, secularism, and the integrity of the nation needed to be proclaimed in order for the ideals of the Constitution to be fully realized. Against the risk of the "virtual atrophy" of the Constitution, the Statement proclaimed the need "to spell out expressly the high ideals of socialism, secularism, and the integrity of the nation, to make the directive principles more comprehensive and give them precedence over those fundamental rights which have been allowed to be relied upon to frustrate socio-economic reforms for implementing the directive principles."

Thus secularism was proclaimed in order to contrast the allegedly abusive advocacy of fundamental rights. The two rivals, Krishna Iyer and Indira Gandhi, both advocated secular India without plainly defining what *secular* meant. Certainly for the judge whose decision had prompted Indira Gandhi to declare the Emergency in 1975, secular India implied the "dharma of politics," the independence of the judiciary, the rule of law, and the supremacy of fundamental rights. For Indira, secular India rather conveyed the ideology of a strong state entrusted with changing society and defending the unity and integrity of the nation, no matter the democratic orthodoxy of the means to which she resorted.

250. Ibid.

There Is No Right to Convert

In two major decisions of 1977 and 1978, the Supreme Court tested the newly proclaimed secularism on account of the emerging issues of conversions and women's rights.

On January 17, 1977, nearly four months after the Forty-second Amendment, the Supreme Court decided on the controversy over conversions in the states of Orissa and Madhya Pradesh. Against a judiciary arm wrestling with the government for independence, Chief Justice A. N. Ray had been appointed in 1973, thanks to pressure applied by Indira Gandhi. In his opinion, the judge adamantly dismissed the contention of the counsel for the appellant that "the right to 'propagate' one's religion means the right to convert a person to one's own religion."[251] In fact, for Justice Ray, religious freedom meant "not the right to convert another person to one's own religion, but to transmit or spread one's religion by an exposition of its tenets."[252]

Justice Ray further clarified that no matter how important conversions for Christianity, the right to propagate religion could not include the right to convert: "It has to be appreciated that the freedom of religion enshrined in the Article 25 is not guaranteed in respect of one religion only, but covers all religions alike, and it can be properly enjoyed by a person if he exercises his right in a manner commensurate with the like freedom of persons following the other religions. What is freedom for one, is freedom for the other, in equal measure, and there can therefore be no such thing as a fundamental right to convert any person to one's own religion."[253]

The anticonversion vision of Ray's Supreme Court was fed by anxieties about public disorder and communal conflicts. This was Emergency time, after all. Chief Justice Ray spoke out in favor of the Anti-conversion Acts in Madhya Pradesh and Orissa as a matter first of all of public order: "if forcible conversion had not been prohibited, that would have created public disorder in the States."[254] Faced with the risk of mounting "communal passions," the judge wrote, the Acts were indispensable "to avoid disturbances to the public order by prohibiting conversion from one religion to another in a manner reprehensible to the conscience of the community."[255]

On January 17, 1977, the Supreme Court dismissed the appeal and upheld the Madhya Pradesh Anti-conversion Act of 1968, thus paving the way for similar legislation in the future, including the Arunachal Pradesh Freedom of Religion Act of 1978.

The following week, on January 23, 1977, Indira Gandhi called new elections and announced that political prisoners would be released. Emergency rule was at an end. The same day, the Janata Party was officially presented. On January 28, eleven days after his momentous anticonversion judgment, Justice Ray stepped down as chief justice.

251. *Rev. Stainislaus* (1977) [16].
252. Ibid. [20].
253. Ibid. [21].
254. Ibid. [23].
255. Ibid. [25].

Legal Sanctity

After the electoral defeat of Indira Gandhi in 1977, under the new government led by the Janata Party, the right to maintenance of divorced Muslim women was again challenged before the Supreme Court. Five years earlier, through the reform of Sections 125 and 127 of the Criminal Procedure Code, Indira Gandhi had tried first to push women's rights forward against religious laws and then to appease heated factions in the Muslim community. The result was contradictory. Under the new Section 125, divorce did not allow the Muslim husband to disown maintenance to the ex-wife beyond the *iddat* period. Under the new Section 127, the order of mandatory maintenance could be canceled, if the "whole of the sum payable" to the woman according to Muslim law was accorded to the divorcee.

In the case of Bai Tahira, lower courts denied a divorced Bombay woman with a child the monthly maintenance allowance she sought, on the grounds that Rs. 5000 of *mehar*, and Rs. 180 of *iddat* had been paid at the time of divorce, and that the husband had no further obligation under Muslim law.

Justice Krishna Iyer, the paladin of a judiciary devoted to secular India, allowed Bai Tahira's appeal on October 6, 1978, and awarded monthly maintenance of Rs. 300 for the son and Rs. 400 for the mother. Justice Krishna Iyer's opinion for the Supreme Court proved less concerned with strict legal interpretation then with the spirit of the reform of 1973. New provisions, the judge wrote, were intended "to ameliorate the economic condition of neglected wives and discarded divorcees,"[256] to "help women in distress cast away by divorce,"[257] to ensure that "ill-used wives and desperate divorcees shall not be driven to material and moral dereliction to seek sanctuary in the streets."[258] This was precisely the case of Bai Tahira. The interest from a *mehar* of Rs. 5000, according to the judge, "could not keep the woman's body and soul together for a day, even in that city where 40 percent of the population are reported to live on pavements, unless she was ready to sell her body and give up her soul!"[259]

This language echoed that of the British judges who decided similar issues thirty years earlier and debated about rescuing distressed Indian "damsels." But this was independent India. Moreover, this was socialist, secular India.

Faced with the conflict between the "social purpose"[260] of the state's law and the "ritual" repetition of religious laws, Justice Krishna Iyer stood for the "fulfilment of the social obligation."[261] This was the constitutional heart of the statutory project of 1973.

256. *Bai Tahira*, 318 [1].
257. Ibid., 320 [7].
258. Ibid., 321 [11].
259. Ibid.
260. Ibid.
261. Ibid., 321 [12].

"No construction which leads to frustration of the statutory project," the judge wrote, "can secure validation if the court is to pay true homage to the Constitution."[262]

The statutory project prevailed over Muslim law because, as Justice Krishna Iyer stated, the "legal sanctity" of an effective maintenance of a divorced wife was superior to customs and beliefs: "the payment of illusory amounts by way of customary or personal law requirement will be considered in the reduction of maintenance rate but cannot annihilate that rate . . . The legal sanctity of the payment is certified by the fulfilment of the social obligation, not by a ritual exercise rooted in custom."[263]

The reform of maintenance in 1973, as interpreted by Justice Krishna Iyer in 1978, reopened the debate on the coexistence of the secular law of the land and religious personal laws, especially Muslim law. A balance proved extremely difficult to reach. Reform of Muslim law was not contemplated. The actual introduction of the uniform civil code was set aside. But measures enforcing women's rights conflicted with customs and made many Muslims feel they were under pressure. The debate about women's rights and personal laws was, in fact, also a debate about religious communities and communal tensions. The legal and political conflict captured public attention. Real conditions of women mattered less than politics. The gap increased between what was decided in courts and legislative assemblies, and the everyday degradation of millions of women, before which secular laws and religious laws appeared powerless, if not insensitive. There was increasing concern over issues of dowry and rape, alcoholism and domestic violence among husbands, family oppression and cruel labor conditions. In 1978, several groups of women activists gathered in Bombay at the initiative of local "Socialist Feminists."[264] This was a momentous step for a movement that had been growing since the midseventies. By reappropriating a legacy of feminist endeavor going back to the struggle for liberation, Indian women mobilized and became a strong though often unheard voice in society.

The Pilgrim

At the end of the seventies, the Cold-War pattern in India and South Africa seemed to be changing. While the United States of Nixon and Kissinger had been on the side of anticommunist Pakistan and South Africa, the leftist British opinion of the seventies supported secular India and anti-apartheid strugglers in South Africa. Nevertheless, the British international influence had dramatically declined, and the Labour government did not dare break with Pretoria, the UK remaining South Africa's primary foreign investor and commercial partner.

In 1978, US President Jimmy Carter visited India and gave a speech to the Lok Sabha. The president was confronted with deep-rooted anti-American sentiments

262. Ibid.
263. Ibid.
264. Guha, *India after Gandhi*, 542.

and with a country heading to the left. Since 1977, a leftist coalition with a strong Communist Party of India (Marxist) was in power in West Bengal. Marxist views were powerfully represented in the new cabinet led by Morarji Desai. The gap in the economy between the Indian option for public enterprise and the American preference for private enterprise also challenged US-Indian relations. Minister of Industries George Fernandes, a trade unionist jailed under the Emergency, fought multinationals that did not comply with limits imposed upon foreign shares in Indian companies, eventually pushing IBM and Coca-Cola to leave the country.

Looking for a way to overcome the anti-American prejudice, President Carter resorted to democracy. He praised the determination showed by Indians in the 1977 elections, when democratic rule had been regained. He emphatically stressed the common allegiance to popular sovereignty in both America, the second biggest democracy in the world, and of India, the first. Principles and values united the two countries. Jimmy Carter said, "the motto of my country is 'In God We Trust'; India's is Satyameva Jayte—'Truth Alone Prevails.' I believe that such is the commonality of our fundamental values that your motto could be ours, and perhaps our motto could also be yours."[265]

Commonality was not just about principles though. It was also about business. President Carter acknowledged India as both a developing country and an industrial power and complained that "only a few American business leaders are now involved, on a daily basis, in the economic and commercial life of your country."[266]

President Carter announced the marriage between the capitalist God and the liberating God, but most Christians in India stood for the position expressed in 1967 by the pope, Paul VI, who at section 26 of his Encyclical on the Development of Peoples, *Populorum Progressio*, had condemned "unbridled liberalism." And many Indians simply believed Christian missionaries exploited poverty to convert the natives for the ultimate sake of satisfying the West's lust for money and power.

Capitalism and liberation were the two sides of the same coin of American Christianity, which spread in India in the seventies. In 1972, evangelical leader Billy Graham, a close acquaintance of Carter's, visited the Indian region of Nagaland. A highly Christian population, the Nagas had been seeking secession from Delhi on the grounds of their religion, among other things, since the fifties. The violent struggle for independence and the brutal response of the state had ravaged the region. During his visit in 1972, Graham addressed crowds of thousands in Kohima with sermons on oppression and poverty, the need for conversion and the liberating power of Christ's love. "God is searching for you tonight,"[267] Billy Graham proclaimed as he closed his

265. Carter, "India Remarks before the Indian Parliament."

266. Ibid.

267. Pollock, *Billy Graham*, 24.

last sermon on November 22, "so you can repent of your sin, and be willing to give up all sins. He wants you to receive Jesus, and serve Him as you go back home."[268]

In his speech to the Lok Sabha of January 2, 1978, President Carter personified the entanglement of the God of liberation and the God of capitalism. When he spoke of friendship between the United States and India, he spoke "from the heart as well as the head."[269] He referred to the American struggle with racial segregation, and to the inspiration drawn from Gandhi. In this regard, he said, "I come also as a pilgrim."[270] He explained: "The nonviolent movement for racial justice in the United States, a movement inspired in large measure by the teachings and examples of Gandhi and other Indian leaders—some of whom are here today—changed and enriched my own life and the lives of many millions of my countrymen."[271]

What Carter said in Delhi that day detonated a blast in Pretoria. For the first time in the Cold War, the US administration was not ready to turn a blind eye to apartheid in the name of anticommunism. If Gandhi's disciple Martin Luther King Jr. had changed America, Reverend King's disciple Jimmy Carter was now threatening to change South Africa.

The Chains of History

In the second half of the seventies, as the Labour experiment failed, and Margaret Thatcher rose, the clash in England deepened between the ambition to enjoy unlimited freedom in religious matters and the sensitivity of the traditional faithful.

After the cases of Richard Handyside, Yvonne Van Duyn, and Pat Arrowsmith, the *Gay News* case, the first court case of blasphemy in fifty years, emphasized such a clash.

Since her crusade against *The Little Red Schoolbook*, Mary Whitehouse had never ceased monitoring British pop culture in her fight against immorality, obscenity, corruption, and blasphemy. Denis Lemon, also a publisher in London, became her new target when, in June 1976, he published in his newspaper *Gay News* a poem by a certain Professor Kirkup titled "The Love that Dares to Speak Its Name." According to the summary given later by Lord Justice Diplock, the poem and the accompanying illustrative drawing jointly purported to describe "in explicit detail acts of sodomy and fellatio with the body of Christ immediately after His death and to ascribe to Him during His lifetime promiscuous homosexual practices with the Apostles and with other men."[272]

The usual pattern of the British seventies followed: outcries of scandal and protests on the one hand; the counterculture milieu mobilizing to defend the increasingly provocative freedom of expression on the other. Finally, Mary Whitehouse brought a

---

268. Ibid.
269. Carter, "India Remarks before the Indian Parliament."
270. Ibid.
271. Ibid.
272. *Whitehouse*, 632.

private criminal prosecution against Denis Lemon and against his publishing house, Gay News Ltd. On July 11, 1977, the Central Criminal Court convicted both. Lemon was sentenced to nine months' imprisonment, was suspended for eighteen months, and was heavily fined. The Court of Appeal, Criminal Division, confirmed the conviction on March 17, 1978. Lemon and Gay News Ltd. were allowed to appeal to the House of Lords, because their conviction raised legal issues "of general public importance" pertaining to the definition of the crime of blasphemy.

After more than fifty years, this was the first case of blasphemy brought before an English court. The problem faced by the lords was not whether the publication was blasphemous or not. Of course it was. Instead the problem was if and how the real intention of the publisher had to be taken into account. The lower courts had deemed the objective blasphemy of the publication a sufficient element for convicting Denis Lemon, regardless of his specific motives. Were the lords of the same opinion, and thus did they dismiss the appeal? Or did they believe that the crime of blasphemy needed not only a blasphemous act but also a blasphemous intention, which had not been proved in the case of Lemon?

In their judgment of February 21, 1979, the five lords split.

They all shared the awareness that the case was about a different religion in a different country. Blasphemy law could not bear the same meaning now as at the time of the Act of Supremacy. This was no longer the age of Henry VIII, Cardinal Wolsey, and Thomas More.

Lord Edmund-Davies underlined that blasphemy in the origins consisted of "*any* attack upon the Christian Church, as part of the State."[273] Lord Diplock elaborated:

> In the post-Restoration politics of 17th and 18th century England, Church and State were thought to stand or fall together. To cast doubt on the doctrines of the established church or to deny the truth of the Christian faith upon which it was founded was to attack the fabric of society itself; so blasphemous and seditious libel were criminal offences that went hand in hand.[274]

Since the 1880s, since Gandhi's New Age London, the focus had moved from religious dissension to the manner of dissent. The subjective dimension had gained importance; the personal attitude had started to matter. Lord Diplock quoted Lord Coleridge in the 1883 case, *R v. Ramsay and Foote*:

> The law visits not the honest errors, but the malice of mankind. A wilful intention to pervert, insult, and mislead others, by means of licentious and contumelious abuse applied to sacred subjects, or by wilful misrepresentations or artful sophistry, calculated to mislead the ignorant and unwary, is the criterion and test of guilt. A malicious and mischievous intention, or what is equivalent to

273. Ibid., 654.
274. Ibid., 633–34.

such an intention, in law, as well as moral,—a state of apathy and indifference to the interests of society—is the broad boundary between right and wrong.[275]

Precisely: the boundary between right and wrong had been as much an issue in 1883 as it was now, with Richard Handyside, Pat Arrowsmith, and Denis Lemon one century later.

Lord Edmund-Davies summarized the threefold historical development of the legal doctrine on blasphemy:

> In the earliest stage, it was clearly a crime of strict liability and consisted merely of any attack on the Christian Church and its tenets. In the second stage, the original harshness of the law was ameliorated, and the attack was not punishable unless expressed in intemperate or scurrilous language. In the third stage, opinions were mixed. Some judges held that the subjective intention of author or publisher was irrelevant, others that it was of the greatest materiality.[276]

Such a development led Justice Diplock to accept, against the lower courts, that the crime of blasphemy could not subsist without the specific intention "to shock and arouse resentment among those who believe in or respect the Christian faith."[277] He concluded that Lemon's appeal had to be allowed. Lord Edmund-Davies shared Justice Diplock's view, believing that "to treat as irrelevant the state of mind of a person charged with blasphemy would be to take a backward step in the evolution of a humane code."[278] He also allowed Lemon's appeal, despite his "strong feelings of revulsion over this deplorable publication."[279]

Lord Scarman departed from the strict legal interpretation given by the two colleagues. In his opinion, he argued that precedents did not provide any definitive guidance and that the issue was "one of legal policy in the society of today."[280] He looked at the latest developments, in particular the Race Relations Act of 1976, which "made it unnecessary to prove an intention to provoke a breach of the peace in order to secure a conviction for incitement to racial hatred."[281] The judge also referred to Article 9 of the European Convention of Human Rights, the article invoked by Pat Arrowsmith and Richard Handyside, the correct interpretation of which implied "a duty on all of us to refrain from insulting or outraging the religious feelings of others."[282]

Lord Leslie Scarman was a privileged witness of the turbulences of the seventies. He had chaired inquiries on the 1969 fights in Northern Ireland, and on the

275. Ibid., 635.
276. Ibid., 654–55.
277. Ibid., 636.
278. Ibid., 656.
279. Ibid.
280. Ibid., 664.
281. Ibid., 665.
282. Ibid.

Red Lion Square clash of 1975, when Kevin Gately, a Marxist sympathizer, had been the first demonstrator to be murdered in England in half a century. With the case of Denis Lemon, he was adamant. No skillful evocation of subjectivity could prevent blasphemy from being blasphemous and offense from being offensive. Were the appeal to be allowed, what state of mind could Lemon possibly invoke to diminish the gravity of his act? Lord Scarman held firm:

> It would be intolerable if by allowing an author or publisher to plead the excellence of his motives and the right of free speech he could evade the penalties of the law even though his words were blasphemous in the sense of constituting an outrage upon the religious feelings of his fellow citizens. This is no way forward for a successful plural society . . . The character of the words published matters; but not the motive of the author or publisher.[283]

The assessment by liberal Lord Scarman went well beyond the case of Lemon and conveyed a strong vision of what modern and plural Britain needed. His colleagues handled blasphemy law as an embarrassing, outdated residue of an ancient past. He went in the opposite direction, calling for the common law offense of blasphemy to be fully applied and even extended:

> I do not subscribe to the view that the common law offence of blasphemous libel serves no useful purpose in the modern law. On the contrary, I think that there is a case for legislation extending it to protect the religious beliefs and feelings of non-Christians. The offence belongs to a group of criminal offences designed to safeguard the internal tranquillity of the kingdom. In an increasingly plural society such as that of modem Britain, it is necessary not only to respect the differing religious beliefs, feelings, and practices of all, but also to protect them from scurrility, vilification, ridicule, and contempt.[284]

Lord Scarman believed there were lessons to be learned from the past that made perfect sense for the present. India was the best example he could offer:

> When . . . Lord Macaulay protested in Parliament against the way the blasphemy laws were then administered, he added: "If I were a judge in India, I should have no scruple about punishing a Christian who should pollute a mosque." When Macaulay became a legislator in India, he saw to it that the law protected the religious feelings of all. In those days, India was a plural society: today the United Kingdom is also.[285]

Lord Scarman admitted that this belief of his was crucial in determining his approach to the *Gay News* case. Indeed history suggested not that the law of blasphemy needed to be discarded, but that it had to be freed from the chains of the past: "I will

283. Ibid.
284. Ibid., 658.
285. Ibid.

not lend my voice to a view of the law relating to blasphemous libel which would render it a dead letter, or diminish its efficacy to protect religious feeling from outrage and insult. My criticism of the common law offence of blasphemy is not that it exists but that it is not sufficiently comprehensive. It is shackled by the chains of history."[286]

Lord Russell of Killowen joined with Lord Scarman, and declared: "speaking for myself as an ordinary Christian, I found the publication quite appallingly shocking and outrageous."[287] Lord Viscount Dilhorne also joined. The appeal was dismissed by three votes to two.

After fifty years, the struggle over blasphemy had been reignited. Also in 1979, the release of Monthy Python's *Life of Brian*, a satirical critique of religious fanaticism and leftist sectarianism, contributed to persuading Mary Whitehouse and her camp that Jesus was under attack, though the film was only locally banned and no prosecution for blasphemy was initiated. Only ten years later, with the Rushdie and the Wingrove cases, would the issue fully blow, culminating after two more decades, in 2008, in the abolition of the offense of blasphemy.

A few months after Denis Lemon's conviction, the general elections put an end to Labour's almost twenty-year rule, while triggering the revolution of Margaret Thatcher. In India, the Janata Party government was in trouble, and Indira Gandhi would soon be back after the 1980 elections. At the end of the seventies, South Africa was a pariah country, isolated from an increasingly decolonized Africa, with Mozambique freed from the Portuguese in 1977 and the imminent defeat of white rulers in Rhodesia, South Africa was isolated also from a West where Gandhi and Martin Luther King Jr. were widely acclaimed. After the United Nations' embargo on arms trade, South Africa was itself a segregated country. New Prime Minister Wilhelm Botha would do everything to perpetuate the system, but the ideology and interests of his constituency would soon be challenged from within the Afrikaner community, because of newly emerging religious and social priorities.

Between the end of the seventies and the beginning of the eighties, a string of major events announced that the picture of religion and politics was changing all over the world. A Polish pope had been elected in late 1978, soon to become a formidable opponent of the atheist Soviet empire. The anti-Western revolution in Iran, the Soviet invasion of Afghanistan, and the Iran–Iraq war brought the Cold War deep into the heart of Islam. The war in Lebanon, the aggravated Israeli–Palestinian conflict, and the murder of President Sadat in Egypt further defined a new international arena.

The cold gods gradually transformed first into the explosive gods of the post-1989 age, and then into the national gods of the late nineties. By the beginning of the new millennium, the Rushdie affair and tensions over multicultural Britain, the Indian polarization over faiths after the Babri mosque case, and Tutu's rainbow nation of God all rubbed out the memory of cold gods. Still their legacy endured. The

286. Ibid.

287. Ibid., 657.

socio-legal context framed from 1948 to 1978, the conflict between man's law and God's law, and the new boundaries between right and wrong would all deeply influence the struggle of Sushmita, Gareth, and Shabina. Despite the world's tendency to forget, the Cold War would linger in the DNA of the global gods that would emerge from 2001 onward.

Chapter 5

Global Gods (2001–2009)

No Exception

ON NOVEMBER 23, 2001, Mary Whitehouse, aged ninety-one, died. Many years had elapsed since her most famous victory. That day in July 1977 at the Old Bailey, her private prosecution for blasphemy achieved the conviction of Denis Lemon and *Gay News* and announced the reaction of conservative-Christian Britain against the decline prompted by the secular left.

In the sixties and seventies, Mary Whitehouse resisted permissive new media, television in particular, which spilled out violence, indecency, and blasphemy. And she championed the causes of chastity and fidelity, and the need for homosexuals to be cured. Protesters in the street vilified her as a fascist. In a time when younger generations endeavored to subvert a hierarchical, unequal, and oppressive society, stink bombs against Whitehouse and pies in her face were an obvious response to her views, though she also managed to gain remarkable popular support.

More than twenty years after her victory in the *Gay News* case, from the viewpoint of the postmodern and multicultural new Britain, both the nostalgic Victorians and the liberal sixties seemed outdated.

And yet, two months after 9/11, Mary Whitehouse's call for the puritan soul of Britain, her struggle for the moral fiber of the nation, her defense of a threatened legacy, sounded plausible. In the aftermath of the destruction of the Twin Towers, the alarm she sounded for the survival of Western civilization and her opposition to the conspiracy against values and faith went beyond an old-fashioned opposition between conservatives and liberals. Whitehouse came from the age of Margaret Thatcher's famous 1978 remark on foreigners "swamping" British culture. Her fight made sense to the many concerned with a scattered society, and, in particular, to those who believed the new enemy consisted of uncompromising alien cultures—first of all, Islamists. In a post-mortem portrait of Whitehouse for the *Spectator*, Mary Kenny asked, "One wonders whether Geoffrey Robertson, QC, would now be as eager to defend a poem about a Roman centurion's homosexual desire for the Prophet Muhammad, as he was in 1977 to perform the same service on behalf of James Kirkup's verses on the centurion's longing for Christ."[1]

After the *Gay News* case, over the eighties and the nineties, the explosive gods and the national gods followed the cold gods of Mary Whitehouse. The New York attack announced a new generation of gods. Global gods featured prominently in the most extreme religious challenge of the time: Islamist terrorism. In the *Guardian* on September 18, 2001, Martin Amis saw 9/11 as "the apotheosis of the postmodern era—the era of images and perceptions."[2] This applied to the new generation of deities as well: global gods were the gods of "images and perceptions."

In the same article, Amis called for the development of "species consciousness, something over and above nationalisms, blocs, religions, ethnicities."[3] New gods hit locally but thought globally. Like their predecessors, global gods made no distinction between politics, economics, and religion. They also shared with their predecessors the same ambivalence: the equal potential either for division and violence or for unity and dialogue. Far more than prior gods, global gods operated in an interconnected world, and had the ambition to be universal players.

Global gods interacted with South African and Indian developments as well. After the transition to democracy and majority rule, persisting social and economic divisions made the South African rainbow nation of God more a dream than a reality. With the BJP in power, the national gods of Hindutva also proved unable to deliver their promises to Indians. Muslim global dynamics affected both countries.

The passing of Mary Whitehouse, a devout Christian and aggressive initiator of lawsuits, was also a reminder that gods loved courts and that this established a fundamental continuity between cold gods, together with imperial, explosive, and national gods, and the post-2001 global gods. In this period, the three stories of Sushmita Ghosh, Gareth Prince, and Shabina Begum came to an end. In India, Sushmita's legal victories in 1995 and 2000 were again tested before the Supreme Court and in society. In South Africa, the Constitutional Court decided on Prince's application. In Britain, the House of Lords adjudicated Shabina Begum's appeal.

Seventeen Days Later

At the time of explosive gods, in 1986, the counsel of Shah Bano, Danial Latifi, filed a petition before the Supreme Court in support of the Shah Bano ruling and against the Muslim Women Bill, the piece of legislation meant to neutralize Shah Bano. Defending the extension of full maintenance of wives to Muslims, Danial

1. Kenny, "In Defence of Mary Whitehouse."
2. Amis, "The Second Plane," 5.
3. Ibid., 9–10.

Latifi argued that the Bill was unconstitutional for three reasons: it fostered gender injustice, it was "un-Islamic,"[4] and it undermined the "secular character, which is the basic feature of the Constitution."[5]

For twenty-five years, the Court left the petition pending. As Sushmita Ghosh's case witnessed, the issue of personal laws and the uniform code was extremely controversial and had the potential to occasion Hindu-Muslim riots. It also polarized politics, with the Congress Party trying to secure its traditional minority-vote banks by standing as the guarantor of personal laws, and with the BJP promoting the end of the principle of the state's non-interference in personal laws and championing for a uniform civil code. Civil society mobilized to pressure the Court. The All India Muslim Personal Law Board attacked the interpretation of the Islamic law given by the Court in Shah Bano. The National Commission for Women underlined that the Bill's provisions, which made the Wakf Boards responsible for supporting destitute women instead of the women's husbands, proved immaterial because of the Boards' lack of means.

After 9/11, the supreme Indian judiciary estimated that the time was ripe for deciding against a Muslim exception to women's maintenance rights and in favor of a full liability of Muslim husbands.

On September 28, 2001, seventeen days after the crumbling of the Twin Towers, a bench of five judges for the Supreme Court dismissed Danial Latifi's appeal and confirmed the constitutionality of the Muslim Women Bill but stated that the Bill could not be interpreted as allowing for a Muslim exception to the duty of maintenance. The Shah Bano ruling was substantially confirmed. Danial Latifi had won despite the dismissal of his appeal.

The overarching argument of the Court rested on the necessity of affirming women's rights beyond "religion or religious faith or beliefs or national, sectarian, racial, or communal constraints."[6] Given the importance of wedlock for Indian women, the social and material inequality they experienced, and the dramatic loss they suffered in cases of breakdown, it was "a small solace,"[7] Justice Rajendra Babu wrote, to know that the woman will be compensated in terms of money. According to the judge,

> such a relief which partakes basic human rights to secure gender and social justice is universally recognized by persons belonging to all religions, and it is difficult to perceive that Muslim law intends to provide a different kind of responsibility by passing on the same to those unconnected with the matrimonial life such as the heirs who were likely to inherit the property from her or the Wakf Boards. Such an approach appears to us to be a kind of distortion of the social facts. Solutions to such societal problems of universal magnitude

4. *Danial Latifi*, 753 [9].
5. Ibid.
6. Ibid., 758 [20].
7. Ibid., 757 [20].

pertaining to horizons of basic human rights, culture, dignity, and decency of
life and dictates of necessity in the pursuit of social justice should be invariably
left to be decided on considerations other than religion or religious faith or
beliefs or national, sectarian, racial, or communal constraints.[8]

In particular, the Court found unacceptable that the Bill had the effect of making
a divorced Muslim woman "run from pillar to post in search of her relatives, one after
the other, and ultimately to knock at the doors of the Wakf Board."[9] Such an outcome
would amount to an unreasonable discrimination of Muslim women with respect
to the protection "available to Hindu, Buddhist, Jain, Parsi or Christian women or
women belonging to any other community."[10]

The Court argued that the Bill was constitutional only if interpreted in conformity with Shah Bano, thus holding the husband responsible for the maintenance of
the ex-wife even after the *iddat* period, and concluded that "the Act actually and in
reality codifies what was stated in Shah Bano case."[11] Of course, this went against the
political purpose of the Parliament in 1986. At that time, the adoption of the Bill was
meant precisely to neutralize the Shah Bano ruling. By contrast, in September 2001,
Justice Rajendra Babu stated the Bill had to follow the constitutional standard set in
Shah Bano, and not vice versa. Somewhat ironically, he added, "the legislature does
not intend to enact unconstitutional laws."[12]

A few weeks after the ruling, the American paramount expert of the Indian
Constitution, Granville Austin, pointed out that ever since the Hindu Code Bills of
the 1950s, the relation between personal law and religious identity for Hindus had
become "attenuated,"[13] while "for Muslims, the connection between the two is very
strong."[14] He stressed tensions within the Muslim community and pointed to the reluctance to change from "Muslim professionals" in legal and political affairs; for them,
Austin wrote, "the personal law is not only sacred but is also their job security and the
source of their power, religious and political."[15]

If the 9/11 atmosphere made it easier for the Supreme Court to impinge on Muslim
specificities, or "privileges," as the BJP put it, the ruling had two deeper implications.

First, the Court felt entitled to put gender rights and social emancipation above
religious sensitivities. Though this responded to Hindu nationalist propaganda for the
need to bring Muslims into the fold, the Court also satisfied a true demand from non-
conservative Muslims and women's associations. Beyond the Hindu-Muslim fray, a

8. Ibid., 757–58 [20].

9. Ibid., 763 [33].

10. Ibid., 763–64 [33].

11. Ibid., 763 [32].

12. Ibid., 764 [33].

13. Austin, "Religion, Personal Law, and Identity in India," 15.

14. Ibid.

15. Ibid., 21–22.

broader assertion of gender justice was the priority, and not only for the Court. Confirmation came also in the wake of 9/11 on September 24, 2001, when the Parliament passed three crucial acts. Act no. 49 amended Hindu, Parsi, and Christian personal laws, and the Special Marriage Act with them, so as to allow for wider maintenance rights. Act no. 50 introduced interim maintenance, accelerated the procedure, and removed the earlier ceiling for maintenance: litigation became meaningful for middle-class wives. Simultaneously, Act no. 51 removed an age-old disparity on divorce rights between the generality of Indians and Indian Christians, who were still bound by the extremely restrictive legislation of 1869. Divorce could be sought on eleven grounds, including adultery and conversion to another faith. This brought Christian personal law in line with the other personal laws.

As a second implication of Danial Latifi, the Court confirmed the ruling of 2000 on the case of Sushmita Ghosh and did not reiterate the plea for a uniform civil code. The political implications of the advocacy of the code had changed considerably. Since the mid eighties the BJP had advocated the uniform code, while opposing the Muslim Women Bill and supporting the pro–Ram Mandir platform. However, coalition politics had not allowed the BJP to hold the promise: in order not to alienate the support of partners reluctant to stand against personal laws, the Vajpayee government had taken no initiative to enforce the uniform code thus far. At the same time, women's-rights activists were changing their views and strategy. As Nivedita Menon had shown in 2000, the uniform code was no longer the only option; the theoretical framework of legal pluralism pushed toward the rejection of uniformity, homogenization, and statism, in favor of more flexible ways to promote gender justice.

The need to understand "the limits within which the modern Indian nation-state has been struggling to deal with the incredibly difficult but important issues of religious pluralism and what might be called legal pluralism"[16] was particularly strong at the turn of the millennium. The author of this sentence, Indian studies professor Gerald Larson, edited and published at the end of 2001 the proceedings of a conference held in 1999 at Indiana University in Bloomington. Larson pointed to the problematic role of a "secular state in a religious society"[17] and underlined the two conflicting dimensions of secular India. On the one hand, he saw the constitutional project of the secular elite, focused on neutrality, equality, and the exclusion of a public role for religion; on the other, he acknowledged the pervasive salience of religion and the dominant role of communities. Larson asked whether such a dilemma was the sign of India's unique "ability to reconcile [and] harmonize,"[18] or rather the square contradiction denounced in 1987 by Lloyd and Susanne Rudolph, for whom the Indian concept

---

16. Larson, "Introduction," 1.

17. Ibid. 2.

18. Ibid., 3.

of secularism was undermined by the contradiction of "its simultaneous commitment to communities and to equal citizenship."[19]

The cold gods shaped the dilemma of secular and religious India as a response to imperial gods; subsequently, the explosive and the national gods did not solve the conundrum and, in fact, made it even more contentious, with Hindu nationalists belittling the "pseudo-secularists," and with the intellectual elite joining forces with the minorities to blame backward Hindutva ideologists. Like their predecessors, the global gods of the new millennium could not avoid struggling with the many faces of secular and religious India.

Abstract Rationality

The Constitutional Court of South Africa heard the case of Gareth Prince four months before 9/11, on May 17, 2001.

Former human rights fighters and now constitutional judges Arthur Chaskalson and Albie Sachs placed a different emphasis on the methodology of the Court.

In his opinion, Chaskalson simply mentioned the view he had adhered to in the Christian Education case of 2000 about the importance of the proportionality test through which the judges assessed the gravity of the restriction imposed upon a fundamental right in the relevant context.

More explicitly, Albie Sachs warned against the risk of an abstract and ineffective interpretation of the Constitution resulting in the perpetuation of injustice and in-equality. Constitutionalism, he maintained, implied that the Parliament and the government acknowledged the superiority of a set of fundamental principles enshrined in the Constitution. In order for this approach to transcend the merely theoretical, the Constitutional Court had to take into account the context of the case and avoid a purely abstract legal analysis. As he put it,

> Although notional and conceptual in character, the weighing of the respective interests at stake does not take place on weightless scales of pure logic pivoted on a friction-free fulcrum of abstract rationality. The balancing has always to be done in the context of a lived and experienced historical, sociological and imaginative reality.[20]

Therefore Sachs acknowledged the very difficult conditions in which the Rastafari community had to live because of its status as a "vulnerable minority."[21] He believed that the Constitution provided for that condition to be mitigated as much as possible in the name of tolerance, openness, and respect for diversity. He claimed the duty of the Court was to "cast a flicker of constitutional light into the murky moral

19. Rudolph and Rudolph, *In Pursuit of Lakshmi*, 39.
20. *Prince* (2002) [151].
21. Ibid. [146].

catacombs in which they exist and secure to them a modest but meaningful measure of dignity and recognition."[22]

In his fight against the systematic abuse of power in South African apartheid, Chaskalson opted for a rigorous legal perspective based on evidence and argumentation. Sachs was more political. He vividly opposed a formalistic legal approach denying substantial justice. The political implications of justice were unavoidable; the judiciary operated within reality. He wrote in his opinion: "Even if for purposes of making its judgment the Court is obliged to classify issues in conceptual terms and abstract itself from such reality, it functions with material drawn from that reality and has to take account of the impact of its judgment on persons living within that reality."[23]

Sachs and Chaskalson had shared the same struggle against racist rulers but had followed different legal paths. They still adopted different methodologies now in their capacity as constitutional judges. So far, their divergence had been mitigated. While Chaskalson did not qualify his adherence to Sachs's opinion in the Christian Education case, Sachs departed from Chaskalson's analysis of religious equality in the Solberg case, but concurred in his opinion. In the case of Prince, their divergence became plain.

An Orderly, Dagga-Free World

The proportionality test put emphasis on the concrete circumstances of the case. The judges needed to appreciate the impact of the prohibition of cannabis consumption on Gareth Prince's religious freedom. They needed to grasp the significance of Ethiopian crosses, dreadlocks, dietary requirements and dagga itself in the economy of the Rastafari.

In reality, Prince's difference was not confined to religion. It was about new generations and new cultures springing from freedom. In Nadine Gordimer's novel *The House Gun*, when the parents of Duncan, the main character of the novel, meet his closest friend, Khulu, in the underground parking of the prison, they see him as the symbol of the rising diversity of the country:

> A curved tooth of some captured feline set in gold tangled with an ornate Ethiopian cross on the broad breast in the opening of a shirt left unbuttoned. A gleam of cuff-links and a red-stone ring, these elaborations along with the other, anti-materialist convention of frayed jeans and sneakers, he was normality, a variety of contemporary ordinariness made surprising, simple freedom appearing in the sterility of this space before blind walls, like a daisy pushing up through the stones.[24]

22. Ibid.[148].
23. Ibid. [151].
24. Gordimer, *The House Gun*, 107.

The Constitutional Court asked an expert to clarify the terms of the controversy with respect to Rastafarianism. The expert made clear that Rastafari considered cannabis, or holy herbs—commonly known in South Africa by the term *dagga*—to be a sacred, God-given plant, which put human beings in contact with the inner part of themselves, with others, and ultimately with God. In her affidavit, Professor Carole Diane Yawney explained that the use of the herb served "to create unity and to assist them in re-establishing their eternal relationship with their Creator."[25] According to the expert, the consumption of cannabis "was central to Rastafari spiritual practice:"[26] "the ingestion of herbs encourages inspiration and insight through the process of sudden illumination."[27]

Justice Sachs argued that such an understanding of the place of cannabis consumption among the Rastafari was essential in order to assess the restriction. Preventing the members of the group from licit consumption of dagga was not a marginal limitation to their freedom; it represented a very high "degree of prejudice"[28] to which Rastafari were subject. Their existence as a community of believers under the law of the land was threatened. Sachs summed up: "prohibit the use of dagga, and the mystical connection is destroyed."[29]

The Rastafari reasonably claimed, Sachs argued, that they were subject to suppression by the "implacable reach"[30] of the measures forcing them to choose between their faith and the law.

Justice Sachs's deductions from Professor Yawney's affidavit concerned the doctrinal and theological dimension of the case. But the political context also needed to be weighed. South African history and society, as well as more recent conflicts, were at stake.

The strong African connection of the Rastafari religion was embedded in its Jamaican origins. The Rastafari included dagga in their rituals, and more broadly in their life, also in the sense of reestablishing a broken Afro-centred mystical communion with the universe. Deeply rooted in the African diaspora, the Rastafari spirituality was linked with the redemption of the black man from slavery and humiliation. Thus, the Rastafari developed as a black-consciousness movement defying the law and seeking to overthrow colonialism and white oppression. The ritual use of cannabis was part of the endeavor to achieve freedom. As Albie Sachs pointed out, dagga was "rooted both in South African soil and in indigenous South African social practice."[31] Its use was widespread and unrestricted in the precolonial period. Well before Des-

25. *Prince* (2002) [20].
26. Ibid. [152].
27. Ibid.
28. Ibid. [163].
29. Ibid. [152].
30. Ibid. [145].
31. Ibid. [153].

mond Tutu's invocation of the healing power of faith, generations of natives had used "the God-given plant . . . for healing of the nation."[32]

Sachs looked back toward imperial gods. He recalled religious conflicts in nineteenth-century Cape Town, when the Muslim community rebelled against a municipal sanitation policy including public-health measures contrary to its customary practices. According to David Chidester, South African history featured "legal conflicts in which religious pluralism has been suppressed by the force of law."[33]

The restriction on free use of dagga, Sachs underlined, was tied to the historical transformation of South Africa into a colonial and racist country ruled according to the principles and habits of the whites. The judge referred to the work of legal historian Martin Chanock. A crucial turn took place in the 1920s, when an obsession arose concerning interracial sex, the provision of alcohol by whites to blacks, and the reverse flow of dagga. It was essential for the rulers to avoid circumstances in which, through sharing the consumption of dagga, blacks and whites could cross the social borders on which the South African society was built.

Social stigmatization was advanced through sectarian regulations on alcohol consumption. Albie Sachs recalled how racist liquor laws granted Christian churches an exemption for the use of communion wine while Africans who brewed beer for their traditional religious ceremonies were prosecuted.

Albie Sachs held that the Rastafari were not "unique as a religious group having had to fight against incomprehension and prejudice when seeking protected space for their religious practices in South Africa."[34] The racist state imposed upon the whole South African society the "vision of an orderly, dagga-free world."[35] If this were perpetuated in present times, the Rastafari would be prevented from respecting simultaneously the law of God and the law of the land.

Dictatorial Past

On October 23, 2001, the English Court of Appeal judged on the application by Paul Taylor, a Rastafari convicted to twelve months imprisonment for possession of cannabis. Mr. Hehir, on behalf of the Crown, solicited the judges to dismiss the application. He relied on the 1990 decision by the US Supreme Court in which the American judges denied a similar application. The counsel for the British Rastafari unsuccessfully attempted to downplay the US precedent. In the end, the Court of Appeal substantially conformed to the American template, holding that Taylor's religious motives did not justify an acquittal; however, it found the sanction not proportionate and shortened the term of detention to five months.

32. Ibid.
33. Chidester, *Religions of South Africa*, 235.
34. *Prince* (2002) [159].
35. Ibid. [159].

The South African judges were also confronted with the unavoidable American precedent of 1990. This forced Sachs and Chaskalson to take notice of a different jurisdiction from a different period. They struggled on the one hand with the transnational law of the global gods, and on the other with the cold and the explosive gods presiding over the American discussion of the case in 1990.

The American case concerned Alfred Smith and Galen Black, two members of the Native American Churches in Oregon convicted for use of peyote and, consequently, fired by their employer. The US Supreme Court held that the exclusion from unemployment compensation did not infringe their religious freedom. In the momentous decision, Justice Scalia for the majority emphasized that the ruling against Smith and Black was necessary to fight against "the prospect of constitutionally required religious exemptions from civic obligations of almost every conceivable kind."[36]

Ten years later, the case of Prince looked like a repetition of the Smith case. If Smith and Black claimed peyote was a sacrament of the Native American Church, Gareth Prince defended the principle that dagga was essential for the practice of his faith. The decision on Prince depended on how the South African judges evaluated their American colleagues' judgment.

Arthur Chaskalson limited himself to noticing that the US Supreme Court's approach to the Smith case proved too rigid compared to the proportionality- and balancing-based methodology of the South African Constitutional Court.

Justice Sachs took a more substantial position against Justice Scalia and the conclusion of the US Supreme Court in the Smith case. Endorsing the minority opinions by American Justices Blackmun and O'Connor, Albie Sachs especially rejected the view that "it is an inevitable outcome of democracy that in a multi-faith society minority religions may find themselves without remedy against burdens imposed upon them by formally neutral laws."[37]

The history of the two countries played a fundamental role in shaping the opinions of the judges. In the aftermath of the fall of the Berlin Wall, the Smith case marked a considerable progovernment turn in the case law of the US Supreme Court. Antonin Scalia voiced the American concern about potentially excessive tolerance of diversities.

Against the South African background, Albie Sachs placed himself in a completely different position. The memory of repression of indigenous beliefs and practices embedded in South African colonial history fed his disagreement with Scalia. He saw intolerance in the social standard safeguarded by the general law "through a set of rigid mainstream norms which do not permit the possibility of alternative forms of

36. *Employment Division*, 888.
37. *Prince* (2002) [155].

conduct."[38] For Sachs, Scalia's approach was simply about "the use of power to crush beliefs and practices considered alien and threatening."[39]

Sachs believed the freedom of individuals and minorities had to be preserved against the will of the majority. This principle had been laid down in the jurisprudence of the US Supreme Court, first in the aftermath of World War II, when Justice Black in the famous Everson case held that the wall between church and state "must be kept high and impregnable"[40] and "could not approve the slightest breach,"[41] a position subsequently reinforced in the sixties and seventies. Albie Sachs borrowed the key expression for his criticism, "conformity to majoritarian standards" from Chief Justice Burger's majority opinion in the famous Yoder case of 1972, when the US Supreme Court allowed the Amish to be exempted from compulsory public education.

In the name of South African history, Sachs took inspiration from the same US Supreme Court's jurisprudence of the sixties and the seventies that Antonin Scalia rejected in 1990. Contrary to the "conservative" Rehnquist Court, the "liberal" Warren Court was closer to Sachs as a judge and as a citizen of post-apartheid South Africa.

Since his opinions on the cases of Solberg and Christian Education, Albie Sachs had distanced himself from an anachronistically rigid conception of the wall of separation like the one Justice Black had proclaimed for the US Supreme Court in the Everson case in 1947. The South African judge rather adhered to the elaboration of Justice Brennan for the US Supreme Court in the Sherbert case of 1963, namely, that "no State may exclude individual Catholics, Lutherans, Mohammedans, Baptists, Jews, Methodists, Non-believers, Presbyterians, or the members of any other faith, because of their faith, or lack of it, from receiving the benefits of public welfare legislation."[42]

Following that doctrine, Justice Sandra Day O'Connor dissented from Justice Scalia on Smith in 1990, underlining the "harsh impact majoritarian rule has had on unpopular or emerging religious groups such as the Jehovah's Witnesses and the Amish."[43] Justice Sachs imported her view in his judgment on Prince.

The "right to be different" was what the Prince case and the Smith case were all about. Sachs had no doubt over what to stand for, in response to the history of his country: "given our dictatorial past, in which those in power sought incessantly to command the behaviour, beliefs, and taste of all in society, it is no accident that the right to be different has emerged as one of the most treasured aspects of our new constitutional order."[44]

38. Ibid. [145].
39. Ibid.
40. *Everson*, 18.
41. Ibid.
42. *Sherbert*, 410.
43. *Employment Division*, 902.
44. *Prince* (2002) [170].

Also the "dictatorial past" made Sachs value "the vast experiential dimensions of faith,"[45] and to recall his own passionate advocacy of religion in the Christian Education case of 2000.

The reason why the Rastafari were asked to give up either their spirituality or their loyalty to the state, Albie Sachs argued, was simply that they did not conform. Their diversity lay, first of all, in that their beliefs and practices were socially marginal and easily stigmatized; but it ultimately resided in the spontaneous and nonhierarchical organization of the Rastafari, and in their consequent ineptitude to mount effective lobbies.

Accommodating religious difference, Sachs wrote, was thus not just a matter of "astute jurisprudential technique, which facilitates settlement of disputes."[46] Rather, it was essential to the "whole constitutional enterprise."[47]

At the same time, respect for diversity and religious tolerance mattered not only to those directly involved, who were saved from "excruciating choices between their beliefs and the law."[48] In Sachs's view, it was also "deeply meaningful to all of us because religion and belief matter, and because living in an open society matters."[49]

The Rastafari Island

Arthur Chaskalson had a different view. From the outset, he stressed that the case was not about compatibility with the constitution of the antidrug legislation in general. Accordingly, in his joint opinion with Justices Ackermann and Kriegler, the president of the Court dismissed any consideration on the history of the antidagga fight as irrelevant to the judgment. "Whatever that history might have been,"[50] he assumed, the laws prohibiting the use of dagga could not be considered "an illegitimate inheritance from the past."[51] In fact, the legislation was based on the urgent and pressing need to suppress the use, possession, and trafficking of drugs. It also incorporated the international obligations of the state.

For Albie Sachs, the case pertained to the "dictatorial past" with its inherently racist and discriminatory vision of a white society crushing all possible indigenous or alternative ways of life. He saw the marginalization and persecution of the Rastafari as the legacy of the apartheid system. To Arthur Chaskalson, the war on drugs demanded the prohibition of the use of dagga, no matter what dagga meant to the Rastafari. Sachs drew the context of the case from the anti-apartheid struggle. Chaskalson drew

45. Ibid. [151].
46. Ibid. [171].
47. Ibid.
48. Ibid. [170].
49. Ibid.
50. Ibid. [105].
51. Ibid.

it rather from the violent South African society, which had grown increasingly illegal in the post-apartheid years.

President Chaskalson did not underestimate the right to be different. Neither did he underestimate how sensitive religious freedom was. He recognized that the vulnerability of the Rastafari as a very small group within the larger South African community meant that the Bill of Rights had "particular significance to them."[52] To him, the crucial question was again the one Justice Sachs himself had asked in his opinion for the unanimous Court in Christian Education: how far a democracy "can and must go in allowing members of religious communities to define for themselves which laws they will obey and which not."[53]

Arthur Chaskalson pointed out the contradiction between the hypothetical exemption, which should be granted to the Rastafari, and the prohibition still incumbent on those non-Rastafari who might happen to be in the same bona fide condition.

President Chaskalson did not dispute that certain Rastafarian uses of cannabis were not harmful. He argued instead that the nature of the prohibition was not based on the effective harm caused by the use of cannabis: the law forbade the possession of prohibited substances per se, no matter how harmful the use. Had it not been so, granting the Rastafari an exemption on the basis of their harmless use of dagga would have been discriminatory against the non-Rastafari: "subject to the limits of self-discipline, the use may or may not be harmful, but that holds also for non-Rastafarians who are prohibited from using or possessing cannabis, even if they use it sparingly and without harming themselves."[54]

Arthur Chaskalson did not believe that an exemption could be granted to the Rastafari without seriously undermining the antidrug legislation. No reasonable accommodation of Rastafarian practices seemed compatible with an effective war on drugs.

Rather then being the reason why an exemption should be granted, as Justice Sachs claimed, the lack of a stable and structured organization of the Rastafari, the "looseness"[55] of their structures, was to Chaskalson the reason why an exemption would not have been manageable. The Rastafari claimed their bona fide use of cannabis was not harmful, but Justice Chaskalson stressed that there was "no set norm or generally accepted pattern"[56] as to the conditions in which dagga could or must be used in compliance with Rastafari spirituality.

Justices Ngcobo and Sachs suggested that designated priests could officially receive dagga for sacramental use; but such priests did not exist in the Rastafari community, objected Chaskalson, and furthermore the community itself did not regulate the use or possession of cannabis by its members, nor was there any body capable of

52. Ibid. [112].
53. *Christian Education* [35].
54. *Prince* (2002) [118].
55. Ibid. [137].
56. Ibid. [100].

providing internal supervision. Therefore no exemption could be designed in order to protect the interests of the Rastafari and, at the same time, the interests of the state. Chaskalson concluded:

> There is no objective way in which a law enforcement official could distinguish between the use of cannabis for religious purposes and the use of cannabis for recreation . . . Nor is there any objective way in which a law enforcement official could determine whether a person found in possession of cannabis, who says that it is possessed for religious purposes, is genuine or not. Indeed, in the absence of a carefully controlled chain of permitted supply, it is difficult to imagine how the island of legitimate acquisition and use by Rastafari for the purpose of practising their religion could be distinguished from the surrounding ocean of illicit trafficking and use.[57]

The impossibility of designating an impermeable Rastafari island isolated from the surrounding illegal ocean of drug trafficking meant to President Chaskalson that permitting an exemption for use of drugs for religious purposes substantially impaired the state's ability to enforce its law.

On December 16, 2001, one month before giving the judgment, Arthur Chaskalson took part in a reunion at the Liliesleaf Farm in Rivonia, now an exclusive area of Johannesburg. Together with their relatives and friends, the men who were arrested in 1963 and were convicted in the famous Rivonia trial together with Nelson Mandela returned to the place in great honor to celebrate alongside the lawyers who defended them.

Forty years later, so much of the old days remained. The past was inextricably part of the biographies of the men called to adjudicate Gareth Prince's demand for justice. At the same time, the Prince case was also very much about present South Africa. Political and cultural diversity; the status of minorities; freedom and security; the cohesion of the country, the war on drugs, violence, and religion—all interwove to form an intricate tapestry. Endless connections kept linking the new to the old gods.

Decided, Five to Four

The Court decided the case on January 25, 2002. The nine judges split, following the two distinct judgments of Arthur Chaskalson and Albie Sachs.

In her 1998 novel *The House Gun*, Nadine Gordimer drew a portrait of the two of them. They both wore green robes with black sashes and red-and-black bands on the sleeves, "a sort of judo outfit with frilly white bib,"[58] Gordimer observed, "which must have been designed to distinguish this court from any other."[59]

57. Ibid. [130].
58. Gordimer, *The House Gun*, 135.
59. Ibid.

Albie Sachs looked like "a swarthy man (Italian or Jew?) with a scarred grin, and eyes, one dark brilliant, one blurred blind, from whom radiant vitality comes impudently since he is gesticulating with a stump in place of one arm."[60]

The Judge President, in Gordimer's description, was a man "with one of those rare faces—easy to forget they exist—which present no projection of ego to impose upon others, upon the world."[61]

When appearing from behind the curtains for a public hearing in *The House Gun*, Arthur Chaskalson "seems to be handsome, but perhaps he is not; it is the calm without solemnity that harmonizes his features into that impression. He looks directly out at the public in acknowledgment that he is one of them."[62]

Sachs and Chaskalson came from the same fight against the old regime. They both partook in the drafting of the new Constitution. They contributed in the momentous decision against the death penalty as well as in the orders in the Magdalene Solberg and the Christian Education cases. Still they differed a lot.

In Gordimer's fiction, the physical difference of the two judges was the mirror of the internal diversity of the Court. In the Prince case, it mirrored two different judgments.

Albie Sachs stood for a jurisprudence based on the explicit rejection of the "dictatorial past" and the promotion of freedom no matter the risk and the cost. This vision decisively steered Albie Sachs's opinion: "exemptions from general laws always impose some cost on the state, yet practical inconvenience and disturbance of established majoritarian mind-sets are the price that constitutionalism exacts from government."[63]

A vulnerable and marginalized minority, the Rastafari deserved a "constitutional light." It was Justice Sachs's view that in order to achieve a reasonable accommodation of their difference, the Constitution obliged "the state to walk the extra mile."[64]

Sachs adhered to Justice Ngcobo's opinion that an exemption granting the Rastafari a certain measure of licit possession and use of cannabis was not only constitutionally necessary but also practically possible.

Justice Ngcobo gave the example of officially appointed Rastafari representatives who could have been given dagga by the state for ceremonial burning on specific occasions. The state could easily manage an exemption, Justice Sachs wrote, that would be "understood publicly as being intensely and directly related to religious use."[65] Together with Ngcobo, Sachs believed this could be the starting point of a continuum leading to a broader exemption concerning smoking dagga at designated places on designated occasions and possibly to an even broader one coinciding with the ultimate freedom Gareth Prince stood for.

60. Ibid.
61. Ibid.
62. Ibid.
63. *Prince* (2002) [147].
64. Ibid. [149].
65. Ibid. [148]

The impossibility of granting the Rastafari all they needed, Justice Sachs believed, was "not a reason for giving them nothing at all."[66] He admitted that they were antagonistically defiant to the law; nonetheless Gareth Prince was fighting in court, and this testified that the Rastafari were able "to accommodate themselves to the institutions of the state."[67] Rather, Gareth's fight reminded Sachs of Gandhi when he was "expelled from his Inn in London because of his stand in defying laws that he regarded as unjust,"[68] and of Nelson Mandela's struggle with the Law Society of the Transvaal. Sachs concluded: "The legal profession has never suffered from having persons of honour and integrity in its ranks."[69]

The Constitution required that an effort be made in the direction of "a reasonable measure of give and take from all sides"[70] as well as in the process of accommodation and mutual recognition. Albie Sachs concluded that Gareth Prince was right in claiming that the state was called upon "to walk the extra mile."

In his joint opinion with Justices Ackermann and Kriegler, President Chaskalson held that no exemption could be designed without impairing the state's war on drugs. He also remarked that Gareth Prince neither asserted nor had "established authority to act on behalf of any person other than himself."[71] Prince's claim was not for a limited exemption for the ceremonial use of cannabis on special occasions such as the one Justices Ngcobo and Sachs proposed. Under the present conditions, there was no evidence that granting a limited exemption would satisfy Gareth Prince himself or more generally the Rastafari: nothing suggested that any such exemption would enable the Rastafari to practice their religion in accordance with their beliefs or would stop them from consuming dagga outside the scope of the exemption.

Chaskalson therefore concluded along with Justices Ackermann and Kriegler that the restriction of Prince's religious freedom did not infringe upon the Constitution: "the failure to make provision for an exemption in respect of the possession and use of cannabis by Rastafari is thus reasonable and justifiable under our Constitution."[72]

In the ruling of January 25, 2002, Justices Mokgoro and Madlanga concurred in the opinion given by Justice Sandile Ngcobo, upholding the application. Albie Sachs stood with them. On the other side Justices Goldstone and Yacoob concurred in the joint opinion of Chaskalson, Ackermann and Kriegler against Gareth Prince. All the white judges but Sachs were against Gareth. All the black judges but Yacoob were with him.

66. Ibid. [148].
67. Ibid. [162].
68. Ibid. [171] at footnote 61.
69. Ibid.
70. Ibid. [161].
71. Ibid. [142].
72. Ibid. [139].

By a five-to-four margin, the Court dismissed Gareth Prince's application. The majority deemed reasonable and justifiable under the South African Constitution the restriction to his religious freedom. No exception was granted.

No Guts, No Change

The BBC interviewed Gareth Prince immediately after the verdict. Prince stressed the unmistakably political nature of the decision. He said that by refusing the Rastafari people "humanity and dignity,"[73] the Court had gone against the "first nation or indigenous people of this country."[74] Further change was needed, Gareth declared, but the judges apparently did not "have the guts to embrace the change which is inevitable in this country."[75]

Prince did not go any further in the interview. But he was sure politics had undermined the regularity of the decision. Initially a full bench of eleven judges was in charge of his case. In fact, nine months after the hearing, the decision was taken in the absence of two of them, Justice O'Regan and Justice Langa. This was regular procedure, nine judges being enough to secure the quorum. But the profile of the two absent judges made them likely to have sided with Albie Sachs. Prince did not believe that waiting for nine months before giving the decision on a day when the two were on leave had been purely coincidental. All had been fixed, Prince thought, in order to avoid a momentous ruling for the freedom of the indigenous people. "It was a cheap cop-out," he commented.[76]

Later that year, on October 30, 2002, former National Research Director in the South African Truth and Reconciliation Commission, Charles Villa-Vicencio lectured in Chicago on "God, the Devil, and Human Rights." One of the most committed theologians in the anti-apartheid struggle, Villa-Vicencio warned the audience against the risk "that we begin to use God, that we fit God into our agenda."[77] He pleaded for "a cautious human response to a gracious and restoring God who is beyond our ability to name or control and who continually calls us beyond ourselves and beyond our own dogma."[78]

Villa-Vicencio also spoke against an abstract and absolute notion of human rights and justice. "The quest for human rights," he said, "involves settling for what is reasonably possible . . . in pursuit of an ideal that cannot be realized immediately."[79] In this respect, he underlined the constructive potential of international courts.

73. "SA blocks Rasta cannabis plea."
74. Ibid.
75. Ibid.
76. Interview with the author, Glencairn, Western Cape, 11 April 2011.
77. Villa-Vicencio, "God, the Devil, and Human Rights."
78. Ibid.
79. Ibid.

Unintentionally, the lecture set the context for Gareth Prince's reaction to the defeat in Cape Town. Though the majority of the Constitutional Court had judged it not reasonably possible to accommodate his claim, Prince deemed it utterly reasonable; moreover, he believed his idea could and should be "realized immediately" if the gods of all South Africans were to be honored. His fight had not come to an end. In the time of global gods, Gareth Prince decided to bring his case to the African Commission on Human and Peoples' Rights and to the Human Rights Committee of the United Nations.

Or We Will All Go Down

On February 27, 2002, one month after the rejection in Cape Town of Gareth Prince's appeal, a train of activists of the Vishwa Hindu Parishad returning home from a political ceremony in Ayodhya in support of the construction of the Ram Temple, stopped at the station of Godhra in Gujarat. Militants came in contact with Muslim travelers, and a fight started. The driver quickly moved the train out of the station, where some unidentified people attacked it. A coach caught fire. Fifty-eight men, women, and children died, having been asphyxiated and burned.

The BJP prime minister and the government of the state of Gujarat, also in the hands of a prominent BJP militant, reacted by applying the consolidated anti-Muslim, and indeed antiminority, Hindu nationalist doctrine. Despite the unclear dynamics of the fact, and well before the submission of the investigation's findings, Gujarat Chief Minister Narendra Modi explained the event through the pattern of Muslim terrorism directly inspired by Pakistan or under the influence of the "jihadi mentality."[80]

What journalist Siddharth Varadarajan called the BJP's "need for conspiracy"[81] unleashed massive retaliation, resulting in the killing of two thousand Muslims. Many Hindus died as well in the riots.

Siddharth Varadarajan read the deadly events in Gujarat as the example of the grim effect of "pseudo-Hindu separatism:"[82]

> Gujarat provides a chilling glimpse into the Hindutva dystopia, a land were hatred and irrationality rule the roost, where minorities are terrorized and killed, where aggressive, economically powerful social groups are able to use the State—and State-sponsored mass violence—to further their own business interest, where disadvantaged social groups like dalits and tribals are politically mobilized against their own interests, and where a major section of civil society is fast losing the moral capacity to distinguish between right and wrong.[83]

80. Varadarajan, "Chronicle of a Tragedy Foretold," 5.

81. Ibid.

82. Ibid., 15.

83. Ibid.

During riots in Ahmedabad on March 25, 2002, a Sangh Parivar mob attacked and killed Geetaben, a Hindu woman whose sin was to have fallen in love with a Muslim. On April 19, 2002, Varadarajan published an article in the *Times of India* expressing his shock at the reception of the photo of the naked body of the woman lying in blood on the asphalt, her dress stripped away. The journalist carved out of his personal emotion a call for the reaction of the people of India against the project "to establish a state where all Indians, including Hindus, will be devoid of rights except those which will be bestowed upon them as a privilege."[84] He dramatically concluded: "Gujarat has thrown a challenge to the country. The writing is on the wall. Either we stand up to defend the rights of all citizens; or we will all go down eventually."[85]

With tenants of Hindutva exploiting international Islamist violence, and with British governments allowing London to grow as a world center of radical Islam while making huge profits from the large quantities of arms sold to both Pakistan and India, global gods tightened the link between India and Britain. It was up to Indian citizens, Varadarajan pledged, to prevent Hindu fundamentalists from making use of Kashmiri terrorists and to shape a country open to diversity. Global gods challenged the British public opinion in quite a similar way: while Britons were faced with their own responsibilities in fueling radical Islam, they needed to set the boundaries of their new multireligious identity.

A Young Man Came into School

On September 3, 2002, the first day of the term, a nearly fourteen-year-old Shabina Begum went to school in Luton, Bedfordshire. This was her third year at the Denbigh High School, and so far she had contentedly worn the school uniform for Muslim female pupils, a *shalwar kameeze*. However, that day, as her brother Shuweb Rahman and another young man accompanied her in, she wore a jilbab, a long coat-like garment. The assistant head teacher asked Shabina to go back home and return dressed according to the school's regulations. The three explained that Shabina did not intend to comply with the uniform code of the school. The assistant head teacher did not let Shabina enter the classroom in her present dress. As the three left the school, the young man warned they were not ready to compromise.

Head teacher Mrs. Bevan wrote to Shabina's mother the same day, expressing her concern over what had happened that morning:

> You will be aware that a young man came into school today, with your daughter . . . The young man claimed to be your representative and demanded that we allow your daughter to wear the skirt to school. He claimed that this was a religious requirement and began quoting human rights . . . He was told that

84. Varadarajan, "I Salute You, Geetaben," 449.

85. Ibid.

our school uniform had been agreed with the governing body and that we allowed girls to wear shalwar kameeze or trousers . . . The young man did not accept this and took your daughter away saying that he was not prepared to compromise on this issue and that he would return with a letter from you giving him permission to act as the girl's legal guardian. I have to say that the staff who dealt with your representative were not impressed with his manner which appeared unreasonable and threatening.[86]

Mrs. Bevan further stated the uniform policy of the school had been agreed upon after large consultation with the local imams. Through the policy, she maintained, cultural or religious concerns were reasonably accommodated.

Shabina did not return to school. When the assistant teacher called home, her brother replied he wouldn't let Shabina go back to school in the ordinary uniform. One year after 9/11, on September 11, 2002, the school wrote to the family expressing concern over Shabina's nonattendance. The following October, solicitors on Shabina's behalf wrote back that they held the school accountable for having "excluded/suspended"[87] her from school "because she refused to remove her Muslim dress comprising of a head scarf and a long over garment."[88]

Also in September 2002 the British police started an official investigation on terrorist fundraising and suspect activities at the Finsbury Park Mosque. At least seven times in the past, Muslim community leaders had complained in vain to the police about Abu Hamza's tenure at the mosque. For years the authorities had turned a blind eye to Abu Hamza and the many others who transformed London into Londonistan, the hub of international Islamic terrorism.

Central to the pattern of Britain's ambiguous relations with radical Islam was the "covenant of security." Journalist and writer Mark Curtis reported on a Special Branch officer who summed up the covenant in the following terms: "There was a deal with these guys. We told them that if you don't cause us any problem, then we won't bother you."[89] A few weeks after 9/11, in October 2001, the covenant was exposed in a statement by Omar Bakri's al-Muhajiroun, the Islamist organisation founded in Saudi Arabia at the time of explosive gods and transferred to Britain in 1986: "For the moment, Muslims in UK have a covenant of security which prevents them from attacking the lives and wealth of anyone here . . . However . . . the Blair regime is today sitting on a box of dynamite and have only themselves to blame if, after attacking the Islamic movements and the Islamic scholars, it all blows up in their face."[90]

The question of why the British authorities allowed London to earn the derogatory title of Londonistan encapsulated the whole journey of Britain through the

86. *R. (Begum)* (2004) [9].

87. Ibid., [13].

88. Ibid.

89. Curtis, *Secret Affairs*, 257.

90. Ibid., 258.

different generations of gods. Indeed, Londonistan was nothing but the latest incarnation of a long-standing collusion with radical Muslim countries and groups for the sake of British foreign policy.

In Mark Curtis's analysis, British authorities saw the covenant as "encouraging certain individuals to act as informants on the activities of Islamist groups."[91] By hosting extremist groups in London and allowing them to prepare and carry out violent acts abroad, British officials believed they could cultivate relations with potential future leaders and influence strategic countries. Under the age-old policy of divide and rule, support of radical Muslims was crucial, Curtis noticed, in order "to foment unrest both within and between states."[92]

By the time the police raided Finsbury Park Mosque in January 2003, Blairite rhetoric on "ethical foreign policy" and the trauma of 9/11 had not substantially changed the policy. If the former allies were now presented as enemies, ambiguous relationships were still entertained with Saudi Arabia and Pakistan, and the "control of key energy-rich regions"[93] was still the priority along with the promotion of a "pro-Western global financial order."[94] Underlying this approach was the other consolidated pattern that short-term geopolitical goals "needed to be achieved at all costs, irrespective of the longer-term implications."[95]

Of course, the rule of law, freedom of speech, and freedom of religion were certainly factors, and most probably pretexts for the British police not to act. Violent preachers like Abu Qatada, Omar Bakri, and Abu Hamza himself, relied on the deference traditionally paid by the British authorities to places of worship in general and to mosques in particular. This explained Abu Hamza's surprise at the famous raid to Finsbury Park on January 20, 2003 and his ominous comment, "The police have violated the sacredness of the mosque."[96] Indeed, journalists Sean O'Neill and Daniel McGrory noticed that on the occasion of the raid

> All officers entering the mosque were issued with plastic overshoes to make sure their boots did not come into contact with the floor areas where worshippers prayed . . . Copies of the Koran in the building were to be handled only by Muslim officers, who were to accompany search teams and advise them on how to proceed.[97]

Against this background, the case of Shabina Begum grew into the emblem of an unresolved Muslim question for Britain at home and abroad. With defiant Shabina

---

91. Ibid., 259.
92. Ibid., 263.
93. Ibid., 249.
94. Ibid., xvi.
95. Ibid., 82.
96. O'Neill and McGrory, *The Suicide Factory,* 253.
97. Ibid., 256.

refusing to return to school, the school's authorities defending their ground, and the intervention of the Education Welfare Service proving unsuccessful, the matter was eventually referred to court.

In 2001, the Supreme Court of India confirmed the ruling on Shah Bano and Sushmita Gosh: being a Muslim did not exonerate any man in the land from respecting the basic rights of women, including the right to maintenance. In 2002, the Constitutional Court of South Africa denied Gareth Prince and the Rastafari the right to "puff the holy herb." The two supreme courts had tried the gods and ruled that they deserved no exception. Would the global gods change the picture and make the English courts and ultimately the House of Lords rule differently in the case of Shabina Begum?

They Are Both Women

"The world is ever more interdependent,[98] Tony Blair proclaimed to the House of Commons on March 18, 2003, while demanding that the MPs vote on the motion allowing for the invasion of Iraq. The British prime minister explained: "stock markets and economies rise and fall together. Confidence is the key to prosperity. Insecurity spreads like contagion."[99] He pointed at two "begetters"[100] of the supreme threat, chaos: "tyrannical regimes with weapons of mass destruction and extreme terrorist groups who profess a perverted and false view of Islam."[101]

Blair dramatically ended by summoning "the strength to recognize the global challenge of the 21st century and beat it."[102] He finally got the vote he sought. Britain was off to war in a Muslim land.

In England, from 2003 to 2006, the High Court, the Court of Appeal and finally the House of Lords judged Shabina Begum's claim. While Britain struggled with Islam and with multicultural tensions, the country also underwent a momentous renewal of its own tradition in church-and-state matters, through the House of Lords' redefinition of the establishment of the Church of England and the adoption of the Civil Partnership Act.

Over the same period, Gareth Prince froze his ambition to become a lawyer and started working as a legal advisor on matters of social justice, while carrying on his battle with South African law beyond national borders. At the same time, the South African Constitutional Court further refined its doctrine on religious freedom in the case of Marié Adriaana Fourie and Cecelia Johanna Bonthuys. Indians continued to

---

98. Blair, "Speech in the House of Commons."

99. Ibid.

100. Ibid.

101. Ibid.

102. Ibid.

struggle with the uniform code, personal laws, secularism, and the debate on the Hinduization of the country.

Private Chancels

On June 26, 2003, a judgment in the House of Lords brought new life to England's old, obsolete ecclesiastical law and reshaped the establishment of the Church of England.

The case concerned the liability of a lay rector for the repair of the chancel of a church belonging to a parish of the Church of England. From the outset of his opinion for the Judicial Committee of the House, Lord Nicholls of Birkenhead acknowledged the "arcane . . . anachronistic, even capricious, nature of this ancient liability"[103] and referred to a 1985 statement by the Law Commission recommending the abolition of a "no longer acceptable . . relic of the past."[104] The controversy had started at the time of explosive and national gods: between 1994 and 1996, Mr. and Mrs. Wallbank, the owners of Glebe Farm at Aston Cantlow in Warwickshire, refused to pay the Parochial Church Council notices for almost £100,000 for repair of the chancel of the local church. Ecclesiastical law undoubtedly required the couple to pay, but Mr. and Mrs. Wallbank objected on two grounds. First, with the notices coming from the established Church of England, a public institution, their alleged liability amounted to an arbitrary tax. Second, the common law singled them out with respect to any other landowner in an unjustifiably discriminatory manner. Their status as nonmembers of the Church of England was also problematic. The clash between the old fabric and a new legal system based on individual human rights, equality, and the accountability of public authorities concerned vital patrimonial interests of the Church of England and, at the same time, its very foundation as the established church of the country.

On March 28, 2000, Justice Ferris in the High Court found for the Parochial Church Council and held the defendants liable for the cost of the chancel repairs. On October 2, 2000, the 1998 Human Rights Act came into effect. Since 1966 British private individuals and associations had been able to bring complaints against the UK to the European Court in Strasbourg. The 1998 Act secured that bodies discharging functions of government in the United Kingdom abided by the rights and freedoms enshrined in the Convention. In their appeal, Mr. and Mrs. Wallbank further resorted to the provisions of the Act, Section 6 (1) of which made it unlawful for "a public authority" to act in a way that was incompatible with any right guaranteed by the Convention.

On May 17, 2001, a unanimous Court of Appeal allowed the Wallbanks' appeal on grounds that "a private individual who has no necessary connection with the church [was being] required by law to pay money to a public authority for its upkeep."[105]

---

103. *Parochial Church Council* (2003), 37 [2].
104. Ibid.
105. *Parochial Church Council* (2001), [40].

The judges underlined the unacceptable inconsistency between an outdated ecclesiastical law provision lacking any justification in present English society, and the principles of contemporary British law: "To defend . . . a considered system, voted upon by a representative legislature familiar with contemporary social conditions, is one thing. To defend . . . a residual common law liability to a special local tax, which has long since lost its factual and legal basis is another."[106]

When the Parochial Church Council's appeal reached the House of Lords, the stakes were extremely high. If it was unlawful for a parochial church council to enforce a lay rector's obligation to meet the cost of chancel repairs, one-third of the parishes in the land were in trouble and the whole structure of the Church of England was threatened. The qualification of the Church of England's bodies as "public authorities" or as entities exercising a "public function" was also a terrible blow for the church. In fact it excluded her from resorting to the European Convention of Human Rights and to the Human Rights Act if any of her rights were to be violated, since those instruments protected private individuals and associations only, and public entities did not themselves enjoy Convention rights. Even worse, such qualification made the Church of England accountable for acting in accordance with the Convention rights, thus impairing, the Church's defenders argued, its ability to engage freely in its spiritual mission.

On June 26, 2003, the House of Lords unanimously reversed the Court of Appeal's decision, holding the liability of Mr. and Mrs. Wallbank as lay rectors utterly compatible with the Human Rights Act.

The key argument of the judgment was that the Parochial Church Council could not be deemed a "public authority," and that the entertainment of the parish patrimony could not be considered a "public function" for the purposes of the Human Rights Act. Thus the Council enjoyed the same freedom as any private entity to stipulate contracts and obligations.

The lords asserted the obligation of a lay rector to pay for chancel repairs on grounds not of the exceptional public law nature of the established Church of England, but to the contrary, of the private nature of the relevant obligation. The distinction between the public relevance of the church and the private dimension of the disputed obligation was the key for safeguarding the whole fabric of privileges based on the status of established church, while adjusting to the new era of human rights, governmental accountability, and global law. The lords led the church's interests into the safe harbor of stipulations among private citizens; at the same time, they avoided putting the principle of the church's establishment in jeopardy.

Though the Court of Appeal had extensively quoted from Hill's *Ecclesiastical Law* textbook, Mark Hill, a practicing barrister and judge in both the secular and ecclesiastical courts in England, featured among the fiercest critics of the decision appealed to the House of Lords. In 2000, he had warned against the "litany of unintended consequences"[107]

---

106. Ibid., [44].

107. Hill, "The Impact for the Church of England," 439.

deriving for the Church of England from the enforcement of the Human Rights Act. In 2001, in a footnote to his comment on the Court of Appeal's decision, Hill found "regrettable that the wider interests of the Church of England were not ventilated"[108] and anticipated the line the House of Lords was to follow in its 2003 judgment. With regard to the nature of a Parochial Church Council, Mark Hill wrote that

> whilst it may be arguable that certain of its functions are of a public nature . . . it is not to be treated as a public authority in relation to acts which are private. The recovery of the costs of chancel repairs, the burden of which runs with rectorial land, is self-evidently a private act akin to the enforcement of any other encumbrance on land.[109]

Two years later, the lords followed. The Parochial Church Council's appeal succeeded because, as Lord Nicholls wrote, "a parochial church council is not a core public authority, nor does it become such . . . when enforcing a lay rector's liability for chancel repairs."[110]

Such a conclusion was reached through an extensive discussion of the simultaneously civil and religious nature of the Church of England. The lords shared the view that despite its prominent social and political role throughout history, the Church essentially remained a religious entity. In this regard, they emphasized the peculiar spiritual mission of the church and construed accordingly the relation of the church to the state as one based on the mutual independence of the two.

Lord Hope of Craighead took a robust stand for this doctrine: "The state has not surrendered or delegated any of its functions or powers to the Church. None of the functions that the Church of England performs would have to be performed in its place by the state if the Church were to abdicate its responsibility . . . The relationship which the state has with the Church of England is one of recognition, not of the devolution to it of any of the powers or functions of government."[111]

With an expression that would have become famous, the lord also set clear that "the Church of England as a whole has no legal status or personality:"[112] "There is no Act of Parliament that purports to establish it as the Church of England . . . What establishment in law means is that the state has incorporated its law into the law of the realm as a branch of its general law."[113]

On the same track, Lord Rodger of Earlsferry acknowledged the "somewhat amorphous"[114] juridical nature of the Church, but stood for the distinction be-

---

108. Hill, "Recent Ecclesiastical Cases," 173 (note).

109. Ibid.

110. *Parochial Church Council* (2003) [17].

111. Ibid. [61].

112. Ibid.

113. Ibid.

114. Ibid. [154].

tween the "religious mission"[115] of the Church and the distinct "secular mission of government:"[116]

> Founding on scriptural and other recognized authority, the Church seeks to serve the purposes of God, not those of the government carried on by the modern equivalents of Caesar and his proconsuls. This is true even though the Church of England has certain important links with the state. Those links, which do not include any funding of the Church by the government, give the Church a unique position, but they do not mean that it is a department of state ... In so far as the ties are intended to assist the Church, it is to accomplish the Church's own mission, not the aims and objectives of the government of the United Kingdom.[117]

After the defeat in the appeal, Mark Hill had stepped in as the counsel for the Parochial Church Council. The victory of the Church in the House of Lords was his victory. Hill saluted the Aston Cantlow judgment as a momentous step for ecclesiastical law in Britain, arguing that the "distillation"[118] of the five lords' opinions would "prove a fertile source of debate for years to come."[119] The multireligious dimension of Britain was in the background, when Hill emphasized that "not being classified a public authority, the Church of England will remain free to engage in its mission and witness and, in doing so, it will be on an equal footing with all other denominations and faith communities in the United Kingdom."[120]

Still, the matter was not entirely settled. Lord Nicholls made clear that the judgment did not detract from the need for reform. Law professor Julian Rivers underlined that the case had been straitjacketed into an unsatisfactory opposition between the state and the individual: "The Court of Appeal thought that the Church of England was the 'State' and the lay rectors the 'individual.' The House of Lords thought that the Church of England was on the individual side as a potential victim of human rights violations by the State. Neither construction is adequate."[121]

Is He on to God?

That same month, June 2003, *Vanity Fair* featured a lengthy article on Tony Blair and his partnership with George W. Bush. Two months after the visit of the two to Ulster, where Blair renewed his commitment to the "Good Friday agreement," between

115. Ibid. [156].
116. Ibid.
117. Ibid.
118. Hill, "Editorial," (2004) 246.
119. Ibid.
120. Ibid., 248.
121. Rivers, *The Law of Organized Religions*, 322 n. 14.

Catholics and Protestants, and one month after President Bush's victory speech from the aircraft carrier the USS Abraham Lincoln, Blair enjoyed a large measure of success on both sides of the Atlantic and was about to become the first Labour prime minister ever to complete two terms.

David Margolick, author of the *Vanity Fair* article, recalled Blair's awakening to Christian social justice, the kind Blair had encountered through Australian Anglican pastor Peter Thomson during his time at Oxford in the early 1970s and later promoted at the core of the New Labour in the 1990s. Blair's interest in faith, Margolick suggested, was far from irrelevant in his seemingly unnatural affinity with George Bush, Jr.

The article pointed out divisions in Britain over the prime minister's focus on religion. Margolick explains: "To the secular, [Blair's faith] makes him seem flaky and sanctimonious. To those more religious than he, it is inconsistent, superficial, and, oddly enough in the context of Iraq, unilateral: they say Blair does what he pleases, ignoring religious authorities and teachings."[122]

In an interview in mid-March 2003 aboard "Blairforce One," on the way back home from Blair's meeting with President Bush in the Azores, when David Margolick approached the theme of Blair's and Bush's respective religious beliefs, Blair referred to religion as "something we share."[123] But when the journalist tried to push the conversation further, Blair's director of communications, Alastair Campbell, stepped in. David Margolick related the anecdote, making it a famous example of the Blair staff's uneasiness regarding the religious feelings of the prime minister: "'Is he on to God?' Campbell asks Blair—the 'he' being me. 'We don't do God,' Campbell declares. 'I'm sorry. We don't do God.'"[124]

In fact, Blair had being "doing" a lot of God and was not about to stop. Ending his article, Margolick reported Blair's impressions as a passionate reader of the Koran. Blair told about how much the Muslim holy text had in common with the Jewish and the Christian traditions, expressing his sadness at the "huge misunderstanding between these religious beliefs that, in fact, share so many common values and so much common heritage."[125] The fact that "the best motivations of people from our religion and the best motivations of people from the Muslim religion"[126] were in the same "line of tradition"[127] was the main reason Blair considered "doing God" necessary if a new world order was to be built. And there, in Margolick's view, lay the main difference between the Christian Bush and the Christian Blair: while Bush saw Osama Bin Laden

---

122. Margolick, "Blair's Big Gamble."
123. Ibid.
124. Ibid.
125. Ibid.
126. Ibid.
127. Ibid.

and Saddam Hussein as "threats to American security,"[128] Blair saw them "as excuses to remake the world."[129]

Deathbed Bequests

If global gods presided over Blair's indulgence in "doing religion" and over his ambition to "remake the world," they were no less decisive in shaping the philosophy of the House of Lords in Aston Cantlow.

Indeed, what at first appeared a limitedly English judgment was, in fact, the response to a twofold global challenge. On the one hand, the lords had successfully protected the established Church of England from the tightening of European law and global human rights. On the other hand, the emphasis on the independence and the religious nature of the Church of England was instrumental in asserting its leadership in the worldwide Anglican Communion, again a response to the rising global gods.

While impacting British law and politics, global gods also affected the Indian Supreme Court and the South African Constitutional Court. Following the explosive and national gods' challenge to the secular and multireligious dimension of Britain, South Africa, and India, global gods were on the attack over equality and difference. In Aston Cantlow, the lords protected the difference of the Church of England by accentuating its equality with any other faith organization. But in the name of equality, Shabina Begum would soon ask them to assert her insubordinate difference too.

Shortly after the Aston Cantlow judgment, the trouble with the global gods' call for equality and difference dominated two simultaneous decisions: one in India and one in South Africa.

On July 21, 2003, the Supreme Court of India ruled unconstitutional the discriminatory law of succession, which prevented Christians from disposing of their property by testament for religious and charitable purposes.

The case was yet another reminder of the postcolonial hangover. The petitioner, Roman Catholic priest John Vallamattom, objected to the persistency in Indian law of a relic of the British Raj: the Statute of Mortmain of 1888. Restrictions on disposition of property by succession in favor of religious bodies were meant to avoid ill-considered deathbed bequests under religious influence. Though the British Parliament repealed the Statute of Mortmain only in 1960, already in 1925, the Indian Succession Act excluded from the scope of the law the testamentary succession to the property of non-Christians, including Muslims, Hindus, Buddhists, Sikhs, and Parsis. Discrimination was the key contention John Vallamattom put forward, and, in particular, discrimination against Christians vis-à-vis non-Christians.

The petition succeeded under the constitutional principle of equality. Justice Khare for the Court found unreasonable the construction of Christians as a separate

128. Ibid.
129. Ibid.

category deserving a more restrictive regulation; he thus found the relevant section of the 1925 Indian Succession Act arbitrary and discriminatory and declared it unconstitutional. As for the House of Lords in Aston Cantlow, the Supreme Court of India grounded the decision not only on domestic law but on comparative law and human rights law as well.

Beyond the redress of the anti-Christian discrimination, Justice Khare's vision of an expanding global law prompted a plea for the adaptation of the law to historical changes. The Indian judge quoted Albert Camus's "the wheel turns, history changes" and delivered his dynamic concept of the two-sided "law-coin": "Stability and change are the two sides of the law-coin. In their pure form they are antagonistic poles; without stability the law becomes not a chart of conduct, but a game of chance; with only stability the law is as the still waters in which there is only stagnation and death."[130]

In his concurring opinion, Justice Sinha signified that the passage of time had caused the purpose of the disputed legislation to lose its significance: the need was no more to protect those illiterate people who "used to blindly follow the preachers of the religion."[131]

India's struggle with the "two sides of the law-coin," with "stability and change," was at the heart of the whole issue of personal laws. Eight years after the 1995 victory of Sushmita Ghosh in court, Justice Khare recalled the Sarla Mudgal judgment and reiterated Justice Kuldip Singh's plea that "there is no necessary connection between religious and personal law in a civilized society."[132] He added that matters "of a secular character" like marriage and succession should not be treated as practices protected under the constitutional guarantee of religious freedom. Hence Justice Khare's regret that Parliament was "still to step in for framing a common civil code in the country"[133] and his support of the Court's argument in Shah Bano, almost twenty years earlier, that such code would "help the cause of national integration by removing the contradictions based on ideologies."[134]

One Impediment

The civil code issue was not alone in connecting Sushmita Ghosh's struggle to the Vallamattom judgment. Echoing the global gods' offensive on equality, Justice Khare took the assertion of women's rights in Indian law as an example that the world "witnessed a sea-change"[135] and that the legal response needed to follow accordingly: "The right of equality of women vis-à-vis their male counterpart is accepted worldwide. It will

130. *John Vallamattom* [35].
131. Ibid. [56].
132. Ibid. [44].
133. Ibid.
134. Ibid.
135. Ibid. [36].

be immoral to discriminate a woman on the ground of sex. It is forbidden both in our domestic law as also international law."[136]

On the other side of the Indian Ocean, ten days after the Vallamattom ruling, the South African Constitutional Court also faced a sea change in equality and gender rights.

The Court received the application from a couple whose history appeared ordinary at first glance. In his opinion, Justice Albie Sachs presented the facts in an almost literary style: "Finding themselves strongly attracted to each other, two people went out regularly and eventually decided to set up home together. After being acknowledged by their friends as a couple for more than a decade, they decided that the time had come to get public recognition and registration of their relationship, and formally to embrace the rights and responsibilities they felt should flow from and attach to it."[137]

Then the novelist judge surprised the reader: "Like many persons in their situation, they wanted to get married. There was one impediment. They are both women."[138]

Marié Adriaana Fourie and Cecelia Johanna Bonthuys had first applied to the Pretoria High Court asking that the Marriage Act of 1961 be interpreted so as to allow same-sex marriages. On October 18, 2002, Justice Roux in the High Court dismissed the application, maintaining that the reference of the law to a "marriage between a male and a female and no other" was peremptory. In July 2003, the constitutional judges had to decide on the request of the two women to be granted leave for direct appeal to the Constitutional Court. Justice Moseneke for the Court refused the application, prescribing a further appeal to the Supreme Court of Appeal. Only in 2005, with a momentous one-hundred-page opinion by Justice Sachs, would the Constitutional Court rule in the case.

As the Supreme Court of Appeal in South Africa started examining the Fourie case, Queen Elizabeth announced on November 26, 2003, that her government "will maintain its commitment to increased equality and social justice by bringing forward legislation on the registration of civil partnerships between same sex couples."[139]

No matter the country, equality was decidedly what the global gods were after.

She Chose

Following the day in September 2002 when Shabina Begum arrived at school wearing her jilbab, the Begum case snowballed, progressively involving an ever larger panoply of people and actions: school authorities and committees wrote letters and released statements, imams gave a wide array of contradicting opinions, newspapers exposed the alarming sides of the story, proactive agents of the Education Welfare Service did all they could to bring Shabina back to the Denbigh High School or to find a viable alternative.

136. Ibid.
137. *Minister of Home Affairs* [1].
138. Ibid.
139. Elizabeth, "Queen's Speech."

Muslim radicals at the gates of the school demonstrated against the education of Muslim children in secular schools. Several Muslim girls reported to their teachers that they felt they were being pressured to wear the jilbab. Parents of Denbigh High School's pupils showed their worries for what radical Muslims viewed as a conflict between "better" Muslims wearing the jilbab and second-class, hypocritical Muslims.

The particular case of Shabina Begum assumed broader significance. It also grew in terms of legal intricacy, as counsels progressively took the stage. On September 11, 2003, Shabina's counsel, Ms. Spencer, advanced two proposals. Shabina would attend school wearing the jilbab but would be educated in the Inclusive Learning Room, away from the main school community. Alternatively, she would attend school wearing a modified version of the uniform: she would still wear a white shirt and tie, but her arms and legs would be covered by one dark garment in accordance with the school's colors.

On September 15, Mrs. Bevan wrote back. She replied that Shabina had been offered the option of returning to school wearing the *shalwar kameeze* "in a form which covers most of her legs, which would also be covered by the loose trousers worn underneath."[140] The head teacher explained that in addition to the full consultation with the parents, pupils, and local mosques, which led to the adoption of the uniform policy, four additional opinions from independent Muslim scholarly sources had been sought, all of them confirming that the *shalwar kameeze* satisfied the Islamic dress code. In conclusion, anticipating the decision taken by the chair of the governors on September 23, 2003, she stated that the school was unable to accommodate "individuals' interpretations of religious codes."[141]

Eventually, Shabina Begum's lawyer issued claim for judicial review on February 13, 2004. As in Aston Cantlow, the European Convention played a central part. Based on the Convention, the counsel for Shabina claimed the decision not to admit her while wearing a jilbab infringed Shabina's right to "manifest [her] religion . . . in . . . practice and observance" (Article 9) and her right not to "be denied the right to education" (Article 2 of the First Protocol).

In her statement to the High Court, Mrs. Bevan highlighted the stakes of the attack on the uniform policy of the school. With the case being given wide publicity, with Muslim activists picketing the school and with the High Court now in charge, Mrs. Bevan felt entitled to put on the table the most sensitive arguments. Muslim and non-Muslim students were extremely concerned that a change in the uniform policy might make room for extremist views. A number of girls in the school were "resisting the efforts of others to recruit them to extreme Muslim groups."[142] Allowing the jilbab, Mrs. Bevan declared, would deprive these girls of "proper protection"[143] and would make them feel abandoned "by those upon whom they were relying to preserve their

140. *R. (Begum)* (2004) [27].
141. Ibid.
142. Ibid. [82].
143. Ibid.

freedom to follow their own part of the Islamic tradition."[144] The refusal to accommodate Shabina went beyond the particular case. Ultimately it was about inclusion and social cohesion. Mrs. Bevan wrote to the judges:

> If the school were to allow pupils to wear a variety of different forms of clothing there would be the potential for the forming of groups and cliques who would be identified by the clothes that they wear. In my view, that would make the delivery of the curriculum more difficult, as well as undermining the strong positive and inclusive ethos of the school.[145]

The head teacher underlined this was the very project she had been undertaking since her appointment. Under such guidelines, the school had changed from being "well below national averages and viewed negatively within the community to being well above average and oversubscribed."[146]

Against such a background, Justice Bennett for the High Court handed down his verdict on June 15, 2004. He dismissed Shabina Begum's application for two reasons. First, he did not find evidence proving the alleged exclusion of Shabina from school. "What to my mind is abundantly clear,"[147] the judge wrote, "is that the Defendant [Mrs. Bevan] earnestly and sincerely wanted the Claimant [Shabina] to attend school."[148] He added:

> The reality of the situation was and still is that the Claimant, entirely of her own volition, chose not to attend Denbigh High School unless the Defendant agreed to her wearing the jilbab. The Defendant did not so agree. The Claimant had a choice, either of returning to school wearing the school uniform or of refusing to wear the school uniform knowing that if she did so refuse the Defendant was unlikely to allow her to attend. She chose the latter.[149]

The judge concluded that nothing in the school's action amounted to exclusion, "either formal, informal, unofficial, or in any way whatsoever."[150]

The second reason for dismissal was that the restriction on Shabina's freedom of religion because of the uniform policy was legitimate and proportionate. The legitimate aim, Justice Bennett found, was "the proper running of a multi-cultural, multi-faith, secular school."[151] The restriction was proportionate since it had been "specifically devised with the advice of the Muslim community."[152] Accordingly, the judge considered

---

144. Ibid.
145. Ibid.
146. Ibid.
147. Ibid. [60].
148. Ibid.
149. Ibid.
150. Ibid.
151. Ibid. [91].
152. Ibid.

the school uniform policy was "reasoned, balanced" and proportionate and found no breach of Shabina's religious freedom.

Hands Off

During 2004, under the leadership of Thabo Mbeki, who commenced his second term in power, South Africa celebrated the tenth anniversary of the first racially inclusive elections. The big point of contention had to do with delivery. Poverty and deprivation were still huge. Violence, crime, and AIDS ravaged the country. Affirmative actions aiming at the creation of a black middle class proved immaterial. The Black Economic Empowerment program, noticed journalist Alec Russell, encouraged "a culture of dependency and expectation."[153] In a context where the easiest way to flourish was, Russell quipped, "to trade political contacts for shareholdings,"[154] the new class of black rich people, most of them African National Congress veterans, were "more adept at parlaying influence than building businesses."[155] Political corruption and incompetence were blatant. Promises had not been fulfilled.

Desmond Tutu gave voice to the widespread disappointment. In the famous 1990 speech in Rustenburg, in which Willie Jonker confessed the complicity of the Dutch Reformed Church with the apartheid regime, Jonker himself foresaw the challenge ahead: "Churches are always in danger of relaxing their critical vigilance when, after a period of strife, the political power is taken over by a party or movement to which they are favourably disposed. They are then tempted to bless it and offer religious sanctioning."[156]

Fifteen years later, Jonker's words, "the Church may never forfeit its critical role in society,"[157] were certainly recalled by Tutu as he rebuked Mbeki for the self-interested and nondemocratic government style of the African National Congress (ANC) and criticized the emergence of an exiguous, rich black elite against the backdrop of the persisting deprivation of large sectors of the population. Mbeki responded with an adamant defense of the ANC. His entourage belittled Tutu for being an icon of white elites. The archbishop fought back, declaring he would pray for Mbeki as he had prayed for the officials of the apartheid government.

Shortly afterward, at its thirty-sixth ordinary session from November 23 to December 7, 2004, in Dakar, the African Commission on Human and Peoples' Rights examined Gareth Prince's petition against the 2002 adverse ruling by the Constitutional Court.

153. Russell, *After Mandela*, 169.

154. Ibid., 172.

155. Ibid., 171.

156. Jonker, "Understanding the Church Situation," 96.

157. Ibid.

Based on the African Charter of Human Rights of 1981, Gareth Prince summoned the Commission to declare that South Africa had violated his right to dignity (Article 5), to religious freedom (Article 6), to occupational choice (Article 15), and to a cultural life (Article 17 §2). Gareth Prince's submission echoed Albie Sachs's opinion in 2002. The Rastafari complained he belonged to a vulnerable "political minority not able to use political power to secure favourable legislation for themselves."[158] Prince also clarified he did not seek an overall decriminalization of cannabis but only a "reasonable accommodation."[159] The point was that statutes failed "to distinguish between Rastafari and drug abusers, thereby grouping genuine religious observation with criminality."[160]

Another Rastafari, Reuben Phillip Andrews, had made the same point a few months earlier before the Court of Appeal in London. Andrews had been arrested at Heathrow Airport on his way back from Jamaica. Two large brown taped packages were found in his blue Adidas carry-on containing 11.7 kilos of cannabis, for a street value in England of more than 35,000 pounds. Andrews had been subsequently sentenced to thirty months in prison. In the judgment of March 5, 2004, the British judges confirmed the conviction, maintaining that Andrews's religious defense should succumb to the international obligations of Britain in the antidrug fight.

While the Court of Appeal in London proved impregnable to Andrews's arguments, the African Commission in Dakar did not listen to Prince's either. If the right to hold a religious belief should be absolute, the decision read, "the right to act on those beliefs should not."[161] In some circumstances, the right to practice one's religion had to "yield to the interests of society."[162] It was legitimate to restrict individual freedom for the sake of the fight on the abuse and traffic of drugs. Cultural rights could not be protected as to endanger the "overall good of society,"[163] the Commission held: "Minorities like the Rastafari may freely choose to exercise their culture, yet, that should not grant them unfettered power to violate the norms that keep the whole nation together. Otherwise . . . the result would be anarchy, which may defeat everything altogether."[164]

Again, as in the Constitutional Court of South Africa, avoidance of anarchy was the reason, or the pretext, for not granting Prince the exception he sought.

As for the occupational choice, the Commission argued along the same line as Justice Bennett had in the English High Court's dismissal of Shabina Begum's application. As Shabina had chosen either the wrong attire or the wrong school, Gareth had chosen

158. *Prince* (2004) [31].
159. Ibid.
160. Ibid. [30].
161. Ibid. [41].
162. Ibid.
163. Ibid. [48].
164. Ibid.

either the wrong religious practice or the wrong job. Gareth therefore suffered not from an immoderate restriction on the part of the state but as the result of his own volition.

The Commission found no violation of Gareth Prince's rights and upheld the South African state's view. In the time of global gods, the decision was about the competition between the South African and the pan-African dimensions, between the national Constitutional Court and the supranational African Commission. The government bullied the African Commissioners, urging them not to contradict such "an esteemed judicial body" as the South African Constitutional Court. An adverse ruling, the government alleged, "will inevitably carry seeds of possible conflict between domestic and international legal systems, and will upset the careful balances struck within the young and developing human rights system of member states of the African Union."[165]

The government of South Africa pleaded for the principle of subsidiarity and required the Commission to acknowledge the margin of appreciation, which allowed the state a wide discretion. Such discretion, the government alleged, rested "on its [the state's] direct and continuous knowledge of its society, its needs, resources, economic, and political situation, legal practices, and the fine balance that need to be struck between the competing and sometimes conflicting forces that shape a society."[166]

The African Commission recognized its own limited scope and acknowledged that subsidiarity and the margin of appreciation were two key principles. At the same time, the commissioners expressed their disagreement with an approach from the South African government, which "would be tantamount to ousting the African Commission's mandate to monitor and oversee the implementation of the African Charter."[167] They further asserted the mandate of the Commission "to guide, assist, supervise, and insist upon member states on better promotion and protection standards should it find domestic practices wanting."[168] Hence the contrast with the South African government, which the Commission blamed for advocating a "hands-off approach by the African Commission on the mere assertion that its domestic procedures meet more than the minimum requirements of the African Charter."[169]

Nearly twenty years had elapsed since Alex Boraine and Albie Sachs, together with other white South Africans, met a delegation of exiled African National Congress militants in Dakar. The international dimension of the anti-apartheid struggle was crucial. In 2004, in Dakar again, before the African Commission, the ANC-led South African government successfully defended internal policies against the global spreading of human rights. This was the reverted picture under the global gods. While advocating a "hands-off approach" by international human-right actors, Thabo Mbeki's

---

165. Ibid. [37].
166. Ibid.
167. Ibid. [53].
168. Ibid.
169. Ibid.

government also applied the same approach against domestic critics, including an ever-defiant Desmond Tutu.

Sparing the Rod

The play *Behzti* ("Dishonour") opened at the Birmingham Repertory Theatre on December 9, 2004. Its script, written by a British-born woman of Sikh background named Gurprett Kaur Bhatti, was set in the context of the precincts of a Sikh *gurdwara*. It focused on religious, especially Sikh, hypocrisy in relation to corruption, violence, and failure in relationships across racial and social lines. The theater's management did not accede to requests by Sikh authorities to restage the play in a community center rather than in the *gurdwara*, a place of worship. Consultations by the theater's manager with the local Sikh community did not avoid an outraged protest against the desecration of the sacred *gurdwara*.

The initially peaceful protest turned wild on December 19, 2004, when around four hundred Sikhs, most of them from outside the local area, stormed the theater. Doors and windows were destroyed, the foyer attacked. Five police officers were injured and two rioters were arrested. As a result, the play was canceled indefinitely.

Religious-studies professor Paul Weller stressed an analogy between the case of Salman Rushdie, and that of the playwright Gurprett Kaur Bhatti, threatened and forced to go into hiding. In the time of global gods, demonstrations mobilized Sikhs beyond Britain. Paul Weller noticed "the issue reached the global media and many Sikhs in other parts of the world expressed concern and outrage."[170]

Along with the alien gods of immigrant communities with international networks, Christian global gods also challenged Britain. After trying the global Anglican-establishment gods in Aston Cantlow in 2003, the House of Lords tried the global non-mainstream Christian gods in 2005 in the Williamson case.

That case concerned corporal punishment at school. The applicants were head teachers, teachers, and parents of children at four independent schools, the Christian Fellowship School at Edge Hill, Liverpool; Bradford Christian School at Idle, Bradford; Cornerstone School at Epsom, Surrey; and King's School at Eastleigh, Hampshire.

The applicants claimed the statutory ban on corporal correction imposed in 1986 and extended in 1998 infringed their belief that "part of the duty of education in the Christian context is that teachers should be able to stand in the place of parents and administer physical punishment to children who are guilty of indiscipline."[171] They interpreted the Bible as justifying and requiring the use of "loving corporal correction."[172] Did not Proverbs 13:24 read, "He who spares the rod hates his son"? In practice, boys would be punished with "a thin, broad flat 'paddle' to both buttocks

---

170. Weller, *Religious Diversity in the UK*, 172.

171. *R. (Williamson)* (2005) [9].

172. Ibid [10].

simultaneously in a firm controlled manner"[173] and girls by being strapped upon the hand. This would take place in a separate room. After the punishment, a member of the staff would comfort the child and encourage him or her to pray.

In 1982 the European Court of Human Rights had condemned the UK on the same issue, but on a converse claim. Mrs. Campbell and Mrs. Cosans held that the use of corporal correction against their children at school was incompatible with their worldview. Their success in Strasbourg prompted Britain to ban corporal punishment. Twenty years later, the claimants in Williamson advanced the opposite claim, holding that their belief commanded them to have their children educated in a school where corporal correction was administered. Accordingly, they opposed the UK's blanket ban on physical chastisement and requested to be exempted from the ban.

In the Christian Education case judged in 2000, the South African Constitutional Court had dismissed an identical claim, with Albie Sachs delivering his momentous opinion for a unanimous court.

On December 12, 2002 the English Court of Appeal dismissed the application in the Williamson case. The main argument was about "the nature of religious belief itself."[174] The judges objected to the construction of the claim as pertaining to religious freedom: they did not accept that the claimants had given evidence that corporal correction in education was a manifestation of their religious belief. Justice Rix went so far as to emphasize the inherent threat of religion for social stability: "it is impossible to shut one's eyes to the great dangers which exist and have always existed in the very potency of religious belief and in its potential for conflict."[175]

Justice Buxton challenged the biblical foundation of the applicants' option for mild corporal correction. Paradoxically, he argued, a literal interpretation of the Bible required a far more extensive application of corporal punishment than the applicants demanded.

Counsel for the applicants, Paul Diamond, argued that "assertions by believers that their belief had been infringed by particular state or secular arrangements had to be taken as given."[176] The judges of the Court of Appeal did not agree. First, they asserted a distinction needed to be drawn between an act expressing a belief and one that was merely motivated by it. Second, the judges accepted the Secretary of State's argument that the appellants' belief, "albeit accepted as a genuine one, was not a religious belief."[177]

On February 24, 2005, a unanimous bench of the House of Lords also dismissed the appeal. The lords, however, did not follow the approach of the Court of Appeal,

---

173. Ibid.
174. *R. (Williamson)* (2002) [114].
175. Ibid. [95].
176. Ibid. [58].
177. Ibid. [96].

based on the denial that the requested exemption served the purpose of allowing the manifestation of a religious belief in the sense of Article 9 of the European Convention.

Like Albie Sachs five years earlier, the lords did not question the sincerity of the claimants' religious motives. Nor did they challenge the assumption that their claim was based on a religious belief. Instead they dismissed the claim because the state's restriction to the claimants' freedom was accurately prepared through "an array of international and professional support"[178] and fully justified in view of the state's obligation to protect children from inhumane or degrading punishment.

Counsel Paul Diamond had challenged the lords not to "show liberal tolerance only to tolerant liberals."[179] In fact, the appeal failed not because the lords did not accept the opposition to the ban on corporal correction as based on a religious belief, but because they held as justified the restriction to the freedom of the applicants. Indeed, though the House of Lords rejected the application, the decision became a victory as for the applicants' claim that corporal punishment was a true manifestation of their faith.

Lord Walker of Gestingthorpe articulated the reluctance of the lords to engage with the definition of religious belief. Quoting Justices Wilson and Deane for the High Court of Australia in the 1983 Church of the New Faith case, the English judge first referred to the global trend towards a broader understanding of religion: "The trend of authority (unsurprisingly in an age of increasingly multicultural societies and increasing respect for human rights) is towards a 'newer, more expansive, reading' of religion."[180]

It went beyond the Court's legitimate role, he asserted, "to adjudicate on the seriousness, cogency, and coherence of theological beliefs."[181]

Furthermore, the judge stressed that it was not disputed "that Christianity is a religion, and that the appellants are sincere, practising Christians."[182] Diversity among Christians was obvious, Lord Walker emphasized, and spurred a huge variety of beliefs and practices:

> Those who profess the Christian religion are divided among many different churches and sects, sometimes hostile to each other, which is a cause of both sadness and scandal. That some Christians should believe that the Bible not merely permits but enjoins them to have corporal punishment administered to their children may be surprising to many, but it is by no means an extreme instance. Some sects claiming to be Christian believed that polygamy was not merely permitted but actually enjoined by the Bible . . . Others believe that medical treatment by blood transfusion is forbidden by the Bible and is sinful, even if it is the only means of saving life . . . Countless thousands have suffered

178. R. (Williamson) (2005) [86].
179. Ibid. [60].
180. Ibid. [55].
181. Ibid. [57].
182. Ibid. [56].

cruel deaths because at different periods during the last two thousand years parts of the Christian Church thought that the Bible not merely permitted but enjoined them to torture and kill apostates, heretics, and witches . . . By comparison with these horrors a belief in a scriptural basis for smacking children is fairly small beer.[183]

With his carefully motivated denial of an exception, as well as his care for the beliefs of the applicants, Albie Sachs in 2000 paved the way for the decision of the House of Lords in 2005.

Lord Walker explicitly endorsed Albie Sachs's nuanced and contextual approach. Referring to Sachs, the British judge affirmed that "this is an area in which a rigidly analytical approach, dividing the case into watertight issues, to be decided *seriatim*, may not always be the best way forward."[184]

Moreover, Lord Walker also quoted at length the substantial position adopted by Sachs.

Going back to his opinion of 2000, years later Albie Sachs recalled how difficult had been to judge a case so intimately linked to his experience as a detainee with fellow black youngsters beaten by wardens. Yet, he wrote in 2009, "I felt it necessary to explain the issues not in terms of my particular experiences, but in relation to the constitutional values involved."[185] In the end, if Sachs's opinion went against the applicants, the South African judge paid deep respect to their position. He wrote in 2009: "I like to think that disappointed as they might have been by the result, the School felt that the depth of their convictions had been appreciated and taken seriously."[186]

By endorsing Albie Sachs's approach in 2005, the House of Lords could hope to express a similar sentiment with regard to the Williamson ruling.

Shabina's Victory

On March 2, 2005, a few days after the Williamson decision by the House of Lords, the Court of Appeal allowed Shabina Begum's appeal and held that the young lady had been unlawfully excluded from school. A new advocate, Cherie Booth—Britain's First Lady—had joined Shabina's legal team. Starting in September 2004, Shabina had attended at Putteridge High School, where she was allowed to wear a jilbab. By the time of the appeal, Shabina had decided not to pursue a claim for damages. The case was about a point of principle. All she sought at this stage was a declaration that her exclusion had been unlawful.

183. Ibid.
184. Ibid. [66].
185. Sachs, *The Strange Alchemy of Life and Law*, 272.
186. Ibid.

Against the school's version, Lord Justice Brooke held that yes, Shabina had been excluded from school, and yes, such exclusion had limited Shabina's religious freedom. The judge stated that if the uniform policy suited a majority of mainstream "liberal Muslims,"[187] this was no reason not to take into account the freedom of belief of a minority of "very strict Muslims."[188]

The Court held the Denbigh High School, "as an emanation of the state,"[189] had not justified the limitation on Shabina's freedom created by "the uniform code and by the way in which it was enforced."[190] Lord Justice Scott Baker recalled that the United Kingdom was not "a secular state" and therefore allowed for the broadest respect of religious feelings: "The United Kingdom is not a secular state; there is no principle of denominational neutrality in our schools. Provision is made for religious education and worship in schools under Chapter VI of the School Standards and Framework Act 1998. Every shade of religious belief, if genuinely held, is entitled to due consideration under Article 9."[191]

He then remarked the school had "regrettably . . . decided that because the *shalwar kameeze* was acceptable for the majority of Muslims the claimant should be required to toe the line."[192] By this, the school had failed to correctly approach the case of Shabina in light of Article 9 of the European Convention: "What went wrong in this case was that the School failed to appreciate that, by its action, it was infringing the claimant's Article 9 (1) right to manifest her religion."[193]

In the time of global gods and global law, the British judges quoted the Court of Strasbourg. Recently, the Court had upheld the Turkish refusal to exempt Leyla Şahin, a student at the University of Ankara, from the obligation to take off her head scarf while on campus. Justice Brooke stressed that the European ruling was based on the neutrality of public universities in Turkey, which responded to the Turkish constitutional principle of secularism. By contrast, the judge underlined that Britain was not a secular state and thereby excluded the notion that the European ruling could apply in the case of Shabina. Religious Britain was singled out as opposed to secular Turkey.

Finally, Shabina Begum was found entitled to the declaratory relief she sought. However, Lord Justice Scott Baker expressed "considerable sympathy with the School and its governors in the predicament that they faced,"[194] and drew the difference between the unlawfulness of their decision and the quality of their approach:

187. *R. (Begum)* (2005) [31].
188. Ibid. [31]
189. Ibid. [49]
190. Ibid.
191. Ibid. [94].
192. Ibid. [92].
193. Ibid. [94].
194. Ibid. [91].

It is perhaps understandable that a school that can rightly be proud of its contribution to the welfare of members of a multicultural society should have taken the line that it did, albeit one that on careful analysis has been shown to be erroneous in law.[195]

Unfortunately the school bodies "did not appreciate that they faced foursquare an issue that engaged"[196] the protection of religious freedom under Article 9 of the European Convention. Nevertheless, Lord Justice Mummery pointed out, the expression of religious freedom was not an absolute and certainly not "necessarily a valid reason for overriding the social responsibilities of the individual holder of the right to others living in the community."[197] Justice Brooke concluded sympathetically with the school that "nothing in this judgment should be taken as meaning that it would be impossible for the School to justify its stance if it were to reconsider its uniform policy in the light of this judgment and were to determine not to alter it in any significant respect."[198]

Shabina Begum's victory was therefore strictly procedural and very limited in scope. But it was a victory anyway. According to British justice, the school had been three times unlawful: first, in excluding Shabina from school; second, in denying her the right to manifest her religion; and third, in preventing her from accessing an appropriate education. The Denbigh High School's bodies were not pleased. For them the case was not closed. They appealed to the House of Lords.

By Gandhi's Statue

On July 7, 2005, in London, Hasib Hussain detonated his rucksack bomb at 9:47 a.m., on the top deck of the No. 30 bus. Thirteen people died, in addition to the suicide bomber himself.

Witnesses reported that on his way from King's Cross the bomber repeatedly tried to detonate the explosive. He only succeeded at the junction of Tavistock Square and Upper Woburn Place. A few meters away, in the square's gardens, stood a statue of Gandhi. Unveiled in 1968, this was the monument to pacifism, nonviolence, and the postcolonial British optimism for diversity, there in the heart of the very Bloomsbury that had helped Gandhi clarify his dharma. There was a much more dramatic Indian element in the killings that day. Among the passengers of the No. 30 bus, Neetu Jain, thirty-seven, a Hindu woman born in Delhi, was killed in the blast, as was Shahara Islam, twenty, a British Bengali Muslim who attended the local mosque. According to

195. Ibid.
196. Ibid.
197. Ibid. [86].
198. Ibid. [81].

the statement issued by the family, "She was an Eastender, a Londoner and British, but above all a true Muslim and proud to be so."[199]

In the four explosions that day, fifty-two were killed in addition to the four home-grown suicide attackers, and about seven hundred were wounded.

The London bombings affected the British debate on multiculturalism, religious diversity and Islam. Explanations of 7/7 were deeply polarized: on the one extreme, many pointed out the failure of integration of an increasingly alienated and marginalized Muslim sector of the population. On the other, blame fell on the Iraqi war, the role of which, as a motive for the attack, Prime Minister Blair clumsily denied. Mark Curtis saw the whole British foreign policy and the long-lasting partnership with radical Islamists, especially in Pakistan, as "the dirty secret at the heart of 7/7:"[200]

> The bombings were, to a large extent, a product of British foreign policy, not mainly since they were perpetrated by opponents of the war in Iraq, but because they derived from a terrorism infrastructure established by a Pakistani state long backed by Whitehall and involving Pakistani terrorist groups which had benefited from past British covert action.[201]

The bombings had a close connection with an English judiciary that was just starting to try the explosive gods. In their biography of Abu Hamza, Sean O'Neill and Daniel McGrory underscore the coincidence between the bombings and the start of the trial against the sheikh of Finsbury Park:

> At the moment the first three explosions occurred beneath the streets of London, Abu Hamza was arriving at the Old Bailey courthouse to stand trial for inciting his followers to kill and be killed, to carry out what he liked to call "martyrdom operations." . . . Abu Hamza was sitting in the dock as news filtered through to the court of the carnage that had occurred in the city outside. The trial judge decided that it would be simply impossible to find a jury that week or in the immediate future to conduct a fair trial of Abu Hamza. The preacher was taken back to the cells, knowing that holy warriors had brought the bloody jihad he advocated to London.[202]

With the country growing anxious over its multicultural and multireligious character, the question of discrimination and equality touched upon society as a whole and reached well beyond the uneasiness within immigrant communities.

A couple weeks after the London bombings, the bishops of the Church of England issued a statement on the Civil Partnership Act due to go into effect on December 5, 2005.

---

199. Rai, 7/7, 49.

200. Curtis, *Secret Affairs*, 285.

201. Ibid.

202. O'Neill and McGrory, *The Suicide Factory*, xxi.

In the "pastoral statement" of July 25, 2005, the House of Bishops stayed firm on two aspects: one theological and one legal. Following on the *Issues on Human Sexuality*, the guidelines published in 2003, bishops stated first of all that the Church's teaching on sexual ethics was unchanged. According to n. 27, lifelong union between a man and a woman remained the "proper context for sexual activity," and the Act did not alter the balance between preference for heterosexuality within marriage and tolerance of a faithful, committed homosexual relation for those who, in conscience, felt unable to accept a life of sexual abstinence.[203] Second, at n. 8 bishops underlined the Act did not amend matrimonial law and did not introduce same-sex marriage:

> The new legislation makes no change to the law of the land in relation to marriage. It remains the case that, in law, as in the eyes of the Church, marriage can be entered into only by a man and a woman. The Government has stated that it has no intention of introducing "same–sex marriage." Civil partnerships are not a form of marriage.[204]

The matter was not settled with the same clarity on more divisive aspects of the legislation, with the bishops holding principles that allowed a considerable grey area. According to n. 17, "the Church will continue . . . to affirm the value of committed, sexually abstinent friendships between people of the same sex and to minister sensitively and pastorally to those Christians who conscientiously decide to order their lives differently."[205]

In particular, n. 17 of the statement forbade the clergy from performing services of blessing of civil partnerships, but recognized that people "in a variety of relationships," some possibly consistent with the Church's teaching, could approach clergy asking for prayer. In such case, n. 18 of the statement acknowledged the clergy large discretion "in the light of the circumstances of each case." On another controversial issue, the statement did not issue an absolute prohibition to ordained ministers to register a civil partnership; at n. 19 bishops did not consider entering into a civil partnership "as intrinsically incompatible with holy orders," provided the person concerned was "willing to give assurances to his or her bishop that the relationship is consistent with the standards for the clergy set out in *Issues in Human Sexuality*."[206]

If multiculturalism and radical Islam challenged Britain with the London bombings, the issue of same-sex marriages was also a blast, though a metaphorical one, challenging postmodern Christians in Britain and South Africa.

203. Church of England, House of Bishops, "Civil Partnerships."
204. Ibid.
205. Ibid.
206. Ibid.

Fourie Decided

Four days before the Civil Partnerships Act in Britain went into effect, on December 1, 2005, the Constitutional Court of South Africa decided the case of Marié Adriaana Fourie and Cecelia Johanna Bonthuys, the two women who claimed their right to be married.

The decision had been long awaited, inside the country and abroad. Everywhere, the redefinition of the boundaries of marriage and family was a crucial aspect of the global gods' challenge. The Fourie case had been consolidated with a similar case deferred by the Johannesburg High Court, following an application by the Lesbian and Gay Equality Project. Albie Sachs presided the bench and delivered a lengthy opinion for a unanimous court. He later captured the worldwide interest for the moment through an image that recapitulated his entire life: "For the second time in my life, my photograph appeared in the *New York Times*—the first image had been of me recovering from the bomb in a London hospital, swathed in bandages; now it showed me in my green robes, flanked by my law colleagues, with my law clerk sitting below."[207]

One year earlier, on November 30, 2004, the Supreme Court of Appeal had granted the applicants what Sachs described as a "tiny modicum of success."[208]

For Justice Cameron in the Supreme Court, who gave the opinion for the majority, the Bill of Rights implied that the present common-law concept of marriage discriminated unfairly against same-sex couples and should be developed so as to encompass them, but held the court could not intrude in the legislative process and amend the Marriage Act. The Supreme Court judge suggested, however, that since the Act recognized that religious ministers acting as marriage officers could celebrate marriages according to the rites of the relevant community, and since some religious communities approved of same-sex marriages, the present statute could be interpreted as allowing for religious celebrations of same-sex marriages. According to this interpretation, religious couples could hope to find a sympathetic church and get married under the present Marriage Act, while couples seeking a purely secular marriage had no option.

The Court was confronted by discontentment from both parties. Marié Adriaana, Cecelia Johanna, and the others wanted nothing less than true marriage, the full acknowledgment of their equality. The state argued it was for the Parliament to intervene in such a sensitive domain, and emphasized that discrimination against homosexuals was not the result of their exclusion from marriage as such, but of the lack of legal recognition. With such an extensive array of issues, Justice Sachs endeavored to put "the pieces of the puzzle"[209] together. He answered two fundamental questions. First, did the combination of common law and the Marriage Act deny equal protection to and discriminate unfairly against same-sex couples by not allowing them to

207. Sachs, *The Strange Alchemy of Life and Law*, 252–53.

208. Ibid., 241.

209. *Minister of Home Affairs* [43].

get married? Second, in case of an affirmative answer, what appropriate remedy could the Court provide?

Albie Sachs pointed to four basic constitutional features. The first was that South Africa had "a multitude of family formations"[210] in rapid evolution, this being incompatible with the adoption of one single, exclusive social and legal model of family. The second was the "long history in our country and abroad of marginalization and persecution of gays and lesbians."[211] The third was the absence of a "comprehensive legal regulation of the family-law rights of gays and lesbians."[212] The fourth was the constitutional need to break radically "with a past based on intolerance and exclusion,"[213] and to develop a society "based on equality and respect by all for all."[214] The judge summed up the four features in a passionate endorsement of difference. He referred to his own opinion in the Christian Education case, and linked the history of South Africa, where "for centuries, group membership based on supposed biological characteristics such as skin colour has been the express basis of advantage and disadvantage,"[215] to the constitutional commitment to a society based on tolerance and mutual respect:

> South Africans come in all shapes and sizes. The development of an active rather than a purely formal sense of enjoying a common citizenship depends on recognizing and accepting people with all their differences, as they are. The Constitution thus acknowledges the variability of human beings (genetic and socio-cultural), affirms the right to be different, and celebrates the diversity of the nation. Accordingly, what is at stake is not simply a question of removing an injustice experienced by a particular section of the community. At issue is a need to affirm the very character of our society as one based on tolerance and mutual respect.[216]

The judge subsequently accepted the key submission of the applicants, that the exclusion from marriage was discriminatory, not only for its practical, but also for its symbolic meaning. Such exclusion, Justice Sachs wrote,

> represents a harsh if oblique statement by the law that same-sex couples are outsiders, and that their need for affirmation and protection of their intimate relations as human beings is somehow less than that of heterosexual couples. It reinforces the wounding notion that they are to be treated as biological oddities, as failed or lapsed human beings who do not fit into normal society, and, as such, do not qualify for the full moral concern and respect that our

210. Ibid. [59].
211. Ibid.
212. Ibid.
213. Ibid.
214. Ibid.
215. Ibid. [60].
216. Ibid.

> Constitution seeks to secure for everyone. It signifies that their capacity for love, commitment, and accepting responsibility is by definition less worthy of regard than that of heterosexual couples.[217]

At that point the main obstacle to the applicants' claim was religion. For most religions, homosexuality was a sin, not to be encouraged through legal equality. Also, introduction of same-sex marriages was not indifferent to people who believed in the exclusive heterosexual character of marriage: same-sex marriages, many churches held, would inevitably threaten and even undermine traditional heterosexual unions. Other remedies could be found to address the needs of homosexuals, the plurality of family forms guaranteed by the Constitution being an opportunity to shape an ad hoc solution.

Though the British example was not put forward, the solution of the Civil Union Partnerships Act hung over the South African debate.

Albie Sachs gave an articulate response to the religious objection, recapitulating his vision of law and religion in new South Africa.

His starting point was the full acknowledgment of the public role of religion. Religion, he wrote, reached far beyond personal beliefs and doctrines:

> It is part of a people's temper and culture, and, for many believers, a significant part of their way of life. Religious organizations constitute important sectors of national life and accordingly have a right to express themselves to government and the courts on the great issues of the day. They are active participants in public affairs fully entitled to have their say with regard to the way law is made and applied.[218]

This did not mean that religion could be "a source for interpreting the Constitution:"[219]

> It would be out of order to employ the religious sentiments of some as a guide to the constitutional rights of others. Between and within religions there are vastly different and, at times, highly disputed views on how to respond to the fact that members of their congregations and clergy are themselves homosexual. Judges would be placed in an intolerable situation if they were called upon to construe religious texts and take sides on issues which have caused deep schisms within religious bodies.[220]

The Constitution contemplated an open and democratic society in which a "mutually respectful coexistence between the secular and the sacred"[221] was established.

---

217. Ibid. [71].
218. Ibid. [90].
219. Ibid. [92].
220. Ibid.
221. Ibid. [94].

With this goal in mind, the Court had "to recognize the sphere which each inhabits, not to force the one into the sphere of the other."[222]

The Court owed religions and believers not the power to hinder the freedom of others or to impose faith-based prejudice and inequalities on the society as a whole, but the recognition of the right to freely bear their difference. Therefore, if an order of the Court to allow same-sex marriages could not be countered in the name of religion, such order could not impinge on religious rights either. This meant the state had to accommodate religious belief in the event of the introduction of same-sex marriages: "no minister of religion," Sachs wrote, "could be compelled to solemnize a same-sex marriage if such a marriage would not conform to the doctrines of the religion concerned."[223]

Albie Sachs reached the conclusion that the failure of the common law and the Marriage Act to grant same-sex couples access to marriage constituted "an unjustifiable violation of their right to equal protection of the law under section 9 (1), and not to be discriminated against unfairly in terms of section 9 (3) of the Constitution."[224] This was a bold step, pushing the right to difference and the right to equality further than ever in South Africa and beyond.

Indeed, Albie Sachs took the problem of the balance between the Constitutional Court and the Parliament very seriously: should the Court limit its order to a declaration that the law of marriage breached fundamental rights of same-sex couples, or was it for the Court also to dictate a remedy?

The judge took a middle position. He acknowledged that it behooved the Parliament to amend the law in order to address the violation declared by the Court. But he limited the action of the legislature in the interest of the applicants. In fact, he provided that if Parliament failed "to cure the defect within twelve months,"[225] the words "or spouse" would "automatically be read into section 30 (1) of the Marriage Act,"[226] so as to integrate same-sex marriages in the legislation.

The judgment was given. It was now up to the Parliament to act. Commenting on his struggle with such a delicate ruling, Albie Sachs recalled in 2009: "the toughest part of the case for me was not purely technical; it was to take religion seriously as part of public life, and to respond to both the gay and lesbian community and the religious communities in a balanced, principled, and carefully reasoned way."[227]

With the British Civil Partnerships Act going into effect four days after the Fourie ruling, the two countries parted ways on two different levels. As for the substantial response to the issue, South Africa recognized the right of its citizens to marry a partner

222. Ibid.
223. Ibid. [97].
224. Ibid. [114].
225. Ibid. [161].
226. Ibid.
227. Sachs, *The Strange Alchemy of Life and Law*, 240.

of the same sex, while Britain opted for civil partnership, postponing the introduction of same-sex marriages. But difference also lay in the decision-making process. While the Parliament decided in Britain upon the initiative of the government, in South Africa, the Constitutional Court disavowed the government and anticipated the Parliament. Global gods played a role in shaping such a difference. The centrality of the Parliament in Britain had enabled the Church of England, twenty-six bishops of which were members of the House of Lords, to successfully oppose full equality in marriage between heterosexual and homosexual couples. Vice versa in South Africa, the absence of established Christianity and the prevailing role of the Constitutional Court had prevented antigay religious lobbying from having a decisive say.

Albie Sachs accepted the application by the two women Marié Adriaana Fourie and Cecelia Johanna Bonthuys a few weeks before the House of Lords heard the controversy between two other women, both Muslims: the head teacher and moderate Jasmin Bevan and the rebellious and radical Shabina Begum. In the two cases, the protagonists were "both women."[228] In the English case, two women were fighting each other over the inclusiveness of the public space and the competition within the Muslim community in Britain and beyond. In the South African case, two women were fighting on the same side for equality and the enfranchisement of stigmatized minorities. As anticipated in the struggle of Sushmita Ghosh and perpetuated in Indian social tensions over sex equality, women and gender were at the heart of the global quest for a new balance between tradition and modernity, equality and difference. India was again a crucial test as the Supreme Court directed the High Court of Delhi to reexamine the dismissal of a public-interest application by the progay and prolesbian Indian Naz Foundation, challenging the constitutional validity of criminal provisions against "unnatural offences"—essentially homosexual intercourse.

Global gods were a coin with two contradictory sides. One side of the coin coincided with the tightening of majority rule, which commanded courts to grant no exception either to Gareth Prince or to Indian Muslim men who refused to comply with general rules of maintenance. The other side of the coin coincided with the expansion of universal human rights, equality, and antidiscrimination measures—this benefiting to a different extent British and South African same-sex couples. Shabina Begum embodied the ambiguity of global gods, as her litigation had been differently judged according to one or the other side of the coin. The High Court dismissed Shabina's claim because she had refused to obey the uniform policy suiting the majority, but the Court of Appeal acknowledged her right as a radical Muslim to enjoy the same freedom as that enjoyed by moderate Muslims.

The common space of South Africa, India, and Britain grew into a laboratory of problems and solutions, similarities and differences. By trying the global gods, the judges of the three countries experienced the gods' ambivalence. Like their

---

228. *Minister of Home Affairs* [1].

predecessors, global gods had the potential for both inspiration and division: while mostly featuring as *your* gods, they had not renounced the ambition to be *our* gods.

The Moon in the Mirror

"This case concerns a particular pupil and a particular school in a particular place at a particular time."[229] When the House of Lords ruled on Shabina Begum's case, Lord Bingham of Cornhill began his opinion by downplaying the reach of a case that had become the blatant emblem of tensions in multicultural Britain. If global gods liked highly symbolic contentions, if they were the gods of "images and perceptions,"[230] Lord Bingham refused to follow their path. He declared he would not go global himself, he would not lead the House to the dangerous territory of general policies on Islam: "The House is not, and could not be, invited to rule whether Islamic dress, or any feature of Islamic dress, should or should not be permitted in the schools of this country."[231]

Instead, Baroness Hale of Richmond proved more docile to global gods. While trying them, she overtly addressed the questions they raised. She discussed the issue of Islam-based, and generally faith-based, gender inequalities and quoted from the Runnymede Trust's Parekh Report of 2000, *The Future of Multi-Ethnic Britain*, which suggested that "religion often accepts and gives its blessing to gender inequalities."[232] She acknowledged the complexities, and ambiguities, of multiculturalism and feminism. A dress code requiring women "to conceal all but their face and hands, while leaving men much freer to decide what they will wear"[233] would bear the assumption "that women will play their part in the private domestic sphere while men will play theirs in the public world."[234] Still, the judge wrote in her opinion, "from a woman's point of view, this may be a safer and more comfortable place to be,"[235] and though this could offend some people, a woman's free choice should be respected.

The House of Lords' decision on Shabina Begum encapsulated the victory of Sushmita Ghosh and the defeat of Gareth Prince. Whether acknowledged or denied, the fact remained that gender equality, minority rights, and common standards were at the heart of the case as they were at the heart of the global gods' challenge to India, South Africa, and Britain.

229. *R. (Begum)* (2006) [2].
230. Amis, "The Second Plane," 5.
231. *R. (Begum)* (2006) [2].
232. Ibid. [94].
233. Ibid. [95].
234. Ibid.
235. Ibid.

Thoughtful Mrs. Bevan

Shabina's Begum's case had been pending for four years. The young Muslim woman had lost her application to the High Court in 2004 and had moved to another school since. The Court of Appeal had allowed her appeal in 2005. In February 2006, the House of Lords heard the appeal by the governors and the head teacher of Denbigh High School, Yasmin Bevan.

The five lords gave their decision on March 22, 2006. Two of them had judged the Aston Cantlow case on chancel repair. Three of them had been on the bench responsible for the Williamson ruling on corporal correction. Lord Nicholls had judged both cases.

The judges unanimously stood for the school and rejected the procedural approach taken by the Court of Appeal. While that court had allowed Shabina's appeal because of a defective process of reasoning at Denbigh High School, it had not declared unlawful the decision as such. Lord Bingham endorsed the comment by Gareth Davies, a law professor at the University of Groningen, that the Court had followed the pattern of "retreat to procedure"[236] as a "way of avoiding difficult questions."[237] Instead the lord, and the House, believed that what mattered for the judgment was "the practical outcome, not the quality of the decision-making process that led to it."[238] Article 9 of the European Convention, Lord Hoffmann explained, was "concerned with substance, not procedure."[239] Contrary to what the Court had held, head teachers and governors could not be expected "to make such decisions with textbooks on human rights law at their elbows."[240]

Article 9 did not require that, as Lord Hoffmann put it, "one should be allowed to manifest one's religion at any time and place of one's own choosing."[241] In Lord Bingham's words, Article 9 protected both "the right to hold a belief, which is absolute, and a right to manifest belief, which is qualified."[242]

Though unanimous in allowing Mrs. Bevan's appeal, the five lords split on whether to take the more radical stance and declare that Shabina's freedom had not been restricted at all, or to accept that a restriction had taken place, but justifiably. Lord Nicholls and Lady Hale found for the objective existence of a restriction, while the others rather believed that Shabina had an alternative, and thus her freedom had not been hindered. Lord Scott of Foscote summarized the latter view, underlining that according to the Court of Strasbourg's case law, no restriction existed when "the

236. Ibid. [30].
237. Ibid.
238. Ibid. [31].
239. Ibid. [68].
240. Ibid.
241. Ibid. [50].
242. Ibid. [20].

individual has a choice,"[243] and that in the case of Shabina Begum, there were schools in the Luton area "whose rules would permit her to wear a jilbab."[244]

The three judges, however, joined Lord Nicholls and Lady Hale in asserting that the school's dismissal of Shabina's challenge was justified and proportionate. Indeed, the five lords praised the school, its uniform policy, and the handling of the case. The House recognized that Shabina's interest in getting her education had been constantly present to school's authorities, and her religious position had been carefully weighted, in particular when the school sought fresh advice on its uniform policy's consistence with Islamic requirements. Moreover, Lord Bingham emphasized, the school uniform had been designed "to avoid the development of sub-groups identified by dress."[245] Thus the "uniform policy . . . respected Muslim beliefs, but did so in an inclusive, unthreatening, and uncompetitive way."[246] Along the same line, according to Lord Scott, "there was no unnecessary rigidity"[247] in the school's policy. Lady Hale went even further and stressed that Denbigh High School had successfully promoted "the ability of people of diverse races, religions, and cultures to live together in harmony"[248] and fostered "a sense of community and cohesion."[249] Encapsulating the sense of Mrs. Bevan's endeavor, Lady Hale stated that the school's had been "indeed a thoughtful and proportionate response to reconciling the complexities of the situation."[250]

While Lord Bingham explicitly connected his analysis of religious freedom "in a pluralistic, multi-cultural society"[251] to Albie Sachs's opinion in Christian Education, Lady Hale took inspiration from the dissenting opinion by Belgian Judge Françoise Tulkens in the Court of Strasbourg's decision in the Turkish case of Leyla Şahin.

In a case revolving around gender equality and women's rights, a woman, Baroness Hale, endorsed the opinion of another woman, Justice Tulkens, to allow the appeal by a third woman, the "thoughtful" head teacher, Yasmin Bevan, against still another woman, Shabina Begum, defended by former First Lady Cherie Booth.

At the same time, in KwaZulu-Natal, similar litigation divided Anne Martin, the principal of Durban Girls' High School and the adolescent Sunali Pillay, who insisted on wearing a gold nose stud in observance of South Indian culture and religion, thus breaking the school's code of conduct. On July 5, 2006, nearly four months after the decision in the case of Shabina Begum, the High Court of Pietermaritzburg ruled that the denial of an exemption to Sunali had been unfairly discriminatory, with Justice Kondile

243. Ibid. [87].
244. Ibid. [89].
245. Ibid. [18].
246. Ibid. [34].
247. Ibid. [83].
248. Ibid. [97].
249. Ibid.
250. Ibid. [98].
251. Ibid. [2].

ordering that "Hindu/Indian learners"[252] should be entitled to wear a nose stud. Indeed, global gods made Shabina Begum's a global case despite Lord Bingham's attempt to limit it to "a particular pupil and a particular school in a particular place at a particular time."

It Was About Power

In his comment for the *Sunday Times* on the House's decision on Shabina Begum, Jaspar Gerard saw the lords standing with Tony Blair, who had just criticized hard-line Muslims for their "regressive" attitude to women, and against Cherie, who had argued the case for the charities siding with Shabina Begum and her brother.

Gerard lunched with Shabina Begum after the ruling only to find it was "less the 'regressive' forces of Islam leading Shabina astray than the progressive forces of legal aid:"[253]

> Actually, her brother, 23, comes across as her meekest minder and certainly the most charming. It is her white guards who are the real frights. First up: her powerfully built "celebrity consultant" (really: I have her business card). If this man-munching reptile is alarming, the three dragons from the legal charity opposite breathe fire: "You can't ask that," they hiss. "Is that relevant?" Think Cherie without the charm. At times the only one not expressing opinions is poor Shabina, whose dreams of becoming a doctor have been hit by disappointing GCSE results following two years' sulk leave from school.[254]

Gerard described Shabina as "attractive."[255] Of course she wore a jilbab, but this was "fetching, even showy, with purple patterns, offset by a funky multi-coloured bag."[256] "I go shopping a lot with friends and I love bags, shoes, girly stuff," she smiles.[257]

Conversation turned to the crucial point. Shabina insisted the dispute was really about religion: "Our belief in our faith,"[258] she said, "is the one thing that makes sense of a world gone mad."[259] The journalist pushed her. Precisely, the lords drew the line between the absolute right to believe and the qualified right to behave accordingly. Shabina fought back. The following exchange rendered the different mindset of the journalist and of the Muslim woman:

> She stares back for the first time—with a hint of fire hitherto hidden with that downward frown: "Islam is a complete way of life; it is not something you leave

252. *Pillay* [70].
253. Gerard, "Jasper Gerard Meets Shabina Begum," 5.
254. Ibid.
255. Ibid.
256. Ibid.
257. Ibid.
258. Ibid.
259. Ibid.

at home." A good point, but if you are allowed to take your faith to school with your lunch box, could a Rastafarian claim it essential to his religion to smoke skunk in home economics? "I do understand uniforms are important," she counters. "I was even happy to put the school logo on my jilbab. But smoking pot is illegal; wearing the clothes of your religion is not." Hmm: a silky debater. But if schools declared that "anything goes" for religion, think of the ramifications.[260]

Was this the true and only difference between Shabina Begum the British Muslim and Gareth Prince the South African Rastafari?

To the journalist, both a radical-Muslim young lady and a defiant, law-breaking Rastafari represented worrying challenges to the tolerable difference in a plural society. Gerard expressed his unease with Begum's views on arranged marriages, Muslim intolerance, and sectarian separateness. When Begum's brother complained that Denbigh High School did not accept the proposal of letting Shabina be taught in an isolated room, Gerard erupted: "So here is the authentic voice of the extremist: prepared for his bright, giggly sister who loves medicine and handbags to be shut away from life, just so she remains theologically pure."[261] Still, the journalist closed his piece by pointing at the impossibility for anything pure and separate to subsist in the syncretistic context of multicultural England. However extreme the confrontation between radical Shabina and British "secular(ish) society,"[262] the two could not but coexist and intermingle:

> Before Shabina is hauled off to face the cameras by her menagerie of celebrity consultants and lawyers, I ask what she wants to be. "My dream would be a TV presenter," she smiles, eyes blazing once more.[263]

In his leader for the *Telegraph* the day after the Begum decision, the future mayor of London, Boris Johnson, then the Tory MP for Henley, also emphasized the contrast between the Muslim and the British identity of Shabina Begum, this "exceedingly good-looking and confident young woman"[264] who impressively addressed the nation on television after the ruling.

Johnson pointed out the inconsistency between the apparent religious focus of the "ludicrous and lamentable"[265] controversy and its real aim: power. The whole Shabina case, he believed, had been built upon "modesty," but the "media national storm,"[266] the transformation of Shabina's "dress sense and physical form"[267] into "the

260. Ibid.
261. Ibid.
262. Ibid.
263. Ibid.
264. Johnson, "The Shabina Begum Case," 18.
265. Ibid.
266. Ibid.
267. Ibid.

number one subject for conversation in every household in the country,"[268] witnessed that modesty was not the real issue. The case was rather about who was in charge:

> It was about power. It was about who really runs the schools in this country, and about how far militant Islam could go in bullying the poor, cowed, gelatinous, and mentally spongiform apparatus of the British state.[269]

The strategy aiming at pushing girls into a "terrible game of holier-than-thou"[270] had nothing to do with Shabina's or any other young lady's faith or integrity: radical Muslims such as those belonging to the extremist organization Hizb-ut-Tahrir "were doing it to show that they could, and to take another yard of territory in the kulturkampf of modern Britain."[271]

In Johnson's view, the House of Lords' ruling represented an act of resistance, resistance against the variegated front who had assigned Shabina the "starring role in the great Rocky Horror Show of British self-flagellation, featuring Cherie Blair, Matrix Chambers, assorted terrified judges, and a chorus of cretinous articles by retired feminists, famous for living colorful lives in the 1970s, in which they declared that the jilbab was really rather lovely and "empowering," and that they wished they had worn one themselves."[272]

Faced with such an offensive, many British institutions, judges in particular, had demonstrated "a certain leeriness and timorousness about Islam" that had led the appeal-court judges to show "less robust common sense than the judges of Strasbourg."[273] Boris Johnson insisted, "I detect in the Appeal Court ruling in favour of Shabina, that was so ignominiously crushed yesterday, the same hand-wringing wetness that inspired some poor Welsh bishop to resign the editorship of his local church news after he was found to have printed a Danish-type cartoon of positively ovine inoffensiveness."[274]

Multiculturalism, Johnson concluded, was a complete failure. By standing against Shabina, the House of Lords had blown the whistle:

> All around us, in our courts, in the oppressive liberty-destroying Bills being rushed through Parliament, we see the disasters of multiculturalism, the system by which too many Muslims have been allowed to grow up in this country with no sense of loyalty to its institutions, and with a sense of complete apartness. In rejecting Shabina's case, the Law Lords have provided a small

---

268. Ibid.
269. Ibid.
270. Ibid.
271. Ibid.
272. Ibid.
273. Ibid.
274. Ibid.

but important victory for good sense, for British cohesion, and for the right of teachers to run their own schools.[275]

The Dependent Mind

Global gods were not nice. They fought for power. The anxiety Johnson expressed in the comment on Shabina's defeat went beyond his own specific political ideology and strategy. Large sectors of British society shared the same apprehension.

A few months later, on the eve of the fifth anniversary of 9/11, Martin Amis published an essay in the *Observer*. If Johnson had attacked the judges' "leeriness and timorousness about Islam," Amis described a West "enfeebled . . . by 30 years of multicultural relativism."[276] The novelist provocatively imagined what Bin Laden might think of the way Westerners would react to a massive-scale attack:

> They'll think suicide bombing is just an exotic foible, like shame-and-honour killings or female circumcision. Besides, it's religious, and they're always slow to question anything that calls itself that. Within days of our opening outrage, the British royals will go on the road for Islam, and stay on it.[277]

Amis added the ideology of Westerners weakened both their "powers of perception"[278] and their "moral unity and will."[279] This explained the defective reaction to suicide mass murder:

> Suicide-mass murder is astonishingly alien, so alien, in fact, that Western opinion has been unable to formulate a rational response to it. A rational response would be something like an unvarying factory siren of unanimous disgust. But we haven't managed that. What we have managed, on the whole, is a murmur of dissonant evasion.[280]

Johnson had saluted both the House's halt to the Islamists' quest for power and the lords' stance for gender equality. Amis went much further, claiming that the connection between Islam's "manifest failure and the suppression of women"[281] was "unignorable."[282] During his visit to the United States in 1949, Sayyid Qutb, as Amis remarked, came to detest not only American places of worship, which the Egyptian founder of the Muslim Brothers found too similar to cinemas or amusement arcades,

---

275. Ibid.
276. Amis, "The Age of Horrorism, 7."
277. Ibid.
278. Ibid.
279. Ibid.
280. Ibid.
281. Ibid., 9.
282. Ibid.

and "American jazz, ('a type of music invented by Blacks to please their primitive tendencies—their desire for noise and their appetite for sexual arousal')," [283] but also the whole Western approach to sex and gender. Amis wrote:

> Qutb joins a club—where an epiphany awaits him. "The dance is inflamed by the notes of the gramophone," he wrote; "the dance-hall becomes a whirl of heels and thighs, arms enfold hips, lips and breasts meet, and the air is full of lust." You'd think that the father of Islamism had exposed himself to an early version of Studio 54 or even Plato's Retreat. But no: the club he joined was run by the church, and what he is describing, here, is a chapel hop in Greeley, Colorado. [284]

Christopher Hitchens' "Islamist triumvirate" [285] made of "self-righteousness, self-pity, and self-hatred" [286] nurtured the "Islamist's paranoia" [287] and terrorist Islam. Moderates were immaterial. Amis ridiculed the paradigm of a civil war within Islam: "Well, the civil war appears to be over. And Islamism won it. The loser, moderate Islam, is always deceptively well represented on the level of the op-ed page and the public debate; elsewhere, it is supine and inaudible. We are not hearing from moderate Islam. Whereas Islamism, as a mover and shaper of world events, is pretty well all there is." [288]

Amis refined Johnson's "it was all about power" by detailing the kind of power the Islamist mass-murderer bomber was after: in fact, not only did the suicide bomber secure a comfortable place in the afterlife along with some practical gains for his family, but he also achieved a role as protagonist in history:

> To feel that you are a geohistorical player is a tremendous lure to those condemned, as they see it, to exclusion and anonymity. In its quieter way, this was perhaps the key component of the attraction of Western intellectuals to Soviet Communism: "join," and you are suddenly a contributor to planetary events . . . the ghost of Shehzad Tanweer, as it watched the salvage teams scraping up human remains in the rat-infested crucible beneath the streets of London, could be sure that he had decisively outsoared the fish-and-shop back in Leeds. [289]

This brought the author straight to the fundamental question of the place of religion in the impending struggle with Islamist "horrorism." [290] Now that the "innocent

---

283. Ibid., 6.
284. Ibid.
285. Ibid.
286. Ibid.
287. Ibid.
288. Ibid., 4.
289. Ibid., 8.
290. Ibid., 4.

times"[291] before 9/11 were over, now that failures in the Iraqi War had destroyed much more than Blair's credibility, the attitude toward religion was crucial. Amis sensed religion was both decisive and extremely knotty: "Religion is sensitive ground, as well it might be. Here we walk on eggshells. Because religion is itself an eggshell."[292]

Amis attacked the Muslim notion of "submission" as the "surrender of independence of mind."[293] Beyond Islam, the author attacked religious beliefs as such, as he understood the whole struggle with global gods as a "global confrontation with the dependent mind:"[294] "To be clear: the opposite of religious belief is not atheism or secularism or humanism. It is not an 'ism.' It is independence of mind—that's all . . . I mean the global confrontation with the dependent mind."[295]

If Johnson placed Shabina's case in the context of radical Islam's pursuit of power, Amis announced the true clash was with gods, with gods of all kinds: "All religions are violent; and all ideologies are violent. Even Westernism, so impeccably bland, has violence glinting within it. This is because any belief system involves a degree of illusion, and therefore cannot be defended by mind alone. When challenged, or affronted, the believer's response is hormonal, and the subsequent collision will be one between a brain and a cat's cradle of glands."[296]

Martin Amis was a novelist. Historians and social scientists criticized him for his excessive reliance on anti-Islam writers like Bernard Lewis and Paul Berman, for his shortcuts and oversimplifications. Of course, his distinction between Islam and Islamism, between radicals and moderates, was inaccurate. His picture of cowardly Westerners happy with the defeat in Iraq was wrong. And his idea that the "historical emotion"[297] of Muslim hatred belonged to "their history, and not ours"[298] was also flawed, for it neglected the choices the West had made in its relationship with the Muslim world. But Amis, like Boris Johnson, captured the mood of the country.

Among the many who shared his critique, a conspicuous part did not share the all-encompassing blame he placed on religion. In her book *Londonistan*, also published in 2006, Melanie Phillips claimed the traditional Judeo-Christian gods of the country had to be preserved from the attack of "secular nihilists": "British nationhood has been eviscerated by the combination of three things: mass immigration, multiculturalism, and the onslaught mounted by secular nihilists against the country's Judeo-Christian values."[299]

291. Ibid., 5.
292. Ibid., 4.
293. Ibid., 8.
294. Ibid.
295. Ibid.
296. Ibid., 9.
297. Ibid., 6.
298. Ibid.
299. Phillips, *Londonistan*, 281.

Hatemongers

On February 7, 2006, the Central Criminal Court in London delivered its verdict on Abu Hamza, who had been arrested in 2004 and charged with incitement to murder and soliciting racial murder. Hamza was the symbol of Londonistan and of the inextricable knot of Britain's ambiguous and not disinterested relationship to Muslim radicals. By virtue of his trial at the Old Bailey, Hamza also expressed the hardship of trying the global gods of terror.

The jury found Hamza guilty. In their book on the case, journalists Sean O'Neill and Daniel McGrory described how the presiding judge, fifty-seven-year-old Sir Anthony Hughes, betrayed "more than a little impatience"[300] when Hamza, from the dock, "attempted to preach rather than to answer questions."[301] Before pronouncing his sentence, the judge addressed the former sheikh of Finsbury Park:

> You are entitled to your views, and in this country you are entitled to express them up to the point where you incite murder or incite racial hatred. That, however, is what you did. You used your authority to legitimize anger and to encourage your audiences to believe that it gave rise to a duty to murder. You commended suicide bombing, you encouraged them to kill in the cause you set for them . . . No one can say now what damage your words may have caused. No one can say whether your audience, present or wider, acted on your words. I am satisfied that you are and were a person whose views and the manner of expression of those views created a real danger to the lives of innocent people in different parts of the world.[302]

The judge sentenced Abu Hamza to a seven-year term in prison. On behalf of his client, Hamza's solicitor, Muddasar Arani, responded to Sir Hughes's legal universe by paying tribute to Hamza's religious one: "Sheikh Abu Hamza wishes to thank God Almighty for what has been decreed for him . . . We may have lost one battle, but there are many more to be fought yet for Sheikh Abu Hamza. So much for freedom of expression. Sheikh Abu Hamza is a prisoner of faith. The sentence that has been decreed on him constitutes nothing more than slow martyrdom."[303]

In the same months of 2006, Tony Blair tried hard to cope with extreme readings of the London bombings and the failure of multiculturalism. On August 1, the prime minister acknowledged that an "arc of extremism" was discernible and launched an "alliance of moderation that paints a different future in which Muslim, Jew, and Christian; Arab and Western; wealthy and developing nations can make progress in peace and harmony with each other."[304]

300. O'Neill and McGrory, *The Suicide Factory*, 300.
301. Ibid.
302. Ibid., 310.
303. Ibid., 311.
304. Curtis, *Secret Affairs*, 300.

By implication, Blair wanted "moderate, mainstream Islam to triumph over reactionary Islam."[305]

For this to be credible, a dramatic departure from the British alliance with radical Islam was needed: when in March 2006 Blair had attacked the "arc of extremism," and "offshoots of the Muslim Brotherhood, supported by Wahhabi extremists and taught in some of the madrassas of the Middle East and Asia,"[306] he had pointed toward countries and groups the British had supported for ages.

Indeed, Mark Curtis denounced, later that year Blair stopped a Serious Fraud Office's investigation on bribes paid by BAE Systems, Britain's largest arms company, to the Saudi regime. Even more telling of the ambiguities and ties Britain continued to build with governments heavily involved in the "arc of extremism," was Gordon Brown's pledge, also in 2006, "for making Britain the gateway to Islamic trade, to make Britain the global centre for Islamic finance."[307] With energy policies growing increasingly crucial in a global world where rising competitors threatened Britain, the British economy, warned Curtis, "was set to become ever more intertwined with the Islamic financial system, in turn deepening British dependence on the state champions of extremist Islam."[308]

At the end of the year, on December 8, 2006, Tony Blair took a position on the issue of multiculturalism in a speech at Downing Street.

Almost ten years of New Labour rule had reshaped British law accompanying the transformation of Britain into a multicultural country obsessed with equality and nondiscrimination:

> The courts recognize racial offences in a way that was inconceivable [in the past]. We have the most comprehensive panoply of anti-discrimination legislation in the world. We have tough laws outlawing discrimination on the grounds of sexual orientation, religion, race, gender, and disability. The Human Rights Act provides basic protection to ethnic minorities and lays down some minimum standards. It is a matter of some pride to me that it has only been Labour governments that have introduced anti-discrimination legislation.[309]

London bombings, the prime minister acknowledged, had betrayed such development for the sake of "an ideology alien to everything this country stands for,"[310] of values based "on a warped distortion of the faith of Islam."[311] Blair also acknowledged the widespread resentment that "our very openness, our willingness to welcome dif-

---

305. Ibid., 301.
306. Ibid., 312.
307. Ibid., 319.
308. Ibid., 320.
309. Blair, "Speech at Downing Street."
310. Ibid.
311. Ibid.

ference, our pride in being home to many cultures, is being used against us; abused, indeed, in order to harm us."[312]

Finally, he spoke out that a specific problem existed with extremist Muslims. Echoing Lord Bingham's emphasis on Shabina's as a "particular" case, Blair put the blame on "a particular ideology that arises within one religion at this one time."[313]

Forty years after Roy Jenkins's speech on the virtue of diversity, the prime minister's response consisted of underscoring that multicultural Britain "was never supposed to be a celebration of division, but of diversity. The purpose was to allow people to live harmoniously together, despite their difference; not to make their difference an encouragement to discord."[314]

Tolerance, as opposed to religious fanaticism; shared values, as opposed to separated values, made diversity what distinguished Britain:

> Our tolerance is part of what makes Britain, Britain. So conform to it; or don't come here. We don't want the hate-mongers, whatever their race, religion, or creed. If you come here lawfully, we welcome you. If you are permitted to stay here permanently, you become an equal member of our community and become one of us. Then you, and all of us, who want to, can worship God in our own way, take pride in our different cultures after our own fashion, respect our distinctive histories according to our own traditions; but do so within a shared space of shared values in which we take no less pride and show no less respect.[315]

Tony Blair listed specific problems like forced marriages, inflammatory visiting preachers, and intolerant education in madrassahs. While suggesting ad hoc measures, he laid out his view that the duty to integrate meant conforming to common values: "tolerance, solidarity across the racial and religious divide, equality for all and between all . . . obedience to the rule of law, to democratic decision-making about who governs us, to freedom from violence and discrimination."[316] He also demanded "allegiance to the rule of law"[317] and set a barrier against religious laws likely to compete with the law of the land:

> Nobody can legitimately ask to stand outside the law of the nation. There is thus no question of the UK allowing the introduction of religious law in the UK. Parliament sets the law, interpreted by the courts. All criminal matters should be dealt with through the criminal justice system. There may be areas where, in civil proceedings, parties consent to arbitration by a religious body.

312. Ibid.
313. Ibid.
314. Ibid.
315. Ibid.
316. Ibid.
317. Ibid.

But these are arrangements based on consent and, in all cases, parties will have recourse to the UK courts.[318]

In the time of global gods, with both Turkish case law and Muslim jurisprudence brought into the House of Lords' analysis of Shabina's case, Tony Blair championed the legal unity of the country under the sole legitimate law of the land. The legal unity and orthodoxy propounded by the prime minister came with an equivalent doctrine of religious unity and orthodoxy. Interfaith dialogue and religious education stressing shared principles were meant to transform religious diversity into a united force propelling the country towards a bright future. "True religion,"[319] as opposed to "religious bigotry,"[320] was the cornerstone of Blairite religious orthodoxy, in the name of which religious leaders were asked to uphold "the true theology"[321] and "gird themselves up and defeat those that pervert it."[322]

Little Krishna

Martin Amis's struggle against extremist believers in the name of "independence of mind," and Tony Blair's eagerness to reaffirm the unity of British law and religion against the emergence of multiple alternative religious and legal systems both made sense for India as well.

Six years after the decision on Sushmita Ghosh's case, five years after the Danial Latifi decision on Shah Bano, the debate on the uniform civil code was still hot, and the pressure to get Indian Muslims into the fold of family law had not relented. One week before the House of Lords decided on Shabina, a bill was introduced in the Rajya Sabha in order to render compulsory the registration of all marriages solemnized in India. The proposal followed a February 14, 2006 decision by the Supreme Court in which Justice Pasayat, in the interest of the applicant, a woman whose rights were threatened because of the uncertainty of her conjugal status, had advanced "the view that marriages of all persons who are citizens of India belonging to various religions should be made compulsorily registrable."[323] The ideology of legal formality and uniformity imposed itself as the only way to pursue fundamental social aims. In the statement of objects and reasons for the Compulsory Registration of Marriages Bill, the Congress Party–led majority suggested compulsory registration was necessary in order

> to prevent child marriages, check bigamy or polygamy, help women to exercise their rights of maintenance from husband and custody of children, enable

318. Ibid.
319. Ibid.
320. Ibid.
321. Ibid.
322. Ibid.
323. *Seema*, 583 [17].

widows to claim inheritance and to serve as deterrent to husband[s] deserting
their wives and for matters connected therewith or incidental thereto.

Werner Menski, the German professor of Indian law at the School of Oriental
and African studies in London, believed developments in India and Britain should
not be read separately.

In an article for the *Kerala Law Times* published in 2006, at the time of Tony
Blair's speech, Menski argued that legal uniformity was "clearly a fiction, and not a
fact"[324] in multicultural Britain as well as in postmodern India.

Menski explained to legal professionals in Kerala that "silent private opposition
to uniformity"[325] was advancing in Britain. He pointed to an "emerging process of
pluralization," which was "almost inevitable, given the factual scenarios presented
by litigants."[326] Numerous examples pointed to the gap between the formal and the
substantial status of individuals in multicultural Britain. Menski recalled the case of
Mrs. Bath, a Sikh widow from a marriage celebrated in a London *gurdwara* in the
1950s and never registered, to whom the English Court of Appeal in 2000 had granted
pension rights on principles of equity. Prakash Shah, legal scholar at Queen Mary,
had suggested in his 2005 book that "legal pluralism" was the issue to face, as Britain
inevitably struggled to cope "with cultural diversity in law."[327]

Indians had borrowed from the British and from the West the model of legal
centralism and uniformity. But the elevation of the Western model as the superior
standard was based on a false representation of Western laws themselves. Now that the
model was challenged in India as well as in Britain, Menski stressed uniformity was a
myth with regard to both the past and present of the West: "Western laws were never
uniform, and today's Western laws are re-pluralizing as a result of 'ethnic implants.'"[328]

Uneasiness with religion was distinctive of the legal model imposed upon India,
first by the imperialists and then by the Nehruvian and Ambedkarite dream of Indian
modernization by means of a centralized and secularized law. The model, Menski
stressed, looked down on religion-based customary or traditional legal systems as
"evidence of backwardness."[329] Religion, though, had not been "abolished by the predominance of secularism even in the West."[330]

As a result, Menski noticed, Asian and African countries were portrayed as
"tradition-ridden and inferior, dependent on 'religion' and 'tradition' and incapable
of modernization."[331] Tom Bennett made a similar point about South Africa in 2009

324. Menski, "Asking for the Moon," 54.

325. Ibid., 55.

326. Ibid., 56.

327. Shah, *Legal Pluralism in Conflict*.

328. Menski, "Asking for the Moon," 57.

329. Ibid., 58.

330. Ibid.

331. Ibid.

when he illustrated "the old, but immensely damaging, idea that customary normative orders are static and hence somehow primitive,"[332] the assumption being that
"while law is rational and purposive, custom is no more than mindless conformity to
tradition."[333]

Menski believed Indian law in particular was squeezed between two alternatives:
conforming as much as possible to the superior model of English law, or being "an
inferior cousin," "a third-world jurisdiction that better follows the West as fast as possible and gets rid of its vestiges of "religion" and "tradition" when it comes to law. As
though the British had gotten rid of Anglicanism, the Italians of Catholicism, or the
Turks of Islam."[334]

But however strong the paralyzing postcolonial mixture of superiority complexes
and inferiority complexes might be, Indian lawmakers, judges, and practitioners had
not given in. In reality, Menski observed, many aspects of Indian law, as of South
African law, witnessed the rise of a postmodern state, looking for an alternative to
inoperable "state-centric lines of governance."[335]

In India, this meant a state widely delegating traditionally centralistic powers
while maintaining a twofold form of control. First, in accord with Menski, the state kept
enforcing "symbolic legislation"[336] aimed at "changing opinions among the people."[337]
This followed the Nehruvian pattern of social engineering through such educative
measures as antidowry law or anti-child-marriage provisions, or the 2005 prowomen
amendment to the Hindu Succession Act. Second, said Menski, the state operated a
court system allowing for public-interest litigation and the enforcement of basic rules
of "fairness and justice irrespective of "religion," "culture," and "tradition.""[338] This was,
in Menski's view, a new form of equity, of "constitutional dharma."[339]

The case of Sushmita Ghosh represented a vast shift. The previous conflict between the myth of Western secular legal uniformity and resisting religious and customary "backwardness" gave way to a postmodern state pursuing social justice and
equality through a mixture of centralized rule and local and communal self-regula-
tion—of secular standards and religious variations.

Family law was the best illustration of the rise of the postmodern pattern. Against
the backdrop of tensions over gender justice and the reform of Muslim personal law,
Menski affirmed that although India had not achieved the uniform civil code in the
form originally envisioned, in fact the same effect had been virtually obtained by

332. Bennett, "Re-introducing African Customary Law," 9.

333. Ibid.

334. Menski, "Asking for the Moon," 58.

335. Ibid., 59.

336. Ibid., 60.

337. Ibid.

338. Ibid., 61.

339. Ibid.

other means. It was possible to say that ground rules existed across personal laws on the basics of access to and exit from marriage.

As for the entry into the conjugal status, "unity in diversity" was the pattern, the common element being that Indian marriages depended "on customary traditions, which may be new forms of custom rather than ancient traditions laid down in stone."[340] Also, evidence of marriage was traditionally secured without registration by the state. For this reason, Menski opposed the recent emphasis by the Supreme Court and by the government on compulsory registration, which he saw as another unrealistic myth, inapplicable in the context of real India.

In matters of divorce, some common ground had also been achieved in the absence of a uniform code. Real progress, Menski believed, had not come from top-down imposition of gender equality, which could solve very little in "a patriarchally dominated legal system."[341] True achievement came rather from "situation-specific justice"[342] superseding legal uniformity. What the Latifi case taught was that judges posed as "postmodern realists," caring first of all for effective social welfare and substantive justice. Beyond Justice Kuldip Singh's emphasis on the uniform code, this was the ultimate lesson of the case of Sushmita, with her husband's responsibility affirmed beyond religious lines. Thus, what Menski called the "completion of the jigsaw puzzle of post-divorce maintenance"[343] had taken place through the "defeat of legal modernism."[344] The Parliament had played a relevant role. But first of all, the judiciary should be credited, particularly the Supreme Court, the judges of which Menski saw as the "gatekeepers of the Indian welfare state system," as those who "had firmly brought Muslim males back into the postmodern Indian net of social welfare arrangements without insisting on formal legal uniformity."[345]

In his article of 2006 for the *Kerala Law Times*, Werner Menski suggested that India offered an alternative to the kind of "control-freakism that seems typical of the current British government." This was decidedly not the uniform civil code, but a system of legislative measures and court rulings, of central policies and local self-reliance, of secular and religious elements, that achieved some fundamental goals of welfare and justice. Such a solution was certainly less appealing than the myth of legal modernism but also much more realistic and viable. This reminded Menski of the story of Mother Yashoda showing little Krishna, who had asked for the moon, the mirror image of it.

Equating the uniform civil code to the moon, Werner Menski made his case in the following terms: "India has thus achieved a different kind of mirror image of

340. Ibid., 62.
341. Ibid., 64.
342. Ibid.
343. Ibid., 61.
344. Ibid., 73.
345. Ibid., 72.

uniform civil code than originally anticipated. It came in through the back door, so to say, gradually developing more uniform family laws for the nation through a combination of legislative interventions and, where necessary, judicial activism."[346]

So far as "the moon" represented socially engineered equality and radical legal uniformity, its mirror image—common basics arriving "through the back door"—was all that India could have in reality. This meant more consistency and more tools to protect the weak against religion-based abuses, but not the end of religious conflicts. Not the triumph of socialism and secularism or of Hindutva either. Not the magic wand with which to make inequality, violence, and poverty vanish. This was what the case of Sushmita Ghosh had been about.

By contrast, ironically, pragmatic Britain still seemed to yearn for the moon. Serving as the undercurrent to Martin Amis's struggle for the "independent mind," to Melanie Phillips's pledge to traditional Judeo-Christian gods, and to Tony Blair's "no question of religious law in Britain" was the belief the British would never be content with having the actual moon reflected in the mirror.

Also in 2006, Edward Luce, former *Financial Times* correspondent to India, published a best seller on emerging India. The title of the book, *In Spite of the Gods*, was inspired, the author made clear, by "Nehru's contention that India's greatest strengths are not exclusively, or even necessarily, located in its religious traditions."[347] Luce exalted India's "vibrant democracy,"[348] "traditions of pluralism,"[349] and "intellectual capital and technological prowess."[350] The author exposed his surprise to see India "emerging as an important economic and political force on the world stage while remaining an intensely religious, spiritual, and, in some ways, superstitious society."[351]

While Tony Blair invoked "true religion" and interfaith dialogue as the propitious gods for multicultural Britain, Luce, in a nutshell, suggested India was rising "in spite of the Gods." Menski had a different idea. He pointed out the difference between dreaming of the moon and struggling with the illusions and achievements of real life. In this, he believed, India could be a template for Britain.

With the Same Voice

On January 20, 2007, in the Cape Town township of Gugulethu, the African National Congress activist Tony Yengeni celebrated his early release from a four-year prison sentence by slaughtering a bull, a ritual meant to appease the family ancestors.

---

346. Ibid., 52.

347. Luce, *In Spite of the Gods*, 18.

348. Ibid.

349. Ibid., 18–19.

350. Ibid. 19.

351. Ibid.

Human-rights lawyer Jewel Amoah and Cape Town law professor Tom Bennett read the case and the ensuing public outcry and clash between animal-rights activists and African traditionalists as a marker of South African uneasiness with the articulation of culture and religion in the postcolonial and post-apartheid society. Cultural rights were neglected, they denounced, to the advantage of mainstream proselytizing religions such as Islam and Christianity. Separation of religion and culture was based on the dominance of a Western, monotheistic understanding of religion, making no room for the distinctive African overlapping of the two dimensions. The authors blew the whistle on human rights as well: "Those working under the influence of modern human rights seem to take religion more seriously than culture."[352]

One month after the bull slaughtering in Gugulethu, in the midst of the ensuing debate, the Constitutional Court of South Africa heard the case of Sunali Pillay, the girl who wore the nose stud. The adjudication of cultural and religious rights became the major theoretical knot to be solved. But many other aspects of the case recalled the challenge of the global gods.

The case of Sunali Pillay echoed Shabina Begum's in many ways. For Anne Martin, the principal of Durban Girls' High School, and for the governing body, the decision not to grant an exemption to Sunali rested on the need to uphold discipline and deference to authorities, to strengthen rules aimed at cohesion in an extremely diverse society. A code of conduct limiting jewelry served the purpose of avoiding the perverse competition of a commercial society, where, as the principal underlined, "pressures of modern fashion"[353] were "particularly intense as girls try to imitate and out-do each other."[354]

In her submission, Mrs. Martin explained that exemptions had been granted in the past, an example being the case of Hindu pupils who had been allowed, at certain times of the year, to wear red strings in honour of the Goddess Lakshmi. But in Sunali Pillay's case, the principal maintained, the girl and her mother had given no serious reasons for the school to grant any such exemption.

In a letter to the school, Sunali's mother presented the piercing as a "time-honoured family tradition,"[355] coming from "a South Indian family that has sought to maintain a cultural identity by respecting and implementing the traditions of the women before us."[356] She equally submitted that Sunali was "a responsible and emotionally mature young woman capable of making independent choices"[357] and stated that no harm could come from an exemption, both mother and daughter living

---

352. Amoah and Bennett, "The Freedoms of Religion and Culture," 1–2.
353. *MEC for Education* [99].
354. Ibid.
355. Ibid. [131].
356. Ibid.
357. Ibid.

"in a spiritually aware holistic centre based on the values of integrity, respect, and compassion."[358]

School authorities found such a justification to be wanting. Exemption was not sought in the name of religion or culture, but simply on grounds of "family traditions." An expert on Hindu and Tamil culture gave evidence that wearing a nose stud was not a compulsory requirement. The governing body rejected the notion that cultural rights could be involved, based on a strict definition of *culture* derived from British case law in application of the 1976 Race Relations Act.

In the decision of October 5, 2007, the Constitutional Court praised the governing bodies of Durban Girls' High School. Echoing the House of Lords' appreciation for the Denbigh High School in Luton, Justice O'Regan acknowledged that Mrs. Martin ran "an excellent school,"[359] at the "cutting edge of non-racial education, facing the challenges of moving away from its racial past to a non-racial future where young girls, regardless of their colour or background, can be educated."[360]

Still, a unanimous Court upheld the KwaZulu Natal High Court's decision, finding that the refusal to grant an exemption to Sunali Pillay had been unfairly discriminatory.

Chief Justice Pius Langa gave the opinion for nine other judges, including Albie Sachs. The judge struggled with the different protection of culture and religion in the 1996 Constitution, section 15 of which protected individual belief, while sections 30 and 31 protected the right to belong to a cultural and religious community of choice. Langa tentatively distinguished between religion (the equivalent of personal faith) and culture (pertaining to community membership). But he admitted *culture* and *religion* overlapped and defied unambiguous definitions. For this reason, he contested the governing body's use of the definition of *culture* given in 1983 by Justice Fraser for the House of Lords. As he endeavored to interpret the 1976 UK Race Relations Act, Lord Fraser had been mainly concerned with race and ethnicity. More than thirty years later, the Constitutional Court of South Africa stood for a much broader notion of culture. The case of Sunali Pillay, however, went beyond definitions and borders:

> Sunali is part of the South Indian, Tamil and Hindu groups which are defined by a combination of religion, language, geographical origin, ethnicity, and artistic tradition. Whether those groups operate together or separately matters not; combined or separate, they are an identifiable culture of which Sunali is a part.[361]

Justice Langa further underlined the importance of cultural identity for the individual and the peculiar nature of cultures—an associative force but never a monolith.

358. Ibid.
359. Ibid. [125].
360. Ibid.
361. Ibid. [50].

Colonial awareness, and Martin Chanock's warning that cultures were "complex conversations"[362] with "many voices,"[363] made Langa stress both the "danger of falling into an antiquated mode of understanding culture as a single unified entity that can be studied and defined from outside[364] . . . [and the danger of reinforcing] ideas about the respective roles and importance of religion and culture in peoples' lives and fail[ing] to accommodate those who do not conform to that stereotype."[365]

Accordingly, the judge avoided clear-cut definitions and limited himself to the subjective perception of culture, and to the fact that "what is relevant is not whether a practice is characterised as religious or cultural but its meaning to the person involved."[366]

Thus the Court satisfied itself with the evidence that "Sunali held a sincere belief that the nose stud was part of her religion and culture."[367] Despite the constitutional distinction between culture and religion, Justice Langa and the other nine judges of the bench held

> that the borders between culture and religion are malleable and that religious belief informs cultural practice and cultural practice attains religious significance. As noted above, that will not always be the case: culture and religion remain very different forms of human association and individual identity, and often inform peoples' lives in very different ways. But in this matter, culture and religion sing with the same voice and it is necessary to understand the nose stud in that light—as an expression of both religion and culture.

A Pageant of Diversity

In her separate opinion, Justice Kate O'Regan also recognized the unfair discrimination suffered by Sunali but declared herself uncomfortable with the majority's understanding of culture and religion.

Though the judge acknowledged it was not easy "to divine a sharp dividing line"[368] between the two, she nevertheless expressed the conviction that, according to the Constitution, "culture is not the same as religion, and should not always be treated as if it is."[369] In particular, she believed, the Constitution intended for religion and culture to be understood and protected differently. Religion, in O'Regan's view, should

362. Ibid. [54].
363. Ibid.
364. Ibid.
365. Ibid. [91].
366. Ibid.
367. Ibid. [58].
368. Ibid. [143].
369. Ibid.

be "understood in an individualist sense: a set of beliefs that an individual may hold, regardless of the beliefs of others."[370] On the other hand, culture should be protected as expressed through "associative practices."[371] In addition, such collective protection should also apply to collective religious practices.

Based on such a distinction, Justice O'Regan, a PhD graduate from the London School of Economics, dissented from Justice Langa and from the rest of the bench on two aspects.

The first concerned the subjective approach according to which Langa accepted Sunali's practice as individually relevant to the young lady. Justice O'Regan drew on a colonial past that had imposed a false "coherence and unity on a set of customary rules and practices,"[372] and she stressed the need for what the Court itself had called "living customary law."[373] The constitutional value of culture was not in an "individualized and subjective approach to what constitutes culture,"[374] but in the real collective meaning of practices and in what mattered as a "cultural practice"[375] to the relevant community. Cultural rights could only consist of widely shared "associative practices."[376] Hence their meaning held for a society "unified in its diversity"[377] and not threatened by "atomized communities."[378]

The second contentious point was about the entanglement of religion and culture. If Langa and the others had accepted the impossibility of separating the two aspects in the case of Sunali Pillay, Kate O'Regan held that the case was not about religion. She accepted the evidence given by expert Dr. Rambilass that wearing a nose-stud was not "a part of Hindu religion," even though the expert had warned against the difficult distinction between "Hindu culture and Hindu religion,"[379] a distinction which represented a "universal dilemma of all cultures and religions."[380] The judge instead concluded "that the applicant has established that the wearing of the nose-stud is a matter of associative cultural significance, which was a matter of personal choice at least for the learner in this case, but that it is not part of a religious or personal belief of the applicant that it is necessary to wear the stud as part of her religious beliefs."[381]

---

370. Ibid.
371. Ibid. [145].
372. Ibid. [153].
373. *Bhe* [87].
374. *MEC for Education* [154].
375. Ibid.
376. Ibid. [157].
377. Ibid. [155].
378. Ibid.
379. Ibid. [13].
380. Ibid.
381. Ibid. [162].

Pius Langa and Kate O'Regan reached the same conclusion—that the Constitution protected Sunali's wearing of the nose stud. But while for Langa and the majority, it was not necessary to disentangle the cultural from the religious dimension once the genuine attachment of Sunali to the practice had been proven, in O'Regan's view, Sunali's was not the expression of a religious belief but an "associative practice," which only deserved protection as such.

Justice Langa and Justice O'Regan also carried out their assessments of the unfair discrimination in two different ways. Justice Langa and the majority underlined that the lack of a compulsory character in the wearing of the nose stud was not an argument for withdrawing protection from Sunali. On the contrary, the Court emphasized the virtue of voluntary choice: "That we choose voluntarily rather than through a feeling of obligation only enhances the significance of a practice to our autonomy, our identity, and our dignity."[382]

Furthermore, the Court held that the Constitution's "commitment to affirming diversity"[383] was central to the case. Justice Langa reiterated the High Court of Pietermaritzbug's concern for the "vulnerable and marginalized status of Hindus and Indians in South Africa's past and present."[384] He recalled Justice Sachs's emphasis on diversity in Christian Education and in Fourie, though in those cases religion, not culture, had featured prominently. Jewel Amoah and Tom Bennett observed that, in the course of the Christian Education litigation, applicants had given up on their initial claim to culture and kept the sole grounds of freedom of religion, "presumably on an intuitive assumption that this would be perceived as the weightier right."[385] Instead, Justice Langa advanced the protection of culture in all its diversity:

> Cultures, unlike religions, are not necessarily based on tenets of faith but on a collection of practices, ideas or ways of being. While some cultures may have obligatory rules that act as conditions for membership of the culture, many cultures, unlike many religions, will not have an authoritative body or text that determines the dictates of the culture. Any single member of a culture will seldom observe all those practices that make up the cultural milieu, but will choose those which she or he feels are most important to her or his own relationship to and expression of that culture. To limit cultural protection to cultural obligations would, for many cultures and their members, make the protection largely meaningless.[386]

382. Ibid. [64].

383. Ibid. [65].

384. Ibid. [17].

385. Amoah and Bennett, "The Freedoms of Religion and Culture," 3.

386. *MEC for Education* [66]

Drawing on Sachs's opinion in Fourie, Langa underscored that new South Africa did not "tolerate diversity as a necessary evil,"[387] but affirmed it "as one of the primary treasures of our nation."[388]

Chief Justice Langa recalled the English case of Shabina Begum in order to deny application of a principle of deference towards the appreciation of school governing bodies. Langa brusquely rejected the school's argument that a judgment in favor of Sunali would engender chaos in schools, with learners arriving with all sorts of "dreadlocks, body piercing, tattoos, and loincloths."[389] On the contrary, he affirmed, "the display of religion and culture in public" was "a pageant of diversity which will enrich our schools and in turn our country."[390]

Reasonable accommodation could have been possible, Pius Langa concluded, without impairing the school's enforcement of the code of conduct. Because of this, Sunali Pillay had been subject to unfair discrimination. What Justice Langa had called a "storm"[391] revolving around "a tiny gold nose stud"[392] turned into the momentous affirmation of South African cultural rights.

Justice O'Regan reached the same conclusion by affirming the inconsistency between the denial of an exemption to Sunali Pillay and the granting of exemptions for Lakshmi strings and in other similar cases. The judge joined in the unanimous order that the code of conduct be amended accordingly, but did not join in the declaratory order of Langa for the majority that Sunali had been unfairly discriminated.

In Geneva

In the judgment on Sunali Pillay, the Constitutional Court referred repeatedly to the decision of 2002 in the case of Gareth Prince. In particular, Chief Justice Langa explicitly grounded his notion of reasonable accommodation on Justice Ngcobo's sympathetic understanding of Prince's position. Albie Sachs's opinion in favour of Prince was also quoted when Justice Langa discussed the issue of genuine belief. Decidedly, Gareth Prince's defeat had alimented Sunali Pillay's victory.

Nearly one month after the Pillay decision in Cape Town, Gareth Prince's last hope to have his South African ruling reversed sank in Geneva. Before the United Nations' Human Rights Committee, the South African government reiterated its opposition to Prince's claim.

---

387. Ibid. [92]
388. Ibid.
389. Ibid. [107].
390. Ibid.
391. Ibid. [1].
392. Ibid.

The government submitted that the application lacked legal consistency. It also attacked Prince's "misguided approach in the domestic courts,"[393] his leaning for "human rights forum shopping,"[394] and his search for an incremental practical relief, ultimately leading him to ask, the government contended, for legalization of "a whole chain of cultivation, import, transport, supply, and sale of cannabis for Rastafarians."[395] Only a few months earlier, on April 13, 2007, the Metropolitan Police raided a Rastafari center in Kennington, South London. Police alleged that drug dealers had taken over the place, well known for Bob Marley's visit, forcing out peaceful, law-abiding worshipers. A huge quantity of drugs, including cannabis and crack cocaine, was reportedly found, along with six rounds of ammunition hidden under floorboards. The episode was not mentioned in the Geneva proceedings, but the story had a vast echo and certainly did not benefit Gareth Prince's case.

Prince claimed the twelve thousand Rastafarians in South Africa deserved an exemption, for the sake of a way of life with "deep African roots."[396] He replied to the state's reference to the ruling of 2002 that a strong minority of the Court had found that the exemption requested was clearly possible without impairing the state's fight against drugs. He reiterated that "a tailor-made exemption would not open the floodgates of illicit use; and there is no evidence that an exemption would pose substantial health or safety risks to society at large."[397]

Thus Gareth Prince had insisted, but to no avail.

The Committee upheld the government's argument that prohibition was based "on objective and reasonable grounds,"[398] and it flatly dismissed the application. Prince had definitively lost.

Secular Legal Monopoly

The end of the first decade of the new millennium found the global gods particularly active in reshaping law, politics, and religion. No certainty was spared in the exercise or redefining boundaries between culture and religion, between civil and religious laws, between the secular and the sacred, between the traditional and the alien, and between old and new faiths.

Britain was at the forefront. After stepping down from office, Tony Blair announced his conversion to the Roman Catholic Church. New Prime Minister Gordon Brown, himself a Presbyterian, was about to reform the prime minister's prerogatives in the nomination of officials of the Church of England. A 2008 book by Welsh law

393. *Prince* (2007) [4.1].
394. Ibid. [4.3].
395. Ibid. [4.5].
396. Ibid. [3.4].
397. Ibid. [3.2].
398. Ibid. [7.5].

and religion professor Norman Doe described the reaction of the worldwide Anglican Communion to the risk of a schism. Doe illustrated the debate on the adoption of an "Anglican Covenant,"[399] aimed at strengthening the ties between the forty-four autonomous churches while making their structure more suitable to the era of the global gods.

An acute observer of change, then–Archbishop of Canterbury Rowan Williams announced the new picture in a memorable speech on February 7, 2008. Speaking at the Royal Courts of Justice on "Civil and Religious Law in England," he addressed the passage from *your* gods to *our* gods as nobody with the same public authority had ever done before. While Tony Blair in 2006 had denied room for religious laws as threatening competitors to the law of the land, Williams called for a reflection on how to accommodate the increasing number of those in Britain who related to "something other than the British legal system alone."[400] The archbishop exposed a double challenge inherently linked to the "rights of religious groups within a secular state."[401]

One set of issues pertained to faith-based claims in civil courts. Did British secular judges hear the voice of the gods? And how did they adjudicate those requests? While Rowan Williams required British law not to shut the door to the needs of believers, he also warned that the legal process could not be left "at the mercy of . . . vexatious appeals to religious scruple."[402] If the South African Constitutional Court found that culture and religion were hardly dissociable, Williams sharply distinguished "between cultural and strictly religious dimensions."[403] He believed only serious "conscience-related claims"[404] sanctioned by a "recognised authority"[405] on behalf of a religious group deserved to be accommodated.

A second set of issues concerned the place for religious courts in multicultural Britain. Should the religious expectation to "live under more than one jurisdiction"[406] be accommodated? Was the "delegation of certain legal functions to the religious courts of a community"[407] acceptable? If Werner Menski heralded legal pluralism in postmodern Indian and South African law, Rowan Williams pointed out the crisis of "our commitment to legal monopoly."[408] In Williams's words,

> So much of our thinking in the modern world, dominated by European assumptions about universal rights, rests, surely, on the basis that the law is the

399. Doe, *Anglican Covenant*.

400. Williams, "Lecture on Civil and Religious Law in England," 262.

401. Ibid., 263–64.

402. Ibid., 267.

403. Ibid.

404. Ibid.

405. Ibid.

406. Ibid.

407. Ibid.

408. Ibid., 270.

law; that everyone stands before the public tribunal on exactly equal terms, so that recognition of corporate identities or, more seriously, of supplementary jurisdictions, is simply incoherent if we want to preserve the great political and social advances of Western legality.[409]

Williams argued that the legal monopoly had become theoretically and practically unfit to govern a "plural society of overlapping identities"[410] based on "multiple affiliation"[411] and on "different modes and contexts of belonging."[412] Of course "no 'supplementary' jurisdiction could have the power to deny access to the rights granted to other citizens or to punish its members for claiming those rights."[413] But abstract equal citizenship in ethnically, culturally, and religiously diverse societies was conducive to a "ghettoized pattern of social life,"[414] in which "particular sorts of interest and of reasoning are tolerated as private matters but never granted legitimacy in public as part of a continuing debate about shared goods and priorities."[415]

For Williams, the limit to "secular legal monopoly"[416] in a pluralistic society depended on those sources, "religion above all, but also . . . custom and habit,"[417] from which sprang "moral vision in a society."[418] The role of secular law was not the dissolution of such sources, but "the monitoring of such affiliations to prevent the creation of mutually isolated communities in which human liberties are seen in incompatible ways and individual persons are subjected to restraints or injustices for which there is no public redress."[419]

The archbishop referred to Jewish legal theorist Ayelet Shachar. In her 2001 book Shachar proposed "transformative accommodation"[420] as a sound way to articulate competing jurisdictions. According to Williams's summary, under such a scheme, "individuals retain the liberty to choose the jurisdiction under which they will seek to resolve certain carefully specified matters, so that 'power-holders are forced to compete for the loyalty of their shared constituents' . . . Hence 'transformative accommodation': both jurisdictional parties may be changed by their encounter over time, and we avoid the sterility of mutually exclusive monopolies."[421]

---

409. Ibid.
410. Ibid., 271.
411. Ibid.
412. Ibid.
413. Ibid., 268.
414. Ibid., 271.
415. Ibid.
416. Ibid., 273.
417. Ibid., 271.
418. Ibid.
419. Ibid., 272.
420. Shachar, *Multicultural Jurisdictions*, 118.
421. Williams, "Civil and Religious Law in England," 274.

If groups and communities were to contribute to the common good and avoid an unproductive clash between "cultural loyalty and state loyalty,"[422] if citizenship were to be acknowledged as "a complex phenomenon not bound up with any one level of communal belonging but involving them all,"[423] some degree of "competition for loyalty"[424] was "unavoidable."[425] This essentially signified that some applications of religious laws and some space for religious courts, were also "unavoidable." Williams specified that the problem also concerned Orthodox Jewish practices and Roman Catholic adoption agencies. Furthermore he dispassionately discussed Sharia law: its universal dimension and divine foundation, its construction as a repressive and retrograde despotism by "Islamic primitivists,"[426] with terrible implications for the status of women and converts, its evolution through "a fairly muted but nonetheless real debate among Muslim scholars."[427]

Rowan Williams's speech was nuanced and scholarly. It nevertheless provoked scandalized reactions. Critics and the press reduced the discussion to a green light for indiscriminate Sharia and the takeover of the judiciary by Sharia Councils. Williams's alleged stance for "unavoidable Sharia" became yet another label to designate that sector of Western intellectuals and religious leaders who underestimated the Muslim and communal threat, succumbed to multiculturalism, and gave up on legal and civil unity.

In a letter published in the *Times* two days after the speech, on February 9, 2008, ecclesiastical lawyer Mark Hill expressed his astonishment at "the wholly inaccurate coverage of the measured and thoughtful contribution"[428] by Rowan Williams. On religion in courts there was "nothing novel"[429] in the speech, Hill protested:

> While reluctant to engage with matters of doctrine, the courts do so when necessary but have traditionally shown deference to the internal governing instruments of individual faith communities, provided they do not offend the law of the land . . . For centuries Britain has shown toleration to religious minorities and afforded accommodations in laws of general application. Such is the mainstay of a liberal democracy in a plural state.[430]

The editor of the *Times* cut the final sentence of the original letter by Hill: "The threat to social cohesion lies not in the moderate orthodoxy of the Archbishop, but in the misleading and mischievous misreporting of his words in the media."[431]

422. Ibid.
423. Ibid., 269.
424. Ibid., 274.
425. Ibid.
426. Ibid., 265.
427. Ibid., 269.
428. Hill, "Letter to the *Times*," 21.
429. Ibid.
430. Ibid.
431. Hill, "Editorial" (2008) 259.

Mark Hill was right in pointing toward a consolidated pattern in the law of religious organizations in Britain providing for the kind of accommodation he referred to. But the media were also right in exposing that a new game was being played in a new context. The same applied to global gods: they encapsulated the different generations of deities who had come before them, while themselves standing as an original breed of gods.

Over the Phone

From 2007 to 2008, momentous legislative change accompanied the reshaping of British law and religion. In 2007, the Race and Religious Hatred Act set limits to free expression on an equal basis for all faiths. Also in 2007, the High Court endorsed the view of the district judge who had refused to issue summonses against the producers of the allegedly blasphemous theatrical work *Jerry Springer: The Opera* and against the director general of the BBC for the broadcasting of the recorded performance. On May 8, 2008, blasphemy law was repealed in England and Wales. Established Christianity no longer enjoyed special protection under common law. Thirty years after the *Gay News* case and twenty years after the struggle over the *Satanic Verses*, a new balance was found between free speech and hate speech. Fittingly, the reform coincided with the Queen's awarding knighthood to Salman Rushdie.

Equality and antidiscriminatory legislation also contributed to offering gods new tools for faith-based litigation. New concepts of religious freedom were the result of Europe, with the Human Rights Act entrusting British judges with the task of upholding the European Convention's standard. Likewise, the Employment Equality (Religion and Belief) Regulations of 2003 stood as a mark of European integration as it translated European Union antidiscrimination law into British law.

The Employment Tribunal found itself on the front line. On October 3, 2007, the Tribunal dismissed the appeal by a Rastafari driver who claimed he had lost his job because he wore a "rasta tam," the typical multicolored hat, and had dreadlocks. The Company's version of truth held that the man "did not represent the Company well:"[432] he was "sometimes abrasive, flouted dress rules (quite apart from hair), and he had made himself unavailable for work for a period."[433] The Court found the requirement of tidy hair to be a proportionate means to achieving a "presentable appearance to customers"[434] and did not exclude the wearing of dreadlocks, "at least if tidy."[435] Thus the company had not discriminated against the Rastafari.

The Employment Regulations of 2003 encouraged strong-hearted believers to go and fight for their causes in courts. This concerned Christians no less than the Rastafari.

432. *Harris* [5].
433. Ibid. [7].
434. Ibid. [15].
435. Ibid. [22].

Like many other companies, British Airways tried to protect itself by allowing Muslim, Jewish, and Sikh employees to wear the hijab, the skullcap, and the turban, respectively. The policy, British Airways retained, was based on the respect of religious obligations. In the case of Ms. Eweida, though, a practicing Christian claiming the right to wear a silver cross on her uniform, British Airways argued that such a practice was not compulsory for Christians. Upon Ms. Eweida's lawsuit, in 2007 British Airways amended the code of conduct so as to allow for symbols like a cross or the star of David to be worn over the uniform. Ms. Eweida, who had refused the company's offer of an alternative employment not requiring her to wear a uniform, resumed working but did not withdraw her application, claiming back the wages withheld for the time she was not permitted to go to her workplace.

On November 20, 2008, the Employment Appeal Tribunal found for British Airways and decided that Ms. Eweida had not been discriminated against. In the case of Sunali Pillay the South African Constitutional Court had found that voluntary religious practices deserved no less protection than compulsory practices. Instead, the British judges found the same distinction legitimate and upheld the code of conduct.

The case showed that global gods were the protagonists on both sides of the trial: they pushed applicants to fight in the extreme in order to assert their belief, while requiring judges, by consequence, to speak the language of gods. From India to South Africa, from Cape Town to London, courts were asked to define true religion, to discern proper religious obligations, and to distinguish genuine from sham believers. For religious courts, this was not new. They had the mentality and the tools to cope. But in the civil courts, the contradiction emerged between the all-religious world of the applicants and the secular language and culture of the judges.

In 2000, English law professor Anthony Bradney anticipated the friction ahead: "There is an inevitable conflict between the secularism of the argumentative rhetoric in the British courts and the faith-based vision of the obdurate believer . . . Greater numbers of obdurate believers will appear before the courts. A greater weight of cases will make the gap between . . . [strongly held] religious beliefs . . . and the nature of modern British legal discourse even clearer."

At the end of the decade, Mark Hill confirmed Bradney's prescience and added to it: if trying the global gods in British courts was about the confrontation between the secular mind of the law and the religious mind of the faithful, it was also about the difference between extreme and moderate religious claims:

> Respect for religious doctrine is part of the tapestry of the constitutional framework in the United Kingdom, but the adopting of extreme positions by certain litigants, ostensibly in the name of religion, may have a deleterious effect upon those who strive within the confines of the law actively, and successfully, to engage with the delicate balancing of competing rights and freedoms. Measured and moderate submissions are more likely to advance the cause of faith communities. Extreme positions, expressed with hyperbole

and aggression, will serve to alienate public opinion and reinforce the existing prejudices of secularists.[436]

Mark Hill referred to extreme claims where religion had been construed in a particularly aggressive way. In the time of global gods, however, extreme claims were often the simple, unintended effects of intermingling cultures.

One month after Rowan Williams's speech, the English Court of Appeal examined the case of IC, a twenty-seven-year-old British national of Bangladeshi origin with a severe mental disability. The parents of IC asked for civil recognition of a Muslim marriage celebrated by telephone between IC himself and NK, a bride chosen by IC's parents in Bangladesh. The judges accepted Werner Menski's expertise that such a marriage over the telephone was not only in an "Islamically accepted form"[437] but also "increasingly common and accepted as entirely valid."[438] Nevertheless, they dismissed the appeal, holding that English law applied, and that the marriage was "not entitled to recognition in English law."[439] While the decision dealt at length with technicalities and precedents, Justice Wall was adamant on the real issue at stake:

> The appeal throws up a profound difference in culture and thinking between domestic English notions of welfare and those embraced by Islam. This is a clash which, in my judgment, this court cannot side-step or ignore.[440]

Based on expert witness Werner Menski, the judge pointed at the underlying Bangladeshi understanding of the situation: "To the Bangladeshi mind . . . the marriage of IC is perceived as a means of protecting him, and of ensuring that he is properly cared for within the family when his parents are no longer in a position to do so."[441]

Lord Justice Wall countered by illustrating the English perspective: "To the mind of the English lawyer, by contrast, such a marriage is perceived as exploitative and indeed abusive. Under English law, a person in the position of IC is precluded from marriage for the simple reason that he lacks the capacity to marry . . . Furthermore, as IC is incapable of giving his consent to any form of sexual activity, NK would commit a criminal offence in English law by attempting to have sexual intercourse, or indeed having any form of sexual contact with him."[442]

To Rowan Williams's plea for a sensible recognition of diversity, the English judiciary responded by drawing a clear line between cultures and practices. A few months later, on December 24, 2008, Samuel Huntington, the father of *The Clash of Civilizations*, died. The increasingly interconnected global world was very different from the

---

436. Hill, "Editorial" (2011) 130–31.

437. *KC* [34].

438. Ibid.

439. Ibid. [48].

440. Ibid. [44].

441. Ibid.

442. Ibid. [45].

one the American author had prophesied. India had prompted Martha Nussbaum to argue in 2007 that the true clash was rather "between proponents of ethnoreligious homogeneity and proponents of a more inclusive and pluralistic type of citizenship." [443] The rise of global gods, so mobile and multiform in character, was one of the reasons why Huntington's forecast had failed, though the rhetoric of the clash of civilizations still had the power to shape the mind of so many all over the world.

Much more meaningful and real was the clash between the declamatory function of the law and its actual, social implications. This was a clash between powerful collective emotions over clear-cut identities and the problematic reality of intermingling identities, between *our* gods as an ideal uniformity and *our* gods as an inextricable plurality—or, worded differently, between the moon, which people would never possess, and the image of the moon, which, indeed, was already available to them.

We Cannot Turn the Clock Back

On July 15, 2009, the Constitutional Court of South Africa decided on the legal effects of polygynous Muslim marriages. Against the background of the specifically South African context, the decision encapsulated the case of the English-Bangladeshi phone marriage, Rowan Williams's speech, and the ongoing Indian struggle with religious personal laws.

The Court held that the Succession Act had to be interpreted as allowing for more than one widow to succeed to the dead husband. Justice Bess Nkabinde for a unanimous bench, also including Albie Sachs, was cautious in excluding that the ruling directly concerned the constitutionality of Islamic polygynous unions; the judge also clarified that the judgment did not "purport to incorporate any aspect of Sharia law into South African law." [444] The focus of the Court was on granting "appropriate protection" [445] to women. The suffering of wives in Muslim marriages was the reason why equal treatment between women in monogamous and polygynous marriages was essential, thus implying recognition and protection. Justice Nkabinde noted:

> By discriminating against women in polygynous Muslim marriages on the grounds of religion, gender, and marital status, the [Succession] Act clearly reinforces a pattern of stereotyping and patriarchal practices that relegates women in these marriages to being unworthy of protection. [446]

For many in Britain and in India, a legal barrier against polygynous Muslim marriages was a necessity for the sake of destitute Muslim women. For the South African Court, recognition of Muslim widows' rights in polygynous marriages served

443. Nussbaum, *The Clash Within*, 15.
444. *Hassam* [17].
445. Ibid. [35].
446. Ibid. [37].

the purpose of protecting "a particularly vulnerable group in Muslim communities."[447] The Court satisfied itself with the moon in the mirror, believing this was the best application of constitutional principles. South African praise for diversity, the reshaping of customary law, and the lingering post-apartheid hangover played a substantial part. The Court went back to Gandhi's time in South Africa, recalling that white judges, as in the "terrible judgment" by Justice Searle for the Cape Supreme Court in 1913, could decline to recognize a widow from a Muslim marriage as a surviving spouse because the potential polygynous character of such a marriage made it "reprobated by the majority of civilized peoples, on ground of morality and religion."[448] The same mindset had prevailed in 1987, when the Succession Act was framed. Now, in 2009, this was a different country; Justice Bess Nkabinde proclaimed the past was gone: "we cannot turn the clock back."[449]

The Whole Armor of God

Also in 2009, Tom Bennett, the South African law professor and expert in customary law, dealt in two articles with the issue of legal recognition of cultural and religious diversity in South Africa. His approach to customary law was one of cautious endorsement. Both legal pluralism and Marxist deconstructionism had denounced the official version of customary law as shaped by the colonialist and by the racist ruler. If the ethnographer's viewpoint was no less alien, customary law could only be taken as a "living law" needing both "to be revitalized and brought into line with the Bill of Rights."[450] Bennett noticed judges were uneasy with the inherent dynamism of customs, showing often an "uncritical attitude towards the proof of and assumptions underlying the law."[451] Courts, the author denounced, "had no coherent approach and, not surprisingly, they floundered."[452] The "living law," Bennett found, was by its own nature "highly localized and variable."[453] Western-minded formal unification was impossible. But communities were wrong if they believed they could nourish the myth of a "genuine customary law . . . left in a state of pristine innocence, forever beyond the reach of the formal legal system."[454] The "creation of customary law," Bennett concluded, should be seen rather "as a dialectic process involving the communities from which the law springs and official organs of state in which it is applied."[455]

447. Ibid. [41].
448. Ibid. [33].
449. Ibid. [45].
450. Bennett, "Re-introducing African Customary Law," 29.
451. Ibid., 14.
452. Ibid., 13.
453. Ibid., 29.
454. Ibid.
455. Ibid., 30.

Bennett's concern with a fully constitutional understanding of customary law reflected his conviction that the emphasis on the rainbow nation of a monotheistic God and the preference for religion in human-rights litigation went against the reality and diversity of African culture. In the article cowritten with Jewel Amoah, Bennett pointed out the serious risk that the peculiar, inextricable mix of culture and religion in South Africa might succumb to the latest developments. The largely undifferentiated and unstructured traditional African religion, with its holistic worldview and its reluctance to "distinguish the sacred from the secular,"[456] did not fit into the prevailing religious pattern of Islam and Christianity, which coincided with "the model of religion contemplated for human rights advocacy."[457] The active proselytizing of Muslims and Christians superseded African syncretism. Urbanization and the advancing secular attitude in an increasingly consumerist society also impacted negatively. Moreover, colonial prejudice was slow to die, and the "implicit value judgment"[458] that African faiths were "somehow inferior to the main monotheistic religions"[459] was still widely held.

At the same time, traditional African elements proved resilient well beyond the apparent success of proselytizing religions. The authors admitted that culture had the power to transform Christianity and Islam, enculturation being a way through which "traditional African life and beliefs"[460] were revitalized. Furthermore, the success of African independent churches, with the Zionist church, founded in 1895, featuring by now as the largest denomination in South Africa, was also a sign that the line between the traditional and the imported was not so easy to draw.

Still, the authors protested that traditional African religions of South Africa were undervalued and "threatened by forces of secularism and in danger of being eclipsed by Christianity and Islam."[461] With mainstream churches and faith communities drafting a South African Charter of Religious Rights and Freedoms, insistence on cultural rights, the authors suggested, was crucial to secure "not only the elements of belief and practice that comprise traditional African religions, but also the right of adherents to have faiths that differ from the Western construct of religion."[462]

In this perspective, Amoah and Bennett stressed that equality and nondiscrimination were the crucial tools. They had indeed proved ineffective in Gareth Prince's litigation. However, Albie Sachs's construction in the case of Prince and again in the case of same-sex marriage, enabled first Justice Langa to give justice to the woman with the nose stud and then Justice Nkabinde to assert the rights of the polygynous Muslim widow. Equal rights, the authors maintained, were also to be mobilized in

---

456. Amoah and Bennett, "The Freedoms of Religion and Culture," 15.
457. Ibid., 16.
458. Ibid., 14.
459. Ibid.
460. Ibid., 18.
461. Ibid. 17.
462. Ibid., 3.

order for traditional religions "to compete on their own terms, in the free marketplace of faith."[463] Applying equality to traditional religions "will bring culture out from under the shadow of religion, and allow culture to shine in its own right."[464]

Global gods in South Africa were a matter of culture and religion, of past and future, of departure from apartheid and "transformative constitutionalism"[465] in view of a better tomorrow. In his 2009 *The Strange Alchemy of Life and Law*, Albie Sachs delivered a passionate summary of his personal and legal experience. For the cover, he chose the picture of a work by artist Judith Mason, which was placed in the Constitutional Court building. As the artist explained in the preface to Sachs's book, the work was in memory of Phila Ndwandwe, a victim of apartheid:

> Phila Ndwandwe was shot by the security police after being kept naked for weeks in an attempt to make her inform on her comrades. She preserved her dignity by making panties out of a blue plastic bag. This garment was found wrapped around her pelvis when she was exhumed. "She simply would not talk," one of the policemen involved in her death testified. "God . . . she was brave."[466]

The artist's work had been produced in 1995, at the time of transition, and consisted of blue plastic bags collected by the artist and sewn into a dress. On the skirt, Judith Mason had painted this letter:

> Sister, a plastic bag may not be the whole armour of God, but you were wrestling with flesh and blood, and against powers, against the rulers of darkness, against spiritual wickedness in sordid places. Your weapons were your silence and a piece of rubbish. Finding that bag and wearing it until you were disinterred is such a frugal, commonsensical, house-wifely thing to do, an ordinary act . . . At some level you shamed your captors, and they did not compound their abuse of you by stripping you a second time. Yet they killed you. We only know your story because a sniggering man remembered how brave you were. Memorials to your courage are everywhere; they blow about in the streets and drift on the tide and cling to thorn-bushes. This dress is made from some of them. Hambe khale. Umkhonto.[467]

Sachs's choice to set this image and its related message as a seal upon his book summed up the experience of the former communist, who had shaped the constitutional approach of post-apartheid South Africa to religious and cultural diversity.

---

463. Ibid., 19.
464. Ibid.
465. *Hassam* [28].
466. Mason, "The Man Who Sang and the Woman Who Kept Silent," vii.
467. Ibid., vii–viii.

Yielding or Rising

In 2007, the 150th anniversary of the First War of Independence against the British offered an opportunity to tenants of Hindutva. Lal Krishna Advani, the protagonist of the rashtra to Ayodhya, hailed the date of May 10, the day when the uprising began, as a "super-sacred day in the history of India, for it marked . . . the beginning of what subsequently came to be regarded as India's first war of Independence."[468] Hindu nationalist rhetoric was still powerful and influential in politics and society. But the complexity of Indian democracy, and the resilience of the Congress Party in the context of coalition politics along lines of region, caste, and religion had prevented the BJP from prevailing. Advani himself, former home minister from 1998 to 2004 and deputy prime minister from 1999 to 2004, spoke in 2007 as the leader of the opposition in the Lok Sabha. "Saffron terror" was indeed a problem for the middle class. Corruption and infighting also contributed to the political defeats of BJP in the elections of 2004 and 2009, in what journalist Siddharth Varadarajan saw as the "declining salience"[469] of extremist Hindutva politics.

An increasingly ramified and structured worldwide Hindu diaspora, coupled with the threat of global Islamic radicalism, nourished Hindu nationalist gods. They featured prominently among global gods. But global gods formed a hugely diverse galaxy. However prominent they may have been, Hindu nationalist gods had to compete with many other families of global gods. In particular, despite the end of the Cold War, global gods still comprised the gods of capitalist consumerism and, especially in India, the gods of Marxist resistance. As had happened in the case of past generations of deities, no family of gods, not even the powerful gods of Hindutva, could achieve dominance over the others.

In the second half of the decade of the 2000s, the Supreme Court left pending the much-awaited decision on Ayodhya, and tried the Hindu nationalist gods in the field of cow slaughtering. In 2006, Justice Tarun Chatterjee for the Court defended the possibility of permission from the central government to slaughter old and useless buffaloes against hard-line believers in the protection of the procow sentiments of the majority through a total ban on cow slaughtering. Striking a difficult balance, the judge upheld the view expressed by the Court in 2005[470] that total prohibition of cow and cow progeny slaughter may be constitutionally justified; but the judge emphasized at the same time that the Court could not hold "that permitting slaughter of bovine cattle by itself is unconstitutional."[471]

Hindu nationalists were strong and proactive but clashed with the many constituencies of Indian society and politics.

468. Advani. "150 Years of Heroism."

469. Interview with the author, New Delhi. February 15, 2011.

470. *State of Gujarat.*

471. *Akhil*, 204 [100].

In 2007, at the Lord Sri Krishna Temple of Guruvayoor in Kerala, a cabinet minister's Christian wife entered the temple, prompting the head priest to conduct a purification ceremony afterwards. In the ensuing outcry, progressive movements campaigned for the need to push forward the historical struggle of the 1930s, which had led to admitting all Hindus, beyond caste lines, to the temple. Their demand to open the temple to all believers led to confrontations with Hindu organizations protesting the involvement of leftist parties in the affairs of temple. Tensions about conversions in the tribal areas also opposed Christian to Hindu missionaries, in a context where different forms of Marxist militancy still retained a remarkable presence.

The challenge of the global gods to India also concerned Islam. Against the background of violence in Kashmir, the targeting of Muslim youth in the name of the war on "Indian mujahideens," and the strategies of obscurantist Islamic leaders, the editor of the *Hindu*, Varadarajan, exposed "Indian politics exploiting the Muslim community exclusively on the religious line."[472] Varadarayan pointed out the "institutional bias against Muslims"[473] and called for the necessity to "de-toxify the approach of the state to Muslims."[474] A fresh approach was needed at all levels and in particular among the police, the judiciary, and the public service. The 2006 Report by the Sachar Committee on socioeconomic disparities of Indian Muslims called for a national awareness of reality and for a serious response to the alienation of the Muslim community.

As the decade closed, mutual influences and trends connecting India to South Africa and Britain emerged on July 2, 2009, when the Delhi High Court reversed the criminal ban on homosexuality on grounds of invasion of privacy.

If India had been a template for imperial gods, cold gods, explosive gods, and national gods, the case was not different with global gods at the dawn of the new millennium. Indian religious issues had transformed over time, while absorbing and perpetuating the memory of subsequent generations. New generations of Indian gods added new beliefs to the old ones, the past was preserved while shaping the future. In this too India was a template.

History shaped India, South Africa, and Britain as highly distinctive countries, and yet history also interconnected them. By trying the gods, each nation built up its own identity, while participating in a wider dynamism. The three countries experienced together, and through one another, the potential of religion to bring bloodshed or healing, tyranny or liberation, for yielding or rising. While attaining all domains of social life, such ambivalence was crucially experienced in courts. Judges and parties connected principles to practice, ideologies to reality, the general to the specific, the abstract to the actual. Trying the gods was more than just reacting to private litigations; it was also more than just enforcing the will of powers. As a complete experience of invention and memory, of purpose and hazard, of patterns and uniqueness, trying

472. Interview with the author, New Delhi, February 15 2011.

473. Ibid.

474. Ibid.

the gods in the three countries encapsulated the tension between *your* gods and *our* gods, the moon and the mirror image of it.

As in the story of little Krishna and Mother Yashoda, each trial asked for the moon, yet the verdict each time delivered the mirror image of it. The moon was accessible to people only if they acknowledged it was far away, out of reach: if they accepted the illusion of the mirror. At dawn, the moon would disappear anyway.

Sushmita Ghosh, Gareth Prince, and Shabina Begum shared the revelation that whoever the winner or the loser, the moon could only be possessed through the glass.

Sushmita Ghosh's victory was an achievement for all Indian women, but it proved far from final. Her legacy was that Indian women had to struggle every day to carve out new strategies and tools in their quest for justice. By 2009, Justice Kuldip Singh had retired. "You need courage"[475] to be a judge: this was the lesson he drew from a lifetime. His plea for the uniform civil code in the momentous decision of 1995 in the case of Sushmita Ghsosh was defeated. But his dismissal of conversion as a ground for divorcing a wife was a milestone. Thinking back at his judgment, he could affirm: "it has served the purpose."[476] Also in 2009, the Law Commission of India published a Report on "Preventing Bigamy via Conversion to Islam—A Proposal for giving Statutory Effect to Supreme Court" in which the legislation of the outcome of Sushmita Ghosh's struggle was envisaged, along with the amendment of the Hindu Marriage Act of 1955.

Gareth Prince lost his litigation battle but prompted the South African Constitutional Court to shape a unique doctrine of diversity. Like Mandela, Prince never became a barrister. However, he made an excellent legal adviser. In October 2009, four months after President Zuma, in his first address to the nation, had promised serious agrarian reform, Gareth Prince led a group of small-scale South African farmers to lodge a complaint against the government's failure to grant sufficient access to the land. While some farmers did not know "their rights,"[477] as Gareth declared to the press, others simply lived "too far from a courthouse"[478] or could not "afford to press charges."[479] He was there to help.

In Britain, Shabina Begum won in the Court of Appeal, and then lost in the House of Lords. She succeeded anyway in exposing to all Britons the defiant Islam of her generation. Ironically, Shabina outlived the court that dismissed her appeal: on October 1, 2009, judicial authority was taken away from the House of Lords, and a Supreme Court for the United Kingdom was created. In 2009, the Denbigh High School was awarded as the *Times Educational Supplement*'s secondary school of the

475. Interview with the author, Chandigarh, February 16, 2011.

476. Ibid.

477. Mannak, "South Africa. If You Are Landless, You Are Damned."

478. Ibid.

479. Ibid.

year honor. The school was still under the leadership of Yasmin Bevan—Dame Bevan since 2007 for her services to education.

In the end, contrary to the expectations, *our* peaceful gods had not replaced *your* confrontational gods. *Our* gods were there, not in their idealized form, but instead in the everyday experience of mixed identities, hybrid deities, shared fears, and hopes.

Indians, South Africans, and Britons learned together how hard it was to cope with dreams and illusions, with the moon and the mirror image of it. When illusions faded away, all the mirror could reflect was the less exciting but more truthful reality of the three countries. This was the shared reality that gods and men had built together in India, South Africa, and Britain. There, in that reality, gods and men could still find further inspiration, nourishing their struggle for a better future in their countries and beyond.

Bibliography

Advani, L. K. "150 Years of Heroism, via Kala Pani." *The Indian Express*, May 10, 2007. Online: http://www.indianexpress.com/story/30503.html/.

Ahmed Khan, Syed, Sir. *The Causes of the Indian Revolt*. Oxford in Asia Historical Reprints. Oxford: Oxford University Press, 2000.

Alberts, Louw, and Frank Chikane, eds. *The Road to Rustenburg*. Cape Town: Struik Christian Books, 1991.

Ambedkar, B. R. *Annihilation of Caste*. Bombay: Kadrekar, 1936.

———. "Speech on the Hindu Code Bill at the Constituent Assembly of India." April 9, 1948. In Constituent Assembly of India (Legislative) Debates 4:3628–33. Delhi: The Manager of Publications.

Amis, Martin. "The Age of Horrorism." *The Observer Review* September 10, 2006, 4–9.

———. "The Second Plane." In *The Second Plane,* 3–10. London: Cape, 2008.

Amoah, Jewel, and Tom Bennett. "The Freedoms of Religion and Culture under the South African Constitution: Do Traditional African Religions Enjoy Equal Treatment?" *Journal of Law and Religion* 24 (2008–2009) 1–20.

Asmal, Kader. "Foreword." In *Truth, Reconciliation and the Apartheid Legal Order*, by David Dyzenhaus, vii–x. Cape Town: Juta, 1998.

Austin, Granville. "Religion, Personal Law, and Identity in India." In *Religion and Personal Law in Secular India: A Call to Judgment*, edited by Gerald J. Larson 15–23. Bloomington: Indiana University Press, 2001.

B. Pocker Sahib Bahadur. "Speech at the Constituent Assembly." November 23, 1948. In *Constituent Assembly of India Debates* 7:544–46. 12 vols. Delhi: The Manager of Publications.

Ball, Charles. *History of the Indian Mutiny*. Volume 2. London: London Printing and Publishing Co., 1858–1859.

Barber, James. *South Africa in the Twentieth Century*. History of the Contemporary World. Oxford: Blackwell, 1999.

Battersby. John D. "White Foe of Pretoria Injured by a Car Bomb in Mozambique." *New York Times*, April 8, 1988.

Baxi, Upendra. *The Crisis of the Indian Legal System*. Alternatives in Development. Law. New Delhi: Vikas, 1982.

Bennett, Thomas W. "Re-introducing African Customary Law to the South African Legal System." *The American Journal of Comparative Law* 57 (2009) 1–32.

———. *A Sourcebook of African Customary Law for Southern Africa*. Cape Town: Juta, 1991.

Bernstein, Edgar. "Union of South Africa." *American Jewish Year Book* 59 (1958) 366–74.

Biko, Steve. *I Write What I Like*. London: Bowerdean, 1996.

Bizos, George. *No One to Blame? In Pursuit of Justice in South Africa*. Mayibuye History and Literature Series 90. Cape Town: David Philip, 1998.

Blair, Tony. "Foreword." In *Reclaiming the Ground: Christianity and Socialism*, edited by Christopher Bryant, 9–12. London: Spire, 1993.

———. "Speech at Downing Street," December 8, 2006. Online: http://tna.europarchive.org/20070305112605/http:/www.pm.gov.uk/output/Page10563.asp/.

———. "Speech in the House of Commons on the Iraq Crisis," *Guardian*, March 18, 2003. Online: http://www.guardian.co.uk/politics/2003/mar/18/foreignpolicy.iraq1/.

Bocock, Robert. "Religion in Modern Britain." In *Religion and Ideology*, edited by Robert Bocock and Kenneth Thompson, 207–33. An Open University Set Book. Manchester: Manchester University Press, 1985.

Boesak, Allan A. *Farewell to Innocence: A Socio-Ethical Study on Black Theology and Black Power*. Maryknoll, NY: Orbis, 1976.

Bolt, Robert. *A Man for All Seasons*. London: French, 1960.

Boraine, Alex. *A Life in Transition*. Cape Town: Zebra, 2008.

Boraine, Alex et al. *Dealing with the Past: Truth and Reconciliation in South Africa*. Cape Town: Institute for Democracy in South Africa 1994.

Brooke, Stephen. *Reform and Reconstruction: Britain after the War, 1945–51*. Manchester: Manchester University Press, 1995.

Caine, Michael. *What's It All About?* London: Century, 1992.

Calata, Jimmy. "Presidential Address for the ANC (Cape)," July 1948. Online: http://www.sahistory.org.za/pages/library-resources/speeches/1948_address-calata.htm.

Carter, Jimmy. "India Remarks Before the Indian Parliament," January 2, 1978. Website: *The American Presidency Project*, compiled by John Woolley and Gerhard Peters. Online: http://www.presidency.ucsb.edu/ws/?pid=30623.

Chakrabarty, Bidyut. *Indian Politics and Society since Independence*. London: Routledge, 2008.

Chapman, Mark. *Doing God: Religion and Public Policy in Brown's Britain*. London: Darton, Longman & Todd, 2008.

Chaskalson, Arthur. "Law in a Changing Society." *South African Journal on Human Rights* 5 (1989) 293–300.

Chidester, David. *Religions of South Africa*. The Library of Religious Beliefs and Practices. London: Routledge, 1992.

———. *Shots in the Streets: Violence and Religion in South Africa*. Boston: Beacon, 1991.

Church of England, House of Bishops. "Civil Partnerships: A Pastoral Statement from the House of Bishops of the Church of England." 25 July 2005. Online: http://www.churchofengland.org/media-centre/news/2005/07/pr5605.aspx/.

Church of England, Media Centre. "House of Bishops Issues Pastoral Statement on Civil Partnerships" (summary of statement). 25 July 2005. Online: http://www.churchofengland.org/media-centre/news/2005/07/pr5605.aspx/.

Churchill, Randolph. "Speech in Parliament." May 24, 1880. *Hansard Parliamentary Debates*, 3rd series (1830–91). Online: http://hansard.millbanksystems.com/commons/1880/may/24/adjourned-debate#S3V0252P0_18800524_HOC_85/.

Churchill, Winston. "Alone: 'Their Finest Hour.'" In *Blood, Toil, Tears and Sweat: The Great Speeches*, edited by David Cannadine, 166–78. Penguin Classics. London: Penguin, 2007.

Crowther, Bosley. "It's British vs. Natives in Action-Filled 'Zulu.'" *New York Times*, July 8, 1964, 38.

Curtis, Mark. *Secret Affairs: Britain's Collusion with Radical Islam*. London: Serpent's Tail, 2010.

Davie, Grace. "Believing without Belonging: Is this the Future of Religion in Britain?" *Social Compass* 37 (1990) 456–69.

———. *Religion in Britain since 1945: Believing without Belonging*. Making Contemporary Britain. Oxford: Blackwell, 1994.

De Gruchy, John W. *The Church Struggle in South Africa*. Cape Town: David Philip, 1979.

———. "Evidence at the Trial The State v Ashley Forbes & others (charges of terrorism) Cape of Good Hope Supreme Court (Cape Town) 1988." No date. Pages numbered 1917–1939. Courtesy of John de Gruchy.

De Gruchy, John W., and Charles Villa-Vicencio, eds. *Apartheid Is a Heresy*. Cape Town: David Philip, 1983.

De Gruchy, Steve. "Postscript to the Third Edition: Locating *The Church Struggle in South Africa* in the Wider Historiography of the Church in South Africa" In *The Church Struggle in South Africa. Twenty-fifth Anniversary Edition*, by John W. De Gruchy and Steve De Gruchy, xxvii–xxx. London: SCM, 2004.

De Klerk, Willem. *F. W. de Klerk: The Man in His Time*. Johannesburg: Ball, 1991.

Derrett, J. Duncan M. "The Hindu Succession Act, 1956: an Experiment in Social Legislation." *American Journal of Comparative Law* 8 (1959) 485–501.

———. *The Hoysalas: A Medieval Indian Royal Family*. Madras: Oxford University Press, 1957.

———. *Religion, Law and the State in India*. London: Faber & Faber, 1968.

De Smith, S. A. "The London Declaration of the Commonwealth Prime Ministers, April 28, 1949." *The Modern Law Review* 12 (1949) 351–54.

Doe, Norman. *Anglican Covenant: Theological and Legal Considerations for a Global Debate*. Norwich, UK: Canterbury, 2008.

Dyzenhaus, David. *Truth, Reconciliation and the Apartheid Legal Order*. Cape Town: Juta, 1998.

Eckerman, Ingrid. *The Bhopal Saga: Causes and Consequences of the World's Largest Industrial Disaster*. Hyderabad: Universities Press, 2005.

Edwardes, Michael. "The Mutiny and Its Consequences." In William H. Russell, *My Indian Mutiny Diary*, edited by Michael Edwardes, xiii–xxviii. London: Cassell, 1957.

Elizabeth II, Queen of Great Britain. "Queen's Speech," November 26, 2003. Commons Journal 260. Session 2003–2004. Online: http://www.publications.parliament.uk/pa/cm200304/cmjournal/260/001.htm/.

Endfield, Cy, director. *Zulu*. Produced by Stanley Baker and Cy Endfield. Diamond Films, 1964. 1 DVD. United States: MGM, 2003.

Fischer, Louis. *The Life of Mahatma Gandhi*. London: HarperCollins, 1997.

Forster, E. M. *A Passage to India*. Penguin Classics. London: Penguin, 2005.

Fukuyama, Francis. "The End of History." *The National Interest* 16 (1989) 3–18.

Galanter, Marc. *Law and Society in Modern India*. Edited with an introduction by Rajeev Dhavan. Delhi: Oxford University Press, 1989.

Gandhi, Mohandas K. *An Autobiography: Or the Story of My Experiments with Truth*. London: Penguin, 1982.

———. *Satyagraha in South Africa*. Ahmedabad: Navajivan, 1961.

Garrett, Herbert L. O. *The Trial of Muhammad Bahadur Shah.* Lahore: Research and Publication Centre, National College of Arts, 2003.

Gerard, Jasper. "Jasper Gerard Meets Shabina Begum: Faith, the Veil, Shopping, and Me." *Sunday Times*, March 26, 2006, 5.

Gevisser, Mark. "ANC Was His Family, the Struggle Was His Life: A Tribute to Govan Mbeki." *Sunday Times* [South Africa]September 2, 2001. Website of the African National Congress. Online: http://www.anc.org.za/show.php?id=4589/.

———. *Thabo Mbeki: The Dream Deferred.* Johannesburg: Ball, 2007.

Giliomee, Hermann. *The Afrikaners: Biography of a People.* London: Hurst, 2003.

"God." *The Economist*, Millennium Special Edition, December 31, 1999.

Gordimer, Nadine. *The House Gun.* London: Bloomsbury, 1999.

Guha, Ramachandra. *India after Gandhi: The History of the World's Largest Democracy.* London: Pan, 2008.

Gunn, T. Jeremy. *Spiritual Weapons: The Cold War and the Forging of an American National Religion.* Westport, CT: Praeger, 2009.

Hall, Sheldon. *Zulu: With Some Guts behind It; The Making of the Epic Movie.* Sheffield: Tomahawk, 2005.

Hancock, W. K., and Jean van der Poel, eds. *Selections from the Smuts Papers.* Vol. 3, *June 1910—November 1918.* Cambridge: Cambridge University Press, 1966.

Hansen, Randall. *Citizenship and Immigration in Post-war Britain: The Institutional Origins of a Multicultural Nation.* Oxford: Oxford University Press, 2000.

Hasford, Gustav. *The Short-Timers.* Toronto: Bantam, 1985.

Hazarika, Sanjoy. "Twelve Die in Bombay in Anti-Rushdie Riots." *New York Times*, February 25, 1989, 3.

Heredia, Rudolf C. *Changing Gods: Rethinking Conversion in India.* New Delhi: Penguin, 2007.

Herman, Arthur. *Gandhi & Churchill: The Epic Rivalry That Destroyed an Empire and Forged Our Age.* London: Hutchinson, 2008.

Hill, Mark. "Editorial." *Ecclesiastical Law Journal* 7 (2004) 246–50.

———. "Editorial." *Ecclesiastical Law Journal* 10 (2008) 259–61.

———. "Editorial." *Ecclesiastical Law Journal* 13 (2011) 129–31.

———. "The Impact for the Church of England of the Human Rights Act 1998." *Ecclesiastical Law Journal* 5 (2000) 431–39.

———. "Letter to the *Times*." *Times* February 9, 2008, 21.

———. "Recent Ecclesiastical Cases." *Ecclesiastical Law Journal* 6 (2001) 162–74.

Hobhouse, Arthur. *Native Indian Judges.* London: Reeves, 1883.

Huntington, Samuel P. "The Clash of Civilizations?" *Foreign Affairs* 3 (1993) 22–49.

Husain, Iqbal, ed. *Karl Marx on India.* New Delhi: Tulika, 2006.

Huttenback, Robert A. *Gandhi in South Africa: British Imperialism and the Indian Question, 1860–1914.* Ithaca, NY: Cornell University Press, 1971.

Jacobsohn, Gary J. *The Wheel of Law: India's Secularism in Comparative Constitutional Context.* Princeton: Princeton University Press, 2003.

Jaffrelot, Christophe. *Dr. Ambedkar and Untouchability: Fighting the Indian Caste System.* New York: Columbia University Press, 2005.

Jenkins, Roy. "Racial Equality in Britain. Speech to the National Committee for Commonwealth Immigrants," May 23, 1966. In *Essays and Speeches*, by Roy Jenkins, 267–73. London: Collins, 1967.

Jinnah, Muhammad Ali. "Presidential Address at the All-India Muslim League," Lahore, 22 March 1940. In *Some Recent Speeches and Writings of Mr. Jinnah*, edited by Jamil-Ud-Din, Ahmad, 1:159–81. Lahore: Shaikh Muhammad Ashraf, 1952.

Joffe, Joel. *The State vs. Nelson Mandela: The Trial that Changed South Africa*. Oxford: Oneworld, 2007.

Johnson, Boris. "The Shabina Begum Case Never Had Anything to Do with Modesty." *The Daily Telegraph*, March 23, 2006, 18. Online: http://www.telegraph.co.uk/comment/personal-view/3623879/The-Shabina-Begum-case-never-had-anything-to-do-with-modesty.html/.

Jonker, Willie. "Understanding the Church Situation and Obstacles to Christian Witness in South Africa." In *The Road to Rustenburg*, edited by Louw Alberts and Frank Chikane. 87–98. Cape Town: Struik Christian Books, 1991.

Karapin, Roger. "Major Anti-Minority Riots and National Legislative Campaigns against Immigrants in Britain and Germany." In *Challenging Immigration and Ethnic Relations Politics: European Perspectives*, edited by Ruud Koopmans and Paul Statham. 312–47. Oxford: Oxford University Press, 2000

Keble, John. *National apostasy considered in a sermon preached in St. Mary's, Oxford before His Majesty's Judges of Assize on Sunday, July 14, 1833*. London: Mowbray, 1931.

Kenny, Mary. "In Defence of Mary Whitehouse." *The Spectator Online*, June 7, 2010. Online: http://blogs.spectator.co.uk/coffeehouse/2010/06/in-defence-of-mary-whitehouse/.

Kipling, J. Rudyard. *Kim*. Penguin Popular Classics. London: Penguin, 1994.

Krishna Iyer, V. R. "Emergency: Darkest Hour in India's Judicial History." June 27, 2000. Online: http://www.expressindia.com/news/ie/daily/20000627/ina27053.html/.

Kubrick, Stanley, director and producer. *Full Metal Jacket*. Great Britain: Warner Bros., 1987.

Kugle, Scott A. "Framed, Blamed, and Renamed: the Recasting of Islamic Jurisprudence in Colonial South Asia." *Modern Asia Studies* 35 (2001) 257–313.

Larson, Gerald J. "Introduction. The Secular State in a Religious Society." In *Religion and Personal Law in Secular India: A Call to Judgment*, edited by Gerald J. Larson, 1–11. Bloomington: Indiana University Press, 2001.

Ling, Trevor. *Religious Change and the Secular State*. Calcutta: Research India Publications, 1978.

Luce, Edward. *In Spite of the Gods: The Strange Rise of Modern India*. London: Little, Brown, 2006.

Lynch, Owen M. "Rioting as Rational Action: An Interpretation of the April 1978 Riots in Agra." *Economic and Political Weekly* 16 (1981) 1951–56.

Macaulay, Thomas B. "Government of India. A Speech delivered in the House of Commons on the 10th of July, 1833." In *Macaulay: Prose and Poetry*, selected by George M. Young, 688–718. London: Rupert Hart-Davis, 1952.

———. "Indian Education. Minute of the 2nd of February, 1835." In *Macaulay. Prose and Poetry*, selected by George M. Young, 719–30. London: Hart-Davis, 1952.

MacDonald, Ian. *Revolution in the Head: The Beatles' Records and the Sixties*. London: Vintage, 2008.

Macmillan, M. Harold. "Speech to the South African Parliament." February 3, 1960. Online: http://africanhistory.about.com/od/eraindependence/p/wind_of_change2.htm/.

Mahboob Ali Baig Sahib Bahadur. "Speech at the Constituent Assembly." November 23, 1948. In *Constituent Assembly of India Debates*, 7:543–44. 12 vols. Delhi: The Manager of Publications.

Mahmood, Tahir. *Uniform Civil Code: Fictions and Facts*. New Delhi: India & Islam Research Council, 1995.

Major, John. *The Autobiography*. London: HarperCollins, 2000.

Malik, Kenan. *From Fatwa to Jihad: The Rushdie Affair and Its Legacy*. London: Atlantic, 2009.

Mandal Commission. *Report of the Backward Classes Commission, 1980*. Delhi: Akalank Publications, 1991.

Mandela, Nelson. *Long Walk to Freedom*. London: Abacus, 1995.

———. *The Struggle Is My Life*. London: International Defence and Aid Fund, 1978.

Mannak, Miriam. "South Africa: If You Are Landless, You Are Damned." Inter Press Service, October 16, 2009. Online: http://www.ipsnews.net/2009/10/south-africa-quotif-you-are-landless-you-are-damnedquot.

Manzo, Kathryn A. *Creating Boundaries: The Politics of Race and Nation*. Boulder, CO: Lynne Rienner, 1998.

Margolick, David. "Blair's Big Gamble." *Vanity Fair*, June 2003. Online: http://www.vanityfair.com/politics/features/2003/06/blair-200306/.

Marley, Bob, Peter Tosh. "Get Up, Stand Up." On *Burnin'*, by Bob Marley and the Wailers. Los Angeles: Island Records, 1973.

Mason, Judith. "The Man Who Sang and the Woman Who Kept Silent." In *The Strange Alchemy of Life and Law,* by Albie Sachs, vii–viii. Oxford: Oxford University Press, 2009.

McSmith, Andy. *No Such Thing as Society: A History of Britain in the 1980s*. London: Constable, 2010.

Meintjes, Johannes. *Sandile, the Fall of the Xhosa Nation*. Cape Town: Bulpin, 1971.

Menon, Nivedita. "State, Community, and the Debate on the Uniform Civil Code in India." In *Beyond Rights Talk and Culture Talk: Comparative Essays on the Politics of Rights and Culture*, edited by Mahmood Mamdani, 75–95. New York: St Martin's, 2000.

Menski, Werner. "Asking for the Moon: Legal Uniformity in India from a Kerala Perspective." *Kerala Law Times* 2 (2002) 52–78.

———. "Legal Pluralism in the Hindu Marriage." In *Hinduism in Great Britain: The Perpetuation of Religion in an Alien Cultural Milieu*, edited by Richard Burghart, 181–200. London: Tavistock, 1987.

Meredith, Martin. *Coming to Terms. South Africa's Search for Truth*. New York: Public Affairs, 1999.

———. *Nelson Mandela: A Biography*. London: Hamish Hamilton, 1997.

Modood, Tariq. "British Asian Muslims and the Rushdie Affair." *Political Quarterly* 61 (1990) 143–60.

Mohammad Ismail Sahib. "Speech at the Constituent Assembly." November 23, 1948. In *Constituent Assembly of India Debates*, 7:540–41. 12 vols. Delhi: The Manager of Publications.

Mohammed, Jan, director. *International Guerillas*. Written by Nasir Adib et al. Starring Afzaal Ahmad et al. Produced by Evernew Pictures. DVD. Tampa: Revengeismydestiny.com, 1990.

The Monty Python Partnership. *The Meaning of Life*. Directed by Terry Jones. Starring Graham Chapman et al. United States: Universal, 1983. DVD. United States: Universal Home Entertainment, 2005.

Moosa, Ebrahim. "Muslim Family Law in South Africa: Paradoxes and Ironies." In *Muslim Family Law in Sub-Saharan Africa: Colonial Legacies and Post-colonial Challenges*, edited by Shamil Jeppie et al., 331–54. Amsterdam: Amsterdam University Press, 2010.

Naipaul, V. S. *A Writer's People*. London: Picador, 2008.

Nayar, Pramod K., ed. *The Penguin 1857 Reader*. New Delhi: Penguin, 2007.

Nehru, Jawaharlal. "Ends and Means: Address on the Occasion of the Conferment of the Degree of Doctor of Laws at Columbia University, New York," October 17, 1949. In *Jawaharlal Nehru's Speeches, 1949–1953*, 395–401. Delhi: The Publications Division. Ministry of Information and Broadcasting. Government of India, 1954.

———. "Changing Hindu society. III. The Hindu Marriage Bill. Speech during the debate on the Third Reading of the Hindu Marriage Bill in Lok Sabha." May 5, 1955. In *Jawaharlal Nehru's Speeches, March 1953–August 1957*, 446–54. Delhi: The Publications Division. Ministry of Information and Broadcasting. Government of India, 1958.

Nussbaum, Martha C. *The Clash Within: Democracy, Religious Violence and India's Future*. Cambridge, MA: Belknap, 2007.

O'Neill, Sean, and Daniel McGrory. *The Suicide Factory: Abu Hamza and the Finsbury Park Mosque*. London: Harper Perennial, 2006.

Paton, Alan. *Apartheid and the Archbishop*. New York: Scribner, 1973.

———. "Foreword." In *The Church Struggle in South Africa*, by John W. De Gruchy, vii–xii. Cape Town: David Philip, 1979.

Pattabhi Sitaramayya, Bhogaraju. "Speech on the Hindu Code Bill at the Constituent Assembly of India," April 9, 1948. In *Constituent Assembly of India (Legislative) Debates* 4:3633–39.

Pauw, Jacques. *Into the Heart of Darkness: Confessions of Apartheid's Assassins*. Johannesburg: Ball, 1997.

Pearce, Malcolm, and Geoffrey Stewart. *British Political History 1867–2001: Democracy and Decline*. 3rd ed. London: Routledge, 2002.

Peires, Jeffrey B. *The Dead Will Arise*. Johannesburg: Ball, 2003.

Phillips, Melanie. *Londonistan: How Britain is Creating a Terror State Within*. London: Gibson Square, 2006.

Pollock, John. *Billy Graham, Evangelist of the World: An Authorised Biography of the Decisive Years*. San Francisco: Harper & Row, 1979.

Rai, Milan. *7/7: The London Bombings, Islam and the Iraq War*. London: Pluto, 2006.

Rivers, Julian. *The Law of Organized Religions: Between Establishment and Secularism*. Oxford: Oxford University Press, 2010.

Robson, Mark, director. *Nine Hours to Rama*. Starring Horst Buchholz et al. Written by Nelson Gidding and Stanley Wolpert. United Kingdom: Red Lion and Twentieth Century Fox Productions, 1963. 1 DVD. Spain: n.p.

Rocher, Rosane. "The Creation of Anglo-Hindu Law." In *Hinduism and Law: An Introduction*, edited by Timothy Lubin et al., 78–87. New York: Cambridge University Press, 2010.

Rudolph, Lloyd I., and Susanne H. Rudolph. *In Pursuit of Lakshmi: The Political Economy of the Indian State*. Chicago: University of Chicago Press, 1987.

Rule, Sheila. "Khomeini Urges Muslims to Kill Author of Novel." *New York Times*, February 15, 1989, A-1, A-10. Online: http://www.nytimes.com/books/99/04/18/specials/rushdie-khomeini.html/.

Rushdie, Salman. "Mohandas Gandhi." *Time* April 13, 1998, 70–74. Online: http://content.time.com/time/magazine/article/0,9171,988159,00.html/.

———. "Outside the Whale." *Granta* 11 (1984) 123–38. Online: http://www.granta.com/Archive/11/Outside-the-Whale/Page-1/.

Russell, Alec. *After Mandela: The Battle for the Soul of South Africa*. London: Windmill, 2010.

Russell, William H. *My Indian Mutiny Diary*. Edited by Michael Edwardes. London: Cassell, 1957.

"SA blocks Rasta cannabis plea" *BBC News*, January 25, 2002. Online: http://news.bbc.co.uk/1/hi/world/africa/1782694.stm.

Sachs, Albie. *The Soft Vengeance of a Freedom Fighter*. London: Paladin, 1991.

———. *The Strange Alchemy of Life and Law*. Oxford: Oxford University Press, 2009.

Said, Edward W. *Culture and Imperialism*. London: Vintage, 1994.

Scott, G. Michael. "Statement in Court." 27 June 1946. Online: http://v1.sahistory.org.za/pages/library-resources/onlinebooks/passive-resistance/1946-NIC%20meeting.htm/.

Shachar, Ayelet. *Multicultural Jurisdictions: Cultural Differences and Women's Rights*. Contemporary Political Theory. Cambridge: Cambridge University Press, 2001.

Shah, Prakash. *Legal Pluralism in Conflict: Coping with Cultural Diversity in Law*. London: Cavendish, 2005.

Shri, K. Hanumanthaiya. "Speech to the Constituent Assembly." November 17, 1949. In *Constituent Assembly of India Debates*, 10:616–18. 12 vols. Delhi: The Manager of Publications.

Singh, Bhagat. *Select Speeches & Writings*. Edited by D. N. Gupta. New Delhi: National Book Trust, 2007.

Smith, David James. *Young Mandela*. London: Weidenfeld & Nicolson, 2010.

Som, Reba. "Jawaharlal Nehru and the Hindu Code: A Victory of Symbol over Substance?" *Modern Asian Studies* 28 (1994) 165–94.

South Africa Truth and Reconciliation Commission. "Institutional Hearing: The Faith Community." In *Truth and Reconciliation Commission Report*, 4:59–92. Cape Town: The Commission, 1998.

———. "The Pan Africanist Congress." In *Truth and Reconciliation Commission Report* 6: 375–441. 7 vols. Cape Town: The Commission, 1998.

———. "Political Violence in the Era of Negotiations and Transition (1990-1994)." In *Truth and Reconciliation Commission Report* 2:583–710. 7 vols. Cape Town: The Commission, 1998.

———. "The State inside South Africa between 1960 and 1990." In *Truth and Reconciliation Commission Report* 2:165–312. 7 vols. Cape Town: The Commission, 1998.

Srinivasan, Rajeev. "Interview with Stanley Wolpert." The Rediff Interview. 1996. Online: http://www.rediff.com/news/mar/01nehru.htm/.

Storey, Peter. "There Comes a Time." Address at a Service of Solidarity to Mark the Trial of Rev. Ecclesia de Lange, Rosebank Methodist Church, February 8, 2010. Online: http://www.goodhopemcc.org/news/ghmcc-news/593-there-comes-a-time-solidarity-to-mark-the-trial-of-rev-ecclesia-de-lange.html.

Swan, Maureen. *Gandhi: The South African Experience*. New History of Southern Africa Series. Johannesburg: Ravan, 1982.

Thapar, Romila. *Cultural Pasts: Essays in Early Indian History*. New Delhi: Oxford University Press, 2000.

Thatcher, Margaret. "Speech at lunch for Indian Prime Minister." March 22, 1982. Margaret Tatcher Foundation Website. Online: http://www.margaretthatcher.org/document/104899/.

Thompson, Leonard. *A History of South Africa*. 3rd ed. New Haven: Yale University Press, 2001.

Tutu, Desmond. "Foreword by Chairperson." In *Truth and Reconciliation Commission Report* 1:1–23. 7 vols. Cape Town: The Commission, 1998.

———. *The Rainbow People of God*. Edited by John Allen. London: Doubleday, 1994.

Van der Veer, Peter. *Religious Nationalism: Hindus and Muslims in India*. Berkeley: University of California Press, 1994.

Varadarajan, Siddharth. "Chronicle of a Tragedy Foretold." In *Gujarat, the Making of a Tragedy*, edited by Siddharth Varadarajan, 3–44. New Delhi: Penguin, 2002.

———. "I Salute You, Geetaben, from the Bottom of My Heart" In *Gujarat: the Making of a Tragedy*, edited by Siddharth Varadarajan, 446–49. New Delhi: Penguin, 2002.

Verwoerd, Hendrik F. "Address to the South African Club in London." March 17, 1961. *Hendrik Verwoerd Blog*. Online: http://hendrikverwoerd.blogspot.com/2010/12/march-17-1961-prime-minister-verwoerd.html/.

Victoria, Queen of Great Britain, 1819–1901. "Proclamation in Council, to the princes, chiefs, and people of India." British Library, India Office Records. European Manuscripts. MSS. Eur. D 620. Printed by Thomas Jones. Calcutta: Office of the Bengal Secretariat, 1858.

Villa-Vicencio, Charles. "God, the Devil, and Human Rights." Lecture given at the University of Chicago Divinity School. October 30, 2002. Online: http://pewforum.org/Politics-and-Elections/God-the-Devil-and-Human-Rights-A-South-African-Perspective.aspx/.

———. "South Africa's Theologized Nationalism" *The Ecumenical Review* 29 (1977) 373–82.

Villa-Vicencio, Charles, and Peter Grassow. *Christianity and the Colonisation of South Africa: A Documentary History*. Vol. 1, *1487–1883*. Hidden Histories Series. Pretoria: Unisa, 2009.

Viswanathan, Gauri. *Outside the Fold: Conversion, Modernity and Belief*. New Delhi: Oxford University Press, 2001.

Weller, Paul. *Religious Diversity in the UK*. London: Continuum, 2008.

Williams, Rina V. *Postcolonial Politics and Personal Laws: Colonial Legal Legacies and the Indian State*. New Delhi: Oxford University Press, 2006.

Williams, Rowan. "Civil and Religious Law in England: A Religious Perspective." *Ecclesiastical Law Journal* 10 (2008) 262–82.

Wilson, Harold. "Speech at Labour Party Conference." October 1, 1963. *Labour Party Annual Conference Report* (1963) 139–40.

Wolpert, Stanley. *Nine Hours to Rama*. New York: Random House, 1962.

———. *Shameful Flight: The Last Years of the British Empire in India*. Oxford: Oxford University Press, 2006.

Zinneman, Fred, director. *A Man for All Seasons*. Starring Paul Scofield. Based on the play by Robert Bolt. Produced by Fred Zinneman and William N. Graf. London: Highland Films, 1966. 1 DVD. United States: Sony Pictures Home Entertainment, 1999.

Case Law

Akhil Bharat Goseva Sangh v. State of A.P.& Ors. Supreme Court of India. Decided on March 29, 2006. (2006) 4 SCC 162.

Arrowsmith v. UK. European Commission of Human Rights. Decided on May 16, 1977. App. no. 7050/75.

Arrowsmith v. UK. European Commission of Human Rights. Report of October 12, 1978. App. no. 7050/75.

Bai Tahira v. Ali Hussain Fidaalli Chothia. Supreme Court of India. Decided on October 6, 1978. (1979) 2 SCC 316.

Bhe and Others v Magistrate, Khayelitsha, and Others (Commission for Gender Equality as Amicus Curiae); Shibi v Sithole and Others; South African Human Rights Commission and Another v. President of the Republic of South Africa and Another. Constitutional Court of South Africa. Decided on October 15, 2004. 2005 (1) SA 580 (CC); 2005 (1) BCLR 1 (CC).

Choudhury v. UK. European Commission of Human Rights. Decided on March 5, 1991. App. no. 17439/90.

Christian Education South Africa v. Minister of Education. Constitutional Court of South Africa. Decided on August 18, 2000. (CCT4/00) [2000] ZACC 11; 2000 (4) SA 757; 2000 (10) BCLR 1051.

Danial Latifi and Anr. v. Union of India. Supreme Court of India. Decided on September 28, 2001. (2001) SCC 7 740.

Durgah Committee, Ajmer and Another v. Syed Hussain Ali and Ors. Supreme Court of India. Decided on March 17, 1961. (1962) SCR (1) 383.

Employment Division, Department of Human Resources of Oregon v. Smith. Supreme Court of the United States. Decided on April 17, 1990. 494 U.S. (1990) 872.

Esop v. Union Government (Minister of the Interior). Cape Supreme Court. Decided on March 13-14, 1913. 1913 CPD 133.

Everson v. Board of Education. Supreme Court of the United States. Decided on February 10, 1947. 330 U.S. (1947) 1.

Fuzlunbi v. K. Khader Vali & Anr. Supreme Court of India. Decided on May 8, 1980. (1980) 4 SCC 125.

Handyside v. UK. European Court of Human Rights. Decided on November 7, 1976. App no. 5493/72.

Harris v. NKL Automotive Ltd & Anor. United Kingdom Employment Appeal Tribunal. Decided on October 3, 2007. [2007] UKEAT/0134/07/DM; 2007 WL 2817981.

Hassam v. Jacobs NO and Others. Constitutional Court of South Africa. Decided on July 15, 2009. (CCT83/08) [2009] ZACC 19; 2009 (11) BCLR 1148 (CC); 2009 (5) SA 572 (CC).

John Vallamattom and Anr. v. Union of India. Supreme Court of India. Decided on July 21, 2003. (2003) 6 SCC 611.

Jorden Diengdeh v. S.S. Chopra. Supreme Court of India. Decided on May 10, 1985. (1985) 3 SCC 62.

KC & NNC v. City of Westminster Social & Community Services Department & Anor. Court of Appeal. Civil Division. Decided on March 19, 2008. [2008] EWCA Civ 198.

Krishna Singh v. Mathura Ahir and Ors. Supreme Court of India. Decided on December 21, 1979. AIR (1980) SC 707.

Lily Thomas and Ors v. Union of India and Ors. Supreme Court of India. Decided on May 5, 2000. (2000) 6 SCC 224.

MEC for Education: Kwazulu-Natal and Others v. Pillay, Constitutional Court of South Africa. Decided on October 5, 2007. [2007] ZACC 21; 2008 (1) SA 474 (CC); 2008 (2) BCLR 99 (CC).

Minister of Home Affairs and Another v. Fourie and Another. Constitutional Court of South Africa. Decided on December 1, 2005. [2005] ZACC 19; 2006 (3) BCLR 355 (CC); 2006 (1) SA 524 (CC).

Mohd. Ahmed Khan v. Shah Bano Begum and Ors. Supreme Court of India. Decided on April 23, 1985. (1985) 2 SCC 556.

Mrs. Yulitha Hyde and Ors. v. State of Orissa and Ors. Orissa High Court. Decided on October 24, 1972. AIR Orissa (1973) 116.

Musstt. Ayesha Bibi v. Subodh Ch. Chakravarty. Court of Calcutta. Decided on March 2, 1945. (1945) 49 C. W. N. 439.

National Textile Workers' Union and Ors. v. P.R. Ramkrishnan and Ors. Supreme Court of India. Decided on December 10, 1982. (1983) SCC 1 228.

Pannalal Bansilal Pitti & Ors v. State of Andhra Pradesh & Anr. Supreme Court of India. Decided on January 17, 1996. (1996) SCC 2 498.

Paras Ram and Ors. v. State of Punjab. Supreme Court of India. Decided on October 9, 1973. (1981) 2 SCC 508.

Parochial Church Council of the Parish of Aston Cantlow and Wilmcote with Billesley, Warwickshire. Court of Appeal (Civil Division). Decided on May 17, 2001. [2001] EWCA Civ 713.

Parochial Church Council of the Parish of Aston Cantlow and Wilmcote with Billesley, Warwickshire v. Wallbank & Anor. UK House of Lords. Decided on June 26, 2003. [2003] UKHL.

Pillay v. MEC for Education, KwaZulu-Natal, and Others. High Court of South Africa. Natal Provincial Division. Decided on July 5, 2006. 2006 (6) SA 363 (EqC) 2006 (10) BCLR 1237 (N).

Prince v. President of the Law Society of the Cape of Good Hope and Others. Constitutional Court of South Africa. Decided on January 25, 2002. [2002] ZACC 1; 2002 (2) SA 794; 2002 (3) BCLR 231.

Prince v. South Africa. African Commission on Human and Peoples' Rights. Decided in December 2004. (2004) AHRLR 105 (ACHPR 2004).

Prince v. South Africa, UN Human Rights Committee. Decided on October 31, 2007. (2007) AHRLR 40 (HRC 2007).

R. (Begum) v. Governors of Denbigh High School, Court of Appeal. Civil Division. Decided on March 2, 2005. [2005] EWCA Civ 199.

R. (Begum) v. Governors of Denbigh High School, High Court of Justice. Administrative Court. Decided on 15 June 2004. [2004] EWHC 1389 (Admin).

R. (Begum) v Governors of Denbigh High School. UK House of Lords. Decided on March 22, 2006. [2006] UKHL 15.

R. (Williamson and ors) v. Secretary of State for Education and Employment and others. Court of Appeal (Civil Division). Decided December 12, 2002. [2002] EWCA Civ 1926.

R. (Williamson and ors) v. Secretary of State for Education and Employment and others. UK House of Lords. Decided on February 24, 2005. [2005] UKHL 15.

R v. Chief Metropolitan Stipendiary Magistrates ex parte Choudhury. Queen's Bench Division. April 9, 1990. [1991] 1 QB 429.

Ram Kumari. High Court of Calcutta. Decided on February 18, 1891. ILR (1891) 18 Cal 264.

Ratilal Panachand Gandhi v. The State of Bombay and Ors. Supreme Court of India. Decided on March 18, 1954. AIR (1954) SC 388.

Rev. Stainislaus v. State of Madhya Pradesh and Ors. Madhya High Court. Decided on April 23, 1974. AIR Madhya Pradesh (1975) MP 163.

Rev. Stainislaus v. State of Madhya Pradesh and Ors. Supreme Court of India. Decided on January 17, 1977. (1977) SCC (1) 677.

Robasa Khanum v. Khodadad Bomanji Irani. Court of Bombay. Decided on December 14, 1945. Text reported in the decision on the appeal. See *Robasa Khanum v. Khodadad Bomanji Irani.* High Court of Bombay. Decided on August 22, 1946.

Robasa Khanum v. Khodadad Bomanji Irani. High Court of Bombay. Decided on August 22, 1946. (1946) 48 Bom. L. R. 864.

S v. Lawrence, S v Negal, S v Solberg. Constitutional Court of South Africa. Decided on October 6, 1997. (CCT38/96, CCT39/96, CCT40/96) [1997] ZACC 11; 1997 (10) BCLR 1348; 1997 (4) SA 1176.

S v. Makwanyane and Another. Constitutional Court of South Africa. Decided on June 6, 1995. (CCT3/94) [1995] ZACC 3; 1995 (6) BCLR 665; 1995 (3) SA 391; [1996] 2 CHRLD 164; 1995 (2) SACR 1 (6 June 1995) [384].

S v. Nkosi and Others. High Court of South Africa. Transvaal Provincial Division. Decided on March 17, 1972. 1972 (2) SA 753 (T).

Sarla Mudgal, President, Kalyani and Ors v. Union of India and Ors. Supreme Court of India. Decided on May 10, 1995. (1995) 3 SCC 635.

Sayeda Khatoon alias A.M. Obadiah v. M. Obadiah, Calcutta Civil Court. Decided on August 10, 1945. (1945) 49 C. W. N. 745.

Seema v. Ashwani Kumar. Supreme Court of India. Decided on February 14, 2006. (2006) 2 SCC 578.

Sherbert v. Verner. Supreme Court of the United States. Decided on June 17, 1963. 374 U.S. (1963) 398.

Skinner v. Orde. Her Majesty's Privy Council. December 1871. (1871–72) 14 Moore's I. A., 309.

State of Gujarat v. Mirzapur Moti Kureshi Kassab Jamat & Ors. Supreme Court of India. Decided on October 26, 2005. (2005) 8 SCC 534.

UK v. Council. Court of Justice of the European Communities. Decided on November 12, 1996. Case C-84/94.

Vilayat Raj Alias Vilayat Khan v. Smt. Sunila. Delhi High Court. Decided on February 17, 1983. AIR (1983) Delhi 351.

Whitehouse v. Gay News Ltd. UK House of Lords. Decided on February 21, 1979. [1979] AC 617, HL.

Wingrove v. UK. European Court of Human Rights. Decided on November 25, 1996. App no. 17419/90.

Wisconsin v. Yoder. Supreme Court of the United States. Decided on May 15, 1972. 406 U.S. (1972) 205.

Yvonne van Duyn v. Home Office. Court of Justice of the European Communities. Decided on December 4, 1974. Case 41–74.

INDEX

Explanatory note. Judges for whom it has been impossible to provide the first name are listed by the family name, followed by "Justice" (e.g., Roch, Justice). Honorary titles have been omitted, except in the case of deities (e.g., Lord Rama), Kings or Queens (e.g., Queen Victoria) and judges at the House of Lords (e.g., Dilhorne, Viscount). In some cases the distinction between family name and first name would have been improper (e.g., Chinnappa Reddy). Initials have been used instead of the full first name when this corresponded to the common use (e.g. Naipaul, V. S.).

Abortion, 205, 209, 228
Abu Hamza. *See* Mustafa, Mustafa Kamal
Ackermann, Dawie, 154–55
Ackermann, Laurie, 274, 278
Action Committee on Islamic Affairs, United Kingdom, 43
Adventists, 63
Afghanistan, 5, 6, 72–73, 105, 182, 261
African Charter on Human and Peoples' Rights, 296–97
  see also African Commission on Human and Peoples' Rights
African Commission on Human and Peoples' Rights, 17, 280
  Prince, 295–97
African Methodist Episcopal Church, 32
African National Congress, 5, 28–30, 35, 38–39, 40, 107, 123, 126, 154, 161, 172, 181, 185–86, 205, 207, 213, 222–24, 231, 295, 297, 327
African nationalists, 207
African traditional religion / culture, 34, 124, 126–27, 173, 232, 242, 269–71, 279, 327–28, 334, 342–44
African Union, 297
Agra riots, 9
Afrikaans Protestant Church, 68
Afrikaner Weerstand Beweging, 68

Afrikaners, 2, 7, 30–34, 68, 77, 79, 82, 96, 106–7, 126–27, 184–86, 220–21, 223, 240–46, 261
  Christians, 30–34, 40–42, 68, 77, 83, 89, 98, 126, 144, 184–86, 201–2, 232, 243–46
  Nationalists, 31, 68, 77, 126–27, 130, 144, 161–62, 166, 184–86, 196, 243–45
  see also Afrikaans Protestant Church; Great Trek; Nederduitse Gereformeerde Kerk; Retief, Piet
Ahmad. *See* Court of Appeal, United Kingdom, Ahmad
Ahmad, Saghir, 173–76
Ahmed Khan, Syed, 91, 93
Ahmedabad, 123, 232, 281
AIDS, 295
Akhil. *See* Supreme Court of India, Akhil
Al-Muhajiroun, 282
Al-Qaeda, 73
Al-Quds Al Arabi, 162
Alcohol, 163–66, 255, 271
Alderson, Justice, 83
Alipore, 99
All India Anti-Hindu Code Bill Committee, 191
All India Muslim Personal Law Board. *See* Muslim Personal Law Board
Allahabad, 92, 197

Ambedkar, Bhimrao Ramji, 9, 111, 127–29, 161, 187, 189–91, 192–94, 197, 200–201, 324

Amis, Martin, 264, 317–19, 323, 327

Amish, 64, 273

Amoah, Jewel, 328, 332, 343–44

Amritsar
Massacre (1919), 111
Massacre (1984), 247

Andrews, Reuben Phillip. *See* Court of Appeal, United Kingdom, Andrews

Anglican Communion, 170–71, 179, 202, 234, 290, 335

Anglicans
Anglican Catholics, 77, 97
Evangelicals, 77, 78–80, 82–88, 97–98, 104
Missionaries, 2, 11, 77, 78–80
see also Anglican Communion; Church of England; Clayton, Geoffrey; Lambeth Conference of 1998; Puritan divines; Scott, Michael; South Africa, Anglicans; Tutu, Desmond; Williams, Rowan

Anglo-Boer War, 105, 106–7, 184, 216–22

Anglo-Hindu Law, 11

Anglo-Zulu wars, 105, 216

Angola, 7, 29, 39

Ansari, Zia-ur-Rahman, 25

Anti-conversion laws, India, 205, 226–27, 248–51, 253
see also Conversions

Anti-semitism, 134

Apartheid, 29, 39, 70, 106–7, 112, 123–24, 126–27, 151–55, 171, 179, 184–86, 196, 201–4, 213–16, 218–24, 230, 240–46, 271–74, 342–
Christians, 30–34, 40–42, 123–24, 201–4, 230, 240–47
Judiciary, 37–38
Law, 20
Violence, 20, 32–34, 68–69, 123, 144, 146–47, 151–55, 196, 207, 220, 231, 344
see also Theology, Apartheid

Apostasy, 53
Christians, 83, 84, 91, 103
Hindus, 133
Muslims, 53, 125

Apple, 169–70

Appropriation Bill, South Africa, 245

Arab-Israeli conflict / wars, 5, 234, 261

Arab nationalists, 200

Arani, Muddassar, 320

Arnold, Edwin, 103

Arrowsmith, Pat. *See* European Commission of Human Rights, Arrowsmith

Arunachal Pradesh, 253

Arunachal Pradesh Freedom of Religion Act, 253

Arya Samaj, 59

Asiatic Land Tenure and Indian Representation Bill, South Africa, 123, 126

Asmal, Kader, 37

Assam, 25

Aston Cantlow. *See* Court of appeal, United Kingdom, Parochial Church Council; High Court, United Kingdom, Parochial Church Council; House of Lords, Parochial Church Council

Atheists, 4, 5, 97–99, 102–103, 105, 130, 180, 206, 225, 242, 273, 319
see also Bradlaugh, Charles; London Secular Society; National Secular Society, United Kingdom; United Kingdom, Atheists

Atlantic alliance, 5, 7

Attenborough, Richard, 18

Attlee, Clement, 127, 184

Australia, 178, 289

Ayesha Bibi. *See* Court of Calcutta, Musstt. Ayesha Bibi

Ayodhya. *See* Babri Mosque

Azam, Sher, 43

Azanian People's Liberation Army, 68, 154–55

Azhar, Ali Muhammed, 45–50, 55–56, 74

B. Pocker Sahib Bahadur, 188–89

Babri Mosque, 26–27, 62, 64–67, 70, 74, 89, 162, 261, 267, 280, 345

Babu, Rajendra, 265–66

Bachan Singh. *See* Supreme Court of India, Bachan Singh

BAE Systems, 321

Bai Tahira. *See* Supreme Court of India, Bai Tahira

Baker, Diane, 217

Baker, Stanley, 219, 221

Bakri, Omar, 282–83

Bal Mariam, 108

Balkans, 72–73

Ball, Charles, 90–91

Bambata, 223

Banerjee, Justice, 100–102

Bangalore, 105, 136

Bangladesh, 17, 67, 174, 247, 340–41

Bantu Administration Act, 15

Bantu courts. *See* South Africa, Bantu courts

Bantu law. *See* South Africa, Bantu law

Baptist Union of Southern Africa, 33

Baptists, 33, 273

Bath. *See* Court of Appeal, United Kingdom, Bath

Battle of Britain, 113

Battle of Mandalay, 114

Battle of Plassey / Plassy, 58, 81, 201

Baxi, Upendra, 13

BBC, 279, 338

Beatles, The, 204, 227–31

   Eleanor Rigby, 227–31

   see also Harrison, George; Lennon, John; Maharishi Mahesh Yogi; McCartney, Paul

Bedfordshire. *See* Denbigh High School

Begum, Shabina, 3, 4, 16–17, 67, 74–75, 76, 99–100, 134, 160, 162, 179–83, 204, 206, 212, 231, 234, 262, 264, 281–84, 290, 292–96, 301–3, 310–17, 319, 322–23, 328, 333, 347

   see also Court of Appeal, United Kingdom, R. (Begum); High Court, United Kingdom, R. (Begum); House of Lords, R. (Begum)

Begum of Oude, 90

Bhatti, Gurprett Kaur, *Behzti*, 298

Behzti. See Bhatti, Gurprett Kaur, *Behzti*

Benares, 99

Bengal, 17, 81, 86, 303

   see also Bangladesh; West Bengal

Bennett, Justice, 294–96

Bennett, Thomas, 14–15, 324–25, 328, 332, 342–44

Bentinck, William, 84, 104

Berlin blockade, 185

Berlin wall, 38–40, 45, 64, 178, 180, 181–82, 205

Berman, Paul, 319

Besant, Annie, 98, 103

Bethel Synagogue, Kolkata, 116

Bevan, Yasmin, 17, 180, 281–82, 292–95, 310, 312–13, 348

Beveridge, Justice, 99–100

Bhagavad Gita, 2, 103

Bhakti, 194

Bharatiya Janata Party, 10, 65–67, 136, 157, 161–62, 170, 264–7, 345

Bhindranwale, Jarnail Singh, 19

Bhopal disaster, 21–22

Bhutto, Zulfikar Ali, 43

Bible, 2, 31, 40, 80, 82, 87, 89, 113, 140, 144, 154, 170, 176, 185, 202, 226, 241, 298–301

Big M. Drug Mart. *See* Supreme Court of Canada, Big M. Drug Mart

Bigamy. *See* Polygamy

Bihar, 9, 25, 232

Bijnor district, 91

Biko, Steve, 147, 241–42, 245

Bilal, Mohammad, 179

Bin Laden, Osama, 73, 162, 182, 200, 289

Bingham of Cornhill, Baron, 311–14, 322

Birmingham, 44, 298

   Birmingham Repertory Theatre, 298

Bizos, George, 39, 153

BJP. *See* Bharatiya Janata Party

Black, Hugo, 273

Black consciousness/power, 21, 29, 32, 34, 41, 74, 79–80, 88, 186, 207, 213, 226, 241–42, 245–46, 270

Black courts. *See* South Africa, Black courts

Black Economic Empowerment Program, South Africa, 295

Black, Galen. *See* Supreme Court of the United States, Employment division

Black theology. *See* Theology, Black theology

Blackmun, Harry, 63, 272

Blagden, Justice, 118–22, 124, 135–36

Blair, Tony, 8, 70, 71–72, 160–61, 200, 282–84, 288–90, 304, 314, 319–24, 327, 334–35

Blasphemy, 8, 21, 42–56, 71, 74, 91–92, 97–99, 158–59, 167, 257–61, 263–64, 338

Blavatsky, Helena, 2, 102, 127

Bloody Sunday

   1887, 103

   1972, 237

Bloomington, 267

Bocock, Robert, 18

Boer War. *See* Anglo-Boer War

Boesak, Alan, 244–45

Bogside, Battle of the, 231

Boipatong massacre, 151

Bolt, Robert, *A Man for All Seasons*, 208–13, 219, 229–30, 244

Bolton, 42

Bombay. *See* Mumbai

Bombay bombings, 62

Bonthuys, Cecelia Johanna

   See Constitutional Court of South Africa, Minister of Home Affairs; High Court of Pretoria, Minister of Home Affairs; Supreme Court of Appeal, South Africa, Minister of Home Affairs

Booth (Blair), Cherie, 301, 313–14, 316

Bophuthatswana, 16

Boraine, Alex, 30, 68–69, 151–55, 201, 213–15, 219–23, 230, 240–46, 297

Bosnia, 72–73

Botha, Pieter Willem, 7, 20, 39, 171–72, 261

Bradford

   Bradford Christian School, Idle, 298

   Council of Mosques, 42–43

Bradford Christian School, Idle, Bradford, 298

   See also Court of Appeal, United Kingdom, R. (Williamson); House of Lords, R. (Williamson)

Bradlaugh, Charles, 98–99, 102–3, 105

Bradney, Anthony, 339

Brahmins, 93, 114

Brennan, Harold Andrew, 63, 273
Brighton hotel bombing, 19
Briley, John, 18
Britain. *See* United Kingdom
British Airways, 339
British Board of Film Classification, 46–48, 50–54
　　See also Rushdie, Salman, *International Guerillas*; Wingrove, Nigel
British Cape Colony, South Africa, 78, 79, 84, 106, 242
British Empire, 8, 10–12, 14–15, 55, 74–75, 76–78, 81–99, 105, 113, 122, 129–30, 184–85, 199, 202, 208–13
　　See also East India Company
British National Party, 134, 161–62
　　See also Griffin, Nick
British Nationality Act, 129, 184
British Race Relations Act, 205
British Raj, 11, 12, 15, 55, 75, 76, 81–99, 100–101, 104, 105, 118–19, 122, 124–25, 137, 290
Brixton riots, 8, 43
Brooke, Justice, 302–3
Brown, Gordon, 8, 160, 321, 334
Buchholz, Horst, 217
Budapest, 200
Buddha, 47
　　See also Buddhists
Buddhists. *See* Buddha; India, Buddhists
Bulganin, Nikolai, 196
Burger, Warren E., 64, 273
Burma, 114
Bush, George W., 288–90
Buthelezi, Mangosuthu, 217
Buxton, Justice, 299

Caine, Michael, 218–21
Calata, Fort, 151
Calata, James, 185–86
Calata, Nomonde, 151
Calcutta. *See* Kolkata
Calvinists, 2, 98
Cambridge, 99
Cameron, Justice, 306
Campbell, Alastair, 289
Campbell and Cosans. *See* European Court of Human Rights, Campbell and Cosans
Camus, Albert, 291
Canada, 214, 217
Cannabis, 4, 16, 160, 178, 242–43, 268–80, 284, 296, 334
Cape Town, 3, 20, 34, 67, 68, 74, 78, 80, 82, 84, 154, 181, 202, 207, 208, 271, 280, 327

Cape Town Fourteen. *See* Forbes, Ashley and the Cape Town Fourteen
Carter, Jimmy, 255–57
Castes, India, 9–12, 58–59, 65, 81, 86, 92, 100, 127, 200, 232, 345
Cattle killing, South Africa, 75, 80, 88–89, 111, 129, 201
Cawnpore, 87
Central Criminal Court, United Kingdom (England and Wales)
　　Mustafa, 320
　　Whitehouse, 263
　　See also Hughes, Anthony
Central Mosque, Birmingham, 44
Cetshwayo. *See* King Cetshwayo
Chagla, Justice, 117–18, 124–25, 135, 139, 194
Chakrabarty, Bidyut, 65, 67
Chandrachaud, Y, V., 22–25
Chanock, Martin, 271, 330
Charar-e-Sharif, 142
Charter Act. *See* Missionaries, Charter Act
Chaskalson, Arthur, 36–39, 69, 145–48, 149, 163–66, 168, 176–78, 204, 224, 268–69, 272, 274–78
Chatterjee, Nirmal Chandra, 197
Chatterjee, Tarun, 345
Chattri, 100
Chaudhuri, J. N., 196
Chicago, 279
Chicane, Frank, 31
Chidester, David, 144, 271
Child marriage, 325
Children rights, 234–36, 325
　　See also Constitutional Court of South Africa, Christian Education; Court of Appeal, United Kingdom, R. (Williamson); European Court of Human Rights, Campbell and Cosans; House of Lords, R. (Williamson)
China, 65, 69, 196, 217, 223
Chinnappa Reddy, 24
Choudhury, Abdul Hussain, 44–56, 74, 97
　　See also European Court of Human Rights, Choudhury; Queen's Bench, R. v. Chief Metropolitan
Christian Education. *See* Constitutional Court of South Africa, Christian Education
Christian Fellowship School, Edge Hill, Liverpool, 298
　　See also Court of Appeal, United Kingdom, R. (Williamson); House of Lords, R. (Williamson)
Christian law. *See* India, Christian law
Christian social justice, 31, 206, 209, 212, 230, 232, 250, 289

Christian socialists, 8, 71–72

Christians, 28, 30–31, 52, 71–72, 74, 79–80, 85, 88–90, 95, 106, 112–13, 130, 159, 171, 180, 206, 221–22, 225, 227–28, 241, 243, 249–50, 289, 320, 327

See also Adventists; Afrikaans Protestant Church; Afrikaners, Christians; Amish; Anglicans; Apartheid, Christians; Baptist Union of Southern Africa; Baptists; Christian socialists; Church of England; Dutch Reformed Church in the Netherlands; India, Christians; Kairos document; Methodists; Missionaries, Christians; Nederduitse Gereformeerde Kerk; NG Sending Church; Orthodox Christians; Presbyterians; Protestants; Puritan divines; Reformed Christians; Roman Catholics; Rustenburg conference; South Africa, Christians; South African Council of Churches; United Kingdom, Christians

Church (building), 75, 82, 84, 90, 140, 154

Church and State, 40–56, 62–64, 163–68, 194, 201–4, 208–13, 229–30, 257–61, 268–80, 284–88, 298–301, 304–10

Church of England, 11, 18, 42–56, 72, 77, 78, 82–83, 99, 121, 134, 179, 208–13, 229–30, 234, 247, 258, 284–88, 290, 304–5, 310, 325, 334–38

  Ecclesiastical law, 230, 285–88

  Synodical Government Measure (1969), 230

  See also Keble, John; Sheppard, David; Williams, Rowan

Church of Scientology, 16, 50, 234, 236–7

  See also United Kingdom, Scientologists

Churchill, Randolph, 98–99, 105

Churchill, Winston, 75, 105, 113, 122, 129–30, 160, 195, 206, 226

Civil disobedience, 103, 106–7, 169, 194, 203

Civil Partnership Act, United Kingdom, 284, 292, 304–10

Civil Rights Act, United States, 222

Clayton, Geoffrey, 202–3, 223, 243

Clive, Robert, 81

Coca Cola, 256

Code Napoleon, 198

Code of Civil Procedure, India, 11, 92

Code of Criminal Procedure, India, 11, 13, 22–24, 92, 247–48, 254–55

Cold War, 4, 5, 6, 28–30, 35, 39, 180–83, 185, 191–93, 200, 204, 206, 240, 255, 261–62

Coleridge, Lord, 258–59

Colonial rule. See Colonialism

Colonialism, 5, 11, 13, 14, 15, 28–30, 58, 75, 76–78, 78–80, 85, 122, 130, 180, 199, 232, 271–74, 342

Colorado, 318

Columbia Law School, 35

Columbia University, 35, 38–39, 127, 191–93

Commonwealth, 74, 129–30, 184, 195, 205, 207, 214–16, 228

Commonwealth Immigrants Act, 205, 216

  See also India, Communists; South Africa, Communists; South African Communist Party; Soviet Union, Communist Party

Communist Party. See Communist Party of India; South African Communist Party; Soviet Union, Communist Party

Communist Party of India, 196, 256

Communists, 4, 27, 28–30, 39–40, 64, 130, 180–81, 222–24, 230, 256, 318

Compulsory Registration of Marriages Bill, India, 323–24, 326

Concordats. See Roman Catholics, Concordats

Constituent Assembly, India, 9, 126–27, 183, 186–91, 193–94, 204, 230

Constitution of India, 126–29, 145, 156–57, 193–94, 204, 252

  Article 14, 191

  Article 25, 194, 249–51, 253

  Article 44. See Uniform Civil Code

  Forty-second amendment, 252

Constitution of South Africa, 145–46, 148–50, 165–66, 177, 308–9

Constitutional Court of South Africa, 3, 173, 330–31

  Christian Education, 176–78, 268–69, 273–75, 277, 299–301, 307, 313, 332

  Fraser, 167

  Hassam, 341–44

  MEC for Education, 328–33, 335, 339, 343

  Minister of Home Affairs, 284, 292, 306–10, 332–33

  Prince, 17, 110, 131, 169, 268–80, 295–7, 347

  S. v. Lawrence, 163–68, 176, 201, 269

  S. v. Makwanyane, 76, 84, 143–50, 165

  See also Ackermann, Laurie; Chaskalson, Arthur; Didcott, John; Goldstone, Richard; Kriegler, Johann; Langa, Pius; Madala, Tholie; Madlanga, Mbuyiseli; Mahomed, Ismail; Mokgoro, Yvonne; Moseneke, Dikgang; Nkabinde, Bess; Ngcobo, Sandile; O'Regan, Kate; Sachs, Albie; Yacoob, Zak

Constitutionalism, 36–39

Convention for the Protection of Human Rights and Fundamental Freedoms. See European Convention for the Protection of Human Rights and Fundamental Freedoms

Conversions, 11, 16, 56–62, 78, 84, 88–89, 92–97, 99–102, 111, 113–22, 132–43, 173–76,

194–95, 200, 205, 226–27, 247, 248–51, 253, 267, 334, 346–47
See also Anti-conversion laws
Cornerstone School, Epsom, Surrey, 298
See also Court of Appeal, United Kingdom, R. (Williamson); House of Lords, R. (Williamson)
Corporal punishment, 16, 176–78, 298–301
See also Death penalty; Torture
Council of Europe, 195
See also European Convention for the Protection of Human Rights and Fundamental Freedoms
Council of India, 100
Council of Mosques. *See* Bradford, Council of Mosques
Court of Alipore
Ram Kumari, 99–100
Also see Beveridge, Justice
Court of Appeal, United Kingdom (England and Wales)
Ahmad, 16
Andrews, 296
Bath, 324
K.C., 340
Khan, 16
Parochial Church Council, 134, 284–88
R (Begum), 284, 301–4, 310, 312, 316, 347
R. (Williamson), 299–300
Taylor, 271
See also Brooke, Justice; Buxton, Justice; Mummery, Justice; Rix, Justice; Scott Baker, Justice; Wall, Justice
Court of Bombay
Robasa Khanum, 117–22, 135
See also Blagden, Justice
Court of Calcutta
Musstt. Ayesha Bibi, 113–16, 119, 121–22
Sayeda Khatoon, 116–18, 119–22
See also Lodge, Justice; Ormond, Justice
Court of Justice of the European Communities
UK. v. Council, 158–59
Van Duyn, 234–37, 240
Courts. *See*
African Commission on Human and Peoples' Rights; Bantu courts; Black courts; Central Criminal Court, United Kingdom; Constitutional Court of South Africa; Court of Alipore; Court of Appeal, United Kingdom; Court of Bombay; Court of Calcutta; Court of Justice of the European Communities; Employment Appeal Tribunal, United Kingdom; European Commission of Human Rights; European Court of Human Rights; High Court of Judicature for

the North-Western Provinces; High Court of Bombay; High Court of Calcutta; High Court of Delhi; High Court of Judicature for the North-Western Provinces; High Court of Madhya Pradesh; High Court of Orissa; High Court of Pietermaritzburg; High Court of Pretoria; High Court of South Africa; High Court, United Kingdom; House of Lords, United Kingdom; Human Rights Committee, United Nations; Queen's Bench Division, United Kingdom; Supreme Court of Appeal, South Africa; Supreme Court of Canada; Supreme Court of India; Supreme Court of South Carolina; Supreme Court of the Cape; Supreme Court of the United States
Coventry Four, 19
Cowdry, Roy, 203
Cradock Four, 152
Criminal Law Report on Offences against Religion and Public Worship, United Kingdom, 50
Cromwell, Oliver, 33
Cromwell, Thomas, 209–10, 212
Crowther, Bosley, 222
Cuba, 39
Cultural rights, 328–33, 335, 343–44
Curtis, Mark, 6, 72–73, 282–83, 304, 321
Customary law, 2, 12, 14–16, 58, 84–85, 324–26, 331, 336, 342–44
India, 12, 58, 85, 92, 140, 198–99, 248, 255
South Africa, 14–16, 271, 342–43
See also Cultural rights; Personal laws

Dagga. *See* Cannabis
Daily Mirror, The, 234
Daily Telegraph, The, 105, 234
Dakar, 30, 295, 297
Dalai Lama, 196
Dalasile, 223
Dalhousie, The Earl of, 84, 104
Dalits, 9, 10, 28, 59, 127–29, 187, 191, 193, 280
See also Ambedkar, Bhimrao Ramji; Poona Pact; Reserved seats, India
Dancing, 167, 201, 318
Danial Latifi. *See* Supreme Court of India, Danial Latifi
Darwin, Charles, 91, 99, 104–5
On the Origin of Species, 91
Davie, Grace, 7, 70–72
Davies, Gareth, 312
De Gruchy, John, 31–34
De Gruchy, Steve, 31–32
De Klerk, Frederick Willem, 39–40, 70, 154, 172

De Klerk, Willem, 40
De Kock, Eugene, 172
De Meyer, Jan, 158–59
Deane, Justice, 300
Death penalty, 83–84, 143–50, 165, 222–24
Decline and Fall of the Roman Empire. See Gibbon, Edward
Deekshabhoomi, 200
Delhi, 66, 74–75, 87, 91, 183, 254–57, 303
Denbigh High School, 17, 67, 134, 160, 195, 281–82, 292–95, 303, 312–13, 315, 329, 347–48
Denmark, 234, 316
Department of Native Affairs, South Africa, 15
Derrett, Duncan, 58–59, 198
Derry, 231, 237
Desai, Morarji, 256
Devi, 251
Diamond, Paul, 299–300
Dickson, Brian, 163–4
Didcott, John, 147
Dilhorne, Viscount, 261
Dingane, 223
Diplock, Baron, 257–59
Disraeli, Benjamin, 85–86, 88
Discrimination, 163–66, 176–78, 290–91, 306–10, 338
Dissolution/invalidity of marriage, 58–59, 99–102, 113, 116–20, 122, 125, 132, 167, 173, 208–13, 247–48, 254–55, 264–67, 340
    See also Court of Alipore, Ram Kumari; Court of Bombay, Robasa Khanum; Court of Calcutta, Musstt. Ayesha Bibi; Court of Calcutta, Sayeda Khatoon; High Court of Bombay, Robasa Khanum; High Court of Calcutta, Ram Kumari; Supreme Court of India, Bai Tahira; Supreme Court of India, Lily Thomas; Supreme Court of India, Sarla Mudgal; United Kingdom, Privy Council, Skinner
Dissolution of Muslim Marriage Act, India, 125
Divorce. *See* Dissolution/invalidity of marriage; India, Divorce; United Kingdom, Divorce
Doe, Norman, 334–35
Dowry, 22, 255, 325
Dulles, John Foster, 200
Durban, 106, 123, 202, 213, 230, 243
Durban Girls High School, 313–14, 328
    See also High Court of Pietermaritzburg, MEC for Education; Constitutional Court of South Africa, MEC for Education
Durgah Committee. *See* Supreme Court of India, Durgah Committee
Dutch East India Company, 82

Dutch Reformed Church in South Africa. *See* Nederduitse Gereformeerde Kerk
Dutch Reformed Church in the Netherlands, 31, 33
Dutch rule, South Africa 37, 82–84
Dyzenhaus, David, 38

Ecclesiastical law. *See* Church of England, Ecclesiastical law
Economist, The, 179
Eden, Anthony, 200
Edmund-Davies, Baron, 258–59
Education Welfare Service, United Kingdom, 284, 292–93
Edwardes, Michael, 84, 87–89
East India Company, 11, 77, 81–82, 84, 86, 89–90, 103
Egypt, 5, 6, 43, 73, 200, 261, 317
Eisenhower, Dwight, 4, 191
Emergency rule, India, 18, 43, 245–47, 251–53, 256
Employment, 338–39
Employment Appeal Tribunal, United Kingdom
    Eweida, 339
    Harris, 338
Employment division. *See* Supreme Court of the United States, Employment division
Employment Equality (Religion and Belief) Regulations, United Kingdom, 338–39
Endfield, Cy, 218
Equality, 290–92, 304–314, 338–39
Equity, 11–12, 85, 121–22, 135–36, 324–25
Esop. *See* Supreme Court of the Cape, Esop
Established churches / religions, 73–74, 83, 163–68, 194, 208–13, 229, 284–88, 298, 310, 338
    See also Church of England; United States, First amendment to the United States Constitution
Ethiopia, 269
European Commission of Human Rights, 56, 235–36
    Arrowsmith, 234, 237–40, 257–59
European Communities / Community. *See* European Union
European Convention for the Protection of Human Rights and Fundamental Freedoms, 56, 179
    Article 9, 195, 235, 238–40, 293, 300, 302–3, 312
    Human Rights Act, United Kingdom, 285–86
    See also European Commission of Human Rights; European Court of Human Rights; Human Rights Act, United Kingdom
European Court of Human Rights

Campbell and Cosans, 16, 299

Choudhury, 56, 234, 261

Handyside, 234–35, 257, 259

Human Rights Act, United Kingdom, 285–86

Leyla Şahin, 302, 313

Wingrove, 46–48, 158–59, 234, 261

See also De Meyer, Jan; Tulkens, Françoise

European Union, 56, 157–59, 234–37, 338

See also Court of Justice of the European Communities; Treaty of Maastricht

Evangelicals, 176, 256–57

See also Anglicans, Evangelicals

Everson. *See* Supreme Court of the United States, Everson

Eweida. *See* Employment Appeal Tribunal, United Kingdom, Eweida

Fagan Commission, South Africa, 124, 184

Falklands War, 18

Farlam, Ian, 167

Fascism, 113

Fatwa. *See* Islamic law, Fatwa

Fernandes, George, 256

Ferris, Justice, 285

Festival of India (1982), United Kingdom

Fifth Pay Commission, India, 70

Financial Times, 327

Finsbury Park Mosque, London, 73, 283–84, 304, 320

First amendment to the United States Constitution. *See* United States, First amendment to the United States Constitution

Fischer, Louis, 123

Foot, Michael, 247

Forbes, Ashley and the Cape Town Fourteen, 32

Foreign Office, United Kingdom, 72–73

Forster, Edward Morgan, *A Passage to India*, 58–59, 101, 120

Fourie, Marié Adriaana. *See* Constitutional Court of South Africa, Minister of Home Affairs; High Court of Pretoria, Minister of Home Affairs; Supreme Court of Appeal, South Africa, Minister of Home Affairs

France, 198, 200, 225

Fraser. *See* Constitutional Court of South Africa, Fraser

Fraser of Tullybelton, Baron, 329

Free Mandela concert, 39

Free speech. *See* Freedom of expression

Freedom of culture, 328–33

See also Cultural rights

Freedom of expression, 45–46, 49–50, 53, 56, 74, 97, 158–59, 181, 205, 234–40, 257–61, 263–64, 283, 338

Freedom of religion, 41–42, 42–56, 62–64, 89–90, 130, 139–41, 155–56, 158–59, 160, 163–68, 176–78, 194–95, 201–4, 208–13, 226–27, 229, 234–40, 248–51, 253, 257–61, 263–64, 268–82, 284, 285–88, 290–91, 292–95, 298–301, 304–10, 328–33, 335–42

Fukuyama, Francis, 180–82

Full Metal Jacket. See Kubrick, Stanley, *Full Metal Jacket*

Fuzlunbi. *See* Supreme Court of India, Fuzlunbi

Gaitskell, Hugh, 216

Galanter, Marc, 199

Gandhi (film), 18–19

Gandhi, Karamchand Mohandas, 1–3, 7, 16, 17, 18, 19, 27–28, 29, 58, 75, 97, 105, 106–10, 111–13, 127–30, 133, 167, 169–70, 179–80, 181, 183–84, 193–94, 204, 206, 225, 238, 257, 261, 303

Ambedkar, 111, 127–30

Death / Murder, 183, 193, 216–17

Economy, 64

Kasturba, 109

Legal practice, 3, 17, 35, 37, 107

London, 2, 102–3, 225, 258

Mother, 2

Nonviolence, 20, 207, 231, 238

Rushdie, 18–19, 169–70

South Africa, 19, 106–10, 123, 144, 342

Upbringing, 2

Women, 109

Yeravda Jail, 128

See also Gandhi (film); Poona Pact; Salt March; Satyagraha

Gandhi, Indira, 5, 7, 9, 10, 13, 17–18, 19, 21–22, 24, 43, 225, 232, 245–8, 252–54, 261

Gandhi, Rajiv, 14, 19, 22, 25–27, 64–66

Gandhi, Sanjay, 43

Ganges, 99

Gately, Kevin, 260

Gathercole. *See* Queen's Bench Division, Gathercole

Gay News. *See* House of Lords, Whitehouse

Gcoba, William, 80

Gender. *See* Women rights

Geneva, 333–34

Gerard, Jaspar, 314–15

Germany, 324

Get Up, Stand Up. See Marley, Bob, *Get Up, Stand Up*

Geyser, A. S., 201–2

Ghosh, Shri, 56–57, 132–33, 174

Ghosh, Sushmita, 3–4, 16–17, 56–57, 61–62, 67, 74–75, 76–77, 102, 120, 129, 131, 132–43, 150, 155–56, 160–62, 173–76, 179,

181–83, 190, 197, 200, 204, 206, 212, 231, 247–48, 262, 264, 267, 284, 291, 310–11, 323, 325–27, 347

   See also Supreme Court of India, Lily Thomas; Supreme Court of India, Sarla Mudgal

Gibbon, Edward, *Decline and Fall of the Roman Empire*, 105

Godhra massacre, 280–81

Godse, Nathuram, 183, 193, 216–17

Goldstone, Richard, 165, 278

Gorbachev, Mikhail, 39, 64

Gordimer, Nadine, *The House Gun*, 3, 146–48, 150, 163, 269, 276–77

Government of India Act, 111, 118–19

Graham, Billy, 256–57

Grahamstown, 202

Granville, Austin, 266

Great Britain. *See* United Kingdom

Great Game, 96, 113

Great Trek, 79

Griffin, Nick, 134

Guardian, The, 264, 317

Guha, Ramachandra, 65–66

Gujarat, 2, 17, 65, 106, 280–81

Gulf war, 70

Gurdwara, 75, 140, 298, 324

Guru Granth Sahib, 140

Guru Nanak, 183

Guruvayoor, 346

Hale of Richmond, Baroness, 311–13

Hall, Sheldon, 218

Handyside, Richard, *The Little Red Schoolbook*, 234–36, 238–40, 257, 259

Hani, Chris, 68–69

Hansen, Randall, 216–17

Hanuman, 86

Hare Krishna. *See* United Kingdom, Hare Krishna

Harijan, 9, 127

Harris. *See* Employment Appeal Tribunal, United Kingdom, Harris

Harrison, George, 230

   See also Beatles, The

Harvard Law School, 35

Hassam. *See* Constitutional Court of South Africa, Hassam

Hastings, Warren, 11, 90, 103

Headscarves. *See* Religious symbols/dress

Hegel, Georg Wilhelm Friedrich, 86

Henry VIII. *See* King Henry VIII

Herman, Arthur, 105, 109–10, 112, 130

Heyns, Johan, 68

High Court of Judicature for the North-Western Provinces, 92

High Court of Australia, New Faith, 300

   See also Deane, Justice; Wilson, Justice

High Court of Bombay, Robasa Khanum, 117–18, 124–25, 135, 139, 194

   See also Chagla, Justice; Stone, Justice

High Court of Calcutta, Ram Kumari, 99–102, 103, 104, 134

   See also Banerjee, Justice; Macpherson, Justice

High Court of Cape Town, Ryland, 167–68

   See also Farlam, Ian

High Court of Delhi.

   Naz Foundation, 310

   Vilayat Raj, 60

   See also Leela Seth

High Court of Madhya Pradesh, 22, 251

   Rev. Stainislaus, 251

High Court of Orissa, Mrs. Yulitha Hyde, 248–51

High Court of Pietermaritzburg (KwaZulu Natal), MEC for Education, 313–14, 329, 332

   See also Kondile, Justice

High Court of Pretoria, Minister of Home Affairs, 292

   See also Roux, Justice

High Court of South Africa, Transvaal Provincial Division, S. v. Nkosi, 242–43

High Court, United Kingdom (England and Wales)

   Parochial Church Council, 134, 284–85

   R (Begum), 284, 293–96, 310, 312

   See also Bennett, Justice; Ferris, Justice

Hill, Mark, 286–88, 337–38, 339–40

Hillsborough tragedy, 70–71

Hindu, The, 141–43, 346

Hindu Adoptions and Maintenance Act, India, 198

Hindu Code Bills, India, 12, 13, 26, 186–91, 194, 197–200, 247–48, 266

Hindu law, 11–13, 16, 60

   See also India, Hindu law; United Kingdom, Hindu Law

Hindu Mahasabha, 183, 191, 194, 197

Hindu Marriage Act, India, 60, 132, 140–43, 198, 347

Hindu Minority and Guardianship Act, India, 198

Hindu-Muslim conflict, 10, 22–27, 64–67, 77, 86, 112, 114, 123, 124, 136, 142, 205, 207, 226, 232, 265–66, 346

Hindu nationalists, 10, 26–27, 58–59, 64–67, 70, 133, 136, 157, 161–62, 170, 178, 194, 196–97, 205, 245, 248, 266–68, 280–81, 285

See also Arya Samaj; Babri Mosque; Hindu-Muslim conflict; Hindu Mahasabha; Hindutva; Ramakrishna Mission; Rashtriya Swayamsevak Sangh; Ritambara, Sadhvi; Sangh Parivar; Vishva Hindu Parishad

Hindu Succession Act, India, 140, 198, 325

Hindus, 331, 345

   See also Hindu nationalists; India, Hindus; South Africa, Hindus; United Kingdom, Hindus

Hindustan Times, 60

Hindutva, 10, 66, 143, 161, 264, 268, 280–81, 327, 345

   See also Hindu nationalists

Hintsa, 223

Hitchens, Christopher, 318

Hitler, Adolf, 113, 151, 169, 211

Hizb-ut-Tahrir, 316

Hobhouse, Arthur, 101

Hoffmann, Baron, 312

Hollywood, 19, 217–18

Holy Spirit, 41

Home Office, United Kingdom, 236

Homelands, South Africa, 15–16, 20, 195–96

Homosexuality, 68, 170, 179, 205, 209, 228, 257, 263–64, 284, 292, 304–10, 346

Hope of Craighead, Baron, 287

Hopkin, David, 45

Hottentots. *See* Khoikhoi

House Gun, The. *See* Gordimer, Nadine, *The House Gun*

House of Commons, United Kingdom, 78, 84, 97–98, 113, 284

House of Lords, United Kingdom

   Parochial Church Council, 134, 285–91, 293, 298, 312

   R (Begum), 17, 110, 284, 303, 310–17, 322–23, 333, 347

   R. (Williamson) 298–301

   Ramsay, 258–59

   Whitehouse, 8, 257–61, 263–64, 338

   See also Bingham of Cornhill, Baron; Coleridge, Lord; Dilhorne, Viscount; Diplock, Baron; Edmund-Davies, Baron; Fraser of Tullybelton, Baron; Hale of Richmond, Baroness; Hoffmann, Baron; Hope of Craighead, Baron; Nicholls of Birkenhead, Baron; Rodger of Earlsferry, Baron; Russell of Killowen, Baron; Scarman, Baron; Scott of Foscote, Baron; Walker of Gestingthorpe, Baron

Hoysalas, 198

Huddlestone, Ernest, 247

Hughes, Anthony, 320

Human Rights, 30, 36–39, 41, 69, 140, 144, 150, 153, 177, 179, 181, 240, 265–66, 268, 275, 279, 281, 285–88, 290–91, 296–97, 300, 306–10, 312, 321, 328–34, 335–38, 343, 347

   See also African Charter on Human and Peoples' Rights; Discrimination; Equality; European Convention for the Protection of Human Rights and Fundamental Freedoms; Freedom of expression; Freedom of religion; Human Rights Act, United Kingdom; Human Rights Committee, United Nations; Universal Declaration of Human Rights; Women rights

Human Rights Act, United Kingdom, 179, 285–88, 321, 338

Human Rights Committee, United Nations, 17, 280

   Prince, 333–34

Hungarian revolution, 200

Hunger strikers. *See* Irish Republican Army, Hunger strikers

Huntington, Samuel, 113, 182, 340–41

Hurd, Douglas, 44

Hussain, Hasib, 303

Hussein, Saddam, 70, 200, 289

Huttenback, Robert, 110

Huxley, Aldous, 1

IBM, 256

Ilbert, Courtenay, 100–101

Ilbert Bill, India, 100–101

Immorality Act, South Africa, 20, 195, 220–21

Independent, The, 71

India

   Atheists, 23, 225

   Buddhists, 9, 10, 12, 59, 70, 93, 139, 191, 198, 200, 266, 290

   Christian law, 117, 121, 267

   Christians, 10, 23, 24, 59, 70, 74, 82–97, 112, 117, 120–21, 125, 127, 135, 139, 178, 190, 198, 245, 248–51, 253, 255–57, 266–67, 290–91

   Communists, 196–97, 225, 256

   Divorce, 12, 14, 22–24, 57, 60, 113, 116, 122, 247–48, 254–55, 264–67

   Feminists, 255

   Free market, 64–65

   Green revolution, 21

   Hindu law, 56–62, 85, 99–102, 103, 104, 113–15, 117, 121–22, 132–43, 155–57, 173–76, 186–91, 197–200, 247–48, 267

   Hindu trusts, 155–56

   Hindus, 5, 23, 70, 81–82, 84–90, 99–102, 111–12, 113–16, 121–22, 124–29, 132–43, 155–57, 161, 173–76, 178, 183, 186–91,

197–200, 205, 232, 245, 247–48, 264–67, 280–81, 290, 303

Islamic law, 56–62, 85, 92–95, 99–102, 103, 104, 113–22, 124–25, 132–43, 173–76, 247–48, 254–55, 264–67

Jains, 12, 139, 191, 198, 266

Jewish law, 116–18

Jews, 116–18

Judges, 75, 76

Maintenance rights, 12, 14, 22–27, 247–48, 254–55, 264–67, 284, 323, 326

Marxists, 5, 10, 68, 70, 128, 178, 180, 196, 245, 256, 345–46

Muslims, 5, 14, 22–24, 70, 81–82, 85–97, 99–102, 111–12, 124–26, 127, 132–43, 161, 173–76, 178, 183, 186–91, 198, 232, 245, 247–48, 254–55, 264–67, 280–81, 284, 291, 304–5, 326, 346

Parsi law, 85, 93, 120, 267

Parsis, 23, 85, 96, 120, 190, 198, 266–67, 291

Satanic Verses, The (ban in India), 42, 49

Secular state/Secularism, 17, 19, 23, 27, 58, 67, 113, 127, 128–30, 133, 136, 139–43, 157, 161, 170, 175–76, 189–91, 197, 204–5, 225–26, 232–33, 245, 247–55, 265–68, 285, 290–91, 325, 327

Sikhs, 9, 12, 18, 19, 24, 26, 52, 70, 93, 127, 139, 182–83, 190, 205, 232, 247, 291

Social justice, 122, 178, 181, 251–52, 265–66, 325

Socialism, 39, 58, 113, 128–30, 180, 190, 196–97, 204, 225, 233, 247–55, 327

Wakf Boards, 265–66

Zoroastrians, 107, 118–22

Indian Home Ministry, 42

Indian Independence Act, 126

Indian National Congress, 1, 25–26, 101, 111–12, 125, 129, 133, 157, 161, 194, 197, 225, 233, 247, 265, 323, 345

Indian nationalists, 114, 125–26, 130, 133, 157, 161

Indian Penal Code, 11, 92, 99, 110, 133, 148, 174

Indian Succession Act, 290–91

Indiana University, 267

Indians Relief Bill, South Africa, 109–10

Indissolubility, 58, 95, 121–22, 208–13

See also Dissolution/invalidity of marriages

Indo-Pakistani wars, 183, 205, 226, 246–47

Indres Naidoo, 172

Inheritance. *See* Succession

Inkatha Freedom Party, 154

International Guerillas. See Rushdie, Salman

IRA. *See* Irish Republican Army

Irish Republican Army, 8, 19, 70, 232

Brighton hotel bombing, 19

Hunger strikers, 8

Sands, Bobby, 8

Iran, 5, 6, 42–56, 173, 261

Iran-Iraq War, 5, 261

Iraq, 5, 70, 200, 261, 284, 289–90, 304

Iraq War, 289–90, 304

Ireland, 86, 97, 103, 195

See also Northern Ireland

Islam, Shahara, 303–4

Islamic finance, 321

Islamic law, 11–12, 14, 16, 22–27, 43, 60, 340

Abduction, 16

Fatwa, 42–43, 52

Iddat, 22–24, 247–48, 254–55, 266

Mahr, 22–24

Repudiation, 58, 60, 167

Sexual intercourse, 16

Talaq, 22–24, 60

See also India, Islamic law; India, Maintenance rights; Mahmood, Tahir; South Africa, Islamic law; United Kingdom, Islamic law

Israel, 5, 200, 234, 261

See also Arab-Israeli conflict / War

Italy, 86, 325

Jabalpur riots, 207

Jacobsohn, Gary Jeffrey, 143

Jadavpur University, 75

Jaganmohan Reddy Commission of Inquiry, India, 232

Jagannath, 84

Jains. *See* India, Jains

Jain, Neetu, 303

Jamaica, 270, 296

James, Justice, 93–96, 104

Jamat-e-Ulema Hind, 160–61, 173–74, 190

Jammur, 183

Janata Party, 5, 7, 9, 10, 253–54, 261

Japan, 114

Jatavs, 9

Jenkins, Roy, 228–29, 322

Jehovah's Witnesses, 234, 273

Jerry Springer: The Opera, 338

Jesus Christ, 27, 41, 47, 50, 159, 221, 225, 229, 241, 257, 261, 264

Jews. 273, 289, 320, 327, 336

See also India, Jews; Israel; South Africa, Jews; United Kingdom, Jews

Jilbab. *See* Religious symbols/dress

Jinnah, Muhammad Ali, 112–13, 124, 126

Jis Desh Men Ganga Behti Hai, 217

Joffe, Joel, 38, 224

Johannesburg, 106, 123, 144, 202–3, 222, 224, 241, 276, 306

John Paul II, Saint, 5, 261
Johnson, Boris, 315–19
Jonker, Willie, 40–42, 295
Jorden Diengdeh. *See* Supreme Court of India, Jorden Diengdeh
Joshi, Subhadra, 198

K.C. *See* Court of Appeal, United Kingdom, K.C.
Kairos document, 32
Kalyani, 61
Kanpur, 1
Kashmir, 42, 70, 72, 142, 179, 183, 281, 346
Kasturba. *See* Gandhi, Karamchand Mohandas, Kasturba
Kathrada, Ahmed, 224
Keble, John, 83–84, 103
Kenilworth. *See* Saint James Church massacre
Kenny, Courtney Stanhope, 99
Kenny, Mary, 263–64
Kentucky Fried Chicken, 136
Kerala, 68, 70, 225, 324, 346
Kerala Law Times, 324–27
Kerkbode, Die, 186
Khalistan, 9
Khan. *See* Court of Appeal, United Kingdom, Khan
Khan, Arif Muhammad, 25
Khare, V. N., 290–91
Khoikhoi, 21, 78, 223
Khomeini, Ruhollah Mustafavi Moosavi, 42–45, 70
Khotso House, 31, 171–72
Khrushchev, Nikita, 196
Kim. See Kipling, Rudyard, *Kim*
King, Martin Luther, 7, 221, 230, 238, 257, 261
King Cetshwayo, 217, 219
King Henry VIII, 208–10, 258
King's College London, 230
King's School, Eastleigh, Hampshire, 298
    See also Court of Appeal, United Kingdom, R. (Williamson); House of Lords, R. (Williamson)
Kipling, Rudyard, *Kim*, 82, 87, 96–97, 104
Kirkup, James, 257, 264
Kissinger, Henry, 255
Knysna High School, 21
Kolkata, 27, 75, 99, 101, 124
    Bethel Synagogue, 116
    Nakhoda Mosque, 116
Kondile, Justice, 313–14
Koran. *See* Quran
Korea, 196
Kriegler, Johann, 274, 278
Kripalani, J.B., 197

Kripalani, Sucheta, 198
Krishna. *See* Lord Krishna
Krishna Iyer, V.R. 23, 246, 251–52, 254–55
Krishna Menon, V.K., 200
Krishna Singh. *See* Supreme Court of India, Krishna Singh
Kubrick, Stanley, *Full Metal Jacket*, 27–28
Kugle, Scott, 119
Kuwait, 70
KwaZulu-Natal, 313–14

Labour Party, United Kingdom, 70, 127, 160, 161, 178, 180–82, 184, 204, 216, 220, 225, 228, 233, 247, 255, 261, 289, 321
Lahore, 42, 111–12, 128
Lakshmi, 268, 328, 333
Lal Krishna Advani, 345
Lambeth Conference (1998), 170–71
Lancashire, 86
Langa, Pius, 149, 279, 329–33, 343
Larson, Gerald, 267
Latifi, Danial, 26, 264–67
    See also Supreme Court of India, Danial Latifi
Law Society of the Cape of Good Hope, 159–60, 178
Law Society of the Transvaal, 278
League of the Nations, 184
Lebanon, 5, 261
Leeds, 318
Leela Seth, 60
Legal Resources Center, South Africa, 37–39
Legislative Council, India, 91, 93
Lemon, Denis, 234, 257–61
Lenin, 225
Leninism, 5, 64
Lennon John, 204
    See also Beatles, The
Lesbian and Gay Equality Project, South Africa, 306
Lesotho, 29
Lester, Anthony, 50
Lewis, Bernard, 319
Leyla Şahin. *See* European Court of Human Rights, Leyla Şahin
Liberation theology. *See* Theology, Liberation
Life of Brian (The). See Monty Python, *The Life of Brian*
Lily Thomas. *See* Supreme Court of India, Lily Thomas
Lincoln, Abraham, 192–93
Ling, Trevor, 73
Liquor Act, South Africa, 163–66
Little Red Schoolbook, The. See Handyside, Richard, *The Little Red Schoolbook*

Liverpool, 233
    Anfield Road Stadium, 71
    Christian Fellowship School, Edge Hill, 298
    St. Peter's Church, Woolton, 204
    See also Beatles, The; Hillsborough tragedy;
        Sheppard, David; Worlock, Derek
Lodge, Justice, 116–18, 119, 121–22
Lok Sabha, 157, 198, 246, 255–57, 345
London, 2, 3, 11–12, 17, 27, 39, 42, 43, 44, 58,
    73, 74, 78, 81, 85, 91, 102–3, 170, 184–85,
    200, 214, 220, 228, 233, 282–83, 303–5,
    315, 318, 324, 334–35
    Bloomsbury, 303
    Brookwood Cemetery, 102–3
    Globe Theatre, 208
    Heatrow Airport, 296
    King's Cross, 303
    Lancaster House, 214
    New Age, 102–3, 106, 258
    Tavistock Square, 303
    Trafalgar Square, 103
    Upper Woburn Place, 303
    Warehouse Theatre, 246
    Wembley, 73
    See also Gandhi, London; London bombings;
        London Secular Society; Londonistan;
        Missionaries, London Missionary Society
London bombings, 303–5, 318, 320–21
London Missionary Society. *See* Missionaries,
    London Missionary Society
London School of Economics, 127, 331
London Secular Society, 98–99
Londonistan, 73, 282–83, 319–20
Lord Krishna, 326, 346–47
Lord Rama, 26, 66
Lord Vishnu, 26
Luce, Edward, 327
Lutherans, 32, 211, 273
    See also South African, Lutherans
Luton. *See* Denbigh High School
Lynch. *See* Supreme Court of the United States,
    Lynch

Macaulay, Thomas Babington, 79, 84–85,
    91–92, 97, 99, 101, 119, 148, 260
Macdonald, Ian, 227–29
MacDonald, James Ramsey, 128
Macmillan, Harold, 200, 207–8, 209, 214
Macpherson, Justice, 100–102
Mad cow disease, 159
Madala, Tholie, 165
Madikizela Mandela, Winnie, 154
Madlanga, Mbuyiseli, 278
Madhya Pradesh, 21–22, 25, 205, 248–51, 253

Madhya Pradesh Dharma Swatantrya Adhini-
    yam, 227, 248–51, 253
Magna Carta, 229
Maharashtra, 27
Maharishi Mahesh Yogi, 230
Mahars, 200
Mahboob Ali Baig Sahib Bahadur, 189
Mahmood, Tahir, 25, 60, 141–43
Mahomed, Ismail, 144–46, 167
Major, John, 70, 134, 157, 161
Makana, 223
Makoma, Gcinikhaya Christopher, 154–55
Makwanyane, Themba. *See* Constitutional
    Court of South Africa, S. v. Makwanyane
Malakand campaign, 105
Malan, Daniel François, 69, 126–27, 184–86
Malik, Kenan, 173
Mamdani, Mahmood, 14
Man for All Seasons, A. See Bolt, Robert, *A Man
    for All Seasons*
Manchester, 73
    See also Manchester No Breakfast Association
Manchester No Breakfast Association, 1
Mandal Commission, India, 9, 65, 67
Mandal Mandir. *See* Babri Mosque
Mandela, Mphakanyiswa Gadla Henry, 15
Mandela, Nelson, 15, 16, 69, 70, 75, 107, 145,
    151, 171, 179, 221, 231, 276, 347
    Childhood, 15
    Education, 35
    Free Mandela concert, 39
    Legal practice, 35, 37
    Release from prison, 40, 55
    Rivonia trial, 107, 150, 205, 222–24, 225,
        231, 243, 276
Mandela, Winnie. *See* Madikizela Mandela,
    Winnie
Manu, 23
Mao, 196
Maoists, 4, 70
Maputo, 28–29, 31, 35–36, 38, 69, 76, 145, 172,
    192, 306
Margolick, David, 288–90
Marley, Bob, 21, 334
    Get Up, Stand Up, 21
Marriage. *See* Dissolution/Invalidity of mar-
    riage; Divorce; Indissolubility; Polygamy;
    Registration; Same sex marriage
Marriage Act, South Africa, 292, 306–10
Martin, Anne. *See* High Court of Pietermaritz-
    burg, MEC for Education; Constitutional
    Court of South Africa, MEC for Education
Marx, Karl, 81–82, 86–87, 95, 105, 113
    See also Marxism/Marxists

Marxism/Marxists, 4, 5, 6, 29, 64, 68, 72, 206, 225–27, 230, 232–33, 242, 245, 256, 260, 342
    See also Communists; India, Marxists; Marx, Karl; Socialists; South Africa, Marxists
Mason, Judith, 344
Mathur, Jitender/Meena, 61–62
Mbeki, Thabo, 29, 37, 154, 179, 230, 295, 297–98
McCartney, Paul, 204
    See also Beatles, The
McGrory, Daniel, 283, 304, 320
Mchunu, Mvuso, *See* Constitutional Court of South Africa, S. v. Makwanyane
Meerut, 87, 92
Meaning of Life (The). *See* Monty Python, *The Meaning of Life*
Meintjes, Johannes, 80, 242
Menon, Nivedita, 199, 267
Menski, Werner, 27, 58–59, 324–27, 335, 340
Meredith, Martin, 69, 153
Methodists, 30, 32, 35, 68, 151, 154, 201, 213, 240–241, 273
    See also African Methodist Episcopal Church
Middle East, 6, 72, 321
    See also Arab-Israeli conflict / War
Midnight Children. *See* Rushdie, Salman
Missionaries
    Charter Act, 84
    Christians, 2, 11, 59, 77, 78–80, 126, 178, 187, 218–20, 226, 238, 242, 248–51, 346
    Hindus, 59, 346
    London Missionary Society, 78
Mlanjeni, 79–80, 242
Modood, Tariq, 46
Moghuls, 11
Mohammad Ismail Sahib, 188
Mohammed. *See* Muhammad, The Prophet of Islam
Mokgoro, Yvonne, 149, 178, 278
Mokotimi, Seth, 213
Monty Python
    The Life of Brian, 8, 261
    The Meaning of Life, 8
Mookerji, Radha Kumud, 198
Moosa, Ebrahim, 167–68
More, Thomas, Saint, 208–13, 219, 229, 244, 258
Mortimer, John, 235
Moscow, 196
Moseneke, Dikgang, 292
Moses, Annie. *See* Court of Calcutta, Sayeda Khatoon
Moshoeshoe, 149, 223
Mosque, 55, 75, 92, 140

    See also Babri Mosque; Central Mosque, Birmingham; Finsbury Park Mosque, London; Nakhoda Mosque, Kolkata
Mother India, 217
Mozambique, 7, 28–29, 261
Mphahlele, Es'kia, 223
Mrs. Yulitha Hyde. *See* High Court of Orissa, Mrs. Yulitha Hyde
Mughal rule, 85
Muhammad, The Prophet of Islam, 42, 44, 47, 50, 264
Muhammad Bahadur Shah, 87
Mukherjea, Bijan Kumar, 13, 248–49
Mumbai, 42, 66, 74, 254–55
    See also Bombay bombings
Mummery, Justice, 303
Muslim Brotherhood, 6, 73, 317–18, 321
Muslim-Hindu conflict. *See* Hindu-Muslim conflict
Muslim League, India, 111–12
Muslim Marriages Act, India, 119
Muslim Nationalists, India, 111–12, 119, 124–26, 133
    See also Jinnah, Muhammad Ali
Muslim Personal Law Board, India, 160–61, 174, 190, 265
Muslim Women (Protection of Rights on Divorce) Bill, India, 25–26, 264–67
Muslims, 2, 4, 5, 42–56, 264, 273, 282–83, 310, 317–23
    See also India, Muslims; South Africa, Muslims; United Kingdom, Muslims
Mustafa, Mustafa Kamal (Abu Hamza), 73, 282–83, 304, 320
    See also Central Criminal Court, United Kingdom, Mustafa
Mutiny. *See* War of independence, India
    See also White Mutiny, India

Naga/Nagaland, 256
Nagpur, 200
Naicker, Gagathura "Monty," 123
Naipaul, V. S., 1–3, 17
Namibia, 39
Nana Sahib, 87
Narajan, J. P., 225
Napakade, 80
Narashima Rao, P. V., 66
Narendra Modi, 280
Narula, Sunita, 61–62
Nasser, Gamal Abdel, 200
Natal, 2, 35, 84, 106–7, 112, 167, 217, 313–14
Natal Indian Congress, 107, 123, 126
National Commission for Women, India, 265

National Committee for Commonwealth Immigrants, United Kingdom, 228

National Conference of Church Leaders. *See* Rustenburg conference

National Party, South Africa, 39, 75, 111, 112–13, 126–27, 130, 184–86, 196, 202, 204, 208, 243–44

National Secular Society, United Kingdom, 98

Nationalists. *See* African nationalists; Afrikaners, Nationalists; Arab nationalists; Hindu nationalists; India, Muslim nationalists; Indian nationalists

Native African religion. *See* African traditional religion

Native American church / religion, 62–64, 272

Native Laws Amendment Bill, South Africa, 201–4

Native Representative Council, South Africa, 123

Naudé, Beyers, 40, 244

Naxalites, 70, 225

Naz Foundation, India, 310

Nazism, 113, 151, 169, 211

Ndwandwe, Phila, 344

Nederduitse Gereformeerde Kerk, 31, 33, 40–42, 68, 186, 201, 226, 232, 243–44, 295

Nehru, Jawaharlal, 9, 12–13, 23, 26, 39, 64, 70, 111, 130, 133, 139, 140, 161, 178, 181, 186, 191–93, 196, 197–200, 214, 216, 220, 225, 246, 248, 324–25

Nehruvian. *See* Nehru.

Netherlands, 236

New York, 6, 38, 72, 86, 95
    See also Nine Eleven

New York Daily Tribune, 81, 86

New York Times, 28–29, 222, 306

Newman, John Henry, 77

NG Sending Church, 32

Ngcobo, Sandile, 275, 277–78, 333

Nicholls of Birkenhead, Baron, 285–88, 312–13

Nicholson, John, 87

Nietzsche, Friedrich, 70

Nine Eleven, 263–67, 282, 317
    See also World Trade Center bombing (1993)

Nine Hours to Rama, 216–17

Nixon, Richard, 247, 255

Nkabinde, Bess, 341–44

Nongqawuse, 80

Nonviolence. *See*
    Gandhi, Nonviolence
    Pacifists

Norfolk, Duke of, 209–11

Northern Ireland, 8, 9, 18, 43, 50, 97, 103, 205, 231–32, 235, 237–40, 259–60, 288–89

Protestants, 8, 9, 18, 43, 50, 97, 205, 231–32, 288–89

Roman Catholics, 8, 9, 18, 43, 50, 205, 231–32, 288–89

See also Bloody Sunday; Bogside, Battle of the; Gately, Kevin; Ireland; Sands, Bobby

Notting Hill riots, 204, 207

Nuremberg trial, 38, 151

Nussbaum, Martha, 341

O'Connor, Sandra Day, 63, 165–66, 272–73

O'Neill, Sean, 283, 304, 320

O'Regan, Kate, 165–6, 279, 329–33

Oath, 97–99, 224, 229

OBC. *See* Other Backward Classes, India

Obscene Publications Act, United Kingdom, 234–36

Observer, The, 317

Oil, 200, 234

Old Bailey, 263, 304, 320
    See also Central Criminal Court, United Kingdom

On the Origin of Species. See Darwin, Charles, *On the Origin of Species*

Operation Blue Star. *See* Amritsar, Massacre (1984)

Orange Free State, 167

Oregon, 62–64

Orissa, 178, 205, 248–51, 253

Orissa Freedom of Religion Act, 226–27, 248–51, 253

Ormond, Justice, 113–16, 119–22, 134–35

Orthodox Christians, 77

Other Backward Classes, India, 9–10, 65

Othman, Omar Mahmoud (Qatada, Abu), 283

Ottoman Empire, 112

Outside the Whale. See Rushdie, Salman

Oxford, 83, 213–14, 219, 240, 289

Pacifists, 218–19, 237–40, 303
    See also Gandhi, Nonviolence

Pakistan, 5, 6, 17, 42, 72, 105, 111–12, 124, 126, 182–83, 205, 208, 228, 246–47, 255, 280–81, 283, 304
    See also Indo-Pakistani wars; Jinnah, Muhammad Ali; Bhutto, Zulfikar Ali; Kashmir; Rushdie, Salman, *International Guerillas*

Palestine, 5, 234, 261

Pan-Africanist Congress, 154

Pannalal Bansilal Pitti. *See* Supreme Court of India, Pannalal

Paras Ram. *See* Supreme Court of India, Paras Ram

Parnell, Charles Stewart, 97

Parochial Church Council. *See* Court of appeal, United Kingdom, Parochial Church Council; High Court, United Kingdom, Parochial Church Council; House of Lords, Parochial Church Council

Parsis. *See* India, Parsi

Parsi law. *See* India, Parsi law

Partition, India-Pakistan, 42, 55, 111, 113, 115, 126, 129, 136–37, 183, 217

Pasayat, Arijit, 323

Pass laws, South Africa, 109, 196, 207

Passage to India, A. See Forster, Edward Morgan, *A Passage to India*

Pathans, 105, 120

Paton, Alan, 202–3, 223–24, 243

Pattabhi Sitaramayya, 187–88

Patten, John, 45–46, 48, 158–59

Paul VI, 256

Pedi, 223

Peires, Jeff, 80

Pension rights, 324, 341–43

Personal laws, 11, 12, 13, 22–27, 56–62, 116–17, 122, 124–25, 128–29, 132–43, 160–61, 173–76, 186–91, 197–200, 247–48, 264–67, 285, 290–91, 325–26

Peter, Saint, 229

Peyote, 62–64, 272–73

Philip, John, 78

Phillips, Melanie, 319, 327

Pietermaritzburg, 106, 201

Pillay. *See* High Court of Pietermaritzburg, MEC for Education; Constitutional Court of South Africa, MEC for Education

Pillay, Krishensamy, 123

Pillay, Sunali. *See* High Court of Pietermaritzburg, MEC for Education; Constitutional Court of South Africa, MEC for Education

Plassey / Plassy. *See* Battle of Plassey

Pledge of allegiance. *See* United States, Pledge of allegiance

Poland, 5, 261

Polygamy, 108, 121, 138, 300, 323, 341–43
    See also Court of Alipore, Ram Kumari; High Court of Calcutta, Ram Kumari; Privy Council, Skinner; Supreme Court of India, Lily Thomas; Supreme Court of India, Sarla Mudgal; Supreme Court of the Cape, Esop

Polygyny. *See* Polygamy

Poona Pact, 111, 127–28, 130, 193

Poor laws, United Kingdom

Population Registration Act, South Africa, 20, 195

Port Said, 200

Portugal, 7, 28–29, 261

Post-colonialism, 5, 7, 58, 125

Powell, Enoch, 216, 233

Prabhu Dutt Brahmachari, 197

Prayer, Right to, 16

Presbyterians, 24, 160, 273, 334

Pretoria, 68, 69, 74, 144, 147, 181, 184, 196, 202

Prince. *See* African Commission on Human and Peoples' Rights, Prince; Constitutional Court of South Africa, Prince

Prince, Gareth, 3, 4, 16–17, 21, 34, 39, 62–64, 67, 69, 74–75, 76, 134, 159–60, 161–62, 166, 168–69, 176–79, 181–83, 204, 206, 212, 231, 242, 262, 264, 268–80, 284, 295–97, 310–11, 315, 333–34, 347
    See also African Commission on Human and Peoples' Rights, Prince; Constitutional Court of South Africa, Prince

Princely states, India, 12, 15

Privy Council, United Kingdom, 11–12
    Skinner, 92–96, 104, 134
    See also James, Justice

Proclamation of 1858. *See* Queen Victoria, Proclamation of 1858

Progressive Federal Party, South Africa, 30, 243

Prohibition of Mixed Marriages Act, South Africa, 20, 186

Promotion of Equality and Prevention of Unfair Discrimination Act (Equality Act), South Africa, 177–78

Promotion of National Unity and Reconciliation Act, South Africa, 151

Protestants, 8, 24, 43, 97, 249–51, 273
    Also see Adventists; Afrikaans Protestant Church; Anglicans; Baptists; Baptist Union of Southern Africa; Calvinists; Lutherans; Methodists; Nederduitse Gereformeerde Kerk; NG Sending Church; Northern Ireland, Protestants; Presbyterians; Reformed Christians; United Kingdom, Protestants

Punjab, 4, 9, 18, 26, 51, 111, 247

Purdah, 58

Puri, 84

Puritan divines, 33

Putteridge High School, 301

Qatada, Abu. *See* Othman, Omar Mahmoud

Quarry Men, 204

Quddas, Abdul, 42–43

Queen's Bench Division, United Kingdom, 49–50, 56
    Gathercole, 83
    R. v. Chief Metropolitan 44–56, 83, 91, 97, 99, 110, 234
    See also Alderson, Justice; Roch, Justice; Stuart Smith, Justice; Watkins, Justice

Queen Catherine, 208–10

Queen Elizabeth II, 214–15, 292, 338

Queen Mary University of London, 324

Queen Victoria, 88, 89–93, 94, 97, 104, 106, 111, 121, 125, 206, 220, 246, 263
    Proclamation of 1858, 89–93, 97, 104, 106, 111, 125, 246

Quran, 11, 23–24, 42, 95, 140, 141, 283, 289

Qutb, Sayyid, 317–18

R. (Begum). *See* Court of Appeal, United Kingdom, R. (Begum); High Court, United Kingdom, R. (Begum); House of Lords, R. (Begum)

R. v. Chief Metropolitan. *See* Queen's Bench Division, R. v. Chief Metropolitan

R. v. Ramsay and Foote. *See* House of Lords, Ramsay

R. (Williamson). *See* Court of Appeal, United Kingdom, R. (Williamson); House of Lords, R. (Williamson)

Race and Religious Hatred Act, 338

Race Relations Act, United Kingdom, 239, 259, 329

Racial segregation. *See* Apartheid; United States, Racial segregation

Racism. *See* Apartheid; United Kingdom, Racism; United States, Racial segregation

Ray, A. N., 253

Rajya Sabha, 198, 323

Ram / Rama. *See* Lord Rama
    See also Babri Mosque

Ram Kumari, 99–102, 103, 104, 118
    Dukhi Singh, 100
    Guzaffer Ali, 100, 102
    See also Court of Alipore, Ram Kumari; High Court of Calcutta, Ram Kumari

Ram Rath Yatra, 65

Ramakrishna Mission, 59

Ramaswamy, K., 156–57, 175–76

Ramayan/Ramayana, 27, 140

Rambilass, Vishram, 331

Ranadive, B. T., 196

Rangoon, 114

Rashtriya Swayamsevak Sangh, 59, 194

Rastafari, 4, 16, 21, 34, 74, 159–63, 268–80, 284, 296, 315, 334, 338
    See also Prince

Rastafarians. *See* Rastafari

Rath Yatra festival, 84

Ratilal Panachand Gandhi. *See* Supreme Court of India, Ratilal Panachand Gandhi

Rau Commission, India, 187

Reade, Winwood, 105

Reagan, Ronald, 39, 64, 69, 227

Red Cross, 106

Reformed Christians. *See* Calvinists; Dutch Reformed Church in the Netherlands; Nederduitse Gereformeerde Kerk; NG Sending Church

Registration of marriages, 107–8, 323–24, 326

Rehnquist, William, 273

Reliance Industries, 64

Religious freedom. *See* Freedom of religion

Religious laws, 23, 26, 58, 74, 94, 103–4, 110–11, 113, 116, 118–19, 121–22, 125, 127, 129, 136–37, 139, 176, 186, 190, 205, 254–55, 322, 334–38
    See also Customary law; Hindu law; India, Christian law; India, Parsi law; Islamic law; Church of England, Ecclesiastical law; Personal law

Religious symbols/dress. *See* Eweida; MEC for Education; R (Begum)

Renamo, 29

Republic of South Africa (proclamation), 215

Repudiation. *See* Islamic law, Repudiation

Reserved seats, India, 9, 28, 128, 130, 193

Retief, Piet, 79

Rev. Stainislaus. *See* High Court of Madhya Pradesh, Rev. Stainislaus; Supreme Court of India, Rev. Stainislaus

Rhodesia. *See* Zimbabwe

Ripon, Marquess of, 100–101

Rishikesh, 230

Ritambara, Sadhvi, 66

Rivers, Julian, 288

Rivonia trial, 107, 150, 205, 222–24, 225, 231, 243, 276

Rix, Justice, 299

Robasa Khanum. *See* Court of Bombay, Robasa Khanum; High Court of Bombay, Robasa Khanum

Robertson, Geoffrey, 49, 264

Robson, Mark, 217

Roch, Justice, 49

Rodger of Earlsferry, Baron, 287–88

Roger, Roy, 218

Roman Catholics, 5, 8–9, 18, 33–34, 47, 77, 96, 97, 113, 202, 208–13, 229, 249–51, 273, 290–91, 325, 334, 337
    Concordats, 113, 211
    See also John Paul II, Saint; Newman, John Henry; Northern Ireland, Roman Catholics; Paul VI; Peter, Saint; Second Vatican Council; Teresa of Avila, Saint; United Kingdom, Roman Catholic disabilities; Worlock, Derek

Roman Empire, 105

Rorke's Drift, 216–22

Ross, Andrew, 78

Roux, Justice, 292
Roy, Raja Ram Mohan, 140
Royal Air Force, United Kingdom, 185
RSS. *See* Rashtriya Swayamsevak Sangh
Rudolph, Lloyd and Susanne, 267–68
Rule of law. *See* South Africa, Rule of law
Rushdie, Salman, 18–19, 42–56, 72, 74, 83, 91,
  97, 99, 167, 169–70, 173, 182, 234, 261, 338
  International Guerillas, 50–54
  Midnight Children, 42–43
  Mohandas Gandhi, 18–19, 169–70
  Outside the Whale, 45
  Satanic Verses, The, 42–56, 67, 83, 91, 97, 99,
    162, 167, 173, 261, 338
  Shame, 43
  See also European Court of Human Rights,
    Choudhury; Queen's Bench, R. v. Chief
    Metropolitan
Ruskin, 1
Russell, Alec, 295
Russell, William Howard, 88, 90
Russell of Killowen, Baron, 261
Russian Empire, 113
Rustenburg conference, 40–42, 68, 295
Ryland. *See* High Court of Cape Town, Ryland

S. v. Lawrence. *See* Constitutional Court of
  South Africa, S. v Lawrence
S. v. Makwanyane. *See* Constitutional Court of
  South Africa, S. v. Makwanyane
S. v. Nkosi. *See* High Court of South Africa, S.
  v. Nkosi
Sabbala, 86
Sachs, Albie, 28–30, 35–39, 68–69, 76, 83–84,
  145–46, 148–50, 163, 165–68, 172,
  176–78, 192, 201, 204, 221, 230, 242, 246,
  268–79, 292, 297, 299–301, 306–10, 313,
  332–33, 343–44
Sacred cows, 81, 86, 226, 345
Sadat, Anwar, 5, 261
Sahai, R. M., 61–62, 132, 134–35, 138–41, 156
Şahin, Leyla. *See* European Court of Human
  Rights, Leyla Şahin
Said, Edward, 96, 104
Saint James Church massacre, 68, 154–55
Salt March, 111
Same sex marriage, 284, 292, 304–310
Sands, Bobby, 8
Sangh Parivar, 66, 281
Sanyasis, 12
Sarla Mudgal. *See* Supreme Court of India,
  Sarla Mudgal
Satanic Verses, The. *See* Rushdie, Salman, *Sa-
  tanic Verses, The*

See also India, see India, *Satanic Verses, The*;
  South Africa, see South Africa, *Satanic
  Verses, The*
Sati, 84, 140
Satyagraha, 106–10, 194
Saudi Arabia, 6, 182, 200, 282–83
Sauer Commission, South Africa, 26
Savarkar, Vinayak Damodar, 2
Savitri, 197
Sayeda Khatoon. *See* Court of Calcutta, Sayeda
  Khatoon
Scalia, Antonin, 62–64, 272–73
Scarman, Baron, 259–61
Scheduled castes, India, 9, 10, 65
Schlebusch/Le Grange Commission, South
  Africa, 244
School for Oriental and African Studies, Lon-
  don, 27, 58–59, 322
School Standards and Framework Act, United
  Kingdom, 302
Schoon, Marius, 153
Scientology. *See* Church of Scientology
Scofield, Paul, 212, 229
Scotland, 16
Scott, Leon, 32
Scott, Michael, 123–24
Scott Baker, Justice, 302–3
Scott of Foscote, Baron, 312–13
Searle, Justice, 107–108, 123, 167, 342
Second Vatican Council, 229, 250
Secular state, 9, 12, 70, 133, 136, 139, 144, 161,
  189, 226, 229, 233, 267, 302, 335–39
  See also India, Secular state/Secularism; South
    Africa, Secular state/Secularism; United
    Kingdom, Secular state / Secularism
Secularism, 225, 228, 319, 324–25, 335–38
  Turkey, 302
  See also India, Secular state/Secularism;
    Secular state; Separation; South Africa,
    Secular state/Secularism; United King-
    dom, Secular state/Secularism
Sekhukhuni, 223
Sen, Ananda Prakash, 12
Senegal, 30, 295, 297
Separation. *See* Church and State; Estab-
  lished churches/religions; United States,
  First amendment to the United States
  Constitution
Serote, Mongane Wally, 223
Sethi, R. P., 173–76
Seven Eleven, 163
Shachar, Ayelet, 336
Shah, Prakash, 324
Shah Bano. *See* Supreme Court of India, Mohd.
  Ahmed Khan

Shahbuddin, Syed, 25

Shame. See Rushdie, Salman, *Shame*

Sharia. *See* Islamic law

Shariat Act, India, 119

Sharpeville massacre, 207, 213–14

Sheffield. *See* Hillsborough tragedy

Sheikh Mohammed Abdullah, 183

Sheppard, David, 71

Sherbert, Adell. *See* Supreme Court of the United States, Sherbert

Shri K. Hanumanthaiya, 193, 204, 230

Sikhs. *See* India, Sikhs; United Kingdom, Sikhs

Singh, Bhagat, 4, 225

Singh, Kalyan, 67

Singh, Kuldip, 61–62, 77, 132–43, 156, 197, 291, 326, 347

Sinha, S. B., 291

Sita, 197

Skinner, Victoria, 92–96, 104, 118

   See also Privy Council, United Kingdom, Skinner

Slavery, 78–79, 86, 270

Smith, Alfred. *See* Supreme Court of the United States, Employment division

Smith, David James, 35

Smuts, Jan, 75, 109–10, 123–24, 126, 130, 184, 206

Social Darwinism. *See* Darwin, Charles

Social justice. 5, 230, 284, 292

   See also Christian social justice; India, social justice

Socialism/Socialists. *See* Christian socialists; India, Socialism; United Kingdom, Socialists

Solberg, Magdalena. *See* Constitutional Court of South Africa, S. v. Lawrence

Som, Reba, 199

Sotho, 149, 223

South Africa

   Anglicans, 32, 40–42, 185–86, 202–4

   Bantu, 14–16, 20, 215, 221, 223, 242

   Bantu courts, 14–16

   Bantu law, 14–16

   Black courts, 14–16

   Chinese, 223

   Christians, 5, 20, 30, 40–42, 68, 112–13, 123–24, 147, 149, 151–55, 161, 163–68, 170–73, 176–79, 185–86, 201–4, 223–24, 232–33, 240–42, 271, 328, 343

   Communists, 28–30, 67–68, 181, 196, 222–24

   Constitution of 1909, 107

   Constitutional reform of 1983, 20, 36

   Customary law, 14–16, 27, 342–44

   Hindu law, 107–109

Hindus, 14, 167, 314, 328–33

Indians, 106–10, 123–24, 144, 167–68, 201, 223, 314, 328–33

Interracial sex, 20, 195, 220–21, 271

Islamic law, 107–9, 167–68, 341–44

Jews, 5, 14, 171

Judges, 37–38, 75, 76

Legal system, 14, 35–39

Lutherans, 32

Marxists, 5, 68, 233

Muslims, 5, 14, 32, 161, 167–68, 171, 271, 328, 341–44

Rule of law, 35–39

Satanic Verses, The (ban in South Africa), 42, 49

Secular state/Secularism, 343

Security forces, 28, 171–72, 240–41

United Kingdom, 19, 20

South African Air Force, 185

South African Charter of Religious Rights and Freedoms, 343

South African Communist Party, 28–30, 40, 67–68, 196

   See also Hani, Chris

South African Council of Churches, 20, 31, 171–72

South African Native College, 35

South African Schools Act, 176

Soviet Union, 5, 6, 30, 39, 40, 64, 66, 72, 73, 113, 180, 182, 192, 196, 200, 225, 261, 318

   Cold War, 205, 261

   Communist Party, 64

   See also Bulganin, Nikolai; Gorbachev, Mikhail; Khrushchev, Nikita

Soweto killings, 244–45

Spain, 225

Special Marriage Act, India, 12, 267

Spectator, The, 263

Squngthi, 223

Srinagar, 179

Staines, Graham, 178

Stalinism, 4

State of Gujarat. *See* Supreme Court of India, State of Gujarat

Statute of Mortmain, 290

Steenkamp, Anna, 79

Stone, Justice, 124, 135

Storey, Peter, 154

Strijdom, Johannes Gerhardus, 69

Stuart Smith, Justice, 49

Succession, 11, 16, 140, 156, 188, 191, 198, 290–91, 324–25

   Also see Hindu Succession Act, India; Indian Succession Act; Succession Act, South Africa

Succession Act, South Africa, 341–42
Sudras, 12
Suez crisis, 200
Sunday, 158–59, 163–68
Sunday Telegraph, The, 160
Sunday Times, The, 234, 314
Suppression of Communism Act, South Africa, 196
Supreme Court of Appeal, South Africa, Minister of Home Affairs, 292, 306
   See also Cameron, Justice
Supreme Court of Canada. Big M. Drug Mart, 163–4
   See also Dickson, Brian
Supreme Court of India.
   Akhil, 345
   Bachan Singh, 148
   Bai Tahira, 12, 22, 254–55
   Danial Latifi, 26, 264–67, 323, 326
   Durgah Committee, 249
   Fuzlunbi, 22
   John Vallamattom, 290–91
   Jorden Diengdeh, 24
   Krishna Singh, 12–13
   Lily Thomas, 57, 61–62, 131, 160–61, 173–76, 190, 267, 284
   Mohd. Ahmed Khan, 14, 22–26, 264–67, 284, 291
   Pannalal, 155–57, 175–6
   Paras Ram, 251–52
   Ratilal Panachand Gandhi, 248–49
   Rev. Stainislaus, 253
   Sarla Mudgal, 16, 56–57, 61–62, 76–77, 110, 122, 129, 131, 132–43, 150, 155–57, 160–62, 173, 190, 197, 284, 291, 326
   Seema, 323–24
   State of Gujarat, 345
   See also Ahmad, Saghir; Babu, Rajendra; Chandrachaud, Y. V.; Chatterjee, Tarun; Chinnappa Reddy; Khare, V. N.; Krishna Iyer, V. R.; Mukherjea, Bijan Kumar; Pasayat, Arijit; Ramaswamy, K.; Ray, A. N.; Sahai, R. M.; Sen, Ananda Prakash; Sethi, R. P.; Singh, Kuldip; Sinha, S. B.; Venkatachaliah, M. N.; Venkataramiah, E. S.;
Supreme Court of Oregon, 62–64
Supreme Court of South Africa, Rivonia trial.
   See Rivonia trial
Supreme Court of South Carolina, 63
Supreme Court of the Cape, Esop, 107–108, 123, 167, 342
   See also Searle, Justice
Supreme Court of the United States.
   Employment division, 62–64, 272–73
   Everson, 194, 273

Lynch, 165–66
Sherbert, 63, 273
Smith, 62–64
Wisconsin, 64, 273
   See also Black, Hugo; Blackmun, Harry; Brennan, Harold Andrew; Burger, Warren E.; O'Connor, Sandra Day; Scalia, Antonin; Warren, Earl
Suttee. *See* Sati
Swan, Maureen, 109
Swaraj, 98, 101, 105, 110–11, 125–26, 194
Sweden, 218
Symbols. *See* Religious symbols
Synagogue, 75
   See also Bethel Synagogue, Kolkata

Table Bay, 82
Taj Mahal, 178
Tamil, 65, 329
Taqui, Abdul, 119
Tata Institute of Social Sciences, 10
Taylor, Paul. *See* Court of Appeal, United Kingdom, Taylor
Teddy boys, 207
Telengana, 196
Temple, 75, 82, 90, 140
Teresa of Avila, Saint
Thapar, Romila, 59, 75
Thatcher, Margaret, 5, 6, 7, 8, 17–18, 19, 20, 39, 43, 55, 69–70, 75, 181, 225–27, 233, 240, 246–47, 257, 261, 263
Thembu, 15, 69
Theology, 77–80, 82, 96–97, 213–14, 240–42
   Afrikaner freedom, 37, 79
   Apartheid, 20–21, 30–34, 37, 40–42, 79, 124, 155, 171, 182, 185–86, 201–4, 219, 230, 240–46, 279
   Black theology, 33, 241–42
   Human rights, 279
   Liberation, 5, 9, 34, 206, 212, 225–28, 230, 232, 238, 240–42, 245, 250, 256–57, 346
   Separation of church and state, 30, 40–42
   Sovereignty, 37, 185
   Violence, 30–34, 68, 88, 144, 147, 151–55, 171–72, 196, 244–45
   See also Bible; Kairos document; Quran; Rustenburg conference
Theosophists, 97–98, 102–103, 105–6
Thompson, Leonard, 29, 69, 80, 82, 109, 151, 195, 223
Thomson, Peter, 289
Thoreau, Henry David, 103
Tibet, 196
Time, 169–70
Times, The, 88, 234, 247, 314, 337, 347

Times of India, The, 281
Tolstoy, Leo, 105–6, 108, 127
Tories, 160, 204, 209, 216, 225, 233–35
Torture, 84, 87–88, 149, 204
Toxteth riots, 8, 43
Transkei, 16, 29, 222
Transvaal, 35, 106, 109
Transvaal Indian Congress, 123, 126
Treaty of Lausanne, 112
Treaty of London, 195
Treaty of Maastricht, 56, 157
Truth and Reconciliation Commission, South
    Africa, 68–69, 134, 151–55, 160, 166,
    171–73, 180, 201, 213, 245, 279
Tswana, 223
Tulkens, Françoise, 313
Turkey, 302, 313, 323, 325
Tutu, Desmond, 20–21, 27–28, 31, 74–75, 134,
    151–55, 161, 171, 179–80, 182, 230, 244,
    261, 270–71, 295, 298
    Rustenburg conference, 40–42
Twain, Mark, 81
Twin Towers. *See* Nine Eleven

Ubuntu, 149, 151, 173, 178
Umkhonto we Sizwe, 231
Uniform Civil Code, India, 12, 13, 24, 128–29,
    137–39, 141–43, 155–57, 175–76, 186–91,
    197–200, 205, 247–48, 265–67, 285, 291,
    325–27, 347
Union of Muslim Organizations, United King-
    dom, 44
Union of South Africa, 107, 184, 186, 214
United Kingdom
    Atheists, 98–99, 102–3, 105, 225–26, 232
    British courts and religion in the early 1980s,
    16
    Brixton and Toxteth riots, 8, 43
    Christians, 17, 41, 42–56, 70–72, 77–78, 78–
    80, 113, 158–59, 170, 178–9, 208–13, 226,
    227–32, 233–40, 257–61, 263–64, 285–90,
    298–301, 304–5, 319, 327, 334–39
    Divorce, 59, 122, 228
    European Union, 157–59, 234–37
    Festival of India (1982), 17–18
    Hare Krishna, 234
    Hindu Law, 27
    Hindus, 234, 303
    Immigrants, 7, 42–56, 184–85, 195, 204–7,
    216, 228, 233–34, 239
    Indians, 102–3, 228, 233
    Islamic law, 16, 17, 179
    Jewish disabilities, 91, 97
    Jews, 50, 83, 88, 91, 97, 234, 289, 319, 327,
    337, 339

Judges, 74–75, 76
Multicultural society, 8, 42–56, 314–23
Muslims, 6, 42–56, 72–73, 83, 179, 234, 281–
    84, 289, 292–95, 301–5, 310–23, 339–40,
    347–48
Pakistani, 228, 233
Poor laws, 83
Protestants, 77–78, 78–80
Racism, 195, 207
Roman Catholic disabilities, 97
Scientologists, 234, 236–7
Secular State/Secularism, 302, 335–40
Sikhs, 233–34, 239, 298, 324, 339
Socialists, 127, 130, 204
South Africa, 19, 20
Suez crisis, 200
Thatcher's reforms, 7–8, 39
Theater censorship, 228
United Kingdom v. Council. *See* Court of Jus-
    tice of the European Union, UK v. Council
United Nations, 123, 184, 195, 200, 261
    See also Human Rights Committee; Univer-
    sal Declaration of Human Rights
United Party, South Africa, 184
United States of America, 4, 6, 27, 39, 113, 208,
    234, 317–18
    Civil rights movement, 221–22, 230, 240
    Communism, 4, 27, 218
    Cold War, 27, 39, 192, 205, 257
    Death penalty, 148
    First amendment to the United States Con-
    stitution, 62–64, 165–66, 194, 272–73
    Marines, 27
    Pledge of allegiance, 4
    Racial segregation, 222, 240, 257
    Union Carbide Corporation, 21–22
    See also Bush, George W.; Carter, Jimmy;
    Civil Rights Act; Dulles, John Foster;
    Eisenhower, Dwight; King, Martin Luther;
    Kissinger, Henry; Nine Eleven; Nixon,
    Richard; Reagan, Ronald; World Trade
    Center bombing (1993)
Universal Declaration of Human Rights, United
    Nations, 195
University College of London, 102
University of Ankara, 302
University of Cape Town, 32
University of Groningen, 312
University of Pretoria, 201
University of Southampton, 230
University of Stellenbosch, 40
University of Sussex, 230
University of the Western Cape, 34, 67
Untouchables. *See* Dalits
USSR. *See* Soviet Union

Uttar Pradesh, 9–10, 26–27, 64–67, 232
Riots, 10, 232
See also Babri Mosque

Vaderland, Die, 201–2
Vajpayee, Atal Bihari, 267
Vallamattom, John. *See* Supreme Court of India, John Vallamattom
Van der Merwe, Johan, 171–72
Van der Veer, Peter, 96
Van der Westhuizen, Henri, 172
Van Duyn, Yvonne, 234–37, 240
See also Court of Justice of the European Communities, Van Duyn
Vanity Fair, 288–90
Varadarajan, Siddharth, 280–81, 345–46
Venkatachaliah, M. N., 57
Venkataramiah, E. S., 13–14, 24
Verwoerd, Hendrik Frensch, 69, 201, 203, 213–15
Victoria. *See* Queen Victoria
Vietnam War, 200
Viking Penguin, 42, 50, 55, 74
Vilayat Raj. *See* High Court of Delhi, Vilayat Raj
Villa-Vicencio, Charles, 32, 37, 245, 279
Virgin Mary, 52, 96–97
Vishnu. *See* Lord Vishnu
Vishva Hindu Parishad, 26, 59, 65–66, 280
Visions of Ecstasy, 46–48, 56, 158–59
Viswanathan, Gauri, 59–60
Vlok, Adriaan, 171–72
Vorster, Balthazar Johannes, 69, 241–42, 244

W. H. Smith, 43
Wahhabi, 321
Walker of Gestingthorpe, Baron, 300–301
Wall, Justice, 340
Wallbank, Gail R./Andrew David. *See* Court of appeal, United Kingdom, Parochial Church Council; High Court, United Kingdom, Parochial Church Council; House of Lords; Parochial Church Council
War of independence, India, 2, 75, 81–82, 85–92, 201, 345
Warren, Earl, 64, 273
Warwickshire, 134, 285
Watkins, Justice, 49–50, 56, 76, 97, 99
Weller, Paul, 298
Wells, Orson, 229
West Bengal, 68, 70, 225, 256
Western Cape, 16, 21
White Mutiny, India, 100–101
Whitehouse, Mary, 8, 234, 257–261, 263–64

See also Central Criminal Court, United Kingdom, Whitehouse; House of Lords, Whitehouse
Williams, Rina, 11, 14, 26, 78, 85, 119, 186, 191, 199–200
Williams, Rowan, 335–38, 340–41
Williamson. *See* Court of Appeal, United Kingdom, R. (Williamson); House of Lords, R. (Williamson)
Williamson, Denys, 33–34
Wilson, Harold, 220, 225, 231–32, 240
Wilson, Justice, 300
Wingrove, Nigel, 46–48, 234, 261
See also European Court of Human Rights, Wingrove
Wisconsin. *See* Supreme Court of the United States, Wisconsin
Witchcraft, 80, 149, 301
Witwatersrand University, 35
Wolsey, Thomas, 208–9, 229, 258
Women rights, 56–62, 113–16, 122, 127–29, 173–76, 179, 186–91, 197–200, 205, 247–48, 254–55, 264–67, 284, 290–91, 311–14, 323–27, 341–44, 347
Wolpert, Stanley, 122, 216–17
World Council of Churches, 241, 243
World Trade Center bombing (1993), 72
See also Nine Eleven
World War I, 111, 128
World War II, 8, 111–14, 116, 120, 123, 182, 273
Worlock, Derek, 71

Xhosa, 75, 78, 79–80, 88, 96, 223, 242

Yacoob, Zak, 278
Yashoda, 326, 347
Yatis, 12
Yawney, Carole Diane, 270
Yengeni, Tony, 327
Yoder. *See* Supreme Court of the United States, Wisconsin
Yutar, Percy, 224

Zambia, 29
Zhou Enlai, 196
Zia-ul-Haq, Muhammad, 5, 43
Zimbabwe, 7, 29, 261
Zionist Church, 343
Zoroastrians. *See* India, Zoroastrians
Zuid-Afrikaanse Republiek, 96
Also see Transvaal
Zulu, 96, 216–22, 223
Zulu (film), 216–22, 228
Zulu wars, 105, 106
Zuma, Jacob, 347

www.ingramcontent.com/pod-product-compliance
Lightning Source LLC
Chambersburg PA
CBHW080129270326
41926CB00021B/4400